Targum Jonathan
of the
Former Prophets

THE ARAMAIC BIBLE
• THE TARGUMS •

PROJECT DIRECTOR
Martin McNamara, M.S.C.

EDITORS
Kevin Cathcart • Michael Maher, M.S.C.
Martin McNamara, M.S.C.

EDITORIAL CONSULTANTS
Daniel J. Harrington, S.J. • Bernard Grossfeld

The Aramaic Bible

Volume 10

Targum Jonathan
of the
Former Prophets

Introduction, Translation and Notes

BY

Daniel J. Harrington, S.J.

and

Anthony J. Saldarini

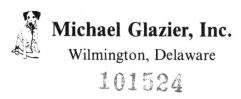

Michael Glazier, Inc.
Wilmington, Delaware

About the Translators:

Daniel J. Harrington, S.J. is Professor of New Testament at Weston School of Theology in Cambridge, Massachusetts, and general editor of *New Testament Abstracts*. He earned his Ph.D. in Near Eastern Languages and Literatures at Harvard University in 1970. He is past president of the Catholic Biblical Association (1985-1986).

Anthony J. Saldarini is Associate Professor in the Department of Theology at Boston College. He earned his Ph.D. from the Department of Near Eastern Languages and Literature at Yale University.

First published in 1987 by Michael Glazier, Inc., 1935 West Fourth Street, Wilmington, Delaware 19805.
©Copyright 1987 by Michael Glazier, Inc. All rights reserved.

Library of Congress Cataloging in Publication Data

Bible. O.T. Former Prophets. English. Harrington.
1987.
Targum Jonathan of the Former Prophets.

(The Aramaic Bible ; v. 10)
Translation of the Aramaic Targum Jonathan of the Former Prophets, which is itself a translation from Hebrew.
Bibliography: p.
Includes indexes.
1. Bible. O.T. Former Prophets. Aramaic. Targum Jonathan. I. Harrington, Daniel J. II. Saldarini, Anthony J. III. Title. IV. Series: Bible. O.T. English. Aramaic Bible. 1986 ; v. 10.
BS895.A72 1986 Vol. 10   221.4'2 s   86-45345
[BS1286.5.A3]   [222'.402]
ISBN 0-89453-479-3

Logo design by Florence Bern.
Printed in the United States of America.

TABLE OF CONTENTS

EDITORS' FOREWORD

While any translation of the Scriptures may in Hebrew be called a Targum, the word is used especially for a translation of a book of the Hebrew Bible into Aramaic. Before the Christian era Aramaic had in good part replaced Hebrew in Palestine as the vernacular of the Jews. It continued as their vernacular for centuries later and remained in part as the language of the schools after Aramaic itself had been replaced as the vernacular.

Rabbinic Judaism has transmitted Targums of all books of the Hebrew Canon, with the exception of Daniel and Ezra-Nehemiah, which are themselves partly in Aramaic. We also have a translation of the Samaritan Pentateuch into the dialect of Samaritan Aramaic. From the Qumran Library we have sections of a Targum of Job and fragments of a Targum of Leviticus, chapter 16, facts which indicate that the Bible was being translated in Aramaic in pre-Christian times.

Translations of books of the Hebrew Bible into Aramaic for liturgical purposes must have begun before the Christian era, even though none of the Targums transmitted to us by Rabbinic Judaism can be shown to be that old and though some of them are demonstrably compositions from later centuries.

In recent decades there has been increasing interest among scholars and a larger public in these Targums. A noticeable lacuna, however, has been the absence of a modern English translation of this body of writing. It is in marked contrast with most other bodies of Jewish literature for which there are good modern English translations, for instance the Apocrypha and Pseudepigrapha of the Old Testament, Josephus, Philo, the Mishnah, the Babylonian Talmud and Midrashic literature, and more recently the Tosefta and Palestinian Talmud.

It is hoped that this present series will provide some remedy for this state of affairs.

The aim of the series is to translate all the traditionally-known Targums, that is those transmitted by Rabbinic Judaism, into modern English idiom, while at the same time respecting the particular and peculiar nature of what these Aramaic translations were originally intended to be. A translator's task is never an easy one. It is rendered doubly difficult when the text to be rendered is itself a translation which is at times governed by an entire set of principles.

All the translations in this series have been specially commissioned. The translators have made use of what they reckon as the best printed editions of the Aramaic Targum in question or have themselves directly consulted the manuscripts.

The translation aims at giving a faithful rendering of the Aramaic. The introduction to each Targum contains the necessary background information on the particular work. In general, each Targum translation is accompanied by an apparatus and notes. The former is concerned mainly with such items as the variant readings in the Aramaic texts, the relation of the English translation to the original, etc. The notes give what explanations the translator thinks necessary or useful for this series.

Not all the Targums here translated are of the same kind. Targums were translated at different times, and most probably for varying purposes, and have more than one interpretative approach to the Hebrew Bible. This diversity between the Targums themselves is reflected in the translation and in the manner in which the accompanying explanatory material is presented. However, a basic unity of presentation has been maintained.

A point that needs to be stressed with regard to this translation of the Targums is that by reason of the state of current targumic research, to a certain extent it must be regarded as a provisional one. Despite the progress made, especially in recent decades, much work still remains to be done in the field of targumic study. Not all the Targums are as yet available in critical editions. And with regard to those that have been critically edited from known manuscripts, in the case of the Targums of some books the variants between the manuscripts themselves are such as to give rise to the question whether they have all descended from a single common original.

Details regarding these points will be found in the various introductions and critical notes.

It is recognised that a series such as this will have a broad readership. The Targums constitute a valuable source of information for students of Jewish literature, particularly those concerned with the history of interpretation, and also for students of the New Testament, especially for those interested in its relationship to its Jewish origins. The Targums also concern members of the general public who have an interest in the Jewish interpretation of the Scriptures or in the Jewish background to the New Testament. For them the Targums should be both interesting and enlightening.

By their translations, introductions and critical notes the contributors to this series have rendered an immense service to the progress of targumic studies. It is hoped that the series, provisional though it may be, will bring significantly nearer the day when the definitive translation of the Targums can be made.

Kevin Cathcart   Martin McNamara, M.S.C.   Michael Maher, M.S.C.

PREFACE

This volume presents the first complete translation of the Aramaic text of Targum Jonathan of the Former Prophets. Unlike some of the other Targums published in this series, Targum Jonathan of the Former Prophets is a fairly close rendering of the Hebrew text, though practically every verse contains at least some point of difference. Except in a few poetic passages, this targum appears to be a careful and systematic adaptation of the Hebrew original. Therefore, our chief goal in translating and commenting on this Aramaic text has been to let shine forth the translation philosophy and achievements of the targumist(s).

In light of the lengthy introductions by C. T. R. Hayward to Targum Jonathan of Jeremiah and Bruce Chilton to Targum Jonathan of Isaiah, our own introduction can be brief and concerned mainly with clarifying the major issues in scholarship on Targum Jonathan of the Former Prophets (especially works by A. Tal, P. Churgin, and L. Smolar and M. Aberbach). Since there are few good parallels in rabbinic literature and the New Testament to Targum Jonathan of the Former Prophets, we have included whatever parallels there are (in this we have been helped greatly by the work of Smolar and Aberbach) in a single apparatus with all our other observations at the foot of the pages.

Harrington translated almost the entire text from Sperber's edition and made notes on the text. Saldarini translated the remaining parts, revised the translation, and added to the notes. Saldarini wrote the "Translation Techniques and Theology" section of the introduction, and Harrington wrote the rest.

We are grateful to Martin McNamara and Michael Glazier for inviting us to be part of this international and interconfessional project and for their encouragement as the work progressed.

Daniel J. Harrington, S.J.
Anthony J. Saldarini

ABBREVIATIONS

JPS   Jewish Publication Society translation of the Bible (1962-1982)

MT   Masoretic Text

RSV   Revised Standard Version of the Bible (1952)

S-A   Leivy Smolar and Moses Aberbach, *Studies in Targum Jonathan to the Prophets.*

Tg   Targum

TO   Targum Onqelos

m.   Mishnah

b.   Babylonian Talmud

y.   Jerusalem or Palestinian Talmud

t.   Tosefta

INTRODUCTION

Title: Targum Jonathan of the Former Prophets

According to the Babylonian Talmud (*b. Megilla* 3a), the Targum of the Prophets was composed by Jonathan ben Uzziel under the guidance of Haggai, Zechariah, and Malachi. Jonathan ben Uzziel was one of Hillel's disciples, and so presumably did his work in Palestine during the first century C.E. But this attribution is suspect on several counts: the silence about Jonathan ben Uzziel in the parallel passage in the Palestinian Talmud (*y. Megilla* 1.9), the mystical note introduced by naming the prophets, and the fanciful suggestion that Onqelos=Aquila and Jonathan=Theodotion.[1] The Talmud's attribution of the Targum of the Prophets to Jonathan ben Uzziel is best interpreted as a late and isolated attempt at enhancing the authority of the Targum by attributing it to a famous disciple of Hillel.

Quotations of Targum Jonathan in talmudic and midrashic writings do not carry the name "Jonathan." Most of the quotations of it in the Babylonian Talmud appear under the name of Rab Joseph, the head of the academy at Pumbeditha in the fourth century C.E. (see *b. Sanhedrin* 94b). But Rab Joseph was not the author of the Targum, since his statements about it signify that he had the Targum before him.[2] Therefore, it is generally agreed that the author of the Targum Jonathan is unknown and that the attribution is not to be taken as historical fact.

Indeed, it is preferable to think in terms of multiple authorship. In the production of these targums that go under the name "Targum Jonathan," there seems to have been an attempt at uniformity in language and translation techniques. Nevertheless, from book to book there is some variety. Even within the relatively homogeneous Targums of the Former Prophets, Joshua is much more literal than 1 Samuel. These targums probably originated in some kind of "school" activity in which there was broad agreement about the philosophy of translation and the ways of rendering Hebrew words in Aramaic. Then individual translators carried out their tasks with some flexibility.

The expression "Former Prophets" refers to the following six biblical books: Joshua, Judges, 1 Samuel, 2 Samuel, 1 Kings, and 2 Kings. These books cover the period in ancient Israel's history from Moses' death (Deuteronomy 34) to the exile. The traditional designation of these books as the Former Prophets[3] serves to distinguish them on the one hand from the Torah (Genesis, Exodus, Leviticus, Numbers, Deuteronomy) and on the other hand from the Latter Prophets (Isaiah, Jeremiah, Ezekiel, etc.) and the Writings (Psalms, Proverbs, Job, etc).

---

[1]See Churgin, pp. 9-18, Smolar-Aberbach, p. xix.

[2]Churgin, p. 146. See the list of rabbinic quotations of Targum Jonathan in Churgin, pp. 147-151.

[3]For a sketch of the history of the designation, see B.S. Childs, *Introduction to the Old Testament as Scripture* (Philadelphia: Fortress, 1979) p. 230.

Witnesses to the Text

This translation is based on MS. Or. 2210 (p) of the British Museum, which Alexander Sperber printed in his edition of the Aramaic text (except for its obvious scribal errors). In his introduction, Sperber divided the representative manuscripts with Babylonian vocalization into two categories:

Biblical Books

> MS. Or. 2210 of the British Museum (p)
> MS. Or. 2371 of the British Museum (y)
> MS. Or. 1472 of the British Museum (m)
> MS. Or. 1471 of the British Museum (w)
> MS. Or. qu. 578 of the Berlin Staatsbibliothek (x).

Haphtaroth

> MS. No. 332 of the S.D. Sassoon Library (j)
> MS. Or. 2364 of the British Museum (k)

He listed three manuscripts with Tiberian (or no vocalization):

> MS. Add. 26879 of the British Museum (a)
> MS. p. 116 of the Montefiore Library at Jews' College in London (c)
> Codex Reuchlinianus of the Badische Landesbibliothek in Karlsruhe (f).

Sperber called attention to some fragmentary texts and some targum quotations in the works of early authors (Aruk of R. Nathan, Yonah ibn Ganah, Rashi, Kimhi).

The present translation follows Sperber's main text (apart from the printing errors). Only in a few cases is notice given to material in Sperber's apparatus. Serious students of the Targums will want to consult that apparatus. The lengthy additions in Codex Reuchlinianus have not been included, since these glosses deserve a separate study. See A. Sperber, *The Bible in Aramaic. Volume IV B: The Targum and the Hebrew Bible* (Leiden: Brill, 1973) 138-43, for descriptions of the individual manuscripts.

Our decision to translate Sperber's text is not simply dictated by convenience. When one inspects the extensive critical apparatus in Sperber's edition and reconstructs what the various manuscripts contained, the impression arises that the manuscript situation described by Peter Schäfer for Hekhalot literature[4] also obtains to some extent in targumic literature. The individual manuscripts of what we call *Targum Jonathan* tend almost to constitute separate works. The process by which these works were shaped was so varied and fluid that the search for the "one" text or the "original" text may be illusory. So in our work we are presenting a new English translation of one Aramaic text (British Museum MS. Or. 2210 as edited by Sperber) without claiming that it is the "one" or "original" text.

---

[4] Schäfer, "Tradition and Redaction in Hekhalot Literature," *Journal for the Study of Judaism* 14 (1983) 172-181.

Language

The only full-scale investigation of the language of Targum Jonathan of the Former Prophets has been carried out by Abraham Tal (Rosenthal). It has been published in Modern Hebrew under the title *Lšwn htrgwm lnby'ym r'šwnym wm'mdh bkll nyby h'rmyt (The Targum of the Former Prophets and its Position within the Aramaic Dialects)*, (Texts and Studies in the Hebrew Language and Related Subjects 1; Tel Aviv: Tel Aviv University, 1975). Tal's major concern is classifying the language of Targum Jonathan of the Prophets in the history of Aramaic.

After summarizing the debate about the character of the Aramaic in Targum Jonathan of the Former Prophets (Palestine in the early Christian period, or Babylonia in the Amoraic period?), Tal examines the vocabulary and grammar of this Targum according to the following outline: pronouns, particles, adverbs, numerals, morphological features, words of meaning (nouns and verbs), lexical material unrecorded in dictionaries, some semantic fields, loan-words, tosefta targum, and unique traits.

Tal takes as his framework the distinction drawn by E. Y. Kutscher between Old Aramaic and Middle Aramaic.[5] He argues that the language of Targum Jonathan of the Former Prophets is closely connected with Old Aramaic, especially in its later strata represented in Nabatean, Palmyrene, and Qumran Aramaic documents. Whatever "Middle-Aramaic" features occur in the targum are also documented in these later strata of Old Aramaic. Tal describes the Aramaic of Targum Jonathan of the Former Prophets (as well as Nabatean, Palmyrene, and Qumran Aramaic) as representing a superdialectical language, comparable to Koine Greek in the Hellenistic era, which was used in a wide geographical expanse: from Palmyra in the Syrian Desert, through Palestine, down to the Sinai Peninsula and the North-Arabian Peninsula. Comparison with Palestinian Aramaic texts leads Tal to place the Aramaic of Targum Jonathan of the Former Prophets in Judea before the crushing of the Bar-Kokhba revolt (135 C.E.). On the other hand, Tal finds no single outstanding linguistic phenomenon to justify the claim that Babylon was the birthplace of this Targum. He maintains that the so-called Palestinian Targums (Neofiti, ps.-Jonathan, Fragmentary Targum) are related to the Middle Aramaic of the Palestinian Talmud and are later than Targums Onqelos and Jonathan, i.e., from the third century C.E. onward.

According to Tal, therefore, the language of Targum Jonathan of the Former Prophets is to be assigned to Judea before 135 C.E. His position seems reasonable, provided that allowance is made for the insertion of later material into the text and the possibility of some editorial activity in Babylonia prior to the Arab invasion.

General Characteristics of the Paraphrase

In his concluding volume (IV B) of *The Bible in Aramaic* (1973), Alexander Sperber maintained that two schools of translators worked on the Targums. One school defined the task as rendering into Aramaic the text before them, adhering to a literal transla-

---

[5] E.Y. Kutscher, "The Language of the 'Genesis Apocryphon.' A preliminary study," in *Scripta Hierosolymitana* 4 (1958) 1-35.

tion as far as possible, and only deviating from it in order to help the readers to get the implied meaning of a phrase or to demonstrate the validity of rabbinic interpretation. Almost all of Targum Jonathan of the Former Prophets is the product of this approach to translation. The second school handled the text quite freely and in more midrash-like fashion. Only a few parts of Targum Jonathan of the Former Prophets (Judges 5; 1 Samuel 2:1-10; 2 Samuel 22:1-23:7) belong to the second category, though there are some passages in which the line between the two kinds of translations is not sharp.

The Hebrew text underlying the Targum of the Former Prophets clearly belonged to the tradition usually known as Masoretic. The most obvious deviations of this Targum from the Masoretic text concern the doctrine of God. Biblical passages suggesting that God has a body or parts of a body are modified. Many actions attributed to God in the Hebrew text are cast in the passive voice. There are no other "gods," only idols. The terms Memra and Shekinah occur frequently in texts that describe God's action or presence in the world. Other modifications of the Hebrew text include place names, descriptions of religious figures ("prophet of the Lord" instead of "man of God"), clarifications of meaning by means of paraphrase or addition, omission or addition of particles, etc. (see the following section).

Since the bulk of Targum Jonathan of the Former Prophets aims to present a literal translation of the Hebrew text, the focus of this volume is the relationship between the Aramaic version and the Hebrew original. To that end, we have indicated every devia-tion of Sperber's edition from the Masoretic Text. The targumist(s) was obviously making great efforts at consistency in rendering the Hebrew, though at some points (e.g., with reference to divine activity) he either failed or was not interested in maintain-ing consistency.

Translation Techniques and Theology

Targum Jonathan of the Former Prophets generally gives a literal translation of the MT of the Hebrew Bible. Unlike most of the other Targums it contains few extended midrashic passages. Many of the changes it makes in vocabulary, idiom, or construc-tion are constantly repeated throughout the entire Former Prophets, and each instance has been recorded in the notes to the translation. This section of the Introduction will sort and categorize the most common characteristics of the translation with a few examples of each and give a few samples of midrashic interpretations which are scat-tered through the text. It will also briefly note the reasons, theological and otherwise, for making the changes. The reader is also referred to Smolar-Aberbach, who group these phenomena under three very general headings: Halacha, Historical and Geo-graphical Allusions, and Theological Concepts.

Eight categories will be used to classify the changes which the Targum makes in the MT. The categories overlap in some cases, and in others they contain phenomena which could be further subdivided. They are proposed as useful organizing devices rather than as the principles or concerns which consciously guided the targumic transla-tors. They are used here to help the reader perceive the range of translational and interpretative activity in the Targum. The eight categories are:

1. Names of people and peoples
2. Place names and their identification
3. Changes in words or grammatical additions for idiomatic reasons or clarity of sense
4. Clarification of an unclear MT text. Substitution of the Qere for the Ketib
5. Anachronistic modernizing
6. Substitution of more literal for metaphoric language
7. Changes in expression to describe God and his activity
8. Midrashic additions, theological interpretations, and halakhic harmonizations.

These categories will be treated in order with a limited selection of examples for each, chiefly from Joshua and Judges.

1. NAMES OF PEOPLE AND PEOPLES

The Targum usually changes the Hebrew collective singular into a plural. "The Canaanite" becomes "the Canaanites" (Josh 7:9; ch. 13), "Moab" becomes "the Moabbites" (2 Kings 3:21), and the names of other ethnic groups are similarly changed. Occasionally, there are variations. "The Gadite" becomes "the tribe of Gad" (Josh 1:12; 18:7), "the Gershonite" becomes "the sons of Gershon" (Josh 21:33), and "Israel" becomes "the sons of Israel" (Josh 6:25). "Naamah the Ammonitess" becomes "Naamah who was from the sons of Ammon" (1 Kings 14:21). Israelite tribes become "the tribe of the house of . . .", for example,"the tribe of Judah" is changed into "the tribe of the house of Judah" (Josh 7:16). When the name of the founder of a tribe is used for the tribe, e.g., "Ephraim," it becomes "the house of Ephraim" (Josh 17:15; 1 Kings 12:25). But that expression can also be changed. "The house of Joseph" becomes "those of the house of Joseph" (Josh 18:15), etc. The changes are idiomatic in that Hebrew collectives generally become Aramaic plurals. But the Targum also tends toward more full expression and precision.

2. PLACE NAMES AND THEIR IDENTIFICATION

Biblical places may have a different name in the Targum. The Targum often gives the contemporary name for a place. Bashan becomes Matnan or less commonly Mattanah (Josh 9:10; 12:4); Chinneroth becomes Ginnesar, which may be a contemporary identification (Josh 11:2; 12:2). If the place is unknown to the targumist, an identification with a known place is sometimes suggested and the suggestion is sometimes inaccurate (see S-A, pp. 119 ff. for many examples). Kadesh-barnea is called Rekam or Rekem, a place in Transjordan (Josh 10:41; 14:6, 7; Judg 11:16). Baal-tamar near Gibeah (Judg 20:33) becomes Jericho through a midrashic reading of its name. Shinar is identified as Babylon on the basis of Gen 10:10; 11:2. Tormah is unknown, so it is translated as a noun meaning "deceit" or "secret" (Judg 9:31). The place name "Moreh" (Judg 7:1) is translated as a participle meaning "facing" or "overlooking." The Targum sometimes translates the Hebrew name, or part of it, into Aramaic. The Arabah is translated into

Aramaic by the equivalent word, *mēšrā*, "plain," but in Aramaic it has a more generic connotation; the Hebrew Beth-arabah becomes Beth-meshra (Josh 18:22). Some place names have been interpreted midrashically. En-rogel becomes En-qarsa, which may have something to do with the place of the camp (Josh 15:7 and the note there). Kiriath-sepher becomes Kiriath-arke because *sēper* (book) was interpreted as records of the court (*arke*) (Josh 15:15 and S-A, p. 124). In general, the theophoric element *ba'al* is avoided (see category 8 below).

3. REGULAR SUBSTITUTIONS AND CHANGES IN WORDS AND PHRASES

The Targum contains dozens of minute changes in words and phrases which are difficult to classify. The following selection is sorted into three broad and overlapping groups:

a. words added to the text, often for grammatical or idiomatic reasons;

b. frequent substitutions of one word or expression for another, often for idiomatic reasons, sometimes for clarity of expression;

c. clarifications of the text, often by a change of phrase or by an addition to the text.

a. Additions: The word "time" is added in Josh 2:5 and the word "out" in 2:19. The relative pronoun "who" is added in Josh 5:7 and "what" in Josh 8:8. These grammatical additions are very common throughout. "Our lives (are) to you" is made more idiomatic and explicit as "Our lives are handed over to you" in Josh 2:14. Similarly, in Josh 9:25 "We are in your hand" becomes "We are given over in your hand." In Josh 6:13 the Targum inserts the implied subject of the sentence and changes the verbal forms to clarify the grammar. In a number of places "the Land" is made specific as "the land of Israel" (Judg 3:11, 30).

b. Substitutions: "Hear" often becomes "accept," a more active word (Josh 1:18; Judg 3:17). S-A (p. 139) suggests that "accept" contains the idea of God accepting prayer, but it is also used among humans (1 Kings 12:15, 16). "Speak in the ears of" becomes "speak before." "A hand" becomes "the hand of a man" (Josh 2:20), and "for us" becomes "coming to our aid" (Josh 5:13). Words and expressions concerning war are often changed. "Men of war" becomes "men waging or making battle" (Josh 5:4; 10:24), "for war" becomes "to wage war" (Josh 8:14), "fight" becomes "wage battle" (Josh 10:29), "struck down" becomes "killed" and "fall [in battle]" becomes "were killed" (Josh 8:24). The Targum often uses "shattered" for other verbs which indicate defeat in battle (e.g., Judg 3:30; 8:28). A number of these substitutions are idiomatic and some are interpretative in that they clarify the meaning of the text.

c. Clarifications: Many of these changes are brief interpretations; some are simply grammatical. For example, "it" becomes "them" because it has a plural antecedent (Josh 7:21), and "he" becomes "they" when the king and his army are meant by the context (Josh 8:14). "His blood" becomes "the guilt of his killing" (Josh 2:19), and "a shameful thing" becomes "what is not fitting" (Josh 7:15). In a more substantive change, Joshua is said to have named the place of circumcision "the hill of foreskins" by the addition of the clause "and he called it" (Josh 5:3); thus the naming is turned into an etiology. The awkward expression that the priests' feet were "lifted up" on dry land is changed to "were drawn up and rested upon" dry land (Josh 4:18). In Josh 6:1 the description of Jericho has two synonyms for "closed up"; the Targum provides a second related but different term: "closed up and fortified." In Josh 6:5 and 20 "and it will be swallowed up" is added to the description of the destruction of the wall to improve the sense. "Before the Lord" becomes more liturgically specific when in some cases it is altered to "before the ark of the Lord." Other clarifications are changes from "wall" to "wall of the city" (Josh 6:20), "youngest" to "youngest of his sons" (6:26), "his reputation was in all the land" to "his reputation was great in all the land" (6:27), and "falling on the ground" to "lying on the ground." "Sustenance" is more fully rendered as "food to sustain life" (Judg 6:4). "[He prepared] unleavened cakes from an ephah of flour" is rendered in a more precise and modern way "he baked a measure of unleavened flour" (Judg 6:19). "A second ox seven years old" for sacrifice becomes "a second ox which has been fattened up for seven years" (Judg 6:25). A unit of currency is specified in Judg 17:3 (and often) where the MT gives none. "The river" in Josh 24:3 is identified as the Jordan and in 24:14-15 as the Euphrates. Some clarifications are more interpretive. In Josh 11:7 the targumist adds that the enemy is camping as an explanation of how Joshua surprised them. "It [a stone] will be among you" becomes "it will be a memorial among you" (Josh 24:27).

4. UNCLEAR MT

Sometimes the Targum translates the Qere rather than the Ketib (1 Sam 27:8; 1 Kings 9:18; 2 Kings 5:12; 8:10). In some cases the MT is unclear and the Targum, in ways similar to other ancient versions, interprets the MT to make it clear. "The third is Naphat" in Josh 17:11 is obscure and the Targum clarifies it by translating the phrase as "three districts." In Josh 24:32 there is an obscure monetary unit (*qesîtâ*), which the Targum replaces with "lambs." In Judges 2:3 the MT "sides," which also means "adversaries," is replaced by the more specific "oppressors." In Judg 3:23 the MT word is uncertain and may mean "dirt," "excrement," or "hole." The Targum has "hall." The Hebrew *ṭabbur* (Judg 9:37) is unclear so the Targum changes it to "strength." *Lālat* in 1 Sam 4:19, which is meaningless, is translated as "to give birth" (*lāledet*; cf. Gen Rab 82:8). An obscure measure of distance in a field (1 Sam 14:14) is rendered as "half the journey of a yoke of oxen in the field." Comparison of the Targum with other ancient versions often shows that all had trouble with passages in the Hebrew and adopted sometimes similar and sometimes varied interpretations.

5. ANACHRONISTIC MODERNIZING

The Targum often modifies biblical things and customs to fit its own time. For example, the biblical expression "go to your tents" is translated as "go to your cities" in the Targum (Josh 22:4, 7, 8; Judg 1:14 and often). People who do forced labor (*mas*) become "bearers of tribute" (Josh 17:13; Judg 1:28, 30) because taxes had generally replaced forced labor. Flint knives for circumcision (Josh 5:2) are replaced by sharp knives, i.e., scalpels. A blessing given by an elder becomes an inheritance (Josh 15:19; Judg 1:15), and a tree becomes a gallows (Josh 8:29; 10:26, 27). The upper chamber of coolness in the palace becomes the upper chamber of the summer house (Judg 3:20, 24), a reflection of the Hellenistic custom of the rich and powerful having summer houses in cool spots. People are said to have reclined to eat rather than sat to eat, another reflection of Hellenistic and Roman customs (Judg 19:6). In the Book of Judges the judges are called "leaders" (*năgôdîn*), a word whose range of meaning in the targumist's day more precisely fits the activities of the judges (2:16 and passim). Deborah is made to reside in a city because that is where courts were in later times (Judg 4:5). Ishmaelites become Arabs (Judg 8:24) because Arabs were thought to be the descendants of Ishmael who settled in the southern wilderness. And "Hebrews" (1 Sam 4:6, 9) become "Jews."

6. SUBSTITUTIONS OF MORE LITERAL FOR METAPHORIC LANGUAGE

The Targum tends to remove metaphoric statements and images in favor of more prosaic, literal, and "clear" expressions. The land flowing with milk and honey becomes a land "producing milk and honey" (Josh 5:6). One's "seed" becomes one's "sons" (Josh 24:3), and the idiomatic Hebrew "hands" is given its meaning "strength" (Josh 8:20). Anger which "burns" or is "hot" becomes anger which is "strong" (Josh 7:26). Samson's charge that the Philistines have "plowed with my heifer" becomes "have examined my wife" (Judg 14:18). "They shall be a snare and a trap for you, a scourge on your sides and thorns in your eyes" (Josh 23:13) becomes "they will be for you for a breach and for a stumbling block and for troops bearing armor opposite you and for camps surrounding you." When God promises Jeroboam a kingdom, he says that he will give one tribe to Solomon's son "that there be a lamp" for David (1 Kings 11:36). The Targum turns the metaphor into descriptive prose with "to establish a kingdom." Proverbs, which are often suggestive and metaphoric, are changed into discursive prose statements. "Is not the gleaning of the grapes of Ephraim better than the vintage of Abiezer?" (Judg 8:2) becomes "Are not the weak ones of the house of Ephraim better than the strong ones of the house of Abiezer?" "My little finger is thicker than my father's loins" (1 Kings 12:10) becomes "My weakness is stronger than the strength of my father."

7. CHANGES IN EXPRESSION TO DESCRIBE GOD AND HIS ACTIVITY

The Targums are well known for avoiding anthropomorphisms, using the passive voice and indirect constructions when referring to God, and protecting monotheism and God's transcendence. Some typical techniques and examples will be cited along with the theological motivation for many of them.

The Targum often modifies God's names. Sometimes "God" is changed into "Lord [=Yahweh]" (Josh 22:33; 24:1; Judg 1:7). In many cases either God's Memra (Word) or Shekinah (Presence) is substituted for his name. "I was with Moses" becomes "My Memra was at the aid of Moses" (Josh 1:5; ch. 22; Judg 1:22). The meaning of the pronoun "with" is made explicit, that is, God helped Moses. The instrumentality of the

Memra is brought out in the translation of "the Lord fought" as "the Lord by his Memra waged battle" (Josh 10:14, 42). The Memra is also used, as would be expected, for God speaking. "The mouth of the Lord" becomes "the Memra of the Lord" (Josh 21:3), "the voice of God" becomes "the Memra of God" (Josh 22:2; Judg 2:2), and "inquired of the Lord" becomes "inquired of the Memra of the Lord" (Judg 1:1).[6] The presence of God is often signified by the name Shekinah: "The living God is in your midst" becomes "The living God has chosen to make his Shekinah reside in your midst" (Josh 3:10).[7] Notice that God's sovereignty is emphasized by the addition of the verb "choose." God's Shekinah is associated with both the heavens (1 Kings 8:23, 30) and the Temple (1 Kings 8:12, 16). God is also designated by the expression "fear of God," that is, by a proper human attitude toward him. For example, "follow after the Lord" becomes "follow after the fear of the Lord" in Josh 14:8, 14; 23:8, etc. The command to "cling to him" becomes "draw near to fear of him" (Josh 22:5). Those who "did not know the Lord" become those who "did not know to fear from before the Lord" (Judg 2:10).

The passive voice, indirect discourse, and deferential expressions are constantly used in reference to God. "From the Lord" becomes "from before the Lord" in numerous instances and "to the Lord" becomes "before the Lord" (Josh 6:17, 19; 7:19). "Before" (*qdm*) has the connotation of "in the presence of" God or "from the presence of" God. It is used in varied constructions; for example, "the Lord heard the voice of a man" becomes "the prayer of a man was accepted before the Lord"; "seek the mouth of the Lord" becomes "seek instruction from before the Lord" (Josh 9:14). The Targum interprets the sense of the Hebrew idioms, but expresses them in a deferential and partly indirect way. For example, "he knows" becomes "before him it is revealed" (Josh 22:22). In other cases, common expressions such as "in the eyes of the Lord" become "before the Lord" (Judg 4:1). Verbal expressions are also modified to the indirect mode. "That the Lord chooses" becomes "that is singled out from before the Lord" (Josh 7:14). "His ways" become "the ways that are good before him" (Josh 22:5). "He will be angry at" becomes "there will be anger upon" (Josh 22:18). It should be noted, however, that some uses of "before" and the passive voice reflect good Aramaic prose style and are used of humans also.[8]

Human relations with God tend to be seen as forms of prayer. "Joshua spoke to the Lord" becomes "Joshua sang praise before the Lord" (Josh 10:12), and "the Lord heard the voice of a man" (Josh 10:14) becomes "the prayer of a man was accepted before the Lord." One does not simply converse with God, but addresses God in prayer. When the people bless God (Josh 22:33), the Targum understands that they "gave thanks before the Lord." When the people turn from the Lord (Josh 22:23, 29; ch. 24), the Targum understands that they "turn from the worship of the Lord" or "abandoned the service of the Lord" (Judg 2:12). When they serve him, the Targum has them "serve before him" (Josh 22:5). God's response to prayer is also made liturgically decorous: "The

---

[6]On Memra, see most recently C.T.R. Hayward, *Divine Name and Presence: The Memra* (Totowa: Allenheld Osmun, 1981).

[7]Shekinah has been most thoroughly studied by A.M. Goldberg, *Untersuchungen über die Vorstellung von der Schekhinah in der frühen rabbinischen Literatur* (Berlin: deGruyter, 1969).

[8]M.L. Klein, "The Preposition *qdm* ('Before'). A Pseudo-Anti-Anthropomorphism in the Targums," *JTS* (n.s.) 30 (1979) 502-507.

Lord was moved to pity by their groaning" becomes "the Lord was turning from what he said and was receiving their prayers and was saving them."

The Targum carefully distinguishes the God of Israel from other gods. When the MT uses the generic term "gods" for pagan gods, the Targum replaces this usage with the clear evaluative term "idols" *(t'wt)* (Josh 24:16; Judg 2:3, 12; Churgin, p. 112; S-A, p. 340). In addition, priests of non-Israelite gods are identified by a separate word, *kwmr* (Judg 17:5), and altars used for worship of other gods are called "mounds" or "heaps" (see Judg 6:25, 28 for this term and the Israelite term; S-A, pp. 36-39; 150-156).

A number of passages protect the transcendence of God from anthropomorphisms and from too close an involvement with human characteristics and affairs. "The Lord God of Israel is their [Levi's] inheritance" seems too stark, and so it is interpreted according to the practice specified in the Bible and rabbinic literature: "The gifts [i.e., sacrifices] that the Lord God of Israel gave to them are their [Levi's] inheritance" (Josh 13:33). Since Israel has sinned, "the hand of the Lord is against them" when they go to battle (Judg 2:15). The Targum makes explicit the effect on Israel and at the same time distances God from it slightly by the formulation "slaughter from before the Lord was upon them." A similar effect is caused by the shift from "I have a word of God for you" to "I have a message of the Lord to speak with you" (Judg 3:20). In other passages an intermediary is substituted for God. When Deborah exhorts Barak: "Does not the Lord go out before you?" (Judg 4:14), the Targum interjects an intermediary and makes specific its effect: "Is not the angel of the Lord going forth to insure success before you?" Often secondary causes replace God as the primary cause so that God is not so directly involved in worldly affairs. But this is not always the case. In 1 Sam 23:14 there is no change in the biblical text. Saul is seeking David, but "God (Tg: the Lord) did not give him into his hand." In 1 Sam 28:18 the Targum retains the expression "The Lord has done this thing to you today."

God is also protected from human effects on him by changes in phraseology. Instead of Israel provoking the Lord, Israel "made provocation before the Lord" (Judg 2:12). "The enemies of the Lord" become "those hating the people of the Lord" (1 Sam 30:26). Finally, the Targum is careful to keep God from the appearance of impropriety. God challenges Israel to go to the other gods they have chosen and concludes with the ironic exhortation: "Let them deliver you in the time of your distress" (Judg 10:14). Targum removes any hint that idols might have power and changes God's irony into a clause with an implied negative answer: "whether they are able to save you in your time of distress."

8. MIDRASHIC ADDITIONS, THEOLOGICAL INTERPRETATIONS, AND HALAKHIC HARMONIZATIONS

This large and disparate category includes numerous interpretations which are made uniquely for one passage, rather than repeated throughout the Targum. Most such interpretations are changes in a word, phrase, clause, or verse. A full study of these passages in the Targum of the Former Prophets would require a book length study. Here the scope of the materials will be sketched and some examples will be given.

The only extended passages that depart from the Masoretic text are several hymns, the Song of Deborah in Judges 5, the Song of Hannah in 1 Samuel 2:1-10 (see the articles on these passages by Harrington, cited in the Select Bibliography), and 2 Samuel 22:1-23:7 (=Ps 18). All these passages are hymns or prayers, and the targumist's sense of proper liturgical expression has influenced his translation of these passages, as can be seen by comparison with the briefer petitions by Hannah (1 Sam 1:11) and Hezekiah (2 Kings 19:15-19) and to a lesser extent in the prayer of Solomon at the Temple (1 Kings 8). The longer hymns are not simply liturgical adaptations, however; each represents a concerted effort by the targumist(s) to render the hymn available to his audience in a special way.

Targum Jonathan of Judges 5 is a good example of interpretative homiletics. Taking his starting point from a difficult biblical passage, the targumist filled out the compact and often mysterious Hebrew poem, used elements already in the text as suggestions for further expansion, made necessary grammatical decisions, and clarified the meaning of many phrases. In these ways, the targumist set the stage for his interpretation. At the same time, he turned Judges 5 into an illustration of Israel's relationship with God: Whenever Israel rejects the Law, its enemies triumph; whenever it returns to the Law, it triumphs over the enemies. By injecting into an ancient text features of his audience's own setting (whatever that may have been historically), the targumist emphasized that the basic principle of Israel's relationship with God applied to their situation also.

The version of Hannah's song (1 Sam 2:1-10) in Targum Jonathan stands out from the material surrounding it by reason of its language, paraphrastic technique, and theology. Whereas Targum Jonathan of 1 Samuel generally uses the imperfect to express the future, this passage often uses the form *ʿātîd* plus *l* with the infinitive (vv. 1, 3, 6) or *ʿātîd* plus *d* with the imperfect (vv. 1, 2, 5). Whereas Targum Jonathan of 1 Samuel (and of the Former Prophets as a whole) generally reflects the Hebrew text rather closely, this passage is very much an expansion and interpretation of the original version. Whereas Targum Jonathan of 1 Samuel generally follows the ideas of the biblical text rather carefully, this targumic passage transforms Hannah's song into an apocalypse that charts the course of Israel's future history and climaxes in a version of the eschaton.

The targumic treatments of the songs of Deborah and Hannah find their methodological counterparts in 2 Sam 22:1-51 and 23:1-7, respectively. The strategy of interpretative homiletics is carried out in 2 Sam 22:1-51 (see Psalm 18); the targumist filled out the difficult Hebrew text, solved various grammatical problems, and tried to clarify obscure phrases. On the other hand, Targum Jonathan of 2 Sam 23:1-7 is an apocalypse in which the Davidic messiah is a central figure.

The Targum consistently carries through some changes in regard to prophets and prophecy. The words prophet, prophecy, and prophesy occur more frequently than they do in the MT. The Targum regularizes the terminology for prophets and eliminates older terms such as "man of God," "seer," and "visionary." Nouns for "vision" and cognate verbs are also translated by prophecy and prophesy. The "word of God" becomes the "word of prophecy from before the Lord" and the "spirit" or "spirit of God" becomes the "spirit of prophecy" (1 Sam 10:10). When a prophet is not speaking God's genuine word, the Targum identifies him as a "lying prophet" (1 Kings 13:11). The Targum treats prophecy as a unified phenomenon which is understood as true contact with God involving revelatory significance. In some cases the Targum changes prophets into scribes (or teachers, since this is what they were in talmudic times). In most instances the prophets who are said to be scribes are either ecstatic prophets (1 Sam 10) who are tamed into a school of teachers or prophetic community leaders (2 Kings 23:1-2 and often in the Latter Prophets) who are "modernized" by the targumist into scribes or teachers, the leaders in his time. (See the article by Saldarini cited in the Select Bibliography.)

Some interpretations and changes in the biblical text are made to harmonize the content of the Bible with later halakhic (legal) practices and requirements. For example, Josh 18:7 says that Levi's inheritance is the priesthood. But other passages in the Bible as well as the Mishnah made a clear distinction between priests and Levites and certain tithes had been assigned to each. In 1 Sam 2:18 Samuel who is a Levite is said to wear the ephod; Targum changes the garment to a sleeved tunic because only priests were supposed to wear the ephod. 1 Sam 3:3 makes clear that Samuel sleeps in his proper place in the Temple, that is, in the court of the Levites and not just in the Temple of the Lord. When water is poured out, the action sounds like a libation taking place outside the Temple (1 Sam 7:6), so the Targum changes the act into a metaphoric expression for repentance: "They poured out their heart in repentance like water." In the aftermath of the sacrifice of Jephthah's daughter, an act which the Targum considers repulsive, the targumist (Judg 11:39) both articulates a law against child sacrifice and suggests that if Jephthah had consulted the priest Phinehas, he would have been correctly instructed not to carry out his vow.

Other changes are brought about by the theology of the targumist; many of these changes have been dealt with under the previous section on expressions concerning God. A few more may be pointed out. The theophoric element "baal" in names is often removed (Josh 11:17; 12:7; 13:5; Judg 3:3; 2 Sam 5:20). *Ba'ālê* meaning "masters of" a town, is interpreted correctly to mean the "inhabitants of" (Josh 24:11; Judg 9:2). The expression of woe, "Alas," addressed to God becomes the more prayerful "Accept my prayer" (Josh 7:7). Any hint of a lack of reverence is guarded against. The question asked of God "What will you do?" becomes the more positive confession, "You are acting (or you will act)" (Josh 7:9). When the Bible notes that Joshua could not drive out the inhabitants of the plain (Judg 1:19), the Targum guards God's omnipotence and Israel's chosen status by explaining "Because they sinned, they were not able to..." In Judg 3:19 and 26 Ehud turned back "at the carved idols which are near Gilgal"; the Targum does not want idols as landmarks in Israel, so it changes them into "quarries."

A variety of other additions, interpretations, regularizations, and clarifications are made in the Targum. The "commander of the army of the Lord" becomes the more normal "angel sent from before the Lord" (Josh 5:14-15). In other places the "angel of the Lord" becomes "the prophet by commission from before the Lord" (Judg 2:1, 4; 5:23). Both are messengers and the Targum interchanges them. The Anakim (Josh 11:21) and Rephaim (Josh 12:4) become "giants." Joshua 6:9, 13 make a cryptic reference to the "rearguard." The Targum identifies the rearguard as the tribe of Dan on the basis of Num 10:25. Some explanations are based on interpretations presumed from the tradition. When Saul is rejected from the kingship by Samuel, his original accession is explained as based on the merit of his tribe, Benjamin, which was the first into the water during the Exodus (1 Sam 15:17). The interpretation that Benjamin was first into the water is found in rabbinic literature, for example Mekilta, Beshallah 6 (Lauterbach 1:232). Sometimes biblical names are translated in a meaningful way by the Targum. "Shebarim," a place where a battle is fought in Josh 7:5, is translated as a clause "until they broke them." "Cushan-rishathaim," a king who is an opponent of Israel, becomes "Cushan the sinner; the root of his name is interpreted as $r\check{s}^\varsigma$ which means wicked. Oddities are also removed. Josh 24:27 has the stone of witness hearing Israel's words and the Targum rewrites the verse to eliminate this. Finally, customs are harmonized. When Samson wishes to marry a Philistine woman, his father goes to speak with the woman (Judg 14:10). The proper procedure is for the parents to confer, so the Targum leaves open this possibility by the more general "his father went down regarding the matter of the woman."

Date and Place of Origin

In his pioneering work *Targum Jonathan to the Prophets* (New Haven: Yale University, 1927; reprinted, New York: Ktav; Baltimore: Baltimore Hebrew College, 1983), Pinkhos Churgin argued that the official Targums (Onqelos and Jonathan) "were formed and reformed through many centuries, gradually, invisibly" (p. 36 = 264) up to the Arab invasion. According to Churgin, several features suggest an early beginning of this process in Palestine and a fairly fixed form by the time of Rabbi Aqiba: textual deviations with respect to the Masoretic text, unacceptable halakhah, elimination of anthropomorphisms, the term Memra, and allusions to historical events.

The review of other research on Targum Jonathan led Leivy Smolar and Moses Aberbach in *Studies in Targum Jonathan to the Prophets* (New York: Ktav; Baltimore: Baltimore Hebrew College, 1983) to the same basic conclusion: Targum Jonathan is "a late first century-early second century work which originated and was first developed in the land of Israel before being brought to Babylonia where it was redacted prior to the Arab invasion. As such, it is a prime resource for the study of early Rabbinic Judaism and early Christianity" (p. xxviii). In the body of their book, Smolar and Aberbach first show that Targum Jonathan retrojected into biblical times the halakhic rulings of the rabbinic period (in particular, those of Rabbi Aqiba and his students) on a variety of issues: legal order, vows, oaths, worship, calendar, education, kingship, idolatry, priests, altars, laws, God, women, sexuality, and the life cycle. Then they explain how Targum Jonathan reflects the Second Temple period and its aftermath by its allusions to historical events from Maccabean times to the third century C.E., its retrojections of contemporary conditions into biblical times, and its identifications of tribes and places with contemporary peoples and places. Finally they argue that the theology of Targum Jonathan is identical with that of orthodox Judaism as developed by the Pharisees and rabbis (especially Rabbi Aqiba).

Thus Churgin and Smolar-Aberbach agree that much of the material contained in Targum Jonathan reflects conditions in second-century C.E. Palestine, especially in the circle of Rabbi Aqiba. But they also admit that the present form(s) of Targum Jonathan is the result of a long process reaching into the Babylonian Jewish community and up to the Arab invasion (seventh century C.E.).[9] The problem is, of course, determining

---

[9]S.H. Levey, "The Date of Targum Jonathan to the Prophets," *Vetus Testamentum* 21 (1971) 186-96. On the basis of the expansion of 2 Samuel 22:32 and the Armilus passage in Isaiah 11:4, L. concludes that the *terminus ad quem* cannot be earlier than the Arab conquest of Babylonia. He suggests that the Targum bears the mark of Saadia Gaon.

which material is early and which is late. It is faulty logic to assume that, since some material in Targum Jonathan is Palestinian and "Aqiban," everything except what is manifestly late is also Palestinian and Aqiban. Churgin and Smolar-Aberbach (and other Targum specialists who work along the same lines) have shown the presence of early traditions in Targum Jonathan. Nevertheless, it is important to bear in mind what they also admit about the long and complex redactional history of the work.

Editions

The edition on which this translation is based is Alexander Sperber's *The Bible in Aramaic. Volume II: The Former Prophets According to Targum Jonathan* (Leiden: Brill, 1959). Sperber took as his basic text MS. Or. 2210 (p) of the British Museum, deviating from it only in cases of obvious scribal errors. In his critical apparatus he gave readings from representative manuscripts and printed texts. These representative manuscripts have been listed above under "Witnesses to the Text." The printed editions ("incunabula and rare books") include *Prophetae priores* (Leiria, 1494), *Biblia Rabbinica* (Bomberg-Venice, 1515/17), and the Antwerp Polyglot Bible (1569/73). There have been no complete English translations of the Targums,[10] nor do we know of complete translations in any other language.

This Translation

This volume provides a literal translation of MS. Or. 2210 of the British Museum, which is the basic text of Sperber's edition. The translation tries to reflect the imagery and syntax of the Aramaic original, thus allowing the reader to get a feel for the Aramaic as opposed to the Hebrew. In some cases, however, where the Aramaic idiom differs slightly from the Hebrew idiom, the difference cannot be reflected well in English. The substantive deviations from the Masoretic Text are printed in italic type, and the wording of the Hebrew original is noted below. Only rarely have we included comments on textual variants; those interested in such matters must consult Sperber's apparatus. (See "Witnesses to the Text" above.)

Our notes at the foot of the pages give special attention to Targum Jonathan's relationship to the Masoretic text. Since Targum Jonathan is a careful translation of the Hebrew original, the best service we can provide is to illustrate specifically and concretely the nature of its translation. We have profited greatly from the material contained in Smolar and Aberbach's *Studies in Targum Jonathan to the Prophets* and included many of their observations; those interested in further research should consult that book. In presenting our single apparatus of numbered notes, we depart somewhat from the usual format of volumes in this project. For these books which are not nearly

---

[10]For translations of 1 Samuel 2:7-10; 2 Samuel 22:28-32; 23:1-5; and 1 Kings 5:13, see S.H. Levey, *The Messiah: An Aramaic Interpretation. The Messianic Exegesis of the Targumim* (Monographs of the Hebrew Union College 2; Cincinnati–New York–Los Angeles–Jerusalem: Hebrew Union College-Jewish Institute of Religion, 1974) 34-42.

so complicated as the Targums of the Pentateuch and have comparatively few ancient parallels, it seemed to be the most efficient procedure.

Select Bibliography

Pinkhos Churgin, *Targum Jonathan to the Prophets* (Yale Oriental Series 14; New Haven, CT: Yale University Press, 1927; reprint, Library of Biblical Studies; New York: Ktav, 1983; Baltimore: Baltimore Hebrew College).

Leivy Smolar and Moses Aberbach, *Studies in Targum Jonathan to the Prophets* (Library of Biblical Studies; New York: Ktav, 1983; Baltimore: Baltimore Hebrew College).

Alexander Sperber, *The Bible in Aramaic. Volume II: The Former Prophets According to Targum Jonathan* (Leiden: Brill, 1959).

_____, *The Bible in Aramaic Based on Old Manuscripts and Printed Texts. Volume IV B: The Targum and the Hebrew Bible* (Leiden: Brill, 1973).

Abraham Tal (Rosenthal). *Lšwn htrqwm lnby'ym r'šwnym wm'mdh bkll nyby h'rmyt (The Targum of the Former Prophets and its Position within the Aramaic Dialects)* (Texts and Studies in the Hebrew Language and Related Subjects 1; Tel Aviv: Tel-Aviv University, 1975).

In connection with our translation, we prepared the following papers:

Daniel J. Harrington, "The Apocalypse of Hannah: Targum Jonathan of 1 Samuel 2:1-10," in Thomas O. Lambdin *Festschrift,* forthcoming.

_____, "The Prophecy of Deborah: Interpretive Homiletics in Targum Jonathan of Judges 5," *CBQ* 48 (1986) (432-42).

Anthony J. Saldarini, "'Is Saul Also Among the Scribes?': Scribes and Prophets in Targum Jonathan," *Essays on Aggadah and Judaica for Rabbi William G. Braude* (New York: Ktav, 1986).

JOSHUA

CHAPTER 1

1. And after Moses the servant of the Lord died, the Lord said to Joshua the son of Nun, the minister of Moses, saying: 2. "Moses my servant is dead. And now arise, cross this Jordan, you and all this people, to the land that I am giving to them, to the sons of Israel. 3. Every place in which the sole of your foot will step, I have given it to you according to what I spoke with Moses. 4. From the wilderness and this Lebanon and unto the great river, the river Euphrates, all the land of the Hittites and unto the great sea toward the setting of the sun will be your territory. 5. No man will take a stand before you all the days of your life. *As my Memra was at the aid of Moses, so my Memra will be at your aid.*[1] I will not forsake you, and I will not reject you. 6. Be strong and be powerful, for you will make this people take possession of the land that I swore to their fathers to give to them. 7. Only be strong and be very powerful to be careful to act according to all the law that Moses my servant commanded you. You shall not turn from it to the right and to the left, in order that you may prosper in every place that you go. 8. Let not this book of the law pass from your mouth, and you shall be meditating on it day and night, in order that you may be careful to act according to everything that is written in it, for thus you will make your ways prosperous and thus you will succeed. 9. Have I not commanded you? Be strong and be powerful. You shall not fear and you shall not be broken, for *the Memra of the Lord your God is at your aid*[2] in every place that you go." 10. And Joshua commanded the leaders of the people, saying: 11. "Pass in the midst of the camp and command the people, saying: 'Prepare for yourselves traveling supplies, for *at the end of*[3] three days you are crossing this Jordan to enter to possess the land that the Lord your God is giving to you to possess it.'" 12. And to *the tribe of Reuben and to the tribe of Gad*[4] and to the half tribe of Manasseh, Joshua said, saying: 13. "*Be mindful of*[5] the word that Moses the servant of the Lord commanded you, saying: 'The Lord your God is giving rest to you and giving to you this land.' 14. Your wives, your children, and your cattle will dwell in the land that Moses gave to you across the Jordan. And you will cross, armed, before your brothers, all the men of valor; and you will help them, 15. until the Lord will give rest to your brothers as to you, and they will also possess the land that the Lord your God is giving to them and you will return to the land of your possession, and you will possess that which Moses

Notes, Chapter One

[1]MT: "As I was with Moses, I will be with you."

[2]MT: "the Lord your God is with you."

[3]MT: "within."

[4]MT: "the Reubenite and the Gadite."

[5]The Aramaic verb is plural, as opposed to the Hebrew singular "remember."

the servant of the Lord gave to you across the Jordan toward the sunrise." 16. And they answered Joshua, saying: "Everything that you have commanded us, we will do; and every place that you will send us, we will go. 17. *As we accepted from Moses, so we will accept from you.*[6] Only may *the Memra of the Lord your God be at your aid as it was at the aid of Moses.*[7] 18. Every man who will rebel against your word and will not accept[8] your words for everything that you will command him, *will be killed.*[9] Only be strong and powerful."

CHAPTER 2

1. And Joshua the son of Nun sent two men from Shittim, as spies in secret, saying: "Go, look at the land and Jericho." And they went and entered the house of the harlot woman, and her name was Rahab; and they slept there. 2. And it was told to the king of Jericho, saying: "Behold men came here by night from the sons of Israel to spy out the land." 3. And the king of Jericho sent unto Rahab, saying: "Bring forth the men who came unto you, who entered your house, for they came to spy out all the land." 4. And the woman took the two men and hid them. And she said: "*In truth*[1] the men came unto me, and I did not know where they were from. 5. And it was *time*[2] to close the gate at dark, and the men went forth. I do not know where the men went. Pursue after them quickly, for you will overtake them." 6. And she brought them up to the roof and hid them in the loads of flax that were arranged for her on the roof. 7. And the men pursued after them by way of the Jordan to the fords. And they closed the gate after the pursuers went forth after them. 8. And when they had not yet fallen asleep, she came up unto them to the roof. 9. And she said to the men: "I know that the Lord has given to you the land, and that fear of you has fallen upon us, and that all the inhabitants of the land are shattered before you. 10. For we heard that the Lord was drying up the waters of the Red Sea before you when you were going forth from Egypt and what you did to the two kings of the Amorite who were across the Jordan, to Sihon and to Og, whom you destroyed utterly. 11. And we heard, and our heart was melted, and there was no spirit left in any man before you, for the Lord your God is the God *whose Shekinah*[3] is in the heavens above and is powerful over the earth below. 12. And now swear now for me by *the Memra of the Lord,*[4] for I have acted kindly with you and you will also act kindly with the house of my father. And you will give to me a sign of truth. 13. And you will let live my father and mother and my brothers and my sisters and everything that is

Notes, Chapter One (Cont.)

[6]The Aramaic verb "accept" is not as concrete as the Hebrew "hear," though the meaning is basically the same. MT: "Just as we listened to Moses, so we will listen to you."

[7]MT: "the Lord your God be with you as he was with Moses."

[8]MT: "hear."

[9]MT: "will be put to death."

Notes, Chapter Two

[1]MT: "thus," meaning "yes."

[2]MT lacks the word.

[3]MT lacks the expression.

[4]MT: "the Lord."

theirs. And you will save our lives from death." 14. And the men said to her: "Our lives *are handed over*[5] in place of your lives to die. If you do not tell this affair of ours, then when the Lord will give us the land, we will do goodness and truth with you." 15. And she let them down by rope from the window, for her house was in the city wall and in the wall she was living. 16. And she said to them: "Go to the hill country, lest the pursuers happen upon you; and hide yourselves there three days until the pursuers return. And afterwards you will go on your way." 17. And the men said to her: "We are innocent regarding this oath of yours that you swore upon us. 18. Behold we are entering the land. This band of red cord you will tie in the window, by which you let us down. And your father and your mother and your brothers and all the house of your father will gather unto you to the house. 19. And everyone who will go forth *out*[6] from the doors of your house to the outside, *the guilt of his killing*[7] will be on his own head; and we will be innocent. And everyone who will be with you in the house, *the guilt of his killing*[8] will be on our head, if *the hand of a man*[9] will be on him. 20. And if you tell this affair of ours, we will be innocent of the oath that you swore upon us." 21. And she said: "According to your words, so it is." And she sent them away, and they went, and she tied a band of red on the window. 22. And they went and entered the hill country and dwelt there three days until the pursuers returned. And the pursuers searched on all the way and did not find (them). 23. And the two men returned and came down from the hill country and crossed over and came unto Joshua the son of Nun. And they told him everything that happened to them. 24. And they said to Joshua that "the Lord has given into our hands all the land," and that "all the inhabitants of the land are shattered before us."

CHAPTER 3

1. And Joshua got up early in the morning, and they moved from Shittim and came unto the Jordan, he and all the sons of Israel; and they spent the night there before they crossed over. 2. And at the end of three days the leaders passed through in the midst of the camp. 3. And they commanded the people, saying: "When you see the ark of the covenant of the Lord your God and the levitical priests carrying it, you will move from your place and go after it. 4. But let there be a distance between you and between it of about 2,000 cubits by measure; you shall not draw near unto it, in order that you may know the way in which you are to go, for you have not passed on the way yesterday or before it." 5. And Joshua said to the people: "*Prepare*[1] yourselves, for tomorrow the

Notes, Chapter Two (Cont.)

[5]MT lacks the verb.
[6]MT lacks the word.
[7]MT: "his blood."
[8]MT: "his blood."

[9]MT: "a hand."

Notes, Chapter Three

[1]MT: "Sanctify." Tg reserves sanctifying to the priests.

Lord will work wonders among you." 6. And Joshua said to the priests, saying: "Take up the ark of the covenant, and pass before the people." And they took up the ark of the covenant and came before the people. 7. And the Lord said to Joshua: "This day I will begin to magnify you in the eyes of all Israel who will know that as *my Memra was at the aid of Moses, so my Memra will be at your aid.*[2] 8. And you will command the priests carrying the ark of the covenant, saying: 'As you reach the edge of the waters of the Jordan, in the Jordan you will stand.'" 9. And Joshua said to the sons of Israel: "Draw near here and hear the words of the Lord your God." 10. And Joshua said: "By this you will know that *the living God has chosen to make his Shekinah reside in your midst.*[3] And he will indeed drive out from before you *the Canaanites and the Hittites and the Hivvites and the Perizzites and the Girgashites and the Amorites and the Jebusites.*[4] 11. Behold the ark of the covenant of the master of all the earth is passing before you in the Jordan. 12. And now take for yourselves twelve men from the tribes of Israel — one man for each tribe. 13. And when the soles of the feet of the priests carrying the ark of the Lord, master of all the earth, rest in the waters of the Jordan, the waters of the Jordan will be cut off. The waters coming down from above will stand in one heap."[5] 14. And when the people moved out from their tents[6] to cross the Jordan, and the priests carrying the ark of the covenant of the Lord were before the people, 15. and when the bearers of the ark reached the Jordan, and the feet of the priests carrying the ark were immersed in the edge of the waters — and the Jordan overflows all its banks all the days of the harvest, 16. the waters coming down from above stood still; they stood in one heap, very far off from Adam, the city that is beside Zarethan. And those (waters) coming down to the sea of *the plain,*[7] the Sea of Salt, were completely cut off. And the people crossed opposite Jericho. 17. And the priests carrying the ark of the covenant of the Lord stood firmly on the dry ground in the midst of the Jordan. And all Israel was crossing on the dry ground, until all the people finished crossing the Jordan.

CHAPTER 4

1. And when all the people finished crossing the Jordan, the Lord said to Joshua, saying: 2. "Take for yourselves from the people twelve men — one man from each tribe. 3. And command them, saying: 'Take up for yourselves from here, from the midst of the Jordan, from the place where the feet of the priests stood firm, twelve stones. And you will take them across with you and put them down in the lodging-place in which you will camp tonight.'" 4. And Joshua called twelve men whom he appointed from the

---

Notes, Chapter Three (Cont.)

[2]MT: "as I was with Moses, so I will be with you."

[3]MT: "the living God is in your midst."

[4]MT has singular (i.e., collective) nouns.

[5]The Aramaic is literally "goatskin, bottle."

[6]A variant has "from their cities," a frequent "modernizing" of the MT "tents." S-A, 99.

[7]MT: "the Arabah." Tg consistently renders this as the generic term "plain" (Josh 8:14; 11:16; etc.).

sons of Israel, one man from each tribe. 5. And Joshua said to them: "Pass before the ark of the Lord your God in the midst of the Jordan; and lift up for yourselves, each man one stone upon his shoulder, according to the number of the tribes of the sons of Israel. 6. For this will be a sign among you, for in the future your sons will ask, saying: 'What are these stones to you?' 7. And you will say to them that the waters of the Jordan were cut off from before the ark of the covenant of the Lord. When it crossed the Jordan, the waters of the Jordan were cut off. And these stones will be for a memorial for the sons of Israel forever." 8. And so the sons of Israel did as Joshua commanded, and they took up twelve stones from the midst of the Jordan, according to what the Lord spoke with Joshua, according to the number of the tribes of the sons of Israel. And they took them across with them to the lodging place, and they deposited them there. 9. And Joshua set up the twelve stones in the midst of the Jordan, in the place where the feet of the priests carrying the ark of the covenant stood. And they are there until this day. 10. And the priests taking up the ark were standing in the midst of the Jordan until every word was fulfilled that the Lord commanded Joshua to speak with the people, according to everything that Moses commanded Joshua. And the people made haste and crossed over. 11. And when all the people finished crossing over, the ark of the Lord crossed, and the priests, before the people. 12. And the sons of Reuben and the sons of Gad and the half-tribe of Manasseh crossed, armed, before the sons of Israel as Moses spoke with them. 13. About 40,000 armed men of war crossed before the people of the Lord for battle to the plains of Jericho. 14. On that day the Lord magnified Joshua in the eyes of all Israel, and they were afraid of him just as they were afraid of Moses all the days of his life. 15. And the Lord said to Joshua, saying: 16. "Command the priests carrying the ark of the testimony, and they will come up from the Jordan." 17. And Joshua commanded the priests, saying: "Come up from the Jordan." 18. And when the priests carrying the ark of the covenant of the Lord *sought to come up*[1] from the midst of the Jordan, the soles of the feet of the priests *were drawn up and rested upon*[2] dry ground. And the waters of the Jordan returned to their place and came as yesterday and before it over all its banks. 19. And the people came up from the Jordan on the tenth of the first month[3] and camped in Gilgal at the eastern borders of Jericho. 20. And those twelves stones that they took from the Jordan, Joshua set up in Gilgal. 21. And he said to the sons of Israel, saying: "In the future your sons will ask their fathers, saying: 'What are these stones?' 22. And you will inform your sons, saying: 'On dry ground Israel crossed this Jordan.' 23. For the Lord your God dried up the waters of the Jordan from before you until you crossed, just as the Lord your God did to the Red Sea which he dried up from before us until we crossed, 24. in order that all the peoples of the earth may know the *might*[4] of the Lord that it is powerful, in order that you may be afraid of the Lord your God all the days."

Notes, Chapter Four

[1]MT: "came up."

[2]MT: "were lifted upon."

[3]A variant specifies "the month of Nisan."

[4]MT: "hand."

CHAPTER 5

1. And when all the kings of the Amorite who were across the Jordan to the west and all the kings of the Canaanite who were on the sea heard that the Lord dried up the waters of the Jordan from before the sons of Israel until they crossed, their heart was melted and no spirit was still left in them from before the sons of Israel. 2. At that time the Lord said to Joshua: "Make for yourself *sharp scalpels,*[1] and circumcise the sons of Israel again a second time." 3. And Joshua made for himself *sharp scalpels*[2] and circumcised the sons of Israel at *the hill, and he called it*[3] the hill of foreskins. 4. And this is the reason that Joshua circumcised: All the people who went forth from Egypt, the males, all the *men waging battle,*[4] died in the wilderness on the way when they went forth from Egypt. 5. For all the people who went forth were circumcised; and all the people who were born in the wilderness on the way when they went forth from Egypt, they did not circumcise. 6. For forty years the sons of Israel walked in the wilderness until all the people, the *men waging battle,*[5] who went forth from Egypt, perished, for *they did not accept the Memra of the Lord;*[6] for the Lord swore to them that he would not let them see the land that the Lord swore to their fathers to give to us, a land *producing*[7] milk and honey. 7. And their sons *who*[8] stood in their place, them Joshua circumcised, because they were uncircumcised, because they did not circumcise them on the way. 8. And when all the people were finished being circumcised, they remained in their place in the camp until they were healed. 9. And the Lord said to Joshua: "This day I have made pass away the *reproaches*[9] of the Egyptians from you." And he called the name of that place Gilgal until this day. 10. And the sons of Israel camped in Gilgal and kept the Passover on the fourteenth day of the month, at evening, in the plains of Jericho. 11. And they ate from the produce of the land *after*[10] the Passover — the unleavened bread and the parched grain, *the first fruits*[11] — *this day.*[12] 12. And the manna ceased on the day that was after the one on which they ate from the produce of the land. And there was no more manna for the sons of Israel. And they ate from the harvest of the land of Canaan in that year. 13. And when Joshua was in Jericho, he lifted up his eyes and saw. And behold a man was standing opposite him, and his sword was drawn in his hand. And Joshua came unto him and said to him: "Are you *coming*

Notes, Chapter Five

[1] MT: "flint knives." In talmudic times surgeons' scalpels were used for circumcision: *y. Shab.* 19.1 (16d); *b. Shab.* 130 a-b; S-A, 54.

[2] MT: "flint knives."

[3] MT: The phrase has been added by the targumist.

[4] MT: "men of war."

[5] MT: "men of war."

[6] MT: "they did not hear the voice of the Lord."

[7] MT: "flowing with."

[8] MT lacks the relative pronoun.

[9] MT has the singular form "reproach."

[10] MT: "on the morrow after." The change reflects the halakhic argument over when the sheaf is offered.

[11] MT lacks the word.

[12] MT: "on this very day."

to our aid[13] or to our enemies?" 14. And he said: "No; for I, *an angel sent from before the Lord,*[14] have come now." And Joshua fell *upon*[15] his face, *upon*[16] the earth, and bowed down and said to him: "What is my master speaking with his servant?" 15. And *the angel who was sent from before the Lord*[17] said to Joshua: "Loosen your shoes from upon your feet, for the place upon which you are standing is holy." And Joshua did so.

CHAPTER 6

1. And Jericho was closed up and *fortified*[1] from before the sons of Israel; no one *of them*[2] was going forth and entering. 2. And the Lord said to Joshua: "See that I have given in your hand Jericho and its king (and) warriors. 3. And you will march around the city, all the *men waging battle;*[3] encircle the city one time. Thus you will do six days. 4. And seven priests will carry seven trumpets of the ram's horn before the ark. And on the seventh day you will march around the city seven times. And the priests will blow on the horns. 5. And at the blast on the ram's horn, *as you hear*[4] the sound of the trumpet, all the people will shout a great shout, and the wall of the city will fall down, *and it will be swallowed up*[5] beneath it, and the people will go up, each man opposite him." 6. And Joshua the son of Nun called to the priests and said to them: "Take up the ark of the covenant." And the seven priests took up the seven trumpets of the ram's horn before the ark of the Lord. 7. And *he said*[6] to the people: "Pass on and encircle the city, and let the armed men pass before the ark of the Lord." 8. And as Joshua said to the people, the seven priests took up the seven trumpets of ram's horn *before the ark of the Lord,*[7] passing by and blowing on the horns. And the ark of the covenant of the Lord was going after them. 9. And the armed men were going before the priests blowing the trumpets. And *the tribe of the house of Dan*[8] was going after the ark, and the priests were going and blowing on the trumpets. 10. And Joshua commanded the people, saying: "You shall not shout, and you shall not make your voice heard, and let not a word go forth from your mouth until the day that I say to you: 'Shout,' and you will shout." 11. And he made the ark of the Lord go around the city, encircling it one

Notes, Chapter Five (Cont.)

[13]MT: "for us."

[14]MT: "the commander of the army of the Lord." In Tg a messenger is ordinarily an angel.

[15]MT: "to."

[16]MT: "to."

[17]MT: "the commander of the army of the Lord."

Notes, Chapter Six

[1]MT has an alternate form of the preceding verb, "closed up."

[2]MT lacks the prepositional phrase.

[3]MT: "men of war."

[4]Some MT mss. have "in (your hearing)." Tg and other MT mss. follow the *qere*.

[5]MT lacks the verb; see 6:20.

[6]MT: "they said." Tg agrees with *qere*.

[7]MT: "before the Lord."

[8]MT: "the rearguard"; see 6:13. In Num 10:25 the tribe of Dan acts as rearguard.

time. And they entered the camp and spent the night in the camp. 12. And Joshua got up early in the morning, and the priests carried the ark of the Lord. 13. And the seven priests took up the seven trumpets of ram's horn before the ark of the Lord, going and blowing on the trumpets. And the armed men were going before them, and *the tribe of the house of Dan,*[9] was going after the ark of the Lord. *And the priests were going and blowing*[10] on the trumpets. 14. And they marched around the city on the second day one time, and they returned to the camp. Thus they did six days. 15. And on the seventh day they got up early at the rising of the morning, and they marched around the city according to this custom, seven times. Only on that day they encircled the city seven times. 16. And at the seventh time, the priests blew on the trumpets. And Joshua said to the people: "Shout, for the Lord has given to you the city. 17. And the city will be a ban, it and everything that is in it, *before*[11] the Lord. Only Rahab the harlot will live, she and everyone who is with her in the house, for she hid the messengers whom we sent. 18. And only you, keep yourselves from the ban lest you declare banned and you take from the ban and you make the camp of Israel for the ban, and you trouble it. 19. And all the silver and the gold and the vessels of bronze and the iron are sacred *before*[12] the Lord. *To the treasury of the house of the sanctuary of the Lord they will be brought in.*"[13] 20. And the people shouted and blew on the trumpets. And when the people heard the sound of the trumpet, and the people shouted a great shout, *the wall of the city*[14] fell down *and it was swallowed up*[15] beneath it. And the people went up to the city, each man opposite him, and they conquered the city. 21. And they destroyed utterly everything that was in the city, from man and unto woman, from young and unto old, and unto cattle and sheep and asses, by the edge of the sword. 22. And to the two men who spied out the land, Joshua said: "Enter the house of the harlot woman, and bring forth from there the woman and all who are hers as you swore to her." 23. And the young men who were the spies entered and brought forth Rahab and her father and her mother and her brothers and everyone who was hers. And all her family they brought forth and had them camp outside the camp of Israel. 24. And they burned the city with fire, and everything that was in it. Only the silver and the gold and the vessels of bronze and the iron they gave in the treasury of *the house of the sanctuary of the Lord.*[16] 25. And Rahab the harlot and the house of her father and everyone who was in it, Joshua let live. And she dwelt in the midst of the *sons of Israel*[17] until this day, for she hid the messengers whom Joshua sent to spy out Jericho. 26. And Joshua made an oath at that time, saying: "Cursed be the man before the Lord who will rise up and build this city, Jericho. By his firstborn he will lay its foundation, and by the youngest *of his sons*[18] he will raise up its gate. 27. And *the Memra of the Lord was at the aid of Joshua,*[19] and his reputation *was great*[20] in all the land.

Notes, Chapter Six (Cont.)

[9]MT: "the rearguard"; see 6:9.

[10]Tg adds a subject ("the priests") and makes the infinitives into plural verbs in order to clarify the grammar.

[11]MT: "to."

[12]MT: "to."

[13]MT: "they will go to the treasury of the Lord.'

Tg anticipates the building of the Temple.

[14]MT: "a wall."

[15]MT lacks the verb; see Judg 6:5.

[16]MT: "the house of the Lord."

[17]MT: "Israel."

[18]MT lacks the word "of his sons."

[19]MT: "the Lord was with Joshua."

[20]The MT verb is simply "was."

CHAPTER 7

1. And the sons of Israel acted falsely in the ban; and Achan the son of Carmi, son of Zabdi, son of Zarah, belonging to the tribe of Judah, took from the ban. And anger of the Lord *was strong*[1] against the sons of Israel. 2. And Joshua sent men from Jericho to Ai, which is near Bethaven, east of Bethel; and he said to them, saying: "Go up and spy out the land." And the men went up and spied out Ai. 3. And they returned unto Joshua and said to him: "Let not all the people go up. Let about two thousand or about three thousand men go up and strike Ai. You shall not move all the people to there, for they are few." 4. And there went up from the people to there about three thousand men, and they fled before the men of Ai. 5. And the men of Ai *killed*[2] from them about thirty-six men and pursued them before the gate *until they broke them,*[3] and they struck them down on the descent. And the heart of the people was melted, and it was like water. 6. And Joshua tore his garments, and he fell on his face *upon*[4] the ground before the ark of the Lord until evening, he and the elders of Israel, and they brought up dust upon their heads. 7. And Joshua said: "*Accept my prayer,*[5] Lord God. Why have you made this people cross Jordan to give us in the hand of the Amorite to destroy us? And would that we had been content and dwelt across the Jordan! 8. Please, Lord, what shall I say after Israel turned their back *to go down*[6] before their enemies? 9. And *the Canaanites*[7] and all the inhabitants of the earth will hear, and they will surround us and destroy our name from the earth. And *you are acting*[8] on account of your great name." 10. And the Lord said to Joshua: "You arise. Why are you *lying*[9] thus upon your face? 11. Israel has sinned. And also they have transgressed against my covenant that I commanded them, and also they have taken from the ban, and also they have stolen, and also they have deceived, and also they have placed (them) in their own possession. 12. And the sons of Israel will not be able to stand before their enemies. They will turn their back *to go down*[10] before their enemies, for they are for the ban. *I will not let my Memra be at your aid anymore,*[11] unless you destroy the ban from among you. 13. Rise up, *prepare*[12] the people, and you will say: '*Prepare your-selves*[13] for tomorrow, for thus says the Lord, the God of Israel: "The ban is among

Notes, Chapter Seven

[1]MT: "burned"; see 7:26.

[2]MT: "struck down."

[3]MT: "as far as Shebarim." Tg is based on the meaning of the Semitic root of the name, "break." S-A, 125.

[4]MT: "to."

[5]MT: "Alas!" Tg turns an expression of dismay into a more reverent prayer.

[6]MT lacks the verb; see 7:12.

[7]MT: "the Canaanite."

[8]MT: "What will you do?" Tg protects God's omnipotence by changing the MT's question, "What will you do?" to an assertion.

[9]MT: "falling."

[10]MT lacks the verb; see 7:8.

[11]MT: "I will not be with you any more."

[12]MT: "sanctify."

[13]MT: "sanctify yourselves."

you, Israel. You will not be able to stand before your enemies until you remove the ban from among you." 14. And *you will draw near*[14] in the morning by your tribes; and let the tribe *that is singled out from before the Lord*[15] be brought near by families; and let the family *that is singled out from before the Lord*[15] draw near by households; and let the household *that is singled out from before the Lord*[15] be brought near by men. 15. And let him who *is singled out*[16] in the ban be burned in the fire, he and everything that is his, because he has transgressed against the covenant of the Lord and because he has done *what is not fitting*[17] in Israel." 16. And Joshua got up early in the morning and brought near Israel by its tribes. And *the tribe of the house of Judah was singled out.*[18] 17. And he brought near the family of Judah, and the family of Zarah *was singled out.*[19] And he brought near the family of Zarah by the men, and Zabdi *was singled out.*[20] 18. And he brought near his household by the men, and Achan the son of Carmi, son of Zabdi, son of Zarah, *was singled out*[21] for the tribe of Judah. 19. And Joshua said to Achan: "My son, now give glory *before*[22] the Lord the God of Israel, and give thanks *before*[23] him. And now tell me what you have done. Do not conceal from me." 20. And Achan answered Joshua and said: "In truth I have sinned *before*[24] the Lord the God of Israel, and thus and so I have done. 21. And I saw in the spoil one beautiful *Babylonian*[25] mantle, and 200 selas of silver, and one bar of gold, 50 selas was its weight. And I coveted them and took them, and behold they are hidden in the ground in the midst of my tent; and the silver is beneath *them.*"[26] 22. And Joshua sent messengers, and they ran to the tent; and behold they were hidden in his tent, and the silver beneath *them.*[27] 23. And they took them from the midst of the tent, and they brought them unto Joshua and unto all the sons of Israel, and they laid them out before the Lord. 24. And Joshua took Achan the son of Zarah, and he took the silver and the mantle and the bar of gold, and he took his sons and his daughters and his cattle and his asses and his sheep and his tent and everything that was his — and all Israel with him — and they brought them up to the valley of Achor. 25. And Joshua said: "Why have you troubled us? The Lord will trouble you on this day." And all Israel pelted him *with*[28] stones and burned them in the fire after they pelted them with stones. 26. And they raised up over him a large heap of stones until this day. And the Lord turned from *the force*[29] of his anger. Therefore he called the name of that place the valley of trouble (=Achor) until this day.

Notes, Chapter Seven (Cont.)

[14]The MT verb is passive, "you will be drawn near."

[15]MT has in all three cases "that the Lord chooses."

[16]MT: "is chosen."

[17]MT: "a shameful thing."

[18]MT: "the tribe of Judah was chosen."

[19]MT: "was chosen."

[20]MT: "was chosen."

[21]MT: "was chosen."

[22]MT: "to."

[23]MT: "to."

[24]MT: "against."

[25]MT: "Shinar." Shinar is Babylon in Gen 10:10 and 11:2.

[26]MT: "it."

[27]MT: "it."

[28]MT lacks the preposition.

[29]MT: "heat."

CHAPTER 8

1. And the Lord said to Joshua: "Do not fear, and do not be shattered. Take with you all *the people making war,*[1] and arise, go up to Ai. See that I have given in your hand the king of Ai and his people and his city and his land. 2. And you will do to Ai and to its king as you did to Jericho and to its king. Only its booty and its cattle you will take as spoil for yourselves. Set for yourself an ambush for the city, from behind it." 3. And Joshua and all the *people making war*[2] arose to go up to Ai. And Joshua chose 30,000 men, warriors, and sent them by night. 4. And he commanded them, saying: "See that you are lying in ambush for the city, from behind the city. Do not be very far from the city, and all of you be prepared. 5. And I and all the people who are with me will draw near to the city. And they will go forth to meet us as in the past, and *we will go forth*[3] before them. 6. And they will go forth after us until we draw them from the city, for they will say: '*They are shattered*[4] before us as in the past.' And *we will go forth*[5] before them. 7. And you will arise from the ambush, and you will seize the city, and the Lord your God will give it in your hand. 8. And when you have taken the city, you will burn the city with fire. According to the word of the Lord you shall act. See *what*[6] I have commanded you." 9. And Joshua sent them, and they went into ambush, and they sat between Bethel and Ai, west of Ai. And Joshua lodged on that night in the midst of the people. 10. And Joshua got up early in the morning and mustered the people. And he and the elders of Israel went up before the people to Ai. 11. And all the *people making war*[7] who were with him went up, and they drew near and came opposite the city. And they camped from the north of Ai, and the valley was between it and Ai. 12. And he took about 5,000 men and set them as an ambush between Bethel and Ai, *west of Ai.*[8] 13. And people set up the whole camp that was north of the city and its *ambush*[9] west of the city. And Joshua came on that night in the midst of the camp. 14. And when the king of Ai saw (it), the men of the city made haste and got up early and went forth to meet Israel, *to wage battle*[10] — he and all his people — at the time that was appointed for him, before the plain. And *they*[11] did not know that there was an ambush for *them*[12] from behind the city. 15. And Joshua and all Israel were shattered before them, and they fled by way of the wilderness. 16. And all

---

Notes, Chapter Eight

[1] MT: "the people of war."
[2] MT: "the people of war."
[3] MT: "we will flee."
[4] MT: "They are fleeing."
[5] MT: "we will flee."
[6] MT lacks the word "what."

[7] MT: "people of war."
[8] Most MT mss. have "the city." Tg agrees with the Vulgate and some Greek mss. here, though some Tg. manuscripts have "the city."
[9] MT: "rearguard."
[10] MT: "for war."
[11] MT: "he."
[12] MT: "him."

the people who were in *Ai*[13] were gathered together to pursue after them, and they pursued after Joshua and were drawn from the city. 17. And there was not a man left in Ai and Bethel who did not go forth after Israel. And they left the city *while it was opened*[14] and pursued after Israel. 18. And the Lord said to Joshua: "Lift up the spear that is in your hand against Ai, for I have given it in your hand." And Joshua lifted up the spear that was in his hand against the city. 19. And the ambush arose in haste from its place, and they ran when he lifted up his hand, and they entered the city and conquered it and made haste and set the city aflame with fire. 20. And the men of Ai turned around behind them and saw. And behold the smoke of the city went up toward the heavens. And there was no *strength*[15] in them to flee here or there. And the people who fled to the wilderness turned back against the pursuer. 21. And Joshua and all Israel saw that the ambush conquered the city and that the smoke of the city went up. And they returned and struck down the men of Ai. 22. And those (others) went forth from the city to meet them, and they were in the middle for Israel — the ones from here, and the others from there — and they struck them down until there was not left for *them*[16] a survivor or a refugee. 23. And they captured the king of Ai *while he was alive*[17] and brought him unto Joshua. 24. And when Israel finished killing all the inhabitants of Ai in the field in the wilderness in which they were pursuing them, all of them *were killed*[18] by the edge of the sword until they were entirely finished off, all Israel returned to Ai and struck it down by the edge of the sword. 25. And all those *who were killed*[19] on that day from man and unto woman were 12,000, all the men of Ai. 26. And Joshua did not turn back his hand with which he had lifted up the spear until he had destroyed completely all the inhabitants of Ai. 27. Only the cattle and the booty of that city Israel took for themselves as spoil according to the word of the Lord that he commanded Joshua. 28. And Joshua set Ai aflame and made it *a mound of ruin*[20] forever to be desolate until this day. 29. And he hanged the king of Ai upon the *gallows*[21] until evening time. And at sunset Joshua commanded, and they took down his corpse from the *gallows*[22] and cast it at the entrance of the gate of the city. And they raised up over it a great heap of stones until this day. 30. Then Joshua built an altar *before*[23] the Lord God of Israel on Mount Ebal, 31. as Moses the servant of the Lord commanded the sons of Israel, as it is written in the book of the law of Moses, an altar of perfect stones over which *the iron was never lifted up*[24] and they brought up upon it holocausts *before*[25] the Lord and sacrificed *holy sacrifices.*[26] 32. And he wrote there upon the stones a copy of the law of Moses, which he wrote before the sons of Israel. 33. And all Israel and its elders and its leaders and its judges were standing on opposite sides of the ark before the levitical priests carrying the ark of the covenant of the Lord,

Notes, Chapter Eight (Cont.)

[13]Tg agrees with other ancient texts against the MT "city," though some Tg mss. have "in the city" or "in the city, in Ai."

[14]MT: simply "open."

[15]MT has the metaphorical term "hands."

[16]MT: "him."

[17]MT: simply "alive."

[18]MT: "fell."

[19]MT: "fell."

[20]MT: simply "a mound."

[21]MT: "tree." S-A, 98 suggest that the "gallows" (*s̆ĕlîbāʾ*) is a cross.

[22]MT: "tree."

[23]MT: "to."

[24]MT: "no (man) has lifted an iron (tool)."

[25]MT: "to."

[26]MT: "peace offerings."

foreigner[27] as well as native citizen, half of them opposite Mount Gerizim and half of them opposite Mount Ebal, as Moses the servant of the Lord commanded formerly to bless the people Israel. 34. And afterwards he read all the words of the law, *blessings and curses*,[28] according to everything that is written in the book of the law. 35. There was no word from everything that Moses commanded that Joshua did not read before all the assembly of Israel and the women and the children and the foreigners who were coming among them.

CHAPTER 9

1. And when all the kings heard, those who were across the Jordan in the hill country and in the lowland and in all the coast of the Gread Sea *which is*[1] toward Lebanon, the Hittites, and the Amorites, the Canaanites, the Perizzites, and the Hivvites and the Jebusites, 2. they gathered together *to wage battle*[2] with Joshua and with Israel as one *company*.[3] 3. And the inhabitants of Gibeon heard what Joshua had done to Jericho and to Ai. 4. And they also acted with *wisdom*.[4] And they came and gathered provisions and took worn-out sacks for their asses and bags of wine — worn-out and torn and mended, 5. and worn-out and patched shoes on their feet, and worn-out clothing upon them; and all the bread of their provisions was dry and crumbling. 6. And they came unto Joshua, to the camp, to Gilgal, and said to him and to the man of Israel: "From a far country we have come, and now cut a covenant for us." 7. And the man of Israel said to the Hivvite: "Perhaps you are dwelling among us; and how *will we cut*[5] a covenant for you?" 8. And they said to Joshua: "We are your servants." And Joshua said to them: "Who are you, and where did you come from?" 9. And they said to him: "From a very far country your servants have come for the name of the Lord your God, for we heard *a report of his power*[6] and all that he did in Egypt, 10. and everything that he did to the two kings of the Amorites who were across the Jordan, to Sihon the king of Heshbon and to Og the king of *Matnan*[7] which is in Ashtaroth. 11. And our elders and all the inhabitants of our land said to us, saying: 'Take in your hands provisions for the way, and go to meet them; and you will say to them: "We are your servants, and now cut for us a covenant." 12. This bread of ours when it was hot, we took it as provisions from our houses on the day of our setting forth to come unto you. And now

Notes, Chapter Eight (Cont.)

[27]The Aramaic *gîyôrā'* also means proselyte. See 8:35 also.

[28]The nouns are singular ("the blessing and the curse") in MT.

Notes, Chapter Nine

[1]MT lacks the relative pronoun "which (is)."

[2]MT: "to fight."
[3]MT: "mouth."
[4]MT: "cunning." Tg uses a less pejorative word.
[5]MT: "will I cut."
[6]MT: "a report of him."
[7]MT: "Bashan." Matnan was probably the Aramaic name for Bashan and another form of Batanaea (S-A, 115). It is used consistently in Tg.

behold it is dry, and it is crumbling. 13. And these bags of wine that we filled when they were new, and behold they are torn; and these shirts of ours and shoes of ours are worn out from the very greatness of the way.' " 14. And the men accepted *their words*[8] and did not seek *instruction from before*[9] the Lord. 15. And Joshua made peace with them and cut a covenant for them to let them live; and the chiefs of the congregation swore to them. 16. And at the end of three days, after they had cut a covenant for them, they heard that they were neighbors to him and they were dwelling in *their*[10] midst. 17. And the sons of Israel set out and came to their cities on the third day. And their cities were Gibeon and Cephirah and Beeroth and Kiriath-jearim. 18. And the sons of Israel did not strike them down, for the chiefs of the congregation swore to them by *the Memra of the Lord*[11] the God of Israel. And all the congregation was murmuring against the chiefs. 19. And all the chiefs said to all the congregation: "We have sworn to them by *the Memra of the Lord*[12] the God of Israel, and now we cannot harm them. 20. This we will do to them, and *we will let them live,*[13] and there will be no wrath against us on account of the oath that we swore to them." 21. And the chiefs said to them: "Let them live; and let them be *gatherers of wood and fillers of water*[14] for all the congregation, as the chiefs spoke to them." 22. And Joshua called to them and spoke with them, saying: "Why did you deceive us saying: 'We are very far from you,' and you are dwelling among us. 23. And now you are cursed, and there will not cease from you *slaves and gatherers of wood and fillers of water for the house of the sanctuary*[15] of my God." 24. And they answered Joshua and said: "Because indeed it was told to your servants that the Lord your God commanded Moses his servant to give to you all the land and to destroy all the inhabitants of the land from before you, we were very much afraid for our lives from before you and we did this thing. 25. And now behold *we are given over*[16] in your hand. According to what is good and what is right in your eye to do to us, do." 26. And so he did to them, and he saved them from the hand of the sons of Israel, and they did not kill them. 27. And Joshua *appointed*[17] them in that time *gatherers of wood and fillers of water*[18] for the congregation and for the altar of the Lord until this day, for the place that *would be chosen.*[19]

CHAPTER 10

1. And when Adoni-zedek the king of Jerusalem heard that Joshua had conquered Ai and destroyed it completely — as he had done to Jericho and to its king, thus he did

Notes, Chapter Nine (Cont.)

[8] MT: "their provisions." The Aramaic term "words" can also mean "things," and so perhaps the difference is not too great.

[9] MT: "the mouth of."

[10] MT: "his."

[11] MT: "the Lord."

[12] MT: "the Lord."

[13] MT: "let him live."

[14] MT: "hewers of wood and drawers of water."

[15] MT: "a slave and hewers of wood and drawers of water for the house."

[16] MT: "we are."

[17] MT: "gave them."

[18] MT: "hewers of wood and drawers of water."

[19] MT: "he will choose."

to Ai and to its king — and that the inhabitants of Gibeon had made peace with Israel, and they were among them, 2. they were very afraid because Gibeon was a great city like one of the cities of the kingdom and because it was greater than Ai and all its men were mighty. 3. And Adoni-zedek the king of Jerusalem sent unto Hoham the king of Hebron and unto Piram the king of Yarmuth and unto Japhia the king of Lachish and unto Debir the king of Eglon, saying: 4. "Come up unto me and help me, and we will strike down Gibeon, because it made peace with Joshua and with the sons of Israel." 5. And the five kings of the Amorite — the king of Jerusalem, the king of Hebron, the king of Yarmuth, the king of Lachish, the king of Eglon — they and all their armies gathered and went up and camped against Gibeon and *waged battle*[1] against it. 6. And the men of Gibeon sent unto Joshua, to the camp, to Gilgal, saying: "Do not loosen your hand from your servants. Come up unto us in haste and save us and help us, for all the kings of the Amorite, the inhabitants of the hill country, have gathered against us." 7. And Joshua went up from Gilgal, he and all *the people making war,*[2] with him, and all the warriors. 8. And the Lord said to Joshua: "Do not be afraid of them, for I have given them in your hand and no man of them will take a stand before you." 9. And Joshua came unto them suddenly; all night he went up from Gilgal. 10. And the Lord *shattered them*[3] before Israel, and *they struck*[4] them a great blow in Gibeon and *pursued*[4] them on the way of the ascent of Beth-horon, and *struck*[4] them down unto Azekah and unto Makkedah. 11. And in their *going forth*[5] from before Israel they were in the descent of Beth-horon, and *from before the Lord great stones were cast down*[6] upon them from the heavens until *they came*[7] to Azekah and they died. There were more who died by the hailstones than the sons of Israel killed by the sword. 12. Then Joshua *sang praise before*[8] the Lord on the day that the Lord gave over the Amorites before the sons of Israel. And he said in the sight of Israel: "Sun, tarry in Gibeon; and moon, in the plain of Aijalon." 13. And the sun tarried, and the moon stood still until *the people of Israel were rescued from their enemies.*[9] Is it not written in the book of *the law?*[10] And the sun stood still in the half of the heavens, and it did not push on to set about a whole day. 14. And there was nothing like that day before it and after it, that *the prayer of a man was accepted before the Lord,*[11] for *the Lord by his Memra waged battle*[12] for Israel. 15. And Joshua and all Israel with him returned to the camp, to Gilgal. 16. And these five kings fled and hid themselves in the cave at Makkedah. 17. And it was told to Joshua, saying: "The five kings have been found, hidden in the cave in Makkedah." 18. And Joshua said: "*Bring near*[13] great stones to the mouth of the cave, and appoint over it men to guard them. 19. And you, do not stay there. Pursue after your enemies and overtake them. Do not let them enter their cities, for the Lord your God had given them in your hand." 20. And when Joshua and the sons of Israel

Notes, Chapter Ten

[1]MT: "fought."

[2]MT: "the people of war."

[3]MT: "confused them."

[4]The plural verbs make it clear that Israel, not the Lord, is directly involved in the battle.

[5]MT: "fleeing."

[6]MT: "the Lord cast down great stones."

[7]MT lacks the verb.

[8]MT: "spoke to."

[9]MT: "the nation took vengeance from its enemies." Tg stresses God's action rather than Israel's.

[10]MT: "Jashar." For rabbinic identifications of the Book of Yashar (Jashar), see *b. A.Z.* 25b; *y. Sota* 1:10 (17c); *Gen. Rab.* 6:9. Genesis and Deuteronomy are both proposed.

[11]MT: "the Lord heard the voice of a man."

[12]MT: "the Lord fought."

[13]MT: "roll."

finished striking them a very great blow until they were wiped out, and those of them who escaped had escaped and entered the fortified cities, 21. all the people returned to the camp, unto Joshua, to Makkedah in peace. *There was no harm for the sons of Israel, for a man to afflict himself.*[14] 22. And Joshua said: "Open the mouth of the cave, and bring forth unto me these five kings from the cave." 23. And they did so and brought forth unto him these five kings from the cave — the king of Jerusalem, the king of Hebron, the king of Yarmuth, the king of Lachish, the king of Eglon. 24. And when they brought forth these kings unto Joshua, Joshua called to all the men of Israel and said to the rulers of the *men making war*[15] who came with him: "Draw near, set your feet upon the necks of these kings." And they drew near and set their feet upon their necks. 25. And Joshua said to them: "Do not be afraid and do not be shattered. Be strong and powerful, for thus the Lord will do to all your enemies against whom you are *waging battle.*"[16] 26. And Joshua struck them down afterwards and killed them and hanged them upon five *gallows,*[17] and they were hanged upon the *gallows*[18] until evening. 27. And at the time of sunset Joshua commanded, and they brought them down from upon the *gallows,*[19] and they cast them into the cave where they hid themselves, and they set great stones upon the mouth of the cave until this very day. 28. And Joshua conquered Makkedah on that day and struck it down by the edge of the sword, and its king. He destroyed completely them and all the living things that were in it. He did not leave a survivor. And he did to the king of Makkedah as he had done to the king of Jericho. 29. And Joshua and all Israel with him crossed from Makkedah to Libnah, and he *waged battle*[20] with Libnah. 30. And the Lord gave it also in the hand of Israel, and its king. And he struck it down by the edge of the sword and all the living things that were in it. He did not leave in it a survivor. And he did to its king as he had done to the king of Jericho. 31. And Joshua and all Israel with him passed from Libnah to Lachish, and he camped against it and *waged battle*[21] against it. 32. And the Lord gave Lachish in the hand of Israel, and he conquered it on the second day, and he struck it down by the edge of the sword and all the living things that were in it, according to all that he had done to Libnah. 33. Then Horam the king of Gezer went up to aid Lachish, and Joshua struck him down and his people until he had not left a survivor for him. 34. And Joshua and all Israel with him passed from Lachish to Eglon, and they camped against it and *waged battle*[22] against it. 35. And they conquered it on that day and struck it down by the edge of the sword. And all the living things that were in it on that day he destroyed completely according to all that he had done to Lachish. 36. And Joshua and all Israel with him went up from Eglon to Hebron, and they *waged battle*[23] against it. 37. And they conquered it and struck it down by the edge of the sword, and its king, and all its towns, and all the living things that were in it. He left no survivor according to all that he had done to Eglon. And he destroyed it completely and all the living things that were in it. 38. And Joshua and all Israel with him turned to Debir and *waged battle*[24] against it. 39. And he conquered it and its king and all its

Notes, Chapter Ten (Cont.)

[14]MT: "No one sharpened his tongue against any of the sons of Israel."

[15]MT: "men of war."

[16]MT: "fighting."

[17]MT: "trees." See note to 8:29.

[18]MT: "trees."

[19]MT: "trees."

[20]MT: "fought."

[21]MT: "fought."

[22]MT: "fought."

[23]MT: "fought."

[24]MT: "fought."

towns, and they struck them down by the edge of the sword. And they destroyed completely all the living things that were in it. He left no survivor. As he did to Hebron, so he did to Debir and to its king; and as he did to Libnah and to its king. 40. And Joshua struck down all the land, the hill-country and the south and the lowland and *the channel from the heights*[25] and all their kings. He left no survivor. And every breathing thing he destroyed completely as the Lord the God of Israel commanded. 41. And Joshua struck them down from *Rekam-Geah*[26] unto Gaza, and all the land of Goshen unto Gibeon. 42. And all those kings and their land Joshua conquered at one time, for the Lord the God of Israel *by his Memra*[27] *waged battle*[28] for Israel. 43. And Joshua and all Israel with him returned to the camp, to Gilgal.

CHAPTER 11

1. And when Jabin the king of Hazor heard, he sent unto Jobab the king of Madon and unto the king of Samaria and unto the king of Achshaph, 2. and unto the kings who were from the north in the hill-country and in the plain south of *Ginnesar*[1] and in the lowland and in the *districts of Dor*[2] on the west, 3. the Canaanite from the east and from the west, and the Amorite and the Hittite and the Perizzite and the Jebusite in the hill country and the Hivvite *in the lowlands of Hermon*[3] in the land of Mizpah. 4. And they and all their armies with them went forth — a people great as the sand that is upon the shore of the sea for greatness, and very many horses and chariots. 5. And all these kings *prepared themselves,*[4] and they came and camped together at the waters of Merom *to wage battle*[5] with Israel. 6. And the Lord said to Joshua: "Do not be afraid of them, for tomorrow at this time I am handing all of them *killed*[6] before Israel. Their horses you will hamstring, and their chariots you will burn with fire." 7. And Joshua and all *the people making war*[7] with him came suddenly upon them; *and they were camping*[8] at the waters of Merom, and they fell on them. 8. And the Lord gave them in the hand of Israel, and they struck them down and pursued them unto Great Sidon and unto *the channels of waters*[9] and unto the valley of Mizpah to the east. And they struck

Notes, Chapter Ten (Cont.)

[25] MT: "slopes." In fact, the complicated Aramaic idiom seems to have the same meaning.

[26] MT: "Kadesh-barnea." Rekam or Rekem is often used for Kadesh. In *m. Giṭṭin* 1:1-2 it is the eastern border of Israel. For other identifications, see S-A, 120.

[27] The phrase "by his Memra" was added by the targumist.

[28] MT: "fought."

Notes, Chapter Eleven

[1] MT: "Chinneroth." Tg identifies this place with a valley near Lake Kinneret. See S-A, 114; Josh 12:3; 13:27; 1 Kgs 15:20.

[2] MT: "Naphoth-dor."

[3] MT: "beneath Hermon."

[4] MT: "assembled."

[5] MT: "to fight."

[6] MT: "slain."

[7] MT: "the people of war."

[8] MT and other ancient versions lack the phrase.

[9] MT: "Misrephoth-maim."

them down until he left no survivor for them. 9. And Joshua did to them as the Lord said to him. Their horses he hamstrung, and their chariots he burned with fire. 10. And Joshua turned back at that time and conquered Hazor, and its king he *killed*[10] by the sword, for Hazor formerly was the head of all these kingdoms. 11. And they struck down all the living things that were in it by the edge of the sword completely. He left no breathing thing, and he burned Hazor with fire. 12. And Joshua conquered all the cities of these kings and all their kings, and he struck them down by the edge of the sword. He destroyed them completely as Moses the servant of the Lord commanded. 13. Only all the cities that were standing on their *strongholds*[11] — Israel did not burn them; only Hazor did Joshua burn. 14. And all the booty of these cities and the cattle the sons of Israel took as spoil for themselves. Only every man did they strike down by the edge of the sword until they had finished them off. They left no breathing thing. 15. As the Lord commanded Moses his servant, so Moses commanded Joshua, and so Joshua did. He did not omit a word from everything that the Lord commanded Moses. 16. And Joshua *took possession of*[12] all this land, the hill country and all the south and all the land of Goshen and the lowland and the plain and the hill country of Israel and its lowland, 17. from Mount *Peligah*[13] that goes up to Seir and unto the *plain of Gad,*[14] in the valley of Lebanon, *the lowlands of*[15] Mount Hermon. And all their kings he conquered, and he struck them down and *killed them.*[16] 18. For many days Joshua did battle with all these kings. 19. There was not a city that made peace with the sons of Israel except the Hivvites inhabiting Gibeon. They took all in battle. 20. For from *before*[17] the Lord it was to harden their heart to engage in battle with Israel in order to destroy them completely, in order that there be no mercy on them, but in order to finish them off as the Lord commanded Moses. 21. And Joshua came at that time and *finished off the giants*[18] from the hill country, from Hebron, from Debir, from Anab, and from all the hill country of Judah and from all the hill country of Israel. With their cities Joshua destroyed them completely. 22. No *giants*[19] were left in the land of the sons of Israel; only in Gaza, in Gath, and in Ashdod they were left. 23. And Joshua took all the land according to everything that the Lord spoke with Moses, and Joshua gave it as an inheritance to Israel according to their divisions by their tribes. And the land was at peace *from the making of war.*[20]

Notes, Chapter Eleven (Cont.)

[10] MT: "struck down."

[11] MT: "mounds" or "tells."

[12] MT: "took."

[13] MT: "Halak," the Hebrew equivalent of *pĕlīgāh* meaning "division."

[14] MT: "Baal-gad." The change of Baal-Gad to the "plain of Gad" probably reflects an objection to the word "Baal." See 12:7. In 2 Sam. 5:20 "Baal-perazim" becomes "the plain of Perazim."

[15] MT: "beneath."

[16] MT: "put them to death."

[17] MT: "with."

[18] MT: "cut off the Anakim."

[19] MT: "Anakim."

[20] MT: "from war."

CHAPTER 12

1. And these are the kings of the land whom the sons of Israel struck down, and they inherited their land on the other side of the Jordan toward the sunrise, from the gorge of the Arnon unto Mount Hermon and all the plain of the east: 2. Sihon the king of the Amorite who dwelt in Heshbon, ruler from Aroer which is upon the edge of the gorge of the Arnon and the middle of the gorge and half *the land of Gilead*[1] and unto the Jabbok, the gorge — the border of the sons of Ammon, 3. and the Arabah unto the sea of *Ginnesar*[2] eastward, and unto the sea of the plain, the Salt Sea eastward by way of Beth-jeshimoth, and southward beneath *the channel from the heights.*[3] 4. And the territory of Og, the king of *Mattanah,*[4] from the remnant of the *giants,*[5] who was dwelling in Ashtaroth and in Edrei, 5. and was ruler in Mount Hermon and in Salecah and in all *Matnan*[6] unto the territory of the Geshurite, and *the Epicaerean*[7] and half *the land of Gilead*[8] — the border of Sihon the king of Heshbon. 6. Moses the servant of the Lord and the sons of Israel struck them down, and Moses the servant of the Lord gave it as an inheritance *to the tribe of Reuben and to the tribe of Gad* [9] and to the half-tribe of Mannaseh. 7. And these are the kings of the land whom Joshua and the sons of Israel struck down on the western side of the Jordan from *the plain of Gad*[10] in the valley of Lebanon and unto Mount *Peligah*[11] that goes up to Seir — and Joshua gave it to the tribes of Israel as an inheritance according to their divisions — 8. in the hill-country and in the lowland and in the plain and in *the channel from the heights*[12] and in the wilderness and in the south — Hittites, Amorites and Canaanites, Perizzites, Hivvites and Jebusites: 9. the king of Jericho, one; the king of Ai which is beside Bethel, one; 10. the king of Jerusalem, one; the king of Hebron, one; 11. the king of Yarmuth, one; the king of Lachish, one; 12. the king of Eglon, one; the king of Gezer, one; 13. the king of Debir, one; the king of Geder, one; 14. the king of Hormah, one; the king of Arad, one; 15. the king of Libnah, one; the king of Adullam, one; 16. the king of Makkedah, one; the king of Bethel, one; 17. the king of Tappuah, one; the king of Hepher, one; 18. the king of Aphek, one; the king of Lasharon, one; 19. the king of Madon, one; the king of Hazor, one; 20. the king of Shimron-meron, one; the king of Achshaph, one; 21. the king of Taanach, one; the king of Megiddo, one; 22. the king of Kedesh, one; the king of Jokneam in Carmel, one; 23. the king of Dor in *the districts of Dor,*[13] one; the king of the nations for Gilgal, one; 24. the king of Tirzah, one; all the kings — thirty-one.

Notes, Chapter Twelve

[1] MT: "Gilead."
[2] MT: "Chinnereth." See 11:2.
[3] MT: "the slopes of Pisgah." See 10:40.
[4] MT: "Bashan."
[5] MT: "Rephaim."
[6] MT: "Bashan."
[7] MT: "Maachite."
[8] MT: "half of Gilead."
[9] MT: "to the Reubenite and to the Gadite."
[10] MT: "Baal-gad"; see 11:17.
[11] MT: "Halak"; see 11:17.
[12] MT: "slopes."
[13] MT: "Naphath-dor"; see 11:2.

CHAPTER 13

1. And Joshua was old, advanced in days, and the Lord said to him: "You are old, advanced in days, and the land remains very great to possess it. 2. This is the land that remains: All the territories of the Philistines; and all the *Geshurites*[1] 3. from *Shihor*[2] which is on the edge of Egypt and unto the territory of Ekron to the north to the land of the *Canaanites*[3] it is reckoned; there are five rulers of the Philistines — *the Gazaites, the Ashdodites, the Ashkelonites, the Gathites, and the Ekronites,*[4] and the Avvites; 4. from the south all the land of the Canaanites and Mearah which belongs to the Sidonians unto Aphek, unto the territory of the Amorite, 5. and the land of the Gebalite and all Lebanon toward the sunrise, from *the plain of Gad,*[5] *the lowlands*[6] of Mount Hermon, unto the entrance of Hamath, 6. all the inhabitants of the hill-country from Lebanon *unto the channels of water,*[7] all the Sidonians, *by my Memra I will dispossess them*[8] from before the sons of Israel; only divide it for Israel in inheritance as I have commanded you. 7. And now divide this land in inheritance for the nine tribes and the half tribe of Manasseh. 8. With it *the tribe of Reuben and the tribe of Gad*[9] received their inheritance that Moses gave to them across the Jordan to the east, as Moses the servant of the Lord gave to them: 9. from the Aroer which is on the edge of the gorge of the Arnon, and the city that is in the midst of the gorge, and all the plain of Medeba unto Dibon; 10. and all the cities of Sihon the Amorite king who was king in Heshbon unto the territory of the sons of Ammon; 11. and *the land of Gilead,*[10] and the territory of the Geshurite, and *Epicaerus,*[11] and all the hill country of Hermon, and all *Matthan*[12] unto Salecah; 12. all the kingdom of Og in *Matthan,*[13] who was king in Ashtaroth and in Edrei (he was left from the remnant of the *giants*),[14] and Moses struck them down and drove them out. 13. And the sons of Israel did not drive out the Geshurite and the *Epicaerite*[15], and the Geshurite and the *Epicaerite*[15] dwell in the midst of Israel unto this day. 14. Only to the tribe of Levi he did not give an inheritance; the *offerings*[16] of the Lord God of Israel are its inheritance as he said to him. 15. And Moses gave to the tribe of the sons of Reuben according to their families. 16. And the territory was for them from Aroer which is on the edge of the gorge of the Arnon, and the city in the midst of the gorge, and all the plain unto Medeba; 17. Heshbon and all its cities which are in the plain — Dibon, and Bamoth-baal, and Beth-baal-maon, 18. and

Notes, Chapter Thirteen

[1] The MT form is singular.
[2] MT: "the Shihor."
[3] MT: "Canaanite."
[4] The forms in MT are singular.
[5] MT: "Baal-gad." See 11:17; 12:7.
[6] MT: "beneath."
[7] MT: "Misrephoth-maim."

[8] MT: "I myself will drive them out."
[9] MT: "the Reubenite and the Gadite."
[10] MT: "Gilead."
[11] MT: "Maachite."
[12] MT: "Bashan."
[13] MT: "Bashan."
[14] MT: "Rephaim."
[15] MT: "Maachite."
[16] MT: "fire offerings."

Jahaz and Kedemoth and Mephaath, 19. and Kiriathaim and Sibmah and Zereth-shahar on the hill of the plain; 20. and Beth-peor, and *the channel from the heights,*[17] and Beth-jeshimoth; 21. and all the cities of the plain and all the kingdom of Sihon, the Amorite king who was king in Heshbon, whom Moses struck down; and the chiefs of Midian — Evi and Rekem and Zur and Hur and Reba, the chiefs of Sihon, the inhabitants of the land. 22. And the sons of Israel killed by the sword Balaam the son of Beor, the diviner, among their killed. 23. And the border of the sons of Reuben was the Jordan and *its territory,*[18] and this was the inheritance of the sons of Reuben according to their families, the cities and their villages. 24. And Moses gave to the tribe of Gad, to the sons of Gad, according to their families. 25. And their territory was Jazer and all the cities of Gilead and half the land of the sons of Ammon unto Aroer which is on the edge of Rabbah; 26. and from Heshbon unto Ramath-mizpeh and Betonim, and from Mahanaim unto the territory of Debir, 27. and in the valley of Beth-haram, and Beth-nimrah, and Succoth, and Zaphon, the rest of the kingdom of Sihon the king of Heshbon, and Jordan and *its territory,*[19] unto the ends of the Sea of *Ginessar,*[20] beyond the Jordan to the east. 28. This is the inheritance of the sons of Gad according to their families, the cities and their villages. 29. And Moses gave to the half tribe of Manasseh, and it was for the half tribe of the sons of Manasseh according to their families. 30. And their territory was from Mahanaim: all *Matnan,*[21] all the kingdom of Og the king of *Matnan*[21] and all the towns of Jair, which are in *Matnan,*[21] sixty cities, 31. and half *the land of Gilead,*[22] and Ashtaroth, and Edrei, the cities of the kingdom of Og in *Matnan,*[23] to the sons of Machir the son of Manasseh, for the half of the sons of Machir, according to their families. 32. These are what Moses gave as an inheritance in the plain of Moab across the Jordan, east of Jericho. 33. And to the tribe of Levi, Moses did not give an inheritance. *The gifts that the Lord God of Israel gave to them are*[24] their inheritance as the Lord spoke to them.

CHAPTER 14

1. And these are what the sons of Israel inherited in the land of Canaan, what Eleazar the priest and Joshua the son of Nun and the heads of the clans of the tribes of the sons of Israel gave them to inherit. 2. By lot their inheritance *was divided to them*[1] as the Lord commanded by the hand of Moses to the nine tribes and the half tribe. 3. For Moses gave the inheritance of the two tribes and the half tribe across the Jordan.

Notes, Chapter Thirteen (Cont.)

[17] MT: "slopes of Pisgah." See 10:40.
[18] MT: "territory."
[19] MT: "territory."
[20] MT: "Chinnereth." See 11:2.
[21] MT: "Bashan."
[22] MT: "of Gilead."

[23] MT: "Bashan."
[24] MT: "the Lord God of Israel is…" "Gifts" refer to the tithes owed the Levites. To say they receive God as an inheritance is too strong for Tg. See also Josh 18:7.

Notes, Chapter Fourteen

[1] MT lacks the phrase.

And he did not give to the Levites an inheritance among them. 4. For the sons of Joseph were two tribes — Manasseh and Ephraim. And they did not give a portion to the Levites in the land, but only cities to dwell in and their open spaces for their cattle and for their possessions. 5. As the Lord commanded Moses, so the sons of Israel did; and they divided the land. 6. And the sons of Judah drew near unto Joshua in Gilgal, and Caleb the son of Jepunneh the Kenizzite said to him: "You know the word that the Lord spoke with Moses *the prophet of the Lord*[2] concerning me and concerning you in *Rekam-geah*.[3] 7. I was forty years old when Moses the servant of the Lord sent me from *Rekam-geah*[4] to spy out the land, and I brought him back the word just as it was with my heart. 8. My brothers who went up with me *shattered*[5] the heart of the people, and I followed wholly after *the fear of the Lord*[6] my God. 9. And Moses swore on that day, saying: 'Surely the land on which *the sole of your foot*[7] has stepped will be yours for an inheritance and your sons forever, for you have followed wholly after *the fear of the Lord*[8] my God.' 10. And now behold the Lord *has sustained me*[9] as he said these forty-five years from the time that the Lord spoke this word with Moses when Israel went about in the wilderness. And now behold this day I am eighty-five years old. 11. Even now this day I am strong as on the day that Moses sent me; as my strength was then, so is my strength now *to wage battle*[10] and to go forth and to come in. 12. And now give to me this hill country of which the Lord spoke on that day; for you heard on that day that there were *giants*[11] there and great *and*[12] fortified cities. *If the Memra of the Lord be at my aid,*[13] I will conquer them as the Lord said." 13. And Joshua blessed him and gave Hebron to Caleb and son of Jepunneh for an inheritance. 14. Therefore Hebron belongs to Caleb the son of Jepunneh the Kenizzite for an inheritance unto this day because he followed wholly after *the fear of the Lord*[14] the God of Israel. 15. And the name of Hebron formerly was "the City of Arba"; he was a great man among the *giants*.[15] And the land had rest *from the making of battle*.[16]

CHAPTER 15

1. And the allotment for the tribe of the sons of Judah for their familes was unto the border of Edom, the wilderness of Zin being at the southernmost ends. 2. Their southern border was from the ends of the Salt Sea, from the *shore*[1] that turns to the

Notes, Chapter Fourteen (Cont.)

[2]MT: "man of God."
[3]MT: "Kadesh-barnea."
[4]MT: "Kadesh-barnea."
[5]MT: "melted."
[6]MT: "the Lord."
[7]MT: "your foot."
[8]MT: "the Lord."
[9]MT: "has kept me alive." The Aramaic is not as specific here.

[10]MT: "for war."
[11]MT: "Anakim."
[12]MT lacks the word "and."
[13]MT: "Perhaps the Lord will be with me."
[14]MT: "the Lord."
[15]MT: "Anakim."
[16]MT: "from war."

Notes, Chapter Fifteen

[1]MT: literally "tongue."

south. 3. And it goes forth southward of the ascent of the Akrabbim, and it passes along to Zin, and it goes up south of *Rekam-geah,*[2] and it passes along to Hezron, and it goes up to Addar, and it turns about to Karka, 4. and it passes along to Azmon, and it goes forth to the gorge of Egypt, and the outlets were the border toward the sea. This will be your southern boundary. 5. And the eastern border — the Salt Sea unto the ends of the Jordan. And the boundary to the northern direction — from the *shore*[3] of the sea, from the ends of the Jordan, 6. and the boundary goes up to Beth-hoglah, and it passes along from the north of *Beth-meshra,*[4] and the border goes up to the Stone of Bohan the son of Reuben. 7. And the border goes up to Debir from the plain of Achor, and it turns northward to Gilgal, which is opposite the ascent of Adummim, which is south of the gorge; and the border passes to the waters of En-shemesh, and its outlet is at *En-qarsa.*[5] 8. And the border goes up to the valley of the son of Hinnom, which is at the southern side of *Jebus,*[6] that is Jerusalem; and the border goes up to the top of the mountain that faces the valley of Hinnom from the west, which is at the ends of the plain of the *giants*[7] toward the north. 9. And the border turns from the top of the mountain to the spring of the waters of Nephtoah, and it goes forth to the cities of Mount Ephron, and the border turns around from Baalah that is, Kiriath-Jearim. 10. And the border turns around from Baalah to the sea, to Mount Seir, and it passes along to the side of Mount Jearim to the north, that is, Chesalon; and it goes down to Beth-shemesh, and it passes along to Timnah. 11. And the border goes forth to the side of Ekron to the north, and the border turns to Shikkeron, and it passes by Mount Baalah, and it goes forth to Jabneel. And the outlets were the border toward the sea. 12. And the western border is the Great Sea and its shore. This is the border of the sons of Judah all round according to their families. 13. To Caleb the son of Jephunneh he gave a portion in the midst of the sons of Judah according to the *Memra*[8] of the Lord to Joshua — the city of Arba the father of *the giants,*[9] that is, Hebron. 14. And Caleb drove out from there the three sons of *the giants,*[9] Sheshai and Ahiman and Talmai, the sons of *the giants.*[10] 15. And he went up from there unto the inhabitants of Debir, and the name of Debir formerly was *Kiriath-arke.*[11] 16. And Caleb said: "Whoever shall strike down *Kiriath-arke*[12] and conquer it, I will give to him Achsah my daughter for a wife." 17. And Othniel, son of Kenaz, brother of Caleb, conquered it; and he gave to him Achsah his daughter for a wife. 18. And when she came, she advised him to ask from her father *an inheritance.*[13] And she got down from upon the ass, and Caleb said to her: "What is it to you?" 19. And she said: "Give to me an *inheritance,*[14] for you have given me to the land of the south. And may you give to me *the place of*[15] the pools of water." And he gave to her the upper pools and the lower pools. 20. This is the

---

Notes, Chapter Fifteen (Cont.)

[2] MT: "Kadesh-barnea."
[3] MT: literally "tongue."
[4] MT: "Beth-arabah."
[5] MT: "En-rogel." "En-qarsa" may mean "En-Castra," that is, "the fountain of the (Roman) camp" or "the fountain of the fuller," a place used for washing clothes at the junction of the Hinnom with the Kidron valleys. See 2 Sam 17:17; 1 Kgs 1:9, and S-A, 112-113.
[6] MT: "the Jebusite."

[7] MT: "Rephaim."
[8] MT: "mouth."
[9] MT: "the Anak."
[10] MT: "the Anak."
[11] MT: "Kiriath-sepher." Kiriath-sepher means City of the Book. "Book" connoted the Bible, so the Canaanite city's name was changed to the City of the Court (records). S-A, 124.
[12] MT: "Kiriath-sepher."
[13] MT: "a field."
[14] MT: "blessing."
[15] MT lacks the word.

inheritance of the tribe of the sons of Judah according to their families. 21. The outermost cities belonging to the tribe of the sons of Judah were upon the border of Edom in the south: Kabzeel and Eder and Jagur 22. and Kinah and Dimonah and Adadah 23. and Kedesh and Hazor and Ithnan 24. and Ziph and Telem and Bealoth 25. and Hazor-hadattah and Keriot-hezron, that is, Hazor, 26. Amam and Shema and Moladah 27. and Hazar-gaddah and Heshmon and Beth-pelet 28. and Hazar-shual and Beersheba and Biziothiah 29. and Baalah and Iim and Ezem 30. and Eltolad and Chesil and Hormah 31. and Ziklag and Madmannah and Sansannah 32. and Lebaoth and Shilhim and Ain and Rimmon — all twenty-nine cities and their villages. 33. In the lowland: Eshtaol and Zorah and Ashnah 34. and Zanoah and En-gannim, Tapuah and Enam, 35. Yarmuth and Adullam, Socoh and Azekah, 36. and Shaaraim and Adithaim and Gederah and Gederothaim — fourteen cities and their villages. 37. Zenan and Hadashah and Migdal-gad 38. and Dilean and Mizpeh and Joktheel 39. *and Cish*[16] and Bozkath and Eglon 40. and Cabbon and *Lahmam*[17] and Chitlish 41. and Gederoth, Beth-dagon, and Naamah and Makkedah — sixteen cities and their villages. 42. Libnah and Ether and Ashan 43. and Iphtah and Ashnah and Nezib 44. and Keilah and Achzib and Maresah — nine cities and their villages. 45. Ekron and its towns and its villages; 46. from Ekron and *westward,*[18] all *the cities*[19] which are upon the border of Ashdod and their villages. 47. Ashdod, its towns and its villages; Gaza, its town and its villages, unto the gorge of Egypt and the *Great*[20] Sea and its shore. 48. And in the hill-country: Shamir and Jattir and Socoh 49. and Dannah and Kiriath-sannah, that is, Debir, 50. and Anab and Eshtemoh and Anim 51. and Goshen and Holon and Giloh — eleven cities and their villages. 52. Arab and *Dumah*[21] and Eshan 53. and Janim and Beth-tapuah and *Aphek*[22] 54. and Humtah and the city of Arba, that is, Hebron, and Zior — nine cities and their villages. 55. Moan, Carmel, Ziph, and Juttah 56. and Jezreel and Jokdeam and Zanoah, 57. Hakain, Gibeah, and Timnah — ten cities and their villages. 58. Halhul, Beth-zur and Gedor 59. and Maarath and Beth-anoth and Eltekon — six cities and their villages. 60. Kiriath-baal, that is, Kiriath-jearim, and Rabbah — two cities and their villages. 61. In the wilderness: *Beth-meshra,*[23] Middin and Secacah, 62. and Nibshan and the City of Salt and En-gedi — six cities and their villages. 63. And the *Jebusites,*[24] the inhabitants of Jerusalem — the sons of Judah were not able to drive them out. And the *Jebusites*[24] dwell with the sons of Judah in Jerusalem unto this day.

Notes, Chapter Fifteen (Cont.)

[16] MT: "Lachish."

[17] MT: "Lahmas."

[18] MT: "to the Sea."

[19] MT lacks the word "cities."

[20] Many MT mss. read *gbwl* ("border") rather than *gdwl* ("great").

[21] Some MT mss. have "Rumah."

[22] MT: "Aphekah."

[23] MT: "Beth-arabah."

[24] The MT forms are singular.

CHAPTER 16

1. The allotment for the sons of Joseph went forth from the Jordan near Jericho, east of the waters of Jericho, *to*[1] the wilderness that goes up from Jericho in the hill country *to*[1] Bethel. 2. And it goes forth from Bethel to Luz, and it passes to the border of the Archites *to*[2] Ataroth. 3. And it goes down to the sea to the border of *Japhlet*[3] unto the border of lower Beth-horon and unto Gezer, and its outlets were toward the sea. 4. And the sons of Joseph — Manasseh and Ephraim — received their inheritance. 5. And the territory of the sons of Ephraim was according to their families: the border of their inheritance was to the east Ataroth-addar unto upper Beth-horon, 6. and the border goes forth to the sea; *to*[4] Michmath from the north; and the border turns around from the north *to*[4] Taanath-shiloh, and it passes *along*[4] it from the east to Janoah. 7. And it goes down from Janoah *to*[5] Ataroth and *to*[5] Naarat, and it touches Jericho and goes forth *to*[5] the Jordan. 8. From Tappuah the border goes to the sea, *to*[6] the gorge of Kanah, and its outlets were toward the sea. This is the inheritance of the tribe of the sons of Ephraim according to their families, 9. and the cities that were set apart for the sons of Ephraim in the midst of the inheritance of the sons of Manasseh, all the cities and their villages. 10. And they did not drive out *the Canaanites who were dwelling*[7] in Gezer; and *the Canaanites*[8] dwell in the midst of the house of Ephraim unto this day, and *they have become bearers of tribute, servants.*[9]

CHAPTER 17

1. And the allotment was to the tribe of Manasseh, for he was the first-born of Joseph. To Machir, the first-born of Manasseh, the father of Gilead; because he was a man *making battles,*[1] he had the land of Gilead and *Matnan.*[2] 2. And it was also to the sons of Manasseh, who were left, according to their families, to the sons of Abiezer and

Notes, Chapter Sixteen

[1] MT lacks the prepositions.
[2] MT lacks the preposition.
[3] MT: "the Japhletite."
[4] MT lacks the prepositions.
[5] MT lacks the prepositions.
[6] MT lacks the preposition.
[7] MT: "the Canaanite who was dwelling."

[8] MT: "Canaanite."
[9] MT: "he (= the Canaanite) has become a labor-band serving."

Notes, Chapter Seventeen

[1] MT: "of war."
[2] MT: "Bashan."

to the sons of Helek and to the sons of Asriel and to the sons of Shechem and to the sons of Hepher and to the sons of Shemida. These were the sons of Manasseh, the son of Joseph, the males, according to their families. 3. And Zelophehad the son of Hapher, son of Gilead, son of Machir, son of Manasseh, had no sons but only daughters. And these were the names of his daughters: Mahlah and Noah, Hoglah, Milcah, and Tirzah. 4. And they drew near before Eleazar the priest and before Joshua the son of Nun and before the chiefs, saying: "The Lord commanded Moses to give to us an inheritance in the midst of our brothers." And he gave to them according to the *Memra*[3] of the Lord an inheritance in the midst of the brothers of their father. 5. And ten lots fell to Manasseh, apart from the land of Gilead and *Matnan*[4] which is on the other side of the Jordan. 6. For the daughters of Manasseh inherited an inheritance in the midst of his sons, and the land of Gilead was allotted to the sons of Manasseh who were left. 7. And the border of Manasseh was from Asher to Michmethath, which is east of Shechem. And the border goes southward unto the inhabitants of En-tappuah. 8. The land of Tappuah belongs to Manasseh, and upon the border of Manasseh belongs to the sons of Ephraim. 9. And the border goes down *to*[5] the gorge of Kanah — to the south of the gorge these cities belong to Ephraim in the midst of the cities of Manasseh, and the border of Manasseh is from the north of the gorge, and its outlets are toward the sea. 10. The south belongs to Ephraim, and the north to Manasseh; and the sea was its border. And they touch Asher northward and Issachar eastward. 11. And Manasseh had in the tribe of Issachar and in Asher Beth-shean and its towns, and Ibleam and its towns, and the inhabitants of Dor and its towns, and the inhabitants of En-dor and its towns, and the inhabitants of Taanach and its towns, and the inhabitants of Megiddo and its towns — three *districts*.[6] 12. And the sons of Manasseh were not able to drive out these cities, and the Canaanite settled to dwell in this land. 13. And when the sons of Israel grew strong, *they appointed*[7] the Canaanites *to be bearers of tribute*,[8] and they did not drive them out completely. 14. And the sons of Joseph spoke with Joshua, saying: "Why have you given *to us*[9] as an inheritance one portion and one allotment. And I am a numerous people so far as the Lord has blessed me *to be numerous*."[10] 15. And Joshua said to them: "If you are a numerous people, go up to the forest, and prepare for yourself there *a place*[11] in the land of *the Perizzites and the giants*,[12] for the hill-country of *the house of Ephraim*[13] is too narrow for you." 16. And the sons of Joseph said: "The hill-country is not enough for us. And among all *the Canaanites who are dwelling*[14] in the land of the plain, those of Beth-shean and its towns, and those of the plain of Jezreel, have chariots of iron." 17. And Joshua said to the house of Joseph, to Ephraim, and to Manasseh, saying: "You are a numerous people, and you have much power. You will not have one allotment. 18. For the hill-country will be yours, for it is a forest; and you will prepare it, and its farthest borders will be yours; for you will drive out *the Canaanites* though *they have* chariots of iron and *they are*[15] strong.

Notes, Chapter Seventeen (Cont.)

[3]MT: "mouth."
[4]MT: "Bashan."
[5]MT lacks the preposition.
[6]The Hebrew term is obscure.
[7]MT: "gave."
[8]MT: "to forced labor."
[9]MT: "to me."
[10]MT: "until now."
[11]MT lacks the word.
[12]MT: "the Perizzite and the Rephaim."
[13]MT: "Ephraim."
[14]MT: "the Canaanite who dwells."
[15]MT: "the Canaanite...he has...he is..."

CHAPTER 18

1. And all the congregation of the sons of Israel were gathered to Shiloh, and they set up there the tent of meeting, and the land lay conquered before them. 2. And there remained among the sons of Israel who had not divided their inheritance seven tribes. 3. And Joshua said to the sons of Israel: "How long are you delaying to enter to inherit the land that the Lord God of your fathers has given you? 4. Pick for yourselves the three men for each tribe, and I will send them, and they will arise and go about in the land, and they will write it up with regard to their inheritance, and they will come unto me. 5. And they will divide it into seven portions. *Those of the house of Judah*[1] will stand on their border from the south, and *those of the house of Joseph*[2] will stand on their border from the north. 6. And you will write out the land according to seven portions, and you will bring to me here, and I will cast the lot for you here before the Lord our God. 7. For the Levites have no portion among you: *only the gifts that the Lord has given them are their inheritance.*[3] And *the tribe of Gad and the tribe of Reuben*[4] and the half tribe of Manasseh have received their inheritance across the Jordan eastward, which Moses the servant of the Lord gave to them." 8. And the men arose and went, and Joshua commanded those who went to write out the land, saying: "Go, and walk about in the land, and write it out and return unto me, and here I will cast lots for you before the Lord in Shiloh." 9. And the men went and passed through the land, and they wrote it out according to cities in seven portions upon a book. And they came unto Joshua, to the camp, to Shiloh. 10. And Joshua cast the lot for them in Shiloh before the Lord, and there Joshua divided up the land for the sons of Israel according to their divisions. 11. And the lot of the tribe of the sons of Benjamin came up according to their families, and the boundary of their allotment went forth between the sons of Judah and the sons of Joseph. 12. And their boundary to the north side is from the Jordan, and the boundary goes up by the side of Jericho on the north, and it goes up in the hill country toward the sea, and its end points were at the wilderness of Beth-aven. 13. And the boundary passed from there to Luz, that is to the south side of Luz, that is Bethel, and the boundary goes down to Ataroth-addar, upon the mountain which is south of lower Beth-horon. 14. And the boundary bends around on the western side to the south from the mountain that faces Beth-horon southward, and its end points were at Kiriath-baal, that is Keriath-jearim, the city of the sons of Judah. This is the western side. 15. And the southern side is from the outskirts of Kiriath-jearim, and the boundary goes forth to the sea, and it goes forth to the spring of the

Notes, Chapter Eighteen

[1] MT: "Judah."
[2] MT: "the house of Joseph."
[3] MT: "for the priesthood of the Lord is his inheritance." Tg changes the MT to fit the later arrangement in which Levites were separate from and subordinate to priests. Thus they receive tithes/gifts, not the priesthood. S-A, 14-15.
[4] MT: "Gad and Reuben."

Waters of Nephtoah. 16. And the boundary goes down to the side of the mountain that faces the valley of the son of Hinnom, which is at the northern end of the plain of the *giants*,[5] and it goes down to the valley of Hinnom which is by the side of Jebus southward, and it goes down to *En-qarsa*.[6] 17. And it bends around northward and goes forth to En-shemesh, and goes forth to *Gelilah*[7] which is opposite the ascent of Adummin, and goes down to the Stone of Bohan the son of Reuben. 18. And it passes by the side opposite the plain to the north, and it goes down to the Arabah. 19. And the boundary passes by the side of Beth-hoglah to the north; and the end points of the boundary are at the shore of the Salt Sea to the north, at the end of the Jordan to the south — this is the southern boundary. 20. And the Jordan is its boundary on the eastern side — this is the inheritance of the sons of Benjamin according to its boundaries round about, according to their families. 21. And the cities that belonged to the tribe of the sons of Benjamin according to their families were Jericho and Beth-hoglah and the Emek-Keziz, 22. and Beth-*meshra*[8] and Zemaraim and Bethel, 23. and Avvim and *Haparah*[9] and Ophrah, 24. and Cephar-ammoni and Ophni and Geba — twelve cities and their villages. 25. *Gaba*[10] and Ramah and Beeroth, 26. and Mizpah and Chephinah and Mozah, 27. and Rekem and Irpeel and Taralah, 28. and Zela and Eleph and *Jebus*,[11] that is Jerusalem, Gibeath, Kiriath — fourteen cities and their villages. And this is the inheritance of the sons of Benjamin according to their families.

CHAPTER 19

1. And the second lot went forth for Simeon, for the tribe of the sons of Simeon according to their families; and their inheritance was in the midst of the inheritance of the sons of Judah. 2. And they had in their inheritance Beer-sheba and Sheba and Moladah, 3. and Hazar-shual and Balah and Ezem, 4. and Eltolad and Bethul and Hormah, 5. and Ziklag and Beth-marcaboth and Hazar-susah, 6. and Beth-lebaoth and Sharuhen — thirteen cities and their villages; 7. Ain, Rimmon and Ether and Ashan —four cities and their village, 8. and all the villages that were in the vicinity of these cities unto Baalath-beer, Ramah of the south — this is the inheritance of the tribe of the sons of Simeon according to their families. 9. The inheritance of the sons of Simeon was from the allotment of the sons of Judah, for the portion of the sons of Judah was too large for them, and the sons of Simeon inherited in the midst of their inheritance. 10. And the third lot came up for the sons of Zebulun according to their families, and the boundary of their inheritance was unto Sarid. 11. And their boundary goes up toward the sea, and to Mareal, and touches Dabbesheth, and touches the gorge that

Notes, Chapter Eighteen (Cont.)

[5]MT: "Rephaim."
[6]MT: "En-rogel." See 15:7.
[7]MT: "Geliloth."

[8]MT: "arabah."
[9]MT: "(ha)-Parah." Aramaic has *Haparah*.
[10]MT: "Gibeon."
[11]MT: "the Jebusite."

faces Jokneam. 12. And it turns from Sarid to the east toward the sunrise to the boundary of Chisloth-tabor, and it goes forth to Daberath and goes up to Japhia. 13. And from there it passes eastward to Gitah-hepher, to Ita-kazin, and it goes forth to Rimmon bending around, and from there it turns around to Neah. 14. And its boundary turns about on the north to Hannathon, and its end points are the valley of Iphtahel, 15. and Kattath and Nahalal and Shimron and Idalah and Bethlehem — twelve cities and their towns. 16. This is the inheritance of the sons of Zebulun according to their families —these cities and their villages. 17. The fourth lot went forth to Issachar, to the sons of Issachar, according to their families. 18. And their boundary was Jezreel and Chesuloth and Shunem, 19. and Hapharaim and Shion and Naharath, 20. and Rabbith and Kishion and Ebez, and 21. Remeth and En-gannim and En-haddah and Beth-pazzez, 22. and the boundary touches Tabor and Shahazumah and Beth-shemesh, and the end points of their boundaries were the Jordan — sixteen cities and their villages. 23. This is the inheritance of the tribe of the sons of Issachar according to their families —the cities and their villages. 24. And the fifth lot went forth for the tribe of the sons of Asher according to their familes. 25. And their boundary was Helkath and Hali and Beten and Achshaph, 26. and Allammelech and Amad and Mishal; and it touches Carmel toward the west and Shihor-libnath. 27. And it turns eastward to Beth-dagon and touches Zebulun and the valley of Iphtahel to the north to *Beth-meshra*[1] and Neiel, and it goes forth to Kabul from the left, 28. and Ebron and Rehob and Hammon and Kanah unto Sidon the Great; 29. and the boundary turns to Ramah and unto the fortified *cities, cities of strength*,[2] and the boundary turns to Hosah, and their end points were the sea — *from the allotment of*[3] Achzib, 30. Ummah and Aphek and Rehob — twenty-two cities and their villages. 31. This is the inheritance of the tribe of the sons of Asher according to their families — these cities and their villages. 32. The sixth lot went forth for the sons of Naphtali, to the sons of Naphtali according to their families. 33. And their boundary was from Heleph, from the oak in Zaanannim, and Adami-nekeb and Jabneel unto Lakkum, and its end points were the Jordan. 34. And the boundary turns to the sea to Aznoth-tabor, and goes forth from there to Hukkok, and touches Zebulun on the south and touches Asher on the west, and Judah at the Jordan on the east. 35. And the fortified cities are Ziddim, Zer and Hammath, Rakkath and Chinnereth, 36. and Adamah and Ramah and Hazor, 37. and Kedesh and Edrei and En-hazor, 38. and Yiron and Migdal-el, Horem and Beth-anath and Beth-shemesh — nineteen cities and their villages. 39. This is the inheritance of the tribe of the sons of Naphtali according to their families — the cities and their villages. 40. To the tribe of the sons of Dan according to their families, the seventh lot went forth. 41. And the boundary of their inheritance was Zorah and Eshtaol and *Kiriath-shemesh*,[4] 42. and Shaalabbin and Aijalon and Ithlah, 43, and Elon and Timnah and Ekron, 44. and Eltekeh and Gibbethon and Baalath, 45. and Jehud and Bene-berak and Gath-rimmon, 46. and Me-jarkon and Rakkon with the territory that is over against Joppa. 47. And the boundary of the sons of Dan went forth from them, and the

Notes, Chapter Nineteen

[1]MT: "Beth-emek."
[2]MT: "city of Tyre."

[3]In the Hebrew the term seems to be a proper name, "Mehebel."
[4]MT: "Ir-shemesh." Tg replaces the Hebrew word for city with the Aramaic.

sons of Dan went up and *waged battle*[5] with Leshem, and they conquered it and struck it down by the edge of the sword, and they inherited it and dwelt in it and called Leshem "Dan" according to the name of Dan their father. 48. This is the inheritance of the tribe of the sons of Dan according to their families — these cities and their villages. 49. And they finished giving out the land as inheritances according to its boundaries, and the sons of Israel gave an inheritance among them to Joshua the son of Nun. 50. According to the *Memra*[6] of the Lord they gave to him the city that he requested —Timnath-serah in the hill country of Ephraim, and he built the city and dwelt in it. 51. These are the inheritances that Eleazar the priest and Joshua the son of Nun and the heads of their clans gave out to the tribes of the sons of Israel by lot in Shiloh before the Lord at the door of the tent of meeting, and they finished dividing up the land.

CHAPTER 20

1. And the Lord spoke with Joshua, saying: 2. "Speak with the sons of Israel, saying: 'Pick out for yourselves the cities of refuge about which I spoke with you by the hand of Moses, 3. where a killer *who will kill*[1] someone by negligence without *his*[2] knowledge may flee. And they will be for you a refuge from the avenger of blood. 4. And he will flee to one of these cities, and he will stand at the entrance of the gate of the city, and he will speak *before*[3] the elders of that city his words, and they will gather him to the city unto them, and they will give to him a place, and he will dwell with them. 5. And if the avenger of blood will pursue after him, they will not hand over the killer in his hand, for without *his*[4] knowing he struck down his neighbor and he was not hating him yesterday and before that. 6. And he will dwell in that city until he will stand before the congregation for judgment, until the high priest in those days will die. Then the killer will return and enter his city and his house, the city from which he fled.'" 7. And *they appointed*[5] Kedesh in Galilee in the hill country of *the house of Naphtali,*[6] and Shechem in the hill country of *the house of Ephraim,*[7] and Kiriath-arba, that is, Hebron, in the hill country of *the house of Judah.*[8] 8. And across the Jordan *which is*[9] east of Jericho, they picked Bezer in the wilderness, in the plain, from the tribe of Reuben, and Ramoth in Gilead from the tribe of Gad, and Golan in *Matnan*[10] from the

Notes, Chapter Nineteen (Cont.)

[5]MT: "fought."
[6]MT: "mouth."

Notes, Chapter Twenty

[1]MT: "striking down."
[2]MT lacks the personal pronoun.

[3]MT: "in the ears of."
[4]MT lacks the personal pronoun.
[5]MT: "they consecrated."
[6]MT: "Naphtali."
[7]MT: "Ephraim."
[8]MT: "Judah."
[9]MT lacks the relative pronoun.
[10]MT: "Bashan."

tribe of Manasseh. 9. And these were the cities that were appointed for all the sons of Israel and for *the sojourners who will sojourn*[11] among them, where anyone *who will kill*[12] someone by negligence may flee, and he will not die by the hand of the avenger of blood until he will stand before the congregation.

CHAPTER 21

1. And the heads of the clans of the Levites drew near unto Eleazar the priest and unto Joshua the son of Nun and unto the heads of the clans of the tribes for the sons of Israel. 2. And they spoke with them in Shiloh in the land of Canaan, saying: "The Lord commanded by the hand of Moses to give to us cities to dwell in and their open spaces for our cattle." 3. And the sons of Israel gave to the Levites from their inheritance according to the *Memra*[1] of the Lord these cities and their open spaces. 4. And the lot went forth for the families of Kohath, and the sons of Aaron the priest from the Levites had in the lot from the tribe of Judah and from the tribe of Simeon and from the tribe of Benjamin thirteen cities. 5. And the sons of Kohath who were left had in the lot from the families of the tribe of Ephraim and from the tribe of Dan and from the half tribe of Manasseh ten cities. 6. And the sons of Gershon had in the lot thirteen cities from the families of the tribe of Issachar and from the tribe of Asher and from the tribe of Naphtali and from the half tribe of Manasseh in *Matnan*.[2] 7. And the sons of Merari according to their families had twelve cities from the tribe of Reuben and from the tribe of Gad and from the tribe of Zebulun. 8. And the sons of Israel gave to the Levites these cities and their open spaces, just as the Lord commanded by the hand of Moses, in the lot. 9. And they gave from the tribe of the sons of Judah and from the tribe of the sons of Simeon these cities which *were set aside by their names*.[3] 10. This went to the sons of Aaron from the family of Kohath from the sons of Levi, for the first lot went to them. 11. And they gave to them the city of Arba, who was the father of the *giants*,[4] that is Hebron, in the hill country of the house of Judah and its open spaces round about it. 12. And the *field*[5] of the city and its villages they gave to Caleb the son of Jephunneh in his inheritance. 13. And to the sons of Aaron the priest they gave the city of refuge of the killer, Hebron, and its open spaces, and Libnah and its open spaces, 14. and Jattir and its open spaces, and Eshtemoa and its open spaces, 15. and Holon and its open spaces, and Debir and its open spaces, 16. and Ain and its open spaces, and Juttah and its open spaces, Beth-shemesh and its open spaces — nine cities from these

Notes, Chapter Twenty (Cont.)

[11] MT: "the sojourner sojourning."
[12] MT: "striking down."

Notes, Chapter Twenty-One

[1] MT: "mouth."

[2] MT: "Bashan."
[3] MT: "one calls them by name."
[4] MT: "the Anak."
[5] MT: "fields."

two tribes; 17. and from the tribe of Benjamin, Gibeon and its open spaces, Geba and its open spaces, 18. Anathoth and its open spaces, and Almon and its open spaces — four cities; 19. all the cities of the sons of Aaron, the priests — thirteen cities and their open spaces. 20. And to the families of the sons of Kohath, the Levites who were left from the sons of Kohath — the cities of their lot were from the tribe of *the house of Ephraim.*[6] 21. And they gave to them the city of refuge of the killer, Shechem, and its open spaces in the hill country of *the house of Ephraim,*[7] and Gezer and its open spaces, 22. and Kibzaim and its open spaces, and Beth-horon and its open spaces —four cities; 23. and from the tribe of Dan, Elteke and its open spaces, Gibbethon and its open spaces, 24. Aijalon and its open spaces, Gath-rimon and its open spaces — four cities; 25. and from the half tribe of Manasseh, Taanach and its open spaces, and Gath-rimmon and its open spaces — two cities. 26. There were ten cities in all and their open spaces for the families of the sons of Kohath who were left. 27. And to the sons of Gershon from the family of the Levites, from the half tribe of Manasseh the city of the refuge of the killer, Golan in *Matnan*[8] and its open spaces, and Beshterah and its open spaces — two cities; 28. and from the tribe of Issachar, Kishion and its open spaces, Daberath and its open spaces, 29. Jarmuth and its open spaces, and En-gannim and its open spaces — four cities; 30. and from the tribe of Asher, Mishal and its open spaces, Abdon and its open spaces, 31. Helkath and its open spaces, and Rehob and its open spaces — four cities; 32. and from the tribe of Naphtali, the city of refuge of the killer, Kedesh in Galilee and its open spaces, and Hammoth-dor and its open spaces, and Kartan and its open spaces — three cities. 33. All the cities of *the sons of Gershon*[9] according to their families — thirteen cities and their open spaces. 34. And to the familes of the sons of Merari, the Levites who were left, from the tribe of Zebulun, Jekneam and its open spaces, and Kartah and its open spaces, 35. Dimnah and its open spaces, Nahalal and its open spaces — four cities; 36. from the tribe of Gad, the city of refuge of the killer, Ramoth in Gilead and its open spaces, and Mahanaim and its open spaces, 37. Heshbon and its open spaces, Jazer and its open spaces — four cities in all. 38. All the cities for the sons of Merari according to their families who were left from the families of the Levites — their allotment was twelve cities. 39. All the cities of the Levites in the midst of the inheritance of the sons of Israel were forty-eight cities and their open spaces. 40. And these were the cities, city by city, and its open spaces round about it — so it was for all these cities. 41. And the Lord gave to Israel all the land that he swore to give to their fathers, and they took possession of it and dwelt in it. 42. And the Lord gave them rest round about according to everything that he swore to their fathers, and no one from all their enemies stood before them; all their enemies the Lord gave in their hand. 43. No word from all the *good words*[10] that the Lord spoke concerning the house of Israel failed; *all of them were fulfilled.*[11]

Notes, Chapter Twenty-One (Cont.)

[6]MT: "Ephraim."
[7]MT: "Ephraim."
[8]MT: "Bashan."

[9]MT: "Gershonite."
[10]MT: "good word."
[11]MT: "everyone came about."

CHAPTER 22

1. Then Joshua called *the tribe of Reuben and the tribe of Gad*[1] and the half tribe of Manasseh. 2. And he said to them: "You have observed everything that Moses the servant of the Lord commanded you, and you have accepted my *Memra*[2] for everything that I commanded you. 3. You did not abandon your brothers these many days until this day, and you have kept the charge of the command of *the Memra of the Lord*[3] your God. 4. And now the Lord your God has given rest to your brothers as he said to them. And now turn around and betake yourselves to your *cities*,[4] to the land of your inheritance that Moses the servant of the Lord gave to you across the Jordan. 5. Only be very careful to do the command and the law that Moses the servant of the Lord commanded you, to love the Lord your God and to walk in all *the ways that are good before him*[5] and to observe his commands and *to draw near to fear of him*[6] and to serve *before him*[7] with all your heart and with all your soul." 6. And Joshua blessed them and sent them away, and they went to their *cities*.[8] 7. And to the half tribe of Manasseh Moses gave in *Matnan*,[9] and to half of them Joshua gave with their brothers on the side of the Jordan to the west. And also when Joshua sent them to their *cities*[10] and blessed them, 8. he said to them, saying: "With many possessions return to your *cities*,[11] and with very much cattle, with silver and with gold and with bronze and with iron and with very many clothes; divide the spoil of your enemies with your brothers." 9. And the sons of Reuben and the sons of Gad and the half tribe of Manasseh turned and went from the sons of Israel, from Shiloh which is in the land of Canaan, to go to the land of Gilead, to the land of their inheritance that they inherited in it, according to the *Memra*[12] of the Lord by the hand of Moses. 10. And they came to the districts of the Jordan that are in the land of Canaan, and the sons of Reuben and the sons of Gad and the half tribe of Manasseh built an altar there upon the Jordan, an altar great to see. 11. And the sons of Israel heard, saying: "Behold the sons of Reuben and the sons of Gad and the half tribe of Manasseh have built an altar opposite the land of Canaan in the districts of the Jordan, on the side that belongs to the sons of Israel." 12. And the sons of Israel heard, and all the congregation of the sons of Israel gathered to Shiloh to go up against them as an army. 13. And the sons of Israel sent unto the sons of Reuben and unto the sons of Gad and to the half tribe of Manasseh, to the land of Gilead,

Notes, Chapter Twenty-Two

[1]MT: "the Reubenite and the Gadite."
[2]MT: "voice."
[3]MT: "the Lord."
[4]MT: "tents."
[5]MT: "his ways."
[6]MT: "to cling to him." The fear of God is highly prized in Tg. See S-A, 156-157. The MT "cling to him" is too anthropomorphic.
[7]MT: "him."
[8]MT: "tents."
[9]MT: "Bashan."
[10]MT: "tents."
[11]MT: "tents."
[12]MT: "mouth."

Phinehas the son of Eleazar the priest, 14. and ten chiefs with him, each one a chief for a family for all the tribes of Israel, and everyone the head of their families for the clans of Israel. 15. And they came unto the sons of Reuben and unto the sons of Gad and unto the half tribe of Manasseh, to the land of Gilead, and they spoke with them, saying: 16. "Thus all the congregation of the Lord said: 'What is this treachery that you have worked against *the Memra of the God*[13] of Israel, to turn this day from after the worship of the Lord in your building for yourselves an altar for your rebelling this day against *the Memra of the Lord*?[14] 17. Is it small to us — the sin of Peor from which we have not cleansed ourselves unto this day, and there was the plague in the congregation of the Lord, 18. that you should turn this day from after the worship of the Lord? And if you rebel this day against *the Memra of the Lord*,[15] tomorrow *there will be anger upon*[16] all the congregation of Israel. 19. But if the land of your inheritance is unclean, cross over to the land of the inheritance of *the people of the Lord*[17] where the tent of the Lord resides, and inherit among us. And do not rebel against *the Memra of the Lord*[18] and do not rebel against us in your building for yourselves an altar besides the altar of the Lord our God. 20. Did not Achan the son of Zerah commit deception in the ban, and there was anger upon all the congregation of Israel? And that man did not *die*[19] alone in his sin.'" 21. And the sons of Reuben and the sons of Gad and the half tribe of Manasseh answered and spoke with the heads of the clans of Israel: 22. "The Mighty One, God, Lord; the Mighty One, God, Lord! *Before him it is revealed,*[20] and Israel will know *in the end;*[21] if in rebellion and if *in deception he deceived against the Memra of the Lord,*[22] do not spare us this day; 23. for building for ourselves an altar to turn from after *the worship of the Lord;*[23] and if to bring up holocausts upon it and cereal offerings and if to make upon it offerings of holy things, may the Lord himself search it out. 24. No, but from fear of something we did this, saying: 'Soon your sons will say to our sons, saying: *"There is no portion for you in the Memra of the Lord*[24] the God of Israel. 25. And the Lord has given as the border between us and between you, sons of Reuben and Gad, the Jordan. There is no portion for you in *the Memra of the Lord."*[25] And your sons will make our sons cease so as not to fear *from before the Lord.*[26] 26. And we said: 'Now we will act to build for ourselves an altar not for holocausts and not for the *offering of holy things,*[27] 27. for it is a witness between us and between you and between our generations after us to worship the worship of the Lord before him with our holocausts and with our sacrifices and with our *offerings of holy things.*[28] And your sons will not in the future say to our sons: 'There is no portion for you in *the Memra of the Lord.'*[29] 28. And we said: "It will happen that if they will speak to us and to our generations in the future, we will say: 'See the copy of the altar of the Lord that our fathers made — not for holocausts and not for the *offering of holy*

Notes, Chapter Twenty-Two (Cont.)

[13] MT: "God."

[14] MT: "the Lord."

[15] MT: "the Lord."

[16] MT: "he will be angry at."

[17] MT: "the Lord."

[18] MT: "the Lord."

[19] MT: "perish."

[20] MT: "he knows."

[21] MT lacks the phrase "in the end."

[22] MT: "in treachery against the Lord."

[23] MT: "the Lord."

[24] MT: "What is there to you and to the Lord."

[25] MT: "the Lord."

[26] MT: "the Lord."

[27] MT: "sacrifice."

[28] MT: "peace offerings."

[29] MT: "the Lord."

things,[30] for it is a witness between us and between you.' 29. Far be it from us *to sin before him,*[31] to rebel against *the Memra of the Lord,*[32] and turn this day from after *the worship of the Lord,*[33] to build an altar for holocausts, for cereal offerings, and for *the offering of holy things*[34] besides the altar of the Lord our God that is before his tent!" 30. And Phinehas the priest and the chiefs of the congregation and the heads of the clans of Israel who were with him heard the words that the sons of Reuben and the sons of Gad and the sons of Manasseh said, and it was pleasing in their eyes. 31. And Phinehas the son of Eleazar the priest said to the sons of Reuben and to the sons of Gad and to the sons of Manasseh: "This day we know that *the Shekinah of the Lord resides*[35] among us, that you have not acted deceitfully against *the Memra of the Lord.*[36] Thus you have saved the sons of Israel from the hand of *the Memra of the Lord.*"[37] 32. And Phinehas the son of Eleazar the priest and the chiefs returned from the sons of Reuben and from the sons of Gad, from the land of Gilead, to the land of Canaan, unto the sons of Israel, and they brought back word to them. 33. And the word was pleasing in the eyes of the sons of Israel, and the sons of Israel *gave thanks before the Lord.*[38] And they did not say to go up against them as an army, to destroy the land in which the sons of Reuben and the sons of Gad were dwelling. 34. And the sons of Reuben and the sons of Gad named the altar: "For it is a witness among us, that the Lord is God."

CHAPTER 23

1. And *at the time of many days*[1] after the Lord gave rest to Israel from all their enemies round about, Joshua was old, advanced in days. 2. And Joshua called to all Israel, to its elders and to its heads and to its judges and to its officers, and he said to them: "I have become old, advanced in days. 3. You have seen everything that the Lord your God has done to all these nations from before you, for the Lord your God — *his Memra*[2a] —was fighting for you. 4. See that I have divided for you these nations that are left in the inheritance for your tribes, from the Jordan and all the nations that I have finished off, and the great sea to the west. 5. And the Lord your God, he will shatter them from before you and drive them from before you, and you will inherit their land as the Lord your God spoke to you. 6. And you shall be very strong to keep doing everything that is written in the book of the law of Moses, so as not to deviate from it to the right and to the left, 7. so as not to be mixed among those nations that are

Notes, Chapter Twenty-Two (Cont.)

[30] MT: "sacrifice."
[31] MT lacks the phrase.
[32] MT: "the Lord."
[33] MT: "the Lord."
[34] MT: "sacrifice."
[35] MT: "the Lord is." Tg avoids expressions which localize God. S-A, 135.

[36] MT: "the Lord."
[37] MT: "the Lord."
[38] MT: "blessed God."

Notes, Chapter Twenty-Three

[1] MT: "after many days."
[2] MT: "he."
[2a] MT: "push them back."

left with you, and that in the name of their *idols*[3] you shall not make mention and you shall not make an oath and you shall not serve them and you shall not worship them, 8. but to the *fear of the Lord*[4] your God you shall cling as you have done unto this day. 9. And the Lord has driven from before you many strong nations; and as for you, no man has stood before you until this day. 10. One man from you will pursue a thousand, for the Lord your God — *his Memra*[5] — fights for you as he spoke to you. 11. And you shall guard yourselves very carefully to love the Lord your God. 12. For if indeed you turn and you cling to the rest of these nations who are left with you and you make marriages with them and *be mixed with them and they be mixed with you,*[6] 13. know assuredly that *the Memra of the Lord*[7] your God will not continue to drive out these nations from before you; and they will be for you *for a breach and for a stumbling block*[8] and for *troops bearing armor opposite you*[9] and for *camps surrounding you*[10] until you perish from upon this good land that the Lord your God has given you. 14. And behold I am going this day in the way of all the earth, and you know in all your heart and in all your soul, that not one word has failed from all the good words that the Lord your God spoke unto you. All of them have come to pass for you; not one word of them has failed. 15. And it will happen that as *all the good words*[11] that the Lord your God spoke unto you *have come to pass,*[12] so the Lord will bring upon you *all the evil words*[13] until he finishes you off from upon this good land that the Lord your God gave you, 16. when you transgress against the covenant of the Lord your God that he commanded you and you go and serve *the idols of the nations*[14] and worship them. And the anger of the Lord *will be strong*[15] against you, and you will perish quickly from upon the good land that he gave you."

CHAPTER 24

1. And Joshua gathered all the tribes of Israel to Shechem, and he called to the elders of Israel and to its heads and to its judges and to its leaders, and they presented themselves before *the Lord.*[1] 2. And Joshua said to all the people: "Thus said the Lord the God of Israel: 'Your fathers dwelt across *the Euphrates*[2] from of old — Terah the father of Abraham and the father of Nahor; and they worshipped *the idols of the*

Notes, Chapter Twenty-Three (Cont.)

[3]MT: "gods."
[4]MT: "the Lord."
[5]MT: "he."
[6]MT: "you go with them, and they go with you."
[7]MT: "the Lord."
[8]MT: "for a snare and a trap." Tg transforms metaphors into concrete realities.
[9]MT: "a scourge on your sides."

[10]MT: "thorns in your eyes."
[11]MT: "every good word."
[12]MT: "has come to pass."
[13]MT: "every evil word."
[14]MT: "other gods."
[15]MT: "will be hot."

Notes, Chapter Twenty-Four

[1]MT: "God."
[2]MT: "the river."

nations.[3] 3. And I took your father Abraham from across *the Jordan,*[4] and I led him into all the land of Canaan, and I multiplied his *sons,*[5] and I gave to him Isaac. 4. And I gave to Isaac Jacob and Esau, and I gave to Esau Mount Seir to inherit it, and Jacob and his sons went down to Egypt. 5. And I sent Moses and Aaron, and I struck down the Egyptians as I did in their midst, and afterward I brought you out. 6. And I brought out your fathers from Egypt, and you came to the sea, and the Egyptians pursued after your fathers with chariots and with horsemen *to*[6] the Red Sea. 7. And they cried out *before*[7] the Lord, and he put darkness between you and between the Egyptians, and he made the sea come over them and covered them. And your eyes saw what I did among the Egyptians, and you dwelt in the wilderness for many days. 8. And I brought you into the land of the Amorite who dwells across the Jordan, and they *waged battle*[8] with you, and I gave them in your hand, and you took possession of their land and finished them off from before you. 9. And Balak the son of Zippor the king of Moab arose and *waged battle*[9] against Israel. And he sent and called to Balaam the son of Beor to curse you. 10. And I was not willing to listen to Balaam, and he blessed you with a blessing, and I saved you from his hand. 11. And you crossed the Jordan, and you came to Jericho, and they *waged battle*[10] against you — the *inhabitants*[11] of Jericho, *the Amorites and the Perizzites and the Canaanites and the Hittites and the Girgashites, the Hivvites and the Jebusites;*[12] and I gave them in your hand. 12. And I sent before you the hornet, and *I*[13] drove them out from before you — the two kings of the Amorite, not by your sword and not by your bow. 13. And I gave to you the land in which you did not toil; and the cities which you did not build, you dwell in them; and the vineyards and the olive groves that you did not plant, you are eating. 14. And now fear *from before the Lord,*[14] and worship *before him*[15] in integrity and in truth. And put away *the idols*[16] that your fathers worshipped across the *Euphrates*[17] and in Egypt, and worship *before the Lord.*[18] 15. And if it is evil in your eyes to worship *before the Lord,*[19] choose for yourselves this day *before whom*[20] you will worship — if it be the *idols*[21] which your fathers who were across the *Euphrates*[22] worshipped, or the *idols of the Amorites*[23] in whose land you are dwelling. But I and *the men of my house*[24] — we will worship *before the Lord.*"[25] 16. And the people answered and said: "Far be it from us to abandon *the worship of the Lord*[26] to worship *the idols of the nations.*[27] 17. For it was the Lord our God who brought us and our fathers up from the land of Egypt, from the house of *slavery,*[28] and who did before our eyes these great signs and guarded us in

Notes, Chapter Twenty-Four (Cont.)

[3]MT: "other gods."
[4]MT: "the river."
[5]MT: "seed."
[6]MT lacks the preposition.
[7]MT: "to."
[8]MT: "fought."
[9]MT: "fought."
[10]MT: "fought."
[11]MT: "lords" = "baals." Tg avoids this word because it is also the title of a chief Canaanite god.
[12]These names are singulars in Hebrew.
[13]MT: "it."

[14]MT: "the Lord."
[15]MT: "him."
[16]MT: "the gods."
[17]MT: "the river."
[18]MT: "the Lord."
[19]MT: "the Lord."
[20]MT: "whom."
[21]MT: "gods."
[22]MT: "the river."
[23]MT: "the gods of the Amorite."
[24]MT: "my house."
[25]MT: "the Lord."
[26]MT: "the Lord."
[27]MT: "other gods."
[28]MT: "slaves."

all the way on which we came and in all the nations among whom we passed. 18. And the Lord drove out all the nations and the Amorite dwelling in the land from before us. We also will worship *before the Lord,*[29] for he is our God." 19. And Joshua said to the people: "You cannot worship *before the Lord,*[30] for he is a holy God, he is a jealous God; *from before the court of truth*[31] he will not forgive your debts and your sins. 20. For you will abandon *the worship of the Lord*[32] and you will serve *the idols of the nations,*[33] and he will turn and do harm to you and finish you off after he did good to you." 21. And the people said to Joshua: "No, but *before the Lord*[34] we will worship." 22. And Joshua said to the people: "You are witnesses against yourselves, that you have chosen for yourselves *the worship of the Lord*[35] to worship *before him.*"[36] And they said: "We are witnesses." 23. "And now put away *the idols of the nations*[37] who are in your midst and turn your heart to *the worship of the Lord*[38] the God of Israel." 24. And the people said to Joshua: "We will serve the Lord our God, and *we will accept his Memra.*"[39] 25. And Joshua cut a covenant for the people on that day, and he deposited for it the covenant and the statue in Shechem. 26. And Joshua wrote these words *and deposited with them*[40] the book of the law of *the Lord,*[41] and he took a great stone and set it up there beneath the oak that was in the sanctuary of the Lord. 27. And Joshua said to all the people: "Behold this stone will be for us *like the two stone tablets of the covenant, for we have made it for a witness, for the words that are written upon it are a reflection of all the words of the Lord that he spoke with us.*[42] And it will be *a memorial*[43] among you for a witness lest you be false *before*[44] your God." 28. And Joshua sent the people, each man to his inheritance. 29. And after these things Joshua the son of Nun, the servant of the Lord, died at the age of 120 years. 30. And they buried him in the territory of his inheritance, in Timnath-serah, which is in the hill country of Ephraim, north of the mountain of Gaash. 31. And Israel worshipped *before the Lord*[45] all the days of Joshua and all the days of the elders who lived on after Joshua and who knew all the work of the Lord that he did for Israel. 32. And the bones of Joseph that the sons of Israel brought up from Egypt, they buried in Shechem in the inheritance of the field that Jacob bought from the sons of Hamor, the father of Shechem, for 100 *lambs,*[46] and they were an inheritance for the sons of Joseph. 33. And Eleazar the son of Aaron died, and they buried him in Gibeah, which belonged to Phinehas his son, which was given to him in the hill country of Ephraim.

Notes, Chapter Twenty-Four (Cont.)

[29]MT: "the Lord."

[30]MT: "the Lord."

[31]MT lacks this phrase.

[32]MT: "the Lord."

[33]MT: "foreign gods."

[34]MT: "the Lord."

[35]MT: "the Lord."

[36]MT: "him."

[37]MT: "foreign gods."

[38]MT: "the Lord."

[39]MT: "we will hear his voice."

[40]MT lacks the phrase. Tg can also mean Joshua "hid" them in the book of the law.

[41]MT: "God."

[42]MT: "a witness, for it has heard all the words of the Lord that he spoke with us."

[43]MT lacks this phrase.

[44]MT: "with."

[45]MT: "the Lord."

[46]MT has an obscure word that refers to money of uncertain value.

JUDGES

CHAPTER 1

1. And after Joshua died, the sons of Israel inquired of *the Memra of the Lord*[1] saying: "Who will go up for us unto the Canaanite first to *wage battle*[2] against him?" 2. And the Lord said: "Judah will go up. Behold I have given *the inhabitants of the land*[3] in his hand." 3. And Judah said to Simeon his brother: "Go up with me in my allotment, and we will *wage battle*[4] against the Canaanite; and I also will come with you in your allotment." And Simeon went with him. 4. And *those of the house of Judah*[5] went up, and the Lord gave *the Canaanites and the Perizzites*[6] in their hand, and they struck down 10,000 men at Bezek. 5. And they found Adoni-bezek at Bezek, and they *waged battle*[7] against him, and they struck down *the Canaanites and the Perizzites.*[8] 6. And Adoni-bezek fled, and they pursued after him and seized him and cut off the joints of his hands and his feet. 7. And Adoni-bezek said: "Seventy kings whose joints of hands and feet were cut off were gathering *bread*[9] beneath my table. As I have done, so *the Lord*[10] has repaid me." And they brought him to Jerusalem, and he died there. 8. And the sons of Judah *waged battle*[11] against Jerusalem and conquered it and struck it down by the edge of the sword, and they set aflame the city with fire. 9. And afterwards the sons of Judah went down to *wage battle*[12] against the Canaanite inhabiting the hill country and *the south*[13] and the lowland. 10. And *those of the house of Judah*[14] went unto the Canaanite who was dwelling in Hebron; and the name of Hebron formerly was Kiriath-arba. And they struck down Sheshai and Ahiman and Talmi. 11. And he went from there unto the inhabitants of Debir, and the name of Debir formerly was *Kiriath-arke.*[15] 12. And Caleb said: "Whoever will strike down *Kiriath-arke*[16] and conquer it, I will give to him Achsah my daughter for a wife." 13. And Othniel, the son of Kenaz, the younger brother of Caleb, conquered it; and he gave to him Achsah his daughter for a wife. 14. And when she came, *she advised*[17] him to ask from her father *the inheritance.*[18] And she let herself down from upon the ass, and Caleb said to her: "What do you want?" 15. And she said to him: "Give to me *the

---

Notes, Chapter One

[1] MT: "the Lord."
[2] MT: "fight."
[3] MT: "the land."
[4] MT: "fight."
[5] MT: "Judah."
[6] MT: "the Canaanite and the Perizzite."
[7] MT: "fought."
[8] MT: "the Canaanite and the Perizzite."
[9] MT lacks the word.
[10] MT: "God."

[11] MT: "fought."
[12] MT: "fight."
[13] MT: "the Negeb" as a place name.
[14] MT: "Judah."
[15] MT: "Kiriath-sepher." In the name "Kiriath-sepher," the element "sepher" is understood as court records by the Tg. See Josh 15:15 and S-A, 124.
[16] MT: "Kiriath-sepher."
[17] MT: "she invited."
[18] MT: "a field."

inheritance.[19] Since you have given me the land of the south, you will give to me the springs of water." And Caleb gave to her the upper springs and the lower springs. 16. And the sons of the *Shalmaite,*[20] the father-in-law of Moses, went up from *the city of Jericho*[21] with the sons of Judah to the wilderness of Judah which is in the south of Arad, and they came and dwelt with the people. 17. And Judah went with Simeon his brother, and they struck down the Canaanite inhabiting Zepath, and they destroyed it; and (people) called the name of the city Hormah. 18. And Judah conquered Gaza and its territory, and Ashkelon and its territory, and Ekron and its territory. 19. And *the Memra of the Lord was at the aid of the house of Judah,*[22] and *they drove out the inhabitants of the hill country.*[23] *Because they sinned, they were not able*[24] to drive out the inhabitants of the plain, for they had chariots of iron. 20. And they gave to Caleb Hebron as Moses said, and he drove out from there the three sons of *the giants.*[25] 21. And the sons of Benjamin did not drive out *the Jebusites*[26] inhabiting Jerusalem, and the Jebusite dwells with the sons of Benjamin in Jerusalem unto this day. 22. And *those of the house of Joseph,*[27] they also went up to Bethel; and *the Memra of the Lord was at their aid.*[28] 23. And *those of the house of Joseph sent spies*[29] to Bethel; and the name of the city formerly was Luz. 24. And the guards saw a man going forth from the city, and they said to him: "Show us now the entrance of the city, and we will act kindly with you." 25. And he showed them the entrance of the city, and they struck down the city by the edge of the sword, and they *saved*[30] the man and all his family. 26. And the man went to the land of the Hittites, and he built a city, and called its name Luz. That is its name until this day. 27. And *those of the house of Manasseh*[31] did not drive out Beth-shean and its villages, and Taanach and its villages, and the inhabitants of Dor and its villages, and the inhabitants of Ibleam and its villages, and the inhabitants of Megiddo and its villages; and the Canaanite began to dwell in this land. 28. And when Israel was strong, it appointed the Canaanite *to bring tribute,*[32] and they did not totally drive them out. 29. And *those of the house of Ephraim*[33] did not drive out the *Canaanites*[34] who were dwelling in Gezer, and the *Canaanites*[35] dwelt in their midst in Gezer. 30. *Those of the house of Zebulun*[36] did not drive out the inhabitants of Kitron and the inhabitants of Nahalol. And the *Canaanites*[37] dwelt in their midst, and they were *bringing tribute.*[38] 31. *Those of the house of Asher*[39] did not drive out the inhabitants of Accho and the inhabitants of Sidon and Ahlab and Achzib and Helbah and Aphik and Rehob. 32. And *those of the house of Asher*[40] dwelt in the midst of the *Canaanites*[41]

Notes, Chapter One (Cont.)

[19]MT: "a blessing."

[20]MT: "Kenite." Talmud also identifies the Kenites with the Shalmaites: *y. Sheb.* 6:1 (36b); *y. Qidd.* 1:9 (61d); *b. B. Bat.* 56a.

[21]MT: "city of palms."

[22]MT: "the Lord was with Judah."

[23]MT: "he conquered the hill country."

[24]MT: "for he could not." Tg explains Joshua's inability to conquer the inhabitants of the plain by sin, as well as chariots of iron.

[25]MT: "Anak."

[26]MT: "the Jebusite."

[27]MT: "the house of Joseph."

[28]MT: "the Lord was with them."

[29]MT: "the house of Joseph spied out."

[30]MT: "let go."

[31]MT: "Manasseh."

[32]MT: "forced labor." In the targumist's time tribute was more common than forced labor.

[33]MT: "Ephraim."

[34]MT: "Canaanite."

[35]MT: "Canaanite."

[36]MT: "Zebulun."

[37]MT: "Canaanite."

[38]MT: "subject to forced labor."

[39]MT: "Asher."

[40]MT: "Asher."

[41]MT: "Canaanite."

inhabiting the land, for they did not drive them out. 33. *Those of the house of Naphtali*[42] did not drive out the inhabitants of Beth-shemesh and the inhabitants of Beth-anath, and they dwelt among *the Canaanites*[43] inhabiting the land; and the inhabitants of Beth-shemesh and of Beth-anath were *bringing tribute*[44] to them. 34. And the Amorites forced the sons of Dan to the hill country, for they did not allow them to come down to the plain. 35. And the Amorite began to dwell in the hill country of Heres, in Aijalon, and in Shaalbim; and the hand of the house of Joseph was strong, and they were *bringing tribute*.[45] 36. And the territory of the Amorite was from the ascent of Akrabbim, from *Kepha*[46] and above.

CHAPTER 2

1. And *the prophet by the commission from before the Lord*[1] went up from Gilgal to Bochim. And he said: "I brought you up from Egypt and brought you into the land that I swore to your fathers. And I said: 'I will not *change*[2] my covenant *that is*[3] with you forever. 2. And you shall not cut a covenant with the inhabitants of this land; their altars you shall break down.' And you did not *accept my Memra*;[4] what is this you have done? 3. And I said also: 'I will not drive them away from before you. And they will be to you as *oppressors,*[5] and their *idols*[6] will be to you as a stumbling block.'" 4. And when *the prophet*[7] of the Lord spoke these words with all the sons of Israel, the people raised their voice and wept. 5. And they called the name of that place "Bochim,"[8] and they sacrificed there *a sacrifice of holy things before the Lord.*[9] 6. And Joshua sent the people, and the sons of Israel went, each man to his inheritance, to possess the land. 7. And the people worshipped *before the Lord*[10] all the days of Joshua and all the days of the elders who lived on a long time after Joshua, who saw all the great work of the Lord that he did for Israel. 8. And Joshua the son of Nun, the servant of the Lord, died at the age of 120 years. 9. And they buried him in the territory of his inheritance in Timnath-heres, in the hill country *of the house of*

Notes, Chapter One (Cont.)

[42] MT: "Naphtali."

[43] MT: "Canaanite."

[44] MT: "subject to forced labor."

[45] MT: "became subject to forced labor."

[46] MT: "Sela," the equivalent of Aramaic *kêpā'* ("rock").

Notes, Chapter Two

[1] MT: "the angel of the Lord." The MT for angel means "messenger," and Tg understands the messenger as a prophet. See Judg 5:23.

[2] MT: "break."

[3] MT lacks the relative pronoun.

[4] MT: "hear my voice."

[5] MT: "sides" (*siddîm*), while other ancient versions have "adversaries" (*ṣārrîm*).

[6] MT: "gods."

[7] MT: "the angel."

[8] In both the MT and Aramaic there is a pun on the root *bkh* ("weep").

[9] MT: "to the Lord."

[10] MT: "the Lord."

Ephraim,[11] north of the hill country of Gaash. 10. And all that generation also was gathered unto its fathers, and another generation arose after them *that did not know to fear from before the Lord*[12] and also the work that he did for Israel. 11. And the sons of Israel did what is evil *before the Lord,*[13] and they served the Baals. 12. And they abandoned *the service of the Lord*[14] the God of their fathers who brought them out from the land of Egypt, and they went astray *after the idols of the nations, from the idols of the nations*[15] that were round about them; and they bowed down to them; and they *made provocation before the Lord.*[16] 13. And they abandoned *the service of the Lord*[17] and served the *Baals*[18] and the Ashtaroth. 14. And the anger of the Lord *was strong*[19] against Israel, and he gave them in the hand of plunderers, and they plundered them. And he gave them in the hand of their enemies round about, and they were not able to stand anymore before their enemies. 15. In every *place*[20] that they went forth, *slaughter from before the Lord*[21] was upon them for evil, as the Lord spoke and as the Lord swore to them; and there was very much distress for them. 16. And the Lord raised up *leaders,*[22] and they saved them from the hand of their plunderers. 17. And also *from their leaders they did not accept,*[23] for they went astray after *the idols of the nations*[24] and bowed down to them. They quickly *turned aside*[25] from the way that their fathers went to *receive*[26] the commandments of the Lord. They did not do so. 18. And when the Lord raised up for them *leaders,*[27] *the Memra of the Lord was at the aid of the leader,*[28] and he saved them from the hand of their enemies all the days of the *leader;*[29] for *the Lord was turning from what he said and was receiving their prayers and saving them*[30] from those *distressing and enslaving them.*[31] 19. And whenever the *leader*[32] died, they were turning and doing worse than their fathers to walk after *the idols of the nations,*[33] to serve them, and to bow down to them. They were not *abandoning*[34] their *evil*[35] deeds and their *corrupt ways.*[36] 20. And the anger of the Lord *was strong*[37] against Israel, and he said: "Because this people has transgressed against my covenant that I commanded their fathers and did not *receive my Memra,*[38] 21. I also will not continue to drive away any man from before them, from the nations that Joshua left when he died, 22. in order to test Israel by them whether they keep *the ways that are good before the*

Notes, Chapter Two (Cont.)

[11] MT: "of Ephraim."

[12] MT: "that did not know the Lord."

[13] MT: "in the eyes of the Lord."

[14] MT: "the Lord."

[15] MT: "after other gods from the gods of the nations."

[16] MT: "provoked the Lord."

[17] MT: "the Lord."

[18] MT: "Baal."

[19] MT: "was hot."

[20] MT lacks the word "place."

[21] MT: "the hand of the Lord."

[22] MT: "judges." Tg uses a term (*nagôdîn*) which more clearly communicates the broad powers of judges.

[23] MT: "to their judges they did not listen."

[24] MT: "other gods."

[25] MT: "prostituted themselves."

[26] MT: "hear."

[27] MT: "judges."

[28] MT: "the Lord was with the judge."

[29] MT: "judge."

[30] MT: "the Lord was moved to pity by their groaning." Tg replaces the emotional interchange with prayer.

[31] MT: "oppressing and distressing them."

[32] MT: "judge."

[33] MT: "other gods."

[34] MT: "dropping."

[35] MT lacks the word.

[36] MT: "stubborn way."

[37] MT: "was hot."

[38] MT: "hear my voice."

Lord[39] to walk in them as their fathers kept (them) or not." 23. And the Lord left those nations in order not to drive them away quickly, and he did not give them in the hand of Joshua.

CHAPTER 3

1. And these are the nations that the Lord left, by which to test Israel, all who did not know all the battles of Canaan, 2. only in order that the generations of the sons of Israel might know, so as to instruct them in war, only those who did not know beforehand. 3. The five rulers of the Philistines and all the *Canaanites*[1] and the *Sidonians*[1] and the *Hivvites*[1] inhabiting the hill country of Lebanon, from the hill country of *the plain of Hermon*[2] unto the entrance of Hamath. 4. And they were to test Israel by them, to know whether they would accept the commandments of the Lord which he commanded their fathers by means of Moses. 5. And the sons of Israel dwelt in the midst of the *Canaanites, Hittites, and Amorites and Perizzites and Hivvites and Jebusites.*[3] 6. And they took their daughters for them for wives, and they gave their daughters to their sons, and they served their *idols.*[4] 7. And the sons of Israel did what was evil *before the Lord.*[5] And they forgot *the service of the Lord*[6] their God, and they worshipped the Baals and the Asheroth. 8. And the anger of the Lord *was strong*[7] against Israel, and he *gave*[8] them in the hand of *Cushan the sinner,*[9] the king of *Aram which is on the Euphrates,*[10] and the sons of Israel served *Cushan the sinner*[11] for eight years. 9. And the sons of Israel cried out *before the Lord,*[12] and the Lord raised up a savior for the sons of Israel, and he saved them — Othniel the son of Kenaz, Caleb's younger brother. 10. *And the spirit of prophecy from before the Lord resided*[13] upon him, and he judged Israel, and he went forth *to wage battle,*[14] and the Lord gave in his hand *Cushan the sinner,*[15] the king of Aram, and his hand prevailed over *Cushan the sinner.*[16] 11. And the land *of Israel*[17] was quiet for forty years, and Othniel the son of Kenaz died. 12. And the sons of Israel continued to do what is evil *before the Lord,*[18] and the Lord strengthened Eglon the king of Moab against Israel because they did what is evil *before the Lord.*[19] 13. And he gathered unto himself the sons of Ammon and Amalek, and he went and struck down Israel, and they took possession of *the city of Jericho.*[20] 14. And the sons of Israel served Eglon the king of Moab for eighteen

Notes, Chapter Two (Cont.)

[39]MT: "the way of the Lord."

Notes, Chapter Three

[1]The MT forms are singular: Canaanite, Sidonian, Hivvite.
[2]MT: "Baal-Hermon." Tg avoids the name Baal, even in a place name.
[3]The MT forms are singular: Canaanite, Hittite, Amorite, Perizzite, Hivvite, Jebusite.
[4]MT: "gods."
[5]MT: "in the eyes of the Lord."
[6]MT: "the Lord."

[7]MT: "was hot."
[8]MT: "sold."
[9]MT: "Cushan-rishathaim." Tg interprets the root meaning of "rishathaim" (*rš* = wicked).
[10]MT: "Aram-naharim."
[11]MT: "Cushan-rishathaim."
[12]MT: "to the Lord."
[13]MT: "And the spirit of the Lord was..."
[14]MT: "to war."
[15]MT: "Cushan-rishathaim."
[16]MT: "Cushan-rishathaim."
[17]MT lacks the word "Israel."
[18]MT: "in the eyes of the Lord."
[19]MT: "in the eyes of the Lord."
[20]MT: "the city of palms."

years. 15. And the sons of Israel cried out *before the Lord,*[21] and the Lord raised up for them a savior—Ehud; the son of Gera, *a son of the tribe of Benjamin,*[22] whose right hand was *withered.*[23] And the sons of Israel sent by his hand an offering to Eglon, the king of Moab. 16. And Ehud made for himself a sword; and it had two edges, a cubit in length. And he tied it beneath his garments upon his right thigh. 17. And he brought the offering to Eglon the king of Moab; and Eglon was a very fat man. 18. And when he finished bringing the offering, he sent away the people bringing the offering. 19. And he himself turned back at *the quarries*[24] that are near Gilgal, and he said: "I have a secret message *to speak with you,*[25] O king." And he said: "Be silent." And all those who were standing by him went forth from him. 20. And Ehud entered unto him, and he was sitting alone in the upper chamber of *his summer house.*[26] And Ehud said: "*I have a message of the Lord to speak with you.*"[27] And he arose from upon his throne. 21. And Ehud reached out his left hand, and he took the sword from upon his right thigh, and he stuck it in his belly. 22. And the handle also went in after the blade, and the fat covered the faces of the blade, for he did not draw out the sword from his belly; and his feces came *pouring*[28] out. 23. And Ehud came forth to *the hall,*[29] and he closed the doors of the upper chamber on himself and locked them. 24. And he went forth, and his servants entered and saw; and behold the doors of the upper chamber were *closed,*[30] and they said: "Perhaps *he is attending to his needs*[31] in the privy of the *summer house.*[32] 25. And they waited *until a long time passed,*[33] and behold he was not opening the doors of the upper chamber. And they took the key, and opened, and behold their master was *struck down, thrown upon*[34] the ground, dead. 26. And Ehud escaped while they were delayed, and he passed *the quarries*[35] and escaped to Seirah. 27. And when he came, he blew on the trumpet in the hill country *of the house of Ephraim,*[36] and the sons of Israel went down with him from the hill country, and he was before them. 28. And he said to them: "Follow after me, for the Lord has given your enemies *the Moabites*[37] in your hand." And they went down after him and seized the fords of the Jordan against Moab, and they did not let any man pass over. 29. And they *killed the Moabites*[38] at that time, about ten thousand men, every one *fearsome*[39] and every man a warrior; and not one man escaped. 30. And *Moabites*[40] were *shattered*[41] on that day beneath the hand of Israel, and the land *of Israel*[42] was quiet for eighty years. 31. And after him was Shamgar the son of Anath, and he *killed*[43] six hundred Philistine men by means of an oxgoad, and he also saved Israel.

Notes, Chapter Three (Cont.)

[21] MT: "to the Lord."

[22] MT: "the Benjamite."

[23] MT: "restricted" (perhaps an idiom for being left-handed).

[24] MT: "the carved idols."

[25] MT: "for you."

[26] MT: "coolness."

[27] MT: "I have a word of God for you."

[28] MT lacks the word.

[29] The MT word is of uncertain meaning. It may mean "excrement" or "dirt" (MT *prš;* Aramaic *prt*) or come from an Akkadian word meaning "hole."

[30] MT: "locked."

[31] MT: "he is covering his feet."

[32] MT: "coolness."

[33] MT: "until they were confounded."

[34] MT: "falling."

[35] MT: "the carved idols."

[36] MT: "of Ephraim."

[37] MT: "Moab."

[38] MT: "struck down Moab."

[39] MT: "stout."

[40] MT: "Moab."

[41] MT: "subdued."

[42] MT lacks the word "Israel."

[43] MT: "struck down."

CHAPTER 4

1. And the sons of Israel continued to do what is evil *before the Lord,*[1] and Ehud was dead. 2. And the Lord *gave*[2] them in the hand of Jabin the king of Canaan who ruled in Hazor; and the chief of his army was Sisera, and he was dwelling *in the strength of the cities of the nations.*[3] 3. And the sons of Israel cried out *before the Lord,*[4] for he had nine-hundred chariots of iron; and he distressed the sons of Israel with might for twenty years. 4. And the woman Deborah the prophetess, the wife of Lapidoth — she was judging Israel in that time. 5. And she was dwelling *in her city at the crowns of Deborah, supporting herself from what was hers. She had palm trees in Jericho, gardens in Ramah, olive trees producing oil in the plain, troughs in Bethel, white dust in the hill country of the king.*[5] And the sons of Israel were coming up unto her for judgment. 6. And she sent and called to Barak the son of Abinoam from Kedesh *of the house of Naphtali,*[6] and she said to him: "Has not the Lord the God of Israel commanded? Go and take your positions on Mount Tabor, and take with you 10,000 men from the sons of Naphtali and from the sons of Zebulun. 7. And *I will turn toward your hand*[7] at the valley of the Kishon Sisera the chief of the army of Jabin and his *chariots*[8] and his army. And I will give him into your hand." 8. And Barak said to her: "If you will go with me, I will go. And if you will not go with me, I will not go." 9. And she said: "Indeed I will go with you. Only your glory shall not be on the road that you are going, for into the hand of a woman the Lord will *give*[9] Sisera." And Deborah arose and went with Barak to Kedesh. 10. And Barak gathered *the tribe of Zebulun*[10] and *the tribe of Naphtali*[11] to Kedesh, and 10,000 men went up *with him,*[12] and Deborah went up with him. 11. And Heber the *Shalmaite*[13] had separated from the *Shalmaites,*[14] from the sons of Hobab, the father-in-law of Moses, and had spread out his tent as far as *the plain of the pools,*[15] which is near Kedesh. 12. And they told Sisera that Barak the son of Abinoam had gone up to Mount Tabor. 13. And Sisera *gathered*[16] all his 900 chariots of iron and all the people who were with him from *the strength of the cities of the*

Notes, Chapter Four

[1]MT: "in the eyes of the Lord."

[2]MT: "sold."

[3]MT: "in Harosheth-ha-goiim." Tg partly translates the MT "ha-goiim" as "of the nations."

[4]MT: "to the Lord."

[5]MT: "under the palm of Deborah between Ramah and Bethel in the hill country of Ephraim." Tg makes Deborah reside in a city because that is where courts were located in talmudic times. The account of her wealth suggests she had no motive to be dishonest. S-A, 89, 114.

[6]MT: "of Naphtali."

[7]MT: "I will draw to you."

[8]MT: "chariot."

[9]MT: "sell."

[10]MT: "Zebulun."

[11]MT: "Naphtali."

[12]MT: "at his feet."

[13]MT: "Kenite."

[14]MT: "Kenites."

[15]MT: "the oak at Za-anannim." See S-A, 127 for similar talmudic interpretations. In Josh 19:33 Tg translates literally. Here it may read the MT letters *as by'y mym,* "pools of water."

[16]MT: "called out."

nations[17] at the valley of the Kishon. 14. And Deborah said to Barak: "Arise, for this is the day on which the Lord has given Sisera into your hand. *Is not the angel of the Lord going forth to insure success before you?*"[18] And Barak came down from Mount Tabor, and 10,000 men were behind him. 15. And the Lord *shattered*[19] Sisera and all the chariots and all the army by the edge of the sword before Barak. And Sisera came down from upon the chariot and fled on foot. 16. And Barak pursued after the chariot and after the army unto *the strength of the cities of the nations.*[20] And all the army of Sisera *was killed*[21] by the edge of the sword. Not even one was left. 17. And Sisera fled on foot to the tent of Jael the wife of Heber the *Shalmaite,*[22] for there was peace between Jabin the king of Hazor and between the house of Heber the *Shalmaite.*[23] 18. And Jael went forth to meet Sisera, and said: "Turn aside, my master, turn aside unto me. Do not fear." And he turned aside unto her to the tent, and she covered him with a blanket. 19. And he said to her: "Give me now a little water to drink, for I am thirsty *to drink.*"[24] And she opened the skin of milk, and she gave him a drink and covered him. 20. And he said to her: "Stand at the entrance of the tent. And if a man comes and asks you and says: 'Is there a man here?,' you will say 'No.'" 21. And Jael the wife of Heber took the peg of the tent and placed the hammer in her hand and entered unto him in secret and drove the peg in this temple and fixed it in the ground. And he was asleep and exhausted, and he died. 22. And behold Barak was pursuing Sisera, and Jael went forth to meet him and said to him: "Come, and I will show you the man whom you are seeking." And he entered unto her, and behold Sisera *was struck down, cast down,*[25] dead; and the peg *was fixed*[26] in his temple. 23. And *the Lord shattered*[27] on that day Jabin the king of Canaan before the sons of Israel. 24. And the hand of the sons of Israel came stronger and stronger upon Jabin the king of Canaan until they had *destroyed*[28] Jabin the king of Canaan.

CHAPTER 5

1. And Deborah and Barak the son of Abinoam *gave praise in that time,*[1] saying: 2. *"When the house of Israel rebelled against the Law, the nations came upon them and banished them from their cities. And when they turned to do the Law, they were*

Notes, Chapter Four (Cont.)

[17]MT: "Harosheth-ha-goiim." See 4:2.
[18]MT: "Is not the Lord going forth before you?"
[19]MT: "confused."
[20]MT: "Harosheth-hagoiim." See 4:2, 13.
[21]MT: "fell."
[22]MT: "Kenite."
[23]MT: "Kenite."
[24]MT lacks "to drink."
[25]MT: "falling."

[26]MT lacks the verb.
[27]MT: "God subdued."
[28]MT: "cut away."

Notes, Chapter Five

[1]MT: "sang in that day." For a full study of the chapter, see D.J. Harrington, "The Prophecy of Deborah: Interpretative Homiletics in Targum Johathan of Judges 5," *CBQ* 48 (1986) 432-442.

victorious over their enemies; they drove them out from upon the territory of the land of Israel. *Therefore on account of the punishment of the breaking of Sisera and his army, and on account of the sign and the redemption that was worked for Israel that the sages returned to sit in the synagogues at the head of the exiles and to teach the people the words of the Law — therefore* bless *and give thanks before* the Lord.[2] 3. Hear, kings; *pay attention*[3] princes. *Deborah speaks in prophecy before the Lord: 'I am praising, giving thanks, and blessing before*[4] the Lord the God of Israel. 4. *Your Law that you gave to them, to Israel, when they transgress it, the nations have power over them; and when they turn to it, they are victorious over their enemies. O Lord, on the day when you revealed yourself so as to teach* from Seir, *when you showed forth your glory upon the territories of Edom,*[5] the earth shook, also the heavens *bent down,*[6] also the clouds *spread rain.*[7] 5. The mountains shook from before the Lord. This Sinai *was shaken up; its smoke went up like the smoke of the furnace because the Lord the God of Israel was revealed upon it.*[8] 6. *When they sinned*[9] in the days of Shamgar the son of Anath, in the days of Jael, *they ceased traveling on roads*[10]*and those who were walking on pathways turned to go in hidden roads.*[11] 7. *The ruin of the unwalled cities where they were dwelling in the land of* Israel *was captured, and their inhabitants were carried off* until *I was commissioned* — *I* Deborah — *I was commissioned to prophesy in the midst of the house of* Israel.[12] 8. *When the house of Israel chose to serve* new *idols, which were made nearby, with which their fathers had not occupied themselves, the nations came against them and drove them from their cities. And whenever they returned to the Law, they could not overpower them, so that when the enemy came against them (and with him were men holding shields and spears) with forty-thousand army-chiefs, they were not able to wage battle in Israel.*[13] 9. *Deborah speaks in prophecy: 'I was sent to give praise to the teachers of Israel who, when that affliction happened, did not cease from studying in the Law; and who, whenever it was proper for them, were sitting in the synagogues at the head of the exiles and were teaching the people the words of the Law and blessing and giving thanks before God.*[14] 10. *Those who were ceasing their labors,* riding *upon* asses *that were saddled with kinds of embroideries, and were going in all the territory of the land of Israel, and were being chosen to sit* for judgment, *they will be going on their ways and talking about the wonders that were done for them.*[15] 11. *From the place were they were assalting them and*

Notes, Chapter Five (Cont.)

[2]MT: "When the leaders acted as leaders in Israel, when the people volunteered themselves...bless the Lord." S-A, 87 connect this verse (and many descriptions in this chapter) with Hadrian's persecution after the Bar-Kokhba War. See Churgin 126-129 (S-A, 354-356) for a discussion of how midrashic elements were added to this chapter.

[3]MT: "give ear."

[4]MT: "I will sing to the Lord, I will chant to."

[5]MT: "O Lord, in your going forth from Seir, in your marching from the field of Edom."

[6]MT: "dripped" or "rained."

[7]MT: "dripped water."

[8]MT: "This Sinai from before the Lord God of Israel."

[9]MT lacks the phrase.

[10]MT: "caravans ceased."

[11]MT: "were going by crooked roads."

[12]MT: "Peasantry ceased, in Israel they ceased, until you arose, Deborah, you arose as a mother in Israel."

[13]MT: "One chose new gods, then war was at the gates. Was shield and spear to be seen among the 40,000 in Israel?"

[14]MT: "My heart is to the commanders of Israel, those volunteering themselves among the people, bless the Lord."

[15]MT: "O riders of tawny asses, those sitting on the judgment seat, and those walking upon the way, tell it." S-A, 87-88, connect this verse with the restoration of the judicial processes after the Hadrianic persecution.

taking what was in their hands — the place of seats of the toll-collectors and the residence of bandits, in back of the water troughs — there *they will give thanks on account of the righteousness of* the Lord, *on account of the righteousness of him who was dwelling in the unwalled cities* in *the land of* Israel. Then they went down *from the strong fortresses to dwell in the unwalled cities —* the people of the Lord.[16] 12. *Give praise, give praise,* Deborah, *give praise, and give thanks;* speak *praise.*[17] Arise, Barak, and capture your captives, son of Abinoam. 13. Then *one from the armies of Israel* went down *and shattered the strength of the* warriors *of the nations. Behold this was not from might, but rather the Lord shattered before his people the strength of the warriors of their enemies.*[18] 14. From *those of the house of* Ephraim, *there arose Joshua the son of Nun; he first waged battle against those of the house of* Amalek. After *him there arose King Saul from those of the house of* Benjamin; *he killed those of the house of Amalek and waged battle against the rest of the* nations. From *those of the house of* Machir, *those who were marked* went down *in battle;* and from *the tribe of* Zebulun *they were writing with the pen of a scribe.*[19] 15. And the captains of Issachar *were listening to the words of* Deborah, and *the rest of the tribe of* Issachar *were serving before* Barak, *being* sent *forth in the cities of the* plain *to every place where there was need in his sending them forth.* In *the clans of* Reuben *there were many crafty of heart.*[20] 16. Why did you sit *apart from the armies of war, to sit* between *the borders,* to hear *good news, to know bad news? My army is victorious with her. Was it right for you to do (so), you of the house of* Reuben? *Did you not know that before me the thoughts of the* heart *are revealed?*[21] 17. *Those of the house of* Gilead camped out across the Jordan. *And those of the house of* Dan *passed over, crossed the Jordan, put their goods in* ships. *Those of the house of* Asher camped out on the shore of the seas; *the cities of the nations that they destroyed — they turned, built them, and* dwelt *in them.*[22] 18. *Those of the house of* Zebulun *opposite to the nations that blasphemed —they handed over their* life *to killing. They* and *those of the house of* Naphtali — *all the inhabitants of the land gave them praise.*[23] 19. The kings came; *they waged battle.* Then they fought the kings of Canaan at Taanach. *They were camping and settling down* by the waters of Megiddo; *wealth* of silver they did not take.[24] 20. From the heavens *the battle was waged with them; from the place where* the stars *go forth,* from the courses *of their movements, there the battle was waged*[25] with Sisera. 21. The Wadi

Notes, Chapter Five (Cont.)

[16]MT: "From the sound of cymbals at the watering places, there they recount the mighty acts of the Lord, the mighty acts of his peasantry in Israel; then the people of Israel went down to the gates."

[17]MT: "Awake, awake, Deborah, awake, awake, words of song."

[18]MT: "Then the survivor went down to the nobles, the people of the Lord went down for me against the warriors."

[19]MT: "Those from Ephraim, their root is in Amalek behind you, Benjamin, among your peoples. Those from Machir the commanders went down, and from Zebulun they draw on the staff of the scribe."

[20]MT: "The chiefs in Issachar were with Deborah; and Issachar was the support of Barak, sent forth in the valley, at his feet. In the divisions of Reuben great were the searchings of heart."

[21]MT: "Why did you sit among the sheepfolds, to listen to the pipings for flocks? For the divisions of Reuben great were the searchings of heart."

[22]MT: "Gilead was dwelling in Transjordan; and Dan, why did he abide with ships? Asher dwelt at the shore of the seas, and at his harbors he was dwelling."

[23]MT: "Zebulun is a people that endangered its life to die. Naphtali upon the heights of the field."

[24]MT lacks the phrases.

[25]MT: "the stars fought; from their courses they fought."

Kishon *shattered* them, the wadi *in which signs and mighty acts were done for Israel from of old — that* Wadi Kishon — *there* my soul crushed their warriors *dead by force.*[26] 22. Then the hoofs of their horses *slipped,*[27] *the galloping that gallops before the chariots of*[28] his warriors. 23. "Curse Meroz" said *the prophet*[29] of the Lord. "Curse, *and*[30] shatter its inhabitants, for they did not come to the aid of *the people of the Lord*[31] to the aid of *the people of the Lord,*[32] *when it waged battle*[33] with warriors." 24. May Jael the wife of Heber *the Shalmaite*[34] be blessed *with the blessing of good women;*[35] may she be blessed *like one of the women who serve in the houses of study.*[36] 25. He asked *her* for water; she gave him milk *to drink; to find out if his pleasure was* in the bowls of warriors, she brought *before him cream-cheese.*[37] 26. She reached out her hand for the tent-peg, and her right hand for the hammer *to shatter wicked men and oppressors. She struck it down into* Sisera; she shattered his head; she crushed *his brain;* she made it pass through in his temple.[38] 27. Between her feet he collapsed, he fell, he lay down. Between her feet he collapsed, he fell. In the place where he collapsed, there *Sisera*[39] fell, plundered. 28. From the window the mother of Sisera looked out *and was gazing from between the laths. She was saying:*[40] "Why are *the chariots of my son*[41] slow to come? Why *are the runners who are bringing to me the letter of victories detained?"*[42] 29. The wisest of her chambermaids were answering her. Even she *according to her wisdom*[43] was answering and saying to her: 30. "Are they not dividing *from what* they are finding, *giving as* spoil *a man and his household to each and every one? Much spoil before* Sisera, spoil of dyed embroidered cloth upon *his* neck, *rich possessions, and delightful things before his warriors who despoiled."*[44] 31. *Like Sisera,* so may all *the haters of your people* perish, Lord; *and may his mercies be ready to give light with the light of his splendor 343 times over,*[45] like the rising of the sun in its might. And the land *of Israel*[46] was at rest forty years."

Notes, Chapter Five (Cont.)

[26]MT: "swept away, the onrushing brook, the brook Kishon; march on, my soul, with strength."

[27]MT: "the horse-hoofs beat loud."

[28]MT: "of his steeds."

[29]MT: "the angel."

[30]MT: "curse bitterly."

[31]MT: "the Lord."

[32]MT: "the Lord."

[33]MT: "against warriors."

[34]MT: "the Kenite."

[35]MT: "among women."

[36]MT: "from the women in the tent."

[37]MT: "He asked water; she gave milk; in the bowl of the warriors she brought curds."

[38]MT: "for the hammer of workmen; and she struck Sisera a blow, she struck his head and his skull, and she pierced his temple."

[39]MT lacks the name.

[40]MT: "she exclaimed by way of the lattice."

[41]MT: "his chariot."

[42]MT: "do the hoofbeats of his chariots tarry."

[43]MT lacks the phrase.

[44]MT: "Are they not finding, dividing the spoil? — a womb, two wombs for each man, spoil of dyed stuffs for Sisera, spoil of dyed stuffs, embroidery, dyed stuff, two pieces of embroidery for the neck as spoil."

[45]MT: "So may all your enemies perish, Lord: and his loved ones." The number 343 is explained by Churgin (125) as 7 x 7 x 7 = 343, an allusion to the light of the seven stars in the seven days of creation.

[46]MT: "the land."

CHAPTER 6

1. And the sons of Israel did what was evil *before the Lord,*[1] and the Lord gave them into the hand of the *Midianites*[2] for seven years. 2. And the hand of the *Midianites*[3] prevailed over Israel. On account of the *Midianites*[4] the sons of Israel made for themselves the hiding places that were in the mountains and the caves and the strongholds. 3. And whenever Israel sowed, *the Midianites and Amalekites*[5] and the sons of the east would come up; and they were coming up against *them.*[6] 4. And they were camping against them and destroying the produce of the land unto the entrance of Gaza, and they were not leaving *food to sustain life*[7] in Israel, and sheep and ox and ass. 5. For they and their herds were coming up, and their tents; *and*[8] they were coming like the locust for number; and for their camels there was no number; and they were entering the land to destroy it. 6. And Israel sunk very low before the *Midianites.*[9] And the sons of Israel cried out *before*[10] the Lord. 7. And when the sons of Israel cried out *before*[11] the Lord on account of the *Midianites,*[12] 8. the Lord sent a man, a prophet, unto the sons of Israel, and he said to them: "Thus said the Lord the God of Israel: 'I brought you up from Egypt and brought you out from the house of *slavery.*[13] 9. And I saved you from the hand of the Egyptians and from the hand of all those oppressing you, and I drove them from before you and I gave to you their land. 10. And I said to you: "I am the Lord your God. Do not fear *the idols of the Amorites*[14] in whose land you are dwelling." And you did not *accept my Memra.*'"[15] 11. And the angel of the Lord came and sat beneath the terebinth, which was in Ophrah, which belonged to Joash the father of *Azar.*[16] And Gideon his son was beating out wheat in the press to hide it from before *the Midianites.*[17] 12. And the angel of the Lord appeared to him, and he said to him: "*The Memra of the Lord is at your aid,*[18] O mighty warrior." 13. And Gideon said to him: "Please, my master, if *the Shekinah of the Lord is at our aid,*[19] why have *all these*[20] happened to us? And where are all his wonders that our fathers recounted to us, saying: 'Did not the Lord bring us up from Egypt?' And now the Lord has abandoned us and given us in the hand of the *Midianites.*"[21] 14. And the Lord turned to him and

Notes, Chapter Six

[1]MT: "in the eyes of the Lord."
[2]MT: "Midian."
[3]MT: "Midian."
[4]MT: "Midian."
[5]MT: "Midian and Amalek."
[6]MT: "it," i.e., Israel.
[7]MT: "sustenance."
[8]MT lacks the word "and."
[9]MT: "Midian."
[10]MT: "to."
[11]MT: "to."

[12]MT: "Midian."
[13]MT: "slaves."
[14]MT: "the gods of the Amorite."
[15]MT: "hear my voice."
[16]MT: "the Ezrite."
[17]MT: "Midian."
[18]MT: "the Lord is with you."
[19]MT: "the Lord is with us."
[20]MT: "all this."
[21]MT: "Midian."

said: "Go in this might of yours, and you will save Israel from the hand of the *Midianites.*[22] Have I not sent you?" 15. And he said to him: "Please, Lord, with what will I save Israel? Behold my family is small in *the tribe of Manasseh,*[23] and I am *weak*[24] in the house of my father." 16. And the Lord said to him: "Since *my Memra will be at your aid,*[25] you will *kill the Midianites*[26] like one man." 17. And he said to him: "If now I have found mercy in your eyes, do for me a sign that you are speaking with me. 18. Now do not depart from here until I come unto you and I bring out my offering and lay (it) before you." And he said: "I will *wait*[27] until you return." 19. And Gideon went and prepared a kid-goat, and *he baked a measure of unleavened flour;*[28] the meat he placed in a basket, and the broth he placed in a pot. And he brought them forth unto him beneath the terebinth, and brought them near. 20. And the angel of the *Lord*[29] said to him: "Take the meat and the unleavened cake, and set them down on this rock; and pour out the broth." And he did so. 21. And the angel of the Lord reached out the tip of the staff that was in his hand, and brought it near the meat and near the unleavened cake. And the fire went up from the stone, and it devoured the meat and the unleavened cake. And the angel of the Lord *was taken up from before*[30] his eyes. 22. And Gideon saw that he was the angel of the Lord. And Gideon said: "*Please, O Lord God,*[31] for so I have seen the angel of the Lord face to face." 23. And the Lord said to him: "Peace to you. Do not fear. You will not die." 24. And Gideon built there an altar *before the Lord,*[32] and *he worshipped upon it before the Lord who made peace for him.*[33] Unto this day, unto now, it is in Ophrah of the father of *Azar.*[34] 25. And on that night the Lord said to him: "Take an ox of your father's oxen and a second ox *which has been fattened up*[35] for seven years; and you shall break up the *mound*[36] of Baal that is your father's, and the Asherah that is by it you shall cut down. 26. And you shall build the altar *before the Lord*[37] your God upon the top of this stronghold in order, and you shall take the second ox and offer it up as a holocaust on the wood of the Asherah that you are to cut down." 27. And Gideon took ten men from his servants and did as the Lord spoke with him. And because he was afraid of the house of his father and of the men of the town to do it by day, he did it by night. 28. And the men of the town got up early in the morning; and behold the *mound*[38] of Baal was broken up, and the Asherah that was by it was cut up, and the second ox was offered up upon the altar that was built. 29. And they said, each man to his neighbor: "Who has done this thing?" And they searched and inquired, and they said: "Gideon the son of Joash has done this thing." 30. And the men of the city said to Joash: "Bring forth your son, and let him *be killed,*[39] for he broke down the *mound*[40] of Baal and cut down the Asherah that was by

Notes, Chapter Six (Cont.)

[22]MT: "Midian."
[23]MT: "Manasseh."
[24]MT: "least."
[25]MT: "I will be with you."
[26]MT: "strike down Midian."
[27]MT: "stay."
[28]MT: "unleavened cakes (from) an ephah of flour."
[29]MT: "God."
[30]MT: "went from."

[31]MT: "Alas, my master, O Lord."
[32]MT: "to the Lord."
[33]MT: "he called it 'the Lord is peace.' "
[34]MT: "the Ezrite."
[35]MT lacks the verb.
[36]Tg uses different Aramaic words to distinguish the altar of Baal (6:25) from the altar before the Lord (6:26).
[37]MT: "to the Lord."
[38]MT: "altar."
[39]MT: "die."
[40]MT: "altar."

it." 31. And Joash said to all those who rose up against him: "Will you *take revenge*[41] for Baal? Will you save him? Whoever *takes revenge*[42] for him, let him *be killed.*[43] *But a time-limit is given to him until morning. If there is need in this, let Baal take revenge for himself,*[44] for he broke down his *mound.*"[45] 32. And he called him on that day "Jerubbaal," saying: "Let Baal *take revenge for himself,*[46] for he tore down his *mound.*"[47] 33. And all *the Midianites and Amalekites*[48] and the sons of the east were gathered together, and they crossed over and camped in the plain of Jezreel. 34. And *the spirit of power from before the Lord*[49] clothed Gideon, and he blew on the trumpet, and *the men of Abiezer*[50] were gathered behind him. 35. And he sent messengers in all *the tribe of Manasseh,*[51] and they also were gathered behind him. And he sent messengers in *the tribe of Asher*[52] and in *the tribe of Zebulun*[53] and in *the tribe of Naphtali,*[54] and they went up toward them. 36. And Gideon said *before the Lord:*[55] "If you are saving Israel by my hand as you have spoken, 37. behold I am setting down the fleece of the wool in the threshing place. If there be dew upon the fleece alone and upon all the ground it be dry, I shall know that you will save Israel by my hand as you have spoken." 38. And it was so. And he got up early on the next day and squeezed the fleece and *shook*[56] the dew from the fleece to fill a *flask*[57] of water. 39. And Gideon said *before the Lord:*[58] "Let not your anger *be strong*[59] against me, and let me speak but this time. Let me test now, only this time with the fleece. Now let it be dry upon the fleece alone, and upon all the land let there be dew." 40. And *the Lord*[60] did so on that night, and it was dry upon the fleece alone and upon all the ground there was dew.

CHAPTER 7

1. And Jerubbaal (that is, Gideon) got up early, and all the people who were with him. And they camped by the spring of Harod; and *the camp of the Midianites was camping opposite him on the north,*[1] on *the hill that faces*[2] the plain. 2. And the Lord

Notes, Chapter Six (Cont.)

[41] MT: "contend."
[42] MT: "contends."
[43] MT: "die."
[44] MT: "until morning. If he is a god, he will contend for himself." The extension of the time limit until morning fulfills the Mishnaic requirement that a trial in a capital case take two days. See *m. Sanh.* 4:1; S-A, 5.
[45] MT: "altar."
[46] MT: "contend against him."
[47] MT: "altar."
[48] MT: "all Midian and Amalek."
[49] MT: "the spirit of the Lord."
[50] MT: "Abiezer."
[51] MT: "Manasseh." Several Tg mss: "the territory of Manasseh."
[52] MT: "Asher."
[53] MT: "Zebulun."
[54] MT: "Naphtali."
[55] MT: "to God."
[56] MT: "wrung."
[57] MT: "bowl."
[58] MT: "to God."
[59] MT: "be not."
[60] MT: "God."

Notes, Chapter Seven

[1] MT: "the camp of Midian was north of him."
[2] MT: "the hill of Moreh in..." Tg understands the name "Moreh" as meaning "showing" and so "overlooking."

said to Gideon: "The people that are with you are too many *to give the Midianites*[3] into their hand, lest Israel boast *before*[4] me, saying: '*Our hand saved us.*'[5] 3. And now proclaim *before*[6] the people, saying: 'Whoever is fearful and trembling, let him return and *separate himself*[7] from Mount Gilead." And 22,000 from the people returned, and 10,000 were left. 4. And the Lord said to Gideon: "The people are still too many. Bring them down to the water, and I will test them for you there. And whomever I say to you 'This one will go with you,' he will go with you; and everyone whom I will say to you 'This one will not go with you,' he will not go." 5. And he brought the people down to the water. And the Lord said to Gideon: "Everyone who will lap with his tongue from the water as the dog laps, you will have stand alone; and everyone who bows down upon his knees to drink." 6. And the number of those who were *pouring*[8] with their hand to their mouth was three-hundred men; and all the rest of the people bowed down upon their knees to drink the water. 7. And the Lord said to Gideon: "With the three-hundred men who were *pouring*[9] I will save you and give *the Midianites*[10] in your hand. And let all the people go, each man to his place." 8. And they took the provisions of the people in their hand and their trumpets; and he sent all the men of Israel, each man to his *town*,[11] and with the three-hundred men he grew strong. And *the camp of the Midianites was encamped opposite him, below*[12] in the valley. 9. And on that night the Lord said to him: "Arise, go down in the camp, for I have given *them*[13] in your hand. 10. And if you are afraid to go down, you and Purah your young man go down to the camp. 11. And you will hear what they are speaking, and afterward your hands will be strong, and you will go down in the camp." And he and Purah his young man went down to beside the armed men who were in the camp. 12. And *the Midianites and the Amalekites*[14] and all the sons of the east were lying in the plain like the locust for multitude; and for their camels there was no number — like the sand that is upon the shore of the sea for multitude. 13. And Gideon came; and behold a man was recounting to his companion a dream, and he said: "Behold the dream I dreamt. And behold a cake of barley bread rolled about in the camp of *the Midianites*,[15] and it came unto the tent, and struck it down, and it fell; and it turned it upside down, and the tent fell." 14. And his companion answered and said: "This is nothing but the sword of Gideon, the son of Joash, the man of Israel. *The Lord*[16] has given in his hand *the Midianites*[17] and all the camp." 15. And when Gideon heard the recounting of the dream and its interpretation, *he gave thanks*[18] and returned to the camp of Israel. And he said: "Arise, for the Lord has given in your hand the camp of *the Midianites*."[19] 16. And he divided the three-hundred men into three companies, and he gave trumpets in the hand of all of them and empty jars and torches inside the jars. 17. And he said to them: "At me you

Notes, Chapter Seven (Cont.)

[3]MT: "for me to give Midian."

[4]MT: "against."

[5]MT: "My hand saved me."

[6]MT: "in the ears of."

[7]MT: "depart."

[8]MT: "lapping." In this and the next verse the chosen men are pictured as pouring water rather than lapping, an undignified process.

[9]MT: "lapping."

[10]MT: "Midian."

[11]MT: "tent."

[12]MT: "the camp of Midian was below him."

[13]MT: "it."

[14]MT: "Midian and Amalek."

[15]MT: "Midian."

[16]MT: "God."

[17]MT: "Midian."

[18]MT: "worshipped."

[19]MT: "Midian."

shall look, and do thus. And when I am coming to the outskirts of the camp, as I do, so you will do. 18. And I will blow on the trumpet — I and all who are with me; and you also will blow on the trumpets round about all the camp. And you will say: '*A sword from before the Lord, and victory by the hands of Gideon.*'"[20] 19. And Gideon and the hundred men who were with him came to the outskirts of the camp at the beginning of the middle watch (but they had just set up the watchmen), and they blew on the trumpets and shattered the jars that were in their hands. 20. And the three companies blew on the trumpets and broke the jars, and they held in their left hand the torches and in their right hands the trumpets to blow. And they said: "A sword *from before the Lord, and victory by the hands of Gideon.*"[21] 21. And they arose, each man in his place, round about the camp, and all the camp ran, and they shouted and fled. 22. And the three-hundred blew the trumpets, and the Lord placed the sword, each man against his fellow, and against all the camp. And the camp fled unto Beth-shittah to Zererah, unto the edge of *the plain of Meholah,*[22] to Tabbath. 23. And the men of Israel were gathered from *the tribe of Naphtali*[23] and from *the tribe of Asher*[24] and from all *the tribe of Manasseh,*[25] and they pursued after *the Midianites.*[26] 24. And Gideon sent messengers in all the hill country *of the house of Ephraim,*[27] saying: "Come down to meet *the Midianites,*[28] and seize against them the *fords*[29] unto Beth-barah and the Jordan." And all the men of Ephraim were gathered, and they seized the *fords*[30] unto Beth-barah and the Jordan. 25. And they seized two chiefs of Midian — Oreb and Zeeb. And they killed Oreb at the cleft of Oreb, and they killed Zeeb at the *plain*[31] of Zeeb. And they pursued after *the Midianites.*[32] And they brought the head of Oreb and Zeeb unto Gideon from across the Jordan.

CHAPTER 8

1. And the men of Ephraim said to him: "What is this thing you have done to us? *Why did you not call*[1] to us when you went to *wage battle*[2] against *the Midianites?*"[3] And they were contending with him with force. 2. And he said to them: "What have I done now compared to you? Are not *the weak ones of the house of Ephraim*[4] better

Notes, Chapter Seven (Cont.)

[20]MT: "For the Lord and for Gideon." Tg keeps Gideon firmly subordinate to Yahweh. See S-A, 141.

[21]MT: "for the Lord and for Gideon."

[22]MT: "Abel (= plain)-meholah."

[23]MT: "Naphtali."

[24]MT: "Asher."

[25]MT: "Manasseh."

[26]MT: "Midian."

[27]MT: "Ephraim."

[28]MT: "Midian."

[29]MT: "waters."

[30]MT: "waters."

[31]MT: "wine press."

[32]MT: "Midian."

Notes, Chapter Eight

[1]MT has an infinitive construction: "not to call."

[2]MT: "fight."

[3]MT: "Midian."

[4]MT: "the gleaning of Ephraim."

than *the strong ones of the house of Abiezer?*[5] 3. In your hand *the Lord*[6] gave the chiefs of Midian, Oreb and Zeeb; and what was I able to do compared to you?" Thus their anger abated from him when he spoke this word. 4. And Gideon came to the Jordan. He and the three-hundred men who were with him crossed over, *when*[7] they were tired and pursuing. 5. And he said to the men of Succoth: "Give now *a piece*[8] of bread to the people who are *with me*,[9] for they are tired and I am pursuing after Zebah and Zalmunna, kings of Midian." 6. And the chiefs of Succoth said: "Are Zebah and Zalmunna *caught now, given*[10] in your hand, that we should give bread to your army?" 7. And Gideon said: "So when the Lord gives Zebah and Zalmunna in my hand, I will thresh your flesh upon the thorns of the wilderness and upon the thistles." 8. And he went up from there to Penuel, and he spoke with them in the same way. And the men of Penuel answered him as the men of Succoth answered. 9. And he also said to the men of Penuel, saying: "When I return in peace, I will break down this tower." 10. And Zebah and Zalmunna were in Karkor, and their armies were with them, about 15,000, all who were left from all the army of the sons of the east; and 120,000 men drawing the sword *had been killed.*[11] 11. And Gideon went up by way *of the camp of the Arabs*[12] who were dwelling in tents in the wilderness east of Nobah and the *height;*[13] and he struck down the camp, and the camp *was encamped for safety.*[14] 12. And Zebah and Zalmunna fled, and he pursued after them and seized the two kings of Midian, Zebah and Zalmunna; and he panicked all the camp. 13. And Gideon the son of Joash returned from the battle *before sunrise.*[15] 14. And he seized a young man from the men of Succoth, and he questioned him; and he wrote down for him the chiefs of Succoth and its elders —seventy-seven men. 15. And he came unto the men of Succoth and said: "Behold Zebah and Zalmunna about whom you jeered at me, saying: 'Behold are Zebah and Zalmunna *caught now, given*[16] in your hand, that we should give bread to your men who are tired?'" 16. And he took the elders of the city and the thorns of the wilderness and the thistles; and he *dragged* the men of Succoth *upon*[17] them. 17. And he broke down the tower of Penuel and killed the men of the city. 18. And he said to Zebah and Zalmunna: "Where are the men whom you killed on Tabor?" And they said: "Like you, so also were they, everyone *of them,*[18] according to the appearance of the sons of the king." 19. And he said: "They were my brothers, the sons of my mother. As the Lord lives, if you let them live, I would not kill you." 20. And he said to Jether his firstborn: "Arise, kill them." And the young man did not draw his sword, for he was afraid, for he was still young. 21. And Zebah and Zalmunna said: "You arise, and *overpower*[19] us, for as the man so his strength." And Gideon arose and killed Zebah and Zalmunna, and he took the *chains*[20] that were on the necks of their camels. 22. And the men of Israel said to Gideon: "Rule over us, both you and your son and your

Notes, Chapter Eight (Cont.)

[5]MT: "the vintage of Abiezer." Tg turns a pastoral proverb into a prose interpretation.

[6]MT: "God."

[7]MT lacks the conjunction "when."

[8]MT: "loaves."

[9]MT: "at my feet."

[10]The MT *hkp* is problematic. Some emend to *h'p* (interrogative particle plus "also").

[11]MT: "those falling were."

[12]MT lacks the phrase. Ms. p. reads "Aroer" rather than "the Arabs."

[13]MT: "Jogbehah."

[14]MT: "was secure" (i.e., off-guard).

[15]MT: "by ascent of Heres," or "by the ascent of the sun."

[16]MT has the same problem as in 8:6.

[17]MT: "taught...by."

[18]MT lacks the word "of them."

[19]MT: "fall upon."

[20]MT: "crescents."

grandson, for you have saved us from the hand of *the Midianites*."²¹ 23. And Gideon said to them: "I will not rule over you, nor will my son rule over you. The Lord *is king*²² over you." 24. And Gideon said to them: "I am asking from you a request; and give to me, every man, *his earring from the spoil*,"²³ for they had earrings of gold, for *they killed the Arabs*."²⁴ 25. And they said: "Indeed we will give them." And they spread out the garment and threw there each man *his earring from the spoil*.²⁵ 26. And the weight of the earrings of gold that he requested was 1,700 of gold apart from the crescents and *crowns*²⁶ and the garments of purple that were upon the kings of Midian, and apart from the chains that were on the necks of their camels. 27. And Gideon made it into an ephod, and he set it up in his city in Ophrah; and all Israel *went astray*²⁷ there after it; and it was a snare for Gideon and for his house. 28. And *the Midianites were shattered*²⁸ before the sons of Israel, and they did not continue to raise up their head. And *the land of Israel*²⁹ was quiet for forty years in the days of Gideon. 29. And Jerubbaal the son of Joash went and dwelt in his house. 30. And Gideon had seventy sons going forth from his loins, for he had many wives. 31. And his concubine who was in Shechem also bore to him a son, and he called his name Abimelech. 32. And Gideon the son of Joash died in good old age, and he was buried in the grave of Joash his father in Ophrah, of *his father, of Azar*.³⁰ 33. And when Gideon died, the sons of Israel turned and *went astray*³¹ after the Baals, and made for themselves Baal-of-the-Covenant for *the idols*.³² 34. And the sons of Israel were not mindful of *the service of the Lord*³³ their God who saved them from the hand of all their enemies round about. 35. And they did not act kindly with the house of Jerubbaal (Gideon) according to all the good that he did with Israel.

CHAPTER 9

1. And Abimelech the son of Jerubbaal went to Shechem unto the brothers of his mother, and spoke with them and with all the family of the house of the father of his mother, saying: 2. "Speak now *before*¹ all the *inhabitants*² of Shechem: 'What is better for you, that seventy men, all the sons of Jerubbaal, should rule over you, or that one man rule over you? And remember that I am your *relative*³ and your flesh.'" 3. And the

---

Notes, Chapter Eight (Cont.)

²¹MT: "Midian."
²²MT: "will rule."
²³MT: "the earring of his spoil."
²⁴MT: "they were Ishmaelites." Tg "modernizes" the Ishmaelites, who lived across the Jordan, into Arabs.
²⁵MT: "the earring of his spoil."
²⁶MT: "pendants."
²⁷MT: "played the harlot."
²⁸MT: "Midian was subdued."
²⁹MT: "the land."

³⁰MT: "the Abiezrite."
³¹MT: "played the harlot."
³²MT: "gods."
³³MT: "the Lord."

Notes, Chapter Nine

¹MT: "in the ears of."
²MT: "masters," i.e., *ba'ălê*, which is similar to the name of the Canaanite god, Baal. Tg avoids it.
³MT: "bone."

brothers of his mother spoke about him *before*[4] all the *inhabitants*[5] of Shechem all these words. And their heart turned after Abimelech, for they said: "He is our brother." 4. And they gave to him seventy (pieces) of silver from the house of Baal-of-the-Covenant; and Abimelech *collected*[6] with them idle and *light-minded*[7] men, and they went after him. 5. And he entered the house of his father to Ophrah, and he killed his brothers, the sons of Jerubbaal, seventy men, upon one stone. And Jotham the youngest son of Jerubbaal was left, for he hid himself. 6. And all the *inhabitants*[8] of Shechem and all Beth-millo were gathered together, and they came and made Abimelech king, *to be the king,*[9] by *the plain of the standing grain*[10] that is in Shechem. 7. And they told Jotham, and he went and stood on the top of Mount Gerizim, and he lifted up his voice and called and said to them: "*Receive from me, inhabitants of Shechem, and the Lord will receive your prayers.*[11] 8. The trees went to *appoint*[12] over them the king, and they said to the olive tree: 'Rule over us.' 9. And the olive tree said to them: 'Shall I leave behind *my oil from which they do honor before the Lord and in which the chiefs are delighted,*[13] and go to *exercise kingship*[14] over the trees?' 10. And the trees said to the fig tree: 'Come, you rule over us.' 11. And the fig tree said to them: 'Shall I leave behind my sweetness and my *beautiful fig cake,*[15] and go to *exercise kingship*[16] over the trees?' 12. And the trees said to the vine: 'Come, you rule over us.' 13. And the vine said to them: 'Shall I leave behind my wine *from which libations are offered before the Lord and in which the chiefs rejoice,*[17] and go to *exercise kingship*[18] over the trees?' 14. And all the trees said to the bramble: 'Come, you rule over us.' 15. And the bramble said to the trees: 'If in truth you are anointing me *to be king*[19] over you, go up, *camp*[20] in my shade. And if not, the fire will go forth from the bramble and devour the cedars of Lebanon. 16. And now if in truth and in sincerity you acted and you made Abimelech king, and if you have acted kindly with Jerubbaal and with his house, and if according to the recompense of his hands you have done to him — 17. for my father fought for you and *gave his life so as to be killed,*[21] and saved you from the hand of *the Midianites;*[22] 18. and you have risen up against the house of my father this day and killed his sons, seventy men, on one stone; and you have made Abimelech, the son of his maidservant, king over the *inhabitants*[23] of Shechem, because he is your brother — 19. and if in truth and in sincerity you have acted with Jerubbaal and with his house this day, rejoice in Abimelech and let him also rejoice in you. 20. And if not, the fire will go forth from Abimelech and devour the *inhabitants*[24] of Shechem and Beth-millo, and

Notes, Chapter Nine (Cont.)

[4]MT: "in the ears of."

[5]MT: "masters," i.e., *ba'ălê.* Tg. avoids this word because of the god Baal.

[6]MT: "hired."

[7]MT: "reckless."

[8]MT: "masters." i.e., *ba'ălê.*

[9]MT: "for king."

[10]MT: "the oak of the pillar." The root meaning of "pillar" is to stand up, hence Tg's "standing grain."

[11]MT: "Listen to me, masters of Shechem; and God will listen to you."

[12]MT: "anoint."

[13]MT: "my fatness by which gods and men are honored."

[14]MT: "hold sway." Tg uses separate verbs for God and humans so that God's superiority is protected.

[15]MT: "good fruit."

[16]MT: "hold sway." Tg uses separate verbs for God and humans so that God's superiority is protected.

[17]MT: "which makes happy gods and men."

[18]MT: "hold sway."

[19]MT: "for king."

[20]MT: "seek refuge."

[21]MT: "risked his life."

[22]MT: "Midian."

[23]MT: "masters."

[24]MT: "masters."

the fire will go forth from the *inhabitants*[25] of Shechem and from Beth-millo and devour Abimelech.'" 21. And Jotham ran away and fled and came to Beer, and he dwelt there because of Abimelech his brother. 22. And Abimelech *was king*[26] over Israel for three years. 23. And *the Lord*[27] sent an evil spirit between Abimelech and the *inhabitants*[28] of Shechem, and the *inhabitants*[29] of Shechem acted treacherously against Abimelech, 24. so that the violence of the seventy sons of Jerubbaal should come and place their blood upon Abimelech their brother who killed them and upon the *inhabitants*[30] of Shechem who strengthened his hands to kill his brothers. 25. And the *inhabitants*[31] of Shechem set for him ambushes upon the tops of the mountains, and *they did violence to*[32] everyone who passed by them on the road. And it was told to Abimelech. 26. And Gaal the son of Ebed and his brothers came and crossed into Shechem. And the *inhabitants*[33] of Shechem entrusted themselves to him. 27. And they went forth to the field and plucked their vineyards and pressed them and held *dances*[34] and entered the house of their *idols,*[35] and ate and drank and cursed Abimelech. 28. And Gaal the son of Ebed said: "Who is Abimelech, and who is Shechem, that we should serve him? Did not the son of Jerubbaal and Zebul his official serve the men of Hamor the father of Shechem? And why should we serve him? 29. And who will give this people in my hand? Then I will remove Abimelech." And he said to Abimelech: "*Amass*[36] your army, and go forth." 30. And Zebul the chief of the city heard the words of Gaal the son of Ebed, and his anger *grew strong.*[37] 31. And he sent messengers unto Abimelech *in secret,*[38] saying: "Behold Gaal the son of Ebed and his brothers are coming to Shechem, and behold they are besieging the city against you. 32. And now arise by night, you and the people who are with you, and set an ambush in the field. 33. And in the morning at sunrise you will get up early and array yourself against the city. And behold he and the people who are with him are going forth unto you, and you will do to him as your hand will find." 34. And Abimelech and all the people who were with him arose by night and set an ambush against Shechem in four companies. 35. And Gaal the son of Ebed went forth and stood at the entrance of the gate of the city, and Abimelech and the people who were with him arose from the ambush. 36. And Gaal saw the people and said to Zebul: "Behold the people is going down from the tops of the mountains." And Zebul said to him: "You are seeing the shadow of the mountains as if they were men." 37. And Gaal continued still to speak and said: "Behold the people are going down from the *strength*[39] of the land, and one company is coming from the way of *the plain*[40] of the diviners." 38. And Zebul said to him: "*Where are those words of yours*[41] that you were saying: 'Who is Abimelech that we should serve him?' Is not this the people that you despised? Go forth, please, now, and *wage battle*[42] against

Notes, Chapter Nine (Cont.)

[25] MT: "masters."

[26] MT: "was chief."

[27] MT: "God."

[28] MT: "masters."

[29] MT: "masters."

[30] MT: "masters."

[31] MT: "masters."

[32] MT: "robbed."

[33] MT: "masters."

[34] MT: "festival."

[35] MT: "gods."

[36] MT: "Prepare."

[37] MT: "grew hot."

[38] MT: "in Tormah." Tormah seems to be a place name in the MT, but the location is unknown and the text may be corrupt. Tg. takes the word as a noun which means "deceit, secret."

[39] The MT *ṭabbûr* was unclear to Tg.

[40] MT: "oak."

[41] MT: "Where then is your mouth?"

[42] MT: "fight."

him." 39. And Gaal went forth before the *inhabitants*[43] of Shechem and *waged battle*[44] against Abimelech. 40. And Abimelech pursued him, and he fled from before him, and many fell *killed*[45] unto the entrance of the gate. 41. And Abimelech dwelt in Arumah, and Zebul drove out Gaal and his brothers from dwelling in Shechem. 42. And on the day after it, the people went forth to the field and they told Abimelech. 43. And he took the people and divided it in three companies, and he laid an ambush in the field and looked. And behold the people was going forth from the city, and he arose against them and *killed them.*[46] 44. And Abimelech and the companies that were with him *drew themselves up*[47] and stood at the entrance of the gate of the city, and the two companies drew themselves up against all that were in the field and *killed them.*[48] 45. And Abimelech fought against the city all that day, and conquered the city, and killed the people that were in it, and broke down the city and sowed it with salt. 46. And all the *inhabitants*[49] of the tower of Shechem heard and came to *the gathering place of the house of God to cut a covenant.*[50] 47. And it was told to Abimelech that all the *inhabitants*[51] of the tower of Shechem were gathered together. 48. And Abimelech went up to Mount Zalmon, he and all the people who were with him; and Abimelech took the axes that were in his hand, and cut a tree bough, and took it up, and placed it upon his shoulder, and said to the people who were with him: "What you saw I did, hurry, do as I did." 49. And all the people cut also, each man his bough; and they went after Abimelech and placed them on the gathering place, and set aflame the gathering place over them by the fire, and all the men of the tower of Shechem *were killed*[52] also, about a thousand men and women. 50. And Abimelech went to Thebez and camped at Thebez and conquered it. 51. And there was a strong tower in the midst of the city, and all the men and women and all the *inhabitants*[53] of the city fled to there and shut themselves up and went up upon the roof of the tower. 52. And Abimelech came unto the tower and *waged battle*[54] against it and drew near unto the gate of the tower to set it aflame by the fire. 53. And a certain woman threw the upper half of a millstone upon the head of Abimelech, and it crushed his skull. 54. And he called quickly to the young man, his armor-bearer, and said to him: "Draw your sword and kill me, lest they say about me: 'A woman killed him.'" And his young man killed him, and he died. 55. And the men of Israel saw that Abimelech was dead, and they went each man to his place. 56. And *the Lord*[55] paid back the evil of Abimelech that he did to his father to kill his seventy brothers. 57. And *the Lord*[56] paid back all the evil of the men of Shechem on their heads, and the curse of Jotham the son of Jerubbaal came unto them.

Notes, Chapter Nine (Cont.)

[43] MT: "masters."

[44] MT: "fought."

[45] MT: "slain."

[46] MT: "struck them down."

[47] MT: "rushed forward."

[48] MT: "struck them down."

[49] MT: "masters."

[50] MT: "the house of the God of the covenant." MT lacks the verb "to cut."

[51] MT: "masters."

[52] MT: "died."

[53] MT: "masters."

[54] MT: "fought"

[55] MT: "God."

[56] MT: "God."

CHAPTER 10

1. And there arose after Abimelech to save Israel Tola the son of Puah the son of Dodo, a man *from the tribe of the house of Issachar.*[1] And he was dwelling in Shamir in the hill country of *the house of Ephraim.*[2] 2. And he judged Israel for twenty-three years, and he died and was buried in Shamir. 3. And there arose after him Jair the Gileadite, and he judged Israel for twenty-two years. 4. And he had thirty sons riding upon thirty asses. And they had thirty towns; they call them *the villages*[3] of Jair unto this day that are in the land of Gilead. 5. And Jair died and was buried in Kamon. 6. And the sons of Israel continued to do *what is evil before the Lord,*[4] and they served the Baals and the Ashtaroth and the *idols*[5] of Syria and the *idols*[5] of Moab and the *idols*[5] of the sons of Ammon and the *idols*[5] of the Philistines, and they abandoned the service of the Lord and did not serve *before him.*[6] 7. And the anger of the Lord *was strong*[7] against Israel, and he *gave*[8] them in the hand of the Philistines and in the hand of the sons of Ammon. 8. And they oppressed and *enslaved*[9] the sons of Israel in that year. (Thus they did)[10] for eighteen years to all the sons of Israel who were across the Jordan, in the land of the Amorite, which is in Gilead. 9. And the sons of Ammon crossed the Jordan to *wage battle*[11] also *against those of the house of Judah and against those of the house of Benjamin and against those of the house of Ephraim.*[12] And there was very great distress for Israel. 10. And the sons of Israel cried out *before*[13] the Lord, saying: "We have sinned *before*[14] you, and so we have forsaken *the service of our God*[15] and served the Baals." 11. And the Lord said to the sons of Israel: "Have I not (saved you)[16] from the Egyptians and from the *Amorites*[17] and from the sons of Ammon and from the Philistines? 12. And the Sidonians and *the Amalekites*[18] and *the men of Maon*[19] oppressed you, and *you prayed before me,*[20] and I saved you from their hand. 13. And you abandoned *my service;*[21] and you served *the idols of the nations.*[22] So I will not continue to save you. 14. Go and *seek from the idols*[23] that you have chosen, *whether*

Notes, Chapter Ten

[1]MT: "of Issachar."

[2]MT: "Ephraim."

[3]MT: "Havvoth," which may mean "tent cities."

[4]MT: "evil in the eyes of the Lord."

[5]MT: "gods."

[6]MT: "him."

[7]MT: "was hot."

[8]MT: "sold."

[9]MT: "crushed."

[10]Both MT and the Aramaic lack the expression, but it must be supplied for reasons of sense.

[11]MT: "fight."

[12]MT: "against Judah and against Benjamin and against the house of Ephraim."

[13]MT: "to."

[14]MT: "against."

[15]MT: "our God."

[16]Both MT and the Aramaic lack the phrase, but it must be supplied.

[17]MT: "Amorite."

[18]MT: "Amalek."

[19]MT: "Maon."

[20]MT: "you cried to me."

[21]MT: "me."

[22]MT: "other gods."

[23]MT: "cry to the gods."

they are able to save you[24] in your time of distress." 15. And the sons of Israel said *before*[25] the Lord: "We have sinned. You do to us according to all that is good *before you.*[26] But save us now this day!" 16 And they put away *the idols of the nations*[27] from their midst, and they served *before*[28] the Lord; and his soul was sick over the suffering of Israel. 17. And the sons of Ammon *were gathered together,*[29] and they camped in Gilead. And the sons of Israel were gathered together, and they camped in Mizpah. 18. And the people, the chiefs of Gilead, said, each man to his fellow: "Whatever man will begin to *wage battle*[30] against the sons of Ammon will be a head for all the inhabitants of Gilead."

CHAPTER 11

1. And Jephthah the Gileadite was a mighty warrior, and he was the son of a harlot woman. And Gilead begat Jephthah. 2. And the wife of Gilead bore to him sons, and the sons of the wife grew up and drove out Jephthah. And they said to him: "You shall not inherit in our father's house, for you are the son of another woman." 3. And Jephthah fled from before his brothers, and he dwelt in the land of Tob. And idle men were gathered unto Jephthah, and they went forth with him. 4. And at *the time of days*[1] the sons of Ammon *waged battle*[2] with Israel. 5. And when the sons of Ammon *waged battle*[3] with Israel, the elders of Gilead went to get Jephthah from the land of Tob. 6. And they said to Jephthah: "Come, and be our leader, and we will *wage battle*[4] against the sons of Ammon." 7. And Jephthah said to the elders of Gilead: "Did you not hate me and drive me out from my father's house? And why have you come unto me now when you are in distress?" 8. And the elders of Gilead said to Jephthah: "Because now we have turned back unto you, may you come with us and *wage battle*[5] against the sons of Ammon, and be our head for all the inhabitants of Gilead." 9. And Jephthah said to the elders of Gilead: "If you bring me back to *wage battle*[6] against the sons of Ammon and the Lord will hand them over before me, I will be your head." 10. And the elders of Gilead said to Jephthah: "*The Memra of the Lord will be a witness*[7] between us if we do not act thus according to your word." 11. And Jephthah went with the elders of Gilead, and the people appointed him over them for head and for the leader. And Jephthah

---

Notes, Chapter Ten (Cont.)

[24] MT: "let them save you." Tg changes the second half of the verse to make sure the hearers do not take God's ironic question literally. S-A, 153.

[25] MT: "to."

[26] MT: "in your eyes."

[27] MT: "foreign gods."

[28] MT lacks the preposition.

[29] MT: "were summoned."

[30] MT: "fight."

Notes, Chapter Eleven

[1] MT: "days."

[2] MT: "fought."

[3] MT: "fought."

[4] MT: "fight."

[5] MT: "fight."

[6] MT: "fight."

[7] MT: "The Lord will be hearing."

arranged[8] all his words before the Lord in Mizpah. 12. And Jephthah sent messengers unto the king of the sons of Ammon, saying: "What is there to me and to you, for you have come unto me to *wage battle*[9] against my land?" 13. And the king of the sons of Ammon said to the messengers of Jephthah: "Because Israel took my land when it went up from Egypt, from the Arnon and unto the Jabbok and unto the Jordan. And now return them in peace." 14. And Jephthah continued again and sent messengers unto the king of the sons of Ammon. 15. And he said to him: "Thus says Jephthah: 'Israel did not take the land of Moab and the land of the sons of Ammon. 16. Because when they went up from Egypt, Israel went in the wilderness unto the Sea of Reeds and came to *Rekem*.[10] 17. And Israel sent messengers unto the king of Edom, saying: 'Let me pass now in your land.' And the kindom of Edom did not *accept*.[11] And again he sent unto the king of Moab, and he was not willing. And Israel dwelt in *Rekem*.[12] 18. And he went in the wilderness and went around the land of Edom and the land of Moab, and they came from east of the land of Moab, and they camped on the other side of the Arnon, and they did not enter within the border of Moab, for the Arnon is the border of Moab. 19. And Israel sent messengers unto Sihon the Amorite king, the king of Heshbon, and Israel said to him: "Let us pass now in your land unto my place." 20. And Sihon did not trust Israel to pass within his border, and Sihon gathered all his people, and they camped at Jahaz, and he *waged battle*[13] with Israel. 21. And the Lord God of Israel gave Sihon and all his people in the hand of Israel, and they struck them down, and Israel inherited all the land of the Amorite inhabiting that land. 22. And they inherited all the territory of the Amorite from the Arnon and unto the Jabbok, and from the wilderness and unto the Jordan. 23. And now the Lord God of Israel has driven out the Amorite from before his people Israel; and *are you thinking to inherit it?*[14] 24. And will not you inherit that which Chemosh your *idol*[15] made you inherit? And everything that the Lord our God drives out before us, we will inherit it. 25. And now are you indeed better than Balak the son of Zippor the king of Moab? Did he ever contend with Israel or *wage battle*[16] against them? 26. When Israel dwelt in Heshbon and in its villages, and in Aroer and in its villages, and in all the cities that are upon the *borders*[17] of the Arnon for three hundred years, why did you not rescue them in that time? 27. And I have not sinned against you, and you are doing evil with me to *wage battle*[18] against me. The Lord who *makes judgment*[19] will judge this day between the sons of Israel and the sons of Ammon." 28. And the king of the sons of Ammon did not *accept*[20] the words of Jephthah that he sent unto him. 29. And *a spirit of power from before the Lord resided*[21] upon Jephthah, and he passed through Gilead and Manasseh, and he passed through Mizpah of Gilead, and from Mizpah of Gilead he passed *unto*[22] the sons of Ammon. 30. And Jephthah vowed a vow *before*[23] the Lord, and said: "If indeed you give the sons of Ammon in my hand, 31. whoever will come forth

Notes, Chapter Eleven (Cont.)

[8] MT: "spoke."
[9] MT: "fight."
[10] MT: "Kadesh."
[11] MT: "listen."
[12] MT: "Kadesh."
[13] MT: "fought."
[14] MT: "will you inherit it."

[15] MT: "god."
[16] MT: "fight."
[17] MT: "banks."
[18] MT: "fight."
[19] MT: "judges."
[20] MT: "listen to."
[21] MT: "the spirit of the Lord was."
[22] MT lacks the preposition.
[23] MT: "to."

outside[24] from the doors of my house to meet me when I return in peace from the sons of Ammon will be *before*[25] the Lord, and I will offer him up as a holocaust." 32. And Jephthah passed unto the sons of Ammon to *wage battle*[26] against them, and the Lord gave them in his hand. 33. And he struck them down from Aroer and unto the entrance of Minnith — twenty cities, and unto *the plain of vineyards,*[27] a very great slaughter. And the sons of Ammon were *shattered*[28] from before the sons of Israel. 34. And Jephthah came to Mizpah to his house. And behold his daughter came forth to meet him with timbrels and with dances. And she was his only child; besides her he had no son or daughter. 35. And when he saw her, he tore his garments and said: "Woe, my daughter, indeed you have saddened me, and you have become my grief, for I opened my mouth *in a vow before the Lord,*[29] and I cannot take it back." 36. And she said to him: "Father, you have opened your mouth *in a vow before the Lord.*[30] Do to me as it went forth from your mouth, after the Lord has worked for you retribution from your enemies, from the sons of Ammon." 37. And she said to her father: "Let this thing be done to me. Leave me alone for two months, and I will go and *withdraw*[31] upon the mountains and weep over my virginity, I and my companions." 38. And he said: "Go." And he sent her away for two months, and she went, she and her companions, and she wept over her virginity upon the mountains. 39. And at the end of two months she returned unto her father, and he did to her his vow that he vowed. And she did not know man. And it was made a rule in Israel *in order that a man not offer up his son and his daughter for a holocaust as Jephthah the Gileadite did. And he was not inquiring of Phinehas the priest; and if he inquired of Phinehas the priest, he would have redeemed her with blood.*[32] 40. From time to time the daughters of Israel were going to lament the daughter of Jephthah the Gileadite four days in a year.

CHAPTER 12

1. And the men of Ephraim were gathered together and crossed to *Ziphon*[1] and said to Jephthah: "Why did you cross *to wage battle*[2] against the sons of Ammon and did not call us *to go*[3] with you? We will set your house aflame over you with fire." 2. And Jephthah said to them: "I was a man of controversy, I and my people, and the sons of

Notes, Chapter Eleven (Cont.)

[24]MT lacks the adverb.

[25]MT: "to."

[26]MT: "fight."

[27]MT: "Abel-keramin." Tg translates the Hebrew name.

[28]MT: "subdued."

[29]MT: "to the Lord."

[30]MT: "to the Lord."

[31]MT: "go down."

[32]MT lacks the italicized material. Tg inserts a general rule against child sacrifice. It suggests

that Phinehas would have advised Jephthah that animal sacrifice could substitute for the human sacrifice of the daughter. It also counsels consulting a competent official concerning the validity of the vow.

Notes, Chapter Twelve

[1]MT: "Zaphon."

[2]MT: "to fight."

[3]MT: "to come."

Ammon, greatly, and I *sought from*[4] you, and you did not save me from their hand. 3. And I saw that you were not saving, and *I gave my soul so as to let myself be killed,*[5] and I crossed unto the sons of Ammon, and the Lord gave them in my hand. And why have you come up unto me this day *to wage battle*[6] against me?" 4. And Jephthah gathered all the men of Gilead and *waged battle*[7] with *those of the house of Ephraim,*[8] and the men of Gilead struck down *those of the house of Ephraim,*[9] for they said: "*Fugitives of the house of Ephraim, how are you considered of the house of Gilead in the midst of the house of Ephraim, in the midst of the house of Manasseh?*"[10] 5. And *those of the house of Gilead*[11] seized the fords of the Jordan against *those of the house of Ephraim;*[12] and *when one of the fugitives of the house of Ephraim*[13] said "Let me cross," the men of Gilead were saying to him: "Are you an Ephraimite?" and he said "No." 6. And they were saying to him: "Say now '*Shubbalta.*'[14] And he said "*Subbalta,*"[15] for he was not prepared to speak thus, and they were seizing him and slaying him at the fords of the Jordan, and there *were killed*[16] at that time 42,000 from *those of the house of Ephraim.*[17] 7. And Jephthah judged Israel for six years; and Jephthah the Gileadite died and was buried in the cities of Gilead. 8. And after him Ibzan from Bethlehem judged Israel. 9. And he had thirty sons. And he sent forth thirty daughters outside, and he brought in thirty *brides*[18] to his sons from outside. And he judged Israel for seven years. 10. And Ibzan died, and he was buried in Bethlehem. 11. And after him Elon *who was from the tribe of Zebulun*[19] judged Israel. And he judged Israel for ten years. 12. And Elon *who was from the tribe of Zebulun*[20] died, and he was buried in Aijalon in the land *of the tribe of Zebulun.*[21] 13. And after him Abdon the son of Hillel, *who was from Pirathon*[22] judged Israel. 14. And he had forty sons and thirty grandsons riding upon seventy asses; and he judged Israel for eight years. 15. And Abdon the son of Hillel *who was from Pirathon*[23] died, and he was buried in Pirathon in the land of *the tribe of Ephraim*[24] in the hill country *of the house of Amalek.*[25]

Notes, Chapter Twelve (Cont.)

[4]MT: "called."
[5]MT: "I put my life in my hand."
[6]MT: "to fight."
[7]MT: "fought."
[8]MT: "Ephraim."
[9]MT: "Ephraim."
[10]MT: "Fugitives of Ephraim, you Gilead, in the midst of Ephraim, in the midst of Manasseh."
[11]MT: "Gilead."
[12]MT: "Ephraim."
[13]MT: "the fugitives of Ephraim."

[14]MT: "Shibboleth" ("current of a river").
[15]MT: "Sibboleth."
[16]MT: "fell."
[17]MT: "Ephraim."
[18]MT: "daughters."
[19]MT: "Zebulunite."
[20]MT: "Zebulunite."
[21]MT: "Zebulun."
[22]MT: "Pirathonite."
[23]MT: "Pirathonite."
[24]MT: "Ephraim."
[25]MT: "Amalekite."

CHAPTER 13

1. And the sons of Israel continued to do *what is evil before the Lord,*[1] and the Lord gave them in the hand of the Philistines for forty years. 2. And there was a certain man from Zorah, from the family of Dan, and his name was Manoah and his wife was sterile, and *she had no child.*[2] 3. And the angel of the Lord appeared to the woman, and he said to her: "Behold now you are sterile, and *you have no child;*[3] and you will become pregnant and give birth to a son. 4. And now be careful, and do not drink *new and old wine,*[4] and do not eat anything unclean. 5. For behold you are pregnant and will give birth to a son. And a razor will not *pass over*[5] his head, for the boy will be from the womb a Nazirite of *the Lord.*[6] And he will begin to save Israel from the hand of the Philistines." 6. And the woman came and said to her husband, saying: "*The prophet of the Lord*[7] came unto me, and his appearance was like the appearance of the angel of *the Lord,*[8] very *powerful.*[9] And I did not ask him from where he was, and he did not tell me his name. 7. And he said to me: 'Behold you are pregnant and will give birth to a son. And now do not drink *new and old wine,*[10] and do not eat anything unclean, for the boy will be a Nazirite of *the Lord*[11] from the womb unto the day of his death.'" 8. And Manoah *prayed before the Lord*[12] and said: "Please, Lord, let *the prophet of the Lord*[13] whom you sent come now once more unto us, and let him teach us what we shall do for the boy who is to be born." 9. And *the Lord received the prayer*[14] of Manoah, and the angel of *the Lord*[15] came once more unto the woman, and she was sitting in the field, and Manoah her husband was not with her. 10. And the woman hastened and ran and told her husband and said to him: "Behold the man who came unto me on *that*[16] day has appeared to me." 11. And Manoah arose and went after his wife and came unto the man and said to him: "Are you the man who spoke with the woman?" And he said: "I am." 12. And Manoah said: "Now let your words *come to fulfillment.*[17] *What shall be proper for the boy, and what shall we do for him?*"[18] 13. And the angel of the Lord said to Manoah: "Of everything that I have said to the woman, let her be careful. 14. From everything that goes forth from the vine of

Notes, Chapter Thirteen

[1]MT: "evil in the eyes of the Lord."
[2]MT: "she had not given birth."
[3]MT: "you have not given birth."
[4]MT: "wine and strong drink."
[5]MT: "come up."
[6]MT: "God."
[7]MT: "the man of God."
[8]MT: "God."
[9]MT: "fearful."
[10]MT: "wine and strong drink."
[11]MT: "God."
[12]MT: "entreated the Lord."
[13]MT: "the man of God."
[14]MT: "God heard the voice."
[15]MT: "God."
[16]MT: "the." MT lacks the word "that." It is in the Septuagint.
[17]MT: "come (to pass)."
[18]MT: "What will be the boy's way of life and his deed(s)?"

wine she shall not eat, and *new and old wine*[19] she shall not drink, and everything unclean she shall not eat. Everything that I commanded her, let her observe." 15. And Manoah said to the angel of the Lord: "Let us detain you now, and let us prepare before you a kid goat." 16. And the angel of the Lord said to Manoah: "If you detain me, I will not eat of your bread. And if you prepare a holocaust, *before*[20] the Lord you shall offer it." For Manoah did not know that he was the angel of the Lord. 17. And Manoah said to the angel of the Lord: "What is your name, so that when your words *come to fulfillment,*[21] we may honor you?" 18. And the angel of the Lord said to him: "Why are you asking for my name? And it is *interpreter.*"[22] 19. And Manoah took the kid goat and the offering, and placed it upon the rock *before*[23] the Lord and the one *who interprets (what) to do;*[24] and Manoah and his wife were looking on. 20. And when the flame went up from upon the altar toward the heavens, the angel of the Lord went up in the flame of the altar. And Manoah and his wife were looking on, and they fell upon their faces upon the ground. 21. And the angel of the Lord did not still continue to appear to Manoah and to his wife. Then Manoah knew that he was the angel of the Lord. 22. And Manoah said to his wife: "We will surely die, for we have seen *the angel of the Lord.*"[25] 23. And his wife said to him: "*If it were pleasing before the Lord that we should die,*[26] he would not have accepted from *us*[27] the holocaust and the cereal offering, and he would not have shown us all these things and would not now have made us hear like this." 24. And the woman gave birth to a son, and she called his name Samson, and the boy grew up and the Lord blessed him. 25. And *a spirit of power from before the Lord*[28] began to *strengthen*[29] him in the camp of Dan between Zorah and Eshtaol.

CHAPTER 14

1. And Samson went down to Timnah, and he saw a woman in Timnah from the daughters of the Philistines. 2. And he went up and told his father and his mother, and he said: "I have seen a woman in Timnah from the daughters of the Philistines; and now get her for me for a wife." 3. And his father and his mother said to him: "Is there not a woman among the daughters of your brethren and among all my people that you are going to take a wife from the uncircumcised Philistines?" And Samson said to his father: "Get her for me, for she is pleasing in my eyes." 4. And his father and his mother did not know that it was *from before the Lord,*[1] for he was seeking *the occasion to*

Notes, Chapter Thirteen (Cont.)

[19]MT: "wine and strong drink."

[20]MT: "to."

[21]MT: "come (to pass)."

[22]The MT *pĕli'y* is obscure; the traditional translation is "wonderful" or "incomprehensible."

[23]MT: "to."

[24]MT: "who is wonderful to do."

[25]MT: "God."

[26]MT: "if the Lord pleased to make us die."

[27]MT: "our hand."

[28]MT: "the spirit of the Lord."

[29]MT: "stir."

Notes, Chapter Fourteen

[1]MT: "from the Lord."

reside as a stranger among the Philistines.[2] And in that time the Philistines were ruling in Israel. 5. And Samson and his father and his mother went down to Timnah and came unto the vineyards of Timnah, and behold *a lion, the son of lions,*[3] roared against him. 6. And *a spirit of power from before the Lord resided*[4] upon him, and he dismembered it as *they dismember*[5] a kid, and there was nothing in his hand. And he did not tell his father and his mother what he did. 7. And he went down and *asked for*[6] the woman, and she was pleasing in the eyes of Samson. 8. And he returned after some time to get her, and he turned aside to see the carcass of the lion, and behold there was a swarm of bees in the carcass of the lion and honey *in it.*[7] 9. And he took it out in his hand, and he went about and was eating. And he went unto his father and unto his mother, and he gave to them, and they ate. And he did not tell them that he took the honey from the carcass of the lion. 10. And his father went down *regarding the matter*[8] of the woman; and Samson held a feast there, for so the young men did. 11. And when they saw him, they took thirty companions and they were with him. 12. And Samson said to them: "Let me tell you a riddle now. If indeed you explain it to me during the seven days of the feast and find it out, I will give to you thirty linen cloaks and thirty coverings of clothing. 13. And if you cannot tell me, you will give to me thirty linen cloaks and thirty coverings of clothing." And they said to him: "Tell your riddle, and we will hear it." 14. And he said to them: "From the eater there came forth something to eat, and from the strong there came forth the sweet." And they could not explain the riddle for three days. 15. And on the seventh day they said to the wife of Samson: "Entice your husband, and let him explain to us the riddle lest we burn you and the house of your father with fire. Have you called us here to *endanger*[9] us?" 16. And the wife of Samson wept to him and said: "You only hate me, and you do not love me. You have told the riddle to the sons of my people, and you have not explained it to me." And he said to her: "Behold I have not explained it to my father and to my mother, and *how*[10] will I explain it to you?" 17. And she wept to him the seven days that they had the feast. And on the seventh day he explained it to her for she pressed him, and she explained it to the sons of her people. 18. And the men of the city said to him on the seventh day before sunrise: "What is sweeter than honey, and what is stronger than the lion?" And he said to them: "If you had not *examined my wife,*[11] you would not have found out my riddle." 19. And *a spirit of power from before the Lord resided*[12] upon him, and he went down to Ashkelon and *killed*[13] thirty men of them and took their garments and gave the coverings to those who explained the riddle. And his anger *was strong,*[14] and he went up to the house of his father. 20. And wife of Samson was (given) to his companion who had been his best man.

Notes, Chapter Fourteen (Cont.)

[2]MT: "an occasion against the Philistines."
[3]MT: "a lion cub."
[4]MT: "the spirit of the Lord came."
[5]MT: "one dismembers."
[6]MT: "spoke to."
[7]MT lacks the phrase "in it."
[8]MT: "to." The proper procedure is for the

father of the man to consult the bride's *parents,* not the bride; so Tg changes the MT.
[9] MT: "impoverish."
[10]MT lacks the word.
[11]MT: "plowed with my heifer."
[12]MT: "the spirit of the Lord came."
[13]MT: "struck down."
[14]MT: "was hot."

CHAPTER 15

1. And after *a period of days*,[1] in the days of the cutting of wheat, Samson *remembered*[2] his wife with a kid-goat and said: "I will go in to my wife to the chamber *of the bedroom*."[3] And her father did not *let*[4] him enter. 2. And her father said, saying: "I said that you indeed hate her, and I gave her to your fellow. Is not her younger sister more beautiful than she? Now let her be yours instead of her." 3. And Samson said to them: "This time I am innocent of the Philistines, for I am doing evil with them." 4. And Samson went and seized three-hundred foxes; and he took torches, and he *tied tail to the end of tail*,[5] and he placed one torch between two tails in the middle. 5. And he kindled the fire in the torches, and he sent them in the standing grain of the Philistines, and he set fire from the stack and unto the standing grain and unto *vineyards and unto the olive groves*.[6] 6. And the Philistines said: "Who did this?" And they said: "Samson the son-in-law of the Timnite, for he took his wife and gave her to his fellow." And the Philistines went up and burned her and her father in the fire. 7. And Samson said to them: "If you act like this, so much the more I will take vengeance from you and afterwards I will desist." 8. And he struck them down, *horsemen along with footmen*,[7] a great slaughter. And he went down and dwelt in the cleft of the rock of Etam. 9. And the Philistines came up and camped in *the land of the house of Judah*,[8] and they were let loose against Lehi. 10. And the men of Judah said: "Why have you come up against us?" And they said: "We have come up to capture Samson, to do to him as he did to us." 11. And 3,000 men from *the house of Judah*[9] went down the cleft of the rock of Etam, and they said to Samson: "Do you not know that the Philistines have power over us?" And he said to them: "As they have done to me, so I have done to them." 12. And they said to him: "We have come down to bind you, to give you in the hand of the Philistines." And Samson said to them: "Swear to me that you yourselves will not *have power*[10] over me." 13. And they said to him, saying: "No, for we will indeed bind you and give you into their hands, and indeed we will not *kill you*."[11] And they bound him with two new ropes and brought him up from the rock. 14. And he came unto Lehi, and the Philistines shouted as they came to meet him. And *a spirit of power from before the Lord resided*[12] upon him, and the ropes that were upon his arms became like flax *in which fire has gone through*[13] and his bonds were *severed off*[14] from upon his

Notes, Chapter Fifteen

[1]MT: "days."
[2]MT: "visited."
[3]MT lacks this phrase.
[4]MT: "give."
[5]MT: "turned them tail to tail."
[6]MT: literally, "vineyard, olive."
[7]MT: "hip and thigh." Tg interprets the MT idiom.
[8]MT: "Judah."
[9]MT: "Judah."
[10]MT: "fall upon."
[11]MT: "put you to death."
[12]MT: "the spirit of the Lord rushed."
[13]MT: "that burned with fire."
[14]MT: "melted off."

hands. 15. And he found the jawbone of an ass *in the mud,*[15] and he reached out his hand and took it and *killed*[16] a thousand men by it. 16. And Samson said: "By the jawbone of an ass *I have thrown them in piles;*[17] by the jawbone of an ass I have *killed*[18] a thousand men." 17. And when he finished speaking, he threw down the jawbone from his hand and called that place "Ramath-Lehi." 18. And he was very thirsty, and he *prayed before*[19] the Lord and said: "And *you have done*[20] this great deliverance by the hand of your servant. And now will I die of thirst and *be given*[21] in the hand of the uncircumcised ones?" 19. And *the Lord*[22] broke open the *molar*[23] which is in the *jawbone,*[24] and waters came forth from it; and he drank, and his spirit revived, and he lived. Therefore he called its name "the spring *that was given at the prayer of Samson." Behold it is standing*[25] in Lehi unto this day. 20. And he judged Israel in the days of the Philistines for twenty years.

CHAPTER 16

1. And Samson went to Gaza, and he saw there a prostitute, and he entered unto her. 2. To the Gazites *it was told,*[1] saying: "Samson has come here." And they surrounded and laid an ambush for him all night at *the entrance of the gate*[2] of the city. And they kept silent all night, saying: "Until *tomorrow at*[3] dawn, and we shall kill him." 3. And Samson slept until midnight, and he arose at midnight and took hold of the doors of the gate of the city and of the two posts, and he took them with the bar and placed them upon his shoulders, and he brought them up to the top of the mountain that faces Hebron. 4. And afterward he loved a woman in the valley of Sorek, and her name was Delilah. 5. And the chiefs of the Philistines went up unto her and said to her: "Entice him and see in what is his great strength and in what we can overcome him and bind him to afflict him; and we each will give to you 1,100 *selas*[4] of silver." 6. And Delilah said to Samson: "Tell me now in what is your great strength and in what you might be bound so as to afflict you?" 7. And Samson said to her: "If they bind me with seven moist cords that are not dried, I will become weak and be like one *of the sons of man."*[5] 8. And the chiefs of the Philistines brought up to her seven moist cords that were not dried, and she bound him with them. 9. And an ambush was sitting for her in *the inner*

Notes, Chapter Fifteen (Cont.)

[15]MT: "fresh." A fresh jawbone (MT) and one in the mud (Tg) — both are moist.
[16]MT: "struck down."
[17]MT: "heap upon heaps."
[18]MT: "struck down."
[19]MT: "called to."
[20]MT: "you have given."
[21]MT: "fall."
[22]MT: "God."
[23]MT may refer to a rocky spring shaped like a molar. Some Tg mss. read "rock."
[24]MT: "Lehi." The Aramaic translates it.
[25]MT: "of him who called, which is."

Notes, Chapter Sixteen

[1]MT lacks the verb.
[2]MT: "the gate."
[3]MT: "the light of."
[4]MT does not specify the kind of currency.
[5]MT: "man."

chamber of the bedroom,[6] and she said to him: "The Philistines *have come*[7] against you, Samson." And he severed the cords as the thread of flax in which *the fire made way*[8] is severed, and his strength was not known. 10. And Delilah said to Samson: "Behold you have deceived me, and you have spoken lies with me now. Tell me now in what you may be bound." 11. And he said to her: "If indeed they bind me with new ropes with which work has not been done, I will become weak and be like one *of the sons of man.*"[9] 12. And Delilah took new ropes and bound him with them, and she said to him: "The Philistines *have come*[10] against you, Samson." And the ambush was sitting in *the inner chamber of the bedroom.*[11] And he broke them from upon his arms like thread. 13. And Delilah said to Samson: "Until now you have deceived me and spoken with me lies. Tell me in what will you be bound." And he said to her: "If you weave the seven locks of my head *with the pin in the web.*"[12] 14. And she drove in with a peg and said to him: "The Philistines *have come*[13] against you, Samson." And he was aroused from his sleep, and he took away *the pin of the weavers*[14] and the web. 15. And she said to him: "How do you say 'I love you,' and your heart is not with me? These three times you have deceived me, and you have not told me in what your great strength is." 16. And when she pained him with her words all the days and pressed him, his soul *was pained*[15] so as to die. 17. And he told her all his heart and said to her: "A razor has not *passed*[16] upon my head, for I have been a Nazirite of *the Lord*[17] from the womb of my mother. If I shave, my strength will pass from me and I will become weak and be like any man." 18. And Delilah saw that he told to her all his heart, and she sent and called to the chiefs of the Philistines, saying: "Go up this time, for he has told me all his heart." And the chiefs of the Philistines went up unto her and brought up silver in their hands. 19. And she had him sleep upon her knees, and she called to the man, and she cut the seven locks of his head and began to afflict him, and his strength passed from him. 20. And she said: "The Philistines *have come*[18] upon you, Samson." And he was aroused from his sleep, and he said: "I will go forth as at the other times, and *I will make myself master.*"[19] And he did not know that *the strength of the Lord*[20] had passed from him. 21. And the Philistines seized him and gouged out his eyes and brought him down to Gaza and imprisoned him in chains of bronze, and he *was grinding in the mill*[21] in the house of prisoners. 22. And the hair of his head began to grow *after*[22] it had been shaved. 23. And the leaders of the Philistines were gathered to sacrifice a great sacrifice to Dagon their *idol*[23] and to rejoice. And they said: "Our *deity*[24] has given in our hands Samson our enemy." 24. And the people saw him and praised their *idol,*[25] for they said: "Our *deity*[26] has given in our hands our enemy and the destroyer of our band and the one who multiplied those of us who are *killed.*"[27] 25. And when their

Notes, Chapter Sixteen (Cont.)

[6] MT: "inner chamber."
[7] MT lacks the verb.
[8] MT: "the fire touches."
[9] MT: "man."
[10] MT lacks the verb.
[11] MT: "the inner chamber."
[12] MT: "with the web."
[13] MT lacks the verb.
[14] MT: "the pin, the loom..."
[15] MT: "was vexed."
[16] MT: "come up."
[17] MT: "God."
[18] MT lacks the verb.
[19] MT: "I will shake myself free."
[20] MT: "the Lord."
[21] MT: "was grinding."
[22] MT: "as."
[23] MT: "god."
[24] MT: "god."
[25] MT: "god."
[26] MT: "god."
[27] MT: "slain."

heart was merry, they said: "Call Samson, and let him make sport for us." And they called Samson from the house of the prisoners, and he made sport before them, and they made him stand between the columns. 26. And Samson said to the young man who was holding onto his hand: "Let me go, and let me feel the columns upon which the house is set, and let me lean on them." 27. And the house was full of men and women, and all the chiefs of the Philistines were there; and upon the roof were about 3,000 men and women who were looking at the sport of Samson. 28. And Samson *prayed before*[28] the Lord and said: "Lord God, *let my memory enter before you;*[29] and strengthen me now but this time, *Lord.*[30] And let me do one act of retribution for my two eyes *that the Philistines knocked out."*[31] 29. And Samson seized the two middle columns upon which the house was set; and he leaned himself upon them, one at his right and one at his left. 30. And Samson said: "Let my soul die with the Philistines." And he stretched with his strength, and the house fell upon the chiefs and upon all the people who were in it. And the ones killed whom he killed in his death were more than he had killed in his life. 31. And his brothers and all the house of his father came down and took him and brought him up and buried him between Zorah and Eshtaol in the tomb of Manoah his father. And he judged Israel for twenty years.

CHAPTER 17

1. And there was a man from the hill country of *the house of Ephraim,*[1] and his name was Micah. 2. And he said to his mother: "The 1,100 *selas*[2] of silver that were taken away from you, and you swore and also spoke *before me*[3] — behold the silver is with me; I myself took it." And his mother said: "Blessed is my son *before*[4] the Lord." 3. And he returned the 1,100 *selas*[5] of silver to his mother. And his mother said: "I have indeed consecrated the silver *before*[6] the Lord from my hand for my son to make a graven image and a molten image; and now I will return it to you." 4. And he returned the silver to his mother, and his mother took 200 *selas*[7] of silver and gave it to the silversmith, and he made it into a graven image and a molten image, and it was in the house of Micah. 5. And the man Micah had a house of *idols,*[8] and he made an ephod and *figures;*[9] and he *consecrated*[10] one of his sons, and he was his *idol priest.*[11] 6. In

Notes, Chapter Sixteen (Cont.)

[28] MT: "called to."
[29] MT: "remember me."
[30] MT: "God."
[31] MT: "from the Philistines.

Notes, Chapter Seventeen

[1] MT: "Ephraim."
[2] MT does not specify the currency.
[3] MT: "in my ears."

[4] MT: "to."
[5] MT does not specify the currency.
[6] MT: "to."
[7] MT does not specify the currency.
[8] MT: "gods."
[9] MT: "teraphim."
[10] MT: "filled the hand."
[11] Here and elsewhere in the chapter, some Tg mss. use the word *kômrā'* in the sense of "idol-priest" as distinguished from *kôhîn*.

those days there was no king in Israel. Each man was doing what was right in his own eyes. 7. And there was a young man from Bethlehem *of the house of Judah*[12] from the family of Judah, and he was a Levite and he resided there. 8. And the man went from *his city,*[13] from Bethlehem *of the house of Judah*[14] to reside in whatever place he might find. And he came to the hill country *of the house of Ephraim*[15] unto the house of Micah to attend to *his need.*[16] 9. And Micah said to him: "From where are you coming?" And he said to him: "I am a Levite from Bethlehem *of the house of Judah,*[17] and I am going to reside in whatever place I find." 10. And Micah said to him: "Dwell with me, and be for me a father and a priest, and I will give to you ten *selas*[18] of silver a year and a set of clothes and your expenses." And the Levite went. 11. And the Levite *chose*[19] to dwell with the man, and the young man was to him like one of his sons. 12. And Micah *consecrated*[20] the Levite, and the young man was his priest, and he was in the house of Micah. 13. And Micah said: "Now I know that the Lord *has done*[21] good for me, for I have the Levite as priest."

CHAPTER 18

1. In those days there was no king in Israel, and in those days the tribe *of the house of Dan*[1] was seeking for *themselves*[2] an inheritance to inhabit, for one had not *been divided*[3] to it until that day in the midst of the tribes of Israel in the inheritance. 2. And the sons of Dan sent from their family five men from part of them, men of strength, from Zorah and from Eshtaol, to spy out the land and to inspect it. And they said to them: "Go, inspect the land." And they went to the hill country *of the house of Ephraim*[4] unto the house of Micah, and they resided there. 3. And they were by the house of Micah, and they recognized the voice of the young man, the Levite, and they turned aside to there and said to him: "Who brought you here? And what are you doing here? And what is there to you here?" 4. And he said to them: "Thus and so Micah has done for me. And he hired me, and I have become priest for him." 5. And they said to him: "Inquire now by *the Memra of the Lord,*[5] and let us know if our way on which we are going will succeed." 6. And the priest said to them: "Go in peace. The Lord has made straight your way on which you are going." 7. And the five men went and came to Laish and saw the people that were dwelling in its midst in security according to the custom of the Sidonians who were quiet and resided in security; *and there was no one*

Notes, Chapter Seventeen (Cont.)

[12]MT: "of Judah."
[13]MT: "the city."
[14]MT: "of Judah."
[15]MT: "of Ephraim."
[16]MT: "his way." The Aramaic is a euphemism for bodily needs.
[17]MT: "of Judah."
[18]MT does not specify the currency.

[19]MT: "was content."
[20]MT: "filled the hand of."
[21]MT: "will do.

Notes, Chapter Eighteen

[1]MT: "the Danites."
[2]MT: "itself."
[3]MT: "fallen."
[4]MT: "of Ephraim."
[5]MT: "God."

who harmed anything in the land. They were small heirs[6] and far removed from the Sidonians, and they had not a word with anyone. 8. And they came unto their brothers, to Zorah and to Eshtaol; and their brothers said to them: "What are you (reporting)?" 9. And they said: "Arise, and let us go up unto them, for we have seen the land, and behold it is very good. And are you silent? Do not be slow to go, to enter, to inherit the land. 10. As you go, you will enter unto a people who reside in security, and the land is wide-open, for *the Lord*[7] has given it in your hands, the place where there is no lack of anything that is in the earth." 11. And they moved from there, from the family of Dan, from Zorah and from Eshtaol, six hundred men armed with the weapons of war. 12. And they went up and camped in Kiriath-jearim in *the land of the house of Judah.*[8] Therefore they call that place the camp of Dan unto this day. Behold it is west of Kiriath-jearim. 13. And they passed from there to the hill country of *the house of Ephraim,*[9] and they came unto the house of Micah. 14. And the five men who went to spy out the land of Laish answered and said to their brothers: "Do you know that there is in these houses an ephod and *figures*[9a] and a grave image and a molten image? And now consider what you will do." 15. And they turned aside to there and entered the house of the young man, the Levite, the house of Micah; and they asked him about his welfare. 16. And the six-hundred men armed with their weapons of war were standing at the entrance of the gate, who were from *the tribe of the sons*[10] of Dan. 17. And the five men who came to spy out the land went up. They entered there *and*[11] took the graven image and the ephod and the figures and the molten image. And the priest was standing at the entrance of the gate, and the six-hundred men who were armed with the weapons of war. 18. And these entered the house of Micah and took the graven image, the ephod, and the *figures,*[11a] and the molten image. And the priest said to them: "What are you doing?" 19. And they said to him: "Be silent. Put your hand upon your mouth, and come with us. And be for us a father and a priest. Is it better that you be a priest for the house of one man, or that you be a priest for a tribe and for a family in Israel?" 20. And the heart of the priest was pleased; and he took the ephod and the *figures*[11b] and the molten image, and he entered in the midst of the people. 21. And they turned and went and set before them the children and the cattle and the *possessions.*[12] 22. And they were some distance from the house of Micah, and the men who were in the houses that were near the house of Micah were gathered together and overtook the sons of Dan. 23. And they called to the sons of Dan, and they turned around; and they said to Micah: "What is it to you that you have assembled?" 24. And he said: "You have taken my *deity*[13] that I made, and *you have led off*[14] the priest, and you have gone away. And what is left to me? And what is this you are saying to me: 'What is it to you?'" 25. And the sons of Dan said to him: "Do not let your voice be heard with us, lest men bitter of soul *overpower*[15] you and you end your life and the life of the men of your house." 26. And

Notes, Chapter Eighteen (Cont.)

[6]MT: "lacking nothing in the land, possessing wealth."

[7]MT: "God."

[8]MT: "Judah."

[9]MT: "Ephraim."

[9a]MT: "teraphim."

[10]MT: "the sons."

[11]MT lacks the word "and."

[11a]MT: "teraphim."

[11b]MT: "teraphim."

[12]MT: "valuables."

[13]MT: "god."

[14]MT lacks the verb.

[15]MT: "comes against."

the sons of Dan went on their way. And Micah saw that they were stronger than he was, and he turned and returned to his house. 27. And they took what Micah made, and *they led off*[16] the priest who was his, and they came upon Laish, upon the people who were quiet and *dwelled in security.*[17] And they struck them down by the edge of the sword, and they set aflame the city with fire. 28. And there was no one who rescued them, for *they were far from the Sidonians,*[18] and they had not a word with anyone. And *they were*[19] in the plain which belongs to Beth-rehob. And they built the city and dwelt in it. 29. And they called the name of the city "Dan" by the name of Dan their father, who was born to Israel. But Laish was the name of the city beforehand. 30. And the sons of Dan set up for themselves the graven image; and Jonathan the son of Gershom the son of Manasseh, he and his sons were *idol priests*[20] for the tribe *of the house of Dan*[21] unto *the day that the inhabitants of the land were exiled.*[22] 31. And they set up the graven image of Micah, which he made, all the days that *the sanctuary of the Lord was standing*[23] in Shiloh.

CHAPTER 19

1. And in those days there was no king in Israel; and a Levite man was sojourning in remote parts of the hill country *of the house of Ephraim.*[1] And he took for himself a woman as concubine from Bethlehem *of the house of Judah.*[2] 2. And his concubine *despised*[3] him and went from him to the house of her father, to Bethlehem *of the house of Judah,*[4] and she was there for four months. 3. And her husband arose and went after her to speak unto her heart for her return; and his young man was with him, and a pair of asses. And she brought him into the house of her father, and the father of the girl saw him and rejoiced to meet him. 4. And his father-in-law, the father of the girl, pressured him; and he stayed with him for three days. And they ate and drank and lodged there. 5. And on the fourth day they got up early in the morning, and he arose to go; and the father of the girl said to his son-in-law: "Strengthen your heart with a piece of bread, and afterwards you may go." 6. And the two of them together *reclined*[5] and ate and drank. And the father of the girl said to the man: "Camp now, and lodge, and let your heart be pleased." 7. And the man arose to go, and his father-in-law pressured him, and he returned and lodged there. 8. And he got up early in the morning on the fifth day to go, and the father of the girl said: "Strengthen now your heart." And they were detained until the turn of the day, and the two of them ate. 9. And the man

Notes, Chapter Eighteen (Cont.)

[16]MT lacks the verb.
[17]MT: "trusting."
[18]MT: "it was far from Sidon."
[19]MT: "it was."
[20]The Aramaic word *kômrîn* is not the same as that used for Jewish priests (*kôhanîn*).
[21]MT: "Danites."
[22]MT: "the day of the captivity of the land."

[23]MT: "the house of God was."

Notes, Chapter Nineteen

[1]MT: "of Ephraim."
[2]MT: "of Judah."
[3]MT: "played the harlot against."
[4]MT: "of Judah."
[5]MT: "sat." Tg assumes one reclines to eat, according to the custom of its own time.

arose to go — he and his concubine and his young man. And his father-in-law, the father of the girl, said to him: "Behold now the day has turned to evening. Lodge here now; *this day only*[6] lodge here, and let your heart be pleased. And you will get up early tomorrow on your way, and you will come to your *city.*"[7] 10. And the man was not willing to lodge, and he arose and went and came unto opposite Jebus, that is, Jerusalem. And with him was a pair of saddled asses, and his concubine was with him. 11. And they were near Jebus, and the day was sunk very low, and the young man said to his master: "Come now, and let us turn aside to this city of the Jebusite and lodge in it." 12. And his master said to him: "We will not turn aside to the city of *the sons of the Gentiles,*[8] who are not from the sons of Israel. And we will travel unto Gibeah." 13. And he said to his young man: "Come, and let us draw near in one of the places, and we will lodge in Gibeah or in Ramah." 14. And they passed on and went, and the sun went down on them beside Gibeah which belongs to *the tribe of Benjamin.*[9] 15. And they turned aside to there to enter to lodge in Gibeah, and he came and sat in the square of the city. And there was no man who was taking them into the house to lodge. 16. And behold an old man came from his work from the field in the evening, and the man was from the hill country *of the house of Ephraim;*[10] and he was sojourning in Gibeah; and the men of the place were *sons of the tribe of the house of Benjamin.*[11] 17. And he lifted up his eyes and saw the man who was taking up lodging in the square of the city. And the old man said: "Where are you going, and from where are you coming?" 18. And he said to him: "We are passing from Bethlehem *of the house of Judah*[12] unto the remote parts of the hill country *of the house of Ephraim;*[13] I am from there. And I went unto Bethlehem *of the house of Judah,*[14] and to *the house of the sanctuary of the Lord*[15] I am going. And there is no one taking me into the house. 19. And there is both straw and fodder for our asses, and also there is bread and wine for me and for your maidservant and for the young man who is with your servant. Nothing at all is lacking." 20. And the old man said: "Peace to you; only everything you lack is up to me; only do not lodge in the square." 21. And he brought him into his house, and he threw down *the fodder*[16] for the asses, and they washed their feet, and they ate and drank. 22. They were making their hearts merry, and behold the men of the city, men of the sons of *wickedness,*[17] surrounded the house beating *so as to break*[18] the door. And they said to the old man, the master of the house, saying: "Bring forth the man who entered your house, and we will know him." 23. And the man, the master of the house, went forth unto them and said to them: "Please, my brothers, do not do evil now after this man entered my house; do not do this shameful thing. 24. Behold my virgin daughter and his concubine; I will bring them forth. Ravish them and do to them what is good in your eyes. And to this man do not do this shameful deed." 25. And the men were not willing *to accept from*[19] him, and the man took hold of his concubine and brought her

Notes, Chapter Nineteen (Cont.)

[6]MT: "(It is) the decline of the day."
[7]MT: "tent."
[8]MT: "of foreigners."
[9]MT: "Benjamin."
[10]MT: "of Ephraim."
[11]MT: "Benjamites."

[12]MT: "of Judah."
[13]MT: "of Ephraim."
[14]MT: "of Judah."
[15]MT: "the house of the Lord."
[16]MT lacks the noun.
[17]MT: "Belial."
[18]MT: "upon."
[19]MT: "listen to."

forth unto them outside, and they knew her and *ridiculed*[20] her all night until morning, and they sent her away at the going up of morning. 26. And the woman came as morning appeared, and she fell at the gate of the house of the man where her master was until it was light. 27. And her master arose in the morning, and he opened the doors of the house, and he went forth to go on his way, and behold his concubine woman was lying at the gate of the house, and her hands *were resting*[21] upon the threshold. 28. And he said to her: "Arise, and let us go." And she was not answering, and he took her upon the ass, and the man arose and went to his place. 29. And he came to his house and took a knife and took hold of his concubine, and he dissected her by her pieces into twelve parts, and he sent her in all the territory *of the land of Israel.*[22] 30. And everyone who saw her said: "There was not, nor was there seen anything like this from the day that the sons of Israel went up from the land of Egypt unto this day. Set your heart upon her, take counsel, and speak."

CHAPTER 20

1. And all the sons of Israel went forth, and the assembly was gathered as one man from Dan and unto Beer-sheba and the land of Gilead *before*[1] the Lord to Mizpah. 2. And the *heads*[2] of all the people, of all the tribes of Israel, readied themselves in the assembly of the people of *the Lord,*[3] 400,000 men on foot drawing the sword. 3. And the sons of Benjamin heard that the sons of Israel had gone up to Mizpah. And the sons of Israel said: "Tell how this wickedness happened." 4. And the Levite man, the *husband*[4] of the woman who was *killed,*[5] answered and said: "I and my concubine entered Gibeah which belongs to *the tribe of Benjamin*[6] to lodge there. 5. And the *inhabitants*[7] of Gibeah arose against me and surrounded the house by night against me; they planned *against*[8] me to kill (me), and they raped my concubine, and she died. 6. And I took hold of my concubine and dissected her and sent her in all the *territory*[9] of the inheritance of *the land of Israel,*[10] for they have done *the counsel of sinners and what is not right*[11] in Israel. 7. Behold all you sons of Israel, give to yourselves a word and counsel here." 8. And all the people arose as one man, saying: "Let no one go to his tent, and let no one turn aside to his house. 9. And now this is the thing that we shall do to Gibeah: *We will be mustered*[12] against it by lot. 10. And we will take ten men for a

Notes, Chapter Nineteen (Cont.)

[20] MT: "abused." Tg is softer here.
[21] MT lacks the verb.
[22] MT: "of Israel."

Notes, Chapter Twenty

[1] MT: "to."
[2] MT: "chiefs."
[3] MT: "God."

[4] MT: "man."
[5] MT: "murdered."
[6] MT: "Benjamin."
[7] MT: "masters" (*ba'ălê*).
[8] MT lacks the preposition.
[9] MT: "field."
[10] MT: "Israel."
[11] MT: "abomination and wantonness."
[12] MT lacks the verb.

hundred for all the tribes of Israel, and a hundred for a thousand, and a thousand for ten thousand, to take provisions to the people, to do to bring[13] them to Gibeah *of the house of Benjamin*[14] according to all the shame that *has been done*[15] in Israel." 11. And all the men of Israel were gathered to the city, joined as one man. 12. And the tribes of Israel sent men in all the tribes of Benjamin, saying: "What is this evil that has happened among you? 13. And now *bring forth*[16] the men, the sons of *wickedness,*[17] who are in Gibeah; and we will kill them and remove *the evildoers*[18] from Israel." And *the sons of Benjamin*[19] were not willing *to accept the word*[20] of their brothers, the sons of Israel. 14. And the sons of Benjamin were gathered from the cities to Gibeah to go forth *to wage battle*[21] with the sons of Israel. 15. And the sons of Benjamin were mustered on that day from the cities 26,000 men drawing the sword; apart from those inhabiting Gibeah where seven hundred *strong*[22] men were mustered. 16. From all this people there were seven hundred *strong*[23] men, men whose right hand was bound, *all these were ones who were shooting the rock in the sling and aiming at a strand of hair, and they were not missing.*[24] 17. And the men of Israel were mustered apart from *those of the house of Benjamin*[25] 400,000 men drawing the sword; *all these were men waging battle.*[26] 18. And they arose and went up to Bethel and inquired of *the Memra of the Lord.*[27] And the sons of Israel said: "Who will go up for us first *to wage battle*[28] with the sons of Benjamin?" And the Lord said: "Judah first." 19. And the sons of Israel arose in the morning and camped against Gibeah. 20. And the men of Israel went forth *to wage battle with those of the house of Benjamin,*[29] and the men of Israel set up battle with them against Gibeah. 21. And the sons of Benjamin went forth from Gibeah and destroyed in Israel on that day 22,000 men, *killed, cast*[30] on the ground. 22. And the people, the men of Israel, strengthened themselves and continued to set up battle in the place where they set it up on the first day. 23. And the sons of Israel went up and wept before the Lord until evening, and they inquired of *the Memra of the Lord,*[31] saying: "Shall I continue to draw near to *wage battle*[32] with the sons of Benjamin my brother?" And the Lord said: "Go up against *them.*"[33] 24. And the sons of Israel drew near unto the sons of Benjamin on the second day. 25. And *those of the house of Benjamin*[34] went forth to meet them from Gibeah on the second day, and destroyed among the sons of Israel another 18,000 men, *killed, cast to*[35] the ground, all those drawing the sword. 26. And all the sons of Israel and all the people went up and came to Bethel and wept and sat there before the Lord and fasted on that day until evening and brought up holocausts and *holy offerings*[36] before the Lord. 27. And the sons of Israel inquired of *the*

Notes, Chapter Twenty (Cont.)

[13] MT also includes the two infinitives.
[14] MT: "of Benjamin."
[15] MT: "he did."
[16] MT: "give."
[17] MT: "Belial."
[18] MT: "evil."
[19] MT: "Benjamin."
[20] MT: "to hear the voice."
[21] MT: "for war."
[22] MT: "chosen."
[23] MT: "chosen."
[24] MT: "everyone slinging with a stone at a hair and not missing."
[25] MT: "Benjamin."
[26] MT: "everyone a man of war."
[27] MT: "God."
[28] MT: "for war."
[29] MT: "for war with Benjamin."
[30] MT lacks the terms.
[31] MT: "the Lord."
[32] MT: "for war."
[33] MT: "him."
[34] MT: "Benjamin."
[35] MT lacks the terms.
[36] MT: "peace offerings."

Memra of the Lord,[37] and the ark of the covenant of *the Lord*[38] was there in those days. 28. And Phinehas, the son of Eleazar, the son of Aaron, was standing before it in those days, saying: "Shall I continue to go forth *to wage battle*[39] with the sons of Benjamin my brother, or shall I hold back?" And the Lord said: "Go up, for tomorrow I will give them in your hand." 29. And Israel set men in ambush against Gibeah round about. 30. And the sons of Israel went out unto the sons of Benjamin on the third day, and they set up *battle*[40] against Gibeah as in the other times. 31. And the sons of Benjamin went forth to meet the people. They were drawn away from the city, and they began to *kill*[41] some of the people, *killed*[42] as in the other times, at *the meeting of the roads*[43] of which one goes up to Bethel and one to Gibeah, in the field, about thirty men in Israel. 32. And the sons of Benjamin said: "They are shattered before us as in the first time." And the sons of Israel said: "*Let us go forth*[44] and draw them from the city to the roads." 33. And all the men of Israel arose from their places and set up *battle in the plains of Jericho,*[45] and the ambush of Israel broke through from its place, from the plain of Geba. 34. And there came *from south*[46] of Gibeah 10,000 *strong*[47] men from all Israel, and *the wagers of battle were strong.*[48] And they did not know that the evil *drew near so as come to*[49] them. 35. And the Lord shattered *those of the house of Benjamin*[50] before Israel, and the sons of Israel destroyed among *those of the house of Benjamin*[51] on that day 25,100 men, all those drawing the sword. 36. And the sons of Benjamin saw that they were shattered. And the men of Israel gave place to *those of the house of Benjamin,*[52] for they entrusted themselves to the ambush that they set against Gibeah. 37. And the ambush made haste and *spread out*[53] against Gibeah; and the ambush *spread out*[54] and struck down all the city by the edge of the sword. 38. And the time was arranged for the men of Israel with the ambush that they would send up *a great column*[55] of smoke from the city, 39. And the men of Israel turned around in battle. And *those of the house of Benjamin*[56] had begun *to kill,*[57] those *killed*[58] among the men of Israel being about thirty men, for they said: "But indeed they are shattered before us as in the first battle." 40. And *the ambush began to send up*[59] from the city a column of smoke; and *those of the house of Benjamin*[60] turned behind them, and behold *the smoke of the city was going up toward the heavens.*[61] 41. And the men of Israel turned around, and the men of Benjamin were agitated, for they saw that the evil *drew near so as to come to*[62] them. 42. And they turned before the men of Israel to the way of the wilderness, and *the wagers of battle*[63] overtook them, and *the men*

Notes, Chapter Twenty (Cont.)

[37] MT: "the Lord."
[38] MT: "God."
[39] MT: "for war."
[40] MT lacks the word.
[41] MT: "strike down."
[42] MT: "slain."
[43] MT: "the paths."
[44] MT: "let us flee."
[45] MT: "in Baal-tamar." Tg avoids the name Baal. "Tamar" means palm tree, and Jericho is the city of palms.
[46] Tg reflects a Hebrew *mnhb,* whereas MT has *mngd.*
[47] MT: "chosen."
[48] MT: "the battle was hard."

[49] MT: "was close upon."
[50] MT: "Benjamin."
[51] MT: "Benjamin."
[52] MT: "Benjamin."
[53] MT: "rushed upon."
[54] MT: "rushed upon."
[55] MT: "a great uprising," i.e., a signal.
[56] MT: "Benjamin."
[57] MT: "strike down."
[58] MT: "slain."
[59] MT: "the uprising/signal began to rise."
[60] MT: "Benjamin."
[61] MT: "the whole of the city went up in smoke heavenward."
[62] MT: "was close upon."
[63] MT: "the war."

of the ambush arose from their cities, killing them from here and there.[64] 43. *They made exiles of those of the house of Benjamin,*[65] they pursued them from *their resting place,*[66] *they troubled them*[67] unto opposite Gibeah from the east. 44. And *there were killed from those of the house of Benjamin*[68] 18,000 men, all those *warriors, wagers of battle.*[69] 45. And they turned and fled to the wilderness, to the rock of Rimmon; and there *were hidden*[70] on the paths 5,000 men; and they pressed after them unto Gidom and *killed*[71] from them 2,000 men. 46. And all those who *were killed from those of the house of Benjamin*[72] were 25,000 men drawing the sword on that day, all of them *warriors, wagers of battle*[73] 47. And they turned and fled to the wilderness, to the rock of Rimmon — 600 men; and they dwelt at the rock of Rimmon for four months. 48. And the men of Israel returned unto the sons of Benjamin, and they struck them down by the edge of the sword; from their cities they destroyed utterly unto the cattle, unto everything that was found; also all the cities that were found, they *set aflame*[74] with fire.

CHAPTER 21

1. And the men of Israel swore in Mizpah, saying: "Let no man from us give his daughter to *those of the house of Benjamin*[1] for a wife." 2. And the people came to Bethel and sat there until evening before *the Lord*[2] and lifted up their voice and wept much weeping. 3. And they said: "Why, O Lord God of Israel, has this happened in Israel that this day one tribe be missing from Israel?" 4. And on the day after this the people got up early and built there the altar and brought up holocausts and *holy offerings.*[3] 5. And the sons of Israel said: "Who was it who did not go up in the assembly from all the tribes of Israel *before*[4] the Lord?" For there was the great oath for whoever did not go up *before*[5] the Lord to Mizpah, saying: "Indeed let him *be killed.*"[6] 6. And the sons of Israel had pity upon *those of the house of Benjamin,*[7] their brothers. And they said: "This day one tribe *is withdrawn*[8] from Israel. 7. What shall we do for wives for those who are left? And we have sworn by *the Memra of the Lord*[9] not

Notes, Chapter Twenty (Cont.)

[64] MT: "those who came out of the cities destroyed them in their midst."

[65] MT: "they surrounded Benjamin."

[66] MT: "Nohah," which can be interpreted as "resting place."

[67] MT: "they trod on him."

[68] MT: "there fell from Benjamin."

[69] MT: "men of might."

[70] MT: "cut down him (Benjamin)."

[71] MT: "struck down from him."

[72] MT: "fell from Benjamin."

[73] MT: "men of might."

[74] MT: "sent forth."

Notes, Chapter Twenty-One

[1] MT: "Benjamin."

[2] MT: "God."

[3] MT: "peace offerings."

[4] MT: "to."

[5] MT: "to."

[6] MT: "die."

[7] MT: "Benjamin."

[8] Tg seems to be translating Hebrew *ngr‘* rather than *ngd‘*.

[9] MT: "the Lord."

to give to them from our daughters for wives." 8. And they said: "What one of the tribes of Israel was there that did not come up *before*[10] the Lord to Mizpah?" And behold no man came to the camp from Jabesh-gilead to the assembly. 9. And the people were mustered, and behold there was no man there from the inhabitants of Jabesh-gilead. 10. And the congregation sent to there 12,000 men, *armed soldiers,*[11] and they commanded them, saying: "Go, and you shall strike down the inhabitants of Jabesh-gilead by the edge of the sword, and the women and children. 11. This is what you will do: Every male and every woman who has known the beds of the male you shall destroy utterly." 12. And they found from the inhabitants of Jabesh-gilead four-hundred young women, virgins who had not known man for the bed of the male; and they brought them to the camp, to Shiloh, which is in the land of Canaan. 13. And all the congregation sent and spoke with the sons of Benjamin who were at the rock of Rimmon. And they proclaimed to them *words of peace.*[12] 14. And *those of the house of Benjamin*[13] returned at that time; and they gave to them the women whom they kept alive from the women of Jabesh-gilead; and *there was not enough*[14] for them thus. 15. And the people had pity *upon those of the house of Benjamin,*[15] for the Lord made the breach in the tribes of Israel. 16. And the elders of the congregation said: "What shall we do for wives for those who are left? For woman *has ceased*[16] from *those of the house of Benjamin.*"[17] 17. And they said: "An inheritance of refuge for *those of the house of Benjamin;*[18] and the tribe will not be wiped out from Israel. 18. And we cannot give to them wives from our daughters, for the sons of Israel swore, saying: Cursed be he *who will give a wife to those of the house of Benjamin.*"[19] 19. And they said: "Behold there is a festival *before*[20] the Lord in Shiloh every year, which is north of Bethel, east of the path that goes up from Bethel to Shechem, and south of Lebonah." 20. And they commanded the sons of Benjamin, saying: "Go, and set an ambush in the vineyards. 21. And you shall see; and behold if the daughters of Shiloh go forth to dance in dances, you shall go forth from the vineyards and seize for yourselves, each man his wife, from the daughters of Shiloh; and you shall go to the land of *the tribe of Benjamin.*[21] 22. And their fathers or their brothers will come *to bring suit before us,*[22] and we will say to them: 'Grant them graciously to *them,*[23] for *we did not have enough to give to them,*[24] each man his wife, in battle; nor were you giving to them then lest you be guilty.' "23. And so the sons of Benjamin did, and they took wives according to their numbers from the dancers whom they took by force, and they came and returned to their inheritances and built cities and dwelt in them. 24. And the sons of Israel went from there in that time, each man to his tribe and to his family; and they went forth from there, each man to his inheritance. 25. In these days there was no king in Israel; each man was doing whatever was right in his own eyes.

Notes, Chapter Twenty-One (Cont.)

[10]MT: "to."

[11]MT: "from the warriors."

[12]MT: "peace."

[13]MT: "Benjamin."

[14]MT: "they did not find."

[15]MT: "for Benjamin."

[16]MT: "has been exterminated."

[17]MT: "Benjamin."

[18]MT: "Benjamin."

[19]MT: "the one giving a wife to Benjamin."

[20]MT: "of."

[21]MT: "Benjamin."

[22]MT: "to complain to us."

[23]MT: "us."

[24]MT: "we did not take." Tg avoids mentioning wives taken in battle.

1 SAMUEL

CHAPTER 1

1. And there was a certain man from *Ramah, from the students of the prophets,*[1] from the hill country of *the house of Ephraim.*[2] And his name was Elkanah, the son of Jehoram, son of Elihu, son of Tohu, son of Zuph, *a man dividing a share in the holy things in the hill country of the house of Ephraim.*[3] 2. And he had two wives. The name of the one was Hannah, and the name of the second was Peninnah. And Peninnah had *sons,*[4] and Hannah had no *sons.*[5] 3. And that man went up from his city *from the time of festival to festival*[6] to worship and to sacrifice *before*[7] the Lord of hosts in Shiloh. And there the two sons of Eli, Hophni and Phinehas, *were serving before*[8] the Lord. 4. And it was *the day of the festival,*[9] and Elkanah sacrificed, and he gave portions to Peninnah his wife and to all her sons and her daughters. 5. And he gave to Hannah one *choice*[10] portion, for he loved Hannah. *And from before the Lord a child was withheld from her.*[11] 6. And her rival was provoking her, also angering her, so as *to make her jealous,*[12] because *from before the Lord a child was withheld from her.*[13] 7. And so it was happening year by year in the time when she went up *to the house of the sanctuary*[14] of the Lord. Thus she was angering her; and she was weeping and not eating. 8. And Elkanah, her husband, said to her: "Hannah, why are you weeping? And why are you not eating? And why is your heart sad to you? *Is not my good will*[15] to you more than ten sons?" 9. And Hannah arose after she had eaten in Shiloh and after *they had drunk.*[16] And Eli the priest was sitting upon the chair *by the side*[17] of the doorpost of the temple of the Lord. 10. And she was bitter of soul and was praying *before*[18] the Lord and weeping very much. 11. And *she swore an oath*[19] and said: "*Lord of hosts, indeed the affliction of your handmaid was uncovered before you, and let my memory come in before you. And may you not keep your handmaid far away. And may you give to your handmaid a son in the midst of the sons of men. And I will hand over him, who will be serving before the Lord all the days of his life. And the dominion of man will not be upon him.*[20] 12. And from the time that she prayed very much before the Lord, Eli *was waiting for her until she stopped.*[21] 13. And Hannah was *praying*[22] in her

Notes, Chapter One

[1] MT: "Ramathaim-Zophim." Tg interprets Zophim to mean "watchmen" (from ṣwp), an image for prophets (see Ezek 3:17; S-A, 125-26).

[2] MT: "Ephraim."

[3] MT: "an Ephr(am)ite."

[4] MT: "children."

[5] MT: "children."

[6] MT: "from days to days."

[7] MT: "to."

[8] MT: "priests to."

[9] MT: "the day."

[10] MT is obscure ("face").

[11] MT: "The Lord had closed her womb."

[12] MT: "to make her complain" or "to make her miserable."

[13] MT: "the Lord had closed her womb."

[14] MT: "in the house."

[15] MT: "Am I not better..."

[16] MT: "drinking."

[17] MT: "by."

[18] MT: "to."

[19] MT: "she vowed a vow."

[20] MT: "Lord of hosts, if indeed you will see the affliction of your handmaid, and you remember me, and you do not forget your handmaid, and you will give your handmaid the seed of men, I will give him to the Lord all the days of his life, and a razor will not come upon his head."

[21] MT: "was watching her mouth."

[22] MT: "speaking."

heart only. Her lips were moving, and her voice was not being heard. And Eli considered her *like a drunken woman.*[23] 14. And Eli said to her: "How long are you *demented?*[24] *Will you not let your wine evaporate*[25] from you?" 15. And Hannah answered and said: "No, my master. I am a woman anguished of spirit. And *new and old wine*[26] I have not drunk. *And I have told the sorrow of my soul in prayer*[27] before the Lord. 16. Do not *rebuke*[28] your handmaid before the daughter of *wickedness,*[29] for from the abundance of my jealousy and my anger *I have prolonged prayer*[30] until now." 17. And Eli answered and said: "Go in peace. And may the God of Israel grant your request that you requested from *before*[31] him." 18. And she said: "Let your handmaid find favor in your eyes." And the woman went on her way, and she ate and her face was no longer *sad.*[32] 19. And they got up early in the morning and worshipped before the Lord and turned and went to their house to Ramah. And Elkanah knew Hannah his wife, and *her memory went in before the Lord.*[33] 20. And it happened at *the time of the completing of the days*[34] that Hannah became pregnant and bore a son. And she called his name "Samuel," *for she said: "From before the Lord*[35] I asked for him." 21. And the man Elkanah and all *the men of his house*[36] went up to sacrifice *before*[37] the Lord the sacrifice of *the festival*[38] and *to fulfill*[39] his vow. 22. And Hannah did not go up, for she said to her husband: "Until the child is weaned and I bring him and he be seen *before*[40] the Lord and live there forever." 23. And Elkanah her husband said to her: "Do what is good in your eyes. *Wait*[41] until you wean him. But may the Lord fulfill his *words.*"[42] And the woman *waited*[43] and nursed her son until she weaned him. 24. And she brought him up with her when she weaned him, with three bulls and one measure of flour and a skin of wine. And she brought him to *the house of the sanctuary*[44] of the Lord, to Shiloh. And the child was very *young.*[45] 25. And they slaughtered the bull and brought the child unto Eli. 26. And she said: "Please, my master, by your life, my master, I am the woman who stood with you here to pray *before*[46] the Lord. 27. For this child I prayed, and the Lord granted me my request that I requested from *before*[47] him. 28. *And I have handed over him who will be serving before the Lord. All the days that he lives, he will be serving before the Lord."*[48] And *he worshipped before*[49] the Lord there.

Notes, Chapter One (Cont.)

[23] MT: "a drunk."
[24] MT: "drunken."
[25] MT: "Put away your wine."
[26] MT: "wine and strong drink."
[27] MT: "And I poured out my soul."
[28] MT: "give."
[29] MT: "Belial."
[30] MT: "I have spoken."
[31] MT: "with."
[32] MT lacks the adjective.
[33] MT: "the Lord remembered her."
[34] MT: "the turning of the days."
[35] MT: "for from the Lord."
[36] MT: "his household."

[37] MT: "to."
[38] MT: "the days."
[39] MT lacks the verb.
[40] MT: "in the presence of."
[41] MT: "remain."
[42] MT: "word."
[43] MT: "remained."
[44] MT: "the house."
[45] MT: "a child."
[46] MT: "to."
[47] MT: "from."
[48] MT: "And I have lent him to the Lord. All the days that he is, he is lent to the Lord."
[49] MT: "they worshipped."

CHAPTER 2

1. And Hannah prayed *in a spirit of prophecy*[1] and said: "*Now Samuel my son is to be a prophet on behalf of Israel. In his days they will be saved from the hand of the Philistines, and by his hands signs and mighty deeds will be done for them. Therefore* my heart *is strong in the portion that* the Lord *has given to me. And also Heman, the son of Joel, the son of my son Samuel who is to arise — he and his fourteen sons are to be speaking in song by means of lyres and lutes with their brothers the Levites to give praise in the house of the sanctuary. Therefore* my horn is exalted *in the gift that* the Lord *has appointed for me. And also concerning the marvelous revenge that will be against the Philistines who are to bring the ark on a new cart, and with it the guilt offering. Therefore the assembly of Israel will say:* 'Let my mouth *be open to speak great things* against my enemies, for I rejoice in your saving power.'"[2] 2. *Concerning Sennacharib the king of Assyria — she prophesied and said that he and all his armies would come up against Jerusalem, and a great sign would be worked on him; there the corpses of his camp would fall. Therefore all the nations, peoples, and language groups will confess and say:* "There is not one *who is* holy *except* the Lord, for there is no one apart from you;" *and your people will say:* "There is no one *who is strong except* our God."[3] 3. *Concerning Nebuchadnezzar the king of Babylon — she prophesied and said:* "*You Chaldeans and all the peoples who are to rule in Israel, do not say many boastful things.* Let not *blasphemies* go forth from your mouth, *for the all-knowing* God is the Lord *and upon all his works he fixes judgment. And also to you he is to repay the revenge of your sins.*" [4] 4. *Concerning the kingdoms of Greece — she prophesied and said:* "The bows of the *Greek* warriors will be broken; *and those of the house of the Hasmonean who were weak — mighty deeds will be done for them.*"[5] 5. *Concerning the sons of Haman — she prophesied and said:* "*Those who were* filled up on bread *and growing in wealth and abounding in money have become poor; they have returned to working as laborers for bread, the food of their mouth. Mordecai and Esther who were needy became rich and forgot their poverty; they returned to being free persons.*

Notes, Chapter Two

[1]MT lacks the phrase. For a full study of 1 Sam 2:1-10, see D. J. Harrington, "The Apocalypse of Hannah: Targum Jonathan of 1 Samuel 2:1-10," in T.O. Lambdin *Festschrift*.

[2]MT: "My heart exults in the Lord; my horn is exalted in the Lord. My mouth is wide against my enemies, for I rejoice in your saving power." For references to Heman, see 1 Chr 6:33; 15:17; 25:5; 2 Chr 5:12.

[3]MT: "There is no one holy like the Lord, for there is no one except you and there is no rock like our God." See 2 Kings 18-19 and Isaiah 36-37 for the biblical accounts about Sennacharib's armies outside Jerusalem.

[4]MT: "Do not continue to speak haughtily; let not arrogance go forth from your mouth. For a God of knowledge is the Lord, and by him actions are weighed."

[5]MT: "The bows of warriors are broken, and the feeble gird on strength." The Tg takes the verse as a prophecy of the Seleucid-Hasmonean war in the second century B.C.

So Jerusalem, which was like a barren woman, *is to be filled with her exiled people. And Rome, which was filled with great numbers of people — her armies will cease to be; she will be desolate and destroyed."*[6] 6. *All these are the mighty works* of the Lord, *who is powerful in the world.* He puts to death *and speaks so as to make alive;* he brings down to Sheol, *and he is also ready* to bring up *in eternal life.*[7] 7. The Lord makes poor and makes rich; he humbles, also he exalts. 8. He raises up the poor from the dust, from the dunghill he exalts the needy one, *to make them dwell* with *the righteous ones,* the chiefs *of the world; and he bequeathes to them* thrones of glory, *for before the Lord the deeds of the sons of men are revealed. He has established Gehenna below for the wicked ones. And the just ones — those doing his good pleasure, he has established the world for them.*[8] 9. He will keep *away from Gehenna the bodies of his servants, the righteous ones. And* the wicked ones *will walk about in Gehenna* in the darkness, *to make it known that there is no one in whom there is strength having claim for the day of judgment.*[9] 10. The Lord will shatter the enemies *who rise up to do harm to his people. The Lord blasts down* upon them *from* the heavens *with a loud voice. He will exact just revenge from Gog and the army of the violent nations who come with him from* the ends of the earth. And he will give power to his king and will magnify *the kingdom of* his anointed one.[10] 11. And Elkanah went to Ramah, to his house. And the boy was serving *before the Lord during the life of Eli*[11] the priest. 12. And the sons of Eli were *evil men.*[12] They did not know *to fear from before the Lord.*[13] 13. And the custom of the priests *from*[14] the people — every man who was slaughtering a sacrificial animal, and the young man of the priest was coming, when the meat was boiling, and his three-pronged fork (was) in his hand, 14. and he set it in the pan or in the cauldron or in the pot or in the cooking vessel. Everything that the fork brought up, the priest took for himself. Thus they were doing to all Israel who were coming *to sacrifice*[15] there in Shiloh. 15. Even before the fat pieces *were brought to the altar,*[16] the young man of the priest was coming and saying to the man who was slaughtering: "Give the meat to the priest to roast. And he will not take from you boiled meat but when it is fresh." 16. And the man said to him: *"Wait until the fat pieces be brought up,*[17] and take for yourself according to the good pleasure of your soul." And he said to him that "Now you will give it; and if not, *they will take from you against your will."*[18] 17. And the sin

Notes, Chapter Two (Cont.)

[6]MT: "The full are hired out for bread, and the hungry cease. The sterile gave birth to seven, and the one with many children is left alone." The first part is applied to Haman versus Esther/Mordecai, and the second is applied to Jerusalem/Rome.

[7]MT: "The Lord puts to death and makes live, brings down to Sheol and raises up." The Tg makes the Lord's word into an agent and specifies "make live" as resurrection.

[8]MT: "He raises the poor from the dust, from the ash-heap he lifts up the needy, to make them sit with princes, and a glorious throne he makes them inherit, for the pillars of the Lord are the earth and on them he set the world." The Tg gives an eschatological interpretation of the biblical text.

[9]MT: "The feet of his pious ones he will guard, and the wicked will be cut off in darkness, for not by might will a man prevail." The eschatological interpretation is continued in the Tg.

[10]MT: "The Lord's enemies will be shattered, against them he will thunder in the heavens. The Lord will judge the ends of the earth and will give strength to his king and will raise up the horn of his anointed one." In the apocalyptic context developed by the Tg, the anointed one is the eschatological Messiah.

[11]MT: "the Lord in the presence of Eli."

[12]MT: "sons of Belial."

[13]MT: "the Lord."

[14]MT: "with."

[15]MT lacks the verb.

[16]MT: "were boiled down." Tg inserts the interpretation that the problem was that the fat had not yet been offered (see verse 16).

[17]MT: "Let them indeed burn the fat pieces."

[18]MT: "I will take it by force."

of the young men was very great before the Lord, for the men *robbed*[19] the sacrifices of the Lord. 18. And Samuel was serving before the Lord; the young man was girt with *a sleeved tunic*[20] of linen. 19. And his mother was making for him a little robe and bringing it up to him *from the time of festival to festival*[21] when she went up with her husband to sacrifice the sacrifice of the *festival.*[22] 20. And Eli blessed Elkanah and his wife. And he said: "May the Lord *raise up*[23] for you *worthy sons*[24] from this woman on account of *the petition that he asked from before*[25] the Lord." And they went to *their*[26] place. 21. For *the memory of Hannah entered before the Lord,*[27] and she became pregnant and bore three sons and two daughters. And the child Samuel grew up, *serving the Lord.*[28] 22. And Eli was very old. And he heard everything that his sons were doing to all Israel and that they were sleeping with the women who *came to pray*[29] at the gate of the tent of meeting. 23. And he said to them: "Why are you acting according to these deeds so that I hear these evil deeds of you from all the people? 24. No, my sons. For the report that I hear the people of the Lord spreading about is not good. 25. If a man will sin against a man, *will he not come before the judge, and he will hear their words, and he will decide between them?*[30] And if the man will sin *before the Lord, from whom will he seek and it will be forgiven to him?*"[31] And *they did not accept the word*[32] of their father, for *it was the good pleasure from before the Lord to kill them.*[33] 26. And the boy Samuel continued to grow, *and his name was good. His ways were right before the Lord, and his works were upright among the sons of man.*[34] 27. And *the prophet of the Lord*[35] came unto Eli and said to him: "Thus says the Lord: 'I indeed revealed myself to the house of your father, when they were in Egypt *and were enslaved to the house*[36] of Pharaoh. 28. And *I took delight in*[37] him from all the tribes of Israel *before me,*[38] to be a priest, to bring up *sacrifice*[39] upon my altar, to burn *sweet-smelling*[40] incense, to *wear*[41] the ephod, *to serve*[42] before me. And I gave to the house of your father all the offerings of the sons of Israel. 29. Why are you *robbing*[43] my *holy*[44] sacrificial offering and *my offering that I appointed to offer before me in my temple?*[45] And you honor your own sons *first of all*[46] to have them eat from the first of all the offering of Israel my people. 30. Thus said the Lord God of Israel: 'Indeed I said: "Your house and the house of your father *will serve*[47] before me forever." And now the Lord says: '*My judgments are truth, for those who act honorably before me I will*

Notes, Chapter Two (Cont.)

[19]MT: "treated with contempt."
[20]MT: "and ephod." Tg keeps Samuel, a Levite, from wearing the ephod. See S-A, 14.
[21]MT: "from days to days."
[22]MT: "the days."
[23]MT: "place."
[24]MT: "offspring."
[25]MT: "the loan that he loaned to." Tg makes Hannah's prayer decisive.
[26]MT: "his."
[27]MT: "the Lord visited Hannah."
[28]MT: "with the Lord."
[29]MT: "were serving." The meaning of the Hebrew is obscure.
[30]MT: "God will intercede for him."

[31]MT: "to the Lord, who will intercede for him?"
[32]MT: "they did not hear the voice."
[33]MT: "the Lord wished to put them to death."
[34]MT: "and he was good both with the Lord and with men."
[35]MT: "the man of God."
[36]MT: "to the house."
[37]MT: "chose."
[38]MT: "for myself."
[39]MT lacks the word.
[40]MT lacks the word.
[41]MT: "carry."
[42]MT lacks the word.
[43]MT: "kicking at."
[44]MT lacks the word.
[45]MT: "my offerings that I commanded."
[46]MT: "more than me."
[47]MT: "will walk."

honor, and those who act despicably against my name will become demented.[48] 31. Behold the days are coming, and I will cut off *the strength of your seed and the strength of the seed*[49] of the house of your father from being old in your house. 32. *And you will be considering and you will be seeing the sorrow that will come upon the men of your house because of the sins that you have sinned in my temple. And afterwards prosperity will come over Israel,*[50] and there will not be an old man in your house all the days. 33. A man I shall not cut off for you from my altar to *darken*[51] your eye and to grieve your soul. And all the multitude of your household, *the young men, will be killed.*[52] 34. And this is the sign to you, which will come unto your two sons, unto Hophni and Phinehas. In one day the two of them will *be killed.*[53] 35. And I will raise up *before*[54] me a faithful priest who will act according to my *Memra*[55] and *according to my good pleasure.*[56] *And I will raise up for him a lasting kingdom, and he will serve*[57] before my anointed one all the days. 36. And everyone who is left in your house will come bow low for himself for a coin of silver and a piece of bread. And he will say: "Appoint me now to one of *the watches of the priests*[58] to eat a piece of bread.'"

CHAPTER 3

1. And the boy Samuel was serving *before the Lord in the life of Eli.*[1] And the word of the Lord was *hidden*[2] in those days. There was *no prophecy revealed.*[3] 2. And on that day Eli was sleeping in his place, and his eye began to be dim. He was not able to see. 3. *And he had not yet put out the lights of the sanctuary of the Lord.*[4] And Samuel was sleeping *in the court of the Levites. And a voice was heard from the temple of the Lord where the ark of the Lord was.*[5] 4. And the Lord called to Samuel. And he said: "Here I am." 5. And he ran unto Eli and said: "Here I am, for you have called to me." And he said: "I did not call. Go back, sleep." And he went and slept. 6. And the Lord called again: "Samuel." And Samuel rose and went unto Eli. And he said: "Here I am, for you have called to me." And he said: "I did not call, my son. Go back, sleep." 7. And Samuel *had not yet learned to know instruction from before the Lord,*[6] and *the word of the*

Notes, Chapter Two (Cont.)

[48]MT: "'Far be it from me, for whoever honors me I will honor, and despises me will be cursed.'"

[49]MT: "your seed and the seed..."

[50]MT: "And you will look in distress with envious eye on all that is good with Israel."

[51]MT: "wear out."

[52]MT: "the men will die."

[53]MT: "will die."

[54]MT: "for me."

[55]MT: "heart."

[56]MT: "according to my soul."

[57]MT: "And I will build for him a lasting house, and he will walk."

[58]MT: "the priesthoods."

Notes, Chapter Three

[1]MT: "the Lord before Eli."

[2]MT: "rare."

[3]MT: "no widespread vision."

[4]MT: "And the lamp of God had not yet gone out."

[5]MT: "in the temple of the Lord, where the ark of God was." Tg has Samuel sleep in the Court of the Levites because sleeping in the Temple with the ark is inconceivable. See S-A, 15.

[6]MT: "did not yet know the Lord."

prophecy of the Lord[7] was not yet revealed to him. 8. And the Lord called again "Samuel" a third time. And he rose and went unto Eli and said: "Here I am, for you have called me." And Eli understood that *from before the Lord it was being called to the boy.*[8] 9. And Eli said to Samuel: "Go, sleep. And if he calls to you, you shall say: 'Speak, O Lord, for your servant hears.'" And Samuel went and slept in his place. 10. And *the glory of the Lord was revealed*[9] and stood forth. And it called as before: "Samuel, Samuel." And Samuel said: "Speak, for your servant hears." 11. And the Lord said to Samuel: "Behold I am doing something in Israel; everyone who will hear it, his two ears will tingle. 12. In that day I will fulfill against Eli everything that I spoke concerning *the men of his house.*[10] *I will consume and destroy.*[11] 13. And I told him that *I am taking vengeance from the men of his house*[12] forever for the *sins*[13] that he knew that his sons were blaspheming for themselves, and he did not restrain them. 14. And thus I have sworn to the house of Eli that the *sins*[14] of the house of Eli will not be *forgiven by the gift of holy things and by offerings*[15] forever." 15. And Samuel slept until morning, and he opened the doors of *the house of the sanctuary of the Lord.*[16] And Samuel was afraid to tell *the vision of prophecy*[17] to Eli. 16. And Eli called to Samuel and said: "Samuel, my son." And he said: "Here I am." 17. And he said: "What is the word that he spoke with you? Now do not hide it from me. May God do thus to you and more so, if you hide from me a word from every word that he spoke with you." 18. And Samuel told him all the words and did not hide from him. And he said: "He is the Lord. Whatever is good *before him,*[18] he will do." 19. And Samuel grew, and *the Memra of the Lord was at his aid,*[19] and *he did not depart*[20] from any one of his words. 20. And all Israel from Dan and unto Beer-sheba knew that Samuel was faithful *in the words of the prophecy of the Lord.*[21] 21. And the Lord continued to reveal himself in Shiloh, for the Lord revealed himself to Samuel in Shiloh by the word of the Lord.

CHAPTER 4

1. And the word of Samuel *was pleasing*[1] to all Israel. And Israel went forth to meet the Philistines *to wage a battle.*[2] And they camped in *Rock of Help,*[3] and the Philistines camped in Aphek. 2. And the Philistines drew up the battle line opposite Israel. And

Notes, Chapter Three (Cont.)

[7]MT: "the word of the Lord."
[8]MT: "the Lord was calling the boy."
[9]MT: "the Lord came."
[10]MT: "his house."
[11]MT: "beginning to end."
[12]MT: "I am judging his house."
[13]MT: "iniquity."
[14]MT: "iniquity."
[15]MT: "expiated by sacrifice or offering."
[16]MT: "the house of the Lord."

[17]MT: "the vision."
[18]MT: "in his eyes."
[19]MT: "the Lord was with him."
[20]MT: "he did not let fall ... to the ground."
[21]MT: "for a prophet to the Lord."

Notes, Chapter Four

[1]MT: "was."
[2]MT: "for war."
[3]The Tg translates into Aramaic the MT place-name "Ebenezer."

the wagers of battle were scattered,[4] and Israel was shattered before the Philistines. And they struck down in the battle line in the field about four thousand men. 3. And the people came to the camp, and the elders of Israel said: "Why has the Lord shattered us this day before the Philistines? Let us take now for ourselves from Shiloh the ark of the covenant of the Lord, and it will come among us. *On account of the glory of his name, we will be saved from the hand*[5] of our enemies. 4. And the people sent to Shiloh, and they took from there the ark of the covenant of the Lord of hosts *whose Shekinah resides above the cherubim*.[6] And the two sons of Eli, Hophni and Phinehas, were there with the ark of the covenant of the Lord. 5. And when the ark of the covenant of the Lord came to the camp, all Israel sounded a loud alarm, and the earth was shaken. 6. And the Philistines heard the sound of the alarm and said: "What is this sound of the great alarm in the camp of the *Jews*?"[7] And they knew that the ark of the Lord had come to the camp. 7. And the Philistines were afraid, for they said: "*The ark of the Lord*[8] has come to the camp." And they said: "Woe to us, for it was not like this yesterday and before that. 8. Woe to us! Who will save us from the hand of *the Memra of the Lord whose works are great*.[9] These are *the mighty acts of the Lord*[10] who struck down the Egyptians with every plague *and did for his people wonders*[11] in the wilderness. 9. Be strong, and be men, *Philistine warriors*,[12] lest you be enslaved to the *Jews*[13] as they have been enslaved to you. And be men, *warriors*,[14] and *wage battle*."[15] 10. And the Philistines *waged the battle*,[16] and Israel was shattered and fled, each man to his own *city*.[17] And there was a very great slaughter, and there *were killed*[18] from Israel 30,000 *men*[19] footsoldiers. 11. And the ark of *the Lord*[20] was captured, and the two sons of Eli, Hophni and Phinehas, *were killed*.[21] 12. And a man *from the tribe of the house of Benjamin*[22] ran from the battle line, and he came to Shiloh on that day. And his garments were torn, and dust *was thrown*[23] on his head. 13. And he came, and behold Eli was sitting on the chair *upon the path of the road of the gateway*,[24] looking out, for his heart was trembling concerning the ark of the *Lord*.[25] And the man came to tell (the story) in the city, and all the city was shaken. 14. And Eli heard the sound of the crying and said: "What is this sound of *agitation*?"[26] And the man hurried and came and told Eli. 15. And Eli was ninety-eight years old, and his eyes were set, and he was not able to see. 16. And the man said to Eli: "I have come from the battle line, and I have fled from the line of battle this day." And he said: "What was the situation, my son?" 17. And the one who was bringing the news answered and said: "Israel has fled from before the Philistines, and there was also a great slaughter among the people. And also your two sons Hophni and Phinehas, *were killed*;[27] and the ark of the *Lord*[28] was

Notes, Chapter Four (Cont.)

[4]MT: "the war was spread."
[5]MT: "And it will save us from the hand."
[6]MT: "sitting (on) the cherubim."
[7]MT: "Hebrews."
[8]MT: "God."
[9]MT: "these mighty gods."
[10]MT: "the gods."
[11]MT lacks the phrase.
[12]MT lacks the word.
[13]MT: "Hebrews."
[14]MT lacks this word.
[15]MT: "fight."
[16]MT: "fought."
[17]MT: "tent."
[18]MT: "there fell."
[19]MT lacks the word.
[20]MT: "God."
[21]MT: "died."
[22]MT: "of Benjamin."
[23]MT lacks the verb.
[24]MT: "by the road."
[25]MT: "God."
[26]MT: "the roaring."
[27]MT: "are dead."
[28]MT: "God."

captured." 18. And when he mentioned the ark of the *Lord*,[29] he fell backwards from upon his chair *onto the path of the road of the gateway*.[30] And his neck was broken, and he died, for he was an old and heavy man. And he judged Israel for forty years. 19. And his daughter-in-law, the wife of Phinehas, was pregnant, about *to give birth*.[31] And she heard the report that the ark of the *Lord*[32] was captured and that her father-in-law was dead and that her husband *was killed*.[33] And she bowed down and gave birth, for her pains agitated her. 20. And about the time of her death, *the women*[34] who were standing around her spoke: "Do not fear, for you have borne *a male child*."[35] And she did not answer and did not pay attention. 21. And she called the boy Ichabod, saying: "Glory has been exiled from Israel," because the ark of the *Lord*[36] was captured and *because her father-in-law was dead and because her husband was killed*.[37] 22. And she said: "Glory has been exiled from Israel, for the ark of the *Lord*[38] has been captured."

CHAPTER 5

1. And the Philistines captured the ark of *the Lord*[1] and brought it back from the *Rock of Help*[2] to Ashdod. 2. And the Philistines took the ark of *the Lord*[3] and brought it into the house of Dagon. And they set it up beside Dagon. 3. And *the men of Ashdod*[4] got up early in the day that was after it. And behold Dagon *was thrown down upon his face*[5] upon the ground before the ark of the Lord. And they took Dagon and returned him to his place. 4. And they got up early in the morning on the day that was after it. And behold Dagon *was thrown down*[6] upon his face upon the ground before the ark of the Lord. And the head of Dagon and the two palms of his hands were cut off, *lying*[7] on the threshold. *Only his trunk*[8] was left upon him. 5. Therefore *the idol priests*[9] of Dagon and all those who enter the house of Dagon do not step upon the threshold of Dagon in Ashdod unto this day. 6. And the *stroke*[10] of the Lord was heavy upon *the men of Ashdod*.[11] And he made them desolate and punished them with hemorrhoids, both Ashdod and its territory. 7. And the men of Ashdod saw that *the*

Notes, Chapter Four (Cont.)

[29] MT: "God."
[30] MT: "by the side of the gate."
[31] The MT (*lālat*) is meaningless.
[32] MT: "God."
[33] MT lacks the verb.
[34] Not in MT, though implied by context and gender of the verbs.
[35] MT: "son."
[36] MT: "God."
[37] MT: "because of her father-in-law and her husband."
[38] MT: "God."

Notes, Chapter Five

[1] MT: "God."
[2] The Tg translates the MT place-name into Aramaic.
[3] MT: "God."
[4] MT: "Ashdodites."
[5] MT: "fell."
[6] MT: "fell."
[7] MT lacks the verb.
[8] MT: "Only Dagon."
[9] The Aramaic word distinguished Dagon's priests from Yahweh's priests.
[10] MT: "hand."
[11] MT: "Ashdodites."

stroke was equally upon them.[12] And they were saying: "Let not the ark of the God of Israel reside with us, for his *stroke*[13] is heavy upon us and upon Dagon our *idol*."[14] 8. And they sent and gathered all the chiefs of the Philistines unto them. And they said: "What shall we do to the ark of the God of Israel?" And they said: "Let the ark of the God of Israel be moved to Gath." And they moved the ark of the God of Israel. 9. And after they moved it, the *stroke*[15] of the Lord was against the city, causing very much agitation. And he struck down the people of the city from the small and unto the great. And they were stricken with hemorrhoids. 10. And they sent the ark of *the Lord*[16] to Ekron. And when the ark of *the Lord*[17] came to Ekron, the Ekronites shouted, saying: "They have moved unto me the ark of the God of Israel so as to kill *us and our people*."[18] 11. And they sent and gathered all the chiefs of the Philistines and said: "Send away the ark of the God of Israel, and let it return to its place. And let it not kill me and my people." For there was a deathly panic on all the city. The *stroke*[19] of the Lord was very heavy there. 12. And the men who did not die were stricken with hemorrhoids. And the crying of the city went up toward the heavens.

CHAPTER 6

1. And the ark of the Lord was in the *cities*[1] of the Philistines for seven months. 2. And the Philistines called to the priests and the diviners, saying: "What shall we do to the ark of the Lord? Inform us with what we shall send it to its place?" 3. And they said: "If you send away the ark of the God of Israel, do not send it away empty, for indeed you should return before it a guilt offering. Thus you will be healed, and *it will be relieved*[2] to you; why will *his stroke not rest*[3] from you?" 4. And they said: "What is the guilt offering that we shall bring back *before*[4] him?" And they said: "The number of the chiefs of the Philistines: Five hemorrhoids of gold and five mice of gold, for the one stroke *is equally*[5] on all of you and on your chiefs. 5. And you shall make graven images of your hemorrhoids and graven images of your mice that are destroying the land. And you shall give glory *before*[6] the God of Israel. Perhaps *his stroke will rest*[7] from you and from your *idols*[8] and from your land. 6. And why shall you harden your heart as the Egyptians and Pharaoh hardened their heart? Did it not happen that *when*

Notes, Chapter Five (Cont.)

[12] MT: "it was so."
[13] MT: "hand."
[14] MT: "god."
[15] MT: "hand."
[16] MT: "God."
[17] MT: "God."
[18] MT: "me and my people."
[19] MT: "hand."

Notes, Chapter Six

[1] MT: "field."
[2] MT: "it will be known."
[3] MT: "his hand not turn."
[4] MT: "to."
[5] MT lacks the verb.
[6] MT: "to."
[7] MT: "he will lighten his hand."
[8] MT: "gods."

he took vengeance from them, afterwards[9] they sent them away and they went? 7. And now take and prepare one new wagon and two milk-cows *which have not been tied in the yoke.*[10] And you will bind the cows to the wagon, and bring back their calves from after them *to the inside.*[11] 8. And you shall take the ark of the Lord, and set it down on the wagon. And the vessels of gold that you are returning *before*[12] him as a guilt offering you will place in the chest at its side. And you shall send it away, and it will go. 9. And you will see, if it goes up on the way of its territory *to*[13] Beth-shemesh, *from before him this great evil has been done to us.*[14] And if not, we will know that *his stroke was not near us.*[15] It was an accident that happened to us." 10. And the men did so. And they took two milk-cows and bound them on the wagon and shut up their calves in the house. 11. And they set the ark of the Lord on the wagon and the chest and the mice of gold and the graven images of their hemorrhoids. 12. And the cows went straight on the road, upon the road to Beth-shemesh. On one path they were going along, and lowing. And they did not turn to the right and to the left. And the chiefs of the Philistines were going after them up to the border of Beth-shemesh. 13. And Beth-shemesh was harvesting the harvest of wheat in the plain. And they lifted their eyes and saw the ark and rejoiced to see it. 14. And the wagon came to the field to Joshua *who was from Beth-shemesh,*[16] and it stopped there. And a great stone was there. And they chopped up the wood of the wagon, and they offered up the cows as a holocaust *before*[17] the Lord. 15. And the Levites brought down the ark of the Lord and the chest that was with it in which were the vessels of gold. And they set it upon the great stone. And the men of Beth-shemesh brought up holocausts and slaughtered *holy*[18] sacrifices on that day *before*[19] the Lord. 16. And the five chiefs of the Philistines saw and returned to Ekron on that day. 17. And these are the hemorrhoids of gold that the Philistines brought as a guilt offering *before*[20] the Lord: *of*[21] Ashdod, one; *of* Gaza, one; *of* Ashkelon, one; *of* Gath, one; *of* Ekron, one. 18. And the mice of gold — the number of all the cities of the Philistines belonging to the five chiefs, from fortified cities and unto the unwalled villages, and unto the great *stone*[22] upon which they put down the ark of the Lord. Unto this day, *behold it is*[23] in the field of Joshua *who was from Beth-shemesh.*[24] 19. And he *killed*[25] some among the men of Beth-shemesh *because they rejoiced,*[26] because they looked in the ark of the Lord *when it was exposed.*[27] And he *killed*[28] among *the elders of the people*[29] seventy men *and among the assembly*[30] fifty

Notes, Chapter Six (Cont.)

[9]MT: "after he made sport of them." Tg does not allow God to make sport.

[10]MT: "upon which there has never come a yoke."

[11]MT: "to the house."

[12]MT: "to."

[13]MT lacks this preposition.

[14]MT: "he has done to us this great evil."

[15]MT: "his hand did not strike us down."

[16]MT: "the Beth-shemeshite."

[17]MT: "to."

[18]MT lacks this word.

[19]MT: "to."

[20]MT: "to."

[21]MT: "for" in all five cases.

[22]MT: "meadow," which must be wrong. A few Hebrew mss. agree with Tg.

[23]MT lacks the phrase.

[24]MT: "the Beth-shemeshite."

[25]MT: "struck down."

[26]MT lacks the phrase. One Tg version reads: "Because they rejoiced at the misfortunes of Israel and despised the ark of the Lord, when it was uncovered." Tg is trying to explain the severe punishment of Beth-shemesh.

[27]MT lacks the phrase.

[28]MT: "struck down."

[29]MT: "the people."

[30]MT lacks the phrase.

thousand men. And the people mourned because the Lord struck a great blow among the people. 20. And the men of Beth-shemesh said: "Who is able to stand before *the ark of the Lord*,[31] this holy God? And *to what place will it be taken up*[32] away from us?" 21. And they sent messengers unto the inhabitants of Kiriath-jearim, saying: "The Philistines have returned the ark of the Lord. Come down, bring it up unto you."

CHAPTER 7

1. And the men of Kiriath-jearim came and took up the ark of the Lord. And they brought it into the house of Abinadab on the hill. And they *appointed*[1] Eleazar his son to care for the ark of the Lord. 2. And from the day that the ark resided in Kiriath-jearim, the days were many and they were twenty years. And all the house of Israel followed eagerly after *the service of the Lord.*[2] 3. And Samuel said to all the house of Israel, saying: "If you are returning with all your heart to *the service of the Lord,*[3] remove the *idols of the nations*[4] from your midst and the Ashtaroth. And set your heart for *the service of the Lord*[5] and worship *before him alone.*[6] And he will save you from the hand of the Philistines." 4. And the sons of Israel removed the Baals and the Ashtaroth, and they worshipped *before the Lord alone.*[7] 5. And Samuel said: "Gather all Israel to Mizpah, and I will pray for you *before*[8] the Lord." 6. And they gathered themselves to Mizpah and *poured out their heart in repentance like water*[9] before the Lord. And they fasted on that day and said there: "We have sinned *before*[10] the Lord." And Samuel judged the sons of Israel in Mizpah. 7. And the Philistines heard that the sons of Israel had gathered themselves to Mizpah, and the chiefs of the Philistines went up against Israel. And the sons of Israel heard and were afraid from before the Philistines. 8. And the sons of Israel said to Samuel: "Do not be silent from us from *praying before*[11] the Lord our God, and he will save us from the hand of the Philistines." 9. And Samuel took one suckling lamb and offered it up as a whole burnt offering *before*[12] the Lord. And Samuel *prayed before*[13] the Lord for Israel, and *the Lord accepted his prayer.*[14] 10. And Samuel was offering up the burnt offering, and the Philistines drew near *to wage battle*[15] against Israel. And the Lord thundered with a

Notes, Chapter Six (Cont.)

[31] MT: "the Lord."
[32] MT: "to whom will it go up."

Notes, Chapter Seven

[1] MT: "consecrated."
[2] MT: "the Lord."
[3] MT: "the Lord."
[4] MT: "the foreign gods."
[5] MT: "the Lord."
[6] MT: "him alone."

[7] MT: "the Lord alone."
[8] MT: "to."
[9] MT: "drew water and poured it out." Tg changes a libation into an act of repentance. It avoids having a libation poured outside the Temple and turns the verse into a simile. See S-A, 18-19.
[10] MT: "to."
[11] MT: "crying out to."
[12] MT: "to."
[13] MT: "cried out."
[14] MT: "the Lord answered him."
[15] MT: "for war."

loud voice on that day against the Philistines and agitated them, and they were shattered before Israel. 11. And the men of Israel went forth from Mizpah and pursued the Philistines, and they struck them down as far as below *Beth-sharon*.[16] 12. And Samuel took one stone and set it between Mizpah and *Shinah*,[17] and he called its name *Rock of Help*[18] and said: "Up to here the Lord helped us." 13. And the Philistines were shattered and did not continue any more to enter in the territory of *the land of Israel*.[19] And the *stroke*[20] of the Lord was on the Philistines all the days of Samuel. 14. And cities that the Philistines took from Israel returned to Israel, from Ekron and unto Gath. And Israel saved their territory from the hand of the Philistines, and there was peace between Israel and the Amorites. 15. And Samuel judged Israel all the days of his life. 16. And he was going year by year and making a circuit to Bethel and to Gilgal and to Mizpah. And he was judging Israel at all these places. 17. And *on*[21] his return to Ramah, for his house was there, he judged Israel there and built there an altar *before*[22] the Lord.

CHAPTER 8

1. And when Samuel became old, he appointed his sons judges *over*[1] Israel. 2. And the name of his firstborn son was Joel, and the name of his second was Abijah. They were judges in Beer-sheba. 3. And his sons did not walk in his ways, and they turned aside after *the mammon of falsehood*[2] and took the bribe and perverted judgment. 4. And all the elders of Israel gathered and came unto Samuel to Ramah. 5. And they said to him: "Behold you have become old, and your sons do not walk in your ways. Now *appoint*[3] for us a king to judge us like all the nations." 6. And the word was evil in the eyes of Samuel when they said: "*Appoint*[4] for us a king to judge us." And Samuel prayed *before*[5] the Lord. 7. And the Lord said to Samuel: "Listen to the *speaking*[6] of the people, to everything that they say to you. For they have not rejected you. For *in serving me they have grown weary of my being king*[7] over them. 8. According to all the deeds that they have done from the day that I brought them up from Egypt and unto this day, they have forsaken *service of me*[8] and have worshipped *the idols of the nations*.[9] Thus they are doing also to you. 9. And now listen to their *speaking*.[10] But you

---

Notes, Chapter Seven (Cont.)

[16]MT: "Beth-car."
[17]MT: "Shen."
[18]The Tg translates the MT words into Aramaic.
[19]MT: "Israel."
[20]MT: "hand."
[21]MT lacks the preposition.
[22]MT: "to."

Notes, Chapter Eight

[1]MT: "for."
[2]MT: "gain."
[3]MT: "set."
[4]MT: "give."
[5]MT: "to."
[6]MT: "voice."
[7]MT: "me they have rejected from ruling."
[8]MT: "me."
[9]MT: "other gods."
[10]MT: "voice."

shall indeed warn them and tell them the law of the king who will rule over them." 10. And Samuel spoke all the words of the Lord to the people who were asking from him a king. 11. And he said: "This will be the law of the king who will rule over you: He will take your sons and appoint them for himself in his chariots and his horsemen, and they will be runners before his chariots. 12. And to appoint for himself commanders of thousands and commanders of fifties, and *farm laborers*[11] to plow his land and to harvest his harvest, and *craftsmen*[12] to make his implements of war and equipment for his chariots. 13. And your daughters he will take for *servants*[13] and for cooks and for bakers. 14. And your fields and your vineyards and your good olive orchards he will take and give to his servants. 15. And your produce and your vineyards *he will take one from ten*[14] and give it to his officers and to his servants. 16. And your servants and your handmaids and your handsome young men and your asses he will take to be doing his own work. 17. And your flocks *he will take one from ten,*[15] and you will be to him for servants. 18. And you will cry out on that day from before your king whom you have chosen for yourselves. And the Lord *will not accept your prayer*[16] on that day." 19. And the people refused to *listen to the word*[17] of Samuel, and they said: "No. But the king will be over us. 20. And we will also be like all the nations, and our king *will take vengeance for us*[18] and go forth *at our head*[19] and wage our battles." 21. And Samuel heard all the words of the people, and *he repeated them before the Lord.*[20] 22. And the Lord said to Samuel: "*Listen to their word,*[21] and appoint for them a king." And Samuel said to the men of Israel: "Go, each man to his city."

CHAPTER 9

1. And there was a man from *the tribe of the house of Benjamin,*[1] and his name was Kish, son of Abiel, son of Zeror, son of Becorath, son of Aphiah, the son of a man *from the tribe of the house of Benjamin,*[2] a man of might. 2. And he had a son, and his name was Saul, young and handsome. And there was no man from the sons of Israel who was more handsome than he. From his shoulders and above he was taller than all the people. 3. And the she-asses belonging to Kish, the father of Saul, were lost. And Kish said to Saul his son: "Take now with you one of the young men; and rise, go, search for

Notes, Chapter Eight (Cont.)

[11] MT lacks the noun.

[12] MT lacks the noun.

[13] MT: "perfumers." According to *b. Qidd.* 82b, the craft of the perfumer was highly respected and desired. Thus it did not fit among the pejorative occupations here. See S-A, 107.

[14] MT: "he will take as tithe."

[15] MT: "he will take as tithe."

[16] MT: "will not answer you."

[17] MT: "hear the voice."

[18] MT: "will judge us."

[19] MT: "before us."

[20] MT: "he spoke them in the ears of the Lord."

[21] MT: "Hear their voice."

Notes, Chapter Nine

[1] MT: "Benjamin."

[2] MT: "Benjamite."

the she-asses." 4. And he passed through the hill country of *the house of Ephraim*,[3] and passed through the land of *the south*,[4] and they did not find them. And they passed through the land of the *breakers*,[5] and they were not there. And he passed through the land of *the tribe of Benjamin*,[6] and they did not find them. 5. They came in the land *in which there was a prophet*.[7] And Saul said to his young man, who was with him: "Come, and let us return, lest my father cease from *the matter of*[8] the she-asses and be afraid for us." 6. And he said to him: "Behold now there is *a prophet of the Lord*[9] in this city, and the man *prophesies the truth*.[10] Everything that he *prophesies*,[11] indeed comes to pass. Now let us go there; perhaps he will tell us our *ways*[12] on which we have come." 7. And Saul said to his young man: "And behold we will go. *If he accepts money, what will we bring to the prophet of the Lord? Also regarding us — provisions have ceased entirely from our food, and there is nothing that is fitting to bring to the prophet of the Lord. And what is there with us to do?*"[13] 8. And the young man answered Saul again and said: "Behold there is found in my hand *one zuz*[14] of silver. And I will give it to *the prophet of the Lord*,[15] and he will tell us our way." 9. In olden times in Israel thus a man said when he went to seek *instruction from before the Lord:*[16] "Come, and let us go unto the seer." For the prophet today was called in olden times the seer. 10. And Saul said to his young man: "Your word is good. Come, let us go." And they went to the city where *the prophet of the Lord*[17] was. 11. They went up by the ascent of the city, and they found young women going forth to fetch water. And they said to them: "Is the seer here?" 12. They answered them and said: "He is here. Behold he is before you. Hurry now, for this day he entered the city, for *they have begun the sacrifice of holy things*[18] this day for the people *in the house of feasting*.[19] 13. As you enter the city, thus you will find him before he goes up to *the house of feasting*[20] to eat. For the people does not eat until his coming, for *he says grace over the food*.[21] Afterward those who have been invited eat. And now go up, for you will find him this day." 14. And they went up to the city. Behold they were entering in the midst of the city, and behold Samuel was going forth toward them, to go up to *the house of feasting*.[22] 15. And *from before the Lord it was said to Samuel*,[23] one day before the coming of Saul, saying: 16. "About this time tomorrow I will send unto you a man from the land of *the tribe of Benjamin*.[24] And you will anoint him to be *king*[25] over my

Notes, Chapter Nine (Cont.)

[3]MT: "Ephraim."

[4]MT: "Shalishah."

[5]MT: "Sha‘alim." The Hebrew word means "hollow," i.e., hollow of the sea between waves.

[6]MT: "Jemina."

[7]MT: "Zuph." See note to 1 Sam 1:1.

[8]MT lacks the word.

[9]MT: "a man of God."

[10]MT: "held in honor." For Tg a prophet is honored if his predictions are true.

[11]MT: "says."

[12]MT: "way."

[13]MT: "And what shall we bring to the man for bread has gone from our sacks, and there is no present to bring to the man of God. What is with us?"

[14]MT: "a quarter of a shekel."

[15]MT: "the man of God."

[16]MT: "God."

[17]MT: "the man of God."

[18]MT: "there is a sacrifice."

[19]MT: "on the high place." Tg eliminates the high place since it smacks of idolatry and turns it into a banquet hall.

[20]MT: "the high place."

[21]MT: "he will bless the sacrifice." Samuel is presented as presiding over a meal rather than as a priest at a sacrifice.

[22]MT: "the high place."

[23]MT: "the Lord uncovered the ear of Samuel."

[24]MT: "Benjamin."

[25]MT: "ruler."

people Israel, and he will save my people from the hand of the Philistines, for *the distress of my people has been revealed before me, for their outcry*[26] has come up *before*[27] me." 17. And Samuel saw Saul, and *from before the Lord it was said to him:*[28] "Behold the man about whom I spoke to you. This one *will take away dominion from*[29] my people." 18. And Saul met Samuel in the midst of the gate. And he said: "Tell me now where is the house of the seer?" 19. And Samuel answered Saul, and said: "I am the seer. Go up before me to *the house of feasting,*[30] and you will eat with me this day. And I will send you off in the morning, and everything that is in your heart I will tell you. 20. And concerning *the matter of*[31] the she-asses that are lost to you *and you have come to search for them*[32] this day these three days, you shall not set your heart upon them, for they have been found. And whose is all the delight of Israel? Is it not yours and all the house of your father?" 21. And Saul answered and said: "Am I not a son of *the tribe of Benjamin,*[33] I from the least of the tribes of Israel? And my family is weaker than all the families of the tribes of Benjamin. And why have you spoken with me according to this word?" 22. And Samuel took Saul and his young man, and brought them up to *the feasting.*[34] And he gave to them the place at the head of those who had been invited, and they were about thirty men. 23. And Samuel said to the cook: "Give the portion that I gave to you, that I said to you: 'Keep it with you.'" 24. And the cook took up the leg *and its thigh,*[35] and put it before Saul. And he said: "Behold what was left aside is put before you. Eat, for it was kept for the time for you, saying: 'I invited the people *for dinner-time.*'"[36] And Saul ate with Samuel on that day. 25. And they came down from *the house of feasting*[37] to the city. And he spoke with Saul upon the roof. 26. And they got up early. And it happened that when morning rose Samuel called Saul to the roof, saying: "Rise up, and I will send you off." And Saul arose, and the two of them — he and Samuel — went forth outside. 27. They were going down on the side of the city, and Samuel said to Saul: "Tell the young man, and he will pass before us. And when he has passed, you stand here this day and I will make you hear the word of the *Lord.*"[38]

CHAPTER 10

1. And Samuel took the *portion*[1] of oil and poured it out upon his head and kissed him and said: "Has not the Lord anointed you over his inheritance *to be the king*?[2] 2. When you come away this day from being with me, you will find two men at the tomb

Notes, Chapter Nine (Cont.)

[26]MT: "I have seen my people, for its outcry."
[27]MT: "to."
[28]MT: "the Lord answered him."
[29]MT: "will restrain."
[30]MT: "the high place."
[31]MT lacks the word.
[32]MT lacks the phrase.

[33]MT: "Benjamin."
[34]MT: "the hall."
[35]MT: "and what was upon it."
[36]MT lacks the word.
[37]MT: "the high place."
[38]MT: "God."

Notes, Chapter Ten

[1]MT: "vial."
[2]MT: "for a prince."

of Rachel in the territory of Benjamin at Zelzah. And they will say to you: 'The she-asses for which you came to seek have been found. And behold your father has left off the matter of the she-asses and is afraid for you, saying: "What shall I do for my son?"' 3. And you shall *go*[3] from there and beyond, and you will come to the *Plain*[4] of Tabor. And three men who are going up *to worship before the Lord*[5] in Bethel will find you there — one carrying three kids, and one carrying three pieces of bread, and one carrying a skin of wine. 4. And they will ask you for peace, and they will give to you *two loaves of bread,*[6] and you will accept from their hand. 5. Afterward you will come to the hill *where the ark of the Lord is,*[7] where the garrisons of the Philistines are. And when you enter there to the city, you will meet a band of *teachers*[8] going down from *the house of feasting*[9] and before them lyres and timbrels and *cymbals*[10] and lutes, and they will be *singing praise.*[11] 6. And *the spirit of prophecy from before the Lord will reside*[12] upon you, and you will *sing praise*[13] with them, and you will be changed into another man. 7. And when these signs come to you, *prepare for yourself the instruments of kingship, for the Memra of the Lord is at your aid.*[14] 8. And you shall go down before me to Gilgal. And behold I am going down unto you to bring up holocausts and to offer the sacrifice of *holy things.*[15] Seven days you shall wait until I come unto you and tell you what you are to do." 9. And *when he turned*[16] to go from being with Samuel, *the Lord*[17] changed for him another heart, and all those signs came on that day. 10. And they came there to the hill, and behold a band of *teachers*[18] met him, and *the spirit of prophecy from before the Lord resided*[19] upon him, and he *sang praise*[20] in their midst. 11. And everyone who knew him yesterday and the day before it saw, and behold *he was singing praise with the teachers.*[21] And the people said, each man to his neighbor: "What is this that has happened to the son of Kish? Is Saul also among the *teachers?*"[22] 12. And a man from there answered and said: "And who is their *master?*"[23] Therefore it became a proverb: "Is Saul also among the *teachers?*"[24] 13. And he ceased from *singing praise*[25] and entered *the house of feasting.*[26] 14. And the uncle of Saul said to him and to his young man: "Where did you go?" And he said: "To seek the she-asses. And we saw that *we had not found them,*[27] and we came to Samuel." 15. And the uncle of Saul said: "Tell me now what Samuel said to you." 16. And Saul said to his uncle: "He indeed told us that the she-asses were to be found." And he did not tell him what Samuel said about the matter of kingship. 17. And Samuel *gathered the people*

Notes, Chapter Ten (Cont.)

[3]MT: "pass through."

[4]MT: "oak."

[5]MT: "to God."

[6]MT: "two of bread."

[7]MT: "of God."

[8]MT: "prophets." Tg tames the ecstatic prophets who do not fit its understanding of prophets, into teachers (scribes, *spry'*), a social role familiar to it.

[9]MT: "the high place."

[10]MT: "flutes."

[11]MT: "prophesying." Tg transforms this group's activity into praise.

[12]MT: "the spirit of the Lord will come."

[13]MT: "prophesy."

[14]MT: "do what your hand will find, for God is with you." Tg is not comfortable with Saul doing whatever he wants, since even kings were to follow the Law (see 1 Sam 10:25; Deut 17:16ff.).

[15]MT: "peace-offerings."

[16]MT: "when he turned his back."

[17]MT: "God."

[18]MT: "prophets."

[19]MT: "the spirit of God came."

[20]MT: "prophesied."

[21]MT: "he was prophesying with the prophets."

[22]MT: "prophets."

[23]MT: "father."

[24]MT: "prophets."

[25]MT: "prophesying."

[26]MT: "the high place."

[27]MT: "they were not."

before[28] the Lord to Mizpah. 18. And he said to the sons of Israel: "Thus says the Lord, the God of Israel: 'I brought Israel up from Egypt and saved you from the hand of the Egyptians and from the hand of all the kingdoms who were oppressing you. 19. And you this day *have grown weary in the service of your God*[29] who rescues you from all your evil and your oppression. And you said *before*[30] him: '*We will not be rescued unless you appoint*[31] over us a king.' And now stand before the Lord by your tribes and by your thousands." 20. And Samuel brought near all the tribes of Israel, and *the tribe of the house of Benjamin was singled out.*[32] 21. And he brought near the tribe *of the house of Benjamin*[33] by its families, and the family of Matar *was singled out.*[34] And Saul the son of Kish *was singled out.*[35] And they sought him, and he was not found. 22. And they inquired again of *the Memra of the Lord:*[36] "*Is the man still*[37] here?" And the Lord said: "Behold he is hidden among the baggage." 23. And they ran and took him from there. And he stood in the midst of the people. And he was taller than all the people from his shoulder and above. 24. And Samuel said to all the people: "Have you seen the one whom the Lord has chosen? For there is no one like him among all the people." And all the people shouted out and said: "May the king *prosper!*"[38] 25. And Samuel spoke with *the people*[39] the law of kingship, and wrote in the book, and deposited it before the Lord. And Samuel sent away all the people, each man to his house. 26. And Saul also went to his house, to Gibeah. And there went with him *part of the people, men fearing sin, in whose hearts fear was given from before the Lord.*[40] 27. And men of *wickedness*[41] said: "*In what*[42] will this one rescue us?" And they despised him and *did not come to ask for his peace.*[43] And he was like one who is silent.

CHAPTER 11

1. And Nahash *the king of the sons of Ammon*[1] went up and camped against Jabesh-gilead. And all the men of Jabesh said to Nahash: "Cut for us a covenant, and we will serve you." 2. And Nahash *the king of the sons of Ammon*[2] said to them: "*If*

Notes, Chapter Ten (Cont.)

[28] MT: "summoned the people to."
[29] MT: "have rejected your God."
[30] MT: "to."
[31] MT: "appoint."
[32] MT: "the tribe of Benjamin was taken by lot."
[33] MT: "of Benjamin."
[34] MT: "was taken by lot."
[35] MT: "was taken by lot."
[36] MT: "the Lord."
[37] MT: "Did the man come."
[38] MT: "live."
[39] MT: "all the people."
[40] MT: "the army whose heart God had touched."

For Tg, men whom God has touched are those who have a proper attitude toward God, that is, fear sin.
[41] MT: "Belial."
[42] MT: "how."
[43] MT: "did not bring to him a present." Tg removes any suggestion that Saul might have been seeking gain. It may refer to the Roman custom of clients paying a daily call to their patron. See S-A, 100.

Notes, Chapter Eleven

[1] MT: "the Ammonite."
[2] MT: "the Ammonite."

you do thus,[3] I will cut *a covenant*[4] for you in digging out for you every right eye. And I will place shame upon all Israel." 3. And the elders of Jabesh said to him: "Wait for us seven days. And we will send out messengers in all the territory *of the land of Israel.*[5] And if there is no one saving us, we will go forth unto you." 4. And the messengers came to Gibeah of Saul, and they spoke the words *before*[6] the people. And all the people lifted up their voice and wept. 5. And behold Saul came behind the oxen from the field, and Saul said: "What is for the people, for they are weeping?" And they told to him the words of the men of Jabesh. 6. And *a mighty spirit from before the Lord rested*[7] upon Saul, when he heard these words. And his anger was very *strong.*[8] 7. And he took the yoke of oxen, and cut it up, and sent it all the territory of Israel by the hand of messengers, saying: "Whoever does not go forth after Saul and after Samuel, thus it will be done to his oxen." And fear *from before the Lord*[9] fell upon the people, and they went forth as one man. 8. And he arranged them in Bezek, and the sons of Israel were three-hundred thousand and the men of Judah were thirty thousand. 9. And they said to the messengers who came: "Thus you will say to the men of Jabesh-gilead: 'Tomorrow you will have deliverance when the *day*[10] grows warm.'" And the messengers came and told the men of Jabesh-gilead, and they rejoiced. 10. And the men of Jabesh said: "Tomorrow we will go forth unto you, and you will do to us according to everything that is good in your eyes." 11. And on the day after it, Saul arranged the people in three companies. And they entered in the midst of the camp at the morning watch, and they struck down *the sons of Ammon*[11] until the day grew warm. And there were some who were left and they were scattered, and there were not left among them two *who fled*[12] together. 12. And the people said to Samuel: "*Who is this who announces, saying: 'Saul is not fit to rule over us?' Bring the men, and we will kill them.*"[13] 13. And Saul said: "Not a man will *be killed*[14] on this day, for this day the Lord has worked deliverance in Israel." 14. And Samuel said to the people: "Come, and let us go to Gilgal, and we will renew there the kingship." 15. And all the people went to Gilgal and there made Saul king before the Lord in Gilgal. And there they offered *the sacrifice of holy things*[15] before the Lord, and Saul and all the people of Israel rejoiced there very much.

Notes, Chapter Eleven (Cont.)

[3]MT: "in this."

[4]MT lacks the word, though it is in the Septuagint and other ancient versions. One Tg m.s. adds to the verse: "in erasing from your Torah the commandment in which it is written that the Ammonites and Moabites shall not be purified to enter the assembly of the Lord." See *m. Yad.* 4:4 and S-A, 56-57.

[5]MT: "of Israel."

[6]MT: "in the ears of."

[7]MT: "the spirit of God came."

[8]MT: "hot."

[9]MT: "of the Lord."

[10]MT: "sun."

[11]MT: "Ammon."

[12]MT lacks the verb.

[13]MT: "Who is he who says: 'Will Saul rule over us?' Give up the men, and we will put them to death."

[14]MT: "die."

[15]MT: "peace-offerings."

CHAPTER 12

1. And Samuel said to all Israel: "Behold *I have listened to your speaking,*[1] to everything that you said to me, and I have made a king over you. 2. And now behold the king *leads at your head.*[2] And I have become *stiff*[3] and old; and behold my sons are with you. And I have walked before you from my youth unto this day. 3. *Behold the witness that I am establishing: Bear witness against me*[4] before the Lord and before his anointed one: Whose ox have I taken, and whose ass have I *confiscated,*[5] and whom have I wronged, and whom have I oppressed, and from whose hand have I received *the mammon of falsehood,*[6] *and from whom have I withheld my eye in judgment?*[7] And I will restore it to you." 4. And they said: "You have not wronged us, and you have not oppressed us, and you have not received anything from the hand of a man." 5. And he said to them: "*The Memra of the Lord*[8] is a witness against you, and his anointed is a witness this day, for you have not found in my hand anything." And they said: "A witness." 6. And Samuel said to the people: "The Lord is the one who *did mighty deeds by the hands of*[9] Moses and Aaron, and who brought up your fathers from the land of Egypt. 7. And now stand, and let me argue with you before the Lord all the righteous deeds of the Lord that he did with you and with your fathers. 8. When Jacob entered Egypt, your fathers called out *before*[10] the Lord. And the Lord sent Moses and Aaron, and they brought up your fathers from Egypt and made them dwell in this place. 9. And they forgot *the service of the Lord*[11] their God, and he delivered them in the hand of Sisera, master of the army of Hazor, and in the hand of the Philistines, and in the hand of the king of Moab. And they *waged battle*[12] against them. 10. And they called out *before*[13] the Lord and said: "We have sinned, for we have forsaken *the service of the Lord*[14] and worshipped the Baals and the Ashtaroth. And now save us from the hand of our enemies, and we will *serve before you.*[15] 11. And the Lord sent *Gideon and Samson*[16] and Jephthah and Samuel, and he saved you from the hand of your enemies round about, and you dwelt in security. 12. And you saw that Nahash the king of the sons of Ammon came against you, and you said to me: 'No, but a king shall reign over us.' And the Lord your God was your king. 13. And now behold the king whom you

Notes, Chapter Twelve

[1] MT: "I have heard your voice."
[2] MT: "walks before you."
[3] MT: "aged."
[4] MT: "Here I am; answer me."
[5] MT: "taken."
[6] MT: "a bribe."
[7] MT: "and blind my eyes with it."
[8] MT: "The Lord."
[9] MT: "made."

[10] MT: "to."
[11] MT: "the Lord."
[12] MT: "fought."
[13] MT: "to."
[14] MT: "the Lord."
[15] MT: "worship you."
[16] MT: "Jeruba'al and Bedan." Gideon is also called Jerubaal (Judg 7:1). Bedan is mentioned as a judge only here. Tg substitutes a more well known figure.

chose, whom you requested. And behold the Lord has *appointed*[17] a king over you. 14. If you will *fear from before the Lord and worship before him and accept his Memra*[18] and do not rebel against *the Memra*[19] of the Lord, both you and the king who will rule over you will *follow eagerly after the service of the Lord*[20] your God. 15. And if you do not *accept the Memra of the Lord*[21] and you rebel against the *Memra*[22] of the Lord, the *stroke*[23] of the Lord will be against you *as it was*[24] against your fathers. 16. Now then stand here and see this great thing that the Lord is doing before your eyes. 17. Is not this day the harvest of wheat? *I will pray before the Lord,*[25] and he will give thunder and rain. And know and see that your evil is great that you have done *before*[26] the Lord to request for yourselves a king." 18. And Samuel *prayed before*[27] the Lord, and the Lord gave thunder and rain on that day. And all the people *were very fearful from before the Lord and from the words of Samuel.*[28] 19. And all the people said to Samuel: "Pray for your *servants before*[29] the Lord your God, and we will not die, for in addition to all our sins we have added the evil to request a king for us." 20. And Samuel said to the people: "Do not fear. You have brought about all this evil, but do not turn from behind *the service of the Lord.*[30] And you shall worship *before the Lord*[31] with all your heart. 21. And do not turn *from behind his service; and do not worship the idols who are good for nothing, and there is no profit in them,*[32] and they do not save for they are good for nothing. 22. For the Lord will not *make distant*[33] his people on account of his great name, for *it was pleasing before the Lord*[34] to make you *before him*[35] into a people. 23. As for me, far be it from me to sin *before*[36] the Lord by refusing to pray on your behalf. And I will teach you *the way that you shall walk in the right and fitting way.*[37] 24. But fear *from before the Lord*[38] and worship *before him*[39] in truth with all your heart, for see how much he has done with you. 25. And if *your works are indeed evil,*[40] both you and your king will be *destroyed completely.*[41]

Notes, Chapter Twelve (Cont.)

[17]MT: "given."

[18]MT: "fear the Lord and serve him and hear his voice."

[19]MT: "mouth."

[20]MT: "be after the Lord."

[21]MT: "hear the voice of the Lord."

[22]MT: "mouth."

[23]MT: "hand."

[24]MT: "and."

[25]MT: "I will cry to the Lord."

[26]MT: "in the eyes of."

[27]MT: "called to."

[28]MT: "feared the Lord and Samuel very much."

[29]MT: "servants to."

[30]MT: "the Lord."

[31]MT: "the Lord."

[32]MT: "because after nothing which does not profit."

[33]MT: "cast away."

[34]MT: "the Lord pleased."

[35]MT: "for himself."

[36]MT: "to."

[37]MT: "in the good and right way."

[38]MT: "the Lord."

[39]MT: "him."

[40]MT: "indeed you do evil."

[41]MT: "swept away."

CHAPTER 13

1. And Saul was *a year old*[1] — *there were no sins in him*[2] — when he became king, and he reigned two years over Israel. 2. And Saul chose for himself three thousand from Israel. And two thousand were with Saul in Michmash and in the hill country of Bethel, and a thousand were with Jonathan in Gibeah of *the house of Benjamin*.[3] And he sent away the rest of the people, each man to his own *town*.[4] 3. And Jonathan struck down the garrison of the Philistines which was in *Gibeah*.[5] And the Philistines heard. And Saul blew on the trumpet in all the land, saying: "Let the *Jews*[6] hear." 4. And all Israel heard, saying: "Saul has struck down the garrison of the Philistines, and Israel *has attacked*[7] the Philistines." And the people *gathered*[8] behind Saul to Gilgal. 5. And the Philistines gathered to *wage battle*[9] with Israel, thirty thousand chariots and six thousand horsemen and people like the sand that is upon the shore of the sea for multitude. And they came up and encamped in Michmash, east of Beth-aven. 6. And the men of Israel saw that they had trouble, for the people were hard pressed; and the people hid themselves in caves and *in strongholds and in clefts of rocks and in caves of flints*[10] and in cisterns. 7. And the *Jews*[11] crossed the Jordan to the land of Gad and Gilead and Saul was still in Gilgal, and all the people *gathered*[12] behind him. 8. And he waited seven days for the time that Samuel said, and Samuel did not come to Gilgal; and the people scattered from him. 9. And Saul said: "Bring near unto me the holocaust and *the sacrifice of holy things*,[13] and *I will offer up*[14] the holocaust." 10. And as he completed offering up the holocaust, behold Samuel came. And Saul went forth to meet him *to ask his peace*.[15] 11. And Samuel said: "What have you done?" And Saul said: "For I saw that the people were scattered from me, and you did not come for the period of the days, and the Philistines were gathered at Michmash. 12. And I said: 'Now *perhaps*[16] the Philistines will come down unto me to Gilgal, and *before the Lord I have not prayed*,'[17] and I took hold of myself and offered up the holocausts." 13. And Samuel said to Saul: "You have acted foolishly. You have not kept the commandment of *the Memra of the Lord*[18] your God, which he commanded you. For the Lord had

Notes, Chapter Thirteen

[1] MT has the same impossible reading; clearly the number has dropped out.

[2] MT lacks the phrase.

[3] MT: "Benjamin."

[4] MT: "tent."

[5] MT: "Geba."

[6] MT: "Hebrews."

[7] MT: "become evil to."

[8] MT: "were summoned."

[9] MT: "to fight."

[10] MT: "in thickets and in rocks and in underground chambers."

[11] MT: "Hebrews."

[12] MT: "trembled." Tg eliminates Israel's fear.

[13] MT: "peace-offering."

[14] MT: "he offered up."

[15] MT: "to bless him."

[16] MT lacks the word.

[17] MT: "the face of the Lord I have not entreated."

[18] MT: "the Lord."

established your kingdom *over*[19] Israel forever. 14. And now your kingdom will not stand. The Lord has *established before himself a man doing his good pleasure*,[20] and the Lord commanded him *to be the king*[21] over his people, for you have not kept what the Lord commanded you." 15. And Samuel arose and went up from Gilgal to Gibeah *of the house of Benjamin*.[22] And Saul *counted*[23] the people who were found with him — about six hundred men. 16. And Saul and Jonathan his son and the people who were found with them were dwelling in Gibeah of *the house of Benjamin*,[24] and the Philistines camped in Michmash. 17. And *the destroyer*[25] went forth from the camp of the Philistines in three companies — one company turned to the way of Ophrah to the land of *the south*,[26] 18. and one company turned to the way of Beth-horon, and one company turned to the way of the border which looks to the Valley of the *Hyenas*[27] toward the wilderness. 19. And *a craftsman making armor*[28] was not found in all *the territory of the land*[29] of Israel, for the Philistines said: "Lest the *Jews*[30] should make *swords or spears*."[31] 20. And all Israel went down to *the land of*[32] the Philistines, each man to sharpen his plowshare and *his colter of his plow, and his axe, and his mattock*.[33] 21. *And they had files to sharpen on it the dullness of every kind of iron — for mattocks and for colters of plows and for the fullers' forks on which there are three teeth and for the axes — and for fastening goads.*[34] 22. And on the day of battle neither a sword nor a spear was found in the hand of all the people who were with Saul and Jonathan. And they were found for Saul and for Jonathan his son. 23. And the garrison of the Philistines went out to the pass of Michmash.

CHAPTER 14

1. And it was day, and Jonathan the son of Saul said to the young man, his armor-bearer: "Come, and we will cross over to the garrison of the Philistines, which is across from here." And he did not tell his father. 2. And Saul was dwelling in the outskirts of Gibeah beneath the pomegranate tree which is in Migron. And the people who were with him were about six hundred men. 3. And Ahijah the son of Ahitub, the brother of Ichabod the son of Phinehas, the son of Eli, *the priest serving before the*

Notes, Chapter Thirteen (Cont.)

[19] MT: "for."

[20] MT: "sought for himself a man according to his own heart."

[21] MT: "for prince."

[22] MT: "of Benjamin."

[23] MT: "mustered."

[24] MT: "Benjamin."

[25] The corresponding MT word also has the meaning "raiding party."

[26] MT: "Shual."

[27] The Tg translates the MT "Zeboim," that is "hyenas."

[28] MT: "a smith." Tg makes the smith's craft more specific.

[29] MT: "the land," though some mss. have "territory."

[30] MT: "Hebrews."

[31] MT: "sword or spear."

[32] MT lacks the phrase.

[33] MT: "his mattock and his axe and his plowshare."

[34] MT is uncertain. "And the charge (?) was a pim for the plowshares and the mattocks (?) and three prongs (?) and axes (?) and for setting the goad."

Lord[1] in Shiloh, was wearing the ephod. And the people did not know that Jonathan had gone. 4. And between the fords that Jonathan sought to cross to the garrison of the Philistines there was a crag of rock from one side and a crag of rock from the other side. The name of the one was *Mashro'itha,*[2] and the name of the other was *Madrukhitha.*[3] 5. One crag looked out from the north toward Michmash, and the other from the south toward Geba. 6. And Jonathan said to the young man, his armor-bearer: "Come and we will cross over to the garrison of those uncircumcised ones. Perhaps the Lord will work *a miracle*[4] for us, for there is no obstacle *before*[5] the Lord to save by many or by few." 7. And his armor-bearer said to him: "Do everything that is in your heart. Direct yourself. Behold I am with you according to your *good pleasure.*"[6] 8. And Jonathan said: "Behold we are crossing over unto the men, and we will show ourselves to them. 9. If thus they say to us: 'Wait until we come unto you,' we will stand *in our place*[7] and we will not go up unto them. 10. And if thus they say: 'Come up toward us,' we will come up for the Lord has handed them over in our hand. And this will be a sign for us." 11. And the two of them showed themselves to the garrison of the Philistines, and the Philistines said: "Behold the *Jews*[8] are coming forth from the holes where they hid themselves." 12. And the watchmen answered Jonathan and his armor-bearer, and said: "Come up toward us, and we will let you know something." And Jonathan said to his armor-bearer: "Come up after me, for the Lord has delivered them in the hand of Israel." 13. And Jonathan went up upon his hands and upon his feet, and his armor-bearer was behind him. And they fell *wounded*[9] before Jonathan, and his armor-bearer was killing after him. 14. And the first blow that Jonathan and his armor-bearer struck was about twenty men in the space of half *the journey*[10] of a yoke *of oxen*[11] in the field. 15. And there was commotion in the camp, in the field, and in all the people. Even the garrisons and the raiding party shook, and the earth shook, and there was shaking *from before the Lord.*[12] 16. And Saul's watchmen in Gibeah of *the house of Benjamin*[13] saw, and behold *the multitude of the camp of the Philistines was broken; its breaking grew more and more.*[14] 17. And Saul said to the people who were with him: "*Go around now*[15] and see who *is missing*[16] from us." And they counted, and behold Jonathan and his armor-bearer were not there. 18. And Saul said to Ahijah: "Bring near the ark of *the Lord.*"[17] For the ark of *the Lord*[18] was *with*[19] the sons of Israel on that day. 19. And while Saul was speaking with the priest, the multitude which was in the camp of the Philistines grew more and more. And Saul said to the priest: "*Bring the ephod near.*"[20]

Notes, Chapter Fourteen

[1]MT: "the priest of the Lord."

[2]MT: "Bozez." The Hebrew name means a swampy place, and the Aramaic means a slippery place.

[3]MT: "Seneh." The Hebrew name means "thorny," and the Aramaic means a "slope." Tg may associate Seneh (*snh*) with Aramaic *msn'y* ("shoes"). Hence, "a well-trodden place." See S-A, 125.

[4]MT lacks the word.

[5]MT: "for."

[6]MT: "heart."

[7]MT: "beneath us."

[8]MT: "Hebrews."

[9]MT lacks the word.

[10]MT: "place for plowing." MT is obscure.

[11]MT lacks the word.

[12]MT: "of God."

[13]MT: "Benjamin."

[14]MT: "the multitude was surging and went hither and thither."

[15]MT: "inspect."

[16]MT: "is gone."

[17]MT: "God."

[18]MT: "God."

[19]MT: "and."

[20]MT: "withdraw your hand." The MT implies that Saul stopped consulting the priest. Tg has him seek his support through the ephod.

20. And Saul and all the people who were with him gathered and came into battle. And behold the sword of each man was against his fellow. There was very great confusion. 21. And the *Jews*[21] who were for the Philistines yesterday and before, who went up with them in the camp round about, they also *turned*[22] to be with Israel, which was with Saul and Jonathan. 22. And all the men of Israel who were hidden in the hill country of *the house of Ephraim*[23] heard that the Philistines fled and they too pressed after them in battle. 23. And the Lord delivered Israel on that day, and *the wagers of battle arrived at*[24] Beth-aven. 24. And the men of Israel were hard pressed on that day, and Saul made the people swear, saying: "Cursed be the man who will eat bread until evening, *until*[25] I be avenged from my enemies." And all the people did not taste bread. 25. And *all the inhabitants of the land*[26] entered in the thicket, and there was honey on the face of the field. 26. And the people came to the thicket, and behold there was a stream of honey. And there was no one who brought his hand back to his mouth, for the people were afraid of the oath. 27. And Jonathan did not hear when his father made the people swear, and he reached out the tip of the staff that was in his hand, and he dipped it in the nest of honey, and brought back his hand to his mouth, and his eyes grew bright. 28. And a man from the people answered and said: "Your father has indeed made the people swear, saying: 'Cursed be the man who will eat bread this day.'" And the people grew faint. 29. And Jonathan said: "My father has troubled the land. See now, for my eyes have grown bright, for I tasted a little of this honey. 30. But it would have been better if the people indeed ate this day from the spoil of its enemies which it found, for the slaughter against the Philistines has not been much." 31. And they *killed*[27] on that day among the Philistines from Michmash to *the plain of Aijalon*,[28] and the people were very wearied. 32. And the people *turned toward*[29] the spoil and took sheep and oxen and calves, and they slaughtered upon the ground, and the people ate with the blood. 33. And they told Saul, saying: "Behold the people are sinning *before*[30] the Lord to eat with the blood." And he said: "You have acted falsely. Bring near unto me this day a large stone." 34. And Saul said: "Disperse yourselves among the people, and you shall say to them: 'Bring near unto me each man his ox and each man his sheep, and you shall slaughter here and eat; and you shall not sin *before*[31] the Lord to eat with the blood." And all the people brought near, each man his ox in his hand by night; and they slaughtered there. 35. And Saul built an altar *before*[32] the Lord. He himself began to build an altar *before*[33] the Lord. 36. And Saul said: "Let us go down after the Philistines by night, and let us *kill*[34] them until the light of morning. And let us not leave a man among them." And they said: "Everything that is good in your eyes, do." And the priest said: "Let us draw near here *and inquire of the Memra of the Lord*."[35] 37. And Saul inquired of *the Memra of the Lord*:[36] "Shall I go down after the Philistines? Will you deliver them in the hand of Israel?" And he did not *receive his prayer*[37] on that day.

Notes, Chapter Fourteen (Cont.)

[21] MT: "Hebrews."
[22] MT lacks the word.
[23] MT: "Ephraim."
[24] MT: "the battle passed by."
[25] MT: "and."
[26] MT: "all the land."
[27] MT: "struck down."
[28] MT: "Aijalon."
[29] MT: "made for."
[30] MT: "to."
[31] MT: "to."
[32] MT: "to."
[33] MT: "to."
[34] MT: "despoil." Tg makes the verb more consistent with the second half of the verse.
[35] MT: "to God."
[36] MT: "God."
[37] MT: "answer him."

38. And Saul said: "Draw yourselves near here, all you *chiefs*[38] of the people, and learn and see in what was this sin this day. 39. For as the Lord who saves Israel lives, that if it be in Jonathan my son, *he will surely be killed.*"[39] And there was no one who was answering him from all the people. 40. And he said to all Israel: "You shall be on one side, and I and Jonathan my son will be on one side." And the people said to Saul: "Whatever is good in your eyes, do." 41. And Saul said: "*Before*[40] the Lord the God of Israel *we are in truth.*"[41] And Jonathan and Saul were taken, and the people went forth. 42. And Saul said: "Cast *lots*[42] between *us*[43] and Jonathan my son." And Jonathan was taken. 43. And Saul said to Jonathan: "Tell me what you did." And Jonathan told him and said: "I have indeed tasted with the tip of the staff that is in my hand a little honey. Behold *I am guilty so as to die.*"[44] 44. And Saul said: "May *the Lord*[45] do thus and still more for you will surely die, Jonathan." 45. And the people said to Saul: "Shall Jonathan be *killed*[46] who worked this great victory in Israel? Far from it! As the Lord lives, if there fall from the hair of his head to the ground, for *before the Lord it was revealed that in carelessness he acted this day.*"[47] And the people saved Jonathan, and he did not die. 46. And Saul went up from after the Philistines, and the Philistines went to their place. 47. Saul *prospered in*[48] the kingdom over Israel, and he *waged battle*[49] round about against all his enemies in Moab and in the sons of Ammon and in Edom and in the kings of Zobah and in the Philistines; and in every place that he was turning, he was condemning. 48. And *he gathered armies*[50] and struck down *those of the house of Amalek*[51] and rescued Israel from the hand of those plundering them. 49. And the sons of Saul were Jonathan and Ishvi and Malchishua; and the name of his two daughters — the name of the *older,*[52] Merab; and the name of the younger, Michal. 50. And the name of the wife of Saul — Ahinoam the daughter of Ahimaaz. And the name of the commander of his army — Abner the son of Ner, the uncle of Saul. 51. And Kish was the father of Saul, and Ner the father of Abner was the son of Abiel. 52. And the battle was strong against the Philistines all the days of Saul; and Saul saw every warrior man and every *man waging battle,*[53] and he gathered him unto him.

CHAPTER 15

1. And Samuel said to Saul: "The Lord sent me to anoint you *to be the king*[1] over his people, over Israel; and now *accept the speaking of the Memra*[2] of the Lord. 2. Thus

Notes, Chapter Fourteen (Cont.)

[38]MT: "leaders."
[39]MT: "he will surely die."
[40]MT: "to."
[41]MT: "give Thummim."
[42]MT lacks the word.
[43]MT: "me."
[44]MT: "I will die."
[45]MT: "God."
[46]MT: "die."
[47]MT: "with God he has worked this day." Tg

provides an extenuating circumstance for Jonathan's offense.
[48]MT: "took hold."
[49]MT: "fought."
[50]MT: "he acted mightily."
[51]MT: "Amalek."
[52]MT: "firstborn."
[53]MT: "strong man."

Notes, Chapter Fifteen

[1]MT: "for a king."
[2]MT: "hear the voice of the words."

said the Lord of hosts: '*I remember*[3] what Amalek did to Israel, that it *ambushed*[4] it on the way in its going up from Egypt. 3. Now go, and you shall strike down *those of the house of Amalek*[5] and destroy utterly all that is *theirs,*[6] and you shall not spare *them,*[7] and you shall kill from man unto woman, from youngster unto infant, from ox unto sheep, from camel unto ass.'" 4. And Saul *gathered*[8] the people and mustered them *by the lambs of Passover*[9] 200,000 men on foot and 10,000 men of Judah. 5. And Saul came unto the city of *those of the house of Amalek*[10] and *set up his camp*[11] in the valley. 6. And Saul said to the *Shalmaite:*[12] "Go, turn aside, *separate yourself*[13] from the midst of the Amalekite lest I destroy you with him. And you did good with all the sons of Israel when they went up from Egypt." And *the Shalmaite separated himself*[14] from the midst of the Amalekite. 7. And Saul struck down *those of the house of Amalek*[15] from Havilah *to the ascent of Hagra*[16] which is facing Egypt. 8. And he took Agag, the king *of those of the house of Amalek,*[17] *while*[18] he was alive, and he destroyed all the people by the edge of the sword. 9. And Saul and the people spared Agag and the best of the sheep and oxen and fatlings and *stout ones*[19] and everything that was good; and they were not willing to destroy them. And everything that was base and that was despised, that they destroyed. 10. And *the word of prophecy from before the Lord was with*[20] Samuel, saying: 11. "I have regretted *my word*[21] that I made Saul king *to be the king,*[22] for he has turned from after *my service*[23] and he has not fulfilled my words." And *it was hard*[24] for Samuel, and he *prayed before*[25] the Lord all night. 12. And Samuel got up early to meet Saul in the morning, and it was told to Samuel, saying: "Saul came to Carmel, and behold he set up for himself there *a place in which to divide up the spoil,*[26] and he turned around and passed over and went down to Gilgal." 13. And Samuel came unto Saul, and Saul said to him: "Blessed are you *before*[27] the Lord; I have fulfilled the word of the Lord." 14. And Samuel said: "And *if you have fulfilled it,*[28] what is the sound of this sheep in my ears and the sound of the oxen that I am hearing?" 15. And Saul said: "From the Amalekite they brought them, for the people spared the best of the sheep and oxen in order to sacrifice *before*[29] the Lord your God; and we destroyed the rest." 16. And Samuel said to Saul: "Wait, and I will tell you *what was spoken from before the Lord with me*[30] by night." And he said to him: "Speak." 17. And Samuel said: "*And were you not from your beginning base and weak in the eyes of*

Notes, Chapter Fifteen (Cont.)

[3]MT: "I have observed."

[4]MT: "set upon."

[5]MT: "Amalek."

[6]MT: "its."

[7]MT: "it."

[8]MT: "summoned."

[9]MT: *tĕlā'îm* ("lambs"), but not "of Passover."

[10]MT: "Amalek."

[11]MT: "struggled." The LXX has "lay in wait."

[12]MT: "Kenite." The Shalmaites are an Arab tribe known in rabbinic literature. See S-A, 48 and 117.

[13]MT: "go down."

[14]MT: "the Kenite turned aside."

[15]MT: "Amalek."

[16]MT: "as you go to Shur." For Hagra, see S-A, 113, and note 335.

[17]MT: "Amalek."

[18]MT lacks the word.

[19]MT: "lambs."

[20]MT: "the word of the Lord was to."

[21]MT lacks the phrase.

[22]MT: "for a king."

[23]MT: "me."

[24]MT: "it was hot," i.e., he was angry.

[25]MT: "cried out to."

[26]MT: "a monument."

[27]MT: "to."

[28]MT lacks the phrase.

[29]MT: "to."

[30]MT: "what the Lord spoke to me."

your own self? But the merit of the tribe of Benjamin your father was the cause for you, for he sought to pass in the sea before the sons of Israel. On account of this the Lord has elevated you to be the king over Israel.[31] 18. And the Lord sent you on the way, and said: 'Go, and destroy the sinners, *those of the house of Amalek,*[32] and you will *wage battle against them*[33] until you put an end to them.' 19. And why did you not *accept the Memra of the Lord?*[34] And you turned yourself to plunder, and you did what was evil *before*[35] the Lord." 20. And Saul said to Samuel that "*I accepted the Memra of the Lord*[36] and went on the way that the Lord sent me, and I brought Agag the king of *the house of Amalek*[37] and destroyed *those of the house of Amalek.*[38] 21. And the people *separated out*[39] from the plunder sheep and oxen *before they destroyed them*[40] to sacrifice *before*[41] the Lord your God in Gilgal." 22. And Samuel said: "Is there delight *before*[42] the Lord in holocausts and *holy offerings*[43] as in *accepting the Memra of the Lord?*[44] Behold accepting his Memra is better than holy offerings; to listen to the words of his prophets is better than the fat of fatlings.*[45] 23. *For like the guilt of men who inquire of the diviner, so is the guilt of every man who rebels against the words of the Law; and like the sins of the people who go astray after idols, so is the sin of every man who cuts out or adds to the words of the prophets. Because you rejected the service of the Lord, he has removed you from being the king."*[46] 24. And Saul said to Samuel: "I have sinned, because I transgressed *against the Memra of the Lord*[47] and *despised your word,*[48] because I feared the people and *accepted their word.*[49] 25. And now *pardon*[50] my sin, and return with me, and I will worship *before*[51] the Lord." 26. And Samuel said to Saul: "I will not return with you, because you rejected the word of the Lord and the Lord *removed*[52] you from being the king over Israel." 27. And Samuel turned around to go, and he took hold of the edge of his robe, and it was torn. 28. And Samuel said to him: "The Lord has *taken away*[53] the kingdom of Israel from you this day and given it to your companion *whose deeds are better*[54] than you. 29. *And if you say: 'I will turn*

Notes, Chapter Fifteen (Cont.)

[31] MT: "Though you are small in your own eyes, you are head of the tribes of Israel, the Lord has anointed you for a king over Israel." See *Mekilta,* Beshallah, 6 (Lauterbach, 1:232) for the interpretation that Benjamin went into the sea first.
[32] MT: "Amalek."
[33] MT: "fight against him."
[34] MT: "hear the voice of the Lord."
[35] MT: "in the eyes of."
[36] MT: "I heard the voice of the Lord."
[37] MT: "Amalek."
[38] MT: "Amalek."
[39] MT: "took."
[40] MT: "the first fruits of the plunder."
[41] MT: "to."

[42] MT: "to."
[43] MT: "sacrifices."
[44] MT: "hearing the voice of the Lord."
[45] MT: "Behold hearing is better than sacrifice; to listen than fat of rams."
[46] MT: "For the sin of divinations is rebellion, and iniquity and idolatry is stubbornness. Because you rejected the word of the Lord, he has rejected you from being king."
[47] MT: "the mouth of the Lord."
[48] MT: "your word."
[49] MT: "heard their voice."
[50] MT: "take away."
[51] MT: the preposition is "to."
[52] MT: "rejected."
[53] MT: "torn away."
[54] MT: "who is better." Tg makes the basis of

from my sins and it will be forgiven to me in order that I and my sons may exercise kingship over Israel forever,' already it is decreed upon you from before the Lord of Israel's glory before whom there is no deception, and he does not turn from whatever he says; for he is not like the sons of men who say and act deceitfully, decree and do not carry out."[55] 30. And he said: "I have sinned; now honor me before the elders of my people and before Israel, and return with me, and I will worship *before*[56] the Lord your God." 31. And Samuel turned back after Saul, and Saul worshipped *before*[57] the Lord. 32. And Samuel said: "Bring near unto me Agag the king of *those of the house of Amalek.*"[58] And Agag came unto him *imperiously.*[59] And Agag said: "*Please, my master, death is bitter.*"[60] 33. And Samuel said: "Just as your sword has left women childless, so your mother will be left childless among women." And Samuel split up Agag before the Lord in Gilgal. 34. And Samuel went to Ramah, and Saul went up to his house to Gibeah of Saul. 35. And Samuel did not see Saul any more until the day of his death, for Samuel grieved over Saul. And the Lord *regretted his Memra*[61] that he made Saul king over Israel.

CHAPTER 16

1. And the Lord said to Samuel: "How long are you grieving over Saul? And I have *removed*[1] him from *being the king*[2] over Israel. Fill your horn with oil, and go; I will send you unto Jesse *who is from Bethlehem,*[3] for *there is revealed before me among his sons one fitting before me to be the king.*"[4] 2. And Samuel said: "How will I go? And *if Saul hears,*[5] he will kill me." And the Lord said: "You shall take a heifer in your hand, and say: 'I have come to sacrifice *before*[6] the Lord.' 3. And you will invite Jesse in the *service,*[7] and I will *tell you*[8] what you will do; and you will anoint *before*[9] me whomever I will tell you." 4. And Samuel did what the Lord said, and he came to Bethlehem; and the elders of the city *gathered*[10] to meet him, and *they*[11] said: "Is your coming peaceful?" 5. And he said: "Peaceful. I have come to sacrifice *before*[12] the Lord. *Prepare*[13]

Notes, Chapter Fifteen (Cont.)

David's goodness explicit.

[55]MT: "And also the glory of Israel will not lie and will not repent, for he is not a man so as to repent."

[56]MT: the preposition is "to."

[57]MT: the preposition is "to."

[58]MT: Amalek.

[59]MT is unclear; it may mean "with delight."

[60]MT: "Surely the bitterness of death has turned aside."

[61]MT: "repented."

Notes, Chapter Sixteen

[1]MT: "rejected."

[2]MT: "ruling."

[3]MT: "Bethlehemite."

[4]MT: "I saw among his sons a king for me."

[5]MT: "Saul will hear and."

[6]MT: "to."

[7]MT: "the sacrifice."

[8]MT: "make you know."

[9]MT: "for."

[10]MT: "trembled."

[11]MT: "he."

[12]MT: "to."

[13]MT: "consecrate."

yourselves and enter with me in the *service*."[14] And he *invited*[15] Jesse and his sons, and he summoned them to *the service for the holy offerings*.[16] 6. And when they entered, he saw Eliab and said: "*Good*[17] before the Lord is his anointed one." 7. And the Lord said to Samuel: "Do not look at his appearance and at the height of his stature, for I have *removed*[18] him; *for not as the sons of men see, for the sons of men see with their eyes and before the Lord are revealed the plans of the heart*."[19] 8. And Jesse called to Abinadab and had him pass before Samuel. And he said: "Also in this one *there is no pleasure before the Lord.*"[20] 9. And Jesse had Shammah pass, and he said: "Also in this one *there is no pleasure before the Lord*."[21] 10. And Jesse had his seven sons pass before Samuel. And Samuel said to Jesse: "*There is no pleasure before the Lord*[22] in these." 11. And Samuel said to Jesse: "Are the young men finished?" And he said: "The youngest is still left, and behold he is tending the sheep." And Samuel said to Jesse: "Send and *bring*[23] him, for we will not dine until his coming here." 12. And he sent and brought him. And he was ruddy; *his eyes were beautiful*,[24] and handsome *in*[25] his appearance. And the Lord said: "Arise, anoint him, for this is he." 13. And Samuel took the horn of oil, and he anointed him in the midst of his brothers. And *a spirit of power from before the Lord resided upon*[26] David from that day and beyond. And Samuel arose and went to Ramah. 14. *And the spirit of power from before the Lord that was with Saul passed from him, and the evil spirit from before the Lord*[27] was agitating him. 15. And the servants of Saul said to him: "Behold now the evil spirit *from before the Lord*[28] is agitating you. 16. Let our master now tell your servants before you, let him seek out a man who knows how to play on the lyre. And it will happen that when the evil spirit *from before the Lord will reside*[29] upon you, he will play with his hand and it will be good for you." 17. And Saul said to his servants: "Search out for me now a man who is good at playing and bring him to me." 18. And one of the young men answered and said: "Behold I have seen a son of Jesse *who is from Bethlehem*[30] who knows how to play; and he is a warrior and a man *waging battle*,[31] and intelligent *in counsel*,[32] and a man *handsome in his appearance*,[33] and *the Memra of the Lord is at his aid*."[34] 19. And Saul sent messengers unto Jesse and said: "Send to me David your son who is with the sheep." 20. And Jesse took an ass-*load*[35] of bread and a skin of wine and one kid-goat, and he sent (them) by the hand of David his son unto Saul. 21. And David came unto Saul, and he *served*[36] before him and loved him very much, and

Notes, Chapter Sixteen (Cont.)

[14]MT: "the sacrifice."
[15]MT: "consecrated."
[16]MT: "the sacrifice."
[17]MT lacks the word.
[18]MT: "rejected."
[19]MT: "for not as man sees, for man sees by eyes and the Lord sees to the heart."
[20]MT: "the Lord has not chosen."
[21]MT: "the Lord has not chosen."
[22]MT: "the Lord has not chosen."
[23]MT: "take."
[24]MT: "with beauty of eyes."
[25]MT: "of."
[26]MT: "the spirit of the Lord came to."
[27]MT: "And the spirit of the Lord departed from Saul, and an evil spirit from the Lord..."
[28]MT: "of God."
[29]MT: "of God is."
[30]MT: "the Bethlehemite."
[31]MT: "of war."
[32]MT: "of word."
[33]MT: "of appearance."
[34]MT: "the Lord is with him."
[35]MT lacks the word.
[36]MT: "stood."

he was his armor-bearer. 22. And Saul sent unto Jesse, saying: "Let David *serve*[37] before me now, for he has found favor in my eyes." 23. And it happened that, when *the evil spirit from before the Lord was residing upon*[38] Saul, David was taking the lyre and playing with his hand, and it was refreshing to Saul and *doing him good*[39] and the evil spirit was *going up*[40] from him.

CHAPTER 17

1. And the Philistines gathered their camps *to wage battle,*[1] and they were gathered to Soco, which belongs to *the tribe of Judah,*[2] and they camped between Soco and Azekah in Ephes-dammim. 2. And Saul and the men of Israel were gathered, and they camped in the *plain*[3] of the Terebinth and drew up battle opposite the Philistines. 3. And the Philistines were standing upon the mountain on one side, and Israel was standing upon the mountain on the other side, and a valley was between them. 4. And *a man from among them*[4] came forth from the camp of the Philistines; Goliath was his name, from Gath; his height was six cubits and a span. 5. And a helmet of bronze was upon his head, and he was dressed with breastplate of scales and the breastplate weighed 5,000 shekels of bronze. 6. And leggings of bronze (were) upon his feet; and the javelin of bronze *coming forth from the helmet, borne between his shoulders.*[5] 7. And the *wood*[6] of his spear was like the beam of weavers, and the point of his spear weighed 600 shekels of iron; and the bearer of the shield was going before him. 8. And he arose and called to the ranks of Israel and said to them: "Why are you coming forth to arrange battle? Am I not the Philistine, and are you not servants to Saul? Choose for yourselves a man, and let him come down unto me. 9. If he is able to *wage battle*[7] with me and *kills*[8] me, we will be servants to you. And if I prevail against him and *kill*[9] him, you will be servants to us and serve us." 10. And the Philistine said: "I put to shame the ranks of Israel this day. *Bring*[10] to me a man, and let us *wage battle*[11] together." 11. And Saul and all Israel heard these words of the Philistine; and they *were shattered*[12] and were very much afraid. 12. And David was the son of a certain Ephraimite man from Bethlehem *of the house of Judah,*[13] and his name was Jesse, and he had eight sons. And in the days of Saul the man was old, *counted among the chosen ones.*[14] 13. And the

Notes, Chapter Sixteen (Cont.)

[37] MT: "stand."
[38] MT: "the spirit of God was to."
[39] MT: "good for him."
[40] MT: "departing."

Notes, Chapter Seventeen

[1] MT: "for war."
[2] MT: "Judah."
[3] MT: "valley."
[4] MT: "a man of the in-between," which may

mean "a champion" or "an infantryman."
[5] MT: "between his shoulders."
[6] MT: "shaft."
[7] MT: "fight."
[8] MT: "strike."
[9] MT: "strike."
[10] MT: "give."
[11] MT: "fight."
[12] MT: "were dismayed."
[13] MT: "of Judah."
[14] MT: "advanced among men." MT probably refer to Jesse's age. Tg interprets the phrase to refer to his status.

three eldest sons of Jesse came and went after Saul *to wage battle;*[15] and the name of his three sons who went in battle: Eliab the first-born, and his second Abinadab, and the third Shammah. 14. And David was young, and the three eldest went after Saul. 15. And David was going and returning from Saul's presence to pasture the sheep of his father at Bethlehem. 16. And the Philistine drew near early and late, and he took up his stand for forty days. 17. And Jesse said to David his son: "Take now to your brothers this measure of grain and these ten *loaves*[16] and *bring*[17] (them) to the camp to your brothers. 18. And you shall bring these ten cheeses of milk to the chief of the thousand. And you shall visit your brothers for peace and bring back a report of them." 19. And Saul and they and all the men of Israel were in the *Plain*[18] of the Terebinth, *waging battle*[19] with the Philistines. 20. And David got up early in the morning, and he left the sheep with the keeper; and he took and went as Jesse commanded him; and he came to *the camp of siegers,*[20] and *the camp of the wagers of war went forth*[21] to the battle line, and they shouted out in battle. 21. And Israel and the Philistines drew up battle line opposite battle line. 22. And David left the things that were upon him at the hand of the keeper of the baggage, and he ran to the battle line and came and greeted his brothers. 23. And he was speaking with them, and behold *a man from their midst*[22] came up, Goliath the Philistine was his name, from Gath, from the battle lines of the Philistines, and he spoke according to these words. And David heard. 24. And all the men of Israel, when they saw the man, fled from before him and were very much afraid. 25. And the men of Israel said: "Have you seen this man who is coming up? For he comes up to jeer at Israel. And whoever will *kill*[23] him, the king will make him rich with great wealth and will give his daughter to him and will make the house of his father *chiefs*[24] in Israel." 26. And David said to the men who were standing with him, saying: "What will be done for the man who will *kill*[25] that Philistine and take away the reproach from upon Israel? For who is this uncircumcised Philistine that he jeers at *the ranks of the people of the living God?*"[26] 27. And the people said to him according to this word, saying: "Thus it will be done to the man who will *kill*[27] him." 28. And Eliab his oldest brother heard while he was speaking with the men, and the anger of Eliab *was strong*[28] against David, and he said: "Why have you come down? And with whom did you leave those few sheep in the wilderness? I know your *thoughtlessness*[29] and the evil of your heart, for you came down in order to see *the wagers of battle.*"[30] 29. And David said: "What have I done? Was it not but a word?" 30. And he turned from him toward another. And he spoke according to this word; and the people answered him a

Notes, Chapter Seventeen (Cont.)

[15] MT: "for war."

[16] MT lacks the word.

[17] MT: "hurry." Some Tg mss. add to the verse: "and take the document of divorce of their wives and give them." Talmudic law suggested that soldiers give conditional divorces to their wives in case they were missing in action. See *b. Šabb.* 56a and S-A, 46.

[18] MT: "valley."

[19] MT: "fighting."

[20] MT: "the encampment."

[21] MT: "the force was going forth."

[22] MT: "a man of the in-between." cf. vs. 4.

[23] MT: "strike."

[24] MT: "free."

[25] MT: "strike."

[26] MT: "the ranks of the living God."

[27] MT: "strike."

[28] MT: "was hot."

[29] MT: "presumption."

[30] MT: "the war."

word like the first word. 31. And the words that David spoke were heard, and they told (them) before Saul, and he took him. 32. And David said to Saul: "Let not the heart of a man *be shattered*[31] on account of him. Let your servant go and *wage battle*[32] with this Philistine." 33. And Saul said to David: "You cannot go against this Philistine to *wage battle*[33] with him, for you are a child, and he is a man *waging battles*[34] from his childhood." 34. And David said to Saul: "Your servant was caring for sheep for his father, and a lion and *even*[35] a bear came and took a lamb from the flock. 35. And I went forth after it and struck it down, and I rescued it from its mouth. And it rose up against me and I took hold by its *jaw*[36] and struck it down and *killed it.*[37] 36. Both lion and bear your servant *has killed,*[38] and this uncircumcised Philistine will be like one of them, for he has defied the ranks of *the people of the living Lord.*"[39] 37. And David said: "The Lord who rescued me from the hand of the lion and from the hand of the bear, he will rescue me from the hand of this Philistine." And Saul said to David: "Go, and *may the Memra of the Lord be at your aid.*"[40] 38. And Saul had David clothed with his clothing, and he put a helmet of bronze upon his head, and he had him clothed with a breastplate. 39. And David girded on his sword over his clothing, and *he was not willing*[41] to go, for he was not so accustomed. And David said to Saul: "I am not able to go in these, for *there is no experience in them.*"[42] And David took them off himself. 40. And he took his staff in his hand, and chose for himself five smooth stones from the wadi, and placed them in the shepherd's clothing that was his and *in his bag,*[43] and his sling was in his hand, and he drew near unto the Philistine. 41. And the Philistine came, coming and drawing near to David; and the man bearing the shield *was coming*[44] before him. 42. And the Philistine looked and saw David, and he despised him, for he was a child and ruddy, *handsome in his appearance.*[45] 43. And the Philistine said to David: "Am I a *despised*[46] dog that you come against me with staffs?" And the Philistine cursed David by his *idol.*[47] 44. And the Philistine said to David: "Come against me, and I will give your flesh to the bird of the heavens and to the beast of the field." 45. And David said to the Philistine: "You are coming against me with sword and with spear and with javelin, and I am coming against you with the name of the Lord of hosts, the God of the ranks of Israel at whom you have jeered. 46. This day the Lord will give you in my hand, and I will *kill*[48] you and take off your head from you; and I will give the corpse of the camp of the Philistines this day to the bird of the heavens and to the wild animals of the earth, and *all those inhabiting the earth*[49] will know that there is a God in Israel. 47. And all this assembly will know that not by the sword and by the spear does the Lord save, for *victory in battles is from before the Lord;*[50] and he will give you in our hand." 48. And when the Philistine arose and came and drew near opposite David, David hurried and ran to the battle line opposite the

Notes, Chapter Seventeen (Cont.)

[31] MT: "fall."
[32] MT: "fight."
[33] MT: "fight."
[34] MT: "of war."
[35] Most MT mss. have accusative marker *'t.*
[36] MT: "beard."
[37] MT: "put it to death."
[38] MT: "struck down."
[39] MT: "of the living God."

[40] MT: "may the Lord be with you."
[41] MT: "he was willing."
[42] MT: "I have not tried them out."
[43] MT: "in a wallet."
[44] MT lacks the word.
[45] MT: "with a handsome appearance."
[46] MT lacks the word.
[47] MT: "gods."
[48] MT: "strike."
[49] MT: "all the earth."
[50] MT: "war is the Lord's."

Philistine. 49. And David sent forth his hand to the bag and took from there a stone, and *he twirled (it) around*[51] and struck the Philistine upon *the house of his eyes,*[52] and the stone sank in *the house of his eyes,*[53] and he fell upon his face to the ground. 50. And David prevailed over the Philistine with the sling and with the stone, and he struck down the Philistine and *killed him,*[54] and there was no sword in the hand of David. 51. And David ran and stood over the Philistine and took his sword and drew it from it sheath and *killed him*[55] and with it cut off his head; and the Philistines saw that their *man*[56] was dead, and they fled. 52. And the men of Israel and Judah arose and shouted and pursued *after*[57] the Philistines unto the entrance of Gai and unto the gates of Ekron; and the Philistines fell *killed*[58] on the road of Shaaraim and unto Gath and unto Ekron. 53. And the sons of Israel turned from *pursuing*[59] after the Philistines, and they plundered their camp. 54. And David took the head of the Philistine and brought it to Jerusalem and put his armor in his tent. 55. And when Saul saw that David was going forth opposite the Philistine, he said to Abner, the chief of the army: "Whose son is this young man, Abner?" And Abner said: "By the life of your soul, O king, I don't know." 56. And the king said: "Ask whose son this young man is." 57. And when David returned from *killing*[60] the Philistine, Abner took him and brought him before Saul, and the head of the Philistine was in his hand. 58. And Saul said to him: "Whose son are you, young man?" And David said: "The son of your servant Jesse, *who is from Bethlehem.*"[61]

CHAPTER 18

1. And when he finished speaking with Saul, the soul of Jonathan *was tied in love*[1] with the soul of David; and Jonathan loved him like his own soul. 2. And Saul took him on that day and he did not let him return to the house of his father. 3. And Jonathan and David cut a covenant because he loved him like his own soul. 4. And Jonathan took off the cloak that was upon him and gave it to David, and his clothing and unto his sword and unto his bow and unto his belt. 5. And David went forth successfully in every place that Saul sent him; and Saul *appointed*[2] him over the men *waging battle,*[3] and this was pleasing in the eyes of all the people and also in the eyes of the servants of Saul. 6. And it happened in their coming in, when David returned from *killing*[4] the Philistine, the women went forth from all the towns of Israel to *praise in*

Notes, Chapter Seventeen (Cont.)

[51] MT: "slung it."
[52] MT: "forehead."
[53] MT: "forehead."
[54] MT: "put him to death."
[55] MT: "put him to death."
[56] MT: "warrior."
[57] MT lacks the preposition.
[58] MT: "slain."

[59] MT: "chasing."
[60] MT: "striking down."
[61] MT: "the Bethlehemite."

Notes, Chapter Eighteen

[1] MT: "was bound."
[2] MT: "placed."
[3] MT: "of war."
[4] MT: "striking down."

dances[5] to meet Saul the king with timbrels, with joy, and with *cymbals*.[6] 7. And the women who *were praising*[7] answered and said: "Saul *killed thousands*,[8] and David *ten thousands*."[9] 8. And this word *was very hard*[10] for Saul and evil in his eyes, and he said: "They have given to David ten thousands, and to me they have given thousands. *And from now on there is not left to him anything except the kingdom*."[11] 9. And Saul *was lying in wait*[12] for David from that day and onward. 10. And on the day after it an evil spirit *from before the Lord resided upon*[13] Saul, and *he became demented*[14] in the midst of the house, and David was playing with his hand day by day, and the spear was in the hand of Saul. 11. And Saul raised up the spear and said: "I will make it strike David, and *I will pin it*[15] in the wall." And David *fled*[16] from before him two times. 12. And Saul was afraid of David, for *the Memra of the Lord was at his aid*[17] and *was far from*[18] Saul. 13. And Saul removed him from his presence and *appointed*[19] him for himself chief of a thousand; and he went forth and came in *at the head*[20] of the people. 14. And David was successful for all his way, and *the Memra of the Lord was at his aid*.[21] 15. And Saul saw that he was very successful, and *he was afraid*[22] of him. 16. And all Israel and Judah were loving David, for he was going forth and coming in *at their head*.[23] 17. And Saul said to David: "Behold my eldest daughter Merab — I will give her to you for a wife; but be for me *a man waging battles*,[24] and *wage the battles of the people of the Lord*."[25] And Saul said: "Let not my hand be on him; and *let him be given in the hand of the Philistines*."[26] 18. And David said to Saul: "Who am I, and what is my life, *indeed*[27] the family of my father in Israel, that I should be the son-in-law to the king?" 19. *And at the time when the giving of Merab the daughter of Saul to David arrived*,[28] she was given to Adriel the Meholathite for a wife. 20. And Michal the daughter of Saul loved David, and they told Saul, and the word was right in his eyes. 21. And Saul said: "I will give her to him, and she will be for him for a stumbling block, and *he will be given in the hand of the Philistines*."[29] And Saul said to David once again: "You will be a son-in-law to me this day." 22. And Saul commanded his servants: "Speak with David in secret, saying: 'Behold the king takes delight in you, and all his servants love you. And now become a son-in-law to the king.'" 23. And the servants of Saul spoke *before*[30] David these words, and David said: "Is it a small thing in your eyes to become a son-in-law to the king? And I am a poor and *common*[31] man." 24. And the servants of Saul told him, saying: "According to these words David spoke." 25. And

Notes, Chapter Eighteen (Cont.)

[5]MT: "singing and dancing."

[6]MT is uncertain; perhaps it means "three-stringed instruments."

[7]MT: "making merry."

[8]MT: "struck down his thousands."

[9]MT: "his ten thousands."

[10]MT: "was very hot."

[11]MT: "And what is left to him but the kingdom?"

[12]MT: "was eying."

[13]MT: "of God came upon."

[14]MT: "he was prophesying." The MT is referring to the ecstatic behavior of certain prophets; Tg interprets this meaning.

[15]MT lacks the verb.

[16]MT: "turned around."

[17]MT: "the Lord was with him."

[18]MT: "turned aside from."

[19]MT: "placed him."

[20]MT: "before."

[21]MT: "the Lord was with him."

[22]MT: "he was in awe."

[23]MT: "before them."

[24]MT: "a man of valor."

[25]MT: "fight the wars of the Lord."

[26]MT: "let the hand of the Philistine be on him."

[27]MT lacks the word.

[28]MT: "And at the time for giving Merab the daughter of Saul to David."

[29]MT: "the hand of the Philistines will be upon him."

[30]MT: "in the ears of."

[31]MT: "small, insignificant."

Saul said: "Thus you will say to David: 'There is no pleasure for the king in bridal presents except in a hundred foreskins of the Philistines so as to be avenged of *those who hate*[32] the king.'" And Saul was planning *to give David*[33] in the hand of the Philistines. 26. And his servants told David these words, and the word was right in the eyes of David to be a son-in-law to the king. And the days were not filled out. 27. And David arose, and he and his men went, and he *killed*[34] among the Philistines two hundred men, and David brought their foreskins and gave them in full number to the king so as to be a son-in-law to the king. And Saul gave to him Michal his daughter for a wife. 28. And Saul saw and knew that *the Memra of the Lord was at the aid of David,*[35] and Michal the daughter of Saul loved him. 29. And Saul continued to be still afraid from before David, and Saul was an enemy to David all the days. 30. And the chiefs of the Philistines went forth, and *at the time*[36] of their going forth David was more successful than all the servants of Saul. And his name *was very great.*[37]

CHAPTER 19

1. And Saul spoke *with*[1] Jonathan his son and *with*[2] all his servants to *kill*[3] David, and Jonathan the son of Saul delighted in David very much. 2. And Jonathan told David, saying: "Saul my father is seeking to *kill you.*[4] And now be careful *now*[5] in the morning and remain in secret and hide. 3. And I will go forth and stand *in the presence of*[6] my father in the field where you are, and I will *speak good words about you before my father,*[7] and I will see whatever and tell you." 4. And Jonathan *spoke good words about David before Saul*[8] his father and said to him: "Let not the king sin against his servant, against David, for he has not sinned against you and because his deeds are very good for you. 5. And *he gave up his life so as to be killed,*[9] and he *killed*[10] the Philistine, and the Lord worked a great victory for all Israel. You saw and rejoiced; and why are you guilty of innocent blood to *kill*[11] David for nothing?" 6. And Saul *accepted the word*[12] of Jonathan, and Saul swore: "As the Lord lives, he will not *be killed.*"[13] 7. And Jonathan called to David, and Jonathan told him all these words, and Jonathan brought David unto Saul, and *he was serving*[14] before him as on yesterday and the day before. 8. And *the wagers of battle*[15] continued to be, and David went forth and *waged battle*[16] against the Philistines, and he struck against them a great blow, and they fled

Notes, Chapter Eighteen (Cont.)

[32]MT: "the enemies of."
[33]MT: "to let David fall."
[34]MT: "struck down."
[35]MT: "the Lord was with David."
[36]MT: "as often."
[37]MT: "was very precious."

Notes, Chapter Nineteen

[1]MT: "to."
[2]MT: "to."
[3]MT: "put to death."

[4]MT: "put you to death."
[5]MT: "please."
[6]MT: "at the hand of."
[7]MT: "speak about you to my father."
[8]MT: "spoke well about David to Saul."
[9]MT: "he placed his life in his hand."
[10]MT: "struck down."
[11]MT: "put to death."
[12]MT: "heard the voice."
[13]MT: "be put to death."
[14]MT: "he was."
[15]MT: "the war."
[16]MT: "fought."

from before him. 9. And an evil *spirit from before the Lord resided upon*[17] Saul, and he was dwelling in his house, and his spear was in his hand; and David was playing by hand. 10. And Saul sought to strike against David with the spear and *to pin it*[18] in the wall; and he slipped away from before Saul, and he *fixed*[19] the spear on the wall; and David fled and escaped on that night. 11. And Saul sent messengers to the house of David to watch him and to *kill him*[20] in the morning. And Michal his wife told David, saying: "If you do not save your life by night, tomorrow you will *be killed.*"[21] 12. And Michal let David down from the window, and he went and fled and escaped. 13. And Michal took the *statues*[22] and placed them upon the bed, and she placed a *goatskin*[23] at its head and covered it with clothes. 14. And Saul sent messengers to take David, and she said: "He is sick." 15. And Saul sent the messengers to *examine*[24] David, saying: "Bring him up on the bed unto me so as to *kill him.*"[25] 16. And the messengers came, and behold the *statue*[26] was on the bed, and a *goatskin*[27] at its head. 17. And Saul said to Michal: "Why have you thus deceived me and sent away my enemy, and he has escaped?" And Michal said to Saul: "He said to me: 'Send me away lest I *kill you.*'"[28] 18. And David fled and escaped and came *unto*[29] Samuel to Ramah, and he told him all that Saul had done to him. And he and Samuel went and dwelt in *the house of study.*[30] 19. And it was reported to Saul, saying: "Behold David is in *the house of study*[31] at Ramah." 20. And Saul sent messengers to take David, and *they saw*[32] the band of *teachers singing,*[33] and Samuel was standing *teaching*[34] them, and *a spirit of prophecy from before the Lord resided*[35] upon the messengers of Saul, and they too *were singing praise.*[36] 21. And they told Saul, and he sent other messengers, and they too *were singing praise.*[37] And Saul again sent a third set of messengers, and they too *sang praise.*[38] 22. And he too went to Ramah and came unto the great cistern that is in Secu. And he asked and said: "Where are Samuel and David?" And he said: "Behold they are in *the house of study*[39] in Ramah." 23. And he came to there to *the house of study*[40] that was in Ramah, and *that spirit of prophecy from before the Lord resided*[41] upon him too, and he went about *singing praise*[42] until he came to *the house of study*[43] that was in Ramah. 24. And he too took off his clothes, and he too *sang praise*[44] before Samuel, and he fell *under those having power*[45] all that day and all night. Therefore they were saying: "Is Saul too among the *scribes?*"[46]

Notes, Chapter Nineteen (Cont.)

[17]MT: "spirit of the Lord was to."
[18]MT lacks the word.
[19]MT: "struck."
[20]MT: "put him to death."
[21]MT: "put to death."
[22]MT: "teraphim."
[23]MT: "goat netting" or "goat pillow."
[24]MT: "see."
[25]MT: "put him to death."
[26]MT: "teraphim."
[27] See 19:13, note 23.
[28]MT: "put you to death."
[29]MT: "to."
[30]MT: "Naioth." The place in the MT is uncertain. As in ch. 10 prophecy is turned into study.
[31]MT: "Naioth."

[32]MT: "he saw."
[33]MT: "prophets prophesying." Tg turns ecstatic prophets into teachers (or scribes). See 10:5-6.
[34]MT: "as head."
[35]MT: "a spirit of God was."
[36]MT: "were prophesying."
[37]MT: "were prophesying."
[38]MT: "prophesied."
[39]MT: "Naioth."
[40]MT: "Naioth."
[41]MT: "that spirit of God was."
[42]MT: "prophesying."
[43]MT: "Naioth."
[44]MT: "prophesied."
[45]MT: "naked." The meaning of the Aramaic word is not certain here. It may mean "naked."
[46]MT: "prophets."

CHAPTER 20

1. And David fled from *the house of study that was*[1] in Ramah, and he came and said before Jonathan: "What have I done? What is my *sin*[2] and what is my *offense*[3] before your father, for he seeks *to kill me?*"[4] 2. And he said to him: "Far from it! You will not die. Behold my father does not do anything great or anything small, and *he does not tell me.*[5] Why should my father hide this thing from me? This is not so." 3. And David swore again and said: "Surely your father knows that I have found favor in your eyes. And he said: 'Let not Jonathan know this lest he be troubled.' And now as the Lord lives and by the life of your soul, there is about *one*[6] step between me and death." 4. And Jonathan said to David: "Whatever *is the will of your soul,*[7] I will do for you." 5. And David said to Jonathan: "Behold the (new) moon is tomorrow, and indeed I must recline with the king to eat. And you will send me away, and I will hide in the field until evening time of the third day. 6. If indeed your father *seeks after*[8] me, you will say: 'David indeed requested of me to *go*[9] to Bethlehem his city, for *they began an offering of holy things this day*[10] there for all the family.' 7. If he says thus: 'Good,' there is peace to your servant. And if there be great anger to him, know that evil is determined from him. 8. And you shall do goodness *with*[11] your servant, for you have brought your servant with you in the covenant of the Lord. And if there is *sin*[12] in me, you *kill me.*[13] And why should you bring me unto your father?" 9. And Jonathan said: "Far be it from you! If indeed I know that evil is determined from my father to come upon you, would I not tell it to you?" 10. And David said to Jonathan: "Who will tell me whether or not your father answers you *harsh words?*"[14] 11. And Jonathan said to David: "Come, and let us go forth to the field." And the two of them went forth to the field. 12. And Jonathan said to David: "By the Lord God of Israel, for I will inquire of my father about this time tomorrow or the third day, and *the words that will be said about David will be good;*[15] and will I not send unto you and *tell you?*[16] 13. Thus may the Lord do to Jonathan and more so, for (if) *evil is determined to come against you from my father, I will tell you*[17] and send you away; and you will go in peace. And *the Memra of the Lord will be at your aid*[18] as it was *at the aid of*[19] my father. 14. And as long as I am alive and

Notes, Chapter Twenty

[1]MT: "Naioth."
[2]MT: "iniquity."
[3]MT: "sin."
[4]MT: "my life."
[5]MT: "he does not open my ear."
[6]MT lacks the word.
[7]MT: "your soul says."
[8]MT: "inspects."
[9]MT: "run."
[10]MT: "the annual sacrifice (is)."
[11]MT: "toward."
[12]MT: "iniquity."
[13]MT: "put me to death."
[14]MT: "harshly."
[15]MT: "behold (it will be) good for David."
[16]MT: "open your ear."
[17]MT: "it pleases my father (to do) evil against you, I will open your ear."
[18]MT: "the Lord will be with you."
[19]MT: "with."

you do not do with me goodness *from before*[20] the Lord, I will not die. 15. And do not cut off your goodness *from the men of my house*[21] forever, and not when the Lord *will put an end to those who hate David,*[22] each man from upon the face of the earth." 16. And Jonathan cut *a covenant*[23] with the house of David, and the Lord *took vengeance for him*[24] from the hand of *those who hated*[25] David. 17. And Jonathan continued to swear to David, for *he loved him,*[26] for with the love of his own soul he loved him. 18. And Jonathan said to him: "Tomorrow is the (new) moon, and *you will be sought out, for your dining place will be empty.*[27] 19. And at the third (day) of the moon *you will be sought out*[28] very much, and you will go to the place where you hid yourself on the *weekday,*[29] and you will dwell near *"Stone Coming."*[30] 20. And *I am to shoot*[31] three arrows *with the bow*[32] so as *to hit*[33] for myself at the target. 21. And behold I will send the young man: 'Go, *get*[34] the arrows.' If indeed I say to the young man: 'Behold *the arrow is*[35] on this side of you; take it and bring (it),' then there is peace for you and *nothing evil*[36] as the Lord lives. 22. And if thus I say to the young man: 'Behold *the arrow is*[37] beyond you,' go, for the Lord has rescued you. 23. And the word that we have spoken — I and you — behold *the Memra of the Lord is a witness*[38] between me and you forever." 24. And David hid in the field, and it was the (new) moon. And the king sat down at the food to eat. 25. And the king sat down upon his seat as at other times, upon the seat *that was prepared for him near the wall.*[39] And Jonathan stood up, and Abner sat down by the side of Saul, and the place of David *was empty.*[40] 26. And Saul did not speak anything on that day, for he said: "*Perhaps an accident has happened to him, and he is not clean; or perhaps he went on the road, and we did not invite him.*"[41] 27. And on *the day after that, which is the intercalation of the second month,*[42] the place of David *was empty,*[43] and Saul said to Jonathan his son: "Why has the son of Jesse not come both yesterday and today for food?" 28. And Jonathan answered Saul: "David earnestly requested from me *to go*[44] unto Bethlehem. 29. And he said: 'Send me away now, for they have begun *an offering of holy things for all our family*[45] in the city, and my brother commanded me. And now if I have found favor in your eyes, let me get away now and see my brothers.' Therefore he did not come to the table of the king." 30. And the anger of Saul *was strong*[46]against Jonathan, and he said to him: "You son of

Notes, Chapter Twenty (Cont.)

[20]MT: "of." In vv. 14-16, the Tg follows the MT, which is confused.

[21]MT: "my house."

[22]MT: "will cut away the enemies of David."

[23]MT lacks the word.

[24]MT: "sought."

[25]MT: "the enemies of."

[26]MT: "out of love for him."

[27]MT: "you will be looked for, for your seat will be inspected."

[28]MT: "you will go down."

[29]MT: "day of the deed," which may be understood as "workday."

[30]MT: "the stone Ha'azel." The Hebrew word, read as an Aramaic word, means "depart."

[31]MT: "I will shoot."

[32]MT: "to its side."

[33]MT: "to send forth."

[34]MT: "find."

[35]MT: "the arrows are."

[36]MT: "no matter."

[37]MT: "the arrows are."

[38]MT: "the Lord is."

[39]MT: "of the wall."

[40]MT: "inspected."

[41]MT: "There was an accident so that he is not clean; for he is not clean."

[42]MT: "on the morrow of the new moon, the second." The word "second" is interpreted as the second (intercalated) month."

[43]MT: "was inspected."

[44]MT lacks the word.

[45]MT: "we have a family sacrifice."

[46]MT: "was hot."

an obstinate woman whose rebellion was harsh,[47] do I not know that you *love*[48] the son of Jesse to your disgrace and to the disgrace of the shame of your mother? 31. For all the days that the son of Jesse is alive upon the earth, neither you nor your kingdom will be established. And now send and bring him unto me, for he is *a man deserving killing.*"[49] 32. And Jonathan answered Saul his father and said to him: "Why shall he *be killed?*[50] What did he do?" 33. And Saul lifted up the spear against him so as to strike him, and Jonathan knew that it was determined from his father to *kill*[51] David. 34. And Jonathan arose from the table in *strong anger,*[52] and he did not eat food *on the day of the intercalation of the second month,*[53] for he grieved over David, for his father shamed him. 35. And in the morning Jonathan went forth to the field at the time *that David said to him,*[54] and a small boy was with him. 36. And he said to his young man: "Run, *get*[55] the arrows that I am shooting." The young man ran, and he shot the arrow beyond him. 37. And the young man came unto the place of the arrow that Jonathan shot, and Jonathan called after the young man and said: "Is not the arrow beyond you?" 38. And Jonathan called after the young man: "Hurry, in haste; do not *delay.*"[56] And Jonathan's young man was gathering the *arrows,*[57] and he came unto his master. 39. And the young man did not know anything. Only Jonathan and David knew the matter. 40. And Jonathan gave his armor to the young man that was his, and he said to him: "Go, bring it to the city." 41. And the young man went, and David arose *from the side of "Stone Coming" that is opposite the south,*[58] and he fell upon his face upon the ground, and *he*[59] bowed down three times, and they kissed each man his fellow, and they wept each man his fellow until David exceeded. 42. And Jonathan said to David: "Go in peace, for the two of us have sworn by the name of the Lord, saying: '*May the Memra of the Lord be a witness*[60] between me and you, and between my *sons*[61] and your *sons*[62] forever.'"

CHAPTER 21

1. And he arose and went; and Jonathan entered the city. 2. And David came to Nob, unto Ahimelech the priest. And Ahimelech was agitated to meet David, and he said to him: "Why are you alone, and there is no man with you?" 3. And David said to Ahimelech the priest: "The king commanded me a word, and he said to me: 'Let no one know anything about the word that I am sending to you and that I have commanded

---

Notes, Chapter Twenty (Cont.)

[47]MT: "a perverse woman of rebellion."
[48]MT: "choose."
[49]MT: "a son of death."
[50]MT: "die."
[51]MT: "put to death."
[52]MT: "heat of anger."
[53]MT: "the second day of the month."

[54]MT: "of David."
[55]MT: "find."
[56]MT: "stand still."
[57]MT: "arrow."
[58]MT: "from beside the south."
[59]MT: "they."
[60]MT: "May the Lord be."
[61]MT: "seed."
[62]MT: "seed."

you.' *And I sent the young men before me to a place concealed and hidden.*[1] 4. And now what is there beneath your hand? Give five *loaves*[2] of bread in my hand or whatever shall be found." 5. And the priest answered David and said: There is no profane bread beneath my hand. Yet there is holy bread. But only if the young men are kept from *the defilement of*[3] woman." 6. And David answered the priest and said to him: "In truth woman is far from us. Both yesterday and the day before it when I go forth, the vessels of these young men were holy; *and that was not on a profane journey it was going. And today it is eaten and not declared unfit in*[4] the vessel." 7. And the priest gave to him the holy (bread), for there was no *common*[5] bread there except the bread of the presence that is removed from before the Lord to replace it with hot bread on the day of its being taken away. 8. And there was a man there from the servants of Saul on that day, *gathered*[6] before the Lord; and his name was Doeg the Edomite, chief of the shepherds that were Saul's. 9. And David said to Ahimelech: "Is there here beneath your hand a spear or sword? For I did not take in my hand both my sword and my armor, for the word of the king was in haste." 10. And the priest said: "The sword of Goliath the Philistine whom you *killed*[7] in the *Plain*[8] of the Terebinth, behold it is wrapped in the cloak *behind which it is inquired for one at the ephod.*[9] If you will take it for yourself, take it for there is no other beside it here." And David said: "There is none like it; give it to me." 11. And David arose and fled on that day from before Saul; and he came unto Achish the king of Gath. 12. And the servants of Achish said to him: "Is not this David the king of the land? Do they not *proclaim*[10] to this one in the dances, saying: 'Saul *killed*[11] thousands, and David ten thousands?'" 13. And David placed these words in his heart, and he was very much afraid from before Achish the king of Gath. 14. And he changed his *intelligence*[12] in their eyes, and he became demented in their hands, and he made marks upon the doors of the gate, and he let his spit run down upon his beard. 15. And Achish said to his servants: "Behold you see that the man is mad. Why did you bring him unto me? 16. Do I lack madmen that you brought this one to be mad before me? Shall this one enter my house?"

Notes, Chapter Twenty-One

[1]MT: "And I informed the young men regarding such and such a place."

[2]MT lacks the word.

[3]MT lacks "the defilement of."

[4]MT: "and that was a profane journey. And much more today their vessel will be holy." Tg changes the end of the verse to refer to the showbread, not the young men. For the halakhic argument, see *b. Men.* 95b and S-A, 1-2.

[5]MT lacks the word.

[6]MT: "detained."

[7]MT: "struck down."

[8]MT: "valley."

[9]MT: "behind the ephod." The rabbinic interpretation of Exod 28:29-30 was that the priest should wear the ephod. Thus, Tg avoids having it hanging in the sanctuary. See S-A, 24.

[10]MT: "sing."

[11]MT: "struck down."

[12]MT: "judgment."

CHAPTER 22

1. And David went from there and escaped to the cave of Adullam, and his brothers and all the house of his father heard and went down unto him there. 2. And there gathered every man troubled *of spirit*[1] and every man against whom *owners*[2] had a claim and every man bitter of soul. And he was chief over them, and there were about 400 men with him. 3. And David went from there to Mizpah of Moab, and he said to the king of Moab: "Let my father and my mother come forth with you until I know what *the Lord*[3] will do for me." 4. And he *had them dwell*[4] before the king of Moab, and they were dwelling with him all the days that David *was hiding*[5] in the stronghold. 5. And Gad the prophet said to David: "Do not dwell in the fortress. Come, and go to the land of *the house of Judah*."[6] And David went and came to the forest of Hereth. 6. And Saul heard that David and the men who were with him were known. And Saul was sitting in Gibeah beneath the tamarisk on the height, and his spear was in his hand and all his servants were standing by him. 7. And Saul said to his servants who were standing by him: "Hear now, *sons of the tribe of the house of Benjamin,*[7] will the son of Jesse give to all of you fields and vineyards? Will he *appoint*[8] from all of you chiefs of thousands and chiefs of hundreds? 8. For all of you have *rebelled*[9] against me. And there was no one *who was telling me*[10] when my son cut (a covenant) with the son of Jesse. And there was no one of you by me feeling pain *for him*[11] and *telling me*[12] that my son raised up my servant against me an ambush as on this day." 9. And Doeg the Edomite answered, and he *was appointed*[13] over the servants of Saul, and he said: "I saw the son of Jesse. He came to Nob, unto Ahimelech the son of Ahitub. 10. And he inquired for him by *the Memra of the Lord,*[14] and he gave to him provisions; and the sword of Goliath the Philistine he gave to him." 11. And the king sent to call Ahimelech, the son of Ahitub, the priest, and all the house of his father, the priests who were in Nob; and all of them came unto the king. 12. And Saul said: "Hear now, son of Ahitub." And he said: "Here I am, my master." 13. And Saul said to him: "Why have you rebelled against me, you and the son of Jesse, in your giving to him food and the sword? And you inquired for him by *the Memra of the Lord*[15] to raise up against me an ambush as on this day." 14. And Ahimelech answered the king and said: "And who among all your servants is like David — faithful and the son-in-law of the king and

Notes, Chapter Twenty-Two

[1] MT lacks the word.
[2] MT: "owner."
[3] MT: "God."
[4] MT: "led them."
[5] MT: "was."
[6] MT: "Judah."
[7] MT: "Benjaminites."
[8] MT: "set."
[9] MT: "conspired."
[10] MT: "opening my ear."
[11] MT lacks the phrase.
[12] MT: "opening my ear."
[13] MT: "stood."
[14] MT: "the Lord."
[15] MT: "God."

chief over[16] your following and honored in your house? 15. Did I begin today to inquire for him by *the Memra of the Lord?*[17] Far be it from me! Let the king not place a word against his servant, against all the house of my father, for your servant did not know in all this a small or a great word." 16. And the king said: "You will surely die, Ahimelech, you and all the house of your father." 17. And the king said to the runners who were standing by him: "Go around and *kill*[18] the priests of the Lord, because their hand is with David also and because they knew that he fled and they did not *tell me*."[19] And the servants of the king were not willing to reach out their hand to *use force*[20] against the priests of the Lord. 18. And the king said to Doeg: "You go around, and use force against the priests." And Doeg the Edomite went around and used force against the priests and *killed*[21] on that day 85 men *who were fit to wear*[22] the ephod of linen. 19. And he struck down Nob, the city of priests, by the edge of the sword, from man and unto woman, from youth and unto suckling, and ox and ass and sheep by the edge of the sword. 20. And one son to Ahimelech the son of Ahitub escaped, and his name was Abiathar; and he fled after David. 21. And Abiathar told David that Saul killed the priest of the Lord. 22. And David said to Abiathar: "I knew on that day that Doeg the Edomite was there, that he would surely tell Saul; and *I was the cause for this to come to pass*[23] against every soul of the house of your father. 23. Dwell with me. Do not fear, for whoever seeks *to kill me*[24] seeks *to kill you*,[25] for you are kept safe with me."

CHAPTER 23

1. And they told David, saying: "Behold the Philistines *are waging battle*[1] against Keilah, and they are plundering the threshing floors." 2. And David inquired of *the Memra of the Lord*,[2] saying: "Shall I go and *kill*[3] these Philistines?" And the Lord said to David: "Go, and you shall *kill*[4] the Philistines and save Keilah." 3. And the men of David said to him: "Behold *when*[5] we are here in *the land of the house of Judah*[6] we are afraid; and so much the more that we should go to Keilah to the battle lines of the Philistines." 4. And David continued once again to inquire of *the Memra of the Lord*,[7] and the Lord *received his prayer*[8] and said: "Arise, go down to Keilah, for I am giving

Notes, Chapter Twenty-Two (Cont.)

[16]MT: "turning aside to." The MT *sār* is related to the MT *śar*, which is related to the Aramaic *rāb*.
[17]MT: "God."
[18]MT: "put to death."
[19]MT: "open my ear."
[20]MT: "strike down."
[21]MT: "put to death."
[22]MT: "bearing."
[23]MT: "I occasioned."

[24]MT: "my life."
[25]MT: "your life."

Notes, Chapter Twenty-Three

[1]MT: "fighting."
[2]MT: "the Lord."
[3]MT: "strike down."
[4]MT: "strike down."
[5]MT lacks the word.
[6]MT: "Judah."
[7]MT: "the Lord."
[8]MT: "answered him."

the Philistines in your hand." 5. And David and his men went to Keilah and *waged battle*[9] against the Philistines, and he took their herds and struck against them a great blow; and David saved the inhabitants of Keilah. 6. And when Abiathar the son of Ahimelech fled unto David to Keilah, he brought down the ephod in his hand. 7. And it was told to Saul that David came to Keilah. And Saul said: "*The Lord has given*[10] him in my hand, for *he has been given*[11] to enter the city *that has*[12] doors and bars." 8. And Saul *gathered*[13] all the people *to wage battle,*[14] to go down to Keilah, to make a siege against David and against his men. 9. And David knew that Saul was plotting evil against him; and he said to Abiathar the priest: "Bring near the ephod." 10. And David said: "Lord God of Israel, your servant has surely heard that Saul seeks to enter Keilah to destroy the city on account of me. 11. *Are the inhabitants of Keilah planning to give me*[15] in his hand? *Is Saul planning to go down*[16] as your servant has heard. Lord God of Israel, tell your servant now." And the Lord said: "*He is planning to go down.*"[17] 12. And David said: "*Are the inhabitants of Keilah planning to give*[18] me and my men in the hand of Saul?" And the Lord said; "*They are planning to give (you) over.*"[19] 13. And David and his men, about 600 men, arose and went forth from Keilah, and they went *in whatever place it was fitting to go.*[20] And it was told to Saul that David had escaped from Keilah, and he withdrew from going forth. 14. And David dwelt in the wilderness in the stronghold, and he dwelt in the hill country in the wilderness of Ziph; and Saul sought him out all the days, and *the Lord*[21] did not give him in his hand. 15. And David saw that Saul went forth to seek *to kill him,*[22] and David was in the wilderness of Ziph in the forest. 16. And Jonathan and the son of Saul arose and went unto David to the forest and strengthened his hand by *the Memra of the Lord.*[23] 17. And he said to him: "Do not fear, for the hand of Saul my father will not find you. And you will be king over Israel, and I will be second to you. And Saul my father also knows thus." 18. And the two of them cut a covenant before the Lord, and David dwelt in the forest and Jonathan went to his house. 19. And *the men of Ziph*[24] went up unto Saul to Gibeah, saying: "Is not David hidden with us in the stronghold *of*[25] the forest, on the hill of Hachilah which is south of Jeshimon? 20. And now come down with all the desire of your soul to come down, O king. And *we will give him*[26] in the hand of the king." 21. And Saul said: "Blessed are you *before*[27] the Lord, for you have had consideration for me. 22. Go now, confirm it again, and learn and see his place *in which he dwells.*[28] Who has seen him there? For *they say*[29] to me that *he is indeed cunning and he goes forth.*[30] 23. And see and learn of all the hiding places where he hides; and return unto me *with truth,*[31] and I will go with you; and if he is in the land, I will search him

Notes, Chapter Twenty-Three (Cont.)

[9]MT: "fought."
[10]MT: "God has sold (*or,* alienated)."
[11]MT: "he has been shut up."
[12]MT: "of."
[13]MT: "summoned."
[14]MT: "for war."
[15]MT: "Will the lords of Keilah deliver me up."
[16]MT: "Will Saul go down."
[17]MT: "he will go down."
[18]MT: "Will the lords of Keilah deliver."
[19]MT: "They will deliver."

[20]MT: "wherever they were going."
[21]MT: "God."
[22]MT: "his life."
[23]MT: "God."
[24]MT: "the Ziphites."
[25]MT: "in."
[26]MT: "it is ours to deliver him."
[27]MT: "to."
[28]MT: "where his foot will be."
[29]MT: "he said."
[30]MT: "he is indeed cunning."
[31]MT: "according to what is certain."

out in all the thousands *of the house of Judah.*"³² 24. And they arose and went to Ziph before Saul. And David and his men were in the wilderness of Maon in the plain which is south of Jeshimon. 25. And Saul and his men went to seek; and they told David, and he went down *to*³³ the rock and dwelt in the wilderness of Maon. And Saul heard and pursued after David *to*³⁴ the wilderness of Maon. 26. And Saul went on one side of the mountain, and David and his men on the other side of the mountain. And David *was anxious*³⁵ to go from before Saul, and Saul and his men *were lying in wait against*³⁶ David and against his men to seize them. 27. And a messenger came unto Saul, saying: "Hurry and go, for the Philistines are spread over the land." 28. And Saul turned from pursuing after David, and he went to meet the Philistines. Therefore they call that place "Rock of Divisions," *the place where the heart of the king was divided to go here and there.*³⁷

CHAPTER 24

1. And David went up from there, and he dwelt in the strongholds of En-gedi. 2. And when Saul returned from after the Philistines, they told him saying: "Behold David is in the wilderness of En-gedi." 3. And Saul took 3000 men chosen from all Israel, and he went to seek David and his men on the face of *the clefts of the rocks.*¹ 4. And he came to the pens of the sheep *that were*² on the road, and there was a cave there, and Saul went in *to do his business,*³ and David and his men were dwelling in the extremities of the cave. 5. And the men of David said to him: "Behold *this is*⁴ the day that the Lord said to you: 'Behold I am giving your enemy in your hand, and you will do to him as is good in your eyes.'" And David arose and cut off the edge of the cloak that was Saul's in secret. 6. And it happened afterward that *David was troubled in his heart*⁵ because he cut off the hem that was Saul's. 7. And he said to his men: "May it be forbidden from *before*⁶ the Lord that I should do this thing to my master, to the anointed of the Lord, to put forth my hand against him, for he is the anointed of the Lord." 8. And David *persuaded*⁷ his men with the words, and he did not let them rise up against Saul; and Saul rose up from the cave and went on the way. 9. And David rose up afterward, and he went forth from the cave, and he called after Saul, saying: "My master, O king."

Notes, Chapter Twenty-Four

Notes, Chapter Twenty-Three (Cont.)

³²MT: "of Judah."
³³MT lacks the word.
³⁴MT lacks the word.
³⁵MT: "was making haste."
³⁶MT: "were surrounding."
³⁷MT lacks the explanation.

¹MT: "the rocks of the mountain goats."
²MT lacks the word.
³MT: "to pour out his feet." As in the MT, a euphemism is used.
⁴MT lacks the word.
⁵MT: "David's heart smote him."
⁶MT lacks the word.
⁷MT seems to have "tore in two," but the meaning is uncertain.

And Saul looked behind him; and David bowed *upon his face upon the ground,*[8] and he did obeisance. 10. And David said to Saul: "Why do you listen to the words of *the sons of men who say:*[9] 'Behold David *plots*[10] your harm.' 11. Behold this day your eyes have seen that the Lord gave you this day in my hand in the cave. And *others*[11] said to kill you, and *I*[12] had pity on you and said: 'I will not put forth my hand against my master, for he is the anointed of the Lord.' 12. And, *my master, look;*[13] see too the edge of your cloak in my hand; for when I cut off the edge of your garment and did not kill you, know and see that there is no *guilt and corruption*[14] in my hand, and I have not sinned against you; and you are lying in wait against my soul *to kill me.*[15] 13. May the Lord judge between me and you, and may the Lord avenge me from you; and my hand will not be against you. 14. As *they say the proverb from olden times:*[16] 'From the wicked comes forth *their guilt.*'[17] And my hand will not be against you. 15. After whom has the king of Israel come forth? After whom are you pursuing? After a *weakling?*[18] After a *common fellow?*[19] 16. May the Lord be for a judge, and *make judgment*[20] between me and you, and *reveal before him whoever will judge my case, and may he avenge my humiliation from you.*"[21] 17. And when David finished speaking these words with Saul, Saul said: "Is this your voice, my son David?" And Saul lifted up his voice and wept. 18. And he said to David: "You are more righteous than I, for you have repaid me good and I have repaid you evil. 19. And you told this day what good you did with me, that the Lord *gave*[22] me in your hand and you did not kill me. 20. For shall a man find his enemy and let him go on the good way? And may the Lord repay you with good on account of what you did to me this day. 21. And now behold I know that you will indeed rule and the kingdom of Israel will be established in your hand. 22. And now swear to me by *the Memra of the Lord*[23] that you will not *destroy*[24] my seed after me and you will not destroy my name from the house of my father." 23. And David swore to Saul, and Saul went to his house, and David and his men went up to the stronghold.

CHAPTER 25

1. And Samuel died, and all Israel gathered and wept *over*[1] him, and they buried him in his house in Ramah. And David arose and went down to the wilderness of Paran.

Notes, Chapter Twenty-Four (Cont.)

[8]MT: "face to the ground."
[9]MT: "a man, saying."
[10]MT: "seeks."
[11]MT: "he."
[12]MT: "you."
[13]MT: "my father, see."
[14]MT: "evil and wrongdoing."
[15]MT: "to take it away."
[16]MT: "the proverb of the ancients says."
[17]MT: "wickedness."

[18]MT: "a dead dog." Tg replaces the metaphor with a descriptive term.
[19]MT: "a flea." See previous note and 26:20.
[20]MT: "judge."
[21]MT: "see and plead my case and judge me from your hand."
[22]MT: "delivered up."
[23]MT: "the Lord."
[24]MT: "cut off."

Notes, Chapter Twenty-Five

[1]MT: "for."

2. And there was a man in Maon, and his business was in Carmel. And the man was very great, and he had 3,000 sheep and 1,000 goats; and he was at the shearing of his sheep in Carmel. 3. And the name of the man was Nabal, and the name of his wife was Abigail; and the woman was *wise*[2] of understanding and beautiful of appearance; and the man was harsh and badly behaving, and he was *from those of the house of Caleb.*[3] 4. And David heard in the wilderness that Nabal was shearing his sheep. 5. And David sent ten young men, and David said to the young men: "Go up to Carmel, and come unto Nabal, and ask him for peace in my name. 6. And thus you shall say: 'To *your*[4] life; and you, peace; and your house, peace; and everything that is yours, peace. 7. Now I heard that you have shearers. Now the shepherds who are yours were with us —we did not harm them. And nothing at all was lost to them all the days that they were in Carmel. 8. Ask your young men, and they will tell you. And let the young men find favor in your eyes, for *we have come*[5] for a holiday. Give now whatever your hand will find to your servants and to your son David.'" 9. And the young men of David came and spoke with Nabal according to all these words in the name of David, and they *ceased.*[6] 10. And Nabal answered the servants of David and said: "Who is David? And who is the son of Jesse? This day there are many slaves *who are fleeing and hiding,*[7] each one from before his master. 11. And shall I take *my food and my drink and my sustenance that I have prepared*[8] for my shearers, and give them to men who I do not know from where they are?" 12. And the young men of David turned around on their way, and they returned and came and told him according to all these words. 13. And David said to his men: "Gird on every man his sword." And every man girded on his sword, and David also girded on his sword. And there went up after David about 400 men, and 200 *were left behind to guard*[9] the equipment. 14. And one young man from the young men told Abigail the wife of Nabal, saying: "Behold David sent messengers from the wilderness to bless our master, and he *loathed*[10] them. 15. And the men were very good to us; we were not harmed, and *nothing at all was lost to us*[11] all the days that we went with them when *we were camping*[12] in the field. 16. They were a wall *surrounding us*[13] both by night and by day all the days that we were with them shepherding the sheep. 17. And now know and see what you will do, for evil is determined *to come*[14] upon our master and upon all his house; and he is *a man too bad*[15] to speak with him." 18. And Abigail hurried and took 200 *loaves*[16] of bread and two skins of wine and five *stuffed*[16a] sheep and five seahs of grain and 100 *clusters*[17] of dried grapes and 200 *cakes*[18] of figs; and she placed them upon asses. 19. And she said to her young men:

Notes, Chapter Twenty-Five (Cont.)

[2]MT: "good."

[3]MT: "a Calebite."

[4]MT lacks the suffix "your."

[5]Some MT mss. have *bnw* ("they built"), though this is probably a mistake for *b'nw* ("we have come") as is presupposed by the Tg.

[6]MT: "were quiet."

[7]MT: "breaking away."

[8]MT: "my bread and my water and my slaughtered meat that I have slaughtered."

[9]MT: "remained by."

[10]MT: "flew at."

[11]MT: "we did not miss anything at all."

[12]MT: "we were."

[13]MT: "for us."

[14]MT lacks the verb.

[15]MT: "a son of Belial."

[16]MT lacks the word.

[16a]Tg associates "ready dressed" with the paschal lamb, which was stuffed with its entrails and legs. See *m. Pesaḥ* 7:1 and S-A, 22.

[17]MT lacks the word.

[18]MT lacks the word.

"Pass before me. Behold I am coming after you." And she did not tell her husband Nabal. 20. And she was riding upon an ass, and she went down *by the side of the mountain.*[19] And behold David and his men were coming down to meet her, and she met them. 21. And David said: "Perhaps in vain did I guard everything that belongs to this fellow in the wilderness, and nothing at all *was lost*[20] from everything that is his; and he has returned to me evil in place of good. 22. May *the Lord*[21] do thus to the enemies of David and more so if I leave from all that is his by morning *anyone knowing knowledge.*"[22] 23. And Abigail saw David, and she hurried and let herself down from upon the ass and fell before David upon her face and bowed down *upon*[23] the ground. 24. And she fell *before*[24] his feet and said: "*Please,*[25] my master, upon me be the guilt *that is mine,*[26] and let your handmaid now speak *before you,*[27] and hear the words of your handmaid. 25. Let my master not set his heart *upon this bad man,*[28] upon Nabal, for as is his name, so is he — Nabal is his name, and *stupidity*[29] is with him; and I your handmaid did not see the young men of my master whom you sent. 26. And now, my master, as the Lord lives and by the life of your soul, the Lord has restrained you *from shedding innocent blood*[30] and your hand from avenging yourself; and now let *those who hate you*[31] and those who seek evil against my master be like Nabal. 27. And now let this be a present that your handmaid brought to my master, and let it be give to the young men *who are serving before*[32] my master. 28. *Forgive now the sins*[33] of your handmaid, for the Lord *will surely establish*[34] for my master *a lasting kingdom,*[35] for my master *is waging the battles of the people of the Lord,*[36] and evil is not found in you from your days. 29. And the man rose up to pursue you and to seek *to kill you,*[37] and the soul of my master *will be hidden in the treasury of eternal life before*[38] the Lord our God; and the soul of your enemies he will make fly off *as they make fly off a stone in the sling.*[39] 30. And it will happen that the Lord *will bring to pass*[40] for my master according to all that he spoke *to bring*[41] good upon you, and he will appoint you to be *king*[42] over Israel. 31. And let this not be to you for regret and for a stumbling of heart for my master to shed *innocent*[43] blood without cause and for my master *to take vengeance*[44] for himself. And *when*[45] the Lord will make things good for my master, you will remember your handmaid." 32. And David said to Abigail: "Blessed be the Lord God of Israel who sent you this day to meet me. 33. And blessed be your

Notes, Chapter Twenty-Five (Cont.)

[19]MT: "by the cover of the mountain."

[20]MT: "was missed."

[21]MT: "God."

[22]A euphemism for "male." MT: "anyone urinating against the wall."

[23]MT lacks the preposition.

[24]MT: "at."

[25]MT lacks the word.

[26]MT lacks the phrase.

[27]MT: "in your ears."

[28]MT: "to this son of Belial."

[29]The Aramaic makes no attempt to preserve the MT pun: *Nābāl/nēbālâ*.

[30]MT: "from going in blood."

[31]MT: "your enemies."

[32]MT: "who go about at the feet of."

[33]MT: "Take away now the transgression."

[34]MT: "will surely make."

[35]MT: "a lasting house."

[36]MT: "is fighting the wars of the Lord."

[37]MT: "your life."

[38]MT: "has been bound in the bundle of the living with." Tg inserts belief in afterlife.

[39]MT: "in the midst of the hollow of the sling."

[40]MT: "will do."

[41]MT lacks the word.

[42]MT: "prince."

[43]MT lacks the adjective.

[44]MT: Literally, "to save (*or, give victory to*)." Aramaic uses a similar literal term: "to redeem, deliver."

[45]MT lacks the word.

knowledge,[46] and blessed are you who have restrained me this day from *shedding innocent blood*[47] and my hand avenging myself. 34. But as the Lord God of Israel lives, who has restrained me from harming you, for if you had not hurried and come to meet me, there would not be left to Nabal by morning *anyone knowing knowledge.*"[48] 35. And David *accepted from her*[49] what she brought to him, and he said to her: "Go up in peace to your house; see that *I have accepted from you*[50] and taken up your request." 36. And Abigail came to Nabal, and behold there was to him a feast in his house like *the feasts of kings;*[51] and the heart of Nabal was *merry*[52] upon him, and he was exceedingly drunk. And she did not tell him a small and big word until morning. 37. And in the morning when the wine *evaporated*[53] from Nabal, his wife told him these words, and his heart died in his innards, and he was *like*[54] a stone. 38. And *in ten days' time*[55] the Lord *broke*[56] Nabal, and he died. 39. And David heard that Nabal died, and he said: "Blessed be the Lord who has judged the case of my shame from the hand of Nabal and restrained his servant from *doing*[57] evil, and the Lord has returned the evil of Nabal on his head." And David sent and *asked*[58] for Abigail to take her for himself for a wife. 40. And the servants of David came unto Abigail to Carmel and spoke with her, saying: "David sent us unto you to take you to himself for a wife." 41. And she arose and bowed *upon her face upon the ground,*[59] and said: "Behold your handmaid is for a handmaid to wash the feet of the servants of my master. 42. And Abigail hurried and arose and rode upon the ass; and her five young women were going *alongside her;*[60] and she went behind the messengers of David, and she was for him a wife. 43. And David took Ahinoam from Jezreel; and the two of them were to him for wives. 44. And Saul gave Michal, his daughter, the wife of David, to Palti the son of Laish who was from Gallim.

CHAPTER 26

1. And *the men of Ziph*[1] came unto Saul to Gibeah, saying: "Is not David hidden on the hill of Hachilah *which is*[2] east of Jeshimon?" 2. And Saul arose and went down to the wilderness of Ziph, and with him were 3,000 chosen men of Israel to seek David in the wilderness of Ziph. 3. And Saul camped in the hill of Hachilah which is east of Jeshimon on the road, and David was dwelling in the wilderness, and he saw that Saul

Notes, Chapter Twenty-Five (Cont.)

[46]MT: "judgment."
[47]MT: "going in blood."
[48]A euphemism for "male." MT: "who urinates against the wall."
[49]MT: "took from her hand."
[50]MT: "I have heard your voice."
[51]MT: "the feast of a king."
[52]MT: "good."
[53]MT: "went forth."
[54]MT: "for."

[55]MT: "in about ten days."
[56]MT: "smote."
[57]MT lacks the verb.
[58]MT: "spoke."
[59]MT: "her face to the ground."
[60]MT: "at her feet."

Notes, Chapter Twenty-Six

[1]MT: "the Ziphites."
[2]MT lacks the relative pronoun.

came after him to the wilderness. 4. And David sent spies, and he knew that Saul had come *in truth*.[3] 5. And David arose and came to the place where Saul camped, and David saw the place where Saul lay sleeping and Abner, the son of Ner, the chief of his army. And Saul lay sleeping in the encampment, and the people were camping around him. 6. And David answered and said to Ahimelech the Hittite and to Abishai the son of Zeruiah, the brother of Joab, saying: "Who will go down with me unto Saul to the camp?" And Abishai said: "I will go down with you." 7. And David and Abishai came unto the people by night, and behold Saul was lying asleep in the encampment, and his spear was stuck in the ground at his head, and Abner and people *were camping*[4] around him. 8. And Abishai said to David: "This day *the Lord*[5] has given your enemy in your hand. And now I will strike him down *now*[6] with the spear and *pin it*[7] in the ground one time, and I will not repeat it for him." 9. And David said to Abishai: "Do not harm him; for who has put forth his hand against the anointed of the Lord and been innocent?" 10. And David said: "As the Lord lives, *from before the Lord he will be struck down*,[8] or his day will arrive and he will die, or he will go down in battle and *be killed*.[9] 11. Far be it from me *from before the Lord*[10] to put forth my hand against the anointed of the Lord. And now take the spear *now*[11] that is at his head and the vessel of water, and let us go." 12. And David took the spear and the vessel of water that were at Saul's head, and they went. And there was no one *who*[12] was seeing and there was no one *who*[12] was knowing and there was no one *who*[12] was awakened, for all of them were sleeping, for a heavy sleep *from before the Lord*[13] fell upon them. 13. And David crossed over to the other side, and he stood upon the top of the mountain far off, a great space being between them. 14. And David called to the people and to Abner the son of Ner, saying: "Will you not answer, Abner?" And Abner answered and said: "Who are you *who are calling at the head of the king?*"[14] 15. And David said to Abner: "Are you not a man? And who is like you in Israel? And why did you not guard your master the king? For one *from*[15] the people came to harm the king your master. 16. This thing that you have done is not good. As the Lord lives, you are *men deserving killing*,[16] who have not guarded your master, the anointed of the Lord. And now look where is the spear of the king and the vessel of water that was at his head." 17. And Saul recognized the voice of David, and said: "Is this your voice, my son David?" And David said: "It is my voice, my master, O king." 18. And he said: "Why does my master pursue after his servant? For what have I done? *And there is not guilt*[17] in my hand. 19. And now let my master the king hear the words of his servant. *If from before the Lord you were stirred up*[18] against me, *let your offering be accepted with delight*.[19] And if it be *from*[20] the sons of man, cursed are they before the Lord, for they have driven me this

Notes, Chapter Twenty-Six (Cont.)

[3]MT: "for certain."
[4]MT: "were sleeping."
[5]MT: "God."
[6]MT lacks the second "now."
[7]MT lacks the word.
[8]MT: "the Lord will smite him."
[9]MT: "perish."
[10]MT: "from the Lord."
[11]MT lacks the second "now."

[12]MT lacks the relative pronouns in all three cases.
[13]MT: "of the Lord."
[14]MT: "you called to the king."
[15]MT: "of."
[16]MT: "sons of death."
[17]MT: "And what evil is."
[18]MT: "if the Lord stirred you up."
[19]MT: "may he accept an offering."
[20]MT lacks the preposition.

day from *dwelling*[21] in the inheritance of *the people of the Lord,*[22] saying: 'Go, *dwell among the nations, the worshippers of idols.* '[23] 20. And now let not my blood *be poured out to the ground from before the Memra of the Lord,*[24] for the king of Israel has gone forth to seek out one *weak man*[25] as a partridge *is pursued*[26] in the mountains." 21. And Saul said: "I have sinned. Return, my son David, for I will not harm you again because my life has been precious in your eyes this day. Behold I have been foolish and exceedingly *stupid.*"[27] 22. And David answered and said: "Behold the spear of the king. And let one of the young men cross over and get it. 23. And may the Lord return to each man his righteousness and his truth. For the Lord gave you this day in my hand, and I was not willing to send forth my hand against the anointed of the Lord. 24. And behold just as your life *was precious*[28] this day in my eyes, so let my life *be precious before*[29] the Lord and let him rescue me from all distress." 25. And Saul said to David: "Blessed are you, my son David. *You will indeed rule and you will indeed be success-ful.*"[30] And David went on his way, and Saul returned to his place.

CHAPTER 27

1. And David said *in*[1] his heart: "Now *perhaps I will be given over*[2] one day in the hand of Saul; there is nothing better for me than that I should escape to the land of the Philistines, and Saul *will rest from me*[3] to search for me anymore in all the territory of *the land of Israel,*[4] and I will be rescued from his hand." 2. And David arose, and he and the 600 men who were with him crossed over unto Achish the son of Maoch, the king of Gath. 3. And David dwelt with Achish in Gath, he and his men, each man and *the men of his house,*[5] David and his two wives, Ahinoam *who was from Jezreel*[6] and Abigail the wife of Nabal *who was from Carmel.*[7] 4. And it was told to Saul that David fled to Gath, and he did not continue to seek him out. 5. And David said to Achish: "If now I have found favor in your eyes, let them give to me a place in one of the cities of the field and I will dwell there. And why should your servant dwell in the royal city with you?" 6. And Achish gave to him on that day Ziklag. Thus Ziklag belonged to the kings of *the house of Judah*[8] unto this day. 7. And the number of days that David dwelt in the

Notes, Chapter Twenty-Six (Cont.)

[21]MT: "sharing."
[22]MT: "the Lord."
[23]MT: "serve other gods."
[24]MT: "fall to the ground away from the face of the Lord."
[25]MT: "flea." See 24:15.
[26]MT: "one pursues."
[27]MT: "mistaken."
[28]MT: "was great."
[29]MT: "be great in the eyes of."

[30]MT: "you will indeed act, and you will indeed prevail."

Notes, Chapter Twenty-Seven

[1]MT: "to."
[2]MT: "I will perish."
[3]MT: "will despair of me."
[4]MT lacks this expression.
[5]MT: "his house."
[6]MT: "the Jezreelite."
[7]MT: "the Carmelite."
[8]MT: "Judah."

*cities*⁹ of the Philistines were a year and four months. 8. And David and his men went up, and they spread out against *the Geshurites and the Gizrites and the Amalekites,*¹⁰ for they were inhabiting the land from of old, the entrance of *Hagra*¹¹ and unto the land of Egypt. 9. And David struck down *the inhabitants of the land,*¹² and he was not letting live a man or a woman, and he was plundering sheep and oxen and asses and camels and garments; and he was returning and coming unto Achish. 10. And Achish said; "*To where*¹³ were you spread out this day?" And David said: "Against the south of Judah and against the south of the Jerachmeelite and to the south of the *Shalmaite.*"¹⁴ 11. And David was not letting live a man or a woman to bring to Gath, saying: "Lest they tell against us, saying: 'Thus David did.'" And thus was his custom all the days that he dwelt in the *cities*¹⁵ of the Philistines. 12. And Achish believed David, saying: "*He has indeed attacked*¹⁶ his own people, Israel; and he will be to me a servant *serving*¹⁷ forever."

CHAPTER 28

1. And in those days the Philistines gathered their armies for a force *to wage battle*¹ against Israel. And Achish said to David: "You know well that you and your men will go forth with me in the army." 2. And David said to Achish: "Thus you know what your servant will do." And Achish said to David: "Thus I will make you guardian for my head all the days." 3. And Samuel died, and all Israel wept over him and buried him in Ramah; *and they wept over him, each man in his own city.*² And Saul removed *lying oracles and necromatic apparitions*³ from the land. 4. And the Philistines gathered and came and camped in Shunem. And Saul gathered all Israel, and they camped in Gilboa. 5. And Saul saw the army of the Philistines, and he was afraid, and his heart shook very much. 6. And Saul inquired of *the Memra of the Lord;*⁴ and the Lord *did not accept his prayer*⁵ both in dreams and in Urim and by *teachers.*⁶ 7. And Saul said to his servants: "Seek for me the woman *who knows how to bring up lying oracles,*⁷ and I will go unto her and inquire of her." And his servants said to him: "Behold the woman *who knows how to bring up lying oracles*⁸ is in En-dor." 8. And Saul *changed himself*⁹ and wore other clothes, and he and two men with him went and came unto the woman

Notes, Chapter Twenty-Seven (Cont.)

⁹MT: "field."
¹⁰MT: "the Geshurite and the Girzite and the Amalekite." The form "Gizrites" corresponds to the MT *qere*.
¹¹MT: "Shur."
¹²MT: "the land."
¹³MT: "against (whom)."
¹⁴MT: "Kenite."
¹⁵MT: "field."
¹⁶MT: "He has indeed done evil."
¹⁷MT lacks the word.

Notes, Chapter Twenty-Eight

¹MT: "fight."
²MT: "and in his city."
³MT: "necromancies and wizards."
⁴MT: "the Lord."
⁵MT: "did not answer him."
⁶MT: "prophets." Aramaic: *spry*'.
⁷MT: "mistress of necromancy." Tg puts in the interpretation that the information received is false, like false prophecy.
⁸MT: "mistress of necromancy."
⁹MT: "disguised himself."

by night. And he said: "Divine now for me by *the lying oracles*[10] and bring up for me whomever I will say to you." 9. And the woman said to him: "Behold you know what Saul has done, that he *put an end to lying oracles and necromantic apparitions*[11] from the land. And why are you *attacking*[12] my soul so as to *kill me?*"[13] 10. And Saul swore to her by *the Memra of the Lord,*[14] saying: "As the Lord lives, no harm will happen to you in this matter." 11. And the woman said: "Whom shall I bring up for you?" And he said: "Bring up Samuel for me." 12. And the woman saw Samuel, and she cried out in a loud voice; and the woman said to Saul, saying: "Why did you deceive me? And you are Saul." 13. And the king said to her: "Do not be afraid. For what did you see?" And the woman said to Saul: "I saw *the angel of the Lord who was coming up*[15] from the earth." 14. And he said to her: "What was his appearance?" And she said: "An old man is coming up, and he is wrapped in a cloak." And Saul knew that it was Samuel, and he bowed *upon his face upon the ground*[16] and did obeisance. 15. And Samuel said to Saul: "Why have you disturbed me so as to bring me up?" And Saul said: "I have very much trouble, and the Philistines *are waging battle*[17] against me, and *the Memra of the Lord is far*[18] from me, and *he does not accept my prayer*[19] anymore both by the hand of *teachers*[20] and by dreams. And I called to you for you to inform me what I should do." 16. And Samuel said: "And why are you asking me? And *the Memra of the Lord is far*[21] from you, and *it is at the aid of the man whose enemy you are.*[22] 17. And the Lord *has established*[23] for him as he spoke *with me,*[24] and the Lord *has made pass*[25] the kingdom *from you*[26] and given it to your fellow, to David. 18. Just as *you did not accept the Memra of the Lord*[27] and did not carry out the *force*[28] of his anger against *those of the house of Amalek,*[29] therefore the Lord has done this thing to you this day. 19. And the Lord will also give Israel with you into the hand of the Philistines. And tomorrow you and your sons will be with me. And the Lord will also give the camp of Israel into the hand of the Philistines." 20. And Saul hurried and fell his full length to the ground, and he was very much afraid of the words of Samuel; there was no strength in him, for he had not eaten bread all day and all night. 21. And the woman came unto Saul and saw that he was very much disturbed. And she said to him: "Behold your handmaid *has accepted from you,*[30] and *I have given my life so as to be killed*[31] and have heard your words that you spoke with me. 22. And now you also *accept the saying*[32] of your handmaid, and let me set before you a piece of bread, and eat; and there will be strength in you that you will go on the way." 23. And he refused and said: "I will not eat." And his servants and the woman also forced him, and *he accepted their word.*[33]

Notes, Chapter Twenty-Eight (Cont.)

[10]MT: "necromancy."

[11]MT: "necromancies and wizards."

[12]MT: "laying a snare for."

[13]MT: "put me to death."

[14]MT: "the Lord."

[15]MT: "a god coming up." Tg protects monotheism by substituting an angel.

[16]MT: "his face to the ground."

[17]MT: "fighting."

[18]MT: "God has turned."

[19]MT: "he does not answer me."

[20]MT: "prophets." Aramaic: *spry'*.

[21]MT: "the Lord has turned."

[22]MT: "he is your enemy."

[23]MT: "has done."

[24]MT: "by my hand."

[25]MT: "has torn away."

[26]MT: "from your hand."

[27]MT: "you did not hear the voice of the Lord."

[28]MT: "heat."

[29]MT: "Amalek."

[30]MT: "has heard your voice."

[31]MT: "I have set my life in my hand."

[32]MT: "hear the voice."

[33]MT: "he heard their voice."

And he arose from the ground and sat upon the bed. 24. And the woman had a fatted calf in the house, and she hurried and slaughtered it. And she took flour and kneaded and baked it as unleavened bread. 25. And she brought it before Saul and before his servants, and they ate. And they arose and went away on that night.

CHAPTER 29

1. And the Philistines gathered all their camps to Aphek, and Israel was camped at the spring which is in Jezreel. 2. And the leaders of the Philistines were passing by hundreds and by thousands, and David and his men were passing in the back with Achish. 3. And the chiefs of the Philistines said: "What are these *Jews*[1] doing there?" And Achish said to the chiefs of the Philistines: "Is not this David, the servant of Saul, the king of Israel, who has been with me these days or these years? And I have found nothing *bad*[2] in him from the day *that he departed unto me*[3] until this day." 4. And the chiefs of the Philistines were angry at him, and the chiefs of the Philistines said to him: "Turn the man back, and let him return to his place where you assigned him, and let him not go down with us in battle, and let him not be for us an adversary in battle. And in what way would this one be reconciled unto his master? Is it not with the heads of these men? 5. Is not this David to whom they sing in the dances, saying: 'Saul *killed thousands,*[4] and David *ten thousands?*'"[5] 6. And Achish called to David and said to him: "As the Lord lives, you are right and good in my eyes *from*[6] your going forth and your coming in with me in the camp, for *I have found nothing that is evil*[7] in you from the day *that you came*[8] unto me unto this day. And in the eyes of the leaders you are not good. 7. And now return and go in peace; and do not do evil in the eyes of the leaders of the Philistines." 8. And David said to Achish: "For what have I done and what have you found in your servant from the day that *I was serving*[9] before you until this day that I should not come and *wage battle against those who hate*[10] my master the king?" 9. And Achish answered and said to David: "I know that you are good in my eyes like the angel of *the Lord.*[11] But the chiefs of the Philistines have said: 'Let him not go up with us in battle.' 10. And now get up early in the morning, (you) and the servants of your master who came with you; and you shall get up early in the morning, and *it will be light for you, and you will go.*"[12] 11. And David, he and his men, got up early to go in the morning, to return to the land of the Philistines. And the Philistines went up to Jezreel.

Notes, Chapter Twenty-Nine

[1]MT: "Hebrews."
[2]MT lacks the word.
[3]MT: "of his falling."
[4]MT: "struck down his thousands."
[5]MT: "his ten thousands."
[6]MT lacks the preposition.
[7]MT: "I have not found evil."
[8]MT: "of your coming."
[9]MT: "I was."
[10]MT: "fight against the enemies of."
[11]MT: "God."
[12]MT: "there will be a light for you, and go."

CHAPTER 30

1. And when David and his men came to Ziklag on the third day, the Amalekites spread out against the south and against Ziklag. And they struck down Ziklag and burned it with fire. 2. And they captured the women who were in it, from small and unto great; and they did not *kill*[1] anyone, and they took and went on their way. 3. And David and his men came to the city, and behold it was consumed in the fire, and their wives and their sons and their daughters were taken captive. 4. And David and the people who were with him raised up their voices and wept until there was no strength in them to weep. 5. And the two wives of David were taken captive — Ahinoam *who was from Jezreel*[2] and Abigail the wife of Nabal *who was from Carmel.*[3] 6. And there was very much trouble to David, for the people said to stone him; for the soul of all the people was bitter, each man over his sons and over his daughters. And David strengthened himself by *the Memra of the Lord*[4] his God. 7. and David said to Abiathar the priest, the son of Ahimelech: "Bring to me now the ephod." And Abiathar brought the ephod unto David. 8. And David inquired by *the Memra of the Lord,*[5] saying: "Shall I pursue after this *army?*[6] Will I overtake it?" And he said to him: "Pursue, for indeed you will overtake and indeed you will rescue." 9. And David, he and the 600 men who were with him, went and came unto the valley of Besor, and *part of them were left behind.*[7] 10. And David, he and 400 men, pursued; and 200 men *were left behind, who were prevented*[8] from crossing the valley of Besor. 11. And they found an Egyptian man in the field; and they brought him unto David and gave to him bread, and he ate; and they made him drink water. 12. And they gave to him a cake of figs and two clusters of dried grapes, and he ate and his spirit returned to him, for he had not eaten bread and he had not drunk water three days and three nights. 13. And David said to him: "Whose are you? And where are you from?" And he said: "I am a young Egyptian man, the servant to an Amalekite man. And my master left me behind because I fell sick *this day three days ago.*[9] 14. We spread out against the south of *Chereth*[10] and against what belongs to Judah and against the south of Caleb, and we burned Ziklag with fire." 15. And David said to him: "Will you bring me down to this *camp?*"[11] And he said: "Swear to me by *the Memra of the Lord*[12] that you will not *kill me*[13] and you

Notes, Chapter Thirty

[1]MT: "put to death."
[2]MT: "the Jezreelite."
[3]MT: "the Carmelite."
[4]MT: "the Lord."
[5]MT: "the Lord."
[6]MT: "band."

[7]MT: "those left behind stayed."
[8]MT: "stayed, who fainted."
[9]MT: "three days ago."
[10]MT: "the Cherethite."
[11]MT: "band."
[12]MT: "God."
[13]MT: "put me to death."

will not give me in the hand of my master, and I will bring you down to this *camp*."[14]
16. And he brought him down, and behold they were spread upon the face of all the earth, eating and drinking and dancing with all the great booty that they *captured*[15] from the land of the Philistines and from the land of *the house of Judah.*[16] 17. And David struck them down from *dark*[17] and unto *the time of evening of the day that was after it,*[18] and no one of them escaped except 400 young men who rode upon *young camels*[19] and fled. 18. And David rescued all that *the Amalekites captured,*[20] and David rescued his two wives. 19. And there was nothing missing for them from small and unto great and unto sons and daughters, and from the spoil and unto everything that they took for themselves. All of it David returned. 20. And David captured all the sheep and oxen; they drove before *those herds*[21] and said: "This is the spoil of David." 21. And David came unto the 200 men who *were prevented*[22] from going after David, and he had them stay at the valley of Besor. And they went forth to meet David and to meet the people who were with him, and David *met*[23] the people and asked for peace for them. 22. And every evil and wicked man from the men who went with David answered and said: "Because they did not go with me, we will not give to them from the booty that we rescued, except that each man may *take*[24] his wife and his sons and go." 23. And David said: "You shall not do thus, my brothers, with what the Lord has given us; and he has guarded us and given over the *army*[25] that came against us into our hand. 24. And who will listen to you in this matter? For according to the share of the one *who went down*[26] in battle, so according to the share of the *one who was left behind to guard*[27] the baggage. They will share alike." 25. And from that day and forward, he made it into a *decree of judgment*[28] for Israel unto this day. 26. And David came to Ziklag, and he sent from the spoil to the elders of *the house of Judah,*[29] to his friends, saying: "Behold a present for you from the spoil of *those hating the people of the Lord.*"[30] 27. (It was) for those in Bethel and for those in Ramoth of the south and for those in Jattir, 28. and for those in Aroer and for those in Siphmoth and for those in Eshtemoa, 29. and for those in Racal and for those in the cities of the Jerachmeelite and for those in the cities of the *Shalmaite,*[31] 30. and for those in Hormah and for those in Borashan and for those in Athach, 31. and for those in Hebron and for all the places that David and his men were going about.

Notes, Chapter Thirty (Cont.)

[14]MT: "band."
[15]MT: "took."
[16]MT: "Judah."
[17]MT: "twilight."
[18]MT: "evening for their next day."
[19]MT: "camels."
[20]MT: "Amalek took."
[21]MT: "that herd."
[22]MT: "fainted."

[23]MT: "drew nearer."
[24]MT: "lead away."
[25]MT: "band."
[26]MT: "going down."
[27]MT: "remaining behind by."
[28]MT: "a statute and an ordinance."
[29]MT: "Judah."
[30]MT: "the enemies of the Lord."
[31]MT: "Kenite."

CHAPTER 31

1. And the Philistines *were waging battle*[1] against Israel, and the men of Israel fled from before the Philistines and fell *killed*[2] on Mount Gilboa. 2. And the Philistines overtook Saul and his sons, and the Philistines *killed*[3] Jonathan and Abinadab and Malchishua, the sons of Saul. 3. And *the wagers of battle pressed hard*[4] against Saul, and the archers — *men who are skilled with the string and bow*[5] — found him, and he was very much afraid of the archers. 4. And Saul said to his armor-bearer: "Draw your sword and *kill*[6] me with it lest these uncircumcised ones come and *kill*[7] me and mock me." And his armor-bearer was not willing, for he was very much afraid; and Saul took the sword and fell upon it. 5. And his armor-bearer saw that Saul was dead, and he too fell upon his sword and died with him. 6. And Saul died, and his three sons and his armor-bearer, also all his men on that day together. 7. And the men of Israel who were on the other side of the plain and who were on the other side of the Jordan saw that the men of Israel fled and that Saul and his sons were dead; and they left the cities and fled, and the Philistines came and dwelt in them. 8. And on the day that was after it the Philistines came to strip *those who were killed,*[8] and they found Saul and his three sons *killed, lying*[9] on Mount Gilboa. 9. And they cut off his head and stripped off his armor and sent around in the land of the Philistines to proclaim it to the house of their idols and the people. 10. And they placed his armor in the house of Ashtaroth, and they hung up his body on the wall of Beth-shean. 11. And the inhabitants of Jabesh-gilead heard about him, what the Philistines did to Saul. 12. And every warrior man arose and went all night, and they took the body of Saul and the bodies of his sons from the wall of Beth-shean; and they came to Jabesh and they burned them *as they burn the kings*[10] there. 13. And they took their bones and buried them beneath the tamarisk tree in Jabesh, and they fasted seven days.

Notes, Chapter Thirty-One

[1] MT: "were fighting."
[2] MT: "slain."
[3] MT: "struck down."
[4] MT: "the battle was heavy against."
[5] MT: "men with the bow."
[6] MT: "stab."
[7] MT: "stab."
[8] MT: "the slain."
[9] MT: "fallen."
[10] MT lacks the phrase. Since cremation was not approved by the Talmud, Tg justifies this act by reference to the special customs associated with kings. See S-A, 8-9.

2 SAMUEL

CHAPTER 1

1. And after Saul died, David returned from striking down *those of the house of Amalek;*[1] and David dwelt in Ziklag two days. 2. And on the third day, behold a man came from the camp from the presence of Saul, and his garments were torn and *dust*[2] was thrown upon his head. And when he came in David's presence, he fell upon the ground and did obeisance. 3. And David said to him: "From where are you coming?" And he said to him: "From the camp of Israel I have been saved." 4. And David said to him: "What was the word? Tell me now." And he said that the people fled from the battle and also many from the people fell and *were killed.*[3] And also Saul and Jonathan his son died. 5. And David said to the young man who was telling him: "How do you know that Saul and Jonathan his son are dead?" 6. And the young man who was telling him said: "I just happened to be on the mountain of Gilboa, and behold *chariots and an army of horsemen*[4] were pressing upon him. 7. And he turned behind him and saw me, and he called to me. And I said: 'Here I am.' 8. And he said to me: 'Who are you?' And I said to him: 'I am an Amalekite.' 9. And he said to me: 'Stand now by me and *kill me,*[5] for the trembling has seized me, for my life *still surrounds*[6] me.' 10. And I stood over him and *killed him,*[7] for I knew that he would not live after he fell. And I took the crown that was upon his head and the bracelet that was upon his arm, and I brought them unto my master here." 11. And David took hold of his garments and tore them, and so too all the men who were with him. 12. And they lamented and wept and fasted until the evening over Saul and over Jonathan his son and over the people of the Lord and over the house of Israel, for they *were killed*[8] by the sword. 13. And David said to the young man who was telling him: "Where are you from?" And he said; "I am the son of a sojourner man, the Amalekite." 14. And David said to him: "How were you not afraid *to stretch out*[9] your hand to harm the anointed of the Lord?" 15. And David called to one of the young men and said: "Draw near, *overpower him.*"[10] And he struck him and *killed him.*[11] 16. And David said to him: "*May your sin of killing be*[12] on your head, for your mouth *bore witness*[13] against you, saying: 'I killed the anointed of the Lord.'" 17. And David lamented this lament over Saul and over Jonathan his son. 18. And he said to teach the sons of Judah *the string on the bow.*[14] Behold it is written upon

Notes, Chapter 1

[1]MT: "Amalek" or "the Amalekite."
[2]MT: "earth."
[3]MT: "died."
[4]MT: "the chariot and masters of horsemen."
[5]MT: "put me to death."
[6]MT is obscure, and the Aramaic reflects its obscurity.

[7]MT: "put him to death."
[8]MT: "fell."
[9]MT: "to send forth."
[10]MT: "strike him down."
[11]MT: "he died."
[12]MT: "your blood."
[13]MT: "answered."
[14]MT: "the bow."

the book of *the Law*.[15] 19. "*You took your stand, O Israel, upon your stronghold; you were cast down, killed.*[16] How the mighty *were killed!*[17] 20. Do not tell it in Gath; do not proclaim it in the streets of Ashkelon, lest the daughters of the Philistines rejoice, lest the daughters of the uncircumcised ones dance about. 21. *O mountains of Gilboa, the dew will not come down upon you and the rain will not be entering in you sufficiently that they might make from it the dough offering, for there were broken the shields of the warriors, the shield of Saul, who was the anointed as with oil.*[18] 22. From the blood of *the killed,*[19] from the fat of the warriors, *the arrows of the bow*[20] of Jonathan were not turning back, and the sword of Saul did not come away empty. 23. Saul and Jonathan, who were loved and dear! In their life and in their death they were not separated *from themselves;*[21] they were swifter than eagles, more powerful than lions. 24. Daughters of Israel, weep over Saul, *who was putting on you garments of colored-stuff and bringing out for you delicacies*[22] and bringing up ornaments of gold upon your clothing. 25. How the mighty *have been shattered*[23] in the midst of battle! Jonathan, *you are killed upon your stronghold.*[24] 26. There is grief to me over you, my brother Jonathan; you were very dear to me; your love *is more wonderful*[25] to me than the love of *two wives.*[26] 27. How the mighty *have been shattered,*[27] and the weapons of war have perished!

CHAPTER 2

1. And afterward David inquired by *the Memra of the Lord*[1] saying: "Shall I go up against one of the cities of *the house of Judah?*[2] And the Lord said to him: "Go up." And David said: "To where shall I go?" And he said: "To Hebron." 2. And David went up *to*[3] there, and also his two wives, Ahinoam *who was from Jezreel*[4] and Abigail the wife of Nabal *who was from Carmel.*[5] 3. And David brought up his men who were with him, each man and the men of his house; and they dwelt in the cities of Hebron. 4. And

Notes, Chapter One (Cont.)

[15]MT: "Jashar." See Josh. 10:13. The unknown "Book of Yashar [the Upright]" is coverted into Torah.

[16]MT: "The beauty (or gazelle), O Israel, upon you high places is pierced." Tg makes the biblical metaphor prosaically descriptive.

[17]MT: "have fallen."

[18]MT: "O mountains in Gilboa, let there be neither dew nor rain upon you, and fields of offerings, for thus the shield of the warriors was defiled, the shield of Saul without anointing with oil."

[19]MT: "the slain."

[20]MT: "the bow."

[21]MT lacks the word.

[22]MT: "who clothed you in scarlet with ornaments."

[23]MT: "have fallen."

[24]MT: "upon your high places slain."

[25]MT: "was more wonderful."

[26]MT: "women."

[27]MT: "have fallen."

Notes, Chapter Two

[1]MT: "the Lord."

[2]MT: "Judah."

[3]MT lacks the preposition.

[4]MT: "the Jezreelite."

[5]MT: "the Carmelite."

men of *the tribe of Judah*[6] came and anointed David there *to be king over those of the house of Judah.*[7] And they told David saying: "Men of Jabesh-gilead are those ones who buried Saul." 5. And David sent messengers unto the men of Jabesh-gilead and said to them: "Blessed are you *before*[8] the Lord, you who did this kindness with your master, with Saul, and you buried him. 6. And now may the Lord do with you goodness and truth; and I also will do this kindness with you who have done this thing. 7. And now let your hands be strong, and be *warrior men,*[9] for your master Saul is dead and *those of the house*[10] of Judah anointed me *to be king*[11] over them." 8. And Abner the son of Ner, commander of the army that was Saul's, took Ishbosheth the son of Saul, and brought him over to Mahanaim. 9. And he made him king *over those of the house of Gilead and over those of the house of Asher and over those of the house of Jezreel and over those of the house of Ephraim and over those of the house of Benjamin and over Israel, all of them.*[12] 10. Ishbosheth the son of Saul was forty years old *when he became king*[13] over Israel, and he was king for two years. But *those of the house*[14] of Judah were after David. 11. And the number of the days that David was king in Hebron over *those of the house*[15] of Judah were seven years and six months. 12. And Abner the son of Ner and the servants of Ishbosheth the son of Saul went forth from Mahanaim to Gibeon. 13. And Joab the son of Zeruiah and the servants of David went forth, and they met them together by the pool of Gibeon. And these camped by the pool on one side, and these by the pool on the other side. 14. And Abner said to Joab: "Let the young men arise now and play before us." And Joab said: "Let them arise." 15. And they arose and crossed over by the number, twelve *from those of the house of Benjamin and from those of Ishbosheth*[16] the son of Saul, and twelve from the servants of David. 16. And each took hold of the head of his fellow, and his sword was in the side of his fellow, and *they were killed*[17] together. And they called that place "*the inheritance of those killed,*[18] which is in Gibeon." 17. And the battle was extremely fierce on that day, and Abner and the men of Israel were shattered before the servants of David. 18. And the three sons of Zeruiah were there, Joab and Abishai and Asahel; and Asahel was swift of foot like one of the gazelles which are in the field. 19. And Asahel pursued after Abner, and he did not turn aside to go to the right and to the left from after Abner. 20. And Abner turned aside to behind him and said: "Are you this Asahel?" And he said: "I am." 21. And Abner said to him: "Turn aside to your right or to your left, and seize for yourself one of the young men, and take for yourself his armor." And Asahel was not willing to turn aside from after him. 22. And Abner continued to say to Asahel: "Turn aside from after me. Why *shall I kill you and cast you down*[19] to the ground? And how shall I lift up my face *and look at*[20] Joab your

Notes, Chapter Two (Cont.)

[6]MT: "Judah."

[7]MT: "for king over the house of Judah."

[8]MT: "to."

[9]MT: "men of might."

[10]MT: "the house."

[11]MT: "for king."

[12]MT: "for Gilead and for the Ashurite and for Jezreel and over Ephraim and over Benjamin and over all Israel."

[13]MT: "at his becoming king."

[14]MT: "the house."

[15]MT: "the house."

[16]MT: "for Benjamin and for Ishbosheth."

[17]MT: "they fell."

[18]MT: "the field of sword-edges (*or,* adversaries, *or* sides)."

[19]MT: "shall I strike you down."

[20]MT lacks the phrase.

brother?" 23. And he *was not willing*[21] to turn aside, and Abner struck him down with the back of the spear *by the side of his loins,*[22] and the spear came forth from in back of him; and he fell there and died *in his place.*[23] And all who were coming to the place where Asahel fell and died were standing still. 24. And Joab and Abishai pursued after Abner, and the sun went down, and they arrived at the hill of Ammah which faces Giah on the way of the wilderness of Gibeon. 25. And the sons of Benjamin gathered after Abner, and they were as one troop, and they stood upon the top of one hill. 26. And Abner called to Joab and said: "Shall the sword *kill*[24] forever? Do you not know that it will be bitter in the end? And how long will you not say to the people to turn from after their brothers?" 27. And Joab said: "As *the Lord*[25] lives, *if you would have spoken,*[26] so from *the time of morning*[27] the people would have gone up, each man from after his brother." 28. And Joab blew on the trumpet, and all the people *rose up*[28] and did not pursue anymore after Israel, and they did not continue to fight. 29. And Abner and his men went about on the plain all that night; and they crossed the Jordan and went all the forenoon and came to Mahanaim. 30. And Joab turned from after Abner and gathered all the people; and there were missing from the servants of David nineteen men and Asahel. 31. And the servants of David *killed from those of the house of Benjamin*[29] and among the men of Abner; 360 men died. 32. And they took up Asahel and buried him in the tomb of his father, which was at Bethlehem; and Joab and his men went all night, and there was daybreak for them in Hebron.

CHAPTER 3

1. And the battle was *fierce*[1] between the house of Saul and the house of David; and *the house of David*[2] was getting stronger, and the house of Saul was getting weaker. 2. And sons were born to David in Hebron; and his firstborn was Amnon, to Ahinoam *who was from Jezreel.*[3] 3. And his second was Chileab, to Abigail the wife of Nabal, *who was from Carmel,*[4] and the third was Absalom the son of Maacah the daughter of Talmai, king of Geshur. 4. And the fourth Adonijah the son of Haggith, and the fifth was Shephatiah the son of Abital. 5. And the sixth Ithream to Eglah, the wife of David. These were born to David in Hebron. 6. And when there was battle between the house of Saul and the house of David, Abner was becoming stronger in the house of Saul. 7. And Saul had a concubine, and her name was Rizpah the daughter of Aiah. And he

Notes, Chapter Two (Cont.)

[21]MT: "refused."
[22]MT: "the belly."
[23]MT: "beneath it."
[24]MT: "devour."
[25]MT: "God."
[26]MT: "If you had not spoken."
[27]MT: "the morning."

[28]MT: "stood up."
[29]MT: "struck down from Benjamin."

Notes, Chapter Three

[1]MT: "long."
[2]MT: "David."
[3]MT: "the Jezreelite."
[4]MT: "the Carmelite."

(Ishbosheth) said to Abner: "Why have you gone into the concubine of my father?" 8. And Abner was very angry over the words of Ishbosheth, and he said: "*Am I not the head? Since when did I become a common man for the remnant of the house of Judah?*[5] This day I am doing kindness with the house of Saul your father, *with*[6] his brothers and *with*[7] his friends. And I did not give you in the hand of David. *And since from this moment*[8] are you visiting upon me the guilt of the woman this day? 9. Thus may *the Lord*[9] do to Abner and thus may he add to him, for as the Lord swore to David, so I will do to him, 10. to make the kingdom pass from the house of Saul and to establish the throne of David over Israel and over Judah from Dan and unto Beer-sheba." 11. And he was not able again to answer Abner a word *because he was afraid*[10] of him. 12. And Abner sent messengers unto David *from his place,*[11] saying: "*We are establishing what he who made the earth*[12] is saying; cut your covenant with me, and behold my hand is with you to turn about all Israel unto you." 13. And he said: "Good. I will cut a covenant with you. But one thing I ask of you, saying: 'You will not see my face unless first you bring Michal the daughter of Saul when you come *to make an appearance before me.*"[13] 14. And David sent messengers unto Ishbosheth the son of Saul, saying: "Give my wife Michal whom I engaged to myself for 100 foreskins of the Philistines." 15. And Ishbosheth sent, and he took her from her husband, from Paltiel the son of Laish. 16. And her husband went along with her, weeping after her unto '*Almat.*[14] And Abner said to him: "Go, turn back." And he turned back. 17. And the word of Abner was with the elders of Israel, saying: "Both yesterday and the day before it you were seeking David *to be king*[15] over you. 18. And now do it, for the Lord said to David, saying: 'By the hand of David my servant *I will save*[16] my people Israel from the hand of the Philistines and from the hand of all their enemies.'" 19. And Abner also spoke *before those of the house of Benjamin,*[17] and Abner also went to speak *before David*[18] in Hebron everything that was good in the eyes of Israel and in the eyes of all *those who were of the house*[19] of Benjamin. 20. And Abner came unto David *to*[20] Hebron, and with him were twenty men. And David made a banquet for Abner and for the men who were with him. 21. And Abner said to David: "I will arise and go and gather unto my master the king all Israel; and they will cut with you a covenant and you will be king in all that your soul desires." And David sent away Abner, and he went in peace. 22. And behold the servants of David and of Joab came from *the camp,*[21] and they brought much booty with them; and Abner was not with David in Hebron, for he sent him away and he went in peace. 23. And Joab and all the army that was with him came. And they told Joab, saying: "Abner the son of Ner came unto the king, and he sent him away and he went in peace." 24. And Joab came unto the king and said:

Notes, Chapter Three (Cont.)

[5]MT: "Am I a dog's head for Judah?" Tg makes the terse proverb more prosaic and clear.

[6]MT: "to."

[7]MT: "to."

[8]MT lacks the word.

[9]MT: "God."

[10]MT: "because of his fear."

[11]MT: "in his place."

[12]MT: "Whose is the land."

[13]MT: "to see my face."

[14]MT: "Bahurim," which means "young (chosen) men." The Aramaic term 'Almat means "youth." See 2 Sam 16:5; 17:18; 1 Kings 2:8.

[15]MT: "for a king."

[16]MT: "he has saved."

[17]MT: "in the ears of Benjamin."

[18]MT: "in the ears of David."

[19]MT: "the house."

[20]MT lacks the preposition.

[21]MT: "the raid."

"What have you done? Behold Abner came unto you. Why did you send him away, and he went off? 25. You know Abner the son of Ner, for he came to lead you astray, and to know your going forth and your coming in, and to know everything that you are doing." 26. And Joab went forth from David, and he sent messengers after Abner, and they brought him back from "the pit of the thorn," and David did not know it. 27. And Abner returned to Hebron, and Joab took him aside to the midst of the gate to speak with him in quiet, and he struck him there *by the side of his loins,*22 and he died for the blood of Asahel his brother. 28. And David heard afterward, and he said: "I and my kingdom are innocent *from before*23 the Lord forever of the blood of Abner the son of Ner. 29. May they hover over the head of Joab and *upon*24 all the house of his father. And may there not cease to be from the house of Joab one who has a flow and one who is leprous and one who holds the spindle and who *is killed*25 by the sword and one who lacks food." 30. And Joab and Abishai his brother killed Abner because he killed Asahel their brother in Gibeon in battle. 31. And David said to Joab and to all the people who were with him: "Rend your garments and tie on sackcloth, and weep before Abner." And King David was going after the bier. 32. And they buried Abner in Hebron, and the king raised up his voice, and he wept over the grave of Abner, and all the people wept. 33. And the king lamented over Abner, and he said: "Should Abner die as *wicked men die?*26 34. Your hands were not tied, and your feet were not drawn near to fetters of bronze; as one falls before wicked men,27 you have fallen." And all the people continued to weep over him. 35. And all the people came to make David eat bread while it was still day. And David swore, saying: "May *the Lord*28 do thus to me and more so if before sunset I taste bread or anything at all." 36. And all the people understood, and *it was pleasing*29 in their eyes; according to everything that the king did was good in the eyes of all the people. 37. And all the people and all Israel knew on that day that it was not *in the plan of the king to kill*30 Abner the son of Ner. 38. And the king said to his servants: "Do you not know that a chief and *powerful one*31 has fallen this day in Israel? 39. I this day am *common and anointed for kingship.*32 And these men, the sons of Zeruiah, are harsher than I am. May the Lord repay to *doers*33 of evil according to his evil."

CHAPTER 4

1. And the son of Saul heard that Abner was dead in Hebron; and his hands became weak, and all Israel was agitated. 2. And two men were *captains, heads, of the two*

Notes, Chapter Three (Cont.)

22MT: "in the belly."
23MT: "from with."
24MT: "for."
25MT: "falls."
26MT: "a fool dies."

27MT: "the sons of wickedness."
28MT: "God."
29MT: "it was good."
30MT: "from the king to put to death."
31MT: "a great one."
32MT: "weak and an anointed king."
33MT: "doer."

armies with the son of Saul.[1] The name of the one was Baanah, and the name of the second was Rechab, the sons of Rimmon, *who were from Beeroth,*[2] from the sons of Benjamin, for Beeroth was also reckoned with *those of the house of Benjamin.*[3] 3. And *the men of Beeroth*[4] fled to Gittaim, and they are sojourning there unto this day. 4. And Jonathan the son of Saul had a son lame in his two feet. He was five years old when the news of Saul and Jonathan came from Jezreel; and his nurse took him up and fled; and in her excitement to flee, he fell and became crippled. And his name was Mephibosheth. 5. And the sons of Rimmon *who were from Beeroth,*[5] Rechab and Baanah, went and came about noontime to the house of Ishbosheth. And he was sleeping *the sleep of kings.*[6] 6. And behold they came unto the middle of the house *like those buying*[7] wheat, and they struck him *by the side of his loins;*[8] and Rechab and Baanah his brother escaped. 7. And they came to the house, and he was sleeping upon his bed in the inner chamber of his bedroom; and they struck him down and *killed him*[9] and cut off his head, and they took his head and went by way of the plain all night. 8. And they brought the head of Ishbosheth unto David to Hebron. And they said to the king: "Behold the head of Ishbosheth the son of Saul, your enemy, who sought *to kill you.*[10] And the Lord has *worked*[11] vengeance for my master the king this day from Saul and from his offspring." 9. And David answered Rechab and Baanah his brother, the sons of Rimmon *who was from Beeroth,*[12] and said to them: "As the Lord lives who saved my life from every grief, 10. the one who told me, saying: 'Behold Saul is dead,' and he was like one bringing good news *in the eyes of his own soul,*[13] and I seized him and killed him in Ziklag, *who was imagining (me) to give to him a present for his good news,*[14] 11. so also wicked men have killed a righteous man in his house upon his bed; and shall I not seek his blood from your hands and remove you from the earth?" 12. And David commanded the young men, and they killed them and cut off their hands and their feet, and they hanged them by the pool in Hebron. And they took the head of Ishbosheth and buried (it) in the tomb of Abner in Hebron.

CHAPTER 5

1. And all the tribes of Israel came unto David to Hebron, and they said, saying: "Behold we are your *kin,*[1] and your flesh are we. 2. Both yesterday and the day before

Notes, Chapter Four

[1]MT: "chiefs of the bands (of) the son of Saul."
[2]MT: "the Beerothite."
[3]MT: "to Benjamin."
[4]MT: "the Beerothites."
[5]MT: "Beerothite."
[6]MT: "noonday rest." Tg associates noonday rest with the upper class.
[7]MT: "fetching."
[8]MT: "into the belly."

[9]MT: "put him to death."
[10]MT: "your life."
[11]MT: "given."
[12]MT: "the Beerothite."
[13]MT: "in his eyes."
[14]MT: "which was the reward I gave him for his good news." Tg makes clear that David did not approve of the murder of Ishbosheth.

Notes, Chapter Five

[1]MT: "bone."

it, when Saul was king over us, *you were going forth and coming in at the head of Israel.*[2] And the Lord said to you: '*You will care for*[3] my people Israel, and you will be *the king*[4] over Israel.'" 3. And all the elders of Israel came unto the king to Hebron, and King David cut a covenant for them in Hebron before the Lord, and they anointed David king over Israel. 4. David was thirty years old when he became king. He reigned for forty years. 5. In Hebron he reigned over *those of the house of Judah*[5] for seven years and six months, and in Jerusalem he reigned for thirty-three years over all Israel and Judah. 6. And the king and his men went to Jerusalem unto the Jebusite inhabiting the land, and he said to David, saying: "You shall not enter here, except by your removing *the sinners and the guilty who were saying:*[6] 'David shall not enter here.'" 7. And David seized the stronghold of Zion — it is, the city of David. 8. And David said on that day: "Everyone *who will kill*[7] the Jebusite, *let him begin to conquer the fortified place.*"[8] And the soul of David *removed the sinners and the guilty.*[9] Therefore they say: "*The sinners and the guilty*[10] shall not enter the house." 9. And David dwelt in the stronghold, and he called it the "city of David." And David built around from the Millo and *inward.*[11] 10. And David became greater and greater, and *the Memra of the Lord the God of hosts was at his aid.*[12] 11. And Hiram the king of Tyre sent messengers unto David, and wood of cedars and *carpenters who were trained to cut the wood and artisans who were trained in the building of walls;*[13] and they built a house for David. 12. And David knew that the Lord had established him *to be the king*[14] over Israel and that *his kingdom was exalted*[15] on account of his people Israel. 13. And David took still more concubines and wives from Jerusalem after he came from Hebron, and there were born to David still more sons and daughters. 14. And these are the names of those who were born to him in Jerusalem: Shammua and Shobab and Nathan and Solomon, 15. and Ibhar and Elishua and Nepheg and Japhia, 16. and Elishama and Eliada and Eliphelet. 17. And the Philistines heard that they had anointed David *to be the king*[16] over Israel, and all the Philistines went up to seek out David. And David heard and went down to the stronghold. 18. And the Philistines came and were spread out in *the plain of the giants.*[17] 19. And David asked by *the Memra of the Lord,*[18] saying: "Shall I go up against the Philistines? Will you give them in my hand?" And the Lord said to David: "Go up, for I will indeed give the Philistines in your hand." 20. And David came *into the plain of breaches,*[19] and David struck them down there, and he said: "The Lord

---

Notes, Chapter Five (Cont.)

[2]MT: "you were leading forth and bringing in Israel."

[3]MT: "you will shepherd."

[4]MT: "leader."

[5]MT: "Judah."

[6]MT: "the blind and the lame, saying." Tg understands the Hebrew verb according to its normal meaning, "remove." The MT uses it to mean "ward off." Tg then gives a moral dimension to the struggle and to the exclusion of sinners and guilty in v. 8.

[7]MT: "who strikes."

[8]MT: "let him approach by the water shaft." Tg makes explicit David's tactic for taking the city.

[9]MT: "hated the lame and the blind."

[10]MT: "the blind and the lame."

[11]MT: "to the house."

[12]MT: "the Lord God of hosts was with him."

[13]MT: "artisans of wood and artisans of the stone of the wall."

[14]MT: "for a king."

[15]MT: "he exalted his kingdom."

[16]MT: "for a king."

[17]MT: "the valley of the Rephaim."

[18]MT: "the Lord."

[19]MT: "upon Baal-perazim." The "perazim" element=Aramaic "breaches."

has broken my enemies before me like the breaking *of a vessel of clay that is filled with water.*[20] Therefore he called the name of that place the *"plain of breaches."*[21] 21. And they left their idols there, and David and his men *burned them.*[22] 22. And the Philistines continued to go up, and they were spread out in *the plain of the giants.*[23] 23. And David asked by *the Memra of the Lord,*[24] and *it*[25] said: "You shall not go up; go around behind them, and you shall come to them opposite *the trees.*[26] 24. And as you hear the sound of the *cry*[27] in the tops of the trees, then you will get stirred up, for then *the angel of the Lord*[28] has gone forth *to prosper before you, to kill*[29] among the camp of the Philistines." 25. And David did so, just as the Lord commanded him. And he *killed*[30] the Philistines from Geba unto the entrance of Gezer.

CHAPTER 6

1. And David once again gathered *all the chosen men of Israel,*[1] 30,000. 2. And David and all the people who were with him arose and went *from the cities of the house of Judah*[2] to bring up from there the ark of *the Lord,*[3] which is called by the name of the Lord of hosts *whose Shekinah resides above*[4] the cherubim upon it. 3. And *they brought down the ark of the Lord by the new cart*[5] and took it up from the house of Abinadab which was on the hill; and Uzzah and Ahio, the sons of Abinadab, were driving the new cart. 4. And they took it up from the house of Abinadab which was on the hill; *they were coming with the ark of the Lord,*[6] and Ahio was going before the ark. 5. And David and all the house of Israel *were praising*[7] before the Lord with all fir-trees and with lyres and with lutes and with timbrels and with sistras and with cymbals. 6. And they came unto *the appointed place,*[8] and Uzzah *reached out his hand on the ark of the Lord*[9] and took hold of it, for the oxen *were swaying it.*[10] 7. And the anger of the

Notes, Chapter Five (Cont.)

[20]MT: "of water."
[21]MT: "Baal-perazim." See note on 5:20.
[22]MT: "took them away." Tg has David and his men dispose of the idols correctly by burning them.
[23]MT: "the valley of the Rephaim."
[24]MT: "the Lord."
[25]MT: "he."
[26]MT: The Hebrew has "the balsam trees."
[27]MT: "marching."
[28]MT: "the Lord."
[29]MT: "before you to strike down."
[30]MT: "struck down."

Notes, Chapter Six

[1]MT: "every chosen man in Israel."
[2]MT: "from Baale-judah." Tg avoids the word "Baal."
[3]MT: "God."
[4]MT: "sitting."
[5]MT: "they carried the ark of God to a new cart."
[6]MT: "with the ark of God."
[7]MT: "were making merry."
[8]MT: "the threshing floor of Nacon." Tg translates Nacon according to its root meaning, "firm, established."
[9]MT: "sent forth to the ark of God."
[10]MT is unclear; perhaps "stumbled."

Lord *was strong*[11] against Uzzah, and *the Memra of the Lord*[12] struck him down there *because he was careless,*[13] and he died there with the ark of *the Lord.*[14] 8. And *it was hard*[15] for David because the Lord made a break on Uzzah. And he called that place "the place in which Uzzah died"[16] unto this day. 9. And David *feared from before the Lord*[17] on that day, and he said; "How shall the ark of the Lord come unto me?" 10. And David was not willing to take aside unto himself the ark of the Lord to the city of David; and David took it aside to the house of Obed-edom the Gittite. 11. And the ark of the Lord resided at the house of Obed-edom the Gittite for three months, and the Lord blessed Obed-edom and all his house. 12. And it was told to King David, saying: "The Lord has blessed the house of Obed-edom and everything that is his on account of the ark of *the Lord.*"[18] And David went and brought up the ark of *the Lord*[19] from the house of Obed-edom to the city of David with joy. 13. And when the bearers of the ark of the Lord *brought (it)*[20] six paces, he *slaughtered*[21] an ox and a fatling. 14. And David *was praising*[22] with all power before the Lord, and David was girded with *a tunic*[23] of linen. 15. And David and all the house of Israel were bringing up the ark of the Lord with shouting and with the sound of the trumpet. 16. And the ark of the Lord was coming to the city of David, and Michal the daughter of Saul was looking out from the window, and she saw King David *dancing and praising*[24] before the Lord, and she despised him in her heart. 17. And they brought in the ark of the Lord and set it up in its place in the midst of the tent that David spread out for it; and David brought up holocausts before the Lord and *offerings of holy things.*[25] 18. And David finished bringing up the holocausts and *offerings of holy things,*[26] and he blessed the people in the name of the Lord of hosts. 19. And he distributed to all the people, to all the multitude of Israel, from man and unto woman, to each one cake of bread, *one portion, and one share;*[27] and all the people went away, each man to his house. 20. And David returned to bless *the men of his house;*[28] and Michal the daughter of Saul went forth to meet David, and she said: "How did the king of Israel honor himself this day, who was revealed this day to the eyes of the handmaids of his servants *as one who strips and exposes himself as one of the idlers does?"*[29] 21. And David said to Michal:

Notes, Chapter Six (Cont.)

[11]MT: "was hot."

[12]MT: "God."

[13]MT is unclear; perhaps "on account of the slip."

[14]MT: "God."

[15]MT: "it was hot."

[16]MT: "the breech of Uzzah."

[17]MT: "David feared the Lord."

[18]MT: "God."

[19]MT: "God."

[20]MT: "stepped."

[21]MT: "sacrificed."

[22]MT: "was dancing." Tg makes David's worship more decorous.

[23]MT: "an ephod." Tg reserves the ephod to priests.

[24]MT: "leaping and dancing."

[25]MT: "peace-offerings."

[26]MT: "peace-offerings."

[27]MT is unclear; perhaps "one portion of meat and one date-cake."

[28]MT: "his house."

[29]MT: "as one of the idlers indeed exposes himself."

"Before the Lord who chose me over your father and over all his house to command me *to be king*[30] over the people of the Lord, over Israel; and *I gave praise*[31] before the Lord. 22. And I will be still *smaller*[32] than this and *lower in the eyes of my soul than this,*[33] and with the handmaids of whom you speak, *in their eyes*[34] I will be honored." 23. And Michal the daughter of Saul had no child until the day of her death.

CHAPTER 7

1. And when the king dwelt in his house, the Lord gave him rest round about from all his enemies. 2. And the king said to Nathan the prophet: "See now *that*[1] I am dwelling *in the house that is covered with panels of cedars,*[2] and the ark of the *Lord*[3] resides *in the tent*[4] in the midst of the curtain." 3. And Nathan said to the king: "Everything that is in your heart, go, do, for *the Memra of the Lord is at your aid.*"[5] 4. And on that night, *the word of prophecy was from before the Lord with Nathan,*[6] saying: 5. "Go, and you will say to my servant, to David: 'Thus said the Lord: Will you build *before me the house for my Shekinah to make its residence in ?*[7] 6. For *I have not made my Shekinah reside*[8] in a house from the day that I brought up the sons of Israel from Egypt and until this day. *And I was making my presence reside in tents and in curtains.*[9] 7. In every *place*[10] that I went with all the sons of Israel, did I speak a word with one of the tribes of Israel which I commanded to provide for my people Israel, saying: "Why have you not built *before me a house that is covered with panels of cedars?*"[11] 8. And now thus you will say to my servant, to David: 'Thus said the Lord of hosts: I have taken you from the *sheepfold,*[12] from after the sheep, to be the *king*[13] over my people, over Israel. 9. *And my Memra was at your aid in every place*[14] that you came, and I destroyed all your enemies from before you, and *I made*[15] for you a great name according to the name of the great ones who are in the earth. 10. And I will appoint a *fixed*[16] place for my people, for Israel; and I will *establish*[17] them, and they will reside *in their place.*[18] And they will not be shaken anymore, and the sons of wickedness will not continue to afflict him as in the past. 11. And from the day that I

Notes, Chapter Six (Cont.)

[30]MT: "as leader."
[31]MT: "I made merry."
[32]MT: "lower."
[33]MT: "more humble in my eyes."
[34]MT: "with them."

Notes, Chapter Seven

[1]MT lacks the word.
[2]MT: "in the house of cedars."
[3]MT: "God."
[4]MT lacks the phrase.
[5]MT: "the Lord is with you."

[6]MT: "the word of the Lord was to Nathan."
[7]MT: "for me a house to dwell in."
[8]MT: "I have not dwelt."
[9]MT: "And I was moving about in a tent and a tabernacle."
[10]MT lacks the word.
[11]MT: "for me a house of cedars."
[12]MT: "pasture."
[13]MT: "ruler."
[14]MT: "And I was with you in every."
[15]MT: "I will make."
[16]MT lacks the word.
[17]MT: "plant." Tg changes the metaphoric term."
[18]MT: "under it."

appointed *leaders*[19] over my people Israel, and I gave you rest from all your enemies. And the Lord told you that the Lord *will establish for you a kingdom.*[20] 12. For your days will be fulfilled, and you will lay down with your fathers. And I will establish *your son after you whom you will sire,*[21] and I will make secure his kingdom. 13. And he will build the house to my name, and I will make secure the throne of his kingdom forever. 14. And I will be to him like a father, and he will be *before*[22] me for a son, *whom if he sins,*[23] I will punish by the *chastisement*[24] of men and by the *correction*[25] of the sons of men. 15. And my goodness will not pass from him as I removed (it) from Saul, whom I removed from before you. 16. And your house and your kingdom will be standing forever before you; *the throne of your kingdom*[26] will be made secure forever." 17. According to all these words and according to all this *prophecy,*[27] thus Nathan spoke with David. 18. And king David came and sat before the Lord, and he said: "*I am not worthy,*[28] *Lord God,*[29] and *what*[30] is my house that you have brought me this far? 19. And this was still something small *before you,*[31] Lord God, and you have spoken also *concerning*[32] the house of your servant *for the age that is coming,*[33] and this is the *vision for the sons of men,*[34] Lord God. 20. And what more will David still speak *before*[35] you? *And you have done the request of your servant,*[36] Lord God. 21. On account of your word and according to your *good pleasure*[37] you have done *all these great things*[38] to make your servant know. 22. Therefore you are great, Lord God, for there is none like you and there is no god apart from you; according to everything that we have heard, *they said before us.*[39] 23. And who is *like your people Israel, one chosen people*[40] in the earth, whom *those sent from before the Lord*[41] went to save for him *a people*[42] and to make for him a name and to do for you *great and mighty deeds until they entered the land of the house of your Shekinah which you gave to them from before your people,*[43] which you saved for yourself from Egypt, *Gentiles*[44] and their gods. 24. And you made secure for yourself your people Israel *before*[45] you for a people forever, and you Lord were for them for God. 25. And now Lord God, confirm the word that you spoke concerning your servant and concerning his house forever, and do as you spoke. 26. And your name will be great forever, saying: 'Lord of hosts, God over Israel;'

Notes, Chapter Seven (Cont.)

[19]MT: "judges."

[20]MT: "will make for you a house."

[21]MT: "your seed after you, who will come forth from your loins."

[22]MT: "to."

[23]MT: "who in his sinning."

[24]MT: "rod."

[25]MT: "stripes."

[26]MT: "your throne."

[27]MT: "vision."

[28]MT: "Who am I."

[29]In David's prayer (vv. 18-29), the Hebrew address "my Lord Yahweh" appears in Aramaic as "Lord (=Yahweh) God."

[30]MT: "who."

[31]MT: "in your eyes."

[32]MT: "to."

[33]MT: "for a great while to come." Tg inserts a messianic reference.

[34]MT: "the law of man." Tg's "vision" suggests the messianic age.

[35]MT: "to."

[36]MT: "you have known your servant."

[37]MT: "heart."

[38]MT: "all this greatness."

[39]MT: "with our ears."

[40]MT: "like your people, like Israel, one people."

[41]MT: "gods." Tg eliminates reference to other gods.

[42]MT: "for a people."

[43]MT: "greatness and fearful deeds, for your land, from before your people."

[44]Tg takes over the MT word *gôyîm*, but in so doing makes its meaning more specific ("Gentiles") than MT.

[45]MT: "for."

and the house of your servant David will be made secure before you. 27. For you, Lord of hosts, God of Israel, *have told*[46] your servant, saying: '*I will establish a kingdom*[47] for you.' *Therefore it was in the heart of your servant to pray before you*[48] this prayer. 28. And now Lord God, you are God: and your words are truth. And you have spoken with your servant *all*[49] this goodness. 29. And now *begin*[50] and bless the house of your servant to be forever before you, for you Lord God have spoken, and from your blessing *the houses of your just servants*[51] will be blessed forever."

CHAPTER 8

1. And afterwards David struck down the Philistines and *shattered*[1] them, and David took *the arrangement of the cubit*[2] from the hand of the Philistines. 2. And he struck down *the Moabites*[3] and measured them with the *lot*,[4] *casting them down*[5] to the ground. And he measured two *lots*[6] *to kill*,[7] and *they filled the lot*[8] to let live. And *the Moabites*[9] were servants to David, bearers of tribute. 3. And David struck down Hadadezer the son of Rehob, the king of Zobah, when he went *to change his border, at the River Euphrates*.[10] 4. And David seized from him 1,700 horsemen and 20,000 men on foot, and David hamstrung all the chariots and left 100 chariots of them. 5. And *the men of Aram-Damascus*[11] came to aid Hadadezer the king of Zobah, and David struck down among Aram 22,000 men. 6. And David set up garrisons in Aram-Damascus; and *the men of Aram were*[12] servants to David, bearers of tribute. And the Lord saved David in every *place*[13] that he sent about. 7. And David took the shields of gold that were on the servants of Hadadezer and brought them to Jerusalem. 8. And from Betah and from *Beroth*,[14] cities of Hadadezer, King David took very much bronze. 9. And Toi the king of Hamath heard that David struck down all the army of Hadadezer. 10. And Toi sent Joram his son unto King David to ask for peace for him and to bless him because he *waged battle*[15] against Hadadezer and *killed*[16] him, for Hadadezer was *a man waging battles with Toi*.[17] And *with him*[18] were vessels of silver and vessels of gold

Notes, Chapter Seven (Cont.)

[46]MT: "have opened the ear of."
[47]MT: "I will build a house."
[48]MT: "therefore your servant found his heart to pray to you."
[49]MT lacks the word.
[50]MT: "be pleased."
[51]MT: "the house of your servant."

Notes, Chapter Eight

[1]MT: "subdued."
[2]MT: "Metheg Ammak" (bridle of the cubit), a place name.
[3]MT: "Moab."
[4]MT: "cord." The MT word *ḥebel* can also mean "lot."
[5]MT: "making them lie down."
[6]MT: "cords."
[7]MT: "to put to death."
[8]MT: "to fill the cord."
[9]MT: "Moab."
[10]MT: "to restore his hand (=power) at the river."
[11]MT: "Aram-Damascus."
[12]MT: "Aram was."
[13]MT lacks the word.
[14]MT: "Berothai."
[15]MT: "fought."
[16]MT: "struck him down."
[17]MT: "a man of wars of Toi."
[18]MT: "in his hand."

and vessels of bronze. 11. And these also King David consecrated *before*[19] the Lord with the silver and the gold that he consecrated from all the nations that he conquered, 12. from Aram and from Moab and from the sons of Ammon and from the Philistines and from the *Amalekites*[20] and from the spoil of Hadadezer the son of Rehob the king of Zobah. 13. And David *gathered forces*[21] when he returned from striking down Aram in the valley of Salt — 18,000. 14. And he set up in Edom garrisons; in all Edom he set up garrisons, and *all the men of Edom*[22] were slaves to David; and the Lord saved David in every *place*[23] that he went. 15. And David was king over all Israel, and David was making *a judgment of truth*[24] and righteousness for all his people. 16. And Joab the son of Zeruiah *was appointed*[25] over the army, and Jehoshaphat the son of Ahilud *was appointed over the records*.[26] 17. And Zadok the son of Ahitub and Ahimelech the son of Abiathar, were priests; and Seraiah was the scribe. 18. And Benaiah the son of Jehoiada *was appointed over the archers and the slingers*;[27] and the sons of David were *chiefs*.[28]

CHAPTER 9

1. And David said: "Is there still here anyone who is left for the house of Saul, and I will do *good*[1] with him on account of Jonathan?" 2. And there was a servant belonging to Saul's house, and his name was Ziba. And they called him unto David. And the king said to him: "Are you Ziba?" And he said: "Your servant." 3. And the king said: "Is there still a man belonging to the house of Saul, and I will do with him *good from before the Lord?*"[2] And Ziba said to the king: "There is still a son of Jonathan, afflicted *in his two feet*."[3] 4. And the king said to him: "Where is he?" And Ziba said to the king: "Behold he is at the house of Machir, son of Ammiel, at Lo-debar." 5. And King David sent and took him from the house of Machir, son of Ammiel, from Lo-debar. 6. And Mephibosheth, son of Jonathan, son of Saul, came unto David and fell on his face and did obeisance. And David said: "Mephibosheth!" And he said: "Behold your servant." 7. And David said to him: "Do not fear, for indeed I will do *good*[4] with you on account of Jonathan your father. And I will restore to you all the *inheritance*[5] of Saul your father. And you will eat the bread on my table always." 8. And he *gave thanks*[6] and said:

Notes, Chapter Eight (Cont.)

[19]MT: "to."
[20]MT: "Amalek."
[21]MT: "made a name."
[22]MT: "all Edom."
[23]MT lacks the word.
[24]MT: "judgment."
[25]MT lacks the word.
[26]MT: "(was) recorder."
[27]MT: "and the Cherethite and the Pelethite." Tg transforms these unfamiliar names into military specializations.

[28]MT: "priests." Tg protects the hereditary nature of the priesthood.

Notes, Chapter Nine

[1]MT: "kindness."
[2]MT: "the kindness of God."
[3]MT: "afflicted of feet" (dual).
[4]MT: "kindness."
[5]MT: "field."
[6]MT: "did obeisance."

"What is your servant that you have turned your face to a *common man*[7] like me?" 9. And the king called to Ziba, the young man of Saul, and said to him: "Everything that belonged to Saul and to all his household, I have given to the son of your master. 10. And you will till for him the land, you and your sons and your servants. And you will bring in (produce), and it will be *food*[8] for the son of your master, *and he will be provided for.*[9] And Mephibosheth, the son of your master, always eats the bread on my table." And Ziba had fifteen sons and twenty servants. 11. And Ziba said to the king: "According to everything that my master the king will command his servant, so your servant will do." And Mephibosheth was eating at *my table,*[10] like one of the king's sons. 12. And Mephibosheth had a small son, and his name was Micah. And all the inhabitants of Ziba's house were servants to Mephibosheth. 13. And Mephibosheth was dwelling in Jerusalem, for at the table of the king he was eating always. And he *had an affliction*[11] in his two feet.

CHAPTER 10

1. And after this the king of the sons of Ammon died, and Hanun his son ruled in his place. 2. And David said: "I will do *good*[1] with Hanun, son of Nahash, as his father did *good*[2] with me." And David sent by the hand of his servants to comfort him regarding his father, and David's servants came to the land of the sons of Ammon. 3. And the chiefs of the sons of Ammon said to Hanun their master: "Is David honoring your father in your eyes because he has sent comforters to you? Is it not to go around the *land*[3] and to spy it out and to search it out that David has sent his servants unto you?" 4. And Hanun took the servants of David and shaved half of their beards and cut their garments in half, *to the place of their shame,*[4] and sent them away. 5. And they told (it) to David, and he sent to meet them, for the men were very ashamed. And the king said: "Stay in Jericho until your beard will grow, and then return." 6. And the sons of Ammon saw that they had attacked David, and the sons of Ammon sent and hired Aram of Beth-rehob and Aram of Zobah (twenty-thousand foot soldiers) and the king of Maacah (a thousand men), and Ish-tob (twelve thousand men). 7. And David heard and sent Joab and *the whole army of warriors.*[5] 8. And the sons of Ammon went forth and drew up the battle line at the entrance of the gate. And Aram of Zobah and Rehob and Ish-tob and Maacah were by themselves in the field. 9. And Joab saw that *the*

Notes, Chapter Nine (Cont.)

[7]MT: "dead dog." Tg translates the metaphor into prosaic language.

[8]MT: "bread."

[9]MT: "and he will eat it."

[10]Tg follows the impossible reading of MT. The Septuagint reads "at the table of the king."

[11]MT: "was lame."

Notes, Chapter Ten

[1]MT: "kindness."

[2]MT: "kindness."

[3]MT: "city." Some MT mss. contain the same reading.

[4]MT: "unto their buttocks."

[5]MT: "the whole army, the warriors."

wagers of battle were strong against him from before him and from behind him.[6] And he chose from all the chosen ones *of*[7] Israel and arrayed (them) opposite *the men of Aram.*[8] 10. And the rest of the people he gave into the hand of Abishai his brother, and he arrayed (them) opposite the sons of Ammon. 11. And he said: "If Aram is stronger than I, then you will be *a rescuer*[9] for me. And if the sons of Ammon are stronger than you, then I will come to rescue you. 12. Be strong! And let us be strong on behalf of our people and on behalf of the cities of our God. And may the Lord do what is good *before him.*[10] 13. And Joab and the people who were with him drew near *to wage battle against the men of Aram,*[11] and they fled before him. 14. And the sons of Ammon saw that *the men of Aram*[12] fled; then they ran from before Abishai, and they came to the city. And Joab returned from the presence of the sons of Ammon and came to Jerusalem. 15. And *the men of Aram*[13] saw that they were shattered before Israel, and they gathered themselves together. 16. And Hadadezer sent and bought forth *the men of Aram*[14] who were from beyond *the Euphrates.*[15] And they came to Helam, and Shobach the commander of the army of Hadadezer was before them. 17. And it was reported to David, and he gathered all Israel and crossed the Jordan and came to Helam. And *the men of Aram*[16] set up ranks opposite David and *waged battle*[17] with him. 18. And *the men of Aram*[18] fled from before Israel, and David killed from *the people of Aram*[19] seven hundred chariots and forty thousand horsemen. And he struck down Shobach the commander of its army, and he died there. 19. And all the kings, the servants of Hadadezer, saw that they were *shattered*[20] before Israel, and they made peace with Israel and served them. And *the men of Aram*[21] were afraid to rescue the sons of Ammon anymore.

CHAPTER 11

1. And *at the time of the end of the year,*[1] at the time when the kings go forth, David sent Joab and his servants with him and all Israel. And they injured the sons of Ammon and besieged Rabbah. And David was dwelling in Jerusalem. 2. And at evening time David arose from his couch and was walking upon the roof of the king's house. And he saw from upon the roof a woman washing herself, and the woman was

Notes, Chapter Ten (Cont.)

[6]MT: "the face of battle was against him from before and from behind."

[7]MT: "in."

[8]MT: "Aram."

[9]MT: "for rescue."

[10]MT: "in his eyes."

[11]MT: "for war against Aram."

[12]MT: "Aram."

[13]MT: "Aram."

[14]MT: "Aram."

[15]MT: "the river."

[16]MT: "Aram."

[17]MT: "fought."

[18]MT: "Aram."

[19]MT: "Aram."

[20]MT: "struck."

[21]MT: "Aram."

Notes, Chapter Eleven

[1]MT: "at the turn of the year."

very beautiful of appearance. 3. And David sent and inquired about the woman. And someone said: "Is not this Bathsheba, daughter of Eliam, wife of Uriah the Hittite?" 4. And David sent messengers and took her, and she came unto him. And he slept with her, and she was purifying herself from her uncleanness. And she returned to her house. 5. And the woman became pregnant and sent and told (it) to David and said: "I am pregnant." 6. And David sent unto Joab: "Sent to me Uriah the Hittite." And Joab sent Uriah unto David. 7. And Uriah came unto him, and David inquired for the health of Joab and for the health of the people and for the health of *the wagers of battle*.[2] 8. And David said to Uriah: "Go down to your house and wash your feet." And Uriah went forth from the king's house, and the king's *meal*[3] went forth after him. 9. And Uriah slept at the gate of the king's house with all the servants of his master, and he did not go down to his house. 10. And they told (it) to David saying: "Uriah did not go down to his house." And David said to Uriah: "Are you not coming off the road? Why did you not go down to your house?" 11. And Uriah said to David: "The ark and Israel and Judah are dwelling in booths, and my master Joab and the servants of my master are camping on the open field. And shall I go up to my house to eat and to drink and to sleep with my wife? By your life and the life of your soul, I will not do this thing." 12. And David said to Uriah: "Stay here also this day, and tomorrow I will send you off." And Uriah stayed in Jerusalem on that day and on the day after it. 13. And David summoned him. And he ate before him and drank, and he got him drunk. And he went forth in the evening to sleep on his couch with the servants of his master, and he did not go down to his house. 14. And in the morning David wrote a letter to Joab and sent it by the hand of Uriah. 15. And he wrote in the letter saying: "Set Uriah opposite the hardest combat, and you will turn from behind him, and he will be struck down and will die." 16. And when Joab *besieged*[4] the city, he set Uriah at the place where he knew that *the mighty men were there*.[5] 17. And the men of the city went forth and *waged battle*[6] with Joab. And some of the people of David's servants *were killed*,[7] and Uriah the Hittite also died. 18. And Joab sent and told to David all the affairs of the battle. 19 And he commanded the messenger saying: "And when you have completed telling the king all the affairs of the battle, 20. and if it happens that the king's anger *burns*[8] and he says to you: 'Why did you draw near to the city to fight? Did you not know that they would throw down *upon you*[9] from the wall? 21. Who *killed*[10] Abimelech, son of Jerubbesheth? Did not a woman throw down upon him half a millstone from the wall, and he died in Thebez? Why did you draw near to the wall?' And you will say: 'Your servant Uriah the Hittite also died.'" 22. And the messenger went and came and told to David everything that Joab sent him (to tell). 23. And the messenger said to David that "the men against us were strong and came forth against us to the field, and *we were driving them back*[11] to the entrance of the gate. 24. And the bowmen shot at your servants from upon the wall, and some of the king's servants *were killed*.[12] And your

Notes, Chapter Eleven (Cont.)

[2] MT: "the battle."
[3] MT: "portion."
[4] MT: "kept watch over."
[5] MT: "the men of might were there."
[6] MT: "fought."
[7] MT: "fell."
[8] MT: "rises."
[9] MT lacks the phrase.
[10] MT: "struck down."
[11] MT: "we were against them."
[12] MT: "died."

servant Uriah the Hittite is dead also." 25. And David said to the messenger: "Thus you will say to Joab: 'Let not this thing be evil in your eyes, for the sword *kills*[13] now this one and now that one. Strengthen your attack against the city, and destroy it.' And make him strong." 26. And the wife of Uriah heard that Uriah her husband was dead, and she mourned over her husband. 27. And the mourning passed, and David sent and took her into his house. And she was a wife for him, and she bore to him a son. And this thing that David did was evil *before*[14] the Lord.

CHAPTER 12

1. And the Lord sent Nathan unto David, and he came unto him and said to him: "There were two men in one city — one rich, and one poor. 2. The rich man had very many sheep and cattle. 3. And the poor man had nothing at all except one small lamb that he bought and raised. And it grew up with him and together with his sons. From his bread it was eating, and from his cup it was drinking, and in his lap it was sleeping. And it was like a daughter to him. 4. And a traveler came to the rich man, and he was unwilling to take from his own sheep and from his own cattle to prepare for the traveler who came to him. And he took the lamb of the poor man, and he prepared it for the man who came unto him." 5. And the anger of David was very *strong*[1] against the man, and he said to Nathan: "As the Lord lives, the man who does this is a man *deserving to be killed.*[2] 6. And he shall make recompense for the lamb four times over on account of the fact that he did this thing and because he had no pity." 7. And Nathan said to David: "You are the man. Thus said the Lord, the God of Israel: 'I anointed you *to be the king*[3] over Israel, and I saved you from the hand of Saul. 8. And I gave to you your master's house and your master's wives in your bosom, and I gave to you the house of Israel and Judah. And if this were small, then I would add for you like these and like these. 9. Why did you despise the word of the Lord to do what is evil *before me?*[4] Uriah the Hittite you *killed*[5] by the sword, and his wife you took to yourself for a wife, and him you killed by the sword of the sons of Ammon. 10. And now the sword will not cease from *the men of your house*[6] forever on account of the fact that you *rejected*[7] me and took the wife of Uriah the Hittite to be to you for a wife.' 11. Thus said the Lord: 'Behold I am raising up evil against you from your house, and I will take your wives before your eyes and will give (them) to your neighbor, and he will sleep with your wives in the sight of this sun. 12. For you acted in secret, and I will do this thing before all Israel and before the sun.'" 13. And David said to Nathan: "I have sinned *before*[8] the

Notes, Chapter Eleven (Cont.)

[13]MT: "devours."
[14]MT: "in the eyes of."

Notes, Chapter Twelve

[1]MT: "hot."
[2]MT: "a son of death."

[3]MT: "for king."
[4]MT: "in his eyes."
[5]MT: "struck down."
[6]MT: "your house."
[7]MT: "despised."
[8]MT: "against."

Lord." And Nathan said to David: "The Lord has also pardoned your sin. You will not die. 14. But because *you have indeed opened the mouth of the enemies of the people of the Lord*[9] by this thing, the son who is born to you will surely die." 15. And Nathan went to his house. And the Lord struck down the boy whom the wife of Uriah bore to David, and he became severely ill. 16. And David sought *mercy from before the Lord*[10] on behalf of the boy, and David fasted a fast and went and spent the night and slept on the ground. 17. And the elders of his house rose up against him to raise him up from the ground, and he was not willing and did not eat bread with them. 18. And on the seventh day the boy died, and David's servants were afraid to tell him that the boy died, for they said: "Behold while the boy was alive, we spoke with him and *he did not receive (word) from us.*[11] And how will we say to him: 'The boy is dead?' And he will do evil." 19. And David saw that his servants were whispering, and David understood that the boy was dead. And David said to his servants: "Is the boy dead?" And they said: "He is dead." 20. And David arose from the ground and washed and anointed himself and changed his clothes and entered the house of the Lord and did obeisance. And he came to his house, and he asked and they put out bread for him, and he ate. 21. And his servants said to him: "What is this thing that you have done? As long as the boy was alive, you fasted and wept. And when the boy died, you arose and ate bread." 22. And he said: "As long as the boy was alive, I fasted and wept, for I said: 'Who knows, *perhaps I will find mercy from before the Lord*[12] and the boy will live.' 23. And now he is dead. Why should I fast? Can I bring him back again? I will go unto him, and he is not returning unto me." 24. And David consoled Bathsheba his wife and entered unto her and slept with her. And she bore a son, and *she called*[13] his name Solomon, and the Lord loved him. 25. And he sent by the hand of Nathan the prophet, and he called his name Jedidiah on account of the Lord. 26. And Joab *waged battle*[14] on Rabbah of the sons of Ammon, and he conquered the city of the kingdom. 27. And Joab sent messengers unto David and said: "I have warred on Rabbah; also I have conquered the city of the *kingdom.*[15] 28. And now gather the rest of the people and encamp against the city and conquer it, lest I conquer the city and my name be called upon it." 29. And David gathered all the people and went to Rabbah and *waged battle*[16] on it and conquered it. 30. And he took the crown of their king from upon his head, and its weight was a talent of gold, and *in it was*[17] a precious stone. And it was on David's head. And he brought forth very many spoils of the city. 31. And he brought forth the people who were in it, and he set them at saws and at picks of iron and at axes of iron. And *he dragged them in the streets.*[18] And thus he would do to all the cities of the sons of Ammon. And David and all the people returned to Jerusalem.

Notes, Chapter Twelve (Cont.)

[9]MT: "you have utterly scorned the enemies of the Lord." Tg clarifies the obscurity of the MT.

[10]MT: "God."

[11]MT: "he did not hear our voice."

[12]MT: "the Lord will have mercy."

[13]MT: "he called."

[14]MT: "fought."

[15]MT: "waters."

[16]MT: "fought."

[17]MT lacks the phrase.

[18]MT: "he had them pass in the brick kilns." Tg substitutes a more usual form of punishment.

CHAPTER 13

1. And afterwards Absalom, son of David, had a beautiful sister and her name was Tamar. And Amnon, son of David, loved her. 2. And it distressed Amnon so that he fell sick on account of Tamar his sister, for she was a virgin and *it was concealed*[1] in the eyes of Amnon to do anything to her. 3. And Amnon had a friend, and his name was Jonadab, son of Shimeah, David's brother. And Jonadab was a very wise man. 4. And he said to him: "Why are you so bleak morning after morning, son of the king? Will you not tell me?" And Amnon said to him: "I love Tamar the sister of Absalom my brother." 5. And Jonadab said to him: "Lie down on your couch and fall sick. And your father will come to see you, and you will say to him: 'Let Tamar my sister come now and let her feed me bread and prepare the meal before my eyes, so that I may see and eat from her hand.'" 6. And Amnon lay down and fell sick. And the king came to see him, and Amnon said to the king: "Let Tamar my sister come now and cook up a couple of dumplings before my eyes, and I will eat from her hand." 7. And David sent unto Tamar, to the house, saying: "Go now *unto*[2] Amnon your brother, and prepare a meal for him." 8. And Tamar went to the house of Amnon her brother, and he was lying down. And she took the dough and kneaded and stirred before his eyes and boiled the dumplings. 9. And she took the pan and emptied before him, and *he was not willing*[3] to eat. And Amnon said: "Make everyone go from me." And everyone went forth from him. 10. And Amnon said to Tamar: "Bring the meal into the inner chamber, *the bedroom,*[4] and I will gain sustenance from your hand." And Tamar took the dumplings that she made and brought them in to Amnon her brother to the inner chamber, *the bedroom.*[5] 11. And she brought (them) near to him, *and he was not willing*[6] to eat. And he seized her and said to her: "Enter in, lie down with me, my sister." 12. And she said to him: "*Please,*[7] my brother, do not violate me, for it is not done this way in Israel. Do not do this disgraceful deed. 13. And as for me, where will I carry my shame, and you will be like one of the *fools*[8] in Israel? And now, speak now with the king, for he will not withhold me from you." 14. And he was not willing *to accept from her,*[9] and he seized her and violated her and lay with her. 15. And Amnon hated her with a very great hatred, for the hatred with which he hated her was greater than the love with which he loved her. And Amnon said to her: "Get up, go." 16. And she said to him: "On account of this very great evil, after what you did with me, *you say*[10] to send me away?"

Notes, Chapter Thirteen

[1] MT: "it seemed beyond his power."
[2] MT lacks the word; it has "the house of."
[3] MT: "he refused."
[4] MT lacks the word.
[5] MT lacks the word.
[6] MT lacks the word.
[7] MT: "No!"
[8] MT: "disgraceful men."
[9] MT: "to hear her voice."
[10] MT lacks the word.

And he was not willing *to accept from*[11] her. 17. And he called his young man who was serving him and said: "Now send that one outside away from my presence, and bolt the door after her." 18. And on her was the tunic with sleeves, for thus the virgin daughters of the king wore tunics. And his servant brought her forth outside and bolted the door after her. 19. And Tamar took ashes upon her head, and the tunic with sleeves that was on her she tore, and she placed her hand upon her head and was going about crying. 20. And Absalom her brother said to her: "Has your brother really been with you? And now my sister, be quiet. He is your brother. Do not set your heart on this matter." And Tamar dwelt *in silence*[12] at the house of Absalom her brother. 21. And king David heard all these matters, and it was very *hard*[13] for him. 22. And Absalom did not speak with Amnon for ill and for good, for Absalom hated Amnon on account of the fact that he violated Tamar his sister. 23. After two full years, Absalom had shearers in *the plain of Hazor,*[14] which is with *the house of Ephraim.*[15] And Absalom invited all the sons of the king. 24. And Absalom came *unto*[16] the king and said: "Behold now, your servant has shearers. May the king and his servants go now with your servant." 25. And the king said to Absalom: "No, my son. Not all of us will go now. And we will not burden you." And he pressed him, and he was not willing to go, and he blessed him. 26. And Absalom said: "If not, let Amnon my brother go now with us." And the king said: "Why will he go with you?" 27. And Absalom pressed him, and he sent with him Amnon and all the king's sons. 28. And Absalom commanded his young men, saying: "See now, when the heart of Amnon *is merry*[17] with wine, and I say to you: '*Kill Amnon,*' you will kill him.[18] Do not fear. Is it not because I commanded you? Be strong, and be warriors." 29. And the young men of Absalom did to Amnon as Absalom commanded. And all the king's sons arose, and each rode upon his mule, and they fled. 30. And while they were on the road, the report came *unto*[19] David, saying: "Absalom *killed*[20] all the king's sons, and not one of them is left." 31. And the king arose and tore his garments and lay upon the ground. And all his servants were standing by *while their garments were torn.*[21] 32. And Jonadab, son of Shimeah, the brother of David, answered and said: " Let not my master say that *they killed* [22] all the young men, the king's sons. *But*[23] Amnon alone is dead, for *in the heart of Absalom was something like this*[24] from the day that he violated Tamar his sister. 33. And now let not my master the king set upon his heart the word, saying: 'All the king's sons *have been killed.*'[25] *But*[26] Amnon alone is dead." 34. And Absalom fled. And the young man, the watchman, lifted up his eyes and saw. And behold many people were coming from the road, *from*[27]

Notes, Chapter Thirteen (Cont.)

[11]MT: "to hear."

[12]MT: "desolate."

[13]MT: "hot."

[14]MT: "Baal-hazor." Tg avoids the name "Baal."

[15]MT: "Ephraim."

[16]MT: "to."

[17]MT: "is good."

[18]MT: "'Strike down Amnon,' you will put him to death."

[19]MT: "to."

[20]MT: "struck down."

[21]MT: "torn of garments."

[22]MT: "they put to death."

[23]MT: "For."

[24]MT: "according to the mouth of Absalom this was determined."

[25]MT: "are dead."

[26]MT: "For."

[27]MT lacks the word.

behind him, from the side of the mountain. 35. And Jonadab said to the king: "Behold the king's sons have come. According to the word of your servant, so it was." 36. And as he finished speaking, behold the king's sons came and raised up their voice and wept. And the king and all his servants also wept a very great weeping. 37. And Absalom fled and went to Talmai, son of *Ammihud*,[28] king of Geshur. And he mourned over his son all the days. 38. And Absalom fled and went to Geshur. And he was there three years. 39. And *the spirit of David*[29] the king desired to go forth to Absalom, for he was consoled over Amnon because he was dead.

CHAPTER 14

1. And Joab, son of Zeruiah, knew that *it was in the heart of the king to go forth to Absalom.*[1] 2. And Joab sent to Tekoa and took from there a wise woman and said to her: "Be in mourning now and put on garments of mourning now, and do not pour on oil, and be like this woman in mourning for many days over a dead one. 3. And you will go unto the king and speak with him according to this word." And Joab placed the words in her mouth. 4. And *the woman who was from Tekoa*[2] spoke to the king and fell upon her face upon the ground and bowed down and said: "Help, O king." 5. And the king said to her: "What is your (problem)?" And she said: "In truth I am a widow woman, and my husband is dead. 6. And your handmaid had two sons. And the two of them quarreled with one another in the field, and there was no one who would save them. And one struck the other and *killed him.*[3] 7. And behold the whole family arose against your handmaid and said: 'Give over the one who *killed*[4] his brother, and *we will kill him because of the guilt of the life*[5] of his brother whom he killed, and we will also destroy the heir." And *they sought to kill the only one*[6] who was left in order not to make for my husband a name and a remnant on the face of the earth." 8. And the king said to the woman: "Go to your house, and I will make a command on your behalf." 9. And *the woman who was from Tekoa*[7] said to the king: "Upon me, *what is mine,*[8] my master the king, be the guilt, and upon my father's house. And may the king and *the throne of his kingdom*[9] be guiltless." 10. And the king said: "*Whoever is there who will speak to you a word*[10] and you will bring him unto me, he will not continue to harm you." 11. And she said: "Let the king remember now *what is written in the book of the*

Notes, Chapter Thirteen (Cont.)

[28] MT: "Ammihur," though many MT mss. and the ancient versions agree with Tg's reading.
[29] MT: "David."

Notes, Chapter Fourteen

[1] MT: "the heart of the king (was) unto Absalom."
[2] MT: "the Tekoan woman."
[3] MT: "put him to death."

[4] MT: "struck down."
[5] MT: "we will put him to death because of the life."
[6] MT: "they quenched my coal." Tg explains the metaphor.
[7] MT: "the Tekoan woman."
[8] MT lacks the phrase.
[9] MT: "his throne."
[10] MT: "whoever speaks to you."

law of the Lord your God so as not to enlarge the road before the avenger of blood to do harm.[11] And let them not destroy my son." And he said; "As the Lord lives, if there will fall from *the hair of the head of your son*[12] to the earth." 12. And the woman said: "Let your handmaid speak a word now *before*[13] my master the king. And he said: "Speak." 13. And the woman said: "And why have you planned like this against the people of *the Lord.*[14] And the king in speaking this word is like *a guilty man,*[15] inasmuch as the king does not bring back his exiled one. 14. For *the death of one dying, behold it is*[16] like waters that are poured out to the ground *that it is not possible for them that they be gathered up.*[17] *Thus it is not possible for judges of the truth to receive the mammon of falsehood, and he devises*[18] plans so as not to scatter from him an exile. 15. And now it is that I have come to speak *before*[19] the king my lord this word, for the people frightened me and your handmaid said: 'I will speak now *before*[20] the king. What if the king should do the word of his handmaid?' 16. For the king will hear so as to save his handmaid from the hand of the man (seeking) to destroy me and my son together from the heritage of *the people of the Lord.*[21] 17. And your handmaid said: 'The word of my master the king will be for comfort, for like the angel of *the Lord,*[22] so is my master the king to hear good and evil. *And the Memra of the Lord your God will at your aid.*'"[23] 18. And the king answered and said to the woman: "Now do not conceal from me the matter that I am asking you." And the woman said: "Let my master the king speak now." 19. And the king said: "Is the hand of Joab with you in all this?" And the woman answered and said: "By the life of your soul, my master the king, if *it is (possible) to turn to the right and to the left*[24] from everything that my master the king has said; for your servant Joab — he commanded me and he put in the mouth of your handmaid all these words. 20. In order to turn around the face of the matter, your servant Joab did this thing. And my master is wise according to the wisdom of the angel of *the Lord*[25] to know everything that is on earth." 21. And the king said to Joab: "Behold now I have done this thing. And go, bring back the young man Absalom." 22. And Joab fell upon his face *upon the ground*[26] and bowed down and blessed the king. And Joab said: "This day your servant knows that I have found favor in your eyes, my master and king, for the king has done the word of *your servant.*"[27] 23. And Joab arose and went to Geshur and brought Absalom to Jerusalem. 24. And the king said: "Let him return to his own house, and let him not see my face." And Absalom returned to his own house and did not see the face of the king. 25. And there was no man as handsome in all Israel as Absalom to praise exceedingly. From the sole of his foot and

Notes, Chapter Fourteen (Cont.)

[11] MT: "the Lord your God, so that the avenger of blood not slay many more." Tg seems to refer to the cities of refuge (Num 35:9-34; Deut 19:1-13) and to later legislation which checked blood vengeance, e.g., *m. Makkot* 2; *b. Makkot* 7a-13a.

[12] MT: "the hair of your son."

[13] MT: "to."

[14] MT: "God."

[15] MT: "a guilty one."

[16] MT: "indeed we die, and we are like."

[17] MT: "that are not gathered up."

[18] MT: "And God will not take away a life, and he devised." The sense of Tg is unclear.

[19] MT: "to."

[20] MT: "to."

[21] MT: "God."

[22] MT: "God."

[23] MT: "And the Lord your God will be with you."

[24] MT: "it is to go right and to go left."

[25] MT: "God."

[26] MT: "to the ground."

[27] MT: "his servant," though many MT mss. also have "your servant."

to his crown there was no blemish in him. 26. And when he cut the hair of his head
—and it was at the end of the year that he was cutting it; for it was heavy upon him,
and he was cutting it — and he was weighing the hair of his head, two hundred *selas*[28]
by the *weight*[29] of the king. 27. And there were born to Absalom three sons and one
daughter, and her name was Tamar. She was a beautiful woman in appearance. 28.
And Absalom lived in Jerusalem two years and did not see the face of the king. 29. And
Absalom sent unto Joab to send him unto the king. And he was not willing to come
unto him. And he sent once more a second time, and he was not willing to come. 30.
And he said to his servants: "See Joab's field that is close to mine, and there he has
barley. Go and set it on fire." And Absalom's servants set the field on fire. 31. And Joab
arose and came unto Absalom to the house, and said to him: "Why have your servants
set the field that is mine on fire?" 32. And Absalom said to Joab: "Behold, I have sent
unto you, saying: 'Come here, and I will send you unto the king, saying: "Why have I
come from Geshur? It would be better that I still be there." And now let me see the face
of the king. And if there be guilt in me, let him *kill me*.'"[30] 33. And Joab came unto the
king and told him. And he called Absalom, and he came unto the king and bowed to
him upon his face upon the ground before the king. And the king kissed Absalom.

CHAPTER 15

1. And after this Absalom made for himself chariots and horses and fifty men
running before him. 2. And Absalom used to get up early and stand *by the ascent of*[1]
the road of the gateway. And every man who had a judgment to bring in before the
king *to judge*,[2] Absalom was calling him and said: "From what town are you?" And he
said: "Your servant is from one of the tribes of Israel." 3. And Absalom said to him:
"See, your affairs are good and fitting. But there is no one to hear you *from before*[3] the
king." 4. And Absalom said: "Who will *appoint me*[4] judge in the land? And *before me*[5]
every man who has *a judgment or a quarrel*[6] will come, and *I will judge him in truth*."[7]
5. And whenever any man drew near to bow to him, he reached out his hand and took
hold of him and kissed him. 6. And Absalom acted in this way for all Israel who were
coming *to make judgment before*[8] the king. And Absalom was stealing the heart of the
men of Israel. 7. And at the end of forty[9] years Absalom said to the king: "Let me go
now and fulfill my vow that I vowed *before*[10] the Lord in Hebron, 8. for your servant

Notes, Chapter Fourteen (Cont.)

[28] MT: "shekels."
[29] MT: "stone."
[30] MT: "put me to death."

Notes, Chapter Fifteen

[1] MT: "beside."
[2] MT: "for judgment."

[3] MT: "from with."
[4] MT: "make me."
[5] MT: "unto me."
[6] MT: "a suit or a legal case."
[7] MT: "I will give him justice."
[8] MT: "for judgment to."
[9] Tg follows the (incorrect) reading of the MT.
Other ancient versions read "four."
[10] MT: "to."

vowed a vow when I was living in Geshur in Aram, saying: 'If indeed the Lord will bring me back to Jerusalem, I will worship *before*[11] the Lord.'" 9. And the king said to him: "Go in peace." And he arose and went to Hebron. 10. And Absalom sent spies among all the tribes of Israel, saying: "When you hear the sound of the trumpet, you will say: 'Absalom reigns in Hebron.'" 11. And with Absalom there went two hundred men summoned from Jerusalem, and they were going in their simplicity and did not know anything at all. 12. And Absalom sent Ahithophel the Gilonite, the counsellor of David, from his city, from Gilo, when he was sacrificing the sacrifices. And the *rebellion*[12] was strong, and the people with Absalom kept increasing. 13. And there came one who was telling unto David, saying: "The heart of the men of Israel *has turned*[13] after Absalom." 14. And David said to all his servants who were with him in Jerusalem: "Arise and let us flee, for there will be no escape for us from before Absalom. Hurry to go, lest he hurry and overtake us and conceal against us the evil and strike the city by the edge of the sword." 15. And the servants of the king said to the king: "According to everything that my master the king *says*,[14] behold your servants (will do)." 16. And the king went forth, and *all the men of his house were with him;* [15] and the king left ten women, concubines, to keep the house. 17. And the king went forth, and all the people *who were with him*.[16] And they stood in a *distant place*.[17] 18. And all his servants were passing beneath his hand, and *all the archers and all the slingers*[18] and all the Gittites — six hundred men who came *with him*[19] from Gath — were passing before the king. 19. And the king said to Ittai the Gittite: "Why do you also go with us? Return and live with the king, for you are a foreigner. *And if you are an exile, go to your own place*.[20] 20. Yesterday you came, and today shall I make you wander to go with us? And I am going *to the place that I know not where I am going*.[21] Return, and bring your brothers back with you, *and do goodness and truth with them*."[22] 21. And Ittai answered the king and said: "As the Lord lives and by the life of my master the king, in the place where my master the king is — whether for death or for life, there your servant will be." 22. And David said to Ittai: "Go, pass on." And Ittai the Gittite passed on, and all his men and all the children who were with him. 23. *All the inhabitants of the land*[23] were weeping in a loud voice, and all the people were passing on, and the king passed on in the brook of Kidron, and all the people were passing over the face of the road *in*[24] the wilderness. 24. And behold also Zadok and all the Levites with him were carrying the ark of the covenant of *the Lord*.[25] And they set down the ark of *the Lord*,[26] and Abiathar went up, until all the people had finished passing from the city. 25. And the king said to Zadok: "Bring the ark of *the Lord*[27] back to the city. If I find favor *before*[28] the Lord, he will bring me back and *make me see before him, and I will worship before him in his sanctuary*.[29] 26. And if thus he will say: '*There is no pleasure before me in*

Notes, Chapter Fifteen (Cont.)

[11]MT lacks the preposition.
[12]MT: "conspiracy."
[13]MT: "is."
[14]MT lacks the word.
[15]MT: "all his household on foot."
[16]MT: "on foot."
[17]MT: "house of the distance."
[18]MT: "all the Cherethites and all the Pelethites."
[19]MT: "on foot."

[20]MT: "and also an exile to your home."
[21]MT: "to where I am going."
[22]MT: "goodness and truth."
[23]MT: "All the land."
[24]MT lacks the preposition.
[25]MT: "God."
[26]MT: "God."
[27]MT: "God."
[28]MT: "in the eyes of."
[29]MT: "and show me himself and his dwelling."

you,'[30] behold here I am. Let him do to me as it is good *before him.*"[31] 27. And the king said to Zadok the priest-seer: "You return to the city in peace, and Ahimaaz your son and Jonathan, son of Abiathar, your two sons with you. 28. See that I am delaying in the plains of the wilderness until the word will arrive from you to inform me." 29. And Zadok and Abiathar brought the ark of *the Lord*[32] back to Jerusalem, and they lived there. 30. And David went up by *the ascent of the Mount of Olives,*[33] going up and weeping, and his head was covered. And he was going up *and*[34] barefoot, and all the people who were with him were covered each man as to his head, and they were going up and weeping as they went. 31. And *it was told to David,*[35] saying: "Ahithophel is among the *rebels*[36] with Absalom." And David said: "Now ruin the counsel of Ahithophel, O Lord." 32. And David came unto the top *of the mount*[37] where one bows *before the Lord,*[38] and behold Hushai the Archite came to meet him with his garment torn and dust *cast*[39] on his head. 33. And David said to him: "If you pass on with me, you will be a burden on me. 34. And if you return to the city and say to Absalom, 'I will be your servant, O king. As I was the servant of your father from them, and now I will be your servant,' you will ruin for me the counsel of Ahithophel. 35. And are not Zadok and Abiathar the priests there with you? And every word that you will hear from the house of the king, you will tell Zadok and Abiathar the priests. 36. And behold there with them are their two sons, Ahimaaz for Zadok and Jonathan for Abiathar. And you will send by their hand unto me everything that you hear." 37. And Hushai, the friend of David, came to the city, and Absalom came to Jerusalem.

CHAPTER 16

1. And David passed on a little from the top *of the mountain,*[1] and behold Ziba the young man of Mephibosheth met him. And there was a pair of saddled asses, and on them were *two hundred loaves of bread and one hundred bunches of dried grapes and one hundred portions of figs*[2] and a skin of wine. 2. And the king said to Ziba: "What are these to you?" And Ziba said: "The asses are for the household of the king to ride, and the bread and *the figs*[3] for the young men to eat, and the wine for those grown weak in the wilderness to drink." 3. And the king said: "And where is the son of your master?" And Ziba said to the king: "Behold he is living in Jerusalem, for he said: 'Today the house of Israel will restore to me the kingdom of my father.'" 4. And the king said to Ziba: "Behold everything that belongs to Mephibosheth is yours." And

Notes, Chapter Fifteen (Cont.)

[30]MT: "I have no pleasure in you."
[31]MT: "in his eyes."
[32]MT: "God."
[33]MT: "the ascent of the Olives."
[34]MT lacks the word.
[35]MT: "David told."
[36]MT: "conspirators."

[37]MT lacks the phrase.
[38]MT: "to God."
[39]MT lacks the word.

Notes, Chapter Sixteen

[1]MT lacks the word.
[2]MT: "two hundred bread and one hundred raisins and one hundred summer fruit."
[3]MT: "summer fruit."

Ziba said: "*I am giving thanks*,[4] may I find favor in your eyes, my master the king." 5. And King David came unto *'Almath*.[5] And behold from there a man from the clan of the house of Saul came forth, and his name was Shimei, son of Gera. And he came along cursing as he went. 6. And he was pelting with stones David and all the servants of king David. And all the people and all the warriors were on his right and on his left. 7. And thus Shimei said when he was cursing him: "Go forth, go forth, you *man guilty of killing and you evil man*.[6] 8. The Lord has brought back upon you all *the sins*[7] of the house of Saul in whose place you reigned. And the Lord *has passed*[8] the kingdom over in the hand of Absalom your son. And behold you are in your evil, for you are *a man guilty of killing*."[9] 9. And Abishai, son of Zeruiah, said to the king: "Why shall this dead dog curse my master the king? Let me pass over now and take off his head." 10. And the king said: "What is it to me and to you, sons of Zeruiah? Thus he curses because the Lord said to him: 'Curse David.' And who will say: 'Why have you done so?'" 11. And David said to Abishai and to all his servants: "Behold my son *whom I have begotten is seeking to kill me*,[10] and also now *the son of the tribe of Benjamin*.[11] Leave him alone and let him curse, for the Lord has told him. 12. *What if the tear of my eye is revealed before the Lord*,[12] and the Lord will repay to me good in place of his curse today?" 13. And David and his men went on the way. And Shimei was going by the side of the mountain opposite him, going and cursing and pelting with stones opposite him and throwing dust. 14. And the king and all the people who were with him came, when they were weary, and he *rested*[13] there. 15. And Absalom and all the people, the men of Israel, came to Jerusalem. And Ahithophel was with him. 16. And when Hushai the Archite, the friend of David, came unto Absalom, Hushai said to Absalom: "May the king *prosper!*[14] May the king *prosper!*"[14] 17. And Absalom said to Hushai: "Is this your goodness that is with your friend? Why did you not go with your friend?" 18. And Hushai said to Absalom: "No, but he whom the Lord and this people and all the men of Israel have chosen, his I will be and I will dwell with him. 19. And again *before*[15] whom will I serve? Shall it not be before his son? As I served before your father, so *I will be serving*[16] before you." 20. And Absalom said to Ahithophel: "Give your counsel. What shall we do?" 21. And Ahithophel said to Absalom: "Go into the concubines of your father whom he left to keep the house, and all Israel will hear that *you have let yourself loose against*[17] your father and the hands of all those who are with you will be strong." 22. And they set up *a curtained couch*[18] on the roof, and Absalom went into the concubines of his father in the eyes of all Israel. 23. And the counsel of Ahithophel that he counseled in those days was as if a man sought the word of *the Lord*.[19] So was all the counsel of Ahithophel, both for David and for Absalom.

Notes, Chapter Sixteen (Cont.)

[4]MT: "I do obeisance."

[5]MT: "Bahurim." The Aramaic and the Hebrew words reflect the root for "youth."

[6]MT: "man of blood and man of Belial."

[7]MT: "blood." MT accuses David of the blood of Saul. Tg changes it to the sins of the house of Saul. S-A, 6.

[8]MT: "has given."

[9]MT: "a man of blood."

[10]MT: "who came forth from my loins is seeking my life."

[11]MT: "the Benjaminite."

[12]MT: "perhaps the Lord will see my affliction."

[13]MT: "refreshed himself."

[14]MT: "live."

[15]MT: "to."

[16]MT: "I will be."

[17]MT: "you have made yourself hateful with."

[18]MT: "tent."

[19]MT: "God."

CHAPTER 17

1. And Ahithophel said to Absalom: "Let me choose now twelve thousand men, and I will arise and pursue after David by night. 2. And I will come upon him while he is weary and his hands are weakened. And I will panic him, and all the people that are with him will flee, and I will *kill*[1] the king alone. 3. And I will bring back all the people unto you. *All of them will return after the man whom you seek will be killed.*[2] All the people will be at peace." 4. And the word was pleasing in the eyes of Absalom and in the eyes of all the elders of Israel. 5. And Absalom said: "Call now to Hushai the Archite also, and let us hear *what he too will say.*"[3] 6. And Hushai came unto Absalom, and Absalom said to him, saying: "According to this word Ahithophel spoke. Shall we do his word? If not, you speak *what is pleasing in your eyes.*"[4] 7. And Hushai said to Absalom: "The counsel that Ahithophel has counselled in this time is not good." 8. And Hushai said: "You know your father and his men, that they are warriors and bitter of soul, like a bear bereft in the field. And your father is a *man waging battles,*[5] and he will not spend the night with the people. 9. Behold now he is hidden in one of the pits or in one of the places. And when he falls on them at first, whoever hears will hear and say: 'There has been a slaughter among the people that are after Absalom.' 10. And even the man who is a warrior, whose heart is like the heart of the lion, will indeed melt; for all Israel knows your father is a warrior and *the men who are with him are warriors.*[6] 11. Thus I counsel: Let there be gathered to you all Israel from Dan and to Beer-sheba like the sand which is on the sea for greatness, and *you will be going at our head.*[7] 12. And we will come upon him in one of the places where he will be found, and we will encamp against him as the dew *encamps*[8] upon the ground. And we will not leave in him and in all the men who are with him even one. 13. And if to the city he be gathered, all Israel *will be gathered against that city and armies will encircle it. And we will root out it and its stones and cast it into the valley until we will not leave there a stone.*"[9] 14. And Absalom and all the men of Israel said: "The counsel of Hushai the Arkite is better than the counsel of Ahithophel." And the Lord ordained to ruin the good counsel of Ahithophel, so that the Lord might bring evil upon Absalom. 15. And Hushai said to Zadok and to Abiathar the priests: "Thus and so Ahithophel counselled Absalom and the elders of Israel, and thus and so I counselled. 16. And now send quickly and tell David, saying: 'You shall not lodge by night in the plains of the wilderness. And by all

Notes, Chapter Seventeen

[1]MT: "strike down."

[2]MT: "like the return of the whole (is) the man whom you seek."

[3]MT: "what is in his mouth too."

[4]MT lacks the phrase.

[5]MT: "a man of war."

[6]MT: "warriors are with him."

[7]MT: "your face (=person) going in battle."

[8]MT: "falls."

[9]MT: "will bring to that city ropes and we will drag it to the valley until not even a pebble is found there." Tg uses more conventional siege language.

means pass over; *perhaps it will be pleasing to*[10] the king and all the people who are with him.'" 17. And Jonathan and Ahimaaz were standing at *the Fuller's Spring,*[11] and a maid went and told them. And they would go and tell King David, for they could not be seen entering the city. 18. And the young man saw them and told Absalom. And the two of them went quickly and entered the house of the man in *'Almath,*[12] and he had a *pit*[13] in his courtyard, and they went down there. 19. And the woman took and spread a covering over the mouth of the well, and sprinkled over it some twigs, and the matter was not known. 20. And the servants of Absalom came unto the woman to the house, and they said: "Where are Ahimaaz and Jonathan?" And the woman said to them: "They have already crossed *the Jordan.*"[14] And they sought and did not find, and they returned to Jerusalem. 21. And after their going, they came up from the *pit*[15] and went and told King David and said to David: "Arise and cross over *the Jordan*[16] quickly, for thus Ahithophel has counselled against you." 22. And David and all the people who were with him arose and crossed over the Jordan. By daybreak there was no one left who had not crossed the Jordan. 23. And Ahithophel saw that his counsel was not *prevailing,*[17] and he saddled the ass and arose and went to his house to his city. And he gave orders to *the men of his house,*[18] and he hanged himself and died, and he was buried in the tomb of his father. 24. And David came to Mahanaim, and Absalom crossed the Jordan, he and all the men of Israel with him. 25. And Absalom placed Amasa in place of Joab over the army. And Amasa was the son of the man whose name was Ithra the Israelite, who had entered unto Abigail, the daughter of Nahash, the sister of Zeruiah, Joab's mother. 26. And Israel and Absalom camped *in*[19] the land of Gilead. 27. And when David came to Mahanaim, Shobi the son of Nahash from Rabbah of the sons of Ammon, and Machir the son of Ammiel from Lo-debar, and Barzilai the Gileadite from Rogelim 28. brought *cushions*[20] and bowls and vessels of *clay*[21] and wheat and barley and flour and parched grain and beans and lentils and parched grain 29. and honey and cream and sheep and *cheeses of the milk*[22] of cattle to David and to the people who were with him to eat, for they said: "The people are hungry and weary and thirsty in the wilderness."

CHAPTER 18

1. And David mustered the people who were with him, and he appointed over them officers of thousands and officers of hundreds. 2. And David sent out the people — one third under the hand of Joab; and one third under the hand of Abishai, the son of

Notes, Chapter Seventeen (Cont.)

[10]MT: "lest he be swallowed up."

[11]The Aramaic is a translation of the place name "En-rogel." See Josh 15:7; 1 Kgs 1:9.

[12]The Aramaic is a translation of the MT "Bahurim" (=youth).

[13]MT: "well."

[14]MT: "brook of water."

[15]MT: "well."

[16]MT: "the waters."

[17]MT: "being done."

[18]MT: "his house."

[19]MT lacks the preposition.

[20]MT: "a bed."

[21]MT: "a potter."

[22]The MT word is obscure, but must mean "cheese" or "cream."

Zeruiah, the brother of Joab; and one third under the hand of Ittai the Gittite. And the king said to the people: "I too will indeed go forth with you." 3. And the people said: "You shall not go forth, for if indeed we flee, they will not pay attention to us; and if half of us be killed, they will not pay attention to us. *For you are able to help ten-thousand like us,*[1] and now it is good that *you pray*[2] for us from the city for help." 4. And the king said to them: "Whatever is good in your eyes, I will do." And the king stood *on the ascent of the road of the gateway,*[3] and all the people came forth by hundreds and by thousands. 5. And the king ordered Joab and Abishai and Ittai, saying: "*Take heed*[4] for me with the young man, with Absalom." And all the people heard when the king ordered all the officers concerning the matter of Absalom. 6. And the people went forth to the field to meet Israel, and the battle was in the forest of *the house of Ephraim.*[5] 7. And the people of Israel were shattered there before the servants of David. And there was a great slaughter there on that day, twenty thousand. 8. And *the wagers of battle*[6] there were scattered over the face of all the land. And *the beast of the forest killed*[7] more among the people than the sword *killed*[8] on that day. 9. And Absalom happened to come before the servants of David. And Absalom was riding upon a mule, and the mule went in under the branches of a great terebinth. And his head was caught in the terebinth, and *he was suspended*[9] between the heavens and the earth. And the mule that was beneath him passed on. 10. And a certain man saw and told Joab and said: "Behold I have seen Absalom suspended in the terebinth." 11. And Joab said to the man who was telling him: "And behold you saw, and why did you not strike him down there *and throw him down*[10] to the ground? And I *would*[11] have given to you ten selas of silver and one belt." 12. And the man said to Joab: "Even if I *were weighted down*[12] upon my hand with a thousand selas of silver, I would not *stretch out*[13] my hand against the son of the king, for *before us*[14] the king ordered you and Abishai and Ittai, saying: 'Take heed for me with the young man, with Absalom.' 13. Otherwise I would have done treachery against my own life — and nothing is hidden from the king — and you would have set yourself on the opposite side." 14. And Joab said: "Not so will I waste time before you." And he took three staffs in his hand and stuck them in the heart of Absalom while he was still alive *in the midst*[15] of the terebinth. 15. And ten young men, Joab's armor-bearers, surrounded and struck Absalom and *killed him.*[16] 16. And Joab blew on the trumpet, and the people turned from pursuing after Israel, for Joab restrained the people. 17. And they took Absalom and threw him in the forest, *in the midst*[17] of the great pit; and they heaped up over him a very great pile of stones. And all Israel fled, each man to his *city.*[18] 18. And Absalom took and erected for himself while he was still alive the pillar that is in the plain of the

Notes, Chapter Eighteen

[1] MT: "For now there are ten-thousand like us."

[2] MT: "you be." Tg sees David as an interessor in prayer rather than one who supplied military help.

[3] MT: "beside the gate."

[4] MT: "Be gentle."

[5] MT: "Ephraim."

[6] MT: "the battle."

[7] MT: "the forest devoured." Tg inserts a beast as subject of the verb "devour."

[8] MT: "devoured."

[9] MT: "he was put."

[10] MT lacks the phrase.

[11] The Aramaic supplies a word not in the Hebrew.

[12] MT: "were weighing out."

[13] MT: "send forth."

[14] MT: "in our ears."

[15] MT: "in the heart."

[16] MT: "put him to death."

[17] MT: "to."

[18] MT: "tent."

king, for he said: "I have no son alive so as to keep my name remembered." And he called the pillar according to his own name, and it is called the "*place*[19] of Absalom" unto this day. 19. And Ahimaaz the son of Zadok said: "Let me run now and announce the news to the king, for the Lord *has taken vengeance for him*[20] from the hand of his enemies." 20. And Joab said to him: "*You are not the right man to announce the news*[21] this day. And you will announce the news on another day. And this day you will not announce *anything, only that*[22] the king's son is dead." 21. And Joab said to the Cushite: "Go, tell to the king what you saw." And the Cushite bowed to Joab and ran. 22. And Ahimaaz the son of Zadok continued on and said to Joab: "And come what may, let me run now after the Cushite." And Joab said: "Why are you running, my son? And no good news *is being given*[23] to you." 23. "And come what may, let me run." And he said to him: "Run." And Ahimaaz ran by the way of the plain and *arrived before*[24] the Cushite. 24. And David was sitting between the two gates. And the watchman was walking upon the roof of the gate upon the wall, and he lifted up his eyes and saw, and behold the man was running by himself. 25. And the watchman called out and told the king. And the king said: "If he is by himself, there is news in his mouth." And he kept coming and drew near. 26. And the watchman saw another man running, and the watchman called to the gatekeeper and said: "Behold the man is running by himself." And the king said: "This one too brings news." 27. And the watchman said: "I see the running of the first one like the running of Ahimaaz the son of Zadok." And the king said: "This is a good man, and *also*[25] good news he will bring." 28. And Ahimaaz called out and said to the king: "Peace." And he bowed down to the king upon his face upon the ground, and he said: "Blessed is the Lord your God who handed over the men who raised their hand against my master the king." 29. And the king said: "Is there peace to the young man, to Absalom?" And Ahimaaz said: "I saw a great crowd *after the king's servant Joab sent your servant,*[26] and I do not know what it was." 30. And the king said: "Turn aside, stand here." And he turned aside and stood. 31. And behold the Cushite came, and the Cushite said: "May my master the king receive the good news, for the Lord *has taken vengeance for you*[27] this day from the hand of all *who have risen up*[28] against you." 32. And the king said to the Cushite: "Is there peace to the young man, to Absalom?" And the Cushite said: "May the enemies of my master the king and all who have risen up against you for evil be like the young man."

Notes, Chapter Eighteen (Cont.)

[19]MT: "monument."
[20]MT: "has judged him."
[21]MT: "You are not to announce."
[22]MT: "because."
[23]MT: "finding."
[24]MT: "passed."

[25]MT: "to" (*'l*) rather than "also" (*'p*).
[26]MT: "to send the servant of the king Joab and your servant."
[27]MT: "has judged you."
[28]MT: "who were rising up."

CHAPTER 19

1. And the king was agitated and went up to the upper chamber of the gate and wept. And thus he said when he was going: "My son, Absalom; my son, my son, Absalom. *Would that I died in place of you, and you were alive this day!*[1] Absalom, my son, my son." 2. And it was told to Joab: "Behold the king is weeping and mourning over Absalom." 3. And in that day the victory was (turned) to mourning for all the people, for the people heard in that day, saying: "The king is grieving over his son." 4. And the people stole away to enter into the city on that day as people steal away *and are ashamed*[2] in their fleeing in battle. 5. And the king covered his face, and the king cried in a loud voice: "My son, Absalom. Absalom, my son, my son." 6. And Joab came unto the king to the house and said: "You have shamed this day the faces of all your servants who have saved your life this day and the life of your sons and your daughters and the life of your wives and the life of your concubines, 7. to love those who hate you and to hate those who love you. For you have made clear this day, that officers and servants are nothing to you, for I know this day that if Absalom were alive and all of us *were killed*[3] this day, it would thus be right in your eyes. 8. And now arise, go forth, and speak to the heart of your servants for by *the Memra of the Lord*[4] I swear that, if you do not go forth, no man will lodge with you in the night. And this evil will be worse for you than all the evil that has come upon you from your youth until now." 9. And the king arose and sat at the gate, and *it was told*[5] to all the people saying: "Behold the king is sitting at the gate." And all the people came before the king. And Israel fled, each man to his *city.*[6] 10. And all the people were arguing in all the tribes of Israel, saying: "The king saved us from the *hand*[7] of our enemies, and he delivered us from the *hand*[8] of the Philistines. And now he has fled from the land from the presence of Absalom. 11. And Absalom whom we anointed over us is dead in battle. And now why are you silent to bring back the king?" 12. And King David sent to Zadok and to Abiathar the priests, saying: "Speak *with*[9] the elders of Judah, saying: 'Why are you the last to bring back the king to his house, and the word of all Israel has come unto the king to his house? 13. You are my brothers, you are my bone and my flesh. And why are you the last to bring back the king?' 14. And to Amasa you will say: 'Are you not my bone and my flesh? May *the Lord*[10] do thus to me and more, if you shall not be chief of the army before me all the days in place of Joab.'" 15. And the heart of all the men of Judah *was turned*[11] as

Notes, Chapter Nineteen

[1]MT: "Who will give my death, I in place of you?"

[2]MT: "ashamed."

[3]MT: "were dead."

[4]MT: "the Lord."

[5]MT: "they told."

[6]MT: "tents."

[7]MT: "palm."

[8]MT: "palm."

[9]MT: "to."

[10]MT: "God."

[11]MT: "he turned."

one man, and they sent to the king: "Return, you and all your servants." 16. And the king returned and came to the Jordan. And *those of the house of Judah*[12] came to Gilgal to go meet the king, to bring the king across the Jordan. 17. And Shimei the son of Gera the son of *the tribe of Benjamin*[13] who was from *'Almath*[14] made haste and went down with the men of Judah to meet King David. 18. And a thousand men from *the tribe of the house of Benjamin*[15] were with him. And Ziba, the young man of Saul's house, and his fifteen sons and his twenty servants with him, and *they crossed*[16] the Jordan before the king. 19. And *they crossed*[17] the ford to bring over the household of the king and to do what was good in his eyes. And Shimei the son of Gera fell before the king when he was passing in the Jordan. 20. And he said to the king: "May my master not hold against me the guilt *that is mine.*[18] And may you not remember that your servant was offensive on the day when my master the king *was exiled*[19] from Jerusalem for the king to place it upon his heart. 21. For your servant knows that I have sinned. And behold I have come this day first for all the house of Joseph to come down to meet my master the king. 22. And Abishai the son of Zeruiah answered and said: "Shall not Shimei *be killed*[20] on account of this, because he cursed the anointed of the Lord?" 23. And David said: "What is it to me and to you, sons of Zeruiah, that you should be to me this day for an adversary? Shall a man *be killed*[21] in Israel this day? For do I not know that this day I am the king over Israel?" 24. And the king said to Shimei: "You shall not die." And the king swore to him. 25. And Mephiboseth the son of Saul went down to meet the king. And he had not *washed*[22] his feet nor *shaved*[23] his upper lip nor whitened his garments from the day *that the king was exiled*[24] until the day that he came in peace. 26. And when he came to Jerusalem to meet the king, the king said to him: "Why did you not go with me, Mephiboseth?" 27. And he said: "My master the king, my servant deceived me, for your servant said: 'I will saddle an ass for myself and ride upon it and go with the king, for your servant is lame.' 28. *And he spoke against your servant words that are not fitting before*[25] my master the king. And my master the king *is wise like the angel of the Lord.*[26] And do what is good in your eyes. 29. For all the house of my father were nothing but *men guilty of killing*[27] to my master the king. And you set your servant among those eating at your table. And what right is there still to complain still *before*[28] the king?" 30. And the king said to him: "Why are you still speaking your words? I have spoken. You and Ziba will divide the property." 31. And Mephibosheth said to the king: "Even let him take all, since my master the king has come in peace to his house." 32. And Barzilai the Gileadite went down from Rogelim and crossed the Jordan with the king, *to escort*[29] him over the Jordan. 33. And Barzilai was very old, a man of eighty years;

Notes, Chapter Nineteen (Cont.)

[12]MT: "Judah."

[13]MT: "Benjaminite."

[14]The Aramaic translated the MT place name "Bahurim" (=youth).

[15]MT: "Benjamin."

[16]MT: "they rushed (to)."

[17]MT: "the ford crossed."

[18]MT lacks the phrase.

[19]MT: "went forth."

[20]MT: "be put to death."

[21]MT: "be put to death."

[22]MT: "done."

[23]MT: "done."

[24]MT: "of the king's going."

[25]MT: "And he slandered your servant too."

[26]MT: "is like the angel of God." Tg tones down the simile.

[27]MT: "men of death."

[28]MT: "to."

[29]MT: "to send off."

and he provided for the king when he was dwelling in Mahanaim, for he was a very great man. 34. And the king said to Barzilai: "You cross over with me, and I will provide for you with me in Jerusalem." 35. And Barzilai said to the king: "How many days of years of my life are there that I should go up with the king to Jerusalem? 36. I am eighty years old this day. Do I know between good and bad? Can your servant taste what I eat and what I drink? Can I still hear the sound of *lutes and songs?*[30] And why should your servant still be a burden *upon*[31] my master the king? 37. A little way your servant will cross over the Jordan with the king. And why will the king repay me this payment? 38. And let your servant return now, and I will die in my city *and I will be buried in the tomb*[32] of my father and my mother. And behold your servant Chimham will cross over with my master the king. And do for him whatever is good in your eyes." 39. And the king said: "Chimham will cross over with me, and I will do for him whatever is good in your eyes. And everything that *you ask from me,*[33] I will do for you." 40. And all the people crossed the Jordan, and the king crossed. And king kissed Barzilai and blessed him, and he returned to his place. 41. And the king crossed over to Gilgal, and Chimham crossed with him. And all the people of the house of Judah brought the king across, and also half of the people of Israel. 42. And behold all the men of Israel were coming unto the king, and they said to the king: "Why have our brothers, the men of Judah, *hidden you away from us*[34] and brought the king and *the men of his house*[35] across the Jordan, and all the men of David with him?" 43. And all the men of Judah answered the men of Israel: "Because the king is closer to me *than to you.*[36] And why are you angry about this matter? Did we ever eat from *the property of the king?*[37] Did he *portion out*[38] any gift to us?" 44. And the men of Israel answered the men of Judah and said: "There are ten shares for me in the king, and also in David *I delight*[39] more than you. And why did you despise me? And was not my word first for me to bring back my king?" And the word of the men of Judah was *stronger*[40] than the word of the men of Israel.

CHAPTER 20

1. And there happened to be there *a wicked man,*[1] and his name was Sheba the son of Bichri, *a man from the tribe of the house of Benjamin.*[2] And he blew on the trumpet and said: "There is no portion for us in David and no inheritance for us in the son of

Notes, Chapter Nineteen (Cont.)

[30]MT: "men singers and women singers." Tg changes to the more innocuous musical instruments.
[31]MT: "to."
[32]MT: "with the tomb."
[33]MT: "you choose for me."
[34]MT: "stolen you away."
[35]MT: "his house."
[36]MT lacks the phrase.

[37]MT: "the king."
[38]MT: "lift up."
[39]MT lacks the word.
[40]MT: "harder."

Notes, Chapter Twenty

[1]MT: "a man of Belial."
[2]MT: "a Benjaminite."

Jesse; each man to his own *city*,[3] Israel." 2. And all the men of Israel *withdrew*[4] from after David to go after Sheba the son of Bichri. And the men of Judah joined with their king from the Jordan and unto Jerusalem. 3. And David came to his house to Jerusalem. And the king took the ten **women** concubines whom he left to keep the house, and assigned them a house **under guard**. And *provision was made for them*.[5] And he did not go unto them. And they were guarded, *and they were called until the day of their death "widows whose husband was alive."*[6] 4. And the king said to Amasa: "*Gather before*[7] me the men of Judah (in) three days, and you stand here." 5. And Amasa went to gather *those of the house of Judah*,[8] and he delayed beyond the time that he *said for him*.[9] 6. And David said to Abishai: "Now lest Sheba the son of Bichri do more evil to us than Absalom, you take the servants of your master and pursue after him, lest he find for himself fortified cities and *cause us trouble*."[10] 7. And there went forth after him the men of Joab and *the archers and the slingers*[11] and all the warriors. And they went forth from Jerusalem to pursue after Sheba the son of Bichri. 8. They were at the great stone which is in Gibeon. And Amasa came before them. And Joab was *bound up, girded as to his clothing*,[12] and upon him was the belt of the sword girded upon his loins in its sheath. And *he went and walked heavily*.[13] 9. And Joab said to Amasa: "Are you well, my brother?" And the right hand of Joab took hold of the beard of Amasa to kiss him. 10. And Amasa did not heed the sword that was in Joab's hand. And he struck him with it *in the side of his thigh*[14] and poured out his bowels to the ground. And he did not do it a second time to him. And he died. And Joab and Abishai his brother pursued after Sheba the son of Bichri. 11. And a man from the young men of Joab was standing over him, and said: "Whoever is there who favors Joab and whoever is there who is for David, *let him come*[15] after Joab." 12. And Amasa was wallowing in blood in the middle of the highway. And the man saw that all the people stopped, and he moved Amasa from the highway to the field and threw over him a garment, since everyone who came upon him saw and stopped. 13. When *he took him aside*[16] from the highway, every man crossed over after Joab to pursue after Sheba the son of Bichri. 14. And he passed through all the tribes of Israel to Abel and Beth-maacah and all the Berites, and they gathered together and also came after him. 15. And they came and made a siege against him in Abel *and*[17] Beth-maacah. And they piled up a rampart against the city, and *armies surrounded it*,[18] and all the people who were with Joab *were planning to destroy the wall*.[19] 16. And a wise woman called from the city: "Listen, listen. Say now to Joab: 'Draw near here, and I will speak with you.'" 17. And he drew near unto her, and the woman said: "Are you Joab?" And he said: "I am." And she said to him: "Listen to the words of your handmaid." And he said: "I am listening." 18. And

Notes, Chapter Twenty (Cont.)

[3] MT: "tent."
[4] MT: "went up."
[5] MT: "he provided for them."
[6] MT: "until the day of their death, widow of life."
[7] MT: "Summon to."
[8] MT: "Judah."
[9] MT: "appointed him."
[10] MT: "snatch away our eyes."

[11] MT: "the Cherethite and the Pelethite."
[12] MT: "girded as to his garments, his clothing."
[13] MT: "and he went forth and it fell out."
[14] MT: "the belly."
[15] MT lacks the verb.
[16] MT: "he was taken aside."
[17] MT lacks the "and."
[18] MT "it/she stood on the wall."
[19] MT: "are causing destruction to make the wall fall down."

she said, saying: "*Remember now what is written in the book of the law, to inquire in this city long ago, saying: 'Was it not here for you to inquire in Abel, if they are at peace?'*[20] 19. *We are at peace in good faith with Israel.*[21] *For you are seeking to destroy the city that is a great capital*[22] and a mother in Israel. Why will you *ruin*[23] the inheritance of *the people of the Lord?"*[24] 20. And Joab answered and said: "Far be it, far be it from me if I should ruin and if I should destroy. 21. The matter is not so. For a man from the mountain of *the house of Ephraim,*[25] Sheba the son of Bichri is his name, has raised up his hand against the king, against David. Give him over by himself, and I will go away from the city." And the woman said to Joab: "Behold his head is being thrown to you *from*[26] the wall." 22. And the woman came unto all the people in her wisdom. And they cut off the head of Sheba the son of Bichri, and threw it at Joab. And he blew on the trumpet, and they were dispersed from the city, each man to his *city.*[27] And Joab returned to Jerusalem unto the king. 23. And Joab *was appointed over*[28] all the army of Israel, and Benaiah the son of Jehoiada *was in command over the archers and over the slingers.*[29] 24. And Adoram *was in command over the raising of taxes,*[30] and Jehoshaphat the son of Ahilud *was in command over the recorders.*[31] 25. And Sheva was the scribe, and Zadok and Abiathar were the priests. 26. And also Ira *who was from Tekoa*[32] was a *great man*[33] for David.

CHAPTER 21

1. And there was a famine in the days of David for three years, year after year. And David sought *mercy from before the Lord,*[1] and the Lord said: "*Because of Saul and because of the house of those guilty of killing, because he killed*[2] the Gibeonites." 2. And the king called to the Gibeonites, and he spoke to them. And the Gibeonites are not from the sons of Israel, but they are from the remnant of the Amorites; and the sons of Israel swore to them, and Saul sought *to kill them*[3] in zeal for the sons of Israel and Judah. 3. And David said to the Gibeonites: "What shall I do to you? And in what

Notes, Chapter Twenty (Cont.)

[20]MT: "They were saying long ago, saying: 'Let them ask counsel in Abel.' And so they settled." See Deut 20:10.

[21]MT: "I am one of the peaceful faithful of Israel."

[22]MT: "You are seeking to put to death a city."

[23]MT: "swallow, destroy."

[24]MT: "the Lord."

[25]MT: "Ephraim."

[26]MT: "over."

[27]MT: "tent."

[28]MT: "(was) for."

[29]MT: "(was) over the Cherethite and the Pelethite."

[30]MT: "(was) over the forced labor." In Roman times, taxes and tribute were a greater burden than the earlier forced labor. See 1 Kings 4:6; 12:18.

[31]MT: "(was) the recorder."

[32]MT: "the Jairite." Jair was across the Jordan in Gilead. Tg makes Ira come from Judah and does not let him be appointed priest, since his lineage is unknown.

[33]MT: "priest."

Notes, Chapter Twenty-One

[1]MT: "the face of the Lord."

[2]MT: "On Saul and on (his) house there is blood because he put to death."

[3]MT: "to strike them down."

way shall I make expiation, and they will bless the inheritance of *the people of the Lord?*[4] 4. And the Gibeonites said to him: "*We do not need to take silver and gold from Saul and from his house;*[5] and also there is no one *to kill*[6] in Israel." And he said: "Whatever you say, I will do for you." 5. And they said to the king: "The man who put an end to us and who was plotting against us that we be put to an end from dwelling in all the territory of the land of Israel, 6. let there be given to us seven men from his sons and let us *hang them before*[7] the Lord in Gibeah of Saul, the chosen of the Lord." And the king said: "I will give (them)." 7. And the king spared Mephibosheth the son of Jonathan the son of Saul because of the oath of the Lord that was between them, between David and between Jonathan the son of Saul. 8. And the king took the two sons of Rizpah, the daughter of Aiah, whom she bore to Saul, Armoni and Mephibosheth; and *the five sons of Merab, whom Michal the daughter of Saul raised,*[8] whom she bore to Adriel the son of Barzilai who was *from Meholath.*[9] 9. And he gave them in the hand of the Gibeonites, and they *hanged*[10] them on the mountain before the Lord, and the seven of them fell together, and those *were killed*[11] on the days of the harvest, on the first days, *in*[12] the beginning of the harvest of barley. 10. And Rizpah the daughter of Aiah took sackcloth and spread it out for herself upon the rock from the beginning of the harvest until *the rain*[13] came down from the heavens upon them; and she did not let the bird of the heavens rest upon them by day and the beast of the field by night. 11. And it was told to David what Rizpah the daughter of Aiah, the concubine of Saul, had done. 12. And David went and took the bones of Saul and the bones of Jonathan his son from the *inhabitants*[14] of Jabesh-gilead who stole them from the *wall*[15] of Beth-shean where the Philistines hanged them on the day that the Philistines *killed*[16] Saul in Gilboa. 13. And he brought up from there the bones of Saul and the bones of Jonathan his son, and they gathered the bones of those who were *hanged.*[17] 14. And they buried the bones of Saul and Jonathan his son in the land of *the tribe of Benjamin,*[18] in Zela, in the tomb of Kish his father; and they did everything that the king commanded, and *the Lord received the prayers of the inhabitants of the land*[19] afterwards. 15. And there was once more war to the Philistines with Israel, and David and his servants with him went down and *waged battle*[20] with the Philistines, and David grew weary. 16. And Ishbinebob was *among the sons of a giant*[21] and the weight of his spear-tip was the weight of 300 *selas*[22] of bronze, and he was girded with a new *belt,*[23] and he said that he would *kill*[24] David. 17. And Abishai the son of Zeruiah aided him, and he struck down the Philistine and *killed*[25] him. Then David's men swore to

Notes, Chapter Twenty-One (Cont.)

[4] MT: "the Lord."

[5] MT: "It is not for us silver and gold with Saul and with his house."

[6] MT: "for us to put to death."

[7] MT: "expose them to."

[8] MT: "the five sons of Michal the daughter of Saul." See 1 Sam 18:19 where Merab is said to have married Adriel. Tg harmonizes the two passages.

[9] MT: "the Meholathite."

[10] MT: "exposed."

[11] MT: "were put to death."

[12] MT lacks the preposition.

[13] MT: "water."

[14] MT: "lords (*Ba'ălê*)." Tg avoids the term "Ba'al."

[15] MT: "square." Tg harmonizes this passage with 1 Sam 31:12.

[16] MT: "struck down."

[17] MT: "exposed."

[18] MT: "Benjamin."

[19] MT: "God was supplicated for the land."

[20] MT: "fought."

[21] MT: "offspring of the Raphah."

[22] MT: "shekels."

[23] MT lacks the word.

[24] MT: "strike down."

[25] MT: "put him to death."

him, saying: "You shall not go forth with us again to battle, and you shall not extinguish *the kingdom*²⁶ of Israel." 18. And afterward there was a battle again in Gob with the Philistines. Then Sibbecai, *who was from Hushath, killed*²⁷ Saph, who was among *the sons of the giant.*²⁸ 19. And there was a battle again in Gob with the Philistines; and *David the son of Jesse, destroying the curtain of the sanctuary, killed*²⁹ Goliath the Gittite; and the wood of his spear was like the beam of the weavers. 20. And there was a battle again in Gath, and there was a man of stature; and his fingers and his toes were six and six, twenty-four the number; and he also was born to the *giant.*²⁹ᵃ 21. And he scoffed at Israel; and Jonathan the son of Shimei, the brother of David, *killed him.*³⁰ 22. And these four were born to the *giant*³¹ in Gath, and *they were given over in*³² the hand of David and in the hand of his servants.

CHAPTER 22

1. And David *gave praise in prophecy before*¹ the Lord the words of this *praise on account of all the days*² that the Lord saved *Israel*³ from the hand of all *their*⁴ enemies and *also for David from the sword of Saul.*⁵ 2. And he said: "The Lord is my *strength*⁶ and my *security*⁷ and the one saving me, 3. *my God, who takes delight in me; he has drawn me near to fear of him; my strength from before whom strength is given to me and redemption to grow strong against my enemies; my security on account of whose Memra I trust in time of distress, shielding me from my enemies." And he said: "For the land — my horn in his redemption; my support that his Memra supported me when I was fleeing from before those pursuing me; my redemption from my enemies; and also from the hand of all robbers he saved me."*⁸ 4. *David said in praise: "I am praying before the Lord who in all times saves me*⁹ from my enemies. 5. For *distress*¹⁰ surrounded me *like a woman who sits upon the birth-stool, and she does not have strength to give birth, and she is in danger of dying.*¹¹ *A company of sinners*¹² terrified me. 6. *An army of evil men*¹³ surrounded me; *those who were girt with weapons of killing*¹⁴ came

Notes, Chapter Twenty-One (Cont.)

²⁶MT: "the lamp."

²⁷MT: "the Hushaite struck down."

²⁸MT: "the offspring of the Raphah."

²⁹MT: "Elhanan the son of Jaareoregim the Bethlehemite struck down." Tg harmonizes MT with the earlier story of David killing Goliath.

²⁹ᵃMT: "Raphah."

³⁰MT: "struck him down."

³¹MT: "Raphah."

³²MT: "they fell by."

Notes, Chapter Twenty-Two

¹MT: "spoke to."

²MT: "song on the day."

³MT: "him."

⁴MT: "his."

⁵MT: "from the hand of Saul."

⁶MT: "rock."

⁷MT: "fortress."

⁸MT: "God of my rock—I trust in him; my shield and horn of my salvation, my stronghold and my refuge, my savior, you save me from violence."

⁹MT: "I call on the Lord, who is to be praised, and I am saved."

¹⁰MT: "the waves of death."

¹¹MT lacks the simile.

¹²MT: "the torrents of Belial."

¹³MT: "the cords of Sheol."

¹⁴MT: "the snares of death."

before me. 7. *David said:*[15] "When I was in distress, *I was praying before*[16] the Lord and *before*[17] my God *I was entreating;*[18] and from his temple *he was receiving my prayers,*[19] and *my petitions were made before him.*[20] 8. The earth was stirred up and shaken; the foundations of the heavens trembled and *bent down, for his anger was strong.*[21] 9. *The haughtiness of Pharaoh went up like smoke before him. Then he sent his anger like a burning fire which was from before him; his wrath was destroying like coals of burning fire from his Memra.*[22] 10. ˙He bent the heavens, and *his glory was revealed,*[23] and a cloud *covered the way before him.*[24] 11. *He was revealed in his might upon the swift cherubim*[25] and *he drove with strength*[26] upon the wings of the wind. 12. *He made his Shekinah reside in thick darkness; a glorious cloud (was) all round about him, bringing down mighty waters from the mass of light clouds in the height of the world.*[27] 13. *From the visage of his splendor the heavens of heavens were shining forth, his wrath like coals of burning fire from his Memra.*[28] 14. The Lord thundered from the heavens, and the Most High *lifted up his Memra.*[29] 15. And he sent forth *his smiting like arrows*[30] and scattered them, *lightnings*[31] and confused them. 16. And the depths of the sea were seen, the foundations of the world were revealed *in the wrath from before the Lord, from the Memra of the strength of his anger.*[32] 17. He sent *his prophets, a strong king who was sitting in the strength of the height; he took me, he rescued me from many nations.*[33] 18. he rescued me *from those hating me, for some of my enemies overpowered me, for they were prevailing against me.*[34] 19. They were coming before me on the day of my *exile*[35] and *the Memra of the Lord*[36] was a support for me. 20. He brought me forth to the open place; he rescued me, for he took delight in me." 21. *David said:*[37] "The Lord rewarded me according to my righteousness; according to the purity of my hands he returned to me. 22. For I have kept ways *that are good before the Lord,*[38] and I have not *walked in evil before*[39] my God. 23. For all his judgments *are revealed for me to do them;*[40] and his statutes—I have not turned aside from them. 24. And I was blameless *in fear of him,*[41] and I was keeping *my soul from sins.*[42] 25. And the Lord returned to me according to my righteousness, according to my purity before *his Memra.*[43] 26. *Abraham who was found pious before you; therefore you did much kindness with his seed. Isaac who was blameless in fear of you; therefore you made*

Notes, Chapter Twenty-Two (Cont.)

[15]MT lacks the phrase.

[16]MT: "I was calling to."

[17]MT: "to."

[18]MT: "I was calling."

[19]MT: "he was hearing my voice."

[20]MT: "my cry was in his ears."

[21]MT: "reeled for he was angry."

[22]MT: "Smoke went up in his nostrils, and fire from his mouth was devouring, and coals burned from him."

[23]MT: "he came down."

[24]MT: "(was) beneath his feet."

[25]MT: "And he rode upon the cherub and flew."

[26]MT: "he was seen."

[27]MT: "He made darkness round about him, canopies, gatherings of water, dark clouds."

[28]MT: "From his splendor, opposite him coals of fire burned."

[29]MT: "gave forth his voice."

[30]MT: "his arrows."

[31]MT: "lightning."

[32]MT: "at the rebuke of the Lord, from the breath of the wind of his nostrils."

[33]MT: "from on high he took me, he drew me out of many waters."

[34]MT: "from my strong enemy, from those hating me, for they were stonger than I."

[35]MT: "calamity."

[36]MT: "the Lord."

[37]MT lacks the phrase.

[38]MT: "of the Lord."

[39]MT: "wickedly departed from."

[40]MT: "opposite me." Tg makes clear that knowing God's law means obeying it.

[41]MT: "to him."

[42]MT: "myself from my guilt."

[43]MT: "his eyes."

perfect the word of your good pleasure with him.[44] 27. *Jacob who was walking in purity before you — you chose his sons from all the nations, you set apart his seed from every blemish. Pharaoh and the Egyptians who plotted plots against your people — you mixed them up like their plans.*[45] 28. *And the people, the house of Israel, who are called in this world*[46] a poor people, you will save; and *by your Memra you will humble the strong who are showing their might against them.*[47] 29. *For you are its Lord; the light of Israel (is) the Lord. And the Lord brings me forth from the darkness to light and shows me the world that is to come for the just ones.*[48] 30. *For by your Memra I will have large armies; by the Memra of my God I will conquer all strong cities.*[49] 31. *God whose way is straight*[50] - the *law*[51] of the Lord is proved; he is *strong*[52] for all who *entrust themselves to his Memra.*[53] 32. *Therefore on account of the sign and the redemption that you work for your anointed one and for the remnant of your people who are left, all the nations, peoples, and language groups will give thanks and say: 'There is no God except the Lord,' for there is none apart from you. And your people will say: 'There is no one who is strong except our God.'*[54] 33. The God *who helps me with might and makes*[55] my way blameless. 34. He makes my feet *light*[56] like the hind, and upon *my stronghold*[57] he establishes me. 35. He instructs my hand *to do battle*[58] and *strengthens my arms*[59] like the bow of bronze. 36. And you have given to me *strength; you have rescued me; and you have made me great by your Memra.*[60] 37. You have made a great space for my step *before me,*[61] and *my knee*[62] did not shake. 38. I pursued those hating me, and I destroyed them; and I did not turn back until *I destroyed them completely.*[63] 39. And I destroyed them and *destroyed them completely, and they were not able to arise,*[64] and they fell *killed*[65] beneath *the soles of my feet.*[66] 40. *And you helped me with might to do battle; you shattered the nations who were arising to do harm to me* beneath me.[67] 41. *And you shattered those hating me before me; my enemies were turning their back,*[68] and I destroyed them. 42. *They were seeking a helper, and there was no deliverer for them; and they were praying before the Lord, and their prayer was not being accepted.*[69] 43. And *I trampled them*[70] like the dust of the earth, like the dirt of the streets *I stepped on them;*[71] *I trampled them down.*[72] 44. And you

Notes, Chapter Twenty-Two (Cont.)

[44]MT: "With a pious one you act piously; with a blameless man you act blamelessly."

[45]MT: "With a pure one you act purely, and with a crooked one you act perversely."

[46]MT lacks the phrase.

[47]MT: "your eyes (are) upon the exalted; you will bring (them) down."

[48]MT: "For you are my lamp, Lord; and the Lord lightens my darkness." Tg interprets the metaphor in the MT as a reference to afterlife.

[49]MT: "For by you I will crush a troop; by my God I will leap a wall."

[50]MT: "This God—straight is his way."

[51]MT: "speaking." For the targumist, the Torah was the speaking of God.

[52]MT: "a shield."

[53]MT: "seek refuge in him."

[54]MT: "For who is a god apart from the Lord, and who is a rock apart from our God? "

[55]MT: "is my strong refuge and sets free."

[56]MT lacks the word.

[57]MT: "my high place."

[58]MT: "for war."

[59]MT: "my arms bend."

[60]MT: "the shield of your salvation, and your help (?) made me great."

[61]MT: "beneath me."

[62]MT: "my ankles."

[63]MT: "they were destroyed completely."

[64]MT: "smote them, and they will not arise."

[65]MT lacks the word.

[66]MT: "my feet."

[67]MT: "And you girded me with might for war; you sank those arising against me beneath me."

[68]MT: "And my enemies you gave to me (their) back; and those hating me."

[69]MT: "They looked, and there was no savior; to God, and he did not answer them."

[70]MT: "I beat them fine."

[71]MT: "I crushed them."

[72]MT: "I stamped them."

rescued me from the strife of *the people;*[73] *you appointed me*[74] head *for*[75] the nations; a people that I did not know were serving me. 45. Sons of *the nations*[76] submitted themselves to me; as soon as the ear heard, they were listening to me. 46. Sons of *the nations perished*[77] and *came trembling*[78] from their fortresses. 47. *Therefore on account of the sign and the salvation that you have done for your people, they confessed and said:*[79] 'May the Lord live and blessed is *the Strong One before whom strength is given to us and salvation;*[80] and exalted be God, the *strength*[81] of *our*[82] salvation, 48. the God who was *making*[83] vengeance for me and *shattering the nations who arose to do harm to me*[84] beneath me, 49. *and saved me from those hating me, and against those who arose to do harm to me you made me more powerful; from Gog and the army of the captured nations — who were with him* [85] — you rescued me. 50. Therefore I will give thanks *before*[86] you, Lord, among the nations; and to your name *I will speak praise.*[87] 51. He works much salvation *with*[88] his king and does goodness to his anointed one, to David and to his seed, forever.

CHAPTER 23

1. And these are *the words of the prophecy of David that he prophesied for the end of the world, for the days of the consolation that are to come. David the son of Jesse spoke;*[1] and the utterance of the man who was raised *to kingship,*[2] the anointed *by the Memra*[3] of the God of Jacob; *and he decided to appoint in your lives*[4] the sweet one of the *praises*[5] of Israel. 2. *David said: "By a spirit of prophecy before the Lord I am speaking these things, and the words of his holiness in my mouth I am ordering."*[6] 3. *David said:*[7] "The God of Israel spoke unto me; *the powerful one*[8] of Israel who has dominion among *the sons of man,*[9] *judging the truth,*[10] said *to appoint for me the king, that is the Messiah to come who will arise and rule*[11] by fear of *the Lord.*[12] 4. *Blessed are you, the just ones. You have done for yourselves good deeds so that you are to shine forth in the splendor of your glory like the light of the dawn that grows stronger and*

Notes, Chapter Twenty-Two (Cont.)

[73] MT: "my people."
[74] MT: "you kept me for."
[75] MT: "of."
[76] MT: "foreigners."
[77] MT: "the foreigners withered."
[78] MT: "girded themselves."
[79] MT lacks the phrases.
[80] MT: "my rock."
[81] MT: "rock."
[82] MT: "my."
[83] MT: "giving."
[84] MT: "bringing down nations."
[85] MT: "and brought me forth from my enemies, and from those arising against me you exalted me; from men of violence."
[86] MT lacks the preposition.

[87] MT: "I will sing."
[88] MT lacks the preposition.

Notes, Chapter Twenty-Three

[1] MT: "the last words of David the son of Jesse."
[2] MT: "on high."
[3] MT lacks the word.
[4] MT lacks the phrase.
[5] MT: "songs."
[6] MT: "A spirit of the Lord speaks in me, and his word in upon my tongue."
[7] MT lacks the phrase.
[8] MT: "the rock."
[9] MT: "man."
[10] MT: "as just."
[11] MT lacks this material.
[12] MT: "God."

stronger, and like the sun that is to shine forth in the splendor of its glory, over the first of three hundred forty-three with the light of seven days. More than this you will be raised, and it will be good for you who long for the years of the consolations that are coming. Behold, like a farmer who hopes during years of scarcity that rain will fall on the earth." [13] 5. *David said: "More than this (is) my house before God, for he established an eternal covenant for me for my kingdom to endure like the orders of creation endure and to be preserved for the world which is coming; for all my needs and all my desire before him are done; therefore every kingdom already opposite it will not be established.* [14] 6. *The evil ones doing sin are like thorns which in their sprouting (are) soft to pluck; and when a man has consideration for them and leaves them alone, they grow stronger and stronger until it is impossible to approach them by hand.* [15] 7. *And also this (is) every man who begins to approach sins; they grow stronger and stronger over him until they cover him like an iron garment which they cannot (pierce) with the wood of lances and spears. Therefore their punishment is not in the hand of man but in the fires destined to be kindled. They will be kindled in the revelation of the great court to sit on the thrones of judgment to judge the world."* [16] 8. These are the names of the mighty men who were *with David: a mighty man, head of the armies, sitting on the thrones of judgment, and all the prophets and elders are surrounding him, anointed with the anointing of holiness, chosen and delicately reared, handsome in his form and fitting in his appearance, wise in wisdom and prudent in counsel, mighty in strength, head of the mighty men, he, prepared with armored equipment,* goes forth with *a loud shout and conquers in battle and cuts down with his spear eight hundred killed in that time.* [17] 9. And after him was Eleazar the son of Dodo the son of Ahdi. He was among the three warriors with David *when the Philistines jeered and* [18] gathered there *to wage battle,* [19] and the men of Israel went up. 10. He arose and *killed* [20] among the Philistines until his hand grew tired, and his hand stuck with the sword; and the Lord worked a great victory on that day, and the people returned after him only to strip *the slain.* [21] 11. And after him was Shammah the son of Agee *the mountain one.* [22] And the Philistines gathered at Lehi, and there was there a plot of land full of lentils; and the people fled from before the Philistines. 12. And he took his stand in the middle of the plot, and he saved it and *killed* [23] the Philistines; and the Lord worked a great victory. 13. And *three warriors from the chief warriors of the armies* [24] went down and came for harvest-time unto David to the cave of Adullam, and the camp of the Philistines was camping in the

Notes, Chapter Twenty-Three (Cont.)

[13] MT: "Like the light of morning the sun shines forth, a morning without clouds, from rain making sprout grass from the land." Three hundred forty-three is 7 x 7 x 7.

[14] MT: "Is not my house so with God? For an eternal covenant he set for me, ordered in all and secure. For all my salvation and all desire—will he not cause to prosper?"

[15] MT: "And Belial in a thorn all thrown away, for no by hand will they be taken."

[16] MT: "And a man touches them; he arms himself with iron and the wood of a spear, and with burning fire they are burned in the sitting."

[17] MT: "for David: Josheb-basshebeth a Tahelemonite; he was chief of the three; he wielded his spear against eight-hundred whom he slew at one time."

[18] MT: "in their defying the Philistines."

[19] MT: "for war."

[20] MT: "struck down."

[21] MT lacks the word.

[22] MT: "Hararite." The Aramaic translates MT as if it were from *har* ("mountain").

[23] MT: "struck down."

[24] MT: "three from the thirty chiefs."

valley of *the warriors.*[25] 14. And David was then in the fortress, and the garrison of the Philistines was then at Bethlehem. 15. And *the soul of David*[26] grew desirous, and he said: "Who will give me waters to drink from the well of Bethlehem which is by the gate?" 16. And the three warriors broke through in the camp of the Philistines and filled up with waters from the well of Bethlehem which was by the gate, and they took it and brought it unto David. And he was not willing to drink it, and *he said to pour it out before the Lord.*[27] 17. And he said: "Far be it from me *from before the Lord*[28] that I should do this! Is not this the blood of the men who went at risk of their lives?" And he was not willing to drink it. The three warriors did these things. 18. And Abishai the brother of Joab the son of Zeruiah — he was head of *the warriors.*[29] And he was wielding his spear over the 300 *killed,*[30] and he had a name among the three *warriors.*[31] 19. He was more renowned than *the warriors,*[32] and he was their captain. But he did not attain to the three warriors. 20. And Benaiah the son of Jehoiada the son of *a man fearing sins, a doer*[33] of deeds, from Kabzeel — he *killed*[34] the two *chiefs*[35] of Moab, and he went down and *killed*[36] a lion in the midst of a pit on a snowy day. 21. And he *killed*[37] an Egyptian man, a handsome man; and in the hand of the Egyptian was a spear, and he went down against him with a staff, and he forced the spear from the hand of the Egyptian, and he killed him with his spear. 22. Benaiah the son of Jehoiada did these things, and he had a name among the three warriors. 23. He was more renowned than *the warriors,*[38] but he did not attain to the three warriors. And David appointed him over his bodyguard. 24. Among the warriors were Asahel the brother of Joab; Elhanan the son of Dodo *who was from*[39] Bethlehem; 25. Shammah *who was from Harod;*[40] Elika *who was from Harod;*[41] 26. Helez *who was from Palat;*[42] Ira the son of Ikkesh *who was from Tekoa;*[43] 27. Abiezer *who was from Anathoth;*[44] Mebunnai *who was from Hushat;*[45] 28. Zalmon *who was from Ahoh;*[46] Maharia *who was from Netophah;*[47] 29. Heleb the son of Baanah *who was from Netophah;*[48] Ittai the son of Ribai from Gibeah of the sons of Benjamin; 30. Benaiah *who was from Pirathon;*[49] Hiddai who was from the brooks of Gaash; 31. Abialbon *who was from Arbath;*[50] Azmaveth *who was from Bahurim;*[51] 32. Eliahba *who was from Shaalbon;*[52] the sons of Jashen; Jonathan; 33. Shammah *the mountain one;*[53] Ahiham the son of Sharar *who was from Yehar-gabwa;*[54] 34. Eliphelet the son of Ahasbai the son of *Maacah;*[55] Eliam

Notes, Chapter Twenty-Three (Cont.)

[25]MT: "Rephaim."

[26]MT: "David."

[27]MT: "he poured it out to the Lord." Tg takes care that David not usurp a priestly function by pouring a libation. So it has David say that he will pour it out before the Lord (back in Jerusalem). See S-A, 19.

[28]MT: "O Lord."

[29]MT: "the three."

[30]MT: "slain."

[31]MT lacks the word.

[32]MT: "the three."

[33]MT: "Ish-hai, chief."

[34]MT: "struck down."

[35]MT: *ări'el*, whose meaning is not known.

[36]MT: "struck down."

[37]MT: "struck down."

[38]MT: "the thirty."

[39]MT lacks the phrase.

[40]MT: "the Harodite."

[41]MT: "the Harodite."

[42]MT: "the Palatite."

[43]MT: "the Tekoan."

[44]MT: "Anathothite."

[45]MT: "the Hushatite."

[46]MT: "the Ahohite."

[47]MT: "the Netophahite."

[48]MT: "the Netophahite."

[49]MT: "the Pirathonite."

[50]MT: "the Arbathite."

[51]MT: "the Bahurimite."

[52]MT: "the Shaalborite."

[53]MT: "the Hararite." See 23:11, note 22.

[54]MT: "the Hararite."

[55]MT: "Maacahite."

the son of Ahithopel the Gilonite; 35. Hezro *who was from Carmel;*[56] Paarai *who was from Arab;*[57] 36. Igal the son of Nathan *who was*[58] from Zobak; Bani *from the tribe of Gad;*[59] 37. Zelek *who was from Ammon;*[60] Naharai *who was from Beeroth,*[61] the armor-bearer of Joab the son of Zeruiah; 38. Ira *who was from Yatir;*[62] Gareb *who was from Yatir;*[63] 39. Uriah the Hittite. In all there were thirty-seven *warriors.*[64]

CHAPTER 24

1. And the anger of the Lord continued *to be strong*[1] against Israel, and it incited David against them, saying: "Go, count Israel and *those of the house of Judah.*"[2] 2. And the king said to Joab, the commander of the army, who was with him: "Go about now in all the tribes of Israel from Dan and unto Beer-sheba, and count the people, and I will know the number of the people." 3. And Joab said to the king: "May the Lord your God add to the people like these and like these a hundred times, and the eyes of my master the king see; and why does my master the king take delight in this matter?" 4. And the word of the king prevailed over Joab and over the chiefs of the army, and Joab and the chiefs of the army went forth before the king to count the people Israel. 5. And they crossed the Jordan and camped in Aroer south of the city, which is in the midst of the valley, *which is in the tribe of Gad,*[3] and in Jazer. 6. And they came to Gilead and to the land *south of Hodshi,*[4] and they came to Dan-jaan, and from there he went around to Sidon. 7. And they entered *the fortified cities*[5] and all the cities of the *Hivvites and Canaanites,*[6] and they went forth to the south of Judah to Beer-sheba. 8. And they went about in all the land and came at the end of nine months and twenty days to Jerusalem. 9. And Joab gave the number of the census of the people to the king; and Israel was 800,000 men, warriors drawing the sword, and the men of Judah were 500,000 men. 10. And *David was troubled in his heart*[7] after he had counted the people, and David said *before*[8] the Lord: "I have sinned very much because I did this; now O Lord, take away the sin of your servant, for I was very foolish." 11. And David arose in the morning, and *the word of prophecy from before the Lord was with*[9] Gad the prophet, David's seer, saying: 12. "Go and speak with David: 'Thus said the Lord:

Notes, Chapter Twenty-Three (Cont.)

[56]MT: "the Carmelite."
[57]MT: "the Arbite."
[58]MT lacks the phrase.
[59]MT: "the Gadite."
[60]MT: "the Ammonite."
[61]MT: "the Beerothite."
[62]MT: "the Yatirite."
[63]MT: "the Yatirite."
[64]MT lacks the word.

Notes, Chapter Twenty-Four

[1]MT: "to be hot."
[2]MT: "Judah."
[3]MT: "of Gad."
[4]MT: "Tahtim-hodshi." The Aramaic takes "Tahtim" as "south of," literally "beneath."
[5]MT: "fortress of Tyre."
[6]MT: "Hivvite and Canaanite."
[7]MT: "the heart of David struck him down."
[8]MT: "to."
[9]MT: "the word of the Lord was to."

"*One of three things*[10] I am holding over you; choose for yourself one of them, and I will do it to you."" 13. And Gad came unto David, and he told him and said to him: "*Shall he give*[11] to you seven years of famine in your land? Or for three months *you will be fleeing*[12] before your enemies, and he will be pursuing you? Or that there be for three days *death*[13] in your land? Now consider and see what word I shall bring to him who sent me." 14. And David said to Gad: "It is very painful to me; *let us be given*[14] now into the hand *of the Memra of the Lord,*[15] for his mercies are great; and *let me not be given*[16] into the hand of man." 15. And the Lord gave *death*[17] in Israel *from the time when the daily burnt offering is slaughtered and until it is removed.*[18] And there died from the people from Dan and unto Beer-sheba 70,000 men. 16. And the angel reached out his hand to Jerusalem to destroy it, and the Lord *turned*[19] from evil, and he said to the angel who was doing harm among the people: "Enough; now stay your hand." And the angel of the Lord *was resting in the threshing floor of Arwan*[20] the Jebusite. 17. And David said *before*[21] the Lord, when he saw the angel who *was killing*[22] among the people, and he said: "Behold I have sinned, and I have done evil; *and these people who are like sheep in the hand of the shepherd,*[23] what have they done? Now let your *blow*[24] be against me and against the house of my father." 18. And Gad came unto David in that day and said to him: "Go up, erect *before*[25] the Lord an altar in the threshing floor of *Arwan*[26] the Jebusite." 19. And David went up according to the word of Gad just as the Lord *spoke.*[27] 20. And *Arwan*[28] looked out and saw the king and his servants passing unto him, and *Arwan*[28] went forth and bowed to the king *upon his face upon the ground.*[29] 21. And *Arwan*[30] said: "Why has my master the king come unto his servant?" And David said: "To buy from you the threshing floor to build an altar *before*[31] the Lord, and the pestilence will cease from upon the people." 22. And *Arwan*[32] said to David: "Let my master the king take and bring up whatever is good in his eyes. See the oxen *fit*[33] for holocausts, and the threshing sledges and the yokes of oxen for wood. 23.

Notes, Chapter Twenty-Four (Cont.)

[10] MT: "three (things)."
[11] MT: "shall there come."
[12] MT: "of your fleeing."
[13] MT: "pestilence."
[14] MT: "let us fall."
[15] MT: "of the Lord."
[16] MT: "let me not fall."
[17] MT: "pestilence."
[18] MT: "from morning until the appointed time." Tg specifies the appointed time.
[19] MT: "repented."
[20] MT: "was at the threshing floor of Araunah."
[21] MT: "to."
[22] MT: "striking down."
[23] MT: "and these sheep."
[24] MT: "hand."
[25] MT: "to."
[26] MT: "Araunah."
[27] MT: "commanded."
[28] MT: "Araunah."
[29] MT: "his face to the ground."
[30] MT: "Araunah."
[31] MT: "to."
[32] MT: "Araunah."
[33] MT lacks the word.

Arwan[34] has given everything to *the king that the king sought from him.*"[35] And *Arwan*[36] said to the king: "May the Lord your God *accept your offering with good pleasure.*"[37] 24. And the king said to *Arwan:*[38] "No, because I will surely buy from you for a price; and I will not offer *before*[39] the Lord my God holocausts for nothing." And David bought the threshing floor and the oxen for the price of fifty *selas.*[40] 25. And David built there an altar *before*[41] the Lord, and he offered holocausts and *holy offerings.*[42] And the Lord *accepted the prayers of the dwellers of the land,*[43] and the pestilence ceased from upon Israel.

Notes, Chapter Twenty-Four (Cont.)

[34] MT: "Araunah."
[35] MT: "the king."
[36] MT: "Araunah."
[37] MT: "favor you."
[38] MT: "Araunah."

[39] MT: "to."
[40] MT: "shekels."
[41] MT: "to."
[42] MT: "peace offerings."
[43] MT: "heeded supplications for the land."

1 KINGS

CHAPTER 1

1. And King David was old, advanced in days; and they were covering him with clothes, and it was not warm for him. 2. And his servants said to him: "Let them seek out for my master the king a young maiden,[1] and she will *serve*[2] before the king, and *she will be brought near*[3] to him and lay *in your presence*,[4] and it will be warm for my master the king." 3. And they sought a beautiful maiden in all the territory of *the land of Israel*,[5] and they found Abishag *who was from Shunem*,[6] and they brought her to the king. 4. And the maiden was extraordinarily beautiful, and *she was brought near to*[7] the king, and she was serving him, and the king did not know her. 5. And Adonijah the son of Haggith was magnifying himself, saying: "I will be king." And he made for himself chariots and horsemen and fifty men running before him. 6. And his father did not rebuke him at any time, saying: "Why *are you doing*[8] thus?" And he too was extraordinarily handsome *in*[9] his appearance; and she gave birth to him after Absalom. 7. And his words were *in counsel with*[10] Joab the son of Zeruiah and with Abiathar the priest, and they were giving aid after Adonijah. 8. And Zakok the priest and Benaiah the son of Jehoiada and Nathan the prophet and Shimei and Rei and David's warriors were not *in the counsel of*[11] Adonijah. 9. And Adonijah sacrificed sheep and oxen and fatlings at *Lookout Rock*,[12] which is beside the *Washer's Well*.[13] And he invited all[14] his brothers, the sons of the king, and all[14] the men of the tribe of Judah, the servants of the king. 10. And he did not invite Nathan the prophet and Benaiah and the warriors and Solomon his brother. 11. And Nathan said to Bathsheba the mother of Solomon, saying: "Have you not heard that Adonijah the son of Haggith has become king, and our master David does not know? 12. And now come, let me give you advice, and you save your life and the life of your son Solomon. 13. Go, and you shall enter unto King David and say to him: 'Did not you, my master the king, swear to your handmaid, saying that "Solomon your son will be king after me, and he will sit upon *the throne of my kingdom*?[15] And why has Adonijah become the king?"' 14. Behold while you are speaking there *before*[16] the king, I will enter after you and *confirm*[17] your words." 15. And Bathsheba entered *before*[18] the king to the inner chamber *of the bedroom*.[19] And

Notes, Chapter One

[1] Some Tg mss: "a virgin."
[2] MT: "stand."
[3] MT: "she will be a nurse for him."
[4] MT: "in your bosom."
[5] MT: "Israel."
[6] MT: "the Shunammite."
[7] MT: "she was nursing."
[8] MT: "have you done."
[9] MT: "of."
[10] MT: "with."
[11] MT: "with."
[12] MT: "Serpent's Stone."
[13] The Aramaic translates the MT "En-rogel." See Josh 15:7; 2 Sam 17:17.
[14] The first "all" is preceded by the accusative marker *yāt*, and the second by *l*.
[15] MT: "my throne."
[16] MT: "with."
[17] MT: "fulfill."
[18] MT: "to."
[19] MT lacks the phrase.

the king was very old, and Abishag *who was from Shunem*[20] was serving *before*[21] the king. 16. And Bathsheba bowed and did obeisance to the king. And the king said: "What is there to you?" 17. And she said to him: "My master, you swore by *the Memra of the Lord*[22] your God to your handmaid that Solomon your son will be king after me, and he will sit upon *the throne of my kingdom.*[23] 18. And now behold Adonijah has become king; and now my master the king, you do not know it. 19. And he has sacrificed oxen and fatlings and sheep in great number; and he has invited all the sons of the king, and Abiathar the priest, and Joab the chief of the army. And he did not invite Solomon your servant. 20. And you, my master the king, the eyes of all Israel *look to you*[24] to tell them who will sit upon *the throne of the kingdom of my master*[25] the king after him. 21. And when my master the king will sleep with his fathers, I and my son Solomon *will be banished.*"[26] 22. And behold while she was speaking *before*[27] the king, Nathan the prophet entered. 23. And they told the king, saying: "Behold Nathan the prophet." And he came before the king and did obeisance to the king upon his face *upon the ground.*[28] 24. And Nathan said: "My master the king, you said: 'Adonijah will be king after me, and he will sit upon *the throne of my kingdom.*'[29] 25. For he went down this day and sacrificed oxen and fatlings and sheep in great number, and he invited all the sons of the king and the chiefs of the army and Abiathar the priest. And behold they are eating and drinking before him, and they said: '*May* King Adonijah *prosper!*'[30] 26. And *me who am your servant*[31] and Zadok the priest and Benaiah the son of Jehoiada and Solomon your servant he did not invite. 27. Was this word from my master the king? And did you not inform your servants who will sit upon *the throne of the kingdom of my master*[32] the king after him?" 28. And King David answered and said: "Call Bathsheba to me." And she came before the king and stood before the king. 29. And the king swore and said: "As the Lord lives who saved my life from all affliction, 30. for just as I swore to you by *the Memra of the Lord*[33] the God of Israel, saying that 'Solomon your son will be king after me and he will sit upon *the throne of my kingdom*[34] in place of me,' thus I will do this day." 31. And Bathsheba bowed *upon her face upon the ground*[35] and did obeisance to the king and said: "May my master King David *endure*[36] forever?" 32. And King David said: "Call to me Zadok the priest and Nathan the prophet and Benaiah the son of Jehoiada." And they came before the king. 33. And the king said to them: "Take with you the servants of your master, and have Solomon my son ride upon the mule that is mine, and bring him down to *Shiloah.*[37] 34. And let Zadok the priest and Nathan the prophet anoint him there *to be the king*[38] over Israel. And you will blow on the trumpet and say: '*May* King Solomon *prosper!*'[39] 35. And you will come up after him, and he will come and sit

Notes, Chapter One (Cont.)

[20]MT: "Shunammite."
[21]MT lacks the preposition.
[22]MT: "the Lord."
[23]MT: "my throne."
[24]MT: "are upon you."
[25]MT: "the throne of my master."
[26]MT: "sinners."
[27]MT: "with."
[28]MT: "to the ground."
[29]MT: "my throne."

[30]MT: "Long live."
[31]MT: "me your servant."
[32]MT: "the throne of my master."
[33]MT: "the Lord."
[34]MT: "my throne."
[35]MT: "her face to the ground."
[36]MT: "live."
[37]MT: "Gihon." The waters of the Gihon flow into the Shiloah pool.
[38]MT: "for king."
[39]MT: "Long live."

upon *the throne of my kingdom,*[40] and he will be king in place of me. And I have commanded him to be *the king*[41] over Israel and over *those of the house of Judah.*"[42] 36. And Benaiah the son of Jehoiada answered the king and said: "Amen. *May there be thus good pleasure from before*[43] the Lord the God of my master the king! 37. Just as *the Memra of the Lord was at the aid of*[44] my master the king, so *may it be as the aid of*[45] of Solomon and make his throne greater than *the throne of the kingdom of my master*[46] King David. 38. And Zadok the priest and Nathan the prophet and Benaiah the son of Jehoida and *the archers and the slingers*[47] went down, and they had Solomon ride upon the mule of King David, and they brought him to *Shiloah.*[48] 39. And Zadok the priest took the horn of oil from the tent, and anointed Solomon. And they blew on the trumpet, and all the people said: "*May* King Solomon *prosper!*"[49] 40. And all the people went up after him, and the people *were praising in the dances*[50] and rejoicing a great joy, and the earth *shook at*[51] their voices. 41. And Adonijah and all the guests who were with him heard, and they had enough to eat; and Joab heard the sound of the trumpet, and he said: "Why is the sound of the city so excited?" 42. While he was speaking, behold Jonathan the son of Abiathar the priest came; and Adonijah said: "Come in, for you are a man *fearing sinners*[52] and you announce good news." 43. And Jonathan answered and said to Adonijah: "*In truth*[53] our master King David has made Solomon king. 44. And the king sent with him Zadok the priest and Nathan the prophet and Benaiah the son of Jehoidia and *the archers and the slingers,*[54] and they had him sit upon the mule of the king. 45. And Zadok the priest and Nathan the prophet anointed him *to be the king in Shiloah.*[55] And they went up from there *while*[56] they were rejoicing, and the city was excited. That was the sound that you heard. 46. And also Solomon sits upon the throne of the kingdom. 47. And also the servants of the king came to bless our master King David, saying: 'May *the Lord*[57] favor the name of Solomon more than your name, and may he exalt his throne more than *the throne of your kingdom.*'[58] And the king did obeisance upon the bed. 48. And also thus said the king: 'Blessed be the Lord the God of Israel who gave this day *a son sitting upon the throne of my kingdom,*[59] and my eyes are seeing it.'" 49. And all the guests that were Adonijah's were afraid, and they arose and went, each one his own way. 50. And Adonijah was afraid of Solomon, and he arose and went and took hold of the horns of the altar. 51. And it was told to Solomon, saying: "Behold Adonijah is afraid of King Solomon, and behold he has taken hold of the horns of the altar, saying: 'Let King Solomon swear to me this day that he will not *kill*[60] his servant with the sword.'" 52.

Notes, Chapter One (Cont.)

[40] MT: "my throne."

[41] MT: "ruler," *nagid.*

[42] MT: "Judah."

[43] MT: "May the Lord God of my lord the king say so."

[44] MT: "the Lord was with."

[45] MT: "may he be with."

[46] MT: "the throne of my master." After David's death, Tg consistently changes "throne of David" to the more accurate "throne of the kingdom of David."

[47] MT: "the Cherethite and the Pelethite."

[48] MT: "Gihon."

[49] MT: "Long live."

[50] MT: "playing on pipes."

[51] MT: "was split."

[52] MT: "of might." Tg sees the highest virtue as fearing sin, not courage.

[53] MT: "Alas" or "But no."

[54] MT: "the Cherethite and the Pelethite."

[55] MT: "for a king in Gihon."

[56] MT lacks the conjunction.

[57] MT: "your God."

[58] MT: "your throne."

[59] MT: "one sitting upon my throne."

[60] MT: "put to death."

And Solomon said: "If he proves to be a man *fearing sinners,*[61] *a hair of his head will not fall to the ground;*[62] if evil shall be found in him, *he will be killed.*"[63] 53. And King Solomon sent and brought him down from upon the altar; and he came and did obeisance to King Solomon, and Solomon said to him: "Go to your house."

CHAPTER 2

1. And the days of David to die drew near, and he commanded Solomon his son, saying: 2. "I am going on the way of all the earth. And may you be strong and be a man *fearing sinners.*[1] 3. And may you keep the charge of *the Memra of the Lord*[2] your God to walk *in the ways that are right before him,*[3] to keep his statutes, his commandments, and his judgments, and his testimonies as it is written in the law of Moses, in order that you may prosper in everything that you will do and in every *place*[4] to which you will turn, 4. in order that the Lord may establish his words that he spoke about me, saying: 'If your sons guard their way to walk before me in truth with all their heart and with all their soul, saying: "A man will not cease for you from upon *the throne of the kingdom*[5] of Israel." 5. And also you know what Joab the son of Zeruiah did to me, what he did to the two chiefs of the armies of Israel, to Abner the son of Ner and to Amasa the son of Jether *whom he killed in his cleverness; and my blood which is reckoned their blood (is) upon him like the blood of the wounded of battle; and he sat for them in an ambush of peace and shed their blood on the belt*[6] that was on his loins and *trampled by the boots*[7] that were on his feet. 6. And may you act according to your wisdom, and do not let his gray head go down in peace *to*[8] Sheol. 7. And to the sons of Barzilai the Gileadite may you act kindly, and let them be among those eating at your table, for they *satisfied my needs*[9] when I was fleeing from before Absalom your brother. 8. And behold there is with you Shimei the son of Gera *the son of the tribe of Benjamin from 'Almat;*[10] and he cursed me with *bitter curses*[11] on the day that I went to Mahanaim, and he went down to meet me to the Jordan; and I swore to him by *the Memra of the Lord,*[12] saying that *I will not kill you*[13] by the sword. 9. And now do not let him go unpunished, for you are a wise man; and you know what you shall do to him and you shall bring his

Notes, Chapter One (Cont.)

[61] MT: "of might." See 1:42.

[62] MT: "there will not fall from his hair to the ground."

[63] MT: "he will die."

Notes, Chapter Two

[1] MT lacks the phrase. Tg provides a spiritual interpretation of the Hebrew idiom "be a man." S-A, 159.

[2] MT: "the Lord."

[3] MT: "in his ways."

[4] MT lacks the word.

[5] MT: "the throne."

[6] MT: "and he murdered them, and he placed the blood of war in peace, and he gave the blood of war on his belt."

[7] MT: "on his sandal."

[8] MT lacks the preposition.

[9] MT: "drew near me."

[10] MT: "the Benjaminite from Bahurim." Tg translates the Hebrew *Bahurim* (young men) into its Aramaic equivalent, *'Almat* (youth).

[11] MT: "a bitter curse."

[12] MT: "the Lord."

[13] MT: "I will not put you to death."

gray head down *to*[14] Sheol *by killing.*"[15] 10. And David slept with his fathers, and he was buried in the city of David. 11. And the days that David was king over Israel were forty years; in Hebron he was king for seven years, and in Jerusalem he was king for thirty-three years. 12. And Solomon sat upon the throne of David his father, and his kingdom was very well established. 13. And Adonijah the son of Haggith came unto Bathsheba the mother of Solomon. And she said: "Is your coming peaceful?" And he said: "It is peaceful." 14. And he said: "I have a word *to speak with*[16] you." And she said: "Speak." 15. And he said: "You know that the kingdom was mine, and upon me all Israel set their faces *to be the king;*[17] and the kingdom has been turned around, and it has become my brother's for it was his *from before the Lord.*[18] 16. And now one request I am requesting from you; do not turn away my face." And she said to him: "Speak." 17. And he said: "Speak now to King Solomon, for he will not turn away your face; and let him give to me Abishag *who is from Shunem*[19] for a wife." 18. And Bathsheba said: "Good. I will speak about you *before*[20] the king." 19. And Bathsheba came *before*[21] King Solomon to speak with him about Adonijah, and the king arose to meet her, and he did obeisance to her and sat upon his throne and set up a throne for the mother of the king, and she sat at his right hand. 20. And she said: "One small request I am requesting from you; do not turn away my face." And the king said to her: "Ask me, my mother, for I will not turn away your face." 21. And she said: "Let Abishag *who is from Shunem*[22] be given to Adonijah your brother for a wife." 22. And King Solomon answered and said to his mother: "And why are you requesting Abishag *who is from Shunem*[23] for Adonijah? And request for him the kingdom, for he is my older brother. *Were they not in one plan*[24] —he and Abiathar the priest and Joab the son of Zeruiah?" 23. And King Solomon swore by *the Memra of the Lord,*[25] saying: "May *the Lord*[26] do thus to me and more so, for at the cost of his life Adonijah has spoken this word. 24. And now as the Lord lives who has established me and seated me upon *the throne of the kingdom*[27] of David my father and who set up for me a *kingdom*[28] as he said, for this day Adonijah *will be killed.*"[29] 25. And King Solomon sent by the hand of Benaiah the son of Jehoida, *and he overpowered him and killed him.*[30] 26. And to Abiathar the priest the king said: "Go *to*[31] Anathoth, *go away to your settlements,*[32] for you are a man *deserving killing.*[33] And on this day *I will not kill you,*[34] because you carried the ark of *the covenant of the Lord God*[35] before David my father and because you suffered in everything that my father suffered." 27. And Solomon drove out Abiathar from being a priest *serving before the Lord*[36] to fulfill the word of the Lord that he spoke about the house of Eli in Shiloh. 28. And *the news reached*[37] Joab, for Joab had

Notes, Chapter Two (Cont.)

[14] MT lacks the preposition.
[15] MT: "in blood."
[16] MT: "for."
[17] MT: "to rule."
[18] MT: "from the Lord."
[19] MT: "the Shunammite."
[20] MT: "to."
[21] MT: "to."
[22] MT: "the Shunammite."
[23] MT: "the Shunammite."
[24] MT lacks the phrase. It does have the prepo-sition "to" before each name.
[25] MT: "the Lord."
[26] MT: "God."
[27] MT: "the throne."
[28] MT: "house."
[29] MT: "will be put to death."
[30] MT: "and he struck him, and he died."
[31] MT lacks the preposition.
[32] MT: "unto your fields."
[33] MT: "a man of death."
[34] MT: "I will not put you to death."
[35] MT: "God the Lord."
[36] MT: "to the Lord."
[37] MT: "the report came."

turned after Adonijah and he had not turned after Absalom; and Joab fled to the tent of the Lord and took hold of the horns of the altar. 29. And it was told to King Solomon that Joab fled to the tent of the Lord and behold he was at the side of the altar; and Solomon sent Benaiah the son of Jehoida, saying: "Go, *overpower him.*"[38] 30. And Benaiah came to the tent of the Lord and said to him: "Thus said the king: 'Come forth.'" And he said: "No, for here *I will be killed.*"[39] And Benaiah brought word back to the king, saying: "Thus Joab spoke, and thus he answered me." 31. And the king said to him: "Do as he said; and *you shall overpower him*[40] and bury him, and you will remove *the guilt of the innocent blood,*[41] which Joab shed without cause, from me and from the house of my father. 32. And the Lord will bring back *the guilt of his killing*[42] on his head, who *overpowered*[43] two men more just and better than him and *killed*[44] them by the sword — and my father David did not know it — Abner the son of Ner the chief of the army of Israel, and Amasa the son of Jether the chief of the army of the house of Judah. 33. And let their blood turn back on the head of Joab and on the head of his *sons*[45] forever; and for David and for his seed and for his house and for his throne let there be peace forever *from before*[46] the Lord." 34. And Benaiah the son of Jehoida went up and *overpowered him and killed*[47] him; and he was buried in his house in the wilderness. 35. And the king *appointed*[48] Benaiah the son of Jehoida instead of him over the army, and he *appointed*[49] Zadok the priest in place of Abiathar. 36. And the king sent and called to Shimei and said to him: "Build for yourself a house in Jerusalem, and you shall dwell there and not go forth from there to here and to there. 37. And on the day that you go forth and you cross the brook Kidron, you know for sure that you will surely die; *the guilt of your killing*[50] will be on your head." 38. And Shimei said to the king: "Good is the word as my master the king spoke it. Thus your servant will do." And Shimei dwelt in Jerusalem many days. 39. And at the end of three years two slaves belonging to Shimei fled unto Achish the son of Maacah the king of Gath; and they told it to Shimei, saying: "Behold your slaves are in Gath." 40. And Shimei arose and saddled his ass and went to Gath unto Achish to seek out his slaves; and Shimei came and brought his slaves from Gath. 41. And it was told to Solomon that Shimei went from Jerusalem to Gath and returned. 42. And the king sent and called to Shimei and said to him: "*Did I not swear about you by the Memra of the Lord*[51] and bear witness against you, saying: 'On the day you go forth and you come to here and to there, you know for sure that you will surely die.' And you said to me: 'Good is the word; I have heard it.' 43. And why have you not kept the oath of the Lord

Notes, Chapter Two (Cont.)

[38]MT: "strike him down."

[39]MT: "I will die."

[40]MT: "strike him down."

[41]MT: "innocent blood."

[42]MT: "his blood."

[43]MT: "struck down."

[44]MT: "murdered."

[45]MT: "his seed."

[46]MT: "from with."

[47]MT: "struck him down and put him to death."

[48]MT: "gave."

[49]MT: "gave."

[50]MT: "your blood."

[51]MT: "Did I not make you swear by the Lord?"

and the commandment that I commanded about you?" 44. And the king said to Shimei: "You know all the evil that your heart knows, what you did to David my father; and the Lord has brought back your evil on your head. 45. And may King Solomon be blessed, and *the throne of the kingdom of David*[52] be established before the Lord forever." 46. And the king commanded Benaiah the son of Jehoiada, and he went forth and *overpowered him and killed him.*[53] And the kingdom was established in the hand of Solomon.

CHAPTER 3

1. And Solomon joined in a marriage alliance with Pharaoh the king of Egypt, and he took the daughter of Pharaoh, and he brought her to the city of David until he had completed building his house and *the house of the sanctuary of the Lord*[1] and the wall of Jerusalem round about. 2. Only the people were sacrificing on the high places because the house was not built to the name of the Lord until those days. 3. And Solomon loved *the service of the Lord,*[2] to go in the *decree*[3] of David his father; only he was sacrificing on the high places and *offering spices.*[4] 4. And the king went to Gibeon to sacrifice there, for it was a great high place. A thousand holocausts Solomon offered up upon that altar. 5. In Gibeon the Lord *revealed himself*[5] to Solomon in a dream of the night. And *the Lord*[6] said: "Ask what I shall give to you." 6. And Solomon said: "You have done great kindness with your servant David my father, just as he was walking before you in truth and in righteousness and in uprightness of heart *before*[7] you; and you have kept for him this great kindness, and you gave to him a son sitting upon his throne according to this day. 7. And now, Lord my God, you have made your servant king in place of David my father. And I am a little child; I do not know how to go forth and to come in. 8. And your servant is in the midst of your people that you have chosen, a great people that you have chosen, a great people that will not be counted and will not be numbered because of greatness. 9. And may you give to your servant a heart *knowing*[8] how to judge your people, to know between good and evil; for who is able to judge this great people of yours?" 10. And the thing *was pleasing before the Lord,*[9] because Solomon asked this thing. 11. And *the Lord*[10] said to him: "Because you have asked this thing, and you did not ask for yourself many days, and you did not ask for yourself wealth, and you did not ask the life of your enemies, and you asked for

Notes, Chapter Two (Cont.)

[52]MT: "the throne of David."
[53]MT: "struck him down, and he died."

Notes, Chapter Three

[1]MT: "the house of the Lord."
[2]MT: "the Lord."
[3]MT: "decrees."

[4]MT: "incensing."
[5]MT: "appeared."
[6]MT: "God."
[7]MT: "with."
[8]MT: "hearing."
[9]MT: "was good in the eyes of the Lord."
[10]MT: "God."

yourself *wisdom*[11] to hear judgment, 12. behold I have done according to your words; behold I have given to you a wise and intelligent heart; one like you there was not before you, and after you there will not arise one like you. 13. And also what you did not ask, I have given to you — both wealth and honor, so that no one among kings was like you, all your days. 14. And if you walk in *the ways that are good before me,*[12] to keep my statutes and my commandments, just as David your father walked, I will lengthen your days." 15. And Solomon awoke, and behold it was a dream. And he came to Jerusalem and stood before the ark of the covenant of *the Lord,*[13] and he offered up holocausts and *sacrificed sacrifices of holy things,*[14] and he made a feast for all his servants. 16. Then two women, prostitutes, came *to argue before the king,*[15] and they stood before him. 17. And one woman said: "Please, my master, I and this woman dwell in one house, and I gave birth with her in the house. 18. And on the third day of my giving birth, this woman also gave birth; and we were together; there was no stranger with us in the house; only the two of us were in the house. 19. And the son of this woman died in the night, because she lay upon him. 20. And she arose in the midst of the night and took my son from me, and your maidservant was sleeping; and she laid him *unto her,*[16] and she laid her dead son *unto me.*[17] 21. And I got up in the morning to nurse my son, and behold he was dead; and I inspected him in the morning, and behold he was not my son to whom I gave birth." 22. And the other woman said: "*Not so!*[18] My son is alive, and your son is dead." And this one was saying: "*Not so!*[19] Your son is dead, and my son is alive." And *they were arguing*[20] before the king. 23. And the king said: "This woman says: 'This is my son who is alive, and your son is dead.' And this woman says: '*Not so!*[21] Your son is dead, and my son is alive.'" 24. And the king said: "*Bring*[22] to me the sword." They brought the sword before the king. 25. And the king said: "Cut the living child in two, and give *half of him*[23] to one woman and *half of him*[24] to the other." 26. And the woman whose son was alive said to the king, for her insides *were moved*[25] for her son; and she said: "Please, my master, give the living child to her, and *do not kill him.*"[26] And this woman was saying: "It shall be neither mine nor yours. Cut." 27. And the king answered and said: "Give the living child to her, and *do not kill him.*[27] She is his mother." 28. And all Israel heard the judgment that the king judged, and they were afraid from before the king, for they saw that the wisdom of *the Lord*[28] was inside of him to make judgment.

Notes, Chapter Three (Cont.)

[11] MT: "understanding."

[12] MT: "my ways."

[13] MT: "Adonai" (rather than the Tetragrammaton).

[14] MT: "he made peace offerings."

[15] MT: "to the king."

[16] MT: "in her bosom."

[17] MT: "in my bosom."

[18] MT: "No, for."

[19] MT: "No, for."

[20] MT: "they were speaking."

[21] MT: "No, for."

[22] MT: "Take."

[23] MT: "half."

[24] MT: "half."

[25] MT: "were feeling compassion."

[26] MT: "do not put him to death."

[27] MT: "do not put him to death." A Tg variant provides absolute proof for Solomon's verdict with the addition: "And a *bath qôl* came down from heaven and said, 'She is his mother.'"

[28] MT: "God."

CHAPTER 4

1. And King Solomon was king over all Israel. 2. And these are the chiefs who were his: Azariah the son of Zadok was the priest; 3. Elihoreph and Ahijah the sons of Shisha were the scribes; Jehoshaphat the son of Ahilud was *put in charge of the records;*[1] 4. and Benaiah the son of Jehoida was *put in charge of*[2] the army; and Zadok and Abiathar were the priests; 5. and Azariah the son of Nathan was *put in charge of the*[3] officers; and Zabud the son of Nathan was the priest, the friend of the king; 6. and Ahishar was *put in charge of*[4] the house; and Adoniram the son of Abda was *put in charge of those bearing tribute.*[5] 7. And Solomon had twelve officers *put in charge of*[6] all Israel, and they are *providing*[7] for the king and *the men of his house;*[8] one month in the year *it comes*[9] to each for making provision. 8. And these are their names: *Bar*[10]-Hur in the hill country of *the house of Ephraim;*[11] 9. *Bar*[12]-Deker in Makaz and in Shaalbim and Beth-shemesh, and Elon *which is from*[13] Beth-hanan; 10. *Bar*[14]-Hesed in Arubboth (to whom belonged Soco and all the land of Hepher); 11. *Bar*[15]-Abinadab, all *the districts of Dor*[16] — Tophath the daughter of Solomon was his wife; 12. Baana the son of Ahilud, Taanach and Megiddo and all Beth-shan which is beside Zarethan below Jezreel, from Beth-shan unto *the plain of Meholah*[17] unto the other side of Jokneam; 13. *Bar*[18]-Geber in Ramoth-Gilead (he had the villages of Jair the son of Manasseh, which are in Gilead; his was the region of *Trachonitis that is in Matthan,*[19] sixty great cities *surrounded with a high wall that had bars of bronze);*[20] 14. Ahinadab the son of Iddo, *to whom Mahanaim belonged;*[21] 15. Ahimaaz in *the tribe of the house of Naphthali*[22] — he too took Basemath the daughter of Solomon for a wife; 16. Baana the son of Hushai in *the tribe of Asher*[23] and in Bealoth; 17. Jehoshaphat the son of

Notes, Chapter Four

[1]MT: "the recorder."
[2]MT: "over."
[3]MT: "over."
[4]MT: "over."
[5]MT: "over the forced labor." See 2 Sam 20:24.
[6]MT: "set over."
[7]MT: "provided."
[8]MT: "his house."
[9]MT: "it would be."
[10]MT: "Ben." In this and the names following Tg translates the Hebrew *Ben* ("son of") into the Aramaic *Bar*.
[11]MT: "Ephraim."
[12]MT: "Ben."
[13]MT lacks the phrase.
[14]MT: "Ben."
[15]MT: "Ben."
[16]MT: "Naphath-dor."
[17]MT: "Abel-meholah." The element "Abel" means "plain."
[18]MT: "Ben."
[19]MT: "Argob which is in Bashan."
[20]MT: "wall and bar of bronze."
[21]MT: "to Mahanaim."
[22]MT: "Naphtali."
[23]MT: "Asher."

Paruah in *the tribe of Issachar;*[24] 18. Shimei the son of Ela in *the tribe of the house of Benjamin;*[25] 19. Geber the son of Uri in the land of Gilead, the land of Sihon the Amorite king and Og the king *of Matthan;*[26] and there was one officer who *was put in charge*[27] in the land. 20. Judah and Israel were numerous, like the sand that is upon the sea for greatness; they were eating and drinking and rejoicing.

CHAPTER 5

1. And Solomon was powerful in all the kingdoms from *the Euphrates,*[1] to the land of the Philistines, and unto the border of Egypt. They were bringing offerings and serving Solomon all the days of his life. 2. And Solomon's bread for one day was thirty measures of fine flour and sixty measures of ordinary flour, 3. ten fatted oxen, and twenty oxen of the pasture, and a hundred sheep, besides deers and gazelles and roebucks and *the birds and the fatling.*[2] 4. For he ruled over all *Trans-Euphrates,*[3] from Tipsah and unto Gaza, over all the kings of *Trans-Euphrates;*[4] and he had peace from all his sides round about. 5. And Judah and Israel dwelt in security, each man beneath *the fruits of his vine*[5] and beneath *the fruits of his fig trees,*[6] from Dan and unto Beersheba all the days of Solomon. 6. And Solomon had forty thousand stalls of horses for his chariots and twelve thousand horseman. 7. And these officials were providing for King Solomon and everyone who approached the table of King Solomon, each man in his month; they were withholding nothing. 8. And barley and straw for the horses, and the harnessed horses they were bringing to the place where he was, each man according to his duty. 9. And *the Lord*[7] gave wisdom to Solomon and very much intelligence and breadth of heart like the sand that is upon the shore of the sea. 10. And the wisdom of Solomon was more than the wisdom of all the sons of the east and than all the wisdom of Egypt. 11. And he was wiser than all the men, than Ethan *the son of Zarah*[8] and Heman and Calcol and Darda, the sons of Mahol; and his name was *great*[9] among all the peoples round about. 12. And he *recited*[10] 3,000 proverbs, and his *songs*[11] were 1,005. 13. *And he prophesied about the kings of the house of David who would rule in this world and in the world of the Messiah;*[12] and he *prophesied*[13] about the beast and about the bird and about the reptile and about the fish. 14. And they came from all the nations to hear the wisdom of Solomon, from all

Notes, Chapter Four (Cont.)

[24]MT: "Issachar."
[25]MT: "Benjamin."
[26]MT: "Bashan."
[27]MT lacks the phrase.

Notes, Chapter Five

[1]MT: "the river."
[2]MT: "fatted fowl."
[3]MT: "Across the River."
[4]MT: "Across the River."

[5]MT: "his vine."
[6]MT: "his fig tree."
[7]MT: "God."
[8]MT: "the Ezrahite."
[9]MT: "was."
[10]MT: "spoke."
[11]MT: "song."
[12]MT: "And he spoke about the trees, from the cedar that is in Lebanon to the hyssop that goes forth in the wall." Some Tg mss. have a more literal rendering of this verse. In midrashic literature Lebanon often symbolizes Jerusalem, David, the Temple, and the Messiah.
[13]MT: "spoke."

the kings of the earth, who were hearing his wisdom. 15. And Hiram the king of Tyre sent his servants unto Solomon, for he heard that they anointed him *to be king*[14] in place of his father, for Hiram loved David all the days. 16. And Solomon sent unto Hiram, saying: 17. "You know David my father that he was not able to build the house to the name of the Lord his God on account of *the wagers of battle*[15] who surrounded him until the Lord gave them beneath the soles of his feet. 18. And now the Lord my God has given rest to me from round about; there is no adversary and no one who causes evil. 19. And behold I propose to build the house to the name of the Lord my God as the Lord spoke *with*[16] David my father, saying: 'Your son whom I will put in your place upon *the throne of your kingdom,*[17] he will build the house to my name.' 20. And now command, and let the cedars be cut for me from Lebanon, and my servants will be with your servants, and the wage of your servants I will give to you according to everything that you say, for you know that there is no man among us who knows how to cut wood like the Sidonians." 21. And when Hiram heard the words of Solomon, he rejoiced very much and said: "Blessed be the Lord this day who has given to David a wise son over this great people." 22. And Hiram sent unto Solomon, saying: "I have heard that you sent unto me; *I will satisfy all your needs*[18] with the cedar wood and with the cypress wood. 23. My servants will bring them down from Lebanon to the sea, and I will make them rafts in the sea unto the place that you shall send me, and I will remove them there, and you will pick them up; and *you will satisfy my needs*[19] to give food to *the men of my house.*"[20] 24. And Hiram was giving to Solomon cedar wood and cypress wood, all *that he needed.*[21] 25. And Solomon gave to Hiram 20,000 cors of wheat as provision for *the men of his house,*[22] and twenty cors of pounded oil; thus Solomon gave to Hiram year by year. 26. And the Lord gave wisdom to Solomon as he spoke to him; and there was peace between Hiram and between Solomon, and the two of them cut a covenant. 27. And King Solomon *appointed bearers of tribute*[23] from all Israel, and there were 30,000 men *bearing tribute.*[24] 28. And he sent them to Lebanon, 10,000 per month, in turn; one month they were in Lebanon, two months *each man*[25] in his house; and Adoniram *was put in charge of the tribute bearers.*[26] 29. And Solomon had 70,000 who were bearing on the shoulder and 80,000 who were hewing in the hill country, 30. besides the 3,300 chiefs of the officers who *were put in charge of*[27] Solomon's work, who were making the people work who were doing the work. 31. And the king commanded, and they removed great stones, *good*[28] stones to lay the foundation of the house, hewn stones. 32. And the *stone-setters*[29] of Solomon and the *stone-setters*[30] of Hiram and *the master-masons*[31] hewed, and they prepared the woods and the stones to build the house.

Notes, Chapter Five (Cont.)

[14]MT: "for king."
[15]MT: "the war."
[16]MT: "to."
[17]MT: "your throne."
[18]MT: "I will do all your desire."
[19]MT: "you will do my desire."
[20]MT: "my house."
[21]MT: "his desire."
[22]MT: "his house."
[23]MT: "raised a levy of forced labor."
[24]MT: "a levy."
[25]MT lacks the phrase.
[26]MT: "was over the levy."
[27]MT: "were over."
[28]MT: "precious."
[29]MT: "builders."
[30]MT: "builders."
[31]MT: "the men of Gebal." The Aramaic for "master-masons" contains the root letters of the name "Gebal."

CHAPTER 6

1. And in the 480th year after the sons of Israel's going forth from the land of Egypt, in the fourth year, in the month of Ziv, *the blossoms,*[1] that is the second month, for Solomon to be king over Israel, he built the house *before*[2] the Lord. 2. And the house that King Solomon built *before*[3] the Lord — sixty cubits was its length, and twenty its width, and thirty cubits its height. 3. And the entrance in front of the nave of the house —twenty cubits its length, in front of the width of the house; ten cubits its width, in front of the house. 4. And he made for the house windows *opened from within and shut from the outside, and covering the beam of the house of the fathers, (the beam) of (=at) the top of the cedar beams.*[4] 5. And he built against the walls of the house the brackets round about; he circled the walls of the house all round, the nave and the house of atonements; and he made extensions all round. 6. The lowest extension was five cubits wide, and the middle was six cubits wide, and the third was seven cubits wide; for he made projections for the house all round *the inside and the outside from the extensions, to be the ends of the beams resting on the brackets, and the beams were not passing through*[5] the walls of the house. 7. And in the building of the house there were used for building perfect, *fitted*[6] stones; and there was not heard hammers and *chisels*[7] and any instrument of iron in the building of the house. 8. The entrance to the lowest extension *opened*[8] to the right side of the house, and by a winding staircase they went up *from the lowest to the highest by way of the middle one.*[9] 9. And he built the house and finished it; and he covered the house *with ceiling panels and above them a row of joined timber, of beams of cedar timbers.*[10] 10. And he built the *gallery*[11] against the whole house, its height five cubits; and he *covered*[12] the house with cedar timbers. 11. And there was *a word of prophecy from before the Lord with*[13] Solomon, saying: 12. "This house that you are building — if you will walk in my statutes and do my ordinances and keep all my commandments to walk in them, then I will establish my *words*[14] with you that I spoke *with*[15] David your father, 13. and *I will make dwell my Shekinah*[16] among the sons of Israel, and I will not *reject*[17] my people, Israel." 14. And Solomon built the house and finished it. 15. And he built the walls of the house inside with boards of cedar; from the floor of the house to the walls *until it reaches the ends of*

Notes, Chapter Six

[1]MT lacks the word.
[2]MT: "for."
[3]MT: "for."
[4]The RSV is "with recessed frames." JPS has "recessed and latticed." Our English version of the Aramaic is not entirely certain.
[5]MT: "outside so as not to join in."
[6]MT: "(at the) quarry."
[7]MT: "axe."

[8]MT lacks the word.
[9]MT: "from the middle to the third."
[10]MT: "beams and planks in cedar."
[11]MT: "structure."
[12]MT: "joined."
[13]MT: "a word of the Lord to."
[14]MT: "word."
[15]MT: "to."
[16]MT: "I will dwell."
[17]MT: "abandon."

the beams he covered with planks of cedar inside;[18] and he covered the *floors*[19] of the house with boards of cypress. 16. And he built twenty cubits from the ends of the house with boards of cedar from the floor to the walls, and he built for it a house inside, for *a house of atonements,*[20] for a holy of holies. 17. The house, that is the nave in front of it, was forty cubits. 18. *He covered the house inside with planks of cedar, and he carved the appearance of eggs and ropes of flowers. The whole house was covered with planks of cedar;*[21] no stone was to be seen. 19. He prepared the *house of atonements*[22] within the house in the inmost part to place there the ark of the covenant of the Lord. 20. And before *the house of atonements*[23] twenty cubits long and twenty cubits wide and twenty cubits high — and he covered it with precious gold and he covered *the house with boards of cedar.*[24] 21. And Solomon covered the house inside with precious gold, and he stretched chains of gold across in front of *the house of atonements,*[25] and he covered it with gold. 22. And he covered the whole house with gold until he finished the whole house; and he covered with gold the whole altar which belongs to the *house of atonements.*[26] 23. And he made *for the house of atonements*[27] two cherubim of olive wood. Its height (was) ten cubits, 24. and one wing of the cherub was five cubits and the second wing of the cherub was five cubits; ten cubits from the ends of its wings, to the ends of its wings. 25. The second cherub (was) ten cubits. (There was) one measure and one *woof*[28] for the two cherubim. 26. The height of one cherub was ten cubits and so was the second cherub. 27. And he placed the cherubim within the innermost part of the house; and they spread the wings of the cherubim, and the wing of one reached the wall and the wing of the second cherub reached the second wall, and their wings in the middle of the house reached each other. 28. And he covered the cherubim with gold. 29. And *he cut figures around all the walls of the house, and he carved reliefs of cherubim and the shape of palm trees and ropes of flowers*[29] inside and outside. 30. And he covered the *floors*[30] of the house with gold inside and outside. 31. And *for*[31] the entrance of *the house of atonements*[32] he made doors of olivewood; *its pilaster, its door-post are joined.*[33] 32. And the two doors of olive wood, he carved on them cherubim and *the shape of palm trees and ropes of flowers,*[34] and he spread gold and he overlaid gold on the cherubim and on *the shape of the palm trees.*[35] 33. And he also made for the entrance of the nave doorposts of olive wood *from their four sides square*[36] 34. and two doors of cypress wood. Two *hinges*[37] of one door are *round,*[38] and

Notes, Chapter Six (Cont.)

[18]MT: "of the ceiling he covered with wood inside."

[19]MT: "floor."

[20]MT: "an inner sanctuary."

[21]MT: "The cedar inside the house was carved as gourds and open flowers; everything was cedar."

[22]MT: "the inner sanctuary."

[23]MT: "the inner sanctuary."

[24]MT: "the altar with cedar."

[25]MT: "the inner sanctuary."

[26]MT: "the inner sanctuary."

[27]MT: "the inner sanctuary."

[28]MT: "shape."

[29]MT: "he carved all the walls of the house round about with carved figures of cherubim and palm trees and open flowers."

[30]MT: "floor."

[31]MT lacks the preposition.

[32]MT: "the inner sanctuary."

[33]MT: "the lintel, the doorposts, five-formed."

[34]MT: "palm trees and open flowers."

[35]MT: "the palm trees."

[36]MT: "in the form of a square."

[37]MT: "leaves."

[38]MT: "folding."

two *hinges*[39] of the second door are *round*.[40] 35. And he carved cherubim and *the shape of palm trees and ropes of flowers*,[41] and he spread *pressed gold over the shapes*.[42] 36. And he built the inner courtyard with three courses of hewn stone and one course of *a beam*[43] of cedar wood. 37. In the fourth year *the house of the holiness of the Lord began to be finished*,[44] in the month of Ziv, *the blossoms*.[45] 38. And in the eleventh year, in the month of *the finishing of ripening*,[46] which is the eighth month, the house was finished according to all his *decrees*[47] and according to *everything which he had revealed to him*.[48] And he built it (in) seven years.

CHAPTER 7

1. And Solomon built his house for thirteen years, and he completed his entire house. 2. And he built *the royal summer-house*[1] — one hundred cubits was its length, and fifty cubits was its width, and thirty cubits was its height — on four rows of pillars of cedars, and *their*[2] beams of cedar upon the pillars. 3. And it was covered with boards of cedar above the extensions that were upon the forty-five pillars, fifteen in each row. 4. And there was *a beam*[3] (in) three rows, and window opposite window three times. 5. And all the doorways and doorposts were squared, and they covered the beam and window opposite window three times. 6. And he made the portico of pillars — fifty cubits was it length, and thirty cubits was its breadth; and there was a portico in front of them; and the pillars and the lintel were in front of them. 7. And the portico *for establishing there the seat of the court that judges there, the enclosure for the court*[4] he made and he covered it with *boards of*[5] cedar from the floors to the floors. 8. And his house where he dwells, the other court outside the hall was of like workmanship. And he made a house for the daughter of Pharaoh, whom Solomon took, like his hall. 9. All these were fine stones, hewn according to measure, sawed with saws inside and outside, and finished with projections, and from the outside to the great court. 10. It was finished with fine stones, large stones, stones of ten cubits and stones of eight cubits. 11. And above were fine stones, hewn according to measure, and *he covered (it) with boards of*[6] cedar. 12. And the great court had three rows of fine stones and one row of

Notes, Chapter Six (Cont.)

[39]MT: "leaves."
[40]MT: "folding."
[41]MT: "the palms and open flowers."
[42]MT: "gold evenly applied over the carved work."
[43]MT lacks the word.
[44]MT: "the house of the Lord was founded," i.e., its foundation was laid.
[45]MT lacks the word. See 6:1.
[46]MT: "Bul."
[47]MT: "words."
[48]MT: "all his statutes."

Notes, Chapter Seven

[1]MT: "the house of the forest of Lebanon." The literal translation of the Aramaic is "the house of the cooling of the kings." Tg understands a summer house, a structure common in Hellenistic-Roman architecture. See 10:17, 21; S-A, 106-07.
[2]MT lacks the possessive element.
[3]The Aramaic (and the MT) is obscure; see 6:4.
[4]MT: "of the throne where he would judge, the portico of judgment."
[5]MT lacks the word.
[6]MT lacks the phrase.

beams of cedar wood all around; and for the inner court of *the house of the sanctuary*[7] of the Lord and for the portico of the house. 13. And King Solomon sent and brought Hiram from Tyre. 14. He was the son of a widow woman from *the tribe of the house*[8] of Naphtali; and his father was a man of Tyre, *a craftsman in working*[9] bronze, and he was filled with wisdom and understanding and knowledge to make any work in bronze. And he came unto King Solomon and did all his work. 15. He cast two pillars of bronze. Eighteen cubits was the height of one pillar, and a *measuring*[10] line of twelve cubits went around *it;*[10] *and thus for*[10] the second column. 16. And he made two capitals to place on the tops of the columns, cast bronze; five cubits was the height of one capital, and five cubits was the height of the second capital. 17. Nets, network, *braids, wreath-work*[11] for the capitals which are on the top of the columns, seven for the first column and seven for the second column. 18. And he made columns and two rows all around on the one netting to cover the capitals which were on the top of the pomegranates; and thus he did for the second capital. 19. And the capitals which were on the top of the columns were lily work relief in the entrance — four cubits. 20. And the capitals were on the two columns also above, next to the *junction*[12] which was beside the netting; and two hundred pomegranates (in) rows *were made for it*[13] all around on the second capital. 21. And he set up the columns at the entrance of the nave; and he set up the pillar on the right and called its name Jachin, and he set up the pillar on the left and called its name Boaz. 22. And on the top of the columns was lily work. And the work of the columns was finished. 23. And he made the cast metal sea, ten cubits from its brim to its brim, round all around, and its height was five cubits and *a measuring line*[14] of thirty cubits went all around it. 24. And *the shape of eggs*[15] below its rim was going all around (for) ten cubits, going all around the sea; two rows *of the shape of eggs*[16] were cast in its casting. 25. It stood on twelve oxen, three *of their faces to* the north and three *of their faces to*[17] the west and three *of their faces to*[17] the south and three *of their faces to*[17] the east; and the sea *was set*[18] upon them from above; and all their hind parts were inward. 26. Its thickness was a handbreadth, and its brim was made like the rim of a cup, *round relief with*[19] lily; two thousand baths with *moisture finishing.*[20] 27. And he made ten stands of bronze. The length of one stand was four cubits, and its width was four cubits, and its height was three cubits. 28. And this was the structure of the *stands:*[21] they had *enclosures*[22] and *enclosures*[23] between the frames. 29. And on the *enclosures*[24] which were between the frames was *the form of*[25] lions, oxen, and cherubim; and on the frames was *a winding*[26] above, and below the lions and oxen *a junction*[27] made of welding. 30. And each stand had four wheels of bronze and *plates*[28] of bronze and its four corners were supports for them from below the laver,

Notes, Chapter Seven (Cont.)

[7]MT: "the house."
[8]MT: "the tribe."
[9]MT: "a worker."
[10]MT lacks the words.
[11]Tg reverses the order of the MT.
[12]MT: "the round projection."
[13]MT lacks the phrase.
[14]The Aramaic uses two words for the one MT word, but the meaning is the same.
[15]MT: "gourds."
[16]MT: "gourds."

[17]MT: "facing."
[18]MT lacks the verb.
[19]MT: "flower of."
[20]MT is obscure.
[21]MT: "stand."
[22]MT: "insets."
[23]MT: "insets."
[24]MT: "insets."
[25]MT lacks the word.
[26]MT: "thus" or perhaps "pedestal" (see 7:31, note 29).
[27]MT: "wreaths."
[28]MT: "axles."

supports (of) cast metal, welded with solder. 31. Its opening was within their crown and above by a cubit and its opening was round, made like a *winding*,[29] a cubit and half; and also on its opening was netting and their *enclosures*[30] were square, not round. 32. And the four wheels were below the *enclosures*,[31] and the axles of the wheels were in the stand; and the height of one wheel was a cubit and a half. 33. And the structure of the wheels was like the structure of *the wheels of an expensive chariot;*[32] their axles and their rims and *their coverings and their connections*[33] all were cast metal. 34. And four supports were at the four corners of each stand; its supports were one with the stand. 35. And on the top of the stand was a band a half cubit high all around and on the top of the stand, its supports and its frames were from it. 36. And on the surfaces, its supports, and on its frames he carved cherubim, lions, and *the shape of*[34] palm trees, *one enclosure and connection*[35] all around. 37. Like this he made the ten stands; one casting, one measure, one *woof*[36] for them all. 38. He made ten lavers of bronze; each laver (held) forty baths *with moisture finishing;*[37] each laver was four cubits; one laver was on each stand for the ten stands. 39. And he set the stands, five on the right side of the house and five on the left side of the house; and he set the sea on the right side of the house, east next to the south. 40. And Hiram made the lavers, the shovels, and the basins; and Hiram finished doing all the work which he did for King Solomon, *the house of the sanctuary*[38] of the Lord: 41. the two columns and the two globes of the capitals which are on the top of the pillars, and the two networks to cover the two globes of the capitals which are upon the columns; 42. and the four hundred pomegranates for the the two networks, two rows of pomegranates for each network, to cover the two globes of the capitals which were upon the columns; 43. and the ten stands and the ten lavers upon the stands; 44. and the one sea and twelve oxen under the sea; 45. and the pots and the shovels and the basins; and all these vessels, *according to the work of the vessels of the tent which Moses made, thus*[39] Hiram made for King Solomon (for) *the house of the sanctuary*[40] of the Lord (out of) burnished bronze. 46. In the plain of the Jordan the king cast (them); in the thickness of the clay between Succoth and Zarethan. 47. And Solomon *put aside*[41] all the vessels because of the great number. *There is no end to*[42] the weight of bronze. 48. And Solomon made all the vessels that are in *the house of the sanctuary*[43] of the Lord, the altar of gold, and the golden table on which is the bread of the presence, 49. and the lampstands (of) pure gold, five on the right and five on the left before *the house of atonements,*[44] and the flowers, and the

Notes, Chapter Seven (Cont.)

[29]MT: "a pedestal."

[30]MT: "insets."

[31]MT: "insets."

[32]MT: "the wheel of a chariot."

[33]MT is unclear; perhaps "their spokes and their hubs."

[34]MT lacks the word.

[35]MT: "according to the space of each, and wreaths."

[36]MT: "shape."

[37]See 7:26, note 20.

[38]MT: "the house."

[39]MT: "of the tent that."

[40]MT: "the house."

[41]MT: "left."

[42]MT: "There was no inquiry as to."

[43]MT: "the house."

[44]MT: "the inner sanctuary."

lamps, and the tongs (of) gold; 50. and the bowls and the snuffers and the basins and the incense dishes and the firepans (of) pure gold; and the hinge sockets for the doors of the innermost house, for the holy of holies, for the doors of the house for the nave, (of) pure gold. 51. And all the work which King Solomon did (for) *the house of the sanctuary*[45] of the Lord was finished. And Solomon brought the holy things of David his father; the gold and the silver and the vessels he put in the treasuries *of the house of the sanctuary*[46] of the Lord.

CHAPTER 8

1. Then Solomon gathered the elders of Israel *and*[1] all the heads of the tribes, the chiefs of the clans for the sons of Israel, unto King Solomon to Jerusalem to bring up the ark of the covenant of the Lord from the City of David, that is Zion. 2. And all the men of Israel were gathered unto King Solomon *in the month that the ancients called the first month (the festival) and now it is the seventh month.*[2] 3. And all the elders of Israel came, and the priests bore the ark. 4. And they brought up the ark of the Lord and the tent of the appointed time, and all the holy vessels that were in the tent; and the priests and the Levites brought them up. 5. And King Solomon and all the assembly of Israel who were joined with him *were standing*[3] with him before the ark, sacrificing sheep and oxen which could not be counted and could not be numbered for greatness. 6. And the priests brought in the ark of the covenant of the Lord to its place, *to the house of atonements that was prepared for it, in the midst of the house,*[4] to the holy of holies, to beneath the wings of the cherubim. 7. For the cherubim spread *their wings*[5] over the place of the ark, and the cherubim made a covering over the ark and over its poles from above. 8. And so long were the poles that the ends of the poles were seen from the holy place facing *the house of atonements*[6] and were not seen outside; and they are there unto this day. 9. In the ark *lay*[7] the two tablets of stones that Moses deposited there on Horeb *upon which were written the ten words of the covenant that the Lord cut*[8] with the sons of Israel in their going forth from the land of Egypt. 10. And when the priests went forth from the holy place, a *dense*[9] cloud filled *the house of the sanctuary*[10] of the Lord. 11. And the priests were not able to stand to minister from before the cloud, for the glory of the Lord filled *the house of the sanctuary*[11] of the

Notes, Chapter Seven (Cont.)

[45]MT: "the house."
[46]MT: "the house."

Notes, Chapter Eight

[1]MT lacks the word.
[2]MT: "in the month Ethanim, at the feast, that is, the seventh month." The reference is to the Feast of Tabernacles.

[3]MT lacks the verb.
[4]MT: "to the inner sanctuary of the house."
[5]MT: the dual "two wings."
[6]MT: "inner sanctuary."
[7]MT: "there was nothing except."
[8]MT: "that the Lord cut."
[9]MT lacks the adjective.
[10]MT: "house."
[11]MT: "house."

Lord. 12. Then Solomon said: "The Lord *has chosen to make his Shekinah reside in Jerusalem.*[12] 13. Indeed I have built *the house of the sanctuary before you, a place prepared for the house of your Shekinah forever.*"[13] 14. And the king turned his face and blessed all the assembly of Israel, and all the assembly of Israel was standing. 15. And he said: "Blessed be the Lord the God of Israel who *decreed by his Memra*[14] with David my father and *by his good pleasure*[15] fulfilled it, saying: 16. 'From the day that I brought forth my people Israel from Egypt I did not choose a city from all the tribes of Israel to build the house *to make my Shekinah reside*[16] there, and I chose David *to be the king*[17] over my people Israel.' 17. And it was in the heart of David my father to build the house to the name of the Lord the God of Israel. 18. And the Lord said to David my father: 'Inasmuch as it was with your heart to build the house to my name, you have done well for it was with your heart. 19. Only you shall not build the house, but *a son whom you will beget*[18] — he will build the house to my name.' 20. And the Lord fulfilled his *words*[19] that he spoke, and I rose up in the place of David my father and sat upon *the throne of the kingdom*[20] of Israel as the Lord spoke, and I built the house to the name of the Lord the God of Israel. 21. And I made a place there *prepared for the ark in which lay the two tablets of stone upon which was the covenant of the Lord*[21] that he cut with our fathers when he brought them out from the land of Egypt." 22. And Solomon stood before the altar of the Lord opposite all the assembly of Israel, and he spread out his hands *in prayer*[22] toward the heavens. 23. And he said: "Lord God of Israel, there is none *except you;*[23] you are the God *whose Shekinah is*[24] in the heavens above and *you are powerful*[25] on the earth below, keeping the covenant and fidelity to your servants who walk before you in all their heart, 24. you who have kept for your servant David my father what you spoke to him and *you decreed by your Memra,*[26] and *by your good pleasure*[27] you have fulfilled it this day. 25. And now Lord God of Israel, keep for your servant David my father what you spoke to him, saying: 'There will not be cut off to you a man before me sitting upon *the throne of the kingdom*[28] of Israel, if only our sons keep their ways to walk before me as you have walked before me.' 26. And now God of Israel, let your words that you spoke to David my father be established. 27. *For who hoped and who thought in truth? The Lord has chosen to make his Shekinah reside in the midst of the sons of men who are dwelling upon the earth.*[29] Behold the heavens and the heavens of the heavens cannot contain *your glory;*[30] so much the less this house that I have built. 28. And may you attend to

Notes, Chapter Eight (Cont.)

[12]MT: "said to dwell in thick darkness." MT could be interpreted as anti-Temple so Tg recasts it totally.

[13]MT: "an exalted house for you, a place for your dwelling forever."

[14]MT: "spoke by his mouth."

[15]MT: "by his hand."

[16]MT: "for my name to be."

[17]MT: "to be."

[18]MT: "your son who goes forth from your loins."

[19]MT: "word."

[20]MT: "the throne."

[21]MT: "the ark where the covenant of the Lord is."

[22]MT lacks the phrase.

[23]MT: "like you." Tg is careful to avoid the possibility of admitting another god exists.

[24]MT lacks the phrase.

[25]MT lacks the phrase.

[26]MT: "you spoke by your mouth."

[27]MT: "by your hand."

[28]MT: "the throne."

[29]MT: "For will God indeed dwell upon the earth?" Tg is more affirmative than the MT.

[30]MT: "you."

the prayer of your servant and to his petition, Lord my God, *to receive the prayer and the petition*[31] that your servant is praying before you this day, 29. that *good pleasure be before you to be a guard over*[32] this house night and day, to the place that you said: 'Let my name be there,' to *receive*[33] the prayer that your servant is praying *toward*[34] this place. 30. And *may you receive*[35] the petition of your servant and your people Israel that they will pray *toward*[36] this place, and *you will receive from the place of the house of your Shekinah, from the heavens; and you will receive their prayers and forgive their sins.*[37] 31. In case a man sins against his neighbor, and he forces him to swear an oath, and he comes, *he swears it*[38] before your altar in this house, 32. *may you receive from*[39] the heavens and act and judge your servants, to condemn the guilty, to give his way on his head, and to acquit the righteous, to give to him according to his righteousness. 33. When your people Israel be struck down before *their enemies*[40] because they are sinning *before*[41] you and they return to *your service*[42] and confess your name and pray and make petition *from before*[43] you in this house, 34. *may you receive from*[44] the heavens and forgive the *sins*[45] of your people Israel and bring them back to the land that you gave to their fathers. 35. *When the heavens are closed up*[46] and there shall not be rain because they will sin *before*[47] you, and they pray *toward*[48] this place and confess your name and turn from their sins because *you will receive their prayers,*[49] 36. *may you receive from*[50] the heavens and forgive the *sins*[51] of your servant and your people Israel, for you will teach them the *right*[52] way in which they will walk and you will give rain upon your land that you have given to your people for an inheritance. 37. If there be famine in the land, if there be pestilence, if there be blight and mildew, locust, caterpillar, if *their enemies attack them in the land of their cities,*[53] whatever affliction *and*[54] whatever sickness; 38. whatever prayer, whatever petition that there may be to any man, to all your people Israel, each man knowing the *afflictions*[55] of his heart, and he will stretch forth his hands *in prayer toward*[56] this house, 39. *then may you receive from the heavens, from the place of the house of your Shekinah, and forgive their sins and act on their petitions and give to each according to all his ways, for his heart is revealed before you, for you are the one, there is none besides you, before you only are the hearts of all the sons of men revealed,*[57] 40. in order

Notes, Chapter Eight (Cont.)

[31] MT: "to hear the cry and the prayer."
[32] MT: "your eyes be opened to."
[33] MT: "hear."
[34] MT: "to."
[35] MT: "may you hear."
[36] MT: "to."
[37] MT: "you will hear at the place of your dwelling, at the heavens; and you will hear, and you will forgive."
[38] MT: "swears."
[39] MT: "may you hear."
[40] MT: "enemy."
[41] MT: "against."
[42] MT: "you."
[43] MT: "to you."
[44] MT: "may you hear."
[45] MT: "sin."

[46] MT: "In the closing of the heavens."
[47] MT: "against."
[48] MT: "to."
[49] MT: "you will answer them."
[50] MT: "may you hear."
[51] MT: "sin."
[52] MT: "good."
[53] MT: "if his enemy attack him in the land of his gates."
[54] MT lacks the word.
[55] MT: "affliction."
[56] MT: "to."
[57] MT: "then may you hear in heaven, the place of your dwelling, and forgive, and act, and give to each according to all his ways, for you know his heart, for you alone know the heart of all the sons of men."

that they might *fear from before you*[58] all the days that they are living upon the face of the land that you have given to our fathers. 41. And also one *from a son of the peoples*[59] that are not from your people Israel and he comes from a far-off land on account of your name, 42. for they will hear of your great name and your mighty hand and your *raised-up*[60] arm, and he will come and pray *toward*[61] this house, 43. *may you receive from the heavens, from the place of the house of your Shekinah,*[62] and act according to all that *the son of the nations will pray before you,*[63] in order that all the nations of the earth may know your name to *fear before you*[64] like your people Israel and to know that your name is called upon this house that I have built. 44. If your people will go forth *to wage battle*[65] against *their enemies*[66] on the way that you will send them and they pray *before*[67] the Lord *toward*[68] the way of the city that you have chosen and the house that I built for your name, 45. *may you receive from the heavens*[69] their prayers and their petitions, and *may you avenge their humiliations.*[70] 46. If they sin *before*[71] you (for there is no man who does not commit sin), and *your anger take effect*[72] against them, and you give them before *their enemies,*[73] and their captors take them captive to the land of *their enemies*[74] whether far-off or near, 47. and they turn to their hearts in the land where they have been taken captive, and they turn and *ask from before*[75] you in the land of their captors, saying: 'We have sinned, and *we been stupid,*[76] we have offended,' 48. and they turn *to your service*[77] with all their heart and with all their soul in the land of their enemies who captured them, and they pray *before you toward*[78] the way of their land that you have given to their fathers, the city that you have chosen, and the house that I built for your name, 49. *may you receive from the heavens, from the place of the house of your Shekinah,*[79] their prayers and their petitions and *may you avenge their humiliations.*[80] 50. And may you forgive your people who have sinned *before*[81] you and all their rebellious acts that they rebelled *against your Memra,*[82] and may you give them mercy before their captors and they have mercy upon them. 51. For they are your people and your inheritance, whom you brought forth from Egypt from the midst of the furnace of iron, 52. *that there be good pleasure before you to receive*[83] the petitions of your servant and the petitions of your people Israel, *to receive their prayers in all the times that they are praying before you.*[84]

Notes, Chapter Eight (Cont.)

[58]MT: "fear you."

[59]MT: "to the foreigner."

[60]MT: "stretched out."

[61]MT: "to."

[62]MT: "may you hear in heaven, the place of your dwelling."

[63]MT: "the foreigner will call out to you."

[64]MT: "to fear you."

[65]MT: "for war."

[66]MT: "his enemy."

[67]MT lacks the preposition.

[68]MT: "to."

[69]MT: "may you hear in heaven."

[70]MT: "may you do their judgment." Tg reflects the later experience of Israel under the empires.

[71]MT: "against."

[72]MT: "you become angry."

[73]MT: "the enemy."

[74]MT: "the enemy."

[75]MT: "make supplication to."

[76]MT: "We have acted perversely."

[77]MT: "to you."

[78]MT: "to you."

[79]MT: "may you hear in the heavens, the place of your dwelling."

[80]MT: "may you do their judgment." See note 70 above.

[81]MT: "against."

[82]MT: "against you."

[83]MT: "that your eyes be opened to."

[84]MT: "to hear them all in their calling out to you."

53. For you have separated them for yourself for an inheritance from all the peoples of the earth as you spoke by the hand of Moses your servant when you brought forth our fathers from Egypt, O Lord God." 54. And when Solomon finished praying *before*[85] the Lord all this prayer and petition, he arose from before the altar of the Lord, from where he was bowed upon his knees and his hands were stretched out *in prayer toward the heavens*.[86] 55. And he arose and blessed all the assembly of Israel in a loud voice, saying: 56. "Blessed be the Lord who has given rest to his people Israel according to everything that he spoke. There has not failed one word from *all his good words*[87] that he spoke by the hand of Moses his servant. 57. *May the Memra of the Lord our God be at our aid as it was at the aid of our fathers!*[88] May it not forsake us, and may it not *reject*[89] us, 58. to direct our hearts *to fear him,*[90] to walk in all *the ways that are good before him*[91] and to keep his commandments and his statutes and his judgments that he commanded our fathers. 59. And may these words of mine that I have asked *from before the Lord be received before*[92] the Lord our God day and night, to carry out the judgment of his servant and *the humiliation*[93] of his people Israel, as needed day by day, 60. in order that all the peoples of the earth may know that the Lord is God; there is no other. 61. And may your heart be peaceful *in the fear of the Lord*[94] our God to walk in his statutes and to keep his commandments according to this day." 62. And the king and all Israel with him were sacrificing *the sacrifice of holy things*[95] before the Lord. 63. And Solomon sacrificed *the sacrifice of holy things*[96] that he sacrificed *before*[97] the Lord — 22,000 oxen and 120,000 sheep, and the king and all the sons of Israel dedicated *the house of the sanctuary*[98] of the Lord. 64. On that day the king consecrated the middle of the court that was before *the house of the sanctuary*[99] of the Lord, for there he made the holocaust and the cereal offering and the fat pieces *of the offering of holy things,*[100] for the altar of bronze that was before the Lord was too small to hold the holocaust and the cereal offering and the fat pieces of *the offering of holy things.*[101] 65. And Solomon made in that time a festival, and all Israel with him, a great assembly, from the entrance of Hamath unto the brook of Egypt, before the Lord our God, *seven days the dedication of the house and seven days the festival*[102] — fourteen days. 66. On the eighth day he sent the people away, and they blessed the king, and they went to their *cities while*[103] rejoicing, and *their heart was pleased*[104] over all the good that the Lord had done to David his servant and to Israel his people.

Notes, Chapter Eight (Cont.)

[85]MT: "to."

[86]MT: "heavenward."

[87]MT: "every good word of his."

[88]MT: "May the Lord our God be with us as he was with our fathers."

[89]MT: "abandon."

[90]MT: "to him."

[91]MT: "his ways."

[92]MT: "before the Lord be brought near."

[93]MT: "the judgment."

[94]MT: "with the Lord." See note 70 above. But the Tg translation does not fit here.

[95]MT: "a sacrifice."

[96]MT: "a sacrifice of peace-offerings."

[97]MT: "to."

[98]MT: "the house."

[99]MT: "the house."

[100]MT: "the peace-offerings."

[101]MT: "the peace-offerings."

[102]MT: "seven days and seven days."

[103]MT: "tents."

[104]MT: "good of heart."

CHAPTER 9

1. And when Solomon finished building *the house of the sanctuary*[1] of the Lord and the house of the king and all the desire of Solomon that he wished to do, 2. the Lord *revealed himself*[2] to Solomon a second time as he *revealed himself*[3] to him in Gibeon. 3. And the Lord said to him: "Your prayers and your petitions that you asked from before me *have been heard before me.*[4] I have consecrated this house that you built *for my Shekinah to reside*[5] there forever, and *my Shekinah will be residing in it, if my good pleasure is done*[6] there all the days. 4. And you, if you walk before me as David your father walked in truthfulness of heart and in uprightness to act according to everything that I have commanded you, my statutes and my judgments you will keep, 5. I will raise up the throne of your kingdom over Israel forever as I spoke *with*[7] David your father, saying: 'There shall not be cut off for you a man from upon the *the throne of the kingdom*[8] of Israel.' 6. If indeed you and your sons turn aside *from after my service*[9] and you do not keep my commandments and my statutes that I gave before you, and you go and serve *the idols of the nations*[10] and you worship them, 7. *I will destroy*[11] Israel from upon the face of the land that I have given to them, and the house that I have consecrated to my name I will remove far *from opposite my Memra,*[12] and Israel will be for a proverb and a by-word among all the nations. 8 *And this house which was high will become ruined.*[13] Everyone who will pass over it *will stop and shake his head,*[14] and they will say: "Why has the Lord done thus to this land and to this house?" 9. And they will say: "Because they forsook *the service of the Lord*[15] their God who brought forth their fathers from the land of Egypt and they held onto *the idols of the nations*[16] and worshipped them and served them. Therefore the Lord brought upon them all this evil." 10. And at the end of twenty years Solomon had built the two houses, *the house of the sanctuary*[17] of the Lord and the house of the king. 11. Hiram the king of Tyre provided Solomon with cedar wood and with cypress wood and with gold for all his needs. Therefore King Solomon gave to Hiram twenty cities in the land of Galilee. 12. And Hiram went forth from Tyre *to visit*[18] the cities that Solomon gave to him, and they were not fitting in his eyes. 13. And he said: "What are these cities that you have

---

Notes, Chapter Nine

[1] MT: "house."
[2] MT: "appeared."
[3] MT: "appeared."
[4] MT: "I have heard."
[5] MT: "to place my name."
[6] MT: "my eyes and my heart will be." Tg qualifies God's promise to be present with the condition that Israel do God's will.
[7] MT: "about."

[8] MT: "the throne."
[9] MT: "from after me."
[10] MT: "other gods."
[11] MT: "I will cut away."
[12] MT: "from my face."
[13] MT: "And this house will be high."
[14] MT: "will be astonished and hiss."
[15] MT: "the Lord."
[16] MT: "other gods."
[17] MT: "the house."
[18] MT: "to see."

given to me, my brother?" And he called them the land of Cabul unto this day. 14. Hiram sent to the king 120 talents of gold. 15. And this is the account of *the tribute bearers*[19] whom King Solomon *appointed*[20] to build *the house of the sanctuary*[21] of the Lord and his house and the Millo and the wall of Jerusalem, and Hazor, and Megiddo, and Gezer 16. (Pharoah the king of Egypt went up and conquered Gezer and set it aflame with fire and killed the Canaanite who was dwelling in the city, and he gave it *as a gift*[22] to his daughter, the wife of Solomon. 17. And Solomon built Gezer), and lower Beth-horon, 18. and Baalath, and *Tadmor*[23] in the wilderness in the land, 19. and all the cities of the storage places that were Solomon's, and the cities of the chariots, and the cities of the horsemen and the desire of Solomon that he wished to build in Jerusalem and in Lebanon and in all the land of his power. 20. All the people who were left from *the Amorites, Hittites, Perizzites, Hivvites, and Jebusites*[24] who were not from the sons of Israel, 21. their sons who were left after them in the land whom the sons of Israel were not able to destroy, Solomon *appointed them to be tribute bearers*[25] serving unto this day. 22. And from the sons of Israel, Solomon did not *appoint to be slaves,*[26] for they were *men waging battle*[27] and his servants and his chiefs *and his warriors*[28] and the chiefs of his chariots and his horsemen. 23. These are the chiefs of the officers who were appointed over the work that was Solomon's: 550 who *were making work*[29] the people who were doing the work. 24. But the daughter of Pharaoh went up from the city of David to her house that he built for her. Then he built the Millo. 25. And Solomon offered three times a year holocausts and *offerings of holy things*[30] upon the altar that he built *before*[31] the Lord and *burned sweet-smelling incense upon it*[32] before the Lord. And he completed the house. 26. And King Solomon made a fleet in Ezion-geber which is near Eloth upon the bank of the Red Sea in the land of Edom. 27. And Hiram sent with the fleet his servants, boatmen *who were skilled to sail in the sea,*[33] along with the servants of Solomon. 28. And they came to Ophir, and they took from there 420 talents of gold, and they brought it unto King Solomon.

Notes, Chapter Nine (Cont.)

[19]MT: "the forced labor."
[20]MT: "brought up."
[21]MT: "the house."
[22]MT: "as dowry."
[23]This is the MT *qere*; the *ketib* is Tamar.
[24]In the MT all these names are in the singular.
[25]MT: "made a slave-levy."

[26]MT: "did not give a slave."
[27]MT: "men of war."
[28]MT lacks the phrase.
[29]MT: "had charge of."
[30]MT: "peace offerings."
[31]MT: "to."
[32]MT: "he burned incense with it which was."
[33]MT: "knowers of the sea."

CHAPTER 10

1. And the queen of Sheba heard a report of Solomon,[1] and she came to test him with riddles. 2. And she came to Jerusalem with very *many retainers,*[2] camels *laden*[3] with spices, and very much gold, and *precious stones.*[4] And she came unto Solomon and spoke with him everything that was with her heart. 3. And Solomon told her all her words; there was nothing *that was hidden*[5] from the king that he did not tell her. 4. And the queen of Sheba saw all the wisdom of Solomon and the house that he built, 5. and the food of his table, and the banqueting of his servants, and the attending of his ministers, and their clothing, and his drink and his holocausts that he was offering at *the house of the sanctuary*[6] of the Lord; and no breath was left in her. 6. And she said to the king: "True was the word that I heard in my land about your words and about your wisdom. 7. And I did not believe the words until I came, and my eyes saw, and behold there was not told to me half *of what I saw.*[7] In wisdom and goodness you have surpassed the report that I heard. 8. Happy are your men, happy are these servants of yours who stand before you always hearing your wisdom. 9. May the Lord your God be blessed, who chose you to give you upon *the throne of the kingdom*[8] of Israel by the Lord's love of Israel forever and appointed you *to be the king to do the judgment of truth*[9] and righteousness." 10. And she gave to the king 120 talents of gold and very many spices and *precious stones.*[10] Never again did so many spices as these come as the queen of Sheba gave to King Solomon. 11. And also the fleet of Hiram, which was bringing gold from Ophir, brought from Ophir very much almug wood and *precious stones.*[11] 12. And the king made of the almug wood a support for *the house of the sanctuary*[12] of the Lord and for the house of the king, and lutes and lyres for *the sons of Levi;*[13] such coral-wood has not come and has not been seen unto this day. 13. And King Solomon gave to the queen of Sheba all her good-pleasure that she asked besides what he *appointed*[14] for her, according to *the wealth of the hand*[15] of King Solomon; and she turned away and went to her land, she and her servants. 14. And the weight of the gold that came to Solomon in one year was 666 talents of gold, 15. apart from *the pay of the craftsmen and the goods of the merchants*[16] and all the kings of *the auxilia-*

Notes, Chapter Ten

[1]MT adds "to the name of the Lord."
[2]MT: "heavy retinue."
[3]MT: "bearing."
[4]MT has the expression in the singular.
[5]MT: "hidden."
[6]MT: "the house."
[7]MT lacks the phrase.
[8]MT: "the throne."

[9]MT: "for a king to do judgment."
[10]MT has the expression in the singular.
[11]MT has the expression in the singular.
[12]MT: "the house."
[13]MT: "the singers." Tg makes the singers Levites, a later arrangement.
[14]MT: "gave."
[15]MT: "the hand."
[16]MT: "the traders and the traffic of the merchants."

ries[17] and the rulers of the land. 16. And King Solomon made 200 large shields of *good*[18] gold; 600 of gold went into one shield. 17. And 300 shields of *good*[19] gold, three minas of gold went into one shield; and the king deposited them in *the summer-house of the kings*.[20] 18. And the king made a throne of much ivory, and covered it with *good*[21] gold. 19. The throne has six steps, and a *round*[22] head in the back, and arms on both sides upon the place of sitting, and two lions standing by the side of the arms, 20. and twelve lions standing there upon the six steps on both sides. Nothing like this was made in any of the kingdoms. 21. And all the drinking vessels of King Solomon were gold, and all the vessels of *the summer-house of the kings*[23] were *good*[24] gold; there was no silver; it was not accounted anything in the days of Solomon. 22. For the king had an *African fleet*[25] in the sea along with the fleet of Hiram. Once every three years *the African fleet*[26] was coming, *laden*[27] with gold and silver, *ivory of the elephant*[28] and apes and peacocks. 23. And King Solomon was greater than all the kings of the earth in wealth and in wisdom. 24. And all *the inhabitants of the earth*[29] were seeking *to see the brightness of Solomon's face,*[30] to hear his wisdom that *the Lord*[31] gave in his heart. 25. And these were bringing, each his offering, vessels of silver and vessels of gold and garments and *armored garments*[32] and spices and horses and mules, *a specified amount*[33] year by year. 26. And Solomon gathered chariots and horsemen, and he had 1,400 chariots and 12,000 horsemen; and he had them reside in the cities of the chariots *except for those who were*[34] with the king in Jerusalem. 27. And the king gave silver in Jerusalem like stones; and he gave cedars like sycamores, which are in the lowland, for multitude. 28. And *they were bringing in*[35] the horses that belonged to Solomon from Egypt and from Kue; the merchants of the king *were buying*[36] from Kue at a price. 29. And a chariot was going up and going forth from Egypt for 600 (pieces) of silver, and *horses*[37] for 150. And they were going forth to all the kings of the Hittites and to the kings of Aram *at their good pleasure*.[38]

Notes, Chapter Ten (Cont.)

[17]MT: "Arabia." Arabs were commonly used as auxiliaries in the Roman army.

[18]MT: "beaten."

[19]MT: "beaten."

[20]MT: "the house of the forest of Lebanon." See 7:12 and 10:21.

[21]MT: "refined."

[22]MT: "a calf's."

[23]MT: "the house of the forest of Lebanon."

[24]MT: "pure."

[25]MT: "the fleet of Tarshish."

[26]MT: "the fleet of Tarshish."

[27]MT: "bearing."

[28]MT: only "ivory."

[29]MT: "the earth."

[30]MT: "Solomon's face."

[31]MT: "God."

[32]MT: "weapons."

[33]MT: "an amount."

[34]MT: "and."

[35]MT: "the import."

[36]MT: "they were taking."

[37]MT: "a horse."

[38]MT: "by their hand."

CHAPTER 11

1. And King Solomon loved many women, *daughters of the nations,*[1] and the daughter of Pharaoh, Moabites, Ammonites, Edomites, Sidonians, Hittites, 2. from the nations that the Lord said to the sons of Israel: "*You shall not be mixed with them, and they shall not be mixed with you lest*[2] they make your heart stray after their *idols.*"[3] Solomon *delighted in loving them.*[4] 3. And he had 700 women (as) *queens*[5] and 300 concubines, and his wives made his heart go astray. 4. And at the time when Solomon was old, his wives made his heart go astray after *the idols of the nations,*[6] and his heart was not perfect *in the fear of the Lord*[7] his God like the heart of David his father. 5. And Solomon went after Ashtoreth *the idol*[8] of the Sidonians and after Milcom the abomination of the Ammonites. 6. And Solomon did what was evil *before*[9] the Lord and did not follow perfectly after *the fear of the Lord*[10] like David his father. 7. Then Solomon built a high place to Chemosh the abomination of *the Moabites*[11] on the mountain that faces Jerusalem and to Moloch the abomination of the sons of Ammon. 8. And thus he did for all his wives, *daughters of the nations, who were offering spices*[12] and sacrificing to *their idols.*[13] 9. And *the anger of the Lord was strong*[14] against Solomon, for his heart turned away from *the fear of the Lord*[15] God of Israel which was revealed to him two times, 10. and commanded him about this matter, in order that he not walk after *the idols of the nations;*[16] and he did not observe what the Lord commanded. 11. And the Lord said to Solomon: "Because this was with you and you did not observe *my commands*[17] and my statutes that I commanded you, I will indeed *make the kingdom pass*[18] from you and give it to your servant. 12. But in your days I will not do this on account of David your father. From the hand of your son *I will make it pass.*[19] 13. Only the whole kingdom *I will not make pass;*[20] I will give one tribe to your son on account of David my servant and on account of Jerusalem which I have chosen. 14. And the Lord raised up an adversary for Solomon, Hadad the Edomite; he was from the seed of the king in Edom. 15. And when David was *in*[21] Edom, when Joab the commander of the army went up *to strip those who had been killed, he killed*[22] every male in Edom. 16. For Joab and all Israel dwelt there for six months until

Notes, Chapter Eleven

[1]MT: "foreigners."

[2]MT: "You shall not go in them, and they shall not go in you, for."

[3]MT: "gods."

[4]MT: "clung to them for love."

[5]MT: "princesses."

[6]MT: "other gods."

[7]MT: "with the Lord."

[8]MT: "god."

[9]MT: "in the eyes of."

[10]MT: "the Lord."

[11]MT: "Moab."

[12]MT: "foreigners, who were incensing."

[13]MT: "their gods."

[14]MT: "the Lord was angry."

[15]MT: "the Lord."

[16]MT: "other gods."

[17]MT: "my covenant."

[18]MT: "tear the kingdom."

[19]MT: "I will tear it."

[20]MT: "I will not tear."

[21]MT: "with."

[22]MT: "to bury the slain, he struck down."

he had destroyed[23] every male in Edom. 17. And Hadad, he and the Edomite men from the servants of his father with him, fled to enter Egypt; and Hadad was a small child. 18. And they arose from Midian and came to Paran, and they took men with them from Paran and came to Egypt unto Pharaoh the king of Egypt; and he gave to him a house, and he assigned food *to supply*[24] him, and he gave land to him. 19. And Hadad found much favor in the eyes of Pharaoh, and he gave him as a wife the sister of his own wife, the sister of Tahpenes *the queen.*[25] 20. And the sister of Tahpenes bore to him Genubath his son; and Tahpenes weaned him in the midst of the house of Pharaoh. And Genubath *was growing up*[26] in the house of Pharaoh in the midst of the sons of Pharaoh. 21. And Hadad heard in Egypt that David slept with his fathers and that Joab the commander of the army was dead; and Hadad said to Pharaoh: "Send me away, and I will go to my land." 22. And Pharaoh said to him: "For what are you lacking with me *that*[27] you are seeking to go to your land?" And he said: "No, send me away." 23. And *the Lord*[28] raised up for him as an adversary Rezon the son of Eliada, who fled from before Hadadezer the king of Zobah his master. 24. And he gathered men about him, and he was chief of a band when David killed them; and they went to Damascus and dwelt in it, and they made him king in Damascus. 25. And he was an adversary to Israel all the days of Solomon, and the evil that Hadad *did;*[29] and *he rebelled against*[30] Israel, and he was king over Aram. 26. Jeroboam the son of Nebat was an Ephraimite from Zeredah, and the name of his mother was Zeruah a widow, and he was a servant of Solomon; and he raised *his hand*[31] against the king. 27. And this is the reason that he raised a hand against the king. Solomon built the Millo; he closed up the breach of the city of David his father. 28. And the man Jeroboam was a man of strength, and Solomon saw the young man, that he was doing the work; and he appointed him for all *the tribute bearers*[32] of the house of Joseph. 29. And at that time Jeroboam went forth from Jerusalem; and Ahijah the Shilonite, a prophet, found him on the road. And he was clothed in a new garment, and the two of them were alone in the field. 30. And Ahijah took hold of the new garment that was upon him, and he tore it into twelve pieces. 31. And he said to Jeroboam: "Take for yourself ten pieces, for thus the Lord God of Israel said: 'Behold I *am making pass*[33] the kingdom from the hand of Solomon, and I will give to you the ten tribes. 32. And one tribe will be his on account of my servant David and on account of Jerusalem, the city that I have chosen from all the tribes of Israel. 33. Because they forsook *my service*[34] and worshipped Ashtoreth *the idol*[35] of the Sidonians, Chemosh *the idol*[36] of the Moabites, and Milcom *the idol*[37] of the sons of Ammon; and they did not walk in *the ways that are right before me*[38] to do what is proper *before me*[39] and my statutes and my judgments, like David his father. 34. And I will not take all the kingdom *from him,*[40] for I will make

Notes, Chapter Eleven (Cont.)

[23]MT: "he cut away."
[24]MT lacks the phrase.
[25]MT: "the lady."
[26]MT lacks the word.
[27]MT: "and behold."
[28]MT: "God."
[29]MT lacks the verb.
[30]MT: "he abhorred."
[31]MT: "a hand."

[32]MT: "forced labor."
[33]MT: "am tearing."
[34]MT: "me."
[35]MT: "the god."
[36]MT: "the god."
[37]MT: "the god."
[38]MT: "my ways."
[39]MT: "in my eyes."
[40]MT: "from his hand."

him *king*[41] all the days of his life, on account of David my servant whom I chose, who kept my commands and my statutes. 35. And I will take the kingdom from the hand of his son and give to you the ten tribes. 36. And to his son I will give one tribe in order *to establish a kingdom*[42] for David my servant all the days before me in Jerusalem, the city in which I chose *to make my Shekinah reside*[43] there. 37. And *I will draw you near,*[44] and you will rule according to all that your soul desires, and you will be king over Israel. 38. And if you *accept*[45] everything that I will command you and you walk in *the ways that are right before me*[46] and do what is proper *before me,*[47] to keep my statutes and my commands just as David my servant did, *my Memra will be at your aid,*[48] and *I will establish for you a lasting kingdom just as I established*[49] for David and I will give to you Israel. 39. And I will afflict the seed of David on account of this; but not all the days.'" 40. And Solomon sought *to kill*[50] Jeroboam, and Jeroboam arose and fled to Egypt unto Shishak the king of Egypt; and he was in Egypt until *Solomon died.*[51] 41. And the rest of the acts of Solomon, and all that he did, and his wisdom, are they not written in the book of the acts of Solomon? 42. And the days that Solomon ruled in Jerusalem over all Israel were forty years. 43. And Solomon slept with his fathers, and he was buried in the city of David his father. And Rehoboam his son ruled in his place.

CHAPTER 12

1. And Rehoboam went to Shechem, for all Israel came to Shechem to make him king. 2. And when Jeroboam the son of Nebat heard, he was still in Egypt where he fled from before King Solomon. And Jeroboam dwelt in Egypt. 3. And they sent and called to him, and Jeroboam and all the assembly of Israel came, and they spoke with Rehoboam, saying: 4. "Your father made harsh our yoke, and you now lighten up from the harsh service of your father and from his heavy yoke that he gave upon us, and we will serve you." 5. And he said to them: "Go, *and wait*[1] until three days, and return unto me." And the people went away. 6. And King Rehoboam took counsel with the elders who *were serving*[2] before Solomon his father while he was alive, saying: "How are you counselling to bring word back to this people?" 7. And they spoke with him, saying: "If this day *you submit yourself*[3] to this people and you serve them and answer them *good*

Notes, Chapter Eleven (Cont.)

[41]MT: "ruler."
[42]MT: "that there be a lamp." Tg translates the metaphor into denotative prose.
[43]MT: "to place my name."
[44]MT: "I will take you."
[45]MT: "hear."
[46]MT: "my ways."
[47]MT: "in my eyes."
[48]MT: "I will be with you."

[49]MT: "I will build for you a sure house just as I built." Tg, like rabbinic literature, stresses the kingdom, rather than the dynasty ("house").
[50]MT: "to put to death."
[51]MT: "the death of Solomon."

Notes, Chapter Twelve

[1]MT lacks the phrase.
[2]MT: "were standing."
[3]MT: "you be a servant."

words[4] and speak with them *right*[5] words, they will be servants to you all the days." 8. And he abandoned the counsel of the elders that they counseled him, and he took counsel with the youngsters who had grown up with him, who *were serving*[6] before him. 9. And he said to them: "What are you counselling that we send word back to this people who are speaking with me, saying: 'Lighten up from the yoke that your father gave upon us?'" 10. And the youngsters who had grown up with him spoke with him, saying: "Thus you will say to this people who spoke with you, saying: 'Your father has made heavy our yoke, and you lighten up from us.' Thus you will speak with them: '*My weakness is stronger than the strength of my father.*'[7] 11. And now my father raised upon you a heavy yoke, and I will add to your yoke. My father chastised you with *rods,*[8] and I will chastise you with *whips.*"[9] 12. And Jeroboam and all the people came unto Rehoboam on the third day just as the king spoke, saying: "Return unto me on the third day." 13. And the king answered the people *in harsh words,*[10] and he abandoned the counsel of the elders that they counselled him. 14. And he spoke with them according to the counsel of the youngsters, saying: "My father made your yoke heavy, and I will add to your yoke. My father chastised you with *rods,*[11] and I will chastise you with *whips.*"[12] 15. And the king *did not accept from*[13] the people, for there was *division from before*[14] the Lord in order to fulfill his word that the Lord spoke by the hand of Ahijah the Shilonite *about*[15] Jeroboam the son of Nebat. 16. And all Israel saw that the king *did not accept from*[16] them, and the people answered the king a word, saying: "What portion is there for us in David? And there is no inheritance in the son of Jesse. *Each man to your cities,*[17] O Israel. Now *rule over the men of*[18] your house, O David." And Israel went to its *cities.*[19] 17. And the sons of Israel who were dwelling in the cities of *the house of Judah*[20] — Rehoboam ruled over them. 18. And King Rehoboam sent Adoram *who was appointed over the tribute bearers,*[21] and all Israel stoned him *with*[22] stone, and he died. And King Rehoboam succeeded to go up on the chariot, *to go forth*[23] to Jerusalem. 19. And Israel rebelled against the house of David unto this day. 20. And when all Israel heard that Jeroboam returned, they sent and called him to the assembly, and they made him king over all Israel. None was after the house of David except the tribe of *the house of Judah*[24] alone. 21. And Rehoboam came to Jerusalem, and he gathered all *those of the house*[25] of Judah and the tribe *of the house of Benjamin*[26] — 180,000, *each a warrior, wagers of battle — to wage battle*[27] with the

Notes, Chapter Twelve (Cont.)

[4]MT lacks the phrase.

[5]MT: "good."

[6]MT: "were standing."

[7]MT: "My little finger is thicker than the loins of my father." The Hebrew proverb is transformed into a clear prose statement.

[8]MT: "whips."

[9]MT: "scorpions."

[10]MT: "harshly."

[11]MT: "whips."

[12]MT: "scorpions."

[13]MT: "did not listen to."

[14]MT: "a turn of affairs from with."

[15]MT: "to."

[16]MT: "did not listen to."

[17]MT: "To your tents."

[18]MT: "see."

[19]MT: "tents."

[20]MT: "Judah."

[21]MT: "who was over the forced labor." See 2 Sam 20:24.

[22]MT lacks the word.

[23]MT: "to flee." Tg avoids the pejorative verb of the MT.

[24]MT: "Judah."

[25]MT: "the house."

[26]MT: "of Benjamin."

[27]MT: "a chosen one, making war—to fight."

house of Israel, to restore the kingdom to Rehoboam the son of Solomon. 22. And *the word of prophecy was from before the Lord with Shemaiah the prophet of the Lord,*[28] saying: 23. "Say to Rehoboam the son of Solomon, the king of *the tribe of the house of Judah,*[29] and to all the house of Judah and Benjamin and the rest of the people, saying: 24. 'Thus said the Lord: "You shall not go up and you shall not *wage battle*[30] with your brothers, the sons of Israel. Return, each man to his house, for *from before my Memra*[31] was the word."'" And they *received*[32] the word of the Lord, and they turned to go according to the word of the Lord. 25. And Jeroboam built Shechem in the hill country *of the house of Ephraim,*[33] and he dwelt in it; and he went forth from there and built Penuel. 26. And Jeroboam said in his heart: "Now *perhaps*[34] the kingdom will return to the house of David, 27. if this people will go up to make *the sacrifice of holy things in the house of the sanctuary*[35] of the Lord in Jerusalem, and the heart of this people will *turn itself after*[36] their master, *after*[37] Rehoboam, the king *of the tribe of the house of Judah,*[38] and they will kill me, and they will turn unto Rehoboam the king *of the tribe of the house of Judah.*"[39] 28. And the king took counsel and made two calves of gold, and he said to them: "Too much for you is the way from going up to Jerusalem. Behold these are *your deities,*[40] O Israel, who brought you up from the land of Egypt." 29. And he set up one in Bethel, and he put one in Dan. 30. And this act was a sin, and the people went before one unto Dan. 31. And he made a house of high places, and he made *idol priests*[41] from a part of the people that were not from the sons of Levi. 32. And Jeroboam made a festival in the eighth month on the fifteenth day of the month, like the festival that was in *the tribe of Judah,*[42] and he went up to the *altar;*[43] thus he did in Bethel to sacrifice to the calves that he made, and he appointed in Bethel the *idol priests*[44] of the high places that he made. 33. And he went up to the *altar*[45] that he made in Bethel, on the fifteenth day of the eighth month, in the month that he *appointed from his own good pleasure,*[46] and he made a festival for the sons of Israel, and he went up to the *altar*[47] to burn incense.

Notes, Chapter Twelve (Cont.)

[28]MT: "the word of God was to Shemaiah, the man of God."

[29]MT: "Judah."

[30]MT: "fight."

[31]MT: "from with me."

[32]MT: "heard."

[33]MT: "of Ephraim."

[34]MT lacks the word.

[35]MT: "sacrifices in the house."

[36]MT: "turn to."

[37]MT: "to."

[38]MT: "of Judah."

[39]MT: "of Judah."

[40]MT: "your gods."

[41]MT: "priests." The Aramaic word distinguishes them from (true) Israelite priests.

[42]MT: "in Judah."

[43]MT: The Aramaic word distinguishes this (false) altar from the (true) altar of the Israelites.

[44]MT: "priests."

[45]As opposed to the Israelite altar.

[46]MT: "devised from his heart."

[47]As opposed to the Israelite altar.

CHAPTER 13

1. And behold *the prophet of the Lord*[1] came from *the tribe of Judah according to*[2] the word of the Lord to Bethel; and Jeroboam was standing at the *altar*[3] to offer incense. 2. And *he prophesied*[4] about the *altar*[5] by the word of the Lord, and he said: "O altar, O altar, thus said the Lord: 'Behold a son is to be born to the house of David, Josiah is his name; and he will slaughter upon you *the idol priests of the high places who offered up spices*[6] upon you, and the bones of men they will burn upon you.'" 3. And he gave a sign on that day, saying: "This is the sign that *you will know that the Lord sent me:*[7] Behold the altar is split, and the ashes that are upon it poured out." 4. And when the king heard the word of *the prophet of the Lord that he prophesied*[8] concerning the altar in Bethel, Jeroboam reached out his hand above the altar, saying: "Seize him." And his hand that he reached forth upon him dried up, and he was not able to draw it back to himself. 5. And the altar was split, and the ashes from the altar were poured out according to the sign that *the prophet of the Lord*[9] gave by the word of the Lord. 6. And the king answered and said *to the prophet of the Lord:*[10] "*Pray now before*[11] the Lord your God, and *ask from before him,*[12] and let my hand return to me." And *the prophet of the Lord prayed before*[13] the Lord, and the hand of the king returned to him, and it became as it was in the first place. 7. And the king spoke *with the prophet of the Lord:*[14] "Enter with me into the house, and eat, and I will give to you a gift." 8. And *the prophet of the Lord*[15] said to the king: "If you give me half of your house, I will not enter with you and I will not eat bread and I will not drink water in this place. 9. For thus he commanded me by the word of the Lord, saying: 'You shall not eat bread, and you shall not drink water, and you shall not return on the way that you came.'" 10. And he went on another way, and he did not return on the way by which he came to Bethel. 11. And one old *lying*[16] prophet was dwelling in Bethel, and his son came and told him all the deed that *the prophet of the Lord*[17] did this day in Bethel, the words that he spoke with the king; and they told them to their father. 12. And their father spoke with them: "By what way did he go?" And his sons showed the way that *the prophet of the Lord*[18] who came from *the tribe of Judah*[19] went. 13. And

Notes, Chapter Thirteen

[1]MT: "the man of God."
[2]MT: "Judah by."
[3]As opposed to the Israelite altar.
[4]MT: "he cried out."
[5]As opposed to the Israelite altar.
[6]MT: "the priests of the high places who were incensing."
[7]MT: "the Lord spoke."
[8]MT: "the man of God that he cried out."
[9]MT: "the man of God."

[10]MT: "the man of God."
[11]MT: "Entreat now the face of."
[12]MT: "pray for me."
[13]MT: "the man of God entreated the face of."
[14]MT: "to the man of God."
[15]MT: "the man of God."
[16]MT lacks the word.
[17]MT: "the man of God."
[18]MT: "the man of God."
[19]MT: "Judah."

he said to his sons: "Saddle the ass for me." And they saddled the ass for him, and he rode upon it. 14. And he went after *the prophet of the Lord*[20] and found him sitting beneath the terebinth, and he said to him: "Are you *the prophet of the Lord*[21] who came from *the tribe of Judah?*"[22] And he said: "I am." 15. And he said to him: "Come with me to the house, and eat bread." 16. And he said: "I cannot return with you and enter with you, and I will not eat bread and I will not drink water with you in this place. 17. For *it was decreed upon me*[23] by the word of the Lord: 'You shall not eat bread, and you shall not drink water there, and you shall not turn to go on the way by which you came.' " 18. And he said to him: "I too am a prophet like you, and the angel spoke with me by the word of the Lord, saying: 'Bring him back with you to your house, and let him eat bread and drink water.' " He lied to him. 19. And he returned with him, and he ate bread in his house and drank water. 20. And *while they were reclining*[24] at the table, *the word of prophecy was from before the Lord with*[25] the prophet who brought him back. 21. And *he prophesied about the prophet of the Lord*[26] who came from *the tribe of Judah,*[27] saying: "Thus said the lord: 'Because you rebelled *against*[28] the *Memra*[29] of the Lord and did not keep the commandment that the Lord your God commanded you, 22. and you returned and ate bread and drank water in the place that he spoke with you: "You shall not eat bread, and you shall not drink water," your corpse *will not be gathered*[30] to the tomb of your fathers.' " 23. And after he ate bread and after he drank, he saddled for him the ass belonging to the prophet who brought him back. 24. And he went, and a lion found him on the way and *killed him;*[31] and his corpse was cast down on the way; and the ass was standing alongside it, and the lion was standing by the side of the corpse. 25. And behold men were passing by, and they saw the corpse cast down on the way and the lion standing by the side of the corpse, and they came and spoke in the city in which the *lying*[32] old prophet was dwelling. 26. And the prophet who brought him back from the way heard and said: "It is *the prophet of the Lord*[33] who rebelled *against*[34] the *Memra*[35] of the Lord, and the Lord gave him over to the lion, and he tore him apart and *killed him*[36] according to the word of the Lord that he spoke to him." 27. And he spoke with his sons, saying: "Saddle for me the ass." And they saddled it. 28. And he went and found his corpse cast down on the way, and the ass and the lion standing by the side of the corpse. The lion had not eaten the corpse and had not torn apart the ass. 29. And the *lying*[37] prophet took the corpse of *the prophet of the Lord*[38] and laid it down upon the ass and brought him back; and *they came*[39] to the city of the *lying*[40] old prophet to mourn *over him*[41] and to bury him. 30. And he laid down his corpse in his tomb, and

Notes, Chapter Thirteen (Cont.)

[20]MT: "the man of God."
[21]MT: "the man of God."
[22]MT: "Judah."
[23]MT: "the word was to me."
[24]MT: "they were sitting."
[25]MT: "the word of the Lord was to."
[26]MT: "he cried out to the man of God."
[27]MT: "Judah."
[28]MT lacks the preposition.
[29]MT: "mouth."
[30]MT: "will not come."

[31]MT: "put him to death."
[32]MT lacks the word.
[33]MT: "the man of God."
[34]MT lacks the preposition.
[35]MT: "mouth."
[36]MT: "put him to death."
[37]MT lacks the word.
[38]MT: "the man of God."
[39]MT: "he came."
[40]MT lacks the word.
[41]MT lacks the phrase.

they mourned over him: "Alas *for* [42] my brother." 31. And after he buried him, he said to his sons, saying: "When I die, you shall bury me in the tomb in which *the prophet of the Lord* [43] is buried; by the side of his bones lay down my bones. 32. For the word that *he prophesied* [44] by the word of the Lord concerning the altar that is in Bethel and concerning all the houses of the high places that are in the cities of Samaria *will surely be fulfilled.* " [45] 33. After this Jeroboam did not turn from his evil way; and he turned and made *part of the people* [46] *idol priests* [47] the high places; whoever so wished *was offering his sacrifice,* [48] and there were *idol priest for* [49] the high places. 34. And *this* [50] was for the sins of the house of Jeroboam and to destroy and annihilate it from upon the face of the earth.

CHAPTER 14

1. In that time Abijah the son of Jeroboam was sick. 2. And Jeroboam said to his wife: "Arise now, and disguise yourself, and let them not know that you are the wife of Jeroboam; and you will go to Shiloh, *and* [1] behold Ahijah the prophet is there; he spoke about me *that I was to be king* [2] over this people. 3. And you will take in your hand ten *loaves of* [3] bread and cakes and a jar of honey, and you will come unto him. He will tell you what will happen to the boy." 4. And the wife of Jeroboam did so, and she arose and went to Shiloh and came to the house of Ahijah. And Ahijah was not able to see because his eyes were dim from his old age. 5. And the Lord said to Ahijah: "Behold the wife of Jeroboam is coming to ask word from you about her son, for he is sick. Thus and so you will speak with her." And when she came in, she was disguised. 6. And when Ahijah heard the sound of her feet as she came in by the door, he said: "Come in, wife of Jeroboam. Why are you so disguised? And I am sent *to prophesy about you harsh words.* [4] 7. Go, say to Jeroboam: 'Thus said the Lord God of Israel: "Because I have set you apart from the midst of the people and *appointed you to be the king* [5] over my people Israel, 8. and *made pass away* [6] the kingdom from the house of David and gave it to you; and you were not like my servant David who kept my commands and who walked *after my service* [7] with all his heart to do only what is proper *before me;* [8] 9. and you have done worse than all who were before you, and you went and made for yourself *the idols of the nations* [9] and molten things so as to cause anger before me, and *you put my service far from opposite your eyes;* [10] 10. therefore

Notes, Chapter Thirteen (Cont.)

[42] MT lacks the word.
[43] MT: "the man of God."
[44] MT: "he cried out."
[45] MT: "will surely be."
[46] MT: "from among the people."
[47] MT: "priests."
[48] MT: "he was filling his hand."
[49] MT: "priests of."
[50] MT: "in this."

Notes, Chapter Fourteen

[1] Most MT mss. lack the word.
[2] MT: "for king."
[3] MT lacks the word.
[4] MT: "to you harshly."
[5] MT: "given you as leader."
[6] MT: "tore away."
[7] MT: "after me."
[8] MT: "in my eyes."
[9] MT: "other gods."
[10] MT: "you cast me behind your back."

behold I am bringing evil *upon*[11] the house of Jeroboam and I will destroy for Jeroboam *whoever knows knowledge*[12] bonded and free in Israel; and *I will glean*[13] after the house of Jeroboam just as *they roll down with threshing rollers until they finish.*[14] 11. Whoever belonging to Jeroboam will die in the city, the dogs will eat; and whoever will die in the field, the birds of the heaven will eat, for *by the Memra of the Lord it is so decreed."*[15] 12. And you, arise, go to your house; when your feet come into the city, the boy will die. 13. And all Israel will mourn *over*[16] him and bury him, for this one alone belonging to Jeroboam *will be gathered*[17] to the tomb, because in him something that is good *before*[18] the Lord God of Israel has been found in the house of Jeroboam. 14. And the Lord will raise up *before*[19] him a king over Israel who will destroy the house of Jeroboam — *whoever is alive this day, and also who will be born from then and forward.*[20] 15. And the Lord will strike down Israel just as one shakes the reed in the waters, and he will root up Israel from upon this good land that he gave to their fathers, and he will banish them across *the Euphrates*[21] because they made their Asherim so as *to cause anger before*[22] the Lord. 16. And *the Lord*[23] will give over Israel on account of the sins of Jeroboam that he sinned and that he made Israel sin." 17. And the wife of Jeroboam arose and went and came to Tirzah. She entered on the threshold of the house, and the boy died. 18. And they buried him, and all Israel mourned over him according to the word of the Lord that he spoke by the hand of his servant Ahijah the prophet. 19. And the rest of the acts of Jeroboam which he fought and which he ruled — behold they are written in the book of the chronicles of the kings of Israel. 20. And the days that Jeroboam ruled were twenty-two years; and he slept with his fathers; and Nadab his son ruled in his place. 21. And Rehoboam the son of Solomon ruled *over those of the house of Judah.*[24] Rehoboam was forty-one years old when he became king, and for seventeen years he ruled in Jerusalem, the city where the Lord chose *to make his Shekinah reside*[25] from all the tribes of Israel. And the name of his mother was Naamah, *who was from the sons of Ammon.*[26] 22. And *those of the house of Judah*[27] did what was evil *before*[28] the Lord and *caused more anger before him*[29] than all their fathers did in their sins that they sinned. 23. And they too built for themselves high places and pillars and Asherim upon every exalted hill and beneath every *leafy*[30] tree. 24. And there were *prostitutes*[31] in the land; they did according to all the abominations of the nations that the Lord drove out from before the sons of Israel. 25. And in the fifth year for King Rehoboam, Shishak the king of Egypt went up against Jerusalem. 26. And he took the treasures of *the house of the sanctuary*[32] of the Lord and the treasures of the house of the king; and he took everything, and he took all the shields of

Notes, Chapter Fourteen (Cont.)

[11] MT "to."

[12] A euphemism for the MT "who urinates against the wall."

[13] MT: "I will burn away."

[14] MT: "one burns away dung until it is gone."

[15] MT: "the Lord has spoken."

[16] MT: "for."

[17] MT: "will come."

[18] MT: "to."

[19] MT: "for."

[20] MT is obscure: "This day and henceforth."

[21] MT: "the river."

[22] MT: "angering."

[23] The subject of the sentence is not explicit in the MT.

[24] MT: "in Judah."

[25] MT: "to place his name."

[26] MT: "the Ammonitess."

[27] MT: "Judah."

[28] MT: "in the eyes of."

[29] MT: "angered him more."

[30] MT: "green."

[31] The Aramaic term has no reference to the cultic aspect of this prostitution. Also the MT specifies them as males.

gold that Solomon made. 27. And King Rehoboam made in their place shields of bronze, and he committed them to the hand of the chiefs of the runners who were guarding the door of the house of the king. 28. And at the time that the king entered *the house of the sanctuary*[33] of the Lord, the runners were taking them and returning them to the hall of the runners. 29. And the rest of the acts of Rehoboam and all that he did, are they not written in the book of the chronicles of the kings of *the house of Judah?*[34] 30. And there was war between Rehoboam and Jeroboam all the days. 31. And Rehoboam slept with his fathers, and he was buried with his fathers in the city of David; and the name of his mother was Naamah *who was from the sons of Ammon.*[35] And Abijam his son ruled in his place.

CHAPTER 15

1. And in the eighteenth year for King Jeroboam the son of Nebat, Abijam ruled over *those of the house of Judah.*[1] 2. For three years he ruled in Jerusalem, and the name of his mother was Maacah the daughter of Abishalom. 3. And he went in all the sins of his father that he did before him, and his heart was not perfect *in the fear of the Lord*[2] his God like the heart of David his father. 4. For on account of David the Lord his God established for him *a kingdom*[3] in Jerusalem so as to appoint his son after him and to establish Jerusalem. 5. For David did what was proper *before*[4] the Lord and did not stray from everything that he commanded him all the days of his life except in the matter of Uriah the Hittite. 6. And there was war between Rehoboam and Jeroboam all the days of his life. 7. And the rest of the acts of Abijam and all that he did — are they not written in the book of the chronicles of the kings of the house of Judah? And there was war between Abijam and Jeroboam. 8. And Abijam slept with his fathers, and they buried him in the city of David. And Asa his son ruled in his place. 9. And in the twentieth year for Jeroboam the king of Israel, Asa ruled as king of *the tribe of the house of Judah.*[5] 10. And for forty-one years he ruled in Jerusalem, and the name of his mother was Maacah the daughter of Abishalom. 11. And Asa did what was proper *before*[6] the Lord like David his father. 12. And he removed the *prostitutes*[7] from the land, and he made pass away all the idols that his fathers made. 13. And he also made Maacah his mother go away from *her kingdom,*[8] for she made an *idol*[9] to Asherah; and

Notes, Chapter Fourteen (Cont.)

[32]MT: "the house."
[33]MT: "the house."
[34]MT: "Judah."
[35]MT: "the Ammonitess."

Notes, Chapter Fifteen

[1]MT: "Judah."

[2]MT: "with the Lord."
[3]MT: "a lamp."
[4]MT: "in the eyes of."
[5]MT: "Judah."
[6]MT: "in the eyes of."
[7]The Aramaic term has no reference to the cultic aspect of this prostitution. Also the MT specifies the prophets as males.
[8]MT: "her being queen-mother."
[9]MT: "abominable image."

Asa cut down her *idol*[10] and burned it in the brook *of*[11] Kidron. 14. And the high places did not cease entirely; only the heart of Asa was perfect *in the fear of*[12] the Lord all his days. 15. And he brought the sacred objects of his father and his own sacred objects to *the house of the sanctuary*[13] of the Lord — silver and gold and vessels. 16. And there was war between Asa and Baasha the king of Israel all their days. 17. And Baasha the king of Israel went up against *those of the house of Judah,*[14] and he built Ramah in order not to *allow*[15] anyone going forth and coming in to Asa the king of *the tribe of the house of Judah.*[16] 18. And Asa took all the silver and gold that were left in the treasuries of *the house of the sanctuary*[17] of the Lord and *in*[18] the treasuries of the house of the king, and he assigned them in the hand of his servants; and King Asa sent them unto the son of Hadad, the son of Tabrimmon, the son of Hezion, the king of Aram who was dwelling in Damascus, saying: 19. "Let there be a covenant between me and you *and*[19] between my father and your father; behold I have sent to you as a gift silver and gold; go, change your covenant with Baasha the king of Israel, and let him withdraw from me." 20. And the son of Hadad *accepted from*[20] King Asa, and he sent the chiefs of the armies that were his against the cities of Israel; and he struck down Ijon and Dan and Abel-beth-Maacah and all Chinneroth, against all the land of the tribe of Naphtali. 21. And when Baasha heard, he ceased from building Ramah and dwelt in Tirzah. 22. And King Asa *gathered all those of the house of Judah;*[21] there was no one who was exempted. And they took up the stones of Ramah and its wood with which Baasha built, and King Asa built with them *Gibeah of the house of Benjamin*[22] and Mizpah. 23. And the rest of all the acts of Asa and all his might and all that he did and the cities that he built — are they not written in the book of the chronicles of the kings of *the house of Judah?*[23] Only at the time of his old age he was diseased *in*[24] his feet. 24. And Asa slept with his fathers, and he was buried with his fathers in the city of David his father, and Jehoshaphat his son ruled in his place. 25. And Nadab the son of Jeroboam ruled over Israel in the second year for Asa the king of *the tribe of the house of Judah,*[25] and he ruled over Israel for two years. 26. And he did what was evil *before*[26] the Lord, and he went in the way of his father and in his sin that he made Israel sin. 27. And Baasha the son of Ahijah belonging to the house of Issachar rebelled against him, and Baasha *killed*[27] him in Gibbethon which belongs to the Philistines. And Nadab and all Israel were laying siege against Gibbethon. 28. And Baasha *killed him*[28] in the third year for Asa the king of *the tribe of the house of Judah,*[29] and he ruled in his place. 29. And as soon as he became king, he *killed*[30] all the house of Jeroboam; he left no breathing thing for Jeroboam until he had destroyed him according to the word of the Lord that he spoke by the hand of his servant Ahijah the Shilonite, 30. on account

Notes, Chapter Fifteen (Cont.)

[10]MT: "abominable image."

[11]MT lacks the word.

[12]MT: "with."

[13]MT: "the house."

[14]MT: "Judah."

[15]MT: "give."

[16]MT: "Judah."

[17]MT: "the house."

[18]Some MT mss. lack the preposition, but it is found in other ancient versions.

[19]MT lacks the conjunction.

[20]MT: "listened to." See Joshua 11:2.

[21]MT: "summoned all Judah."

[22]MT: "Geba of Benjamin."

[23]MT: "Judah."

[24]MT lacks the preposition.

[25]MT: "Judah."

[26]MT: "in the eyes of."

[27]MT: "struck him down."

[28]MT: "put him to death."

[29]MT: "Judah."

[30]MT: "struck down."

of the sins of Jeroboam that he sinned and that he made Israel sin in his causing anger that he caused anger *before*[31] the Lord the God of Israel. 31. And the rest of the acts of Nadab and everything that he did — are they not written in the book of the chronicles of the kings of Israel? 32. And there was war between Asa and Baasha the king of Israel all their days. 33. In the third year for Asa the king of *the tribe of the house of Judah,*[32] Baasha son of Ahijah ruled over all Israel in Tirzah for twenty-four years. 34. And he did what was evil *before*[33] the Lord, and he walked in the way of Jeroboam and in his sins that he made Israel sin.

CHAPTER 16

1. And *a word of prophecy was from before the Lord with*[1] Jehu the son of Hanani concerning Baasha, saying: 2. "Despite the fact that I raised you up from the dust and *appointed you to be the king*[2] over my people Israel, still you went in the way of Jeroboam, and you made my people Israel sin *to cause anger before me*[3] by their sins, 3. behold *I am gleaning*[4] after Baasha and after his house, and I will give your house like the house of Jeroboam the son of Nebat. 4. Whoever belonging to Baasha will die in the city, the dogs will eat; and whoever belonging to him will die in the field, the birds of the heavens will eat." 5. And the rest of the acts of Baasha and what he did and his might — are they not written in the book of the chronicles of the kings of Israel? 6. And Baasha slept with his fathers, and he was buried in Tirzah, and Elah his son ruled in his place. 7. And also by the hand of Jehu the son of Hanani the prophet *a word of prophecy was from before the Lord*[5] concerning Baasha and concerning his house and concerning all the evil that he did *before the Lord to cause anger before him*[6] by the *works*[7] of his hands to be like the house of Jeroboam, and because he *killed it.*[8] 8. In the twenty-sixth year for Asa the king of *the tribe of the house of Judah,*[9] Elah the son of Baasha ruled over Israel in Tirzah two years. 9. And his servant Zimri, *one of the two chiefs of the chariots,*[10] rebelled against him. And he was in Tirzah drinking, getting drunk at the house of Arza *the idol which was in*[11] the house of Tirzah. 10. And Zimri came and struck him down and *killed him*[12] in the twenty-seventy year for Asa the king

Notes, Chapter Fifteen (Cont.)

[31]MT lacks the preposition.
[32]MT: "Judah."
[33]MT: "in the eyes of."

Notes, Chapter Sixteen

[1]MT: "a word of the Lord was to."
[2]MT: "gave you as leader."

[3]MT: "to anger me."
[4]MT: "I am burning away."
[5]MT: "the word of the Lord was to."
[6]MT: "in the eyes of the Lord to anger him."
[7]MT: "work."
[8]MT: "struck him down."
[9]MT: "Judah."
[10]MT: "the commander of half the chariotry."
[11]MT: "who was over." Tg connects inebriation with idolatrous worship. Some Tg mss. follow the MT.
[12]MT: "put him to death."

of *the tribe of the house of Judah,*[13] and he ruled in his place. 11. And when he became king, when he sat upon his throne, *he killed*[14] all the house of Baasha; he did not leave for him *any one knowing knowledge*[15] and *his relatives*[16] and his companions. 12. And Zimri destroyed all the house of Baasha according to the word of the Lord that he spoke against Baasha by the hand of Jehu the prophet, 13. on account of all the sins of Baasha and the sins of Elah his son that they sinned and made Israel sin so as *to cause anger before the Lord*[17] God of Israel by their idols. 14. And the rest of the acts of Elah and all that he did — are they not written in the book of the chronicles of the kings of Israel? 15. In the twenty-seventh year for Asa the king of *the tribe of the house of Judah,*[18] Zimri ruled seven days in Tirzah. And the people were encamped against Gibbethon belonging to the Philistines. 16. And the people who were encamped heard, saying: "Zimri has rebelled, and also he *has killed*[19] the king." And all Israel made Omri, chief of the army, king over Israel in that day in the camp. 17. And Omri and all Israel went up with him from Gibbethon, and they encamped against Tirzah. 18. And when Zimri saw that the city was conquered, he went into *the inner chamber*[20] of the house of the king, and he burned over him the house of the king with fire, and he died, 19. on account of his sins that he sinned to do what is evil *before*[21] the Lord, to go in the way of Jeroboam and in his sins that he made Israel to sin. 20. And the rest of the acts of Zimri and his rebellion that he rebelled — are they not written in the book of the chronicles of the kings of Israel? 21. Then the people of Israel was divided *into two halves.*[22] Half of the people was behind Tibni the son of Ginath to make him king, and half behind Omri. 22. And the people who were behind Omri were stronger than the people who were behind Tibni the son of Ginath; and Tibni died, and Omri ruled. 23. In the thirty-first year for Asa the king of *the tribe of the house of Judah,*[23] Omri ruled over Israel for twelve years. In Tirzah he ruled for six years. 24. And he bought *the fortified place*[24] of Samaria from Shemer for two talents of silver, and he built *the fortified place,*[25] and he called the name of the city that he built by the name of Shemer the lord of the hill country of Samaria. 25. And Omri did what was evil *before*[26] the Lord, and he did worse than all who were before him. 26. And he went in all the way of Jeroboam the son of Nebat and in his sins that he made Israel sin so as *to cause anger before the Lord*[27] God of Israel by their idols. 27. And the rest of the acts of Omri that he did and his might that he did — are they not written in the book of chronicles of the kings of Israel? 28. And Omri slept with his fathers, and he was buried in Samaria. And Ahab his son ruled in his place. 29. And Ahab the son of Omri ruled over Israel in the thirtieth-eighth year for Asa the king of *the tribe of the house of Judah,*[28] and Ahab the son of Omri ruled over Israel in Samaria twenty-two years. 30. And Ahab the son of

Notes, Chapter Sixteen (Cont.)

[13]MT: "Judah."

[14]MT: "he struck down."

[15]A euphemism for the MT "who pisses against the wall."

[16]MT: "his avengers." Tg makes explicit that those responsible for avenging blood guilt would be Baasha's relatives.

[17]MT: "to anger the Lord."

[18]MT: "Judah."

[19]MT: "struck down."

[20]MT: "citadel" or "fortress."

[21]MT: "in the eyes of."

[22]MT: "in half."

[23]MT: "Judah."

[24]MT: "the mountain."

[25]MT: "the mountain."

[26]MT: "in they eyes of."

[27]MT: "to anger the Lord."

[28]MT: "Judah."

Omri did what was evil *before*[29] the Lord more than all who were before him. 31. And it was a light thing *in his eyes*[30] to go in the sins of Jeroboam the son of Nebat, and he took as a wife Jezebel the daughter of Ethbaal the king of the Sidonians, and he went and served Baal and worshipped him. 32. And he erected a pagan altar to Baal (in) the house of Baal that he built in Samaria. 33. And Ahab made the Asherah. And Ahab continued to act so as *to cause anger before the Lord*[31] God of Israel more than all the kings of Israel who were before him. 34. In his days Hiel *of Beth-Mume*[32] built Jericho; *he killed Abiram his firstborn when he began to lay its foundation,*[33] and *Segub his younger son when he erected its gates*[34] according to the word of the Lord that he spoke by the hand of Joshua the son of Nun.

CHAPTER 17

1. And Elijah *who was from Teshub,*[1] from the settlers of Gilead, said to Ahab: "As the Lord God of Israel before whom *we serve*[2] lives, there will not be during these years dew and rain *unless I say so.*"[3] 2. *And there was a word of prophecy from before the Lord with him*[4] saying: 3. "Go from here, and turn aside to the east, and hide yourself by the brook Cherith that faces the Jordan. 4. And you will drink from the brook, and I have commanded the ravens to sustain you there." 5. And he went and did according to the word of the Lord, and he went and dwelt by the brook Cherith that faces the Jordan. 6. And the ravens were bringing to him bread and meat in the morning, and bread and meat in the evening, and he was drinking from the brook. 7. And it happened that at the end of some days the brook dried up because there was no rain in the land. 8. *And there was a word of prophecy from before the Lord with him,*[5] saying: 9. "Arise, go to Zarephath which belongs to *the Sidonians,*[6] and dwell there. Behold I have commanded there a widow woman to sustain you." 10. And he arose and went to Zarephath, and he came to the gate of the city, and behold there a widow woman was gathering wood; and he called to her and said: "Bring me please a little water in a vessel, and let me drink." 11. And she went to get it, and he called to her and said *to her:*[7] "Bring me please a piece of bread in your hand." 12. And she said: "As the Lord your God lives, I have *nothing*[8] except a handful of grain in a vessel and a little oil in a

---

Notes, Chapter Sixteen (Cont.)

[29]MT: "in the eyes."
[30]MT lacks the phrase.
[31]MT: "to anger the Lord."
[32]MT: "the Bethelite." The term "Mume" means "curse."
[33]MT: "he laid its foundation at the cost of Abiram."
[34]MT: "at the cost of Segub his younger son he set up its gates."

Notes, Chapter Seventeen

[1]MT: "the Tishbite."
[2]MT: "I stand."
[3]MT: "except according to my word."
[4]MT: "And the word of the Lord was to him."
[5]MT: "And the word of the Lord was to him."
[6]MT: "Sidon."
[7]MT lacks the phrase.
[8]MT: "nothing baked."

flask; and behold I am gathering two pieces of wood, and I am going and preparing it for myself and for my son; and we will eat it and die." 13. And Elijah said to her: "Do not fear; go in, do according to your word. But prepare for me from there a small cake first of all, and bring it forth to me. And for yourself and for your son prepare afterward. 14. For thus said the Lord God of Israel: 'The vessel of grain will not give out, and the flask of oil will not be lacking until the day that the Lord will give rain upon the face of the earth.' " 15. And she went and did according to the word of Elijah, and she and he and *the people of her house*[9] ate for many days. 16. And the vessel of grain did not give out, and the flask of oil was not lacking according to the word of the Lord that he spoke by the hand of Elijah. 17. And after these things the son of the woman, the mistress of the house, became sick; and his sickness was very powerful until breath was not left in him. 18. And she said to Elijah: "What is there to me and to you, *prophet of the Lord, that*[10] you came unto me to make my sin remembered and to kill my son?" 19. And he said to her: "Give your son to me." And he took him from her bosom, and he brought him up to the upper chamber where he was dwelling, and he laid him out on his bed. 20. And *he prayed before*[11] the Lord, and said: "O Lord my God, *indeed*[12] upon the widow with whom I am residing — *let there not be evil to her, and let her son not die.*"[13] 21. And he stretched himself out upon the boy three times, and *he prayed before*[14] the Lord, and said: "O Lord my God, let the soul of this boy return now to his innards." 22. And the Lord *received the prayer*[15] of Elijah, and the soul of the boy returned to his innards, and he lived. 23. And Elijah took the boy and brought him down from the upper chamber to the house, and he gave him to his mother. And Elijah said: "See *that*[16] your son is alive." 24. And the woman said to Elijah: "Now this I know, that you are *the prophet of the Lord;*[17] and the word of the Lord in your mouth, *they are*[18] truth."

CHAPTER 18

1. And after *the time of*[1] many days *the word of prophecy from before the Lord was with*[2] Elijah, in the third year, saying: "Go, show yourself to Ahab, and I will give rain upon the face of the earth." 2. And Elijah went to show himself to Ahab, and the famine was strong in Samaria. 3. And Ahab called to Obadiah who *was appointed*[3]

Notes, Chapter Seventeen (Cont.)

[9]MT: "her household."
[10]MT: "man of God."
[11]MT: "he cried out to."
[12]MT has an interrogative.
[13]MT: "have you brought evil so as to put to death her son?" Tg changes the MT's challenging question into a prayer petition.
[14]MT: "he cried out."

[15]MT: "heard the voice."
[16]MT lacks the word.
[17]MT: "a man of God."
[18]MT lacks the word.

Notes, Chapter Eighteen

[1]MT lacks the word.
[2]MT: "the word of the Lord was to."
[3]MT lacks the word.

over the house; and Obadiah *was very fearful of sins from before the Lord.*[4] 4. And when Jezebel *killed*[5] the prophets of the Lord, Obadiah took 100 prophets and hid them, *fifty by fifty men*[6] in the cave and supplied them *with*[7] bread and *with*[7] water. 5. And Ahab said to Obadiah: "Go about in the land to all the springs of water and to all the valleys. Perhaps we will find grass and keep alive *horses and mules,*[8] and we will not be cut off from the animals." 6. And they divided the land for themselves to pass about it; Ahab went about on one way alone, and Obadiah went about on one way alone. 7. And Obadiah *was going*[9] on the way, and behold Elijah met him; and he recognized him and fell upon his face and said: "Are you this my master Elijah?" 8. And he said to him: "I am. Go, say to your master: 'Behold Elijah.'" 9. And he said: "How have I sinned, for you are giving your servant over in the hand of Ahab *to kill me?*[10] 10. As the Lord your God lives, there is no people and kingdom where my master has not sent to seek you out; and they said: '*He was not there.*'[11] And he made the kingdom and the people swear that it was not finding you. 11. And now you are saying: 'Go, say to your master: "Behold Elijah."' 12. And it will happen that, *as soon as*[12] I am going *from your presence,*[13] *the spirit from before the Lord*[14] will take you off *to*[15] *a place* that I do not know. And I will go, *I will tell*[16] Ahab, and he will not find you, and he will kill me. And your servant was fearing *from before the Lord*[17] from my youth. 13. Was it not told to my master what I did when Jezebel killed the prophets of the Lord, and I hid 100 from the prophets of the Lord, fifty by fifty men in the cave, and I supplied them *with*[18] bread and *with*[18] water? 14. And now you say: 'Go, say to our master: "Behold Elijah."' And he will kill me." 15. And Elijah said: "As the Lord of hosts before whom *I am serving*[19] lives, this day I will show myself to him." 16. And Obadiah went to meet Ahab and told him; and Ahab went to meet Elijah. 17. And when Ahab saw Elijah, Ahab said to him: "Are you this troubler of Israel?" 18. And he said: "I have not troubled Israel, but you and the house of your father in that you have abandoned the commands of the Lord and gone after the Baals. 19. And now send, gather unto me all Israel to Mount Carmel, and the 450 prophets of Baal and the 400 prophets of Asherah, eating (at) the table of Jezebel." 20. And Ahab sent among all the sons of Israel, and he gathered the *false*[20] prophets to Mount Carmel. 21. And Elijah drew near unto all the people and said: "How long *are you to be divided into two divisions? Is not the Lord God? Serve before him alone. And why are you going astray after Baal in whom there is no profit?*"[21] And the people did not answer him a word. 22. And Elijah said to the people: "I am left alone as the prophet *before*[22] the Lord, and the prophets

Notes, Chapter Eighteen (Cont.)

[4]MT: "was fearing the Lord very much."
[5]MT: "had cut off."
[6]MT: "fifty men."
[7]MT lacks the prepositions.
[8]MT: "horse the mule."
[9]MT: "was."
[10]MT: "to put me to death."
[11]MT: "No" or "There is not."
[12]MT lacks the word.
[13]MT: "from with you."
[14]MT: "the spirit of the Lord."

[15]MT: "unto."
[16]MT: "to tell."
[17]MT: "the Lord."
[18]MT lacks the prepositions.
[19]MT: "I am standing."
[20]MT lacks the word.
[21]MT: "are you to be dancing about on two boughs? If the Lord is God, go after him. And if Baal is, go after him." Tg eliminates the choice offered in the MT and the implied existence granted to Baal.
[22]MT: "to."

of Baal are 450 men. 23. Let there be given to us two oxen, and let them choose for themselves one ox, and let them cut it up and set it upon the wood, and let them not set a fire. And I will prepare one ox and place it upon the wood, and I will not set a fire. 24. And you will call in the name of your *idols and you will not be answered because there is no profit in them. But I will pray in the name of the Lord, and he will send his Memra, and the fire will descend, for the Lord is God."*[23] And all the people answered and said: "The word is good." 25. And Elijah said to the prophets of Baal: "Choose for yourselves one ox, and prepare it first, for you are many; and you will call in the name of your *idols,*[24] and you will not set a fire." 26. And they took the ox that he gave to them, and they prepared it and called on the name of Baal from the morning and unto *the time of midday,*[25] saying: "O Baal, answer us." And there was not a sound, and there was no one who was answering. And they were dancing about the pagan altar that he made. 27. And at *the time of midday,*[26] Elijah was laughing at them, and he said: "Call in a loud voice, for *you say he is a deity.*[27] Perhaps he is having a conversation, or *he is indeed relieving himself,*[28] or he is on a trip, or perhaps he is asleep and will be awakened." 28. And they called in a loud voice, and they mutilated themselves according to their custom with knives and with spears until *blood was poured out*[29] upon them. 29. And as the midday passed, and *they danced around*[30] until the offering of the meal-offering, there was no voice and there was *no one who was answering*[31] and there was *no one who was listening.*[32] 30. And Elijah said to all the people: "Draw near unto me." And all the people drew near unto him, and *he built*[33] the altar of the Lord that had been broken down. 31. And Elijah took twelve stones according to the number of the tribes of the sons of Jacob, *with whom*[34] the word of the Lord was, saying: "Israel will be your name." 32. And he built with stones the altar in the name of the Lord, and he made a trench about two seahs of seed around about the altar. 33. And he arranged the wood and cut up the ox and set it upon the wood. 34. And he said: "Fill four vessels with water, and pour them upon the holocaust and upon the wood." And he said: "Do it a second time." And they did it a second time. And he said: "Do it a third time." And they did it a third time. 35. And the water went around about the altar, and the water even filled the trench. 36. And at the offering of the meal-offering, Elijah the prophet drew near and said: "Lord, God of Abraham, Isaac, and Israel, this day let it be known that you are *the Lord whose Shekinah resides in Israel,*[35] and I am your servant; and according to your words I have done all these things. 37. *Receive my prayer, Lord, with the fire; receive my prayer, Lord, with rain; and may this people know by your doing for them the sign, that you, Lord, are God, and by your loving them you are asking for them by your Memra to bring them back to fear of you. And they gave their divided heart."*[36]

Notes, Chapter Eighteen (Cont.)

[23]MT: "gods, and I will call in the name of the Lord, and the God who will answer in the fire—he will be God."

[24]MT: "gods."

[25]MT: "midday."

[26]MT: "midday."

[27]MT: "he is a god." Tg eliminates a possibility of misunderstanding the MT. See S-A, 153.

[28]MT: "he has gone aside."

[29]MT: "the pouring out of blood."

[30]MT: "they prophesied."

[31]MT: "no one answering."

[32]MT: "no one listening."

[33]MT: "he repaired."

[34]MT: "to whom."

[35]MT: "God in Israel."

[36]MT: "Answer me, Lord, answer me; and may this people know that you Lord are God, and you have turned their heart back." Tg makes Elijah more explicit and more reverent.

38. And *the fire from before the Lord* [37] fell, and it devoured the holocaust and the wood and the stones and the dust and the water, and it licked the water that was in the trench. 39. And all the people saw, and they fell upon their faces and said: "The Lord is God; the Lord is God." 40. And Elijah said to them: "Seize the prophets of Baal; let no man from them escape." And they seized them, and Elijah brought them down to the valley of Kishon and slaughtered them there. 41. And Elijah said to Ahab: "Go up, eat and drink, for there is the sound of the rushing of rain." 42. And Ahab went up to eat and to drink; and Elijah went up the the head of Carmel, and he bent down *upon the ground,* [38] and he put his face between his knees. 43. And he said to his young man: "Go up now, look toward the way of *the west.*"[39] And he went and looked and said: "There is nothing." And he said: "Return seven times." 44. And at the seventh time he said: "Behold a cloud small, like *the palm of the hand of a man* [40] is going up from *the west.*"[41] And he said: "Go up, say to Ahab: 'Ready yourself and go down, so the rain will not prevent you.'" 45. And while *he was readying and coming down,* [42] the heavens were covered with clouds and wind, and there was much rain; and Ahab rode and came to Jezreel. 46. And *a spirit of power from before the Lord was with* [43] Elijah, and he girded his loins and ran before Ahab until he came to Jezreel.

CHAPTER 19

1. And Ahab told Jezebel everything that Elijah did and everything about how he killed all the *false*[1] prophets by the sword. 2. And Jezebel sent a messenger unto Elijah, saying: "Thus may *the deities*[2] do and thus may they add to it unless about this time tomorrow I make your life like the life of one of them." 3. And he saw and arose and went *to save*[3] his life, and he came to Beersheba, which belongs to *the tribe of Judah,*[4] and he left his young man there. 4. And he was walking in the wilderness a day's journey, and he came and sat beneath a single broom-tree, and he asked his life to die, and he said: "*It is long enough for me. How long am I being knocked about like this?*[5] Now, O Lord, take my life, for I am no better than my fathers." 5. And he lay down and slept beneath the single broom-tree, and behold this angel *drew near to*[6] him and said to him: "Rise up, eat." 6. And he looked around, and behold at his head were *a baked cake*[7] and a flask of water. And he ate and drank and lay down again. 7. And the angel of the Lord returned a second time and *drew near to*[8] him and said: "Rise up, eat, for the way will be too much for you." 8. And he arose and ate and drank and went in the strength of that food forty days and forty nights *until he came to the mountain upon which the glory of the Lord had been revealed, to Horeb.*[9] 9. And he went in there to

Notes, Chapter Eighteen (Cont.)

[37] MT: "the fire of the Lord."
[38] MT: "groundward."
[39] MT: "the sea."
[40] MT: "the hand of a man."
[41] MT: "the sea."
[42] MT: "in a little while."
[43] MT: "the hand of the Lord was to."

Notes, Chapter Nineteen

[1] MT lacks the word.
[2] MT: "the gods."
[3] MT lacks the word.
[4] MT: "Judah."
[5] MT: "much," meaning "It is enough."
[6] MT: "was touching."
[7] MT: "a cake baked on hot stones."
[8] MT: "touched."
[9] MT: "unto the mountain of God, Horeb."

the cave, and he lodged there, and behold the word of the Lord was *with*[10] him and said to him: "What is there for you here, Elijah?" 10. And he said: "I have been very jealous *before*[11] the Lord God of hosts, for the sons of Israel abandoned your covenant, they destroyed your altars, and they killed your prophets by the sword; and I alone am left, and they seek my life *to kill me.*"[12] 11. And he said: "Go forth and stand on the mountain before the Lord." And behold the Lord *was revealing himself, and before him were armies of the angels of the wind*[13] breaking apart the mountains and shattering the rocks before the Lord; *not in the army of the angels of the wind was the Shekinah of the Lord. And after the army of the angels of the wind was the army of the angels of the earthquake; not in the army of the angels of earthquake was the Shekinah of the Lord.*[14] 12. *And after the army of the angels of the earthquake was the army of the angels of fire; not in the army of the angels of the fire was the Shekinah of the Lord; and after the army of the angels of the fire was the voice of those who were praising softly.*[15] 13. And when Elijah heard, he wrapped his face in his cloak and went forth and stood at the entrance of the cave; and behold the voice was *with*[16] him, and it said: "What is there for you here, Elijah?" 14. And he said: "I have been very jealous *before*[17] the Lord God of hosts, for the sons of Israel abandoned your covenant, they destroyed your altars, and they killed your prophets by the sword, and I alone am left, and they seek my life *to kill me.*"[18] 15. And the Lord said to him: "Go, return on your way to the wilderness of Damascus, and you will come and anoint Hazael *to be the king*[19] over Aram. 16. And you shall anoint Jehu the son of Nimshi *to be the king*[20] over Israel, and you shall anoint Elisha the son of Shaphat from *the plain of Meholah*[21] to be the prophet in place of you. 17. And whoever will escape from the sword of Hazael, Jehu *will kill;*[22] and whoever will escape from the sword of Jehu, Elisha *will kill.*[23] 18. And I will leave in Israel 7,000, all the knees that did not bend to Baal, and every mouth that was not kissing him." 19. And he went from there and found Elisha the son of Shaphat, and he was driving twelve yokes *of oxen yoked*[24] before him; and he was *on one of the twelve.*[25] And Elijah passed unto him and threw his cloak on him. 20. And he abandoned the oxen and ran after Elijah, and he said: "Let me kiss now my father and my mother, and I will come after you." And he said to him: "Go, return, for what have I done to you?" 21. And he returned from after him and took the yoke of oxen and *cut it up,*[26] and with the implements of the oxen he boiled the flesh *for*[27] them and gave it to the people, and they ate. And he arose and went after Elijah and served him.

Notes, Chapter Nineteen (Cont.)

[10]MT: "to."

[11]MT: "for."

[12]MT: "to take it."

[13]MT: "was passing by, and a great and strong wind was."

[14]MT: "the Lord was not in the wind. And after the wind was an earthquake; the Lord was not in the earthquake." In vv. 11-12 Tg turns the wind and other natural elements into angels.

[15]MT: "And after the earthquake there was fire; the Lord was not in the fire. And after the fire was the sound of a gentle stillness." The final word "softly" is derived from a root meaning "stir (a pot)" and has the the sense of "whisper-

ing" or "stillness." Tg connects God with quiet or silent prayer.

[16]MT: "to."

[17]MT: "for."

[18]MT: "to take it."

[19]MT: "for king."

[20]MT: "for king."

[21]MT: "Abel-meholah." The Aramaic gives a translation of the MT place name.

[22]MT: "will put to death."

[23]MT: "will put to death."

[24]MT lacks this phrase.

[25]MT: "on the twelfth."

[26]MT: "slaughtered it for sacrifice."

[27]MT lacks the preposition.

CHAPTER 20

1. And Ben-Hadad the king of Aram gathered all his army; and thirty-two kings were with him, and *horses and chariots;*[1] and he went up and laid siege against Samaria and *waged battle*[2] against it. 2. And he sent messengers unto Ahab the king of Israel, to the city. 3. And he said to him: "Thus said Ben-Hadad: 'Your silver and your gold are mine, and your beautiful wives and children are mine.'" 4. And the king of Israel answered and said: "According to your word, my master, O king, I and all that is mine are yours." 5. And the messengers returned and said: "Thus said Ben-Hadad, saying: 'Because I sent unto you, saying: "Your silver and your gold and your wives and your children you shall give to me." 6. But about *this*[3] time tomorrow I will send my servants unto you, and they will search your house and the houses of your servants; and every desirable thing of your eyes they will place in their hands and take.'" 7. And the king of Israel called to all the elders of the land and said: "Know now and see that this one seeks evil, for he sent to me for my wives and for my children and for my silver and for my gold; and I did not withhold from him." 8. And all the elders and all the people said to him: "Do not listen, and do not *give.*"[4] 9. And he said to the messengers of Ben-Hadad: "Say to my master the king: 'Everything that you sent to your servant at first, I will do; and this thing I am not able to do.'" And the messengers came and brought word back to him. 10. And Ben-Hadad sent unto him and said: "Thus may *the deities*[5] do to me and thus may they add to it if the dust of Samaria is sufficient *for carrying in the hollows of the soles of the feet of the people who are with me.*"[6] 11. And the king of Israel answered and said: "*Say to him: 'Let not he who girds himself and goes down into battle boast like a warrior who wins and goes up from it.'*"[7] 12. And when he heard this word, he was drinking — he and the kings — in the booths; and he said to his servants: "*Ready yourselves." And they made an ambush against the city.*[8] 13. And behold a prophet drew near unto Ahab the king of Israel and said: "Thus said the Lord: 'Have you seen all this great crowd? Behold I am giving it in your hand this day, and you will know that I am the Lord.'" 14. And Ahab said: "By whom?" And he said: "Thus said the Lord: 'By the young men of the chiefs of the provinces.'" And he said: "Who will arrange the battle?" And he said: "You." 15. And he counted the young men of the chiefs of the provinces, and they were 232; and after them he counted all the people, all the sons of Israel, 7,000. 16. And they went forth at midday, and Ben-Hadad was drinking, getting drunk in the booths — he and the kings, the 32 *kings who*[9] were

Notes, Chapter Twenty

[1]MT: "horse and chariot," i.e., singulars as collective nouns.

[2]MT: "fought."

[3]MT lacks the word.

[4]MT: "consent" or "submit."

[5]MT: "the gods."

[6]MT: "for handfuls for all the people who are at my feet."

[7]MT: "Say: Let not him who girds on boast like one who puts off."

[8]MT: "'Take a position.' And they took a position against the city."

[9]MT has "king" in the singular and lacks the relative pronoun.

aiding him. 17. And the young men of the chiefs of the provinces went forth at first; and Ben-Hadad sent, and they told him, saying: "Men went forth from Samaria." 18. And he said: "If they came forth for peace, seize them alive; and if they came forth for battle, seize them alive." 19. And these went forth from the city, the young men of the chiefs of the provinces, and the army that was behind them. 20. And they *killed,*[10] each man his man; and *the men of Aram*[11] fled, and Israel pursued them; and Ben-Hadad the king of Aram escaped *upon horses, and two horsemen were with them.*[12] 21. And the king of Israel went forth and struck down *the horses, and overturned the chariots,*[13] and struck against *the men of Aram*[14] a great blow. 22. And the prophet drew near unto the king of Israel and said to him: "Go, be strong, and know and see what you shall do; for at *the time of the end*[15] of the year the king of Aram comes up against you." 23. And the servants of the king of Aram said to him: "*The God who has power upon the mountains*[16] is their God. Therefore they have been stronger than us. But let us fight with them in the plain; perhaps we will be stronger than them. 24. And do this thing: Remove the kings, each one from his place, and appoint governors in their places. 25. And you shall muster for yourself *armies that were lost from you, and horses like the horses, and chariots like the chariots;*[17] and we will wage battle with them in the plain; perhaps we will be stronger than them." And *he received their speech*[18] and did so. 26. And at *the time of the end*[19] of the year, Ben-Hadad mustered *the men of Aram*[20] and went up to Aphek *to wage battle*[21] with Israel. 27. And the sons of Israel were mustered and readied themselves and went to meet them, and the sons of Israel encamped opposite them like two flocks of goats, and *the men of Aram*[22] filled the land. 28. And *the prophet of the Lord*[23] drew near and said to the king of Israel. And he said: "Thus said the Lord: 'Because *the men of Aram*[24] said: "*The God who has power upon the mountains is the Lord, and he is not the God who has power upon the plain,*"[25] I will give over all this great crowd in your hand and you will know that I am the Lord.'" 29. And they encamped, these opposite these, for seven days. And on the seventh day, *the wagers of battle*[26] drew near, and the sons of Israel struck down *the men of Aram*[27] 100,000 foot soldiers on one day. 30. And those who were left fled to Aphek, to the city; and the wall fell upon 27,000 men who were left. And Ben-Hadad fled and entered the city, to a chamber in *the midst of chambers.*[28] 31. And his servants said to him: "Behold now we have heard that the kings of the house of Israel *are kings of deeds of loving kindness.*[29] Now *let us gird*[30] sackclothes on our loins and ropes on our heads, and go forth unto the king of Israel. Perhaps he will spare your life." 32. And they girded

Notes, Chapter Twenty (Cont.)

[10]MT: "struck down."
[11]MT: "Aram."
[12]MT: "upon horse and horsemen."
[13]MT: "the horse and chariot."
[14]MT: "Aram."
[15]MT: "the turn."
[16]MT: "The God of the mountains."
[17]MT: "an army like the army that fell away from you, and horse like horse, and chariot like chariot."
[18]MT: "he heard their voice."
[19]MT: "the turn."
[20]MT: "Aram."

[21]MT: "for battle."
[22]MT: "Aram."
[23]MT: "the man of God."
[24]MT: "Aram."
[25]MT: "God of the mountains is the Lord, and not God of the lowlands is he."
[26]MT: "the battle."
[27]MT: "Aram."
[28]MT: "in a chamber."
[29]MT: "that they are kings of loving kindness." Tg uses the familiar rabbinic phrase, "deeds of loving kindness."
[30]MT: "let us put."

sackclothes on their loins and ropes on their heads, and they came unto the king of Israel and said: "Your servant Ben-Hadad said: 'Let my soul live now.'" And he said: "Is he still alive? He is my brother." 33. And the men looked for an omen, and they were quick and seized it from him and said: "Your brother Ben-Hadad." And he said: "Go in, bring him." And Ben-Hadad went forth unto him, and he brought him up *to*[31] the chariot. 34. And he said to him: "The cities that my father took from your father, I will return; and you will establish for yourself markets in Damascus just as my father established in Samaria. And I will send you away in a covenant." And he cut for him a covenant and sent him away. 35. And a certain man from the *students*[32] of the prophets said to his fellow by the word of the Lord: "Strike me now." And the man *was not willing*[33] to strike him. 36. And he said to him: "Because *you have not received the Memra of the Lord,*[34] behold you are going from my presence and a lion *will kill you.*"[35] And he went from his presence, and a lion found him and *killed him.*[36] 37. And he found another man and said: "Strike me now." And the man struck him; he struck him and wounded him. 38. And the prophet went and waited for the king by the way, and he was *wrapped*[37] with a bandage over his eyes. 39. And the king was passing by, and he shouted *before*[38] the king and said: "Your servant went forth in the midst of the battle, and behold a man turned and brought to me a man, and he said: 'Guard this man; if indeed he shall be lost, your life will be in place of his life; or you will weigh out a talent of silver.' 40. And while your servant *was looking about*[39] here and there, behold he was not there." And the king of Israel said to him: "*You have judged your judgment and determined it.*"[40] 41. And he made haste and took away the bandage from upon his eyes, and the king of Israel recognized him that he was from *the students of the prophets.*[41] 42. And he said to him: "Thus said the Lord: Because *you rescued a man deserving killing*[42] from the hand, your life will be in place of his life and your people in place of his people." 43. And the king of Israel went to his house, troubled and *mourning,*[43] and he came to Samaria.

CHAPTER 21

1. And after these things, Nabaoth the Jezreelite who was in Jezreel had a vineyard by the side of the palace of Ahab the king of Samaria. 2. And Ahab spoke with Nabaoth, saying: "Give to me your vineyard, and it will be my vegetable garden, for it is near, by the side of my house; and I will give to you in its place a vineyard that is

Notes, Chapter Twenty (Cont.)

[31]MT: "upon."
[32]MT: "sons."
[33]MT: "refused."
[34]MT: "you have heard the voice of the Lord."
[35]MT: "will strike you down."
[36]MT: "struck him down."

[37]MT: "disguised."
[38]MT: "to."
[39]MT: "was acting."
[40]MT: "Thus you have determined your judgment."
[41]MT: "the prophets."
[42]MT: "you let free a man of destruction."
[43]MT: "sullen" or "enraged."

better than it. If it is good in your eyes, I will give to you silver *whose value is equal.*[1] 3. And Nabaoth said to Ahab: "Far be from me *from before*[2] the Lord to give the inheritance of my fathers to you." 4. And Ahab went to his house, troubled and sullen over the word that Nabaoth the Jezreelite spoke with him, and said: "I will not give to you the inheritance of my fathers." And he lay upon his bed, and he turned his face, and he did not eat bread. 5. And Jezebel his wife came unto him and spoke with him: "Why is your spirit turning around, and you are not eating bread?" 6. And he spoke with her: "Because I spoke with Nabaoth the Jezreelite, and I said to him: 'Give to me your vineyard for silver; or if you wish, I will give to you a vineyard in its place.' And he said: 'I will not give to you my vineyard.'" 7. And Jezebel his wife said to him: "*Are you now succeeding*[3] in the kingship over Israel? Arise, eat bread, and let your heart be happy. I will give to you the vineyard of Nabaoth the Jezreelite." 8. And she wrote *a letter*[4] in the name of Ahab and sealed them with his *signet ring,*[5] and she sent letters to the elders and to the *young nobles*[6] who were in his city, who were dwelling with Nabaoth. 9. And she wrote in the letters, saying: "Proclaim a fast and set up Nabaoth at the head of the people. 10. And set up two men, sons of *wickedness,*[7] opposite him. And let them witness against him, saying: 'You have blasphemed before the Lord, and you have cursed the king.'[8] And take him out and stone him, and *let him be killed.*"[9] 11. And the men of his city, the elders and the young nobles who were dwelling in his city, did just as Jezebel sent unto them, just as it was written in the *letter*[10] that she sent unto them. 12. They proclaimed a fast and set up Nabaoth at the head of the people. 13. And two men, sons of *wickedness,*[11] came, and they sat opposite him. And *the men of the sons of wickedness*[12] witnessed against Nabaoth before the people, saying: "Nabaoth *blasphemed before the Lord and cursed the king.*"[13] And they took him outside the city and stoned him with stones, and he died. 14. And they sent unto Jezebel, saying: "Nabaoth has been stoned, and he is dead." 15. And when Jezebel heard that Nabaoth had been stoned and was dead, Jezebel said to Ahab: "Arise, take possession of the vineyard of Nabaoth the Jezreelite who *was not willing*[14] to give it to you for money, for Nabaoth is not alive but is dead." 16. And when Ahab head that Nabaoth was dead, Ahab arose to go down to the vineyard of Nabaoth the Jezreelite to take possession of it. 17. And *a word of prophecy was from before the Lord with Elijah who was from Teshub,*[15] saying: 18. "Arise, go down to meet Ahab the king of Israel who is in Samaria. Behold he is in the vineyard of Nabaoth where he went down to take possession of it. 19. And you shall speak with him, saying: 'Thus said the Lord: "Have you killed, and also have

Notes, Chapter Twenty-One

[1] MT: "the value of this."

[2] MT: "from."

[3] MT: "Are you now exercising."

[4] MT: the plural, "letters."

[5] MT: "seal."

[6] MT: "freemen." The Aramaic may mean "guardians" or "educators."

[7] MT: "Belial."

[8] MT: "You have blessed (a euphemism for 'cursed') God and king."

[9] MT: "he will die."

[10] MT: "letters."

[11] MT: "Belial."

[12] MT: "the men of Belial."

[13] MT: "blessed God and king," another euphemistic expression.

[14] MT: "refused."

[15] MT: "a word of the Lord was to Elijah the Tishbite."

you taken possession?"' And you shall speak with him, saying: 'Thus said the Lord: "In the place in which the dogs licked the blood of Nabaoth, the dogs will lick your blood also."'" 20. And Ahab said to Elijah: "Have you found me, O my enemy?" And he said: "I have found (you), because *you have planned*[16] to do what is evil *before*[17] the Lord. 21. Behold I am bringing *upon*[18] you evil, and *I will search*[19] after you and destroy for Ahab *everyone knowing knowledge,*[20] bond and free, in Israel. 22. And I will make your house like the house of Jeroboam the son of Nebat and like the house of Baasha the son of Ahijah on account of the provocations that you provoked and you made Israel sin. 23. And also *concerning*[21] Jezebel the Lord *decreed,*[22] saying: 'The dogs will eat Jezebel in the *property*[23] of Jezreel.' 24. Whoever belonging to Ahab will die in the city, the dogs will eat; and whoever will die in the field, the birds of the heavens will eat." 25. Only there was no one like Ahab who *planned to do what is evil before*[24] the Lord, whom Jezebel his wife *led astray.*[25] 26. And he acted *very wickedly*[26] to go after the idols according to all that the Amorites did whom the Lord drove out from before the sons of Israel. 27. And when Ahab heard these words, he rent his garments and *girded*[27] sackcloth on his flesh, and he fasted and slept in *his*[28] sackcloth and was going about *barefoot.*[29] 28. And *a word of prophecy was from before the Lord with Elijah who was from Teshub,*[30] saying: 29. "Have you seen that Ahab *has been broken*[31] from before me? Because *he has been broken*[32] from before me, I will not bring evil in his days; in the days of his son I will bring evil upon his house."

CHAPTER 22

1. And they settled down for three years; there was no battle between Aram and Israel. 2. And in the third year, Jehoshaphat the king of *the tribe of the house of Judah*[1] went down unto the king of Israel. 3. And the king of Israel said to his servants: "Do you know that Ramoth-gilead belongs to us, and we keep quiet from taking it from the hand of the king of Aram?" 4. And he said to Jehoshaphat: "Will you go with me *to wage battle for*[2] Ramoth-gilead?" And Jehoshaphat said to the king of Israel: *"I am like you; my people are like your people; my horses are like your horses."*[3] 5. And

Notes, Chapter Twenty-One (Cont.)

[16] MT: "you have sold yourself."
[17] MT: "in the eyes of."
[18] MT: "to."
[19] MT: "I will consume utterly."
[20] MT: "those who urinate on the wall," meaning males.
[21] MT: "to."
[22] MT: "said."
[23] MT: "rampart." Tg and some MT mss. read *hēliq,* meaning "property" or "field."
[24] MT: "sold himself to do evil in the eyes of."
[25] MT: "incited."
[26] MT: "most abominably."
[27] MT: "put."

[28] MT lacks the preposition.
[29] MT: "softly."
[30] MT: "a word of the Lord was to Elijah the Tishbite."
[31] MT: "has been humbled."
[32] MT: "he has been humbled."

Notes, Chapter Twenty-Two

[1] MT: "Judah."
[2] MT: "for battle."
[3] MT: "like me, like you; like my people, like your people; like my horses, like your horses."

Jehoshaphat said to the king of Israel: "Seek out now this day the word of the Lord." 6. And the king of Israel gathered *the prophets of falsehood*,[4] about 400 men, and he said to them: "Shall I go to Ramoth-gilead to *wage battle*,[5] or shall I *restrain myself*?"[6] And they said: "Go up, and the Lord will *give (it) over*[7] in the hand of the king." 7. And Jehoshaphat said: "Is there not here still another prophet *before*[8] the Lord, and we will seek from him?" 8. And the king of Israel said to Jehoshaphat: "There is still one other man to seek *the Memra of the Lord*[9] from him, and I hate him, for he does not prophesy good about me but evil. He is Micah the son of Imlah." And Jehoshaphat said: "Let not the king speak thus." 9. And the king of Israel called to one eunuch and said: "Bring quickly Micah the son of Imlah." 10. And the king of Israel and Jehoshaphat the king of *the house of Judah*[10] were sitting, each upon his throne, clothed in robes, *and sitting*[11] at the threshing floor, at the entrance of the gate of Samaria; and all *the prophets of falsehood*[12] were prophesying before them. 11. And Zedekiah the son of Chenaanah made for himself horns of iron, and he said: "Thus said the Lord: 'By these *you will kill the men of Aram*[13] until you destroy them completely.'" 12. And all *the prophets of falsehood*[14] were prophesying thus, saying: "Go up to Ramoth-gilead, and triumph. And the Lord will *give (it) over*[15] in the hand of the king." 13. And the messenger who came to call Micah spoke with him, saying: "Behold now the words of *the prophets of falsehood*.[16] One word is *good enough before*[17] the king. Let your word now be like the word of one of them, and you will speak *good words*."[18] 14. And Micah said: "As the Lord lives, whatever the Lord will say to me, I will speak it." 15. And he came unto the king, and the king said to him: "Micah, shall we go to Ramoth-gilead *to wage battle*,[19] or shall we restrain ourselves?" And he said to him: "Go up, and triumph. And the Lord will *give (it) over*[20] in the hand of the king." 16. And the king said to him: "How many times am I adjuring you that you not speak with me anything except truth in the name of the Lord." 17. And he said: "I saw all Israel scattered *upon*[21] the mountains like sheep that have no shepherd; and the Lord said: 'These have no masters; let them return, each to his house, in peace.'" 18. And the king of Israel said to Jehoshaphat: "Did I not say to you: 'He will not prophesy good about me, only evil?'" 19. And he said: "Therefore *receive*[22] the word of the Lord: 'I saw *the glory of the Lord residing*[23] upon his throne and all the armies of the heavens standing *before*[24] him from his right and from his left. 20. And the Lord said: "Who will lead astray Ahab, and he will go up and fall at Ramoth-gilead?" And this one said thus and so, and this one said

Notes, Chapter Twenty-Two (Cont.)

[4]MT: "the prophets."
[5]MT: "for war."
[6]MT: "cease."
[7]MT: "give."
[8]MT: "for."
[9]MT: "the Lord."
[10]MT: "Judah."
[11]MT lacks the word.
[12]MT: "the prophets."
[13]MT: "you will push Aram."
[14]MT: "the prophets."

[15]MT: "give."
[16]MT: "the prophets."
[17]MT: "good to."
[18]MT: "good."
[19]MT: "for war."
[20]MT: "give."
[21]MT: "to."
[22]MT: "hear."
[23]MT: "the Lord sitting."
[24]MT: "by."

thus and so. 21. And a spirit went forth and stood before the Lord and said: "I will lead him astray." And the Lord said to him: "In what way?" 22. And he said: "I will go forth and be *for*[25] a spirit of falsehood in the mouth of all his prophets." And he said: "You shall *lead astray,*[26] and also you will prevail. Go forth and do so." 23. And now behold the Lord gave a spirit of falsehood in the mouth of all these your prophets, and the Lord *decreed to bring evil upon you.*'"[27] 24. And Zedekiah the son of Chenaanah drew near and struck Micah upon the cheek, and said: "*At what time did the spirit of prophecy from before the Lord go up*[28] from me to speak with you?" 25. And Micah said: "Behold you will see on that day as you enter the inner chamber to hide yourself." 26. And the king of Israel said: "Take Micah, and return him unto Amon the chief of the city and unto Joash the son of the king. 27. And you will say: 'Thus said the king: "Put this fellow in jail, and feed him bread *in*[29] scarcity and water *in*[30] scarcity until I come in peace."'" 28. And Micah said: "If indeed you return in peace, *there was no favor before the Lord in me.*"[31] And he said: "Hear, all you peoples." 29. And the king of Israel and Jehoshaphat the king of *the tribe of the house of Judah*[32] went up to Ramoth-gilead. 30. And the king of Israel said to Jehoshaphat: "*I will disguise myself and enter*[33] in battle. And you wear your robe." And the king of Israel disguised himself and entered in battle. 31. And the king of Aram commanded the 32 chiefs of his chariots, saying: "You shall not *wage battle*[34] with the small and with the great, but with the king of Israel alone." 32. And when the chiefs of the chariots saw Jehoshaphat, they said: "Surely he is the king of Israel." And they turned upon him to fight, and Jehoshaphat shouted out. 33. And when the chiefs of the chariots saw that he was not the king of Israel, they turned from after him. 34. And a man drew on his bow *against him*[35] and struck the king of Israel between the scale armor and the breastplate. And he said to his driver: "*Turn me about backward,*[36] and bring me forth from the army for I am wounded." 35. And *the wagers of battle went up*[37] on that day, and the king *was strengthened and stood on the chariot opposite the men of Aram,*[38] and he died in the evening. And the blood of the blow was poured out into the midst of the chariot. 36. And *the herald*[39] passed through in the army about sunset, saying: "Each man to his city, and each man to his land." 37. And the king died, and he came to Samaria, and they buried the king in Samaria. 38. And he washed the chariot by the pool of Samaria, and the dogs licked his blood, and *they washed the implements of war*[40] according to the word of the Lord that he spoke. 39. And the rest of the acts of Ahab and all that he did and the house of ivory that he built and all the cities that he built — are they not

Notes, Chapter Twenty-Two (Cont.)

[25]MT lacks the preposition.

[26]MT: "entice."

[27]MT: "spoke evil against you."

[28]MT: "How did the spirit of the Lord pass."

[29]MT lacks the preposition.

[30]MT lacks the preposition.

[31]MT: "the Lord has not spoken by me."

[32]MT: "Judah."

[33]MT: "Disguise yourself and enter."

[34]MT: "fight."

[35]MT: "in innocence," meaning without taking aim.

[36]MT: "turn your hand about."

[37]MT: "the war grew."

[38]MT: "was stood up in the chariot opposite Aram."

[39]MT: "the cry."

[40]MT: "harlots washed." Tg connects the MT harlotry (*znwt*) with the Aramaic for weapons (*zyn'*) and softens Ahab's fate. S-A, 51.

written in the book of the chronicles of the kings of Israel? 40. And Ahab slept with his fathers, and Ahaziah his son ruled in his place. 41. And Jehoshaphat the son of Asa ruled over *those of the house of Judah*[41] in the fourth year for Ahab the king of Israel. 42. And Jehoshaphat was 35 years old when he ruled, and he ruled 25 years in Jerusalem; and the name of his mother was Azubah the daughter of Shilhi. 43. And he went in all the way of Asa his father; he did not deviate from it, to what is right *before*[42] the Lord. 44. But the high places did not cease; the people were still sacrificing and *offering spices upon*[43] the altar. 45. And Jehoshaphat made peace with the king of Israel. 46. And the rest of the acts of Jehoshaphat and his power that he did and that he waged — are they not written in the book of the chronicles of the kings of *the house of Judah?*[44] 47. And the rest of the *prostitutes*[45] who were left in the days of Asa his father, he drove out from the land. 48. *And no king was appointed in Edom, but there was a prefect for the king.*[46] 49. Jehoshaphat made *an African fleet*[47] to go to Ophir *to bring gold;*[48] and it did not go because *the fleet*[49] was wrecked at Ezion-geber. 50. Then Ahaziah the son of Ahab said to Jehoshaphat: "Let my servants go with your servants in *the fleet.*"[50] And Jehoshaphat was not willing. 51. And Jehoshaphat slept with his fathers, and he was buried with his fathers in the city of David his father. And Jehoram his son ruled in his place. 52. Ahaziah the son of Ahab ruled over Israel in Samaria in the seventeenth year for Jehoshaphat the king of *the tribe of the house of Judah;*[51] and he ruled over Israel for two years. 53. And he did *what was evil before*[52] the Lord, and he went in the way of his father and in the way of his mother and in the way of Jeroboam the son of Nebat who made Israel sin. 54. And he served Baal and worshipped him, and *he caused anger before the Lord*[53] the God of Israel according to all that his father did.

Notes, Chapter Twenty-Two (Cont.)

[41]MT: "Judah."
[42]MT: "in the eyes of ."
[43]MT: "incensing on."
[44]MT: "Judah."
[45]MT: "male cult prostitutes."
[46]MT: "And there was no king in Edom; a deputy was king."

[47]MT: "ships of Tarshish."
[48]MT: "for gold."
[49]MT: "the ships."
[50]MT: "the ships."
[51]MT: "Judah."
[52]MT: "evil in the eyes of."
[53]MT: "he angered the Lord."

2 KINGS

CHAPTER 1

1. And *the Moabites*[1] rebelled against Israel after *Ahab died.*[2] 2. And Ahaziah fell *from*[3] the lattice-work in his upper chamber which was in Samaria, and he took sick; and he sent messengers, and he said to them: "Go, inquire of Baal-zebub *the idol*[4] of Ekron if I will recover from this sickness." 3. And the angel of the Lord was speaking with Elijah *who was from Teshub:*[5] "Arise, go up to meet the messengers of the king of Samaria, and *prophesy*[6] to them: 'Is there no *living God whose Shekinah resides*[7] in Israel that you are going to inquire of Baal-zebub *the idol*[8] of Ekron?' 4. And therefore thus said the Lord: 'The bed where you have gone up, you will not come down from it, for you will surely die.'" And Elijah went away. 5. And the messengers returned unto him, and he said to them: "Why have you returned?" 6. And they said to him: "A man went up to meet us, and he said to us: 'Go, return unto the king who sent you, and you will speak with him: "Thus said the Lord: 'Is there no *living God whose Shekinah resides*[9] in Israel that you are sending to inquire of Baal-zebub *the idol*[10] of Ekron? Thus the bed where you have gone up, you will not come down from it, for you will surely die.'" 7. He spoke with them: "What was the manner of the man who went up to meet you, and spoke with you these words?" 8. And they said to him: "A man of hair and a belt of leather is girded on his lions." And he said: "He is Elijah *who is from Teshub.*"[11] 9. And he sent unto him a chief of fifty and *fifty who were with him.*[12] And he went up unto him, and *he*[13] was sitting upon the top of the mountain; and he spoke with him: "*Prophet of the Lord,*[14] the king says: 'Come down.'" 10. And Elijah answered and spoke with the chief of fifty: "And if I am *a prophet of the Lord,*[15] may the fire come down from the heavens and devour you and *fifty who are with you.*"[16] And the fire came down from the heavens and devoured him and *fifty who were with him.*[17] 11. And once again he sent unto him another captain of fifty and *fifty who were with him.*[18] And he answered and spoke with him: "*Prophet of the Lord,*[19] thus said the king: 'Hasten, come down.'" 12. And Elijah answered and said to them: "If I am *a prophet of the Lord,*[20] may the fire descend from the heavens and devour you and *fifty who are with you.*"[21] And *the fire from before the Lord*[22] descended from the heavens,

Notes, Chapter One

[1] MT: "Moab."
[2] MT: "the death of Ahab."
[3] MT: "through."
[4] MT: "the god."
[5] MT: "the Tishbite."
[6] MT: "speak." The Tg generally makes the MT more explicit by putting in "prophesy."
[7] MT: "God."
[8] MT: "the god."
[9] MT: "God."
[10] MT: "the god."
[11] MT: "the Tishbite."
[12] MT: "his fifty."
[13] MT: "behold."
[14] MT: "man of God." The Tg regularizes various Hebrew expressions such as seer and visionary under one term, prophet.
[15] MT: "a man of God."
[16] MT: "your fifty."
[17] MT: "his fifty."
[18] MT: "his fifty."
[19] MT: "man of God."
[20] MT: "a man of God."
[21] MT: "your fifty."
[22] MT: "the fire of God."

and it devoured him and *fifty who were with him.* [23] 13. And once again he sent a chief of a third fifty and *fifty who were with him,* [24] and the third chief of fifty went up and came and bowed upon his knees opposite Elijah, and he begged *from* [25] him and spoke with him: "*Prophet of the Lord,* [26] may my life and the life of your servants, these fifty, be precious in your eyes. 14. Behold the fire has come down from the heavens and devoured the first two chiefs of fifty and *the fifties who were with them.* [27] And now let my life be precious in your eyes." 15. And the angel of the Lord spoke with Elijah: "Come down with him. Do not fear from before him." And he arose and went down with him unto the king. 16. And he spoke with him: "Thus said the Lord: 'Because you sent messengers to inquire[28] of Baal-zebub *the idol*[29] of Ekron — is there no *living God whose Shekinah resides*[30] in Israel to ask by his word? — therefore the bed where you have gone up, you will not come down from it, for you will surely die.'" 17. And he died according to the word of the Lord that Elijah spoke; and Jehoram ruled in his place in the second year of Jehoram, the son of Jehoshaphat, the king of *the tribe of the house of Judah,* [31] for he had no son. 18. And the rest of the acts of Ahaziah that he did — are they not written in the chronicles of the kings of Israel?

CHAPTER 2

1. And at the Lord's taking up Elijah in the whirlwind *toward*[1] the heavens, Elijah and Elisha came from Gilgal. 2. And Elijah said to Elisha: "Stay here now, for the Lord has sent me unto Bethel." And Elisha said: "As the Lord lives and by the life of your soul, I will not leave you." And they went down to Bethel. 3. And *the students*[2] of the prophets who were in Bethel went forth unto Elisha and said to him: "Do you know that this day the Lord is taking your master *from you?*"[3] And he said: "I too know; be silent." 4. And Elijah said to him: "Elisha, stay here now, for the Lord has sent me to Jericho." And he said: "As the Lord lives and by the life of your soul, I will not leave you." And they came to Jericho. 5. And *the students*[4] of the prophets who were in Jericho drew near unto Elisha and said to him: "Do you know that this day the Lord is taking your master from *you?*"[5] And he said: "I too know; be silent." 6. And Elijah said to him: "Stay here now, for the Lord has sent me unto the Jordan." And he said: "As the Lord lives and by the life of your soul, I will not leave you." And the two of them went away. 7. And fifty men from *the students*[6] of the prophets went and stood

Notes, Chapter One (Cont.)

[23]MT: "his fifty."
[24]MT: "his fifty."
[25]MT lacks the preposition.
[26]MT: "man of God."
[27]MT: "their fifties."
[28]Some Tg mss.: "ask."
[29]MT: "the god."
[30]MT: "God."

[31]MT: "Judah."

Notes, Chapter Two

[1]MT lacks the preposition.
[2]MT: "the sons."
[3]MT: "from upon your head." Ms. y agrees with the MT.
[4]MT: "the sons."
[5]MT: "from upon your head."
[6]MT: "the sons."

opposite, from afar; and the two of them stood by the Jordan. 8. And Elijah took his cloak and rolled it up and struck the waters, and they were divided here and there; and the two of them crossed over on the dry ground. 9. And as they were crossing over, Elijah said to Elisha: "Ask what I will do for you *while I am still not taken from your presence.*"[7] And Elisha said: "May there be a double share *in the spirit of your prophecy with me.*"[8] 10. And he said: "You have asked a hard thing; if you see me *when I am being taken away from your presence,*[9] it will be so to you; and if not, it will not be." 11. And while they were going on and speaking, behold chariots of fire and horses of fire, and they separated the two of them; and Elijah went up in the whirlwind *toward*[10] the heavens. 12. And Elisha was seeing, and he was crying out: *"My master, my master, who did more good for Israel by his prayer than chariots and horsemen."*[11] And he did not see him anymore. And he took hold of his own garments and tore them into pieces. 13. And he lifted up the cloak of Elijah that fell from upon him,[12] and he returned and stood at the bank of the Jordan. 14. And he took the cloak of Elijah that fell from him, and he struck the waters and said: *"Accept my petition, Lord God of Elijah."*[13] And he too struck the waters, and they were divided here and there, and Elisha passed over. 15. And *the students*[14] of the prophets who were in Jericho saw him across the way and said: "The spirit of Elijah has rested upon Elisha." And they came to meet him and bowed to him upon the ground. 16. And they said to him: "Behold now there are with your servants fifty men, sons of might. Let them go now and seek your master; perhaps *the spirit from before the Lord*[15] has taken him up and cast him on one of the mountains or in one of the valleys." And he said: "You shall not send *them.*"[16] 17. And they prevailed on him until *it was too much,*[17] and he said: "Send." And they sent fifty men, and they searched for three days, and they did not find him. 18. And they returned unto him, and he was dwelling in Jericho. And he said to them: "Did I not say to you: 'You shall not go.'" 19. And the men of the city said to Elisha: "Behold now the situation of the city is *fine*[18] as my master sees; but the water is bad, and the land causes bereavement." 20. And he said: "Bring to me a new flask, and put salt there." And they brought it to him. 21. And he went forth to the spring of water, and he threw the salt there and said: "Thus said the Lord: 'I have healed these waters. There will not be from there any more death and miscarriage.'" 22. And the waters have been healed unto this day according to the word of Elisha that he spoke. 23. And he went up from there to Bethel; and he was going up on the road, and small youngsters went forth from the city, and mocked him, and said to him: "Go up, baldy! Go up, baldy." 24. And he turned around behind him and saw them and cursed them in the name of the Lord. And two bears came forth from the forest and tore apart from them forty-two youngsters. 25. And he went from there to Mount Carmel, and he returned from there to Samaria.

Notes, Chapter Two (Cont.)

[7]MT: "before I am taken from with you."

[8]MT: "in your spirit to me."

[9]MT: "When I am being taken from with you."

[10]MT lacks the preposition.

[11]MT: "My father, my father, the chariot of Israel and its horsemen." The word for "my master" in Tg is Rabbi.

[12]Most mss.: "from him."

[13]MT: "Where is the Lord God of Elijah?" The MT sounds too sceptical, so Tg changes it to a prayer.

[14]MT: "the sons."

[15]MT: "the spirit of the Lord."

[16]MT has no pronominal suffix.

[17]MT: "he was ashamed."

[18]MT: "good."

CHAPTER 3

1. And Jehoram the son of Ahab ruled over Israel in Samaria in the eighteenth year for Jehoshaphat the king of *the tribe of the house of Judah.* [1] And he ruled twelve years. 2. And he did what is evil *before* [2] the Lord, only not like his father and like his mother; and he removed the pillar of Baal that his father made. 3. Only *he delighted* [3] in the sins of Jeroboam the son of Nebat who made Israel sin; he did not turn from *them.* [4] 4. And Mesha the king of Moab was *owning flocks,* [5] and he delivered an offering to the king of Israel *year by year* [6] — 100,000 *fatted cattle* [7] and 100,000 rams *of the pasture.* [8] 5. And when Ahab died, the king of Moab rebelled against the king of Israel. 6. And King Jehoram went forth in that day from Samaria, and he mustered all Israel. 7. And he went and sent to Jehoshaphat the king of *the tribe of the house of Judah,* [9] saying: "The king of Moab has rebelled against me. Will you go with me unto Moab *to wage battle?"* [10] And he said: "I will go up — *I like you, my people like your people, my horses like your horses."* [11] 8. And he said: "By what way shall we go up?" And he said: "By the way of the wilderness of Edom." 9. And the king of Israel and the king of *the tribe of the house of Judah* [12] and the king of Edom went; and they travelled around a journey of seven days, and there was no water for the camp and for the beasts that were *with them.* [13] 10. And the king of Israel said: "Alas! For the Lord has appointed for these three kings to give them in the hand of *the Moabites."* [14] 11. And Jehoshaphat said: "Is there not here a prophet *before* [15] the Lord, and we may seek out [16] *the word of the Lord* [17] from him?" And one of *the young men* [18] of the king of Israel answered and said: "Elisha the son of Shaphat who *served Elijah* [19] is here." 12. And Jehoshaphat said: "The word of the Lord is with him." And the king of Israel and Jehoshaphat and the king of Edom went down unto him. 13. And Elisha said to the king of Israel: "What is there to me and to you? Go unto the prophets of your father and unto the prophets of your mother." And the king of Israel said to him: "*Please, do not recall sins in this hour. Beg for mercies upon us,* [20] for the Lord has appointed for these three kings to give them

Notes, Chapter Three

[1] MT: "Judah."

[2] MT: "in the eyes of."

[3] MT: "he clung." TO of Gen 34:3 translates the MT the same way when speaking of Shechem's desire for Dinah. Here it emphasizes Jehoram's involvement in the sin.

[4] MT: "it."

[5] MT: "a herdsman."

[6] MT lacks the phrase.

[7] MT: "lambs."

[8] MT: "wool."

[9] MT: "Judah."

[10] MT: "for war."

[11] MT: "like me, so you; like my people, so your people; like my horses, so your horses."

[12] MT: "Judah."

[13] MT: "at their feet."

[14] MT: "Moab."

[15] MT: "for."

[16] Several Tg mss.: "ask."

[17] MT: "the Lord."

[18] MT: "the servants." So also several Tg mss.

[19] MT: "poured water on the hands of Elijah."

[20] MT: "No." The Tg makes Jehoram, King of Israel, repentant and seeking reconciliation to God.

in the hand of *the Moabites*."²¹ 14. And Elisha said: "As the Lord of hosts *before whom I am serving*²² lives, if I did not regard the face of Jehoshaphat the king of *the tribe of the house of Judah,*²³ I would not look at you and see you. 15. And now bring to me *a man who knows how to play on the lyre*."²⁴ And when the player was playing, *a spirit of prophecy from before the Lord resided*²⁵ upon him. 16. And he said: "Thus said the Lord: 'This brook will be made into *trenches* (and) *trenches.*'²⁶ 17. For thus said the Lord: 'You will not see the wind and you will not see the rain, and that brook will be filled with water; and you and your flocks and your beasts will drink. 18. And this is a light matter *before*²⁷ the Lord, and he will give *the Moabites*²⁸ in your hand. 19. And you will strike down *every strong fortress and every walled city,*²⁹ and every *tree that is fair you will root up,*³⁰ and all the springs of water you will stop up, and every *beautiful piece of land you will fill up*³¹ with stones." 20. And in the morning at the offering of sacrifice, behold waters were coming from the way of Edom, and the land was filled with water. 21. And all *the Moabites*³² heard that the kings went up to *wage battle*³³ against them, and they were gathered from everyone putting on *the sword*³⁴ and above, and they stood upon the border. 22. And they got up early in the morning, and the sun shone upon the waters, and *the Moabites*³⁵ saw from across the waters red like blood. 23. And they said: "This is blood. The kings have surely quarreled, and they have killed, each man his companion. And now *go forth to the spoil, Moabites.*"³⁶ 24. And they came to the camp of Israel, and Israel arose and struck down *the Moabites*³⁷ and they fled from before them, and *they struck them down and killed the Moabites.*³⁸ 25. And they overthrew the cities; and every beautiful piece of land — each man cast his stone, and they filled it in; and they stopped up *all the springs of water, and they rooted up every tree that was fair, until the stone was not left in the wall; whatever they did not overthrow,*³⁹ the slingers surrounded and struck it down. 26. And the king of Moab saw that *the wagers of war were stronger*⁴⁰ than him, and he took with him 700 men, drawers of the sword, *to turn toward*⁴¹ the king of Edom, and they did not prevail. 27. And he took his son, the firstborn, *who was prepared to rule*⁴² in his place, and he offered him up as a holocaust upon the wall. And there was great anger against Israel, and *they went up from him and came*⁴³ to the land of Israel.

Notes, Chapter Three (Cont.)

²¹MT: "Moab."

²²MT: "before whose face I am standing."

²³MT: "Judah."

²⁴MT: "a minstrel."

²⁵MT: "the hand of the Lord."

²⁶MT: "pits/cisterns." The Aramaic *pĕṣîdîn are* something "cut out."

²⁷MT: "in the eyes of."

²⁸MT: "Moab."

²⁹MT: "every fortified city and every choice city."

³⁰MT: "good tree you will fell."

³¹MT: "good property you will ruin."

³²MT: "Moab."

³³MT: "fight."

³⁴MT: "armor."

³⁵MT: "Moab."

³⁶MT: "to the spoil, Moab."

³⁷MT: "Moab."

³⁸The MT is uncertain.

³⁹MT: "every spring of water, and every good tree they felled until only its stones were left in Kir-hareseth." Some Tg. mss. read "city" in place of "wall." The Tg understands Kir (*qyr*) in the name "Kir-hareseth" according to its meaning, "wall." Kir is used to mean "city" in Moabite place names, e.g. Isa 15:1.

⁴⁰MT: "the war was stronger."

⁴¹MT: "to break through to."

⁴²MT: "who would rule."

⁴³MT: "they turned aside from him and returned."

CHAPTER 4

1. And a certain woman from the wives of *the students*[1] of the prophets was crying out *before*[2] Elisha, saying: "Your servant *Obadiah,*[3] my husband, is dead. And you know that your servant was fearing *from before the Lord,*[4] *who, when Jezebel killed the prophets of the Lord, took a hundred men of them and hid them fifty by fifty men in the cave, and he was borrowing and feeding them in order not to feed them from the revenues of Ahab on account of those who were the oppressor.*[5] And now the creditor has come to take my two sons for himself for slaves." 2. And Elisha said to her: "What shall I do for you? Tell me what you have in the house?" And she said: "Your maidservant has nothing at all in the house except a vessel of oil." 3. And he said: "Go, ask for yourself vessels from outside, from all your neighbors, empty vessels. Do not get too few. 4. And go in and shut the door on yourself and on your sons, and *empty the oil*[6] into all these vessels, and set aside *the vessel that is filled up.*"[7] 5. And she went from his presence and shut the door on her and on her sons; they were bringing near to her *the vessels, and she was emptying the oil.*[8] 6. And when the vessels *were finished,*[9] she said to her son: "Bring near to me still another vessel." And he said to her: "There is not another vessel." And the oil stopped. 7. And she came and told *the prophet of the Lord,*[10] and he said: "Go, sell the oil, and repay *the holders of your debts;*[11] and you and your sons *will be provided for* by *whatever will be left over.*"[12] 8. And it was day, and Elisha crossed over to Shunem, and there was *a woman fearing sins*[13] there, and she took hold of him to eat bread. And whenever he was passing by, he was turning aside to there to eat bread. 9. And she said to her husband: "Behold now I know that *the prophet of the Lord*[14] is holy. He turns aside unto us always. 10. Let us make now a small upper chamber with walls, and let us prepare for him there *space for a bed*[15] and a table and a chair and a lamp. And whenever he comes unto us, he will turn aside to there." 11. And it was day, and he came into there, and he turned to the upper chamber and slept there. 12. And he said to Gehazi, his young man: "Call to this Shunamite woman." And he called to her, and she stood before him. 13. And he said to him: "Say now to her: 'Behold you have gone to all this trouble for us. What is there to do for you? Is there *a word*[16] to speak for you with the king or with the chief of the army?"

Notes, Chapter Four

[1] MT: "the sons."
[2] MT: "to."
[3] MT lacks the name.
[4] MT: "the Lord."
[5] The material from "who, when" to "the oppressor" is not in the MT.
[6] MT: "pour."
[7] MT: "the full one."
[8] MT: "and she was pouring out."
[9] MT: "were filled."
[10] MT: "the man of God."
[11] MT: "your creditors."
[12] MT: "will live on the rest."
[13] MT: "a great woman."
[14] MT: "the man of God."
[15] MT: "a bed."
[16] MT lacks the word.

And she said: *"In the midst of the troubles of my people I am carrying on."*[17] 14. And he said: "And what is there to do for her?" And Gehazi said: "In truth she has no son, and her husband is old." 15. And he said: "Call to her." And he called to her. And she stood at the doorway. 16. And he said: "At this time, about the time *that you are living,*[18] you will be embracing a son." And she said: *"Please, my master, prophet of the Lord, let not the word in the case of your maidservant be proved false."*[19] 17. And the woman conceived and gave birth to a son at this time, *about the time that she was living,*[20] which Elisha spoke with her. 18. And the child grew up, and one day he went forth unto his father, unto the harvesters. 19. And he said to his father: "My head, my head." And he said to the young man: "Take him *and bring him*[21] to his mother." 20. And he took him and brought him to his mother, and he sat upon her knees until *the time of noonday,*[22] and he died. 21. And she went up and laid him upon the bed of *the prophet of the Lord,*[23] and she closed the door on him, and went forth. 22. And she called to her husband and said: "Send now to me one of the young men and one of the asses, and *I will arrive in the presence of the prophet of the Lord*[24] and return." 23. And he said: "Why are you going unto him this day? It is not a new moon and not a Sabbath." And she said: "Peace." 24. And she saddled the ass and said to *the young man:*[25] "Lead on, and go. Do not *press upon*[26] me to ride except when I tell you." 25. And she went and came unto *the prophet of the Lord,*[27] to Mount Carmel. And when *the prophet of the Lord*[28] saw her opposite, he said to Gehazi his young man: "Behold that is the Shunamite woman. 26. Now run to meet her and say to her: 'Is there peace to you? Is there peace to your husband? Is there peace to the boy?'" And she said: "There is peace." 27. And she came unto *the prophet of the Lord,*[29] to the mountain; and she took hold of his feet, and Gehazi drew near to push her aside. And *the prophet of the Lord*[30] said: "Leave her alone, for she has a bitter soul; and *from before the Lord it was hidden from me, and it was not shown to me."*[31] 28. And she said: "Did I ask for a son from my master? Did I not say *to you: 'If a son is given to me, he lives; and if not, do not trouble me.'"*[32] 29. And he said to Gehazi: "Gird your loins, and take my staff in your hand, and go; if you will find a man, *you shall not ask for his peace,*[33] and if a man *shall ask for your peace,*[34] you shall not answer him; and you shall place my staff upon the face of the boy." 30. And the mother of the young man[35] said: "As the Lord lives and by the life of your soul, I will not leave you." And he arose and went after her. 31. And Gehazi passed before them and put the staff upon the face of the boy and there was no sound and there was *nothing making a noise,*[36] and he returned to meet him and told him, saying: "The boy *has not been awakened."*[37] 32. And Elisha came to the house, and

Notes, Chapter Four (Cont.)

[17]MT: "In the midst of my people I am dwelling."

[18]MT: "according to the time of life."

[19]MT: "Man of God, do not deceive your maidservant."

[20]MT: "according to the time of her life."

[21]MT lacks the phrase.

[22]MT: "noonday."

[23]MT: "the man of God."

[24]MT: "I will run unto the man of God."

[25]Many Tg mss.: "his young man."

[26]MT: "restrain."

[27]MT: "the man of the Lord."

[28]MT: "the man of the Lord."

[29]MT: "the man of God."

[30]MT: "the man of God."

[31]MT: "the Lord has hidden from me, and he has not told me."

[32]MT: "Do not deceive me."

[33]MT: "you shall not bless him."

[34]MT: "shall bless you."

[35]Most Tg mss.: "the boy."

[36]MT: "attentiveness."

[37]MT: "has not awakened."

behold the boy was dead, laid out upon his bed. 33. And he went and closed the door on the two of them and prayed *before*[38] the Lord. 34. And he went up and lay upon the boy, and he put his mouth upon his mouth and his eyes upon his eyes and his hands upon his hands; and he bent over him, and the flesh of the boy grew warm. 35. And he turned and walked about in the house *one time here and one time there;*[39] and he went up and bent over him, and the boy sneezed up to seven times, and the boy opened his eyes. 36. And he called to Gehazi and said: "Call this Shunamite woman." And he called her, and she came *to meet him,*[40] and he said: "Take your son." 37. And she came and fell *before*[41] his feet, and she bowed down upon the ground; and she took her son and went forth. 38. And Elisha returned to Gilgal, and there was famine in the land. And *the students*[42] of the prophets were sitting before him, and he said to his young man: "Set on the large pot, and boil the soup for *the students*[43] of the prophets." 39. And one went forth to the field to gather herbs and he found *a vine in the field,*[44] and he gathered from it cuttings of the field filling his garment; and he came and *broke them up and threw them*[45] into the pot of soup, for they did not know it. 40. And they poured it out for the men to eat; and as they were eating from the soup, they shouted out and said: "There is death in the pot, *prophet of the Lord."*[46] And they were not able to eat. 41. And he said: "Bring grain and *throw*[47] it into the pot." And he said: "Pour it out to the people." And they were eating and there was nothing bad in the pot. 42. And a man came from *the land of the south,*[48] and he brought to *the prophet of the Lord*[49] bread of first fruits, twenty *loaves*[50] of barley bread, and broken corn in his garment. And he said: "Give to the people, and let them eat." 43. And the one serving him said: "How shall I give this before a hundred men?" And he said: "Give to the people, and let them eat, for thus said the Lord: 'They will eat and have some left over.'" 44. And he gave before them, and they ate and they had some left according to the word of the Lord.

CHAPTER 5

1. And Naaman the chief of the army of the king of Aram was a great man before his master and received favor because *by his hands the Lord worked victory for the men of Aram.*[1] And the man was a warrior, *and he was afflicted with leprosy.*[2] 2. And *the men*

Notes, Chapter Four (Cont.)

[38] MT: "to."
[39] MT: "once here and once there."
[40] MT: "to him."
[41] MT: "at."
[42] MT: "the sons."
[43] MT: "the sons."
[44] MT: "a vine of the field."
[45] MT: "cut them."
[46] MT: "man of God."

[47] MT: "he threw."
[48] MT: "Baal-shalishah."
[49] MT: "the man of God."
[50] MT lacks the word.

Notes, Chapter Five

[1] MT: "by him the Lord gave victory to Aram."
[2] MT: "a leper."

of Aram[3] went forth in companies, and they brought back from the land of Israel a small maidservant, and *she was serving*[4] before the wife of Naaman. 3. And she said to her mistress: "*Happy would my master be if he would go*[5] before the prophet who is in Samaria. Then he would heal him from his leprosy." 4. And he came and told his master, saying: "Thus and so did the maidservant who is from the land of Israel speak." 5. And the king of Aram said: "Come, go. And I will send the letter unto the king of Israel." And he went and took in his hand twenty talents of silver, and 6,000 *denarii of*[6] gold, and ten suits of clothes. 6. And he brought the letter unto the king of Israel, saying; *and thus it was written in it:*[7] "And now as this letter comes unto you, behold I have sent to you Naaman my servant. And you shall heal him from his leprosy." 7. And when the king of Israel read the letter, he was tearing his garments, and he said: "*Is there need from before the Lord*[8] for me to kill and to let live, that this one sends to me to heal the man from his leprosy? But know now and see, for *he is seeking a false accusation to make a quarrel against me.*"[9] 8. And when Elisha *the prophet of the Lord*[10] heard that the king of Israel tore his garments, he sent unto the king, saying: "Why are you tearing your garments? Let him come now unto me, and let him know that there is a prophet in Israel." 9. And Naaman came with his horses and with his chariots, and he stood at the gate of the house belonging to Elisha. 10. And Elisha sent unto him a messenger, saying: "Go and bathe seven times in the Jordan, and your flesh will come back to you and you will be healed." 11. And Naaman grew angry, and he went and said: "Behold I was saying *that*[11] he will surely come forth unto me and stand and pray in the name of the Lord his God and lift up his hand over *the place of the lesion,*[12] and the leprosy would be healed. 12. Are not the *Amana*[13] and the Pharpar, the rivers of Damascus, better than all the waters of *the land of Israel?*[14] Shall I not bathe in them and be healed?" And he turned and went away in anger. 13. And his servants drew near and spoke with him and said: "*My lord,*[15] if the prophet spoke with you a great word, would you not do it? And so much the more that he said to you: 'Bathe, and be healed?'" 14. And he went down and bathed in the Jordan seven times according to the word of *the prophet of the Lord,*[16] and his flesh came back like the flesh of a small infant, and he was healed. 15. And he came back *unto the prophet of the Lord,*[17] he and all his camp, and he came and stood before him and said: "Behold now I know that there is no god *existing*[18] in all the earth except in Israel. And now accept *a present*[19] from your servant." 16. And he said: "As the Lord lives before whom *I am serving,*[20] I will not accept." And he urged him to accept, and *he was not willing.*[21] 17. And Naaman said: "And if not, let there be given now to your servant the loads of a

Notes, Chapter Five (Cont.)

[3]MT: "Aram."

[4]MT: "she was."

[5]MT: "Would that my master were."

[6]No denomination is given in the MT.

[7]MT lacks the phrase.

[8]MT: "Am I God?" Jastrow (p. 1300) gives a freer translation of the Tg: "Does the Lord need me...?"

[9]MT: "he is making a quarrel."

[10]MT: "the man of God."

[11]MT lacks the word.

[12]MT: "the place."

[13]MT: "Abana." Many MT mss. have Amana, which is also the *qere.*

[14]MT: "Israel."

[15]MT: "My father."

[16]MT: "the man of God."

[17]MT: "to the man of God."

[18]MT lacks the word.

[19]MT: "a blessing."

[20]MT: "I am standing."

[21]MT: "he refused."

pair of mules *from the dust of the earth,*[22] for your servant will not anymore make a holocaust and a sacrifice *to the idols of the nations but only to the name of the Lord.*[23] 18. For this matter may the Lord pardon your servant when my master goes into the temple of Rimmon to worship there, and he leans on my hand, and I worship in the temple of Rimon. When I worship in the temple of Rimmon, may the Lord pardon your servant in this matter." 19. And he said to him: "Go in peace."[24] And he went from his presence some distance. 20. And Gehazi *the student of Elisha the prophet of the Lord*[25] said: "Behold my master refused this Aramean Naaman, from accepting *from him*[26] whatever he brought. As the Lord lives, I will run after him and take from him something." 21. And Gehazi pursued after Naaman, and Naaman saw a man running after him and *he let himself down*[27] from the chariot to meet him, and he said: "Is all well?" 22. And he said: "All is well. My master sent me to say: 'Behold just now two young men from the hill country of *the house of Ephraim,*[28] from *the students*[29] of the prophets, came unto me. Give to them now a talent of silver and two changes of clothing." 23. And Naaman said: "Please, take two talents." And he urged him, and he wrapped two talents of silver in two *travelling cloaks*[30] and two changes of clothes, and he gave them to his two young men, and they took them before him. 24. And he went *into a hidden place*[31] and took from their hand and arranged them in the house and sent the men away, and they went. 25. And he himself came and stood *before*[32] his master, and Elisha said to him: "From where *are you coming,*[33] Gehazi?" And he said: "Your servant did not go anywhere." 26. And he said to him: "*In a spirit of prophecy it was revealed to me*[34] when the man turned around from upon his chariot to meet you. Is this the time for you *that you should take*[35] silver and *you should take*[36] clothing? *And you planned in your heart to buy*[37] olives and vineyards and sheep and oxen and slaves and handmaidens. 27. And the leprosy of Naaman will cling to you and to *your sons*[38] forever." And he went forth from him *white*[39] as snow.

Notes, Chapter Five (Cont.)

[22]MT: "earth."

[23]MT: "to other gods but only to the Lord."

[24]MT: /One ms. adds a comment by Elisha after "Go in peace" in order to eliminate the possibility that Elisha gave Naaman permission to offer sacrifice outside Israel. See S-A, 18.

[25]MT: "the young man of Elisha the man of God."

[26]MT: "from his hand."

[27]MT: "alighted."

[28]MT: "Ephraim."

[29]MT: "sons."

[30]MT: "bags."

[31]MT: "to the hill."

[32]MT: "to."

[33]MT lacks the word.

[34]MT: "Did not my heart go."

[35]MT: "to take."

[36]MT: "to take."

[37]MT lacks the phrase.

[38]MT: "your seed."

[39]MT: "a leper."

CHAPTER 6

1. And *the students*[1] of the prophets said to Elisha: "Behold now the place where we dwell before you is too narrow for us. 2. Let us go now unto the Jordan, and let us take from there each man one log, and let us prepare[2] for ourselves there a place to dwell there." And he said: "Go." 3. And one said: "Please now, go with your servants." And he said: "I will go." 4. And he went with them, and they came to the Jordan and cut down the trees. 5. And one *was striking at*[3] a log, and the iron *got loosened and*[4] fell into the water. And he shouted and said: "Please my master, *indeed I borrowed it.*"[5] 6. And *the prophet of the Lord*[6] said: "Where did it fall?" And he showed him the place, and he cut some wood and threw it in there, and the iron floated. 7. And he said: "Take it up for yourself." And he reached out his hand and took it. 8. And the king of Aram *was waging battle*[7] against Israel, and he took counsel with his servants, saying: "*At a hidden and concealed place our camp is.*"[8] 9. And *the prophet of the Lord*[9] sent unto the king of Israel, saying: "Be careful of passing by this place, for there *the men of Aram are hiding.*"[10] 10. And the king of Israel sent to the place that *the prophet of the Lord*[11] said to him. And he warned it, and he took heed there not one time and not two times (only). 11. And the heart of the king of Aram was troubled over this matter, and he called to his servants and said to them: "Will you not tell *us*[12] who from among us *revealed the secret*[13] to the king of Israel?" 12. And one of his servants said: "No, my master the king. For Elisha the prophet who is in Israel tells to the king of Israel the words that you speak in the inner chamber of your bedroom." 13. And he said: "Go and see where he is. And I will send and take him away." And it was told to him, saying: "Behold he is in Dothan." 14. And he sent to there horses and chariots and *many companies,*[14] and they came by night and surrounded the city. 15. And the servant of *the prophet of the Lord*[15] got up early to arise, and he went forth; and behold *companies*[16] surrounded the city, and *horses and chariots.*[17] And his young man said to him: "Please my master, how shall we act?" 16. And he said: "Do not fear, for those who are with us are more numerous than those who are with them." 17. And Elisha prayed and said: "Please, Lord, open his eyes, and let him see." And the Lord opened the eyes of the boy, and he saw, and behold the mountain was full of horses and chariots of fire

Notes, Chapter Six

[1] MT: "the sons."
[2] Many Tg mss.: "make."
[3] MT: "was felling."
[4] MT lacks the phrase.
[5] MT: "and it was borrowed."
[6] MT: "the man of God."
[7] MT: "was fighting."
[8] MT: "At such and such a place our camp will be."
[9] MT: "the man of God."
[10] MT: "Aram has gone down."
[11] MT: "the man of God."
[12] MT: "me."
[13] MT lacks the phrase.
[14] MT: "a strong army."
[15] MT: "the man of God."
[16] MT: "an army."
[17] MT: "horse and chariot."

round about Elisha. 18. And they [the Arameans] went down unto him, and Elisha prayed *before*[18] the Lord and said: "Strike now this people with temporary blindness." And he struck them with temporary blindness according to the word of Elisha. 19. And Elisha said to them: "This is not the way, and this is not the city. Come after me, and I will bring you unto the man whom you are seeking." And he brought them to Samaria. 20. And as they came into Samaria, Elisha said: "O Lord, open now the eyes of these, and let them see." And the Lord opened their eyes, and they saw, and behold *they were*[19] in the midst of Samaria. 21. And the king of Israel said to Elisha when he saw them: *"Shall I kill? Shall I kill, my master?"*[20] 22. And he said: *"You shall not kill! Do you kill*[21] those whom you captured by your sword and by your bow? Set bread and water before them, and let them eat and drink and go unto their master." 23. And he prepared for them a great feast, and they ate and drank and he sent them away, and they went unto their master. And *the army*[22] of Aram did not enter anymore in *the territory of the land*[23] of Israel. 24. And afterwards Ben-Hadad the king of Aram gathered all his army and went up and laid siege against Samaria. 25. And there was a great famine in Samaria, and behold they were laying siege against it until the head of an ass was *being sold*[24] for eighty (pieces) of silver and a quarter of a qab of *dung, the excrement of doves,*[25] for five *selas*[26] of silver. 26. And the king of Israel was passing by upon the wall, and a woman was crying out *before*[27] him, saying: "Save (me), my master the king." 27. And he said: "Will not the Lord save you? From where will I save you? Is it from the threshing floor, or from the vat?" 28. And the king said to her: "What is there to you?" And she said: "A certain woman said to me: 'Give up your son, and let us eat him this day, and we will eat my son tomorrow.'" 29. And we boiled my son and ate him, and I said to her on the next day: 'Give up your son, and let us eat him.' And she hid her son." 30. And when the king heard the words of the woman, he tore his garments; and he was passing upon the wall, and the people saw, and behold sackcloth was girded upon his flesh from underneath. 31. And he said: "Thus may *the Lord*[28] do to me and thus may he add, if the head of Elisha the son of Shaphat *will remain*[29] upon him this day." 32. And Elisha was sitting in *the house,*[30] and the elders were sitting with him. And he sent the man from before him. Before the messenger came unto him, he said to the elders: "Do you see that this *son of killing*[31] has sent to take off my head? Look, when the messenger comes, hold onto the door and close him out by the door. Is not the sound of the feet of his master behind him?" 33. While he was still speaking with them, behold the messenger was coming down unto him and said: "Behold this evil is *from before*[32] the Lord. What more *shall I pray before*[33] the Lord?"

Notes, Chapter Six (Cont.)

[18] MT: "to."

[19] MT lacks the phrase.

[20] MT: "Shall I strike down? Shall I strike down, my father?" "Master" in Aramaic is "Rabbi."

[21] MT: "You shall not strike down. Do you strike down?"

[22] MT: "the troops."

[23] MT: "the land."

[24] MT: lacks the word.

[25] MT: "the dung of doves."

[26] MT lacks the word.

[27] MT: "to."

[28] MT: "God."

[29] MT: "will stand."

[30] MT: "his house."

[31] MT: "the murderer."

[32] MT: "from with."

[33] MT: "shall I wait for." Tg avoids the hopeless tone of the MT.

CHAPTER 7

1. And Elisha said: "*Accept*[1] the word of the Lord: 'Thus said the Lord: "At this time tomorrow a seah of fine flour for *a sela*,[2] and two seahs of barley for *a sela*[3] at the gate of Samaria."'" 2. And *the warrior*[4] upon whose hand the king relied answered *the prophet of the Lord*[5] and said: "*If the Lord was opening windows and making happiness come down from the heavens*,[6] would it be *according to this word?*" [7] And he said: "Behold you are seeing with your eyes, and from there you will not eat." 3. And four leprous men *were sitting*[8] at the entrance of the gate, and they said, each to his fellow: "Why are we sitting here until we die? 4. If we say 'Let us go into the city,' there is famine in the city, and we will die there. And if we sit here, we will die. And now come, and let us desert to the camp of Aram. If they let us live, we will live. And *if they kill us, we will be killed.*"[9] 5. And they arose at dusk to enter the camp of Aram, and they came unto the *edges*[10] of the camp of Aram; and behold there was not a man there. 6. *And from before the Lord a sound of chariots, a sound of horses, a sound of many companies was heard to the camp of Aram;*[11] and they said, each to his brothers:[12] "Behold the king of Israel has hired against us the kings of the Hittites and the kings of the Egyptians to come against us." 7. And they arose and fled at dusk and left their tents and their horses and their asses at the camp as it was, and they fled *to save their lives.*[13] 8. And these lepers came unto the *edges*[14] of the camp and came into *the tent of one,*[15] and they ate and drank and took from there silver and gold and clothes, and they came and hid (them); and they returned and went into another tent, and they took from there and went and hid (them). 9. And they said, each man to his fellow: "What we are doing is not right. This day is a day of good news. And *if*[16] we are silent and waiting until the light of morning, punishment will befall us. And now come, and let us go back and tell the house of the king." 10. And they came and called to *the keepers*[17] of the gate of the city and told them, saying: "We came to the camp of Aram, and behold there was there no man and no sound of a man except *horses tied and asses tied*[18] and tents as they were." 11. And *the keepers of the gates called out,*[19] and they told the house of the

Notes, Chapter Seven

[1]MT: "Hear."
[2]MT: "shekel."
[3]MT: "shekel."
[4]MT: "the captain."
[5]MT: "the man of God."
[6]MT: "Behold the Lord is making windows in the heavens."
[7]MT: "this word."
[8]MT: "were."
[9]MT: "if they put us to death, we will die."

[10]MT: "edge."
[11]MT: "And the lord made the camp of Aram here a sound of a chariot, a sound of a horse, a sound of a great army."
[12]Some Tg mss.: "his fellows."
[13]MT: "for their lives."
[14]MT: "edge."
[15]MT: "one tent."
[16]MT lacks the word.
[17]MT: "the keeper."
[18]MT: "the horse tied and the ass tied."
[19]MT: "gatekeepers."

king inside. 12. And the king arose by night and said to his servants: "I will tell you now what *the men of Aram*[20] have done to us. They know that we are starving, and they went forth from the camp to hide themselves in the field, saying: 'For they will come forth from the city, and we will seize them alive and go into the city.'" 13. And one from his servants answered and said: "Let them take now five from the horses; *the rest*[21] that remain in it, behold those are like all the crowd of Israel who are left in it; and *if they perish,*[22] behold they are like all the crowd of Israel who have come to an end; and let us send and see." 14. And they took two *riders*[23] of horses, and the king sent after the army of Aram, saying: "Go, and see." 15. And they went after them up to the Jordan, and behold all the road was full of clothes and equipment that *the men of Aram*[24] threw down in their haste *to flee;*[25] and the messengers returned and told the king. 16. And the people went forth and despoiled the army of Aram, and a seah of fine flour was for *a sela,*[26] and two seahs of barley were for *a sela*[27] according to the word of the Lord. 17. And the king appointed *the warrior*[28] upon whose hand he relied in charge of the gate; and the people trampled him at the gate, and he died just as *the prophet of the Lord*[29] spoke, who spoke when the king went down unto him. 18. And when *the prophet of the Lord*[30] spoke with the king, saying: "Two seahs of barley for *a sela,*[31] and a seah of fine flour for *a sela*[32] — it will be at this time tomorrow at the gate of Samaria," 19. *the warrior*[33] answered *the prophet of the Lord*[34] and said: "*And if the Lord opens windows and brings happiness down from the heavens,*[35] would it be according to this word?" And he said: "Behold you are seeing with your eyes, and from there you will not eat." 20. And so it was to him, and the people trampled him at the gate, and he died.

CHAPTER 8

1. And Elisha spoke with the woman whose son he restored to life, saying: "Arise and go, you and *the men of your house,*[1] and *dwell in a place where it is good to dwell,*[2] for the Lord *has decreed*[3] a famine, and also *it is ready to come*[4] upon the land for seven years." 2. And the woman arose and did according to the word of *the prophet of the*

Notes, Chapter Seven (Cont.)

[20]MT: "Aram."
[21]MT: "those who are left."
[22]MT lacks the phrase.
[23]MT: "chariots."
[24]MT: "Aram."
[25]MT lacks the word.
[26]MT: "a shekel."
[27]MT: "a shekel."
[28]MT: "the captain."
[29]MT: "the man of God."
[30]MT: "the man of God."

[31]MT: "a shekel."
[32]MT: "a shekel."
[33]MT: "the captain."
[34]MT: "the man of God."
[35]MT: "And behold the Lord makes windows in the heavens."

Notes, Chapter Eight

[1]MT: "your household."
[2]MT: "sojourn where you will sojourn."
[3]MT: "has called for."
[4]MT: "it is coming."

Lord,[5] and she and *the men of her house*[6] went and *she made her dwelling*[7] in the land of the Philistines for seven years. 3. And at the end of seven years the woman returned from the land of the Philistines, and she went forth to complain *before*[8] the king about her house and about her field. 4. And the king was speaking with Gehazi, *the student of the prophet of the Lord,*[9] saying: "Tell me now all the great things that Elisha has done." 5. And he was telling the king that he brought back to life a dead person, and behold the woman whose son he brought back to life was complaining *before*[10] the king about her house and about her field. And Gehazi said: "My master the king, this is the woman, and this is her son whom Elisha brought back to life." 6. And the king asked the woman, and she told him. And the king appointed for her one eunuch, saying: "Return everything that is hers and all the produce of the field from the day that she left the land and until now." 7. And Elisha came to Damascus, and Ben-Hadad the king of Aram was sick, and it was told to him saying: "*The prophet of the Lord*[11] has come unto here." 8. And the king said to Hazael: "Take in your hand the present, and go to meet *the prophet of the Lord,*[12] and ask *the word of the Lord*[13] from him, saying: 'Will I recover from this sickness?'" 9. And Hazael went to meet him, and he took the present in his hand and all the goods of Damascus, the loads of forty camels. And he came and stood before him and said: "Your son, Ben-Hadad, the king of Aram, sent me unto you, saying: 'Will I recover from this sickness?'" 10. And Elisha said to him: "Go, say *to him:*[14] 'You will surely recover,' and the Lord has shown me that he will surely die." 11. And *he turned*[15] his face and *waited for a long time,*[16] and *the prophet of the Lord*[17] wept. 12. And Hazael said: "Why is my master weeping?" And he said: "Because I know the evil that you will do to the sons of Israel. You will burn their fortresses with fire, and you will kill their young men with the sword, and you will dash down their infants, and you will split open their pregnant women." 13. And Hazael said: "For what is your servant a dog that he should do this great thing?" And Elisha said: "The Lord has shown me you as the king over Aram." 14. And he went from the presence of Elisha; and he came unto his master, and he said to him: "What did Elisha say to you?" And he said: "He said to me: 'You will surely live.'" 15. And *on the day after it,*[18] he took a blanket and dipped it in water and spread it over his face, and he died. And Hazael ruled in his place. 16. In the fifth year for Joram the son of Ahab the king of Israel and Jehoshaphat the king of *the tribe of the house of Judah,*[19] Jehoram the son of Jehoshaphat the king of *the tribe of the house of Judah*[20] ruled. 17. He was thirty-two years old when he ruled, and he ruled eight years in Jerusalem. 18. And he went in the way of the kings of Israel just as the house of Ahab did, for a daughter of Ahab was his wife; and he did what was evil *before*[21] the Lord. 19. *There was favor from before the Lord so as not to destroy the house of Judah*[22] on account of David his

Notes, Chapter Eight (Cont.)

[5] MT: "the man of God."
[6] MT: "her household."
[7] MT: "she sojourned."
[8] MT: "to."
[9] MT: "the young man of the man of God."
[10] MT: "to."
[11] MT: "the man of God."
[12] MT: "the man of God."
[13] MT: "the Lord."

[14] MT: "no." Tg follows the *qere*.
[15] MT: "he fixed."
[16] MT: "stared unto shame."
[17] MT: "the man of God."
[18] MT: "on the morrow."
[19] MT: "Judah."
[20] MT: "Judah."
[21] MT: "in the eyes of."
[22] MT: "The Lord was not willing to destroy."

servant, just as he said to him to give to him *a kingdom*[23] to his sons all the days. 20. In his days *the Edomites*[24] rebelled from under the hand of *the men of Judah*,[25] and they made a king rule over them. 21. And Joram passed over to Zair, and all the *chariots*[26] were with him; and he was arising by night, and he struck down *the men of Edom who were surrounding*[27] him and the chiefs of the *chariots*;[28] and the people fled to its cities.[29] 22. And *the Edomites*[30] rebelled from beneath the hand of *the men of Judah*[31] until this day. Then *the inhabitants of Libnah*[32] rebelled at that time. 23. And the rest of the acts of Joram and all that he did, *behold they are*[33] written in the book of the chronicles of the kings of *the house of Judah.*[34] 24. And Joram slept with his fathers, and he was buried with his fathers in the city of David, and Ahaziah his son ruled in his place. 25. In the twelfth year for Joram the son of Ahab the king of Israel, Ahaziah the son of Jehoram the king of *the tribe of the house of Judah*[35] ruled. 26. Ahaziah was twenty-two years old when he ruled, and for one year he ruled in Jerusalem; and the name of his mother was Athaliah, the daughter of Omri the king of Israel. 27. And he was walking in the way of the house of Ahab, and he did what was evil *before*[36] the Lord, like the house of Ahab, for he was the son-in-law of the house of Ahab. 28. And he went with Joram the son of Ahab *to wage battle*[37] with Hazael the king of Aram in Ramoth-gilead, and *the men of Aram*[38] struck down Joram. 29. And Joram the king returned to be healed in Jezreel from the blows that *the men of Aram*[39] struck him in Ramah when *he waged battle*[40] with Hazael the king of Aram. And Ahaziah the son of Jehoram the king of *the tribe of the house of Judah*[41] went down to *visit*[42] Joram the son of Ahab in Jezreel, for he was sick.

CHAPTER 9

1. And Elisha the prophet called to one of *the students*[1] of the prophets, and he said to him: "Gird your loins, and take this vessel of oil in your hand, and go to Ramoth-gilead. 2. And you will come to there, and see there Jehu, the son of Jehoshaphat, the son of Nimshi. And you will come and make him arise from the midst of his brothers and bring him in inside the inner chamber. 3. And you will take the vessel of oil and pour it out upon his head and say: 'Thus said the Lord: "I have anointed you *to be king*[2] over Israel."' And you will open the door and flee, and do not look around." 4. And the young man, *the student of the prophet*,[3] went to Ramoth-gilead. 5. And he

Notes, Chapter Eight (Cont.)

[23]MT: "a lamp."
[24]MT: "Edom."
[25]MT: "Judah."
[26]MT: "chariotry."
[27]MT: "Edom round about."
[28]MT: "chariotry."
[29]MT: "tents."
[30]MT: "Edom."
[31]MT: "Judah."
[32]MT: "Libnah."
[33]MT: "are they not."
[34]MT: "Judah."

[35]MT: "Judah."
[36]MT: "in the eyes of."
[37]MT: "for war."
[38]MT: "the Arameans."
[39]MT: "the Arameans."
[40]MT: "he fought."
[41]MT: "Judah."
[42]MT: "see."

Notes, Chapter Nine

[1]MT: "the sons."
[2]MT: "for king."
[3]MT: "the prophet."

came, and behold the chiefs of the army were sitting, and he said: "I have a word *to speak with you*,[4] chief." And Jehu said: "*With whom*[5] from all of us?" And he said: "*With you*,[6] chief." 6. And he arose and went into the house, and he poured the oil *upon*[7] his head and said to him: "Thus said the Lord God of Israel: 'I have anointed you *to be the king over*[8] the people of the Lord, *over*[9] Israel. 7. And you will strike down the house of Ahab your master, and *the vengeance*[10] of the blood of my servants the prophets and the blood of all the servants of the Lord *will be avenged*[10] from the hand of Jezebel. 8. And all the house of Ahab *is perishing*,[11] and I will destroy for Ahab *him who knows knowledge*,[12] both bond and free, in Israel. 9. And I will make the house of Ahab like the house of Jeroboam the son of Nebat and like the house of Baasha the son of Ahijah. 10. And the dogs will eat Jezebel in the territory of Jezreel, and there will be no one who is burying her." And he opened the door and fled. 11. And Jehu went forth unto the servants of his master, and *they said*[13] to him: "Is all well? Why did this madman come unto you?" And he said to them: "You know the man and his talk." 12. And they said: "*You are telling a lie.*[14] Now tell us." And he said: "Thus and so he said to me, saying: 'Thus said the Lord: "I have anointed you *to be the king*[15] over Israel."'" 13. And they hastened, and each took his garment and they put it beneath him upon *the smooth step*,[16] and they blew on the trumpet and said: "Jehu is king." 14. And Jehu, the son of Jehoshaphat, the son of Nimshi, rebelled against Joram. And Jehoram was guarding at Ramoth-gilead, he and all Israel, from before Hazael the king of Aram. 15. And Jehoram the king returned to be healed in Jezreel from the blows that *the men of Aram*[17] struck him *when he waged battle*[18] with Hazael the king of Aram. And Jehu said: "If *your soul desires*,[19] let no escapee go forth from the city to go to tell it in Jezreel." 16. And Jehu rode and went to Jezreel, for Joram was lying there and Ahaziah the king of *the tribe of the house of Judah*[20] went down *to visit*[21] Joram. 17. And the watchman was standing upon the tower in Jezreel, and he saw the company of Jehu as he came, and he said: "I see a company." And Jehoram said: "Take a rider and send to meet them, and let him say: 'Is it peace?'" 18. And the rider of the horse came to meet him and said: "Thus said the king: 'Is it peace?'" And Jehu said: "What is there to you and to peace? Go around behind me." And the watchman reported, saying: "The messenger came unto them, and he did not return." 19. And he sent a rider of the horse a second time, and he came unto them and said: "Thus said the king: 'Peace.'" And Jehu said: "What is there to you and to peace? Go around behind me." 20. And the watchman reported, saying: "He came unto them, and he did not return. And the driving is like the driving of Jehu the son of Nimshi, for he is

Notes, Chapter Nine (Cont.)

[4]MT: "for you."
[5]MT: "To whom."
[6]MT: "To you."
[7]MT: "to."
[8]MT: "for king for."
[9]MT: "for."
[10]MT: "I will avenge."
[11]MT: "will perish."
[12]MT: "him who urinates against the wall." Tg

avoids this graphic descriptive idiom for males.
[13]MT: "he said."
[14]MT: "A lie."
[15]MT: "for a king."
[16]MT uncertain.
[17]MT: "the Arameans."
[18]MT: "when he fought."
[19]MT: "If it is your soul."
[20]MT: "Judah."
[21]MT: "to see.

driving with *gentleness.*"[22] 21. And Jehoram said: "*Gird yourselves.*"[23] And *he arranged*[24] his chariot, and Jehoram the king of Israel and Ahaziah the king of *the tribe of the house of Judah*[25] went forth, each man in his chariot. And they went forth to meet Jehu, and they found him in the property of Naboth the Jezreelite. 22. And when Jehoram saw Jehu, he said: "Is it peace, Jehu?" And he said: "What peace is there as long as there are the *idols*[26] of Jezebel your mother and her many sorceries?" 23. And Jehoram turned around *behind him,*[27] and he fled and said to Ahaziah: "Deceit, Ahaziah." 24. And Jehu filled his hand with the bow, and he struck down Jehoram between his arms, and the arrow went forth from his heart and stuck in his chariot. 25. And he said to Bidkar his officer: "Take, cast him in the property of the field of Naboth the Jezreelite. For remember, I and you when we were riding, *going as one pair,*[28] after Ahab his father, and *from before the Lord the burden of this prophecy was taken up*[29] against him: 26. '*If there not be revealed*[30] the blood of Naboth and the blood of his sons *before me soon...,*'[31] said the Lord; 'I will pay you back in this property,' said the Lord. And now take, cast him in the property according to the word of the Lord." 27. And Ahaziah the king of *the tribe of the house of Judah*[32] saw and fled on the way of *Beth-ganna,*[33] and Jehu pursued after him and said: "Strike him down too in the *chariots*[34] at the ascent of Gir which is by Ibleam." And he fled to Megiddo and died there. 28. And his servants *brought him down into*[35] Jerusalem, and they buried him in his tomb with his fathers in the city of David. 29. And in the eleventh year of Joram the son of Ahab, Ahaziah ruled over *those of the house of Judah.*[36] 30. And Jehu came to Jezreel, and Jezebel heard, and *she painted*[37] her eyes with eye-paint and adorned her head and looked out *from*[38] the window. 31. And Jehu entered by the gate, and she said: "Is it peace, Zimri, killer of his master?" 32. And he lifted up his face to the window, and he said: "Who is *here?*[39] Who?" And two or three eunuchs looked out unto him. 33. And he said: "Throw her down." And they threw her down, and some of her blood spattered upon the wall and upon the horses, and they trampled her. 34. And he entered and ate and drank and said: "See now to this accursed woman and bury her, for she is the daughter of the king." 35. And they came to bury her, and they did not find on her anything except the skull and the feet and the palms of the hands. 36. And they returned and told him, and he said: "This is the word of the Lord that he spoke by the hand of his servant Elijah *who was from Teshub,*[40] saying: 'In the property of Jezreel the dogs will eat the flesh of Jezebel. 37. And the corpse of Jezebel will be like dung *scattered*[41] upon the face of the field in the property of Jezreel so that they will not say: "This is Jezebel."'"

Notes, Chapter Nine (Cont.)

[22]MT: "frenzy." Tg treats Jehu, who has just been anointed king at God's command, positively.
[23]MT: "Gird" in the singular.
[24]MT: "he girded."
[25]MT: "Judah."
[26]MT: "harlotries."
[27]MT: "his hands."
[28]MT: "side by side."
[29]MT: "the Lord took up this burden."
[30]MT: "If I do not see."
[31]MT: "yesterday."

[32]MT: "Judah."
[33]MT: "Beth-haggan." Tg translated the second half of the name into Aramaic.
[34]MT: "chariot."
[35]MT: "rode him down to."
[36]MT: "Judah."
[37]MT: "she placed."
[38]MT: "by."
[39]MT: "with you."
[40]MT: "the Tishbite."
[41]MT lacks the word.

CHAPTER 10

1. And Ahab had seventy sons in Samaria. And Jehu wrote letters and sent to Samaria unto the chiefs of Jezreel, the elders, and unto the guardians of Ahab, saying: 2. "And now when this letter comes unto you, and the sons of your master are with you, and with you are *chariots*[1] and horses and *fortified cities and kinds of weapons,*[2] 3. you will see who is good and who is fitting from the sons of your master, and you will set (him) upon *the throne of the kingdom*[3] of his father, and *you will wage battle*[4] for the house of your master." 4. And they were very much afraid, and said: "Behold two kings *were not able to stand*[5] before him. And how will we stand?" 5. And he who *was appointed*[6] over the house and he who *was appointed*[7] over the city and the elders and the guardians sent unto Jehu, saying: "We are your servants; and everything that you will tell us, we will do. We will not make any man king. Whatever is good in you eyes, do." 6. And he wrote to them the letter a second time, saying: "If you are for me and *you are accepting from me,*[8] take the heads of the men of the sons of your master, and come unto me about this time tomorrow to Jezreel." And the sons of the king, the seventy men, were with the masters of the city, who were raising them. 7. And when the letter came unto them, they took the sons of the king and slew the seventy men and placed their heads in baskets and sent (them) unto him, to Jezreel. 8. And the messenger came and told him, saying: "They have brought the heads of the sons of the king." And he said: "Place them in two piles at the entrance of the gate until morning." 9. And in the morning he went forth and arose and said to all the people: "You are innocent. Behold I rebelled against my master and killed them. And who *has killed*[9] all these? 10. Know now that nothing from the word of the Lord that the Lord spoke about the house of Ahab *is voided,*[10] and the Lord *has fulfilled*[11] whatever he spoke by the hand of his servant Elijah." 11. And Jehu struck down all those who were left for the house of Ahab in Jezreel and all his chiefs and *his relatives and his companions*[12] until he had left[13] for him no survivor. 12. And he arose and came and went to Samaria. He was at the place of *the assembly*[14] of the shepherds on the way, 13. and Jehu found the brothers of Ahaziah the king of *the tribe of the house of Judah,*[15] and he said: "Who

Notes, Chapter Ten

[1]MT: "chariot."
[2]MT: "fortified city and weaponry."
[3]MT: "the throne."
[4]MT: "you will fight."
[5]MT: "did not stand."
[6]MT: "was."
[7]MT: "was."

[8]MT: "you are hearing my voice."
[9]MT: "has struck down."
[10]MT: "will fall to the ground."
[11]MT: "has done."
[12]MT: "his familiar friends and his priests." Tg removes the priests from the condemned group.
[13]Many Tg mss.: "there was left."
[14]MT: "binding."
[15]MT: "Judah."

are you?" And they said: "We are the brothers of Ahaziah, and we have come down *to inquire about the health*[16] of the sons of the king and the sons of *the queen*."[17] 14. And he said: "Seize them alive." And they seized them alive and slew them at the pit of the place of *the assembly*[18] of forty-two men; and not a man was left from them. 15. And he went from there and found Jehonadab the son of Rechab coming to meet him, and *he asked for his peace*[19] and said to him: "Is your heart right just as my heart is with your heart?" And Jehonadab said: "It is." "If it is, give your hand." And he gave his hand and brought him up unto him to the chariot. 16. And he said: "Come with me, and see my zeal *that I am zealous with before the Lord*."[20] And *they brought him down*[21] in his chariot. 17. And he came to Samaria and struck down all those who were left to Ahab in Samaria until he had destroyed him utterly according to the word of the Lord that he spoke with Elijah. 18. And Jehu gathered all the people and said to them: "Ahab served Baal a little; Jehu will serve him much. 19. And now *summon*[22] to me all the prophets of Baal, all his worshippers, and all his *idol priests.*[23] Let no one be missing, for I am having a great *service*[24] for Baal. Everyone who is missing *will not be left alive.*"[25] And Jehu acted with *wisdom*[26] in order to destroy the worshippers of Baal. 20. And Jehu said: "*Summon*[27] an assembly for Baal." And *they summoned*[28] (it). 21. And Jehu sent in all Israel, and all the worshippers of Baal came, and no one was left over who did not come. And they entered the temple of Baal, and the temple of Baal was filled *doorpost to doorpost.*[29] 22. And he said to him *who was appointed*[30] over *the wardrobes:*[31] "Bring out *garments*[32] for all the worshippers of Baal." And he brought out *garments*[33] for them. 23. And Jehu and Jehonadab the son of Rechab came to the temple of Baal, and he said to the worshippers of Baal: "Search and see lest there be here with you any of the servants of the Lord, but only the worshippers of Baal." 24. And they went in to make *an offering of holy things*[34] and holocausts. And Jehu *stationed*[35] for himself eighty men outside and he said: "The man who will be spared from the men whom I am bringing in under your hands, his life for his life." 25. And when he finished making *the holocausts,*[36] Jehu said to the runners and to the warriors: "Go in, *and*[37] strike them down. Let no man go forth." And they struck them down by the edge of the sword, and the runners and the warriors cast out *those who were killed,*[38] and they went unto the city of the temple of Baal. 26. And they brought out the pillar of the temple of Baal and burned it. 27. And they broke the pillar of Baal and broke the temple of Baal, and they made it into a latrine unto this day. 28. And Jehu destroyed Baal utterly from Israel. 29. Only Jehu did not turn aside from after the sins of Jeroboam the son of Nebat which he made Israel sin; *he enslaved himself to*[39] the

Notes, Chapter Ten (Cont.)

[16]MT: "to visit."

[17]MT: "the queen-mother."

[18]MT: "binding."

[19]MT: "he blessed him."

[20]MT: "for the Lord."

[21]MT: "they drove him."

[22]MT: "call."

[23]MT: "priests."

[24]MT (and some Tg mss.): "sacrifice."

[25]MT: "will not live."

[26]MT: "cunning." Tg uses a clearly positive word to describe Jehu.

[27]MT: "Sanctify."

[28]MT: "they called."

[29]MT: "end to end."

[30]MT lacks the phrase.

[31]MT: "the wardrobe."

[32]MT: "clothing."

[33]MT: "clothing."

[34]MT: "sacrifices."

[35]MT: "placed."

[36]MT: "the holocaust."

[37]MT lacks the word.

[38]MT lacks the phrase.

[39]MT lacks the phrase.

calves of gold that were in Bethel and that were in Dan. 30. And the Lord said to Jehu: "Because you did right to do what was proper *before me,*[40] according to all that is in my *good pleasure*[41] you have done to the house of Ahab, your sons unto the fourth generation will sit upon *the throne of the kingdom*[42] of Israel." 31. And Jehu was not careful to walk in the law of the Lord God of Israel with all his heart. He did not turn away from *all*[43] the sins of Jeroboam that he made Israel sin. 32. In those days *the anger of the Lord began to rest heavily upon*[44] Israel, and Hazael struck them down in all *the territory of the land*[45] of Israel: 33. from the Jordan eastward, all the land of Gilead, *the tribe of Gad and the tribe of Reuben and the tribe of Manasseh;*[46] from Aroer which is by the valley of the Arnon, and the land of Gilead and *Matnan.*[47] 34. And the rest of the words of Jehu and all that he did and all his might, are they not written in the book of the chronicles of the kings of Israel? 35. And Jehu slept with his fathers, and they buried him in Samaria. And Jehoahaz his son ruled in his place. 36. And the days that Jehu ruled over Israel were twenty-eighty years in Samaria.

CHAPTER 11

1. And Athaliah the mother of Ahaziah *saw*[1] that her son was dead, and she arose and destroyed all the seed of the kingdom. 2. And Jehosheba the daughter of King Joram, the sister of Ahaziah, took Joash the son of Ahaziah, and she hid him from the midst of the sons of the kings *who were being killed;*[2] and *she concealed*[3] him and his nurse in the inner chamber of the bedrooms; and they concealed him from before Athaliah, and *he was not killed.*[4] 3. And he was hidden with her *in the house of the sanctuary*[5] of the Lord for six years, and Athaliah ruled over the land. 4. And in the seventh year, Jehoiada sent and took the chiefs of the hundreds for *warriors*[6] and for runners; and he brought them in unto him to *the house of the sanctuary*[7] of the Lord, and he cut for them a covenant and made them swear in *the house of the sanctuary*[8] of the Lord, and he showed them the son of the king. 5. And he commanded them, saying: "This is the thing that you shall do. A third of you are coming in (on) the Sabbath and

Notes, Chapter Ten (Cont.)

[40]MT: "in my eyes."
[41]MT: "heart."
[42]MT: "the throne."
[43]MT lacks the word.
[44]MT: "The Lord began to cut off."
[45]MT: "the territory."
[46]MT: "the Gadite and the Reubenite and the Manassite."
[47]MT: "Bashan."

Notes, Chapter Eleven

[1]MT: "and she saw."
[2]MT: "who were being put to death."
[3]MT lacks the word.
[4]MT: "he was not put to death."
[5]MT: "the house."
[6]MT: "the Carite." Here and in vs. 19 the Carites (or Carians in Asia Minor) are a foreign body guard. Tg identifies them as soldiers, rather than by their ethnic name.
[7]MT: "the house."
[8]MT: "the house."

keeping the guard of the house of the king, 6. and a third at the gate of *the protectors,*[9] and a third at *the gate that is behind it, the gate of the runners,*[10] and you shall keep the guard of the house from what is left over. 7. And two divisions among you, all those going forth (on) the Sabbath, you shall keep the watch of *the house of the sanctuary*[11] of the Lord *upon*[12] the king, 8. and you shall surround the king round about, each man with weapons in his hand; and whoever will enter *to the inside from the ranks will be killed.*[13] And be with the king in his going forth and in his coming in." 9. And the chiefs of the hundreds did according to all that Jehoiada the priest commanded, and each brought his men, those entering (on) the Sabbath with those going forth (on) the Sabbath, and they came unto Jehoiada the priest. 10. And *Jehoiada*[14] the priest gave to the chiefs of the hundreds the spears and the shields that belonged to King David that were in *the house of the sanctuary*[15] of the Lord. 11. And the runners arose, each man with weapons in his hand from the right side of the house unto the left side to the altar and to the house *of atonement*[16] to the king round about. 12. And he brought forth the son of the king and put upon him the crown and the testimonies, and they made him king and anointed him and clapped hands and said: *"May the king prosper."*[17] 13. And Athaliah heard the voice of those *ruling the people;*[18] and she came in unto the people *to the house of the sanctuary*[19] of the Lord. 14. And she saw, and behold the king was standing by the pillar according to the custom, and the chiefs *were with him,*[20] and the trumpets *were before*[21] the king; and all the people of the land were rejoicing and blowing on the trumpets. And Athaliah tore her garments and called: "Rebellion, rebellion." 15. And Jehoiada the priest commanded the chiefs of the hundreds who were appointed over the army, and he said to them: "Bring her forth inside from the ranks. And whoever will go in after her, *let him be killed*[22] by the sword." For the priest said: *"Let her not be killed in the house of the sanctuary*[23] of the Lord." 16. And *they prepared a place for her,*[24] and she went in by way of the entrance of the horses to the house of the king, and *she was killed*[25] there. 17. And Jehoiada cut the covenant between *the Memra of the Lord*[26] and between the king and between the people to be for a people *serving before the Lord*[27] and between the king and between the people. 18. And all the people of the land went in to the temple of Baal and tore it down; his altars and his images they broke properly; and they killed Mattan *the idol priest*[28] of Baal before the altars; and the priest appointed a guard over *the house of the sanctu-*

Notes, Chapter Eleven (Cont.)

[9] MT: "Sur," is unclear.
[10] MT: "the gate behind the runners."
[11] MT: "the house."
[12] MT: "for."
[13] MT: "the ranks will be put to death."
[14] The name is not in the MT and some Tg mss.
[15] MT: "the house."
[16] MT lacks the word.
[17] MT: "May the king live."
[18] MT: "the runners, the people."
[19] MT: "the house."
[20] MT lacks the phrase.
[21] MT: "to."
[22] MT: "he dies."
[23] MT: "Let her not die in the house."
[24] MT: "they laid hands on her."
[25] MT: "she died."
[26] MT: "the Lord."
[27] MT: "for the Lord."
[28] MT: "the priest."

ary[29] of the Lord. 19. And he took the chiefs of the hundreds, *the warriors*[30] and the runners, and all the people of the land; and they brought the king down from *the house of the sanctuary*[31] of the Lord, and they went in by way of the gate of the runners to the house of the king. And he sat upon the throne of the kings. 20. And all the people of the land rejoiced, and the city was at rest, and *they killed*[32] Athaliah by the sword at the house of the king.

CHAPTER 12

1. Jehoash was seven years old when he ruled. 2. In the seventh year of Jehu, Jehoash ruled, and he ruled forty years in Jerusalem, and the name of his mother was Zibiah from Beer-sheba. 3. And Jehoash did what was proper *before*[1] the Lord all his days, whatever Jehoiada the priest taught him. 4. Only the high places did not cease entirely; the people were still sacrificing and *offering sweet spices upon*[2] the high places. 5. And Jehoash said to the priests: "All the silver of the holy things that is brought to *the house of the sanctuary of the Lord, the silver of the shekels that passes according to the number of men, the silver of the assessment of persons that they bring, each man the redemption of his person, also all the silver that each man volunteers in his heart to bring to the house of the sanctuary*[3] of the Lord, 6. let the priests take for themselves, each man from his acquaintance; and let them repair the damage of the house for every place where damage is found. 7. And in the twenty-third year for King Jehoash the priests had not repaired the damage of the house. 8. And King Jehoash called to Jehoiada the priest and to the priests, and he said to them: "Why are you not repairing the damage of the house? And now you shall not take silver from your acquaintances; only you shall give it over for the damage of the house." 9. And the priests agreed not to take silver from the people and not to repair the damage of the house. 10. And Jehoiada the priest took one chest, and he bored a hole in its lid, and he put it at the side of the altar *from*[4] the right when a man goes into *the house of the sanctuary*[5] of the Lord; and the priests-*cashiers*[6] gave in there all the silver that was brought to *the house of the sanctuary*[7] of the Lord. 11. And when they saw that there was much silver in the chest, the scribe of the king and the chief priest went up and tied and counted the silver

Notes, Chapter Eleven (Cont.)

[29]MT: "the house."
[30]MT: "the Carite."
[31]MT: "the house."
[32]MT: "they put to death."

Notes, Chapter Twelve

[1]MT: "in the eyes of."
[2]MT: "incensing at."

[3]MT: "the house of the Lord, the silver passing from each man—the silver from the assessment of persons, all the silver that goes up to the heart of man to bring to the house." Tg identifies the tax in the MT with the later half-shekel tax sent yearly to the Temple by every Jew. After 70 C.E. the Romans collected this tax.
[4]MT: "at."
[5]MT: "the house."
[6]MT: "keepers of the lintel."
[7]MT: "the house."

that was found in *the house of the sanctuary*[8] of the Lord. 12. And they were giving the silver that was collected over to the hands of the workmen who were appointed over *the house of the sanctuary*[9] of the Lord, and they were paying it[10] it out to the carpenters and to the builders who were working at *the house of the sanctuary*[11] of the Lord, 13. and to the masons and to the stonecutters, and to buy wood and hewn stones to repair the damage of *the house of the sanctuary*[12] of the Lord and for everything that might be paid out for the house to repair it. 14. But there was not made (for) *the house of the sanctuary*[13] of the Lord basins of silver, snuffers, bowls, trumpets, any vessel of gold and vessel of silver, from the silver that was brought into *the house of the sanctuary*[14] of the Lord. 15 For they were giving it to the workmen and repairing with it *the house of the sanctuary*[15] of the Lord. 16. And they were not making an accounting with the men who were giving the silver in their hands to give to the workmen, for they were acting with trust. 17. The silver of the guilt offerings and the silver of the sin offerings was not brought into *the house of the sanctuary*[16] of the Lord. They were giving it to the priests. 18. Then Hazael the king of Aram went up and *waged battle*[17] against Gath and conquered it. And Hazael set his face to go up against Jerusalem. 19. And Jehoash the king of *the tribe of the house of Judah*[18] took all the holy things that Jehoshaphat and Jehoram and Ahaziah his fathers, the kings of *the house of Judah,*[19] had sanctified, and his own holy things, and all the gold that was found in the treasuries of *the house of the sanctuary*[20] of the Lord and in *the storerooms of*[21] the house of the king; and he sent (them) to Hazael the king of Aram, and *he removed himself*[22] from Jerusalem. 20. And the rest of the acts of Joash, and all that he did, are they not written in the book of the chronicles of the kings of *the house of Judah?*[23] 21. And his servants rose up and made a rebellion and struck down Joash at the house of Millo that goes down to Silla. 22. And Jozacar the son of Shimeath and Jehozabad the son of Shomer, his servants, struck him down and *killed him.*[24] And they buried him with his fathers in the city of David; and Amaziah his son ruled in his place.

Notes, Chapter Twelve (Cont.)

[8]MT: "the house."
[9]MT: "the house."
[10]The use of the preposition *l* as an accusative marker here and in vv. 15, 17 (*leh* = "it") is rare in this Targum.
[11]MT: "the house."
[12]MT: "the house."
[13]MT: "the house."
[14]MT: "the house."
[15]MT: "the house."
[16]MT: "the house."
[17]MT: "fought."
[18]MT: "Judah."
[19]MT: "Judah."
[20]MT: "the house."
[21]MT lacks the word.
[22]MT: "he went away."
[23]MT: "Judah."
[24]MT: "he died."

CHAPTER 13

1. In the twenty-third year for Joash the son of Ahaziah the king of *the tribe of the house of Judah*,[1] Jehoahaz the son of Jehu ruled over Israel in Samaria for seventeen years. 2. And he did what was evil *before*[2] the Lord, and he went after the sins of Jeroboam the son of Nebat that he made Israel sin. He did not turn aside from them. 3. And the anger of the Lord *was strong*[3] against Israel, and he gave them over in the hand of Hazael the king of Aram and in the hand of Ben-Hadad the son of Hazael all the days. 4. And Jehoahaz *prayed before*[4] the Lord, and the Lord *accepted his prayers, for there was revealed before him*[5] the oppression of Israel, for the king of Aram oppressed them. 5. And the Lord gave to Israel a savior, and they went forth from beneath the hand of *the men of Aram*,[6] and the sons of Israel dwelt in *their cities*[7] as from yesterday *and from before it.*[8] 6. But they did not turn aside from the sins of the house of Jeroboam that he made Israel sin. *In them*[9] he went, and also the Asherah stood in Samaria. 7. For there was not left to Jehoahaz a people except fifty horsemen and ten chariots and 10,000 *men*[10] on foot, for the king of Aram destroyed them and made them like the dust for threshing. 8. And the rest of the acts of Jehoahaz and everything that he did and his might, are they not written in the book of the chronicles of the kings of Israel? 9. And Jehoahaz slept with his fathers, and they buried him in Samaria, and Joash his son ruled in his place. 10. In the thirty-seventh year of Joash the king of *the tribe of the house of Judah*,[11] Jehoash the son of Jehoahaz ruled over Israel in Samaria for sixteen years. 11. And he did what was evil *before*[12] the Lord. He did not turn aside from all the sins of Jeroboam the son of Nebat that he made Israel sin. *In them*[13] he went. 12. And the rest of the acts of Joash and all that he did and his might that he *waged*[14] with Amaziah the king of *the tribe of the house of Judah*,[15] are they not written in the book of the chronicles of the kings of Israel? 13. And Joash slept with his fathers, and Jeroboam sat upon his throne, and Joash was buried in Samaria with the kings of Israel. 14. And Elisha was sick with his sickness by which he was to die, and Joash the king of Israel went down unto him and he wept before his face and said: *"My master, my master, to whom there was more good for Israel in his prayer than chariots and horsemen."*[16] 15. And Elisha said to him: "Take the bow and the

Notes, Chapter Thirteen

[1]MT: "Judah."

[2]MT: "in the eyes of."

[3]MT: "was hot."

[4]MT: "besought the face of."

[5]MT: "heard him, for he saw."

[6]MT: "Aram."

[7]MT: "their tents."

[8]MT: "and the day before."

[9]MT: "In it."

[10]MT lacks the word.

[11]MT: "Judah."

[12]MT: "in the eyes of."

[13]MT: "In it."

[14]MT: "fought."

[15]MT: "Judah." Ms. p omits "the king of the tribe of the house of Judah."

[16]MT: "My father, my father, a chariot of Israel and its horsemen." The Aramaic for "my master" is "Rabbi."

arrows." And he took for him the bow and the arrows. 16. And he said to the king of Israel: "*Bring down*[17] your hand upon the bow." And *he brought down*[18] his hand, and Elisha placed his hands upon the hands of the king. 17. And he said: "Open the window to the east." And he opened (it). And Elisha said: "Shoot." And he shot. And he said: "*This arrow will be made for us salvation from before the Lord, and this arrow will be made for us victory over the men of Aram.*[19] And you will strike down *the men of Aram*[20] in Aphek until you will destroy them utterly." 18. And he said: "Take the arrows." And he took and said to the king of Israel: "Strike the ground." And he struck three times, and he stopped. 19. And *the prophet of the Lord*[21] was angry at him, and he said: "*It is proper for you*[22] to strike five or six times. Then you *would*[23] have struck down *the men of Aram*[24] until you destroyed them utterly. And now three times you will strike down *the men of Aram.*"[25] 20. And Elisha died, and they buried him. And the army of Moab was coming into the land *at*[26] the coming in of the year. 21. And *while*[27] they were burying a man, behold they saw the army and threw the man in the tomb of Elisha. And the man went and *drew near to*[28] the bones of Elisha, and he revived and stood up on his feet. 22. And Hazael the king of Aram oppressed Israel all the days of Jehoahaz. 23. And the Lord had pity upon them and had mercy upon them. And he turned *by his Memra to do good*[29] to them on account of his covenant *that was*[30] with Abraham, Isaac, and Jacob. And he was not willing to destroy them, and *he did not exile them from the land of the house of his Shekinah*[31] until now. 24. And Hazael the king of Aram died, and Ben-Hadad his son ruled in his place. 25. And Jehoash the son of Jehoahaz returned and took the cities from the hand of Ben-Hadad the son of Hazael that he took from the hand of Jehoahaz his father in battle. Three times Joash struck him down, and he recovered the cities of Israel.

CHAPTER 14

1. In the second year for Joash the son of Jehoahaz the king of Israel, Amaziah the son of Joash the king of *the tribe of the house of Judah*[1] ruled. 2. He was twenty-five years old when he ruled, and for twenty-nine years he ruled in Jerusalem, and the name

Notes, Chapter Thirteen (Cont.)

[17]MT: "Grasp."
[18]MT: "he grasped."
[19]MT: "An arrow of victory for the Lord, an arrow of victory in Aram."
[20]MT: "Aram."
[21]MT: "the man of God."
[22]MT lacks the phrase.
[23]MT lacks the word.
[24]MT: "Aram."
[25]MT: "Aram."
[26]MT lacks the word.

[27]MT lacks the word.
[28]MT: "touched." The wicked and the righteous must not be buried together. See *b. Sanh.* 47a and S-A, 59.
[29]MT lacks the phrase.
[30]MT lacks the phrase.
[31]MT: "he did not cast them away from his face." Tg interprets the MT to refer to the later exile and diaspora.

Notes, Chapter Fourteen

[1]MT: "Judah."

of his mother was Jehoaddin from Jerusalem. 3. And he did what was proper *before*[2] the Lord, only not like David his father; according to all that Joash his father did, he did. 4. Only the high places did not cease entirely, while the people were still sacrificing and *offering up sweet spices upon*[3] the high places. 5. And when the kingdom was strong in his hand, *he killed*[4] his servants *who had killed*[5] the king his father. 6. And *he did not kill the sons of the killers*[6] as it was written in the book of the law of Moses that the Lord commanded, saying: "Fathers will not die on account of sons, and sons will not die on account of fathers. But a man will die for his own sin." 7. He struck down *the men of Edom*[7] in the valley of Salt — 10,000 and he conquered *the fortress*[8] in battle, and he called its name Joktheel unto this day. 8. Then Amaziah sent messengers unto Jehoash the son of Jehoahaz the son of Jehu, the king of Israel, saying: "Come, *let us face off in battle.*"[9] 9. And Jehoash the king of Israel sent to Amaziah the king of *the tribe of the house of Judah*[10] saying: "The thistle which is in Lebanon sent to the cedar which is in Lebanon, saying: 'Give your daughter to my son for a wife.' And the beast of the field which is in Lebanon passed by and trampled the thistle. 10. You have indeed struck down *the men of Edom,*[11] and your heart *is high upon you.*[12] Honor yourself and dwell in your house. And why are you becoming hot with evil? And you will fall, you and *those of the house of Judah*[13] with you." 11. And Amaziah did not *accept.*[14] And Jehoash the king of Israel went up, and *they faced off in battle,*[15] he and Amaziah the king of *the tribe of the house of Judah*[16] at Beth-shemesh, which belongs to *the tribe of Judah.*[17] 12. And *the men of Judah were shattered*[18] before Israel, and they fled, each man to *his city.*[19] 13. And Jehoash the king of Israel seized Amaziah the king of *the tribe of the house of Judah,*[20] the son of Jehoash the son of Ahaziah, in Beth-shemesh, and *he came*[21] to Jerusalem, and he split open the wall of Jerusalem *from*[22] the gate of the tribe of Ephraim unto the gate of the Corners four hundred cubits. 14. And he took all the gold and silver and all the vessels that were found in *the house of the sanctuary*[23] of the Lord and in the storerooms of the house of the king, and the sons of *the chiefs;*[24] and he returned to Samaria. 15. And the rest of the acts of Jehoash that he did and his might and what *he waged*[25] with Amaziah the king of *the tribe of the house of Judah,*[26] are they not written in the book of the chronicles of the kings of Israel? 16. And Jehoash slept with his fathers, and he was buried in Samaria with the kings of Israel, and Jeroboam his son ruled in his place. 17. And Amaziah, the son of Joash, the king

Notes, Chapter Fourteen (Cont.)

[2]MT: "in the eyes of."
[3]MT: "incensing at."
[4]MT: "he struck down."
[5]MT: "who struck down."
[6]MT: "he did not put to death the sons of those who had struck down."
[7]MT: "Edom."
[8]MT: "the rock." The MT, Sela, is a place name which Tg interprets.
[9]MT: "let us see faces."
[10]MT: "Judah."
[11]MT: "Edom."
[12]MT: "has exalted you."

[13]MT: "Judah."
[14]MT: "listen."
[15]MT: "faces were seen."
[16]MT: "Judah."
[17]MT: "Judah."
[18]MT: "Judah was struck."
[19]MT: "his tent."
[20]MT: "Judah."
[21]MT: "they came."
[22]MT: "at."
[23]MT: "the house."
[24]MT: "the hostages."
[25]MT: "he fought."
[26]MT: "Judah."

of *the tribe of the house of Judah,*[27] lived fifteen years after Jehoash the son of Jehoahaz the king of Israel died. 18. And the rest of the acts of Amaziah, are they not written in the book of the chronicles of the kings of *the house of Judah?*[28] 19. And they made a rebellion against him in Jerusalem, and he fled to Lachish, and they sent after him to Lachish, and *they killed him*[29] there. 20. And they carried him upon the horses, and he was buried in Jerusalem with his fathers in the city of David. 21. And all the people of *the house of Judah*[30] took Azariah, and he was sixteen years old, and they made him king in place of his father Amaziah. 22. He built Elath, and he restored it to *those of the house of Judah*[31] after the king slept with his fathers. 23. In the fifteenth year for Amaziah, the son of Joash, the king of *the tribe of the house of Judah,*[32] Jeroboam the son of Joash, the king of Israel, ruled in Samaria for forty-one years. 24. And he did what was evil *before*[33] the Lord. He did not turn aside from all the sins of Jeroboam the son of Nebat that he made Israel sin. 25. And he restored the border of Israel from the entrance of Hamath unto the sea of the plain according to the word of the Lord God of Israel that he spoke by the hand of his servant Jonah the son of Amittai, the prophet who was from Gath-hepher. 26. For *the servitude of Israel was revealed before the Lord as very strong, and they were wandering about and left alone,*[34] and there was no one who was helping Israel. 27. *There was good pleasure from before the Lord so as not*[35] to strike out the name of Israel from beneath the heavens, and he saved them by the hand of Jeroboam the son of Joash. 28. And the rest of the acts of Jeroboam and all that he did and his might that *he waged*[36] and that he recovered Damascus and Hamath for *those of the house of Judah*[37] in Israel, are they not written in the book of the chronicles of the kings of Israel? 29. And Jeroboam slept with his fathers, with the kings of Israel; and Zechariah his son ruled in his place.

CHAPTER 15

1. In the twenty-seventh year for Jeroboam the king of Israel, Azariah the son of Amaziah, the king of *the tribe of the house of Judah,*[1] ruled. 2. He was sixteen years old when he ruled, and he ruled fifty-two years in Jerusalem, and the name of his mother was Jecoliah from Jerusalem. 3. And he did what was proper *before*[2] the Lord according to all that Amaziah his father did. 4. Only the high places did not cease entirely,

Notes, Chapter Fourteen (Cont.)

[27]MT: "Judah."
[28]MT: "Judah."
[29]MT: "they put him to death."
[30]MT: "Judah."
[31]MT: "Judah."
[32]MT: "Judah."
[33]MT: "in the eyes of."
[34]MT: "the Lord saw the affliction of Israel as very bitter, and there was no one left, bond and free." Tg avoids the hyperbole of the MT ("there was no one left") and uses Exodus imagery.

[35]MT: "The Lord did not speak."
[36]MT: "he fought."
[37]MT: "Judah."

Notes, Chapter Fifteen

[1]MT: "Judah."
[2]MT: "in the eyes of."

while the people were still sacrificing and *offering sweet spices upon*[3] the high places. 5. And the Lord *brought a sickness upon*[4] the king, and he was a leper unto the day of his death, and he dwelt *outside of Jerusalem,*[5] and Jotham the son of the king *was appointed*[6] over the house, judging the people of the land. 6. And the rest of the acts of Azariah and all that he did, are they not written in the book of the chronicles of the kings of *the house of Judah?*[7] 7. And Azariah slept with his fathers, and they buried him with his fathers, and they buried him with his fathers in the city of David, and Jotham his son ruled in his place. 8. In the thirty-eighth year of Azariah the king of *the tribe of the house of Judah,*[8] Zechariah the son of Jeroboam ruled over Israel in Samaria for six months. 9. And he did what was evil *before*[9] the Lord as his fathers did. He did not turn away from the sins of Jeroboam, the son of Nebat, that he made Israel sin. 10. And Shallum the son of Jabesh rebelled against him, and he struck him down before the people and *killed*[10] him, and he ruled in his place. 11. And the rest of the acts of Zechariah, behold they are written in the book of the chronicles of the kings of Israel. 12. That was the word of the Lord that he spoke with Jehu, saying: "Your sons to the fourth generation will sit upon *the throne of the kingdom*[11] of Israel." And so it was. 13. Shallum the son of Jabesh ruled in the thirty-ninth year for Uzziah[12] the king of *the tribe of the house of Judah,*[13] and he ruled a month of days in Samaria. 14. And Menahem the son of Gadi went up from Tirzah, and he came to Samaria, and he struck down Shallum the son of Jabesh in Samaria, and *he killed him*[14] and ruled in his place. 15. And the rest of the acts of Shallum and his rebellion that he made, behold they are written in the book of the chronicles of the kings of Israel. 16. Then Menahem struck down Tipsah and all that was in it and its territory from Tirzah because it did not open *the gate to make peace;*[15] and he struck it down; all the pregnant women he was ripping up. 17. In the thirty-ninth year of Azariah the king of *the tribe of the house of Judah,*[16] Menahem the son of Gadi ruled over Israel ten years in Samaria. 18. And he did what was evil *before*[17] the Lord. He did not turn aside from the sins of Jeroboam the son of Nebat that he made Israel sin all his days. 19. Pul, the king of Assyria, came against the land; and Menahem gave to Pul 1,000 talents of silver *to entrust*[18] his hand with him, to strengthen the kingdom in his hand. 20. And Menahem *imposed*[19] silver upon Israel, upon all the warriors, to give to the king of Assyria fifty *selas*[20] of silver for each man. And the king of Assyria turned and *did no harm*[21] there in the land. 21. And the rest of the acts of Menahem and all that he did, are they not written in the book of the chronicles of the kings of Israel? 22. Menahem slept with his fathers, and Pekehiah his son ruled in his place. 23. In the fiftieth year of Azariah the king of *the tribe of the*

Notes, Chapter Fifteen (Cont.)

[3]MT: "incensing at."

[4]MT: "smote."

[5]MT: "in a separate house." Tg protects the sanctity of Jerusalem and has Azariah obey biblical law exactly by living outside the city. See Lev 13:46 and 2 Kgs 7:3.

[6]MT lacks the word.

[7]MT: "Judah."

[8]MT: "Judah."

[9]MT: "in the eyes of."

[10]MT: "put him to death."

[11]MT: "the throne."

[12]Some Tg mss. have "Azariah."

[13]MT: "Judah."

[14]MT: "he put him to death."

[15]MT lacks the phrase.

[16]MT: "Judah."

[17]MT: "in the eyes of."

[18]MT lacks the word. The whole Aramaic phrase can be translated: "so that his hand might make peace with him."

[19]MT: "exacted."

[20]MT: "shekels."

[21]MT: "did not stay."

house of Judah,[22] Pekehiah the son of Menahem ruled over Israel in Samaria for two years. 24. And he did what was evil *before*[23] the Lord. He did not turn away from the sins of Jeroboam the son of Nebat that he made Israel sin. 25. And Pekah the son of Remaliah his officer rebelled against him and struck him down in Samaria in the inner chamber of the house of the king and Argob[24] and Arieh, and with him were fifty men from the sons of the Gileadite, and *he killed him,*[25] and he ruled in his place. 26. And the rest of the acts of Pekehiah and all that he did, behold they are written in the book of the chronicles of the kings of Israel. 27. In the fifty-second year of Azariah the king of *the tribe of the house of Judah,*[26] Pekah the son of Remaliah ruled over Israel in Samaria for twenty years. 28. And he did what was evil *before*[27] the Lord. He did not turn away from the sins of Jeroboam the son of Nebat that he made Israel sin. 29. In the days of Pekah the king of Israel, Tiglath-pileser the king of Assyria came and *captured*[28] Ijon, and Abel-beth-maacah, and Janoah, and Kedesh, and Hazor, and Gilead, and Galilee, and *the land of the tribe of*[29] Naphtali, and he exiled them to Assyria. 30. And Hoshea the son of Elah made a rebellion against Pekah the son of Remaliah, and he struck him down and *killed him*[30] and ruled in his place in the twentieth year of Jotham the son of Uzziah. 31. And the rest of the acts of Pekah and all that he did, behold they are written in the book of the chronicles of the kings of Israel. 32. In the second year of Pekah, the son of Remaliah, the king of *the tribe of the house of Judah*[31] ruled. 33. He was twenty-five years old when he ruled, and he ruled for sixteen years in Jerusalem, and the name of his mother was Jerusha the daughter of Zadok. 34. And he did what was proper *before*[32] the Lord; according to all that Uzziah his father did, he did. 35. Only the high places did not cease entirely while the people were still sacrificing and *offering up sweet spices upon*[33] the high places. He built the upper gate of *the house of the sanctuary*[34] of the Lord. 36. And the rest of the acts of Jotham that he did, are they not written in the book of the chronicles of the kings of *the house of Judah?*[35] 37. In those days the Lord began *to arouse against those of the house of Judah*[36] Rezin the king of Aram and Pekah the son of Remaliah. 38. And Jotham slept with his fathers, and he was buried with his fathers in the city of David his father, and Ahaz his son ruled in his place.

Notes, Chapter Fifteen (Cont.)

[22] MT: "Judah."
[23] MT: "in the eyes of."
[24] MT is unclear.
[25] MT: "he put him to death."
[26] MT: "Judah."
[27] MT: "in the eyes of."
[28] MT: "took."
[29] MT: "the land of."
[30] MT: "put him to death."
[31] MT: "Judah."
[32] MT: "in the eyes of."
[33] MT: "incensing at."
[34] MT: "the house."
[35] MT: "Judah."
[36] MT: "to send forth against Judah."

CHAPTER 16

1. In the seventeenth year for Pekah the son of Remaliah, Ahaz the son of Jotham, the king of *the tribe of the house of Judah,*[1] ruled. 2. Ahaz was twenty years old when he ruled, and he ruled for sixteen years in Jerusalem, and he did not do what was proper *before*[2] the Lord his God like David his father. 3. And he went in the way of the kings of Israel. And he even made his son pass in the fire according to the abominations of the nations that the Lord drove out from before the sons of Israel. 4. And he sacrificed and *offered sweet spices*[3] at the high places and upon the heights and beneath every *leafy*[4] tree. 5. Then Rezin the king of Aram and Pekah the son of Remaliah the king of Israel went up to Jerusalem *to wage battle,*[5] and they besieged Ahaz and were not able to fight. 6. At that time Rezin the king of Aram recovered Elath for Aram, and he drove out the Judeans from Elath; and *the men of Edom*[6] came to Elath and dwelt there unto this day. 7. And Ahaz sent messengers unto Tiglath-pileser, the king of Assyria, saying: "I am your servant and your son. Come up and save me from the hand of the king of Aram and from the hand of the king of Israel who have risen up against me." 8. And Ahaz took the silver and the gold that were found in *the house of the sanctuary*[7] of the Lord and in the storerooms of the house of the king, and he sent the bribe to the king of Assyria. 9. And the king of Assyria *accepted from him,*[8] and the king of Assyria went up against Damascus and seized it and exiled *the people who were in it*[9] to *Kerina,*[10] and *he killed*[11] Rezin. 10. And King Ahaz came to meet Tiglath-pileser, the king of Assyria, to Damascus. And he saw the altar[12] that was in Damascus, and King Ahaz sent unto Uriah the priest the model of the altar and its pattern for all its features. 11. And Uriah the priest built the altar according to everything that King Ahaz sent from Damascus. Thus Uriah the priest did before King Ahaz came from Damascus. 12. And the king came from Damascus, and the king saw the altar, and the king drew near to the altar and offered up (sacrifices) upon it. 13. And *he offered*[13] his holocausts and his cereal offerings, and he poured out his libation, and he sprinkled the blood of *the sacrifice of holy things*[14] that was his upon the altar. 14. And the altar of bronze that was before the Lord — he was moving it from before the house, from

Notes, Chapter Sixteen

[1]MT: "Judah."
[2]MT: "in the eyes of."
[3]MT: "incensed."
[4]MT: "green."
[5]MT: "for war."
[6]MT: "the Edomites."
[7]MT: "the house."
[8]MT: "listened to him."

[9]MT: "it."
[10]MT: "Kir." Kir was probably in Mesopotamia. "Kerina" (Tg) is Cyrene, on the North African coast.
[11]MT: "he put to death."
[12]Usually the word for a non-Israelite altar is *'āḡûrā,* a heap of stones. Here the proper word for altar is used *madbĕḥā',* perhaps because it was a model for a Temple altar. See S-A, 154, n. 160.
[13]MT: "he burned."
[14]MT: "the peace offerings."

between the altar and from between *the house of the sanctuary*[15] of the Lord, and he put it on the north side of the altar. 15. And King Ahaz commanded Uriah the priest, saying: "Upon the great altar *offer*[16] the holocaust of the morning and the cereal offering of the evening, and the holocaust of the king and his cereal offering, and the holocaust of all the people of the land and their cereal offerings and their libations; and you shall sprinkle upon it all the blood of the holocaust and all the blood of *the offering of holy things*,[17] and the altar of bronze will be for me to inquire by." 16. And Uriah the priest did according to everything that King Ahaz commanded. 17. And King Ahaz cut off the frames of the stands, and he removed from them the laver, and he took down the sea from upon the oxen of bronze that were beneath it, and he put it upon the pavement of stones. 18. And the covered way of the Sabbath that they built in the house and the entrance of the king outside, he turned to *the house of the sanctuary*[18] of the Lord because of the king of Assyria. 19. And the rest of the acts of Ahaz that he did, are they not written in the book of the chronicles of the kings of *the house of Judah?*[19] 20. And Ahaz slept with his fathers, and he was buried with his fathers in the city of David, and Hezekiah his son ruled in his place.

CHAPTER 17

1. In the twelfth year for Ahaz the king of *the tribe of the house of Judah*,[1] Hoshea the son of Elah ruled in Samaria over Israel for nine years. 2. And he did what is evil *before*[2] the Lord, yet not like the kings of Israel who were before him. 3. Against him Shalmaneser the king of Assyria came up, and Hoshea was a servant to him, and he paid him the tribute. 4. And the king of Assyria found rebellion in Hoshea, who sent messengers unto So, the king of Egypt; and he did not bring up the tribute to the king of Assyria as (he had done) year by year. And the king of Assyria seized him and put him in prison. 5. And the king of Assyria went up in all the land, and he went up to Samaria, and he besieged it for three years. 6. In the ninth year for Hoshea, the king of Assyria conquered Samaria and exiled Israel to Assyria and settled them in Halah and in Habor, the river of Gozan, and the cities of the Mede. 7. And it happened because the sons of Israel sinned *before*[3] the Lord their God, who brought them up from the land of Egypt, from beneath the hand of Pharaoh the king of Egypt; and they feared *the idols of the nations*.[4] 8. And they went in the decrees of the nations that the Lord drove out from before the sons of Israel, and of the kings of Israel that they made.

Notes, Chapter Sixteen (Cont.)

[15]MT: "the house."
[16]MT: "burn."
[17]MT: "the sacrifice."
[18]MT: "the house."
[19]MT: "Judah."

Notes, Chapter Seventeen

[1]MT: "Judah."
[2]MT: "in the eyes of."
[3]MT: "to."
[4]MT: "other gods."

9. And the sons of Israel *said*[5] things that were not *proper before*[6] the Lord their God, and they built for themselves high places in all their cities from a tower of *strength*[7] unto fortified cities. 10. And they erected for themselves pillars and Asherim upon every elevated hill and beneath every *leafy*[8] tree. 11. And *they offered sweet spices*[9] there in all the high places like the nations that the Lord exiled from before them, and they did evil things so as *to produce anger before*[10] the Lord. 12. And they served the idols that the Lord said to them: "You shall not do this thing." 13. And the Lord witnessed against Israel and against Judah by the hand of *every teacher, every instructor,*[11] saying: "Turn from your evil ways, and keep my commands, my statutes, according to all the law that I commanded your fathers and that I sent unto you by the hand of my servants the prophets." 14. And *they did not accept,*[12] and they stiffened their neck like the neck of their fathers who did not believe in *the Memra of the Lord*[13] their God. 15. And they loathed his statutes and *his decrees that he decreed*[14] with their fathers and his witnesses that he witnessed against them; and they wandered after *idols, and they were for nothing,*[15] and after the nations that were in their surroundings that the Lord commanded them so as not to act like them. 16. And they abandoned all the commands of the Lord their God, and they made for themselves molten images — two calves, and they made an Asherah, and they worshipped all the *hosts*[16] of the heavens and served Baal. 17. And they made their sons and their daughters pass in the fire, and they used divination and consulted omens; and *they calculated*[17] to do what is evil *before the Lord so as to cause anger before him.*[18] 18. And there was much *anger from before the Lord*[19] against Israel, and *he exiled them from the land of the house of his Shekinah.*[20] No one was left, only the tribe of Judah[21] alone. 19. Also *against those of the house of Judah — they*[22] did not keep the commands of the Lord their God, and they went in the decrees of Israel that they made. 20. And the Lord loathed all the seed of Israel, and he humbled them and gave them in the hand of the despoilers until *he exiled them from the land of the house of his Shekinah.*[23] 21. For *the house of Israel was divided against those of the house of David,*[24] and they made king Jeroboam the son of Nebat, and Jeroboam *made Israel go astray from after the service of the Lord*[25] and made them sin a great sin. 22. And the sons of Israel went in all the sins of Jeroboam *the son of Nebat*[26] that he did. They did not turn aside from them, 23. until the Lord *exiled Israel from the land of the house of his Shekinah*[27] just as he spoke by

Notes, Chapter Seventeen (Cont.)

[5]MT: "did secretly." The Hebrew root *hp'* occurs only here and its meaning is uncertain.

[6]MT: "right against."

[7]MT: "watchers."

[8]MT: "green."

[9]MT: "they incensed."

[10]MT: "to anger."

[11]MT: "every prophet, every seer." Tg changes the biblical roles into more familiar ones.

[12]MT: "they did not listen."

[13]Israel's unbelief in the Lord their God in MT is mitigated by Tg into unbelief in the Memra of God.

[14]MT: "his covenant that he cut."

[15]MT: "wind, and they became wind."

[16]MT: "host."

[17]MT: "they sold themselves."

[18]MT: "in the eyes of the Lord to anger him."

[19]MT: "the Lord was very angry."

[20]MT: "he turned them from his face."

[21]Many Tg mss.: "the house of Judah."

[22]MT: "Judah—they."

[23]MT: "he cast them from his face."

[24]MT: "he tore Israel from the house of David."

[25]MT: "drove Israel from after the Lord."

[26]MT and some Tg mss. lack the phrase.

[27]MT: "turned Israel from before his face."

means of all his servants the prophets, and Israel was exiled from upon *their land*[28] to Assyria until this day. 24. And the king of Assyria brought (people) from Babylon and from *Cuth*[29] and from Avva and from Hamath and *from*[30] Sepharvaim, and he settled (them) in the cities of Samaria in place of the sons of Israel, and they inherited Samaria and dwelt in its cities. 25. And at the beginning of their dwelling there, they were not fearing *from before the Lord,*[31] and the Lord *aroused*[32] against them the lions, and they were killing them. 26. And they said to the king of Assyria, saying: "The nations that you exiled and settled in the cities of Samaria, they do not know the law of the God of the land, and *he aroused*[33] against them the lions; and behold they are killing them because they do not know the law of the God of the land." 27. And the king of Assyria commanded, saying: "Bring to there one from the priests whom you exiled from there, and let them go and dwell there, and let him teach them the law of the God of the land." 28. And one of the priests who *had been exiled*[34] from Samaria came and dwelt in Bethel, and he was teaching them how they should fear *from before the Lord.*[35] 29. And each nation was still making *its idols,*[36] and they put them down in the house of the high places that the Samaritans had made, each nation in their cities where they were dwelling. 30. And the men of Babylon made Succoth-benoth, and the men of Cuth made Nergal, and the men of Hamath made Ashima, 31. and the Avvites made *Nibhan*[37] and Tartak, and *the men of Sepharvaim*[38] were burning their sons in the fire to Adrammelech and Anamelech *the idols*[39] of the Sepharvaites. 32. And they were fearing *from before the Lord,*[40] and they made for themselves from part of them *idol priests*[41] of the high places, and they were acting for them in the house of the high places. 33. *From before the Lord*[42] they were fearing, and they were serving *their idols*[43] according to the *laws*[44] of the nations from where they had exiled them. 34. Unto this day they are acting according to their former laws. They do not fear *from before the Lord,*[45] and they do not act according to their decrees and according to *their customs*[46] and according to the law and according to the command that the Lord commanded the sons of Jacob whom he named Israel. 35. And the Lord cut with them a covenant and commanded them, saying: "You shall not fear *the idols of the nations,*[47] and you shall not worship them, and you shall not serve them, and you shall not sacrifice to them. 36. But *before the Lord*[48] who brought you up from the land of Egypt with much strength and with *upraised*[49] arm, you shall fear him and worship *before him,*[50] and you shall sacrifice *upon his altars.*[51] 37. And the statutes

Notes, Chapter Seventeen (Cont.)

[28]MT: "its land."
[29]MT: "Cuthah."
[30]MT lacks the preposition.
[31]MT: "the Lord."
[32]MT: "sent."
[33]MT: "he sent."
[34]MT: "they exiled."
[35]MT: "the Lord."
[36]MT: "its gods."
[37]MT: "Nibhaz."
[38]MT: "the Sepharvaim."
[39]MT: "the gods."
[40]MT: "the Lord."

[41]MT: "priests."
[42]MT: "the Lord."
[43]MT: "their gods."
[44]MT: "law." In vv. 33-37 Tg translates the MT *mišpāt* and *hôq* by *nimôsā* (Greek *nomos*) and *gĕzêrā* because they are non-Israelite laws. The usual Aramaic translations are *dînā*'and *qĕyāmā*.'
[45]MT: "the Lord."
[46]MT: "their law."
[47]MT: "other gods."
[48]MT: "the Lord."
[49]MT: "outstretched."
[50]MT: "him."
[51]MT: "to him."

and the judgments and the law and the command that he wrote for you, you shall be careful to do all the days; and you shall not fear *the idols of the nations.*[52] 38. And the covenant that I cut with you, you shall not forget; and you shall not fear *the idols of the nations.*[53] 39. Only *before the Lord*[54] your God you shall fear, and he will save you from the hand of all your enemies." 40. And they did not *accept.*[55] But according to their former laws they were acting. 41. And these nations were fearing *from before the Lord,*[56] and they were serving their graven images — also their sons and their sons' sons — just as their fathers did, they are doing unto this day.

CHAPTER 18

1. And in the third year for Hoshea the son of Elah the king of Israel, Hezekiah the son of Ahaz, king of *the tribe of the house of Judah,*[1] ruled. 2. He was twenty-five years old when he ruled, and for twenty-nine years he ruled in Jerusalem, and the name of his mother was Abi the daughter of Zechariah. 3. And he did what was proper *before*[2] the Lord according to all that David his father did. 4. He removed the high places, and he broke the pillars and cut down the Asherah. And he destroyed the serpent of bronze that Moses made, because unto those days the sons of Israel *were offering sweet spices*[3] to it, and *they were calling*[4] it Nehushtan. 5. In *the Memra of the Lord*[5] God of Israel he trusted; and after him there was none like him among all the kings of *the house of Judah,*[6] nor those who were before him. 6. And he held fast in *the fear of the Lord.*[7] He did not turn aside *from after his service,*[8] and he kept his commands that the Lord commanded Moses. 7. And *the Memra of the Lord was at his aid.*[9] In every place that he went forth, he was successful. And he rebelled against the king of Assyria, and he did not serve him. 8. *He killed*[10] the Philistines unto Gaza and its territories, from the tower of *strength*[11] unto the *fortified cities.*[12] 9. And in the fourth year for King Hezekiah, that is the seventh year for Hoshea the son of Elah the king of Israel, Shalmaneser the king of Assyria went up against Samaria and besieged it. 10. And they conquered it at the end of three years. In the sixth year for Hezekiah, that is the ninth year for Hoshea the king of Israel, Samaria was conquered. 11. And the king of Assyria exiled Israel to Assyria, and he made them reside in Halah and in Habor, the river of

Notes, Chapter Seventeen (Cont.)

[52]MT: "other gods."
[53]MT: "other gods."
[54]MT: "the Lord."
[55]MT: "listen."
[56]MT: "the Lord."

Notes, Chapter Eighteen

[1]MT: "Judah."

[2]MT: "in the eyes of."
[3]MT: "were incensing."
[4]MT: "he called."
[5]MT: "Lord."
[6]MT: "Judah."
[7]MT: "the Lord."
[8]MT: "from after him."
[9]MT: "the Lord was with him."
[10]MT: "He struck down."
[11]MT: "watchers."
[12]MT: "fortified city."

Gozan, and the cities of Media. 12. Because *they did not accept the Memra of the Lord*[13] their God, they transgressed *against*[14] his covenant, all that Moses the servant of the Lord commanded; and *they did not receive his Memra,*[15] and they did not do *his good pleasure.*[16] 13. And in the fourteenth year for King Hezekiah, Sennacherib the king of Assyria went up against all the fortified cities of *the house of Judah,*[17] and he seized them. 14. And Hezekiah the king of *the tribe of the house of Judah*[18] sent unto the king of Assyria to Lachish, saying: "I have sinned. *Withdraw*[19] from me. *According to all that you will impose*[20] upon me, I will accept." And the king of Assyria *imposed*[21] upon Hezekiah the king of *the tribe of the house of Judah*[22] three-hundred talents of silver and thirty talents of gold. 15. And Hezekiah gave all the silver that was found in the house of *the sanctuary of the Lord*[23] and in the storerooms of the house of the king. 16. In that time Hezekiah scraped the doors of the temple of the Lord and the doorposts that Hezekiah the king of *the tribe of the house of Judah*[24] covered, and he gave them to the king of Assyria. 17. And the king of Assyria sent the general and the Rabsaris and the Rabshakeh from Lachish unto King Hezekiah with *many companies*[25] to Jerusalem. And they went up and came to Jerusalem, and they went up and came and stood at the conduit of the upper pool which is on the road of *the spreading field*[26] of the fullers. 18. And they called for the king. And Eliakim the son of Hilkiah who *was appointed*[27] over the house, and Shebna the scribe, and Joah the son of Asaph *who was appointed over the records*[28] came forth unto them. 19. And the Rabshakeh said to them: "Say now to Hezekiah: 'Thus said *the king of our princes,*[29] the king of Assyria: "What is this confidence that you have relied upon? 20. You said: "*Surely a word of the lips with counsel and strength will make battle.*"[30] Now upon whom have you relied that you have rebelled against me? 21. Now behold you have relied upon the help of this broken reed, upon *Pharaoh the king of Egypt;*[31] which if a man leans upon it, it will enter his hand and tear it. So is Pharaoh the king of Egypt to all who rely upon him. 22. And since you say to me: "*Upon the Memra of the Lord*[32] our God we rely," is it not he whose high places and altars Hezekiah rmoved, and who said *to the men of Judah and to the inhabitants of Jerusalem:*[33] "Before this altar you shall worship in Jerusalem." 23. And now make a deal with my master, with the king of Assyria; and I will give to you 2,000 horses if you can *muster*[34] for yourself riders upon them. 24. And how are you planning to turn back the face of one of the officials of the minor servants of my master, and you rely upon the Egyptians for chariots and for

Notes, Chapter Eighteen (Cont.)

[13]MT: "they did not hear the voice of the Lord."

[14]MT lacks the preposition.

[15]MT: "they did not listen."

[16]MT lacks the word.

[17]MT: "Judah."

[18]MT: "Judah."

[19]MT: "Turn."

[20]MT: "Whatever you will give."

[21]MT: "placed."

[22]MT: "Judah."

[23]MT: "the Lord."

[24]MT: "Judah."

[25]MT: "a strong army."

[26]MT lacks the phrase; it refers to the field where the clothes were spread to dry.

[27]MT lacks the word.

[28]MT: "the recorder."

[29]MT: "the great king."

[30]MT: "You said: Surely a word of the lips is counsel and strength for war." An idiomatic translation is: "You must think mere talk is counsel and power for war" (JPS).

[31]MT and some Tg mss.: "Egypt."

[32]MT: "To the Lord."

[33]MT: "to Judah and to Jerusalem."

[34]MT: "give."

horsemen? 25. And now is it apart from *the Memra of the Lord*[35] that I came up against this place to destroy it? The Lord said to me: "Go up against this land, and destroy it."'" 26. And Eliakim the son of Hilkiah and Shebnah and Joah said to the Rabshakeh: "Speak now with your servants in Aramaic, for we are hearing. And do not speak with us in Judean *before*[36] the people who are upon the wall." 27. And the Rabshakeh said to them: "Is it unto your master and unto you that my master sent me to speak these words? Is it not unto the men who are sitting upon the wall, to eat their own excrement and to drink *the waters of their feet in the siege*[37] with you?" 28. And the Rabshakeh arose and called in a loud voice in Judean and spoke and said: "Hear the word of *the king of princes,*[38] of the king of Assyria. 29. Thus said the king: Let not Hezekiah deceive you, for he is not able to save you from *my hand.*[39] 30. And let not Hezekiah make you rely upon *the Memra of the Lord,*[40] saying: 'The Lord will surely save us, and this city will not be given over in the hand of the king of Assyria.' 31. *Do not accept from*[41] Hezekiah, for thus said the king of Assyria: 'Make *peace*[42] with me, and go forth unto me, and eat each man *the fruits of his vines*[43] and each man *the fruits of his fig trees,*[44] and drink each man the waters of his cistern 32. until I come and take you to a land *good*[45] like your land, a land of grain and wine, *a land of farms and vineyards, the land whose olive trees make oil, and it makes honey.*[46] And live, and do not die. And *do not accept from*[47] Hezekiah, for he will deceive you saying: 'The Lord will save us.' 33. Has any of *the deities*[48] of the nations really saved its land from the hand of the king of Assyria? 34. Where are *the deities*[49] of Hamath and Arpad? Where are *the deities*[50] of the Sepharvaim? *Did they not remove them and exile them?*[51] Did they save Samaria from my hand? 35. Who among all *the deities of the provinces*[52] was there who saved their lands from my hand that the Lord might save Jerusalem from my hand?" 36. And the people were silent, and they did not answer him a word, for that was the command of the king, saying: "Do not answer him." 37. And Eliakim the son of Hilkiah who *was appointed*[53] over the house and Shebna the scribe and Joah the son of Asaph who *was appointed over the records*[54] came unto Hezekiah *while tearing their garments,*[55] and they told him the words of the Rabshakeh.

Notes, Chapter Eighteen (Cont.)

[35]MT: "the Lord."

[36]MT: "in the ears of."

[37]MT: "their own urine." The Aramaic translates the *qere* of the Hebrew text.

[38]MT: "the great king."

[39]MT: "his hand." Many mss. agree with Tg.

[40]MT: "the Lord."

[41]MT: "Do not listen to."

[42]MT: "a blessing."

[43]MT: "his vine."

[44]MT: "his fig tree."

[45]MT lacks the word.

[46]MT: "a land of bread and vineyards, a land of olive trees, olive oil, and honey."

[47]MT: "do not listen to."

[48]MT: "the gods." The Aramaic term for "deities" here is *daḥlat* from the root for "fear" (*dḥl*).

[49]MT: "the gods."

[50]MT: "the gods."

[51]MT: "Hena and Ivvah." These words are lacking in Isa 36:19 and the sense of the MT here is difficult."

[52]MT: "the gods of the lands."

[53]MT lacks the word.

[54]MT: "the recorder."

[55]MT: "with torn garments."

CHAPTER 19

1. And when King Hezekiah heard, he tore his *garment*[1] and covered himself with sackcloth and went into *the house of the sanctuary*[2] of the Lord. 2. And he sent Eliakim who *was appointed*[3] over the house and Shebna the scribe and the elders of the priests when they were covered with sackcloths unto Isaiah the prophet, the son of Amoz. 3. And they said to him: "Thus said Hezekiah: 'A day of distress and *disgraces*[4] and insult is this day, *for distress has encompassed us like a woman who sits upon the birth stool and she has no strength to give birth.*[5] 4. Perhaps *there have been heard before the Lord your God*[6] all the words of the Rabshakeh whom the king of Assyria his master sent to disgrace *the people of the living Lord,*[7] and *he will work vengeance over all the words that have been heard before the Lord your God;*[8] and *you will make intercession in prayer*[9] for this remnant that *is left.*'"[10] 5. And the servants of King Hezekiah came unto Isaiah. 6. And Isaiah said to them: "Thus you will say to your master: 'Thus said the Lord: "Do not fear from before the words that you heard that the young men of the king of Assyria *spoke shamefully before me.*[11] 7. Behold I am giving in him the spirit, and he will hear the news, and he will return to his land, and I will make him fall by the sword in his land."'" 8. And the Rabshakeh returned and found the king of Assyria *waging battle with*[12] Libnah, for he heard that he moved from Lachish. 9. And he heard about Tirhak the king of Cush, saying: "Behold he went forth *to wage battle*[13] with you." And he turned and sent messengers unto Hezekiah, saying: 10. "Thus you will say to Hezekiah, king of *the tribe of the house of Judah,*[14] saying: 'Let not your God on whom you rely deceive you, saying: "Jerusalem will not be given in the hand of the king of Assyria."' 11. Behold you have heard what the kings of Assyria did to all *the provinces*[15] to destroy them utterly. *And you are planning to be saved?*[16] 12. Did *the deities*[17] of the nations that my fathers destroyed — Gozan and Haran and Rezeph and the sons of Eden which is in Telassar — save them? 13. Where is the king of Hamath and the king of Arpad and the king *who was*[18] for the city of Sepharvaim? *Did they not*

Notes, Chapter Nineteen

[1] MT: "garments."
[2] MT: "the house."
[3] MT lacks the word.
[4] MT: "reproach."
[5] MT: "for children have come to the birth-stool, and there is no strength to give birth."
[6] MT: "the Lord your God will hear."
[7] MT: "the people of the living God."
[8] MT: "he will rebuke the words that the Lord your God has heard."

[9] MT: "you will raise up a prayer."
[10] MT: "is found."
[11] MT: "blasphemed me."
[12] MT: "fighting."
[13] MT: "to fight."
[14] MT: "Judah."
[15] MT: "the lands."
[16] MT: "Will you be saved?"
[17] MT: "the gods."
[18] MT lacks the phrase.

remove them and exile them?'"[19] 14. And Hezekiah took the letters from the hand of the messengers, and he read them, and he went up *to the house of the sanctuary*[20] of the Lord, and Hezekiah spread them out before the Lord. 15. And Hezekiah prayed before the Lord and said: "Lord God of Israel *whose Shekinah resides up above the cherubim,*[21] you are *Lord. There is none beside you*[22] for all the kingdoms of the earth. You made the heavens and the earth. 16. *It is revealed before you, Lord, and judge; and it is heard before you, and take vengeance. And work vengeance upon all*[23] the words of Sennacherib who sent him *to disgrace the people of the living Lord.*[24] 17. In truth, Lord, the kings of Assyria have laid waste the nations and their lands. 18. *And they burn their idols in the fire, for these are not idols in which there is profit. They are nothing*[25] but the work of the hands of man — wood and stone, and they destroyed them. 19. And now, Lord our God, save us from his hand, and let all the kingdoms of the earth know that you are Lord; *there is none beside you.*"[26] 20. And Isaiah the son of Amoz sent unto Hezekiah, saying: "Thus said the Lord God of Israel: 'What *you sought from before me about*[27] Sennacherib the king of Assyria *was heard before me.*[28] 21. This is the word that the Lord *decreed*[29] about him: "She contemns you, she annoys you, *the kingdom of the assembly*[30] of Zion. After you *they wag their head, the people which are in*[31] Jerusalem. 22. Whom have you disgraced, and *against whom have you made yourself great,*[32] and *before*[33] whom have you raised up the voice and lifted up to the height your eyes? *You have spoken words that are not proper before the Holy One*[34] of Israel. 23. By means of your messengers you have disgraced *the people of the Lord,*[35] and you said: 'With the great number of my chariotry *I have gone up to overpower their fortresses; and also I will seize the house of their sanctuary; and I will kill the best of their warriors, the choice of their officials; and I will conquer the city of their power, and I will destroy utterly many of their camps.*[36] 24. I was digging *wells*[37] and drinking foreign waters, and *I stamped with the sole of the feet of the people that was with me all the waters of the deep rivers.*[38] 25. Have you not heard *from of old what I did to Pharaoh the king of Egypt, over whom he rules.*[39] *Just as the prophets of Israel prophesied about you, and you did not turn, and this was fitting before me from days of old to do to you, so you have established it, now you have brought it about. And that was a stumbling-block*

Notes, Chapter Nineteen (Cont.)

[19]MT: "Hena and Ivvah."

[20]MT: "the house."

[21]MT: "sitting upon the cherubim."

[22]MT: "God, you alone."

[23]MT: "Incline, Lord, your ear, and hear; open, Lord, your eyes, and see; and hear."

[24]MT: "to reproach the living God."

[25]MT: "And they put their gods in the fire, for they are not gods."

[26]MT: "you alone."

[27]MT: "you prayed to me for."

[28]MT: "I have heard."

[29]MT: "spoke."

[30]MT: "virgin daughter." Tg avoids the metaphor in favor of the later designation of Israel, "assembly."

[31]MT: "she wags a head, the daughter of."

[32]MT: "reviled." Tg protects God's dignity by not allowing even Sennacherib to revile him.

[33]MT: "against."

[34]MT: "against the Holy One."

[35]MT: "my Lord."

[36]MT: "I have gone up to the heights of the mountains, the recesses of Lebanon; and I cut down its highest cedars, its choice cypresses; I entered its farthest retreat, its fertile forest." Tg gives the metaphors explicit meaning.

[37]MT lacks the word.

[38]MT: "dried up by the sole of my feet all the streams of Egypt." The biblical verse seems to refer to Israel's crossing the sea in Exod 14. Tg removes the similarity.

[39]MT: "long ago I did it."

for you because it was before you like the noise of waves that destroys fortified cities.[40] 26. And their inhabitants — *their strength is reduced;*[41] they are shattered and ashamed; they are *like*[42] the grass of the fields and like the green of the plant, like the grass of the rooftops that is burned away *without ever becoming ears of corn.*[43] 27. *And your sitting in the council and your going forth to wage battle and your coming to the land of Israel are revealed before me; and what you have done as provocation before me is revealed.*[44] 28. Because you made provocation against *my Memra,*[45] and your noise came up *before me,*[46] I will place my *chain in your jaw*[47] and a bit in your lips, and I will turn you back on the way on which you came. 29. And this will be the sign for you: Eat *in one year*[48] the after-growth, and in the second year the third crop, and in the third year sow and reap and plant vineyards and eat *their fruit.*[49] 30. And the survivors of the house of Judah who will be left will continue *like a tree that sends forth its roots below and raises up its branch above.*[50] 31. Because from Jerusalem the remnant *of the just ones*[51] will go forth and the survival *of those upholding the law*[52] from Mount Zion. *By the Memra of the Lord of hosts this will be done.*[53] 32. Therefore thus said the Lord *about*[54] the king of Assyria: 'He will not come into this city, and he will not shoot an arrow there, and he will not come before it *with shields,*[55] and he will not pile up a siege-mound against it. 33. By the way on which he came he will return, and to this city he will not come in, said the Lord. 34. And I will protect this city to save it *on account of my Memra*[56] and on account of David my servant.'" 35. And on that night the angel of the Lord went forth and *killed*[57] in the camp of *the Assyrians*[58] 185,000; and they got up in the morning, and behold all of them were dead corpses. 36. And Sennacherib the king of Assyria moved and went and returned and dwelt in Nineveh. 37. And he was worshipping at the house of Nisroch *his idol,*[59] and *his sons*[60] Adrammelech and Sharezer *killed him*[61] by the sword and escaped to the land of *Kardu.*[62] And Esarhaddon his son ruled in his place.

Notes, Chapter Nineteen (Cont.)

[40] MT: "From days of old I planned it; now I bring it to pass." Tg rewrites v. 25 to make it plain that Sennacherib, like Pharaoh, is under God's control.

[41] MT: "shorn of strength."

[42] MT lacks the word.

[43] MT: "before becoming standing corn."

[44] MT: "And your sitting and your going forth and your coming I know, and your making provocation against me."

[45] MT: "me."

[46] MT: "in my ears."

[47] MT: "hook in your nose."

[48] MT: "this year."

[49] MT: "fruit."

[50] MT: "as a root below and making fruit above."

[51] MT lacks the phrase.

[52] MT lacks the phrase. Tg makes clear that observance of Torah is the criterion for survival.

[53] MT: "The zeal of the Lord will do this."

[54] MT: "to."

[55] MT: "with the shield."

[56] MT: "on my own account."

[57] MT: "struck down."

[58] MT: "Assyria."

[59] MT: "his god."

[60] At this point the MT has the vowels but not the consonants. Tg follows the *qere.*

[61] MT: "struck him down."

[62] MT: "Ararat." Kardu is northeast of the Tigris, in modern Kurdistan.

CHAPTER 20

1. In those days Hezekiah grew sick to death; and Isaiah the son of Amoz the prophet came unto him and said to him: "Thus said the Lord: Take account over *the men of your house*,[1] for you are dying and *you will not recover from your sickness*."[2] 2. And he turned his face to the wall *of the house of the sanctuary*,[3] and he prayed *before*[4] the Lord, saying: 3. "*Accept my petition*,[5] Lord. Remember now that *I served*[6] before you in truth and with a perfect heart, and I did what is good *before you*."[7] And Hezekiah wept a great weeping. 4. And Isaiah had not gone forth to the middle court, and *a word of prophecy from before the Lord was with him*,[8] saying: 5. "Return, and you shall say to Hezekiah the *king*[9] of my people: 'Thus said the Lord the God of David your Father: *Your prayer has been heard before me, your weeping has been revealed before me*.[10] Behold I am healing you. On the third day you will go up to *the house of the sanctuary*[11] of the Lord. 6. And I will add unto your days fifteen years, and I will rescue from the hand of the king of Assyria you and this city, and I will protect this city *on account of my Memra*[12] and on account of David my servant.'" 7. And Isaiah said: "Take a cake of figs." And they took (it) and placed (it) on the boil, and he was healed. 8. And Hezekiah said to Isaiah: "What sign is there that the Lord will heal me, and I will go up on the third day *to the house of the sanctuary*[13] of the Lord?" 9. And Isaiah said: "This is the sign for you *from before*[14] the Lord that the Lord will bring about the word that he spoke: Shall the shadow go forward ten hours, or shall it turn back ten hours?" 10. And Hezekiah said: "This is easy that the shadow should go forward ten hours, *but a miracle*[15] that the shadow should turn backward ten hours." 11. And Isaiah the prophet *prayed before*[16] the Lord, and he turned back the shadow on *the stone figure of the hours, on which the sun went down on the stairs of Ahaz, backward ten hours*.[17] 12. In that time Berodach-baladan the son of Baladan, the king of Babylon, sent letters and *presents unto*[18] Hezekiah, because he heard that Hezekiah was sick.

Notes, Chapter Twenty

[1]MT: "your house."
[2]MT: "you will not live."
[3]MT lacks the phrase. Turning toward the Temple to pray was a rabbinic custom.
[4]MT: "to."
[5]MT lacks the phrase.
[6]MT: "I prayed."
[7]MT: "in your eyes."
[8]MT: "a word of the Lord was to him."
[9]MT: "prince."

[10]MT: "I have heard your prayer, I have seen your tears."
[11]MT: "the house."
[12]MT: "on my own account."
[13]MT: "the house."
[14]MT: "from with."
[15]MT: "not so." Tg explicitly names the miracle.
[16]MT: "called to."
[17]MT: "And he turned back the shadow on the steps, which it [the sun?] descended on the steps of Ahaz, backward ten steps."
[18]MT: "a present to."

13. And Hezekiah *accepted from*[19] them, and he showed them all his storerooms — the silver and the gold and the sweet spices and the fine oil, and his supply house, and everything that was found in his storerooms. There was nothing that Hezekiah did not show them in his house and in all his realm. 14. And Isaiah the prophet came unto King Hezekiah and said to him: "What did these men say? And where did they come *from?"*[20] And Hezekiah said: "From a far-off land they came, from Babylon." 15. And he said: "What did they see in your house?" And Hezekiah said: "They saw everything that is in my house. There is nothing that I did not show them in my storerooms." 16. And Isaiah said to Hezekiah: "*Accept*[21] the word of the Lord. 17. Behold the days are coming; and everything that is in your house and that your fathers have stored up unto this day will be taken away *and brought*[22] to Babylon. Nothing will be left, said the Lord. 18. And some of your sons who will go forth from you, whom you will sire, *he will take;*[23] and they will be *chiefs*[24] in the palace of the king of Babylon." 19. And Hezekiah said to Isaiah: "Good is the word of the Lord that you spoke." And he said: "Will there not be peace and truth in my days?" 20. And the rest of the acts of Hezekiah and all his might and how he made the pool and the irrigating channel, and he brought the waters to the city, are they not written in the book of the chronicles of the kings of *the house of Judah?*[25] 21. And Hezekiah slept with his fathers, and Manasseh his son ruled in his place.

CHAPTER 21

1. Manasseh was twelve years old when he ruled, and he ruled fifty-five years in Jerusalem, and the name of his mother was Hephzibah. 2. And he did what is evil *before*[1] the Lord according to the abominations of the nations that the Lord drove out from before the sons of Israel. 3. And he turned and built the high places that Hezekiah his father destroyed, and he erected altars to Baal, and he made an Asherah just as Ahab the king of Israel did, and he worshipped all the *hosts*[2] of the heavens, and he served them. 4. And he built altars in *the house of the sanctuary*[3] of the Lord that the Lord said: "In Jerusalem *I will make my Shekinah reside.*"[4] 5. And he built altars to all the *hosts*[5] of the heavens in two courts of *the house of the sanctuary*[6] of the Lord. 6. And he made his son pass in the fire, and he was practicing augury and divination, and

Notes, Chapter Twenty (Cont.)

[19]MT: "listened to."
[20]MT: "from to you."
[21]MT: "Hear."
[22]MT lacks the phrase.
[23]MT: "they will be taken."
[24]MT: "eunuchs." Tg protects the princes from total humiliation.
[25]MT: "Judah."

Notes, Chapter Twenty-One

[1]MT: "in the eyes of."
[2]MT: "host."
[3]MT: "the house." The word for altars, *'ĕgôrîn,* clearly indicated idolatrous altars.
[4]MT: "I will put my name."
[5]MT: "host."
[6]MT: "the house."

he used spiritualists and necromancy. He did much that was evil *before*[7] the Lord so as to provoke (him) to anger. 7. And he placed the image of the Asherah that he made in the house that the Lord said to David and to Solomon his son: "In this house and in Jerusalem that I have chosen from all the tribes of Israel, *I will make my Shekinah reside*[8] forever. 8. And I will not continue *to remove Israel*[9] from the land that I gave to their fathers only if they take care to do according to all that I commanded them and to all the law that my servant Moses commanded them." 9. And *they did not accept,*[10] and Manasseh led them astray to do what was more evil than the nations whom the Lord destroyed utterly from before the sons of Israel. 10. And the Lord spoke by means of his servants the prophets, saying: 11. "Because Manasseh the king of *the tribe of the house of Judah*[11] did those abominations, he did worse than all that the *Amorites*[12] who were before him did, and he also made sin *those of the house of Judah in the service of his idols.*[13] 12. Therefore thus said the Lord God of Israel: Behold I am bringing evil upon Jerusalem and Judah so that every one who will hear it, his two ears will tingle. 13. And I will stretch over Jerusalem *the cord of the destruction*[14] of Samaria and *the plummet of the desolation*[15] of the house of Ahab, and I will wipe away Jerusalem just as the flask *is wiped,*[16] wiped and turned upon its face. 14. And I will drive out the remnant of my inheritance, and I will give them over in the hand of their enemies, and they will be for a spoil and a *misfortune*[17] for all their enemies, 15. because they have done what is evil *before me,*[18] and *they were causing anger before me*[19] from the day that their fathers went forth from Egypt and unto this day." 16. And also Manasseh shed very much innocent blood until he filled Jerusalem end to end, besides his sins that he made sin *those of the house of Judah,*[20] to do what was evil *before*[21] the Lord. 17. And the rest of the acts of Manasseh and all that he did, and his sins that he sinned, are they not written in the book of the chronicles of the kings of *the house of Judah?*[22] 18. And Manasseh slept with his fathers, and he was buried in the garden of his house, in the garden of Uzza. And Amon his son ruled in his place. 19. And Amon was twenty-two years old when he ruled, and for two years he ruled in Jerusalem, and the name of his mother was Meshullemeth the daughter of Haruz from Jotbah. 20. And he did what was evil *before*[23] the Lord just as Manasseh his father did. 21. And he went in the whole way that his father went, and he served the idols that his father served, and he worshipped them. 22. And he abandoned *the worship of the Lord*[24] the God of his fathers, and he did not walk in *the way that was good before the*

Notes, Chapter Twenty-One (Cont.)

[7]MT: "in the eyes of."
[8]MT: "I will put my name."
[9]MT: "to make wander the foot of Israel."
[10]MT: "they did not listen."
[11]MT: "Judah."
[12]MT: "Amorite."
[13]MT: "Judah with his idols."
[14]MT: "the measuring line."
[15]MT: "the plummet."

[16]MT: "one wipes."
[17]MT: "plunder."
[18]MT: "in my eyes."
[19]MT: "they were angering me."
[20]MT: "Judah."
[21]MT: "in the eyes of."
[22]MT: "Judah."
[23]MT: "in the eyes of."
[24]MT: "the Lord."

Lord.[25] 23. And the servants of Amon rebelled against him, and *they killed*[26] the king in his house. 24. And the people of the land *killed*[27] all who rebelled against King Amon, and the people of the land made Josiah his son king in his place. 25. And the rest of the acts of Amon that he did, are they not written in the book of the chronicles of the kings *of the house of Judah?*[28] 26. And he[29] buried him in his tomb in the garden of Uzza. And Josiah his son ruled in his place.

CHAPTER 22

1. Josiah was eight years old when he ruled, and for thirty-one years he ruled in Jerusalem, and the name of his mother was Jedidah the daughter of Adaiah from Bozkath. 2. And he did what was proper *before*[1] the Lord, and he went in all the way of David his father, and he did not turn aside *to the right and to the left.*[2] 3. And in the eighteenth year for King Josiah, the king sent Shaphan the son of Azaliah, son of Meshullam, the scribe, to *the house of the sanctuary*[3] of the Lord, saying: 4. "Go up unto Hilkiah the high priest, and *he will count out the silver that has been brought into the house of the sanctuary*[4] of the Lord that *the cashiers*[5] gathered from the people. 5. And they will give it in the hand of the workmen who are appointed *over the house of the sanctuary*[6] of the Lord and they will give it to the workmen who are in *the house of the sanctuary*[7] of the Lord to repair the breach *that is in the house,*[8] 6. to the carpenters and to the builders and to the masons, and to buy wood and hewn stones to repair the house. 7. But there is to be no accounting with them for the silver that is being given in their hand, for in good faith they are working." 8. And Hilkiah the high priest said to Shaphan the scribe: "I have found the book of the law in *the house of the sanctuary*[9] of the Lord." And Hilkiah gave the book to Shaphan, and he read it. 9. And Shaphan the scribe came unto the king, and he brought word back to the king and said: "Your servants *have counted out*[10] the silver that was found in the house, and they gave it upon the hand of the workmen who are appointed *in the house of the sanctuary*[11] of the Lord." 10. And Shaphan the scribe told the king, saying: "Hilkiah the priest gave to me the book." And Shaphan read it before the king. 11. And when the king heard the words of the book of the law, he tore his garments. 12. And the king commanded Hilkiah the priest, and Ahikam the son of Shaphan, and Achbor the son of Micaiah, and Shaphan the scribe, and Asaiah the servant of the king, saying: 13. "Go, inquire

Notes, Chapter Twenty-One (Cont.)

[25]MT: "thy way of the Lord."
[26]MT: "they put to death."
[27]MT: "put to death."
[28]MT: "Judah."
[29]Some Tg mss.: "they."

Notes, Chapter Twenty-Two

[1]MT: "in the eyes of."

[2]MT: "right and left."
[3]MT: "the house."
[4]MT: "he will give the silver brought to the house."
[5]MT: "the keepers of the threshold."
[6]MT: "in the house."
[7]MT: "the house."
[8]MT: "of the house."
[9]MT: "the house."
[10]MT: "have emptied out."
[11]MT: "the house."

from before the Lord[12] about me and about the people and about all *those of the house of Judah,*[13] about the words of this book that has been found, for much is the anger of the Lord that has been kindled against us on account of the fact that our fathers *did not accept*[14] the words of this book to act according to everything that is written about us." 14. And Hilkiah the priest and Ahikam and Achbor and Shaphan and Asaiah went unto Huldah the prophetess, the wife of Shallum the son of Tikvah, son of Harhas, the keeper of the garments. And she was dwelling in Jerusalem *in the house of instruction,*[15] and they spoke with her. 15. And she said to them: "Thus said the Lord God of Israel: Say to the man who sent you unto me: 16. Thus said the Lord: Behold I am bringing evil *upon*[16] this place and upon its inhabitants, all the words of the book that the king of *the tribe of the house of Judah*[17] read. 17. Because *they abandoned my service and offered up sweet spices to the idols of the nations*[18] in order *to make provocation before me*[19] in all the *works*[20] of their hands, my anger will be kindled on this place, and it will not be extinguished." 18. And to *the king of the tribe of the house of Judah who sent you to inquire instruction from before the Lord,*[21] thus you will say to him: "Thus said the Lord God of Israel: The words that you heard, 19. because your heart *trembled*[22] and you humbled yourself from before the Lord when you heard what *I decreed*[23] about this place and about its inhabitants to be for a desolation and for a curse, and you tore your garments and wept before me; and also *before me it was heard,*[24] said the Lord. 20. Therefore behold I am gathering you[25] unto your fathers, and you will be gathered to your grave in peace; and your eyes will not see all the evil that I am bringing upon this place." And they brought word back to the king.

CHAPTER 23

1. And the king sent, and all the elders of Judah and Jerusalem gathered unto him. 2. And the king went up to *the house of the sanctuary*[1] of the Lord, and all the men of Judah and all the inhabitants of Jerusalem with him, and the priests and *the scribes*[2] and all the people, from small and unto great. And he read *before them*[3] all the words

Notes, Chapter Twenty-Two (Cont.)

[12]MT: "the Lord."
[13]MT: "Judah."
[14]MT: "did not hear."
[15]The MT for "second quarter" is *mišneh*. In rabbinic Hebrew this means "study," hence the Tg translation "house of instruction."
[16]MT: "to."
[17]MT: "Judah."
[18]MT: "they abandoned me and offered incense to other gods."
[19]MT: "to anger me."
[20]MT: "the work."

[21]MT: "the king of Judah who sends you to seek the Lord."
[22]MT: "grew soft."
[23]MT: "I spoke."
[24]MT: "I heard."
[25]MT: "The use of *l* as an accusative marker (*lak* = "you") is noteworthy.

Notes, Chapter Twenty-Three

[1]MT: "the house."
[2]MT: "the prophets."
[3]MT: "in their ears."

of the book of the covenant that was found in *the house of the sanctuary*[4] of the Lord. 3. And the king stood *upon the balcony,*[5] and he cut the covenant before the Lord to walk after *the service of the Lord*[6] and to keep his commands and his testimonies and his statutes with all heart and with all soul, to fulfill the words of this covenant that were written upon this book. And all the people *took upon themselves*[7] the covenant. 4. And the king commanded Hilkiah the high priest and *the prefect of the priests and the cashiers*[8] to bring forth from the temple of the Lord all the vessels that were made for Baal and for Asherah and for all the *hosts*[9] of the heavens; and he burned them outside Jerusalem in the *valley*[10] of the Kidron, and he brought their dust to Bethel. 5. And he made (stop) the idol priests to whom the kings of *the house of Judah*[11] gave and *they offered sweet spices upon*[12] the high places in the cities of *the house of Judah*[13] and in the surroundings of Jerusalem, and those who offered sweet spices to Baal, to the sun and to the moon and to the constellations and to all the *hosts*[14] of the heavens. 6. And he brought forth the Asherah from *the house of the sanctuary*[15] of the Lord outside Jerusalem to the valley of the Kidron, and he burned it in the valley of the Kidron, and he crushed it to dust and cast its dust to *the graves of the idols.*[16] 7. And he broke down the houses of *the sacred property of the idols that were in the house of the sanctuary*[17] of the Lord where the women were weaving *curtains*[18] for the Asherah. 8. And he made all *the idol priests*[19] come from the cities of *the house of Judah,*[20] and he profaned the high places where *the idol priests offered sweet spices*[21] from Geba unto Beer-sheba; and he broke down the high places of the gates that were *before*[22] the gate of Joshua the chief of the city, which were at the left of a man *in his coming*[23] in the gate of the city. 9. But *the idol priests*[24] of the high places were not coming up *to sacrifice upon*[25] the altar of the Lord in Jerusalem; but they ate unleavened bread in the midst of their brothers. 10. And he profaned Topheth which was in the valley of the *son*[26] of Hinnom in order that no man could make his son and his daughter pass in the fire to Molech. 11. And he made stop the horses that the kings of *the house of Judah*[27] gave to the sun at the entrance of *the house of the sanctuary*[28] of the Lord by the chamber of Nathan-melech, *the inner compartment*[29] that was in the courts; and he burned the chariots of the sun in the fire. 12. And the king broke down the altars that were upon the roof of the upper

Notes, Chapter Twenty-Three (Cont.)

[4]MT: "the house."

[5]The MT "pillar" is imagined as supporting a balcony either in the Temple or the King's palace. The Aramaic is similar to words used for the Temple portico found in *b. Pesaḥ* 13b. Only the Second Temple had a portico.

[6]MT: "the Lord."

[7]MT: "stood in" (= "joined", RSV).

[8]MT: "the priests of the second quarter and the keepers of the threshold."

[9]MT: "host."

[10]MT: "fields."

[11]MT: "Judah."

[12]MT: "he offered incense at."

[13]MT: "Judah."

[14]MT: "host."

[15]MT: "the house."

[16]MT: "the grave of the sons of the people." Tg uses *galayā*, for idols here.

[17]MT: "the cult prostitutes that were in the house"; or more literally "the houses of the sacred ones."

[18]MT is uncertain.

[19]MT: "the priests."

[20]MT: "Judah."

[21]MT: "the priests offered incense."

[22]MT: "at the entrance of."

[23]MT lacks the phrase.

[24]MT: "the priests."

[25]MT lacks the phrase.

[26]MT: "sons."

[27]MT: "Judah."

[28]MT: "the house."

[29]MT: "the chamberlain" or "the eunuch." The word means a high military officer, or official in the King's house. The latter was often a eunuch. Eunuchs could not serve in the Temple, so Tg changes the word.

chamber of Ahaz that the kings *of the house of Judah*[30] made and the altars that Manasseh made in two courts of *the house of the sanctuary*[31] of the Lord, and *he removed them far*[32] from there and cast their dust to the valley of Kidron. 13. And the king profaned the high places that were facing Jerusalem, which were from the south to *the Mount of Olives,*[33] that Solomon the king of Israel built for Ashteroth the abomination of the Sidonians and for Chemosh the abomination of the Moabites and for Milcom the disgrace of the sons of Ammon. 14. And he broke in pieces the pillars and cut down the Asherim and filled their places with the bones of men. 15. And also the altar that was in Bethel, the high place that Jeroboam the son of Nebat *built,*[34] who made Israel sin — also that altar and the high place he broke down, and he burned the high place; he crushed it to dust and burned the Asherah. 16. And Josiah turned and saw the tombs that were there on the mountain, and he sent and took the bones from the tombs and burned them upon the altar and profaned it according to the word of the Lord that *the prophet of the Lord who prophesied*[35] these words spoke. 17. And he said: "What is this monument that I see?" And the men of the city said to him: "The tomb of *the prophet of the Lord*[36] who came from *the tribe of Judah;*[37] and *he prophesied*[38] these things that you have done concerning the altar in Bethel." 18. And he said: "Leave him alone. Let no man move his bones." And they saved his bones, *the bones of the prophet of falsehood*[39] who came from Samaria. 19. And also all the houses of the high places that were in the cities of Samaria that the kings of Israel made so as to make provocation — Josiah removed them and did to them according to all the works that he did in Bethel. 20. And he slaughtered all *the idol priests*[40] of the high places who were there at the altars, and he burned the bones of men upon them, and he returned to Jerusalem. 21. And the king commanded all the people, saying: "Make the Passover *before*[41] the Lord your God just as it is written upon the book of the covenant." 22. For it was not done like this Passover from the days of *the leaders*[42] who judged Israel and all the days of the kings of Israel and the kings of *the house of Judah.*[43] 23. Only in the eighteenth year for King Josiah this Passover was made *before*[44] the Lord in Jerusalem. 24. And also the spiritualists and the necromancers and the *graven images*[45] and the idols and all the abominations that were seen in the land of *the house of Judah*[46] and in Jerusalem, Josiah removed in order to fulfill the words of the law that were written upon the book that Hilkiah the priest found in *the house of the sanctuary*[47] of the Lord. 25. And there was no king like him before him who turned to *the service of the Lord*[48] with all his heart and with all his soul and with all his

Notes, Chapter Twenty-Three (Cont.)

[30] MT: "Judah."

[31] MT: "the house."

[32] MT: "he ran." The MT is difficult here.

[33] MT: "the mount of corruption." Tg protects the Mount of Olives, where later Judaism believed the Messiah would appear, from being a place of idolatry.

[34] MT: "made."

[35] MT: "the man of God who proclaimed."

[36] MT: "the man of God."

[37] MT: "Judah."

[38] MT: "he called."

[39] MT: "with the bones of the prophet."

[40] MT: "the priests."

[41] MT: "to."

[42] MT: "the judges."

[43] MT: "Judah."

[44] MT: "to."

[45] MT: "teraphim."

[46] MT: "Judah."

[47] MT: "the house."

[48] MT: "the Lord."

goods[49] according to all the law of Moses. And after him no one like him arose. 26. But the Lord did not turn from the *strength*[50] of his great anger, for his anger *grew strong*[51] against *those of the house of Judah*[52] on account of all the provocations that Manasseh provoked *before*[53] him. 27. And the Lord said: "And also *those of the house of Judah I will exile from the land of the house of my Shekinah just as I exiled Israel;*[54] and *I will cast far off*[55] this city that I chose, Jerusalem, and the house that I said: 'My name will be there.'" 28. And the rest of the words of Josiah and all that he did, are they not written in the book of the chronicles of the kings of *the house of Judah?*[56] 29. In his days Pharaoh *the lame,*[57] the king of Egypt, went up against the king of Assyria to the river Euphrates; and King Josiah went to meet him, and *he killed him*[58] in Megiddo when he saw him. 30. And his servants *brought him down when he died*[59] from Megiddo, and they brought him to Jerusalem and buried him in his tomb. And the people of the land took Jehoahaz the son of Josiah, and they anointed him and made him king in place of his father. 31. Jehoahaz was twenty-three years old when he ruled, and he ruled three months in Jerusalem, and the name of his mother was Hamutal the daughter of Jeremiah from Libnah. 32. And he did what was evil *before*[60] the Lord according to all that his fathers did. 33. And Pharaoh *the lame*[61] imprisoned him in Riblah, in the land of Hamath, from ruling in Jerusalem; and he imposed as a tax upon *the people of the land*[62] a hundred talents of silver and a talent of gold. 34. And Pharaoh *the lame*[63] made king Eliakim the son of Josiah in place of Josiah his father, and *he made*[64] his name Jehoiakim. And he took Jehoahaz, and he came to Egypt, and he died there. 35. And Jehoiakim gave the silver and the gold to Pharaoh, but he *imposed the tax upon the people of the land*[65] to give the silver according to the word[66] of Pharaoh. Each man *as it is proper,*[67] he assessed the silver and the gold *from*[68] the people of the land to give to Pharaoh *the lame.*[69] 36. Jehoakim was twenty-five years old when he ruled, and for eleven years he ruled in Jerusalem, and the name of his mother was *Zebudah*[70] the daughter of Pedaiah of Rumah. 37. And he did what was evil *before*[71] the Lord according to all that his fathers did.

Notes, Chapter Twenty-Three (Cont.)

[49]MT: "might."

[50]MT: "heat."

[51]MT: "grew hot."

[52]MT: "Judah."

[53]MT lacks the preposition.

[54]MT: "Judah I will remove from my face just as I removed Israel."

[55]MT: "I will reject."

[56]MT: "Judah."

[57]MT: "Neco." The consonants of the name Neco are the same as those for the Hebrew "lame."

[58]MT: "he put him to death."

[59]MT: "drove him, dead."

[60]MT: "in the eyes of."

[61]MT: "Neco."

[62]MT: "the land."

[63]MT: "Neco."

[64]MT: "he changed."

[65]MT: "he taxed the land."

[66]The use of *mêmrā* in this context is very unusual.

[67]MT: "according to his assessment."

[68]MT lacks the preposition.

[69]MT: "Neco."

[70]MT: "Zebidah." Tg translates the *qere* of the Hebrew.

[71]MT: "in the eyes of."

CHAPTER 24

1. In his days Nebuchadnezzar the king of Babylon went up; and Jehoiakim was his servant for three years, and he turned and rebelled against him. 2. And the Lord *aroused*[1] against him the *army*[2] of the Chaldeans and the *army*[3] of Aram and the *army*[4] of Moab and the *army*[5] of the sons of Ammon; and he *aroused*[6] them against *those of the house of Judah*[7] to destroy *them*[8] according to the word of the Lord that he spoke by means of his servants the prophets. 3. But *on account of the fact that they made provocation before the Lord this was against those of the house of Judah to exile them from the land of the house of his Shekinah*[9] by the sins of Manasseh according to all that he did. 4. And also the innocent blood that he shed and filled Jerusalem. *The sin of innocent blood was evil from before the Lord so as not to forgive it.*[10] 5. And the rest of the acts of Jehoiakim and all that he did, are they not written in the book of the chronicles of the kings of *the house of Judah?*[11] 6. And Jehoiakim slept with his fathers, and Jehoiachin his son ruled in his place. 7. And the king of Egypt did not continue to come forth from his land, because the king of Babylon *captured*[12] from the valley of Egypt unto the river Euphrates all that belonged to the king of Egypt. 8. Jehoiachin was eighteen years old when he ruled, and for three months he ruled in Jerusalem, and the name of his mother was Nehushta the daughter of Elnathan from Jerusalem. 9. And he did what was evil *before*[13] the Lord according to all that his father did. 10. In that time the servants of Nebuchadnezzar the king of Babylon came up to Jerusalem, and the city underwent siege. 11. And Nebuchadnezzar the king of Babylon came to the city, and his servants were besieging it. 12. And Jehoiachin the king of *the tribe of the house of Judah*[14] went forth against the king of Babylon, he and his mother and his servants and his chiefs and *his warriors.*[15] And the king of Babylon took him in the eighth year *of his kingdom.*[16] 13. And he brought forth from there all the treasures of *the house of the sanctuary*[17] of the Lord and the treasures of the house of the king, and he cut up all the vessels of gold that Solomon the king of Israel made in the temple

Notes, Chapter Twenty-Four

[1]MT: "sent forth."
[2]MT: "troops."
[3]MT: "troops."
[4]MT: "troops."
[5]MT: "troops."
[6]MT: "sent forth."
[7]MT: "Judah."
[8]MT: "him."
[9]MT: "according to the word of the Lord this was against Judah to remove (them) from his face."

[10]MT: "innocent blood—and the Lord was not willing to pardon."
[11]MT: "Judah."
[12]MT: "took."
[13]MT: "in the eyes of."
[14]MT: "Judah."
[15]MT: "his officers." Tg understands the word by its later meaning "eunuch," and changes it because making eunuchs was not permitted.
[16]MT: "of his ruling."
[17]MT: "the house."

of the Lord just as the Lord said. 14. And he exiled all Jerusalem and all the chiefs and all the warriors — ten thousand, *in the exile,*[18] and *all the craftsmen and gatekeepers.*[19] None was left except the poor of the people of the land. 15. And he exiled Jehoiachin to Babylon; and the mother of the king, and the wives of the king, and *his chiefs,*[20] and the chiefs of the land he took away in exile from Jerusalem to Babylon. 16. And all the warriors — seven thousand, and *the craftsmen and the gatekeepers*[21] — a thousand, all of them warriors, men waging battle — the king of Babylon brought them *in exile*[22] to Babylon. 17. And the king of Babylon made Mattaniah his uncle king in his place, and he *made*[23] his name Zedekiah. 18. Zedekiah was twenty-one years old when he ruled, and for eleven years he ruled in Jerusalem, and the name of his mother was *Hamutal*[24] the daughter of Jeremiah from Libnah. 19. And he did what was evil *before*[25] the Lord according to all that Jehoiakim did. 20. For *because they made provocation before the Lord,*[26] so it happened in Jerusalem and in Judah until *he exiled them from the land of the house of his Shekinah.*[27] And Zedekiah rebelled against the king of Babylon.

CHAPTER 25

1. And in the ninth year of his ruling, in the tenth month, on the tenth of the month, Nebuchadnezzar the king of Babylon, he and all his army, came unto Jerusalem; and he encamped against it, and they built against it a siegework round about. 2. And the city came under siege until the eleventh year for King Zedekiah. 3. On the ninth of the month the famine was strong in the city, and there was no food for the people of the land. 4. And the city was broken into, and all the men *waging battle*[1] by night by way of the gate between the walls that were by the garden of the king; and the Chaldeans *were encamped*[2] about the city round about, and he went by way of the plain. 5. And the army of the Chaldeans pursued after the king, and they overtook him in the plains of Jericho, and all his army was scattered from him. 6. And they seized the king and brought him unto the king of Babylon to Riblah, and they spoke with him *words of judgments.*[3] 7. And they slaughtered the sons of Zedekiah before his eyes, and he blinded the eyes of Zedekiah and bound him with *chains of bronze*[4] and brought him to Babylon. 8. And in the fifth month, on the seventh of the month, that is the

Notes, Chapter Twenty-Four (Cont.)

[18]MT: "exiles."
[19]MT: "every craftsman and smith."
[20]MT: "his eunuchs." See note 15.
[21]MT: "the craftsman and the smith."
[22]MT: "exiles."
[23]MT: "changed."
[24]MT: "Hamital."
[25]MT: "in the eyes of."

[26]MT: "because of the anger of the Lord."
[27]MT: "he cast them from his face."

Notes, Chapter Twenty-Five

[1]MT: "men of war." Following this expression the main verb is missing in the MT and Tg; the LXX has "went forth."
[2]MT lacks the word.
[3]MT: "judgment."
[4]MT: "bronze fetters."

nineteenth year for King Nebuchadnezzar the king of Babylon, Nebuzaradan the chief of *the killers*,[5] the servant of the king of Babylon, came to Jerusalem. 9. And he burned *the house of the sanctuary*[6] of the Lord and the house of the king; and all the houses of Jerusalem and *all the houses of the chiefs*[7] he burned with fire. 10. And all the army of the Chaldeans, that of the chief of *the killers*,[8] broke down the walls of Jerusalem round about. 11. And Nebuzaradan, the chief of *the killers*,[9] exiled the rest of the people who were left in the city and the deserters who deserted to the king of Babylon and the rest of the crowd. 12. *And the chief of the killers left some of the poor of the people of the land to be working in the fields and in vineyards.*[10] 13. And the Chaldeans broke up the pillars of bronze that were in *the house of the sanctuary*[11] of the Lord and the stands and the sea of bronze that were in *the house of the sanctuary*[12] of the Lord, and they brought their bronze to Babylon. 14. And they took the pots and the shovels and the snuffers and the incense dishes and all the vessels of bronze that they were using in them, 15. and the fire-pans and the basins. And the chief of *the killers*[13] took whatever was of gold as gold and whatever was of silver as silver. 16. The two pillars, the one sea, and the stands that Solomon made for *the house of the sanctuary*[14] of the Lord, there was no weight for the bronze of all those vessels. 17. Eighteen cubits was the height of one pillar, and the capital upon it was of bronze, and the height of the capital was three cubits; and the lattice-work and the pomegranates were upon the capital round about, all bronze. And like these it was for the second pillar, upon the lattice-work. 18. And the chief of *the killers*[15] took Seraiah the chief priest and Zephaniah *the prefect of the priests*[16] and the three *cashiers*.[17] 19. And from the city he took one eunuch who was appointed over *the men waging battle*,[18] and five men *who were seeing*[19] the face of the king who were found in the city, and the scribe of the chief of the army who gathered the people of the land, and sixty men from the people of the land who were found in the city. 20. And Nebuzaradan the chief of *the killers*[20] took them and brought them unto the king of Babylon to Riblah. 21. And the king of Babylon struck them down and *killed them*[21] in the land of Hamath. And *those of the house of Judah*[22] were exiled from *their land*.[23] 22. And the people who were left in the land of *the house of Judah*[24] that Nebuchadnezzar the king of Babylon left — he appointed over them Gedaliah, the son of Ahikam, the son of Shaphan. 23. And all the chiefs of the armies, they and the men, heard that the king of Babylon appointed Gedaliah; and they came unto Gedaliah to Mizpah; and they were Ishmael the son of Nethaniah, and Johanan the son of Kareah, and Seraiah the son of Tanhumeth *who was from Netopha*,[25] and Jaazaniah

Notes, Chapter Twenty-Five (Cont.)

[5]MT: "the slaughterers."
[6]MT: "the house."
[7]MT: "every great house."
[8]MT: "the slaughterers."
[9]MT: "the slaughterers."
[10]MT: "And the chief of the slaughterers left some of the poor of the land for vinedressers and for plowmen."
[11]MT: "the house."
[12]MT: "the house."
[13]MT: "the slaughterers."
[14]MT: "the house."

[15]MT: "the slaughterers."
[16]MT: "the second priest." Tg substitutes a title familiar in rabbinic literature.
[17]MT: "the keepers of the threshold."
[18]MT: "the men of war."
[19]MT: "from those seeing."
[20]MT: "the slaughterers."
[21]MT: "put them to death."
[22]MT: "Judah."
[23]MT: "its land."
[24]MT: "Judah."
[25]MT: "the Netophathite."

the son of *Maacath,*[26] they and their men. 24. And Gedaliah swore to them and to their men, and he said to them: "Do not fear the servants of the Chaldeans. Dwell in the land, and serve the king of Babylon, and it will be good for you." 25. And in the seventh month, Ishmael, the son of Nethaniah, the son of Elishama, from the seed of the kingdom, came; and ten men were with him; and they struck down Gedaliah; and he died, and the Judeans and the Chaldeans who were with him in Mizpah. 26. And all the people from small and unto great and the chiefs of the armies arose and came to Egypt, because they feared from before the Chaldeans. 27. And in the thirty-seventh year of the exile of Jehoiachin the king of *the tribe of the house of Judah,*[27] in the twelfth month, on the twenty-seventh of the month, Evil-merodach the king of Babylon in the (first) year of his ruling raised the head of Jehoiachin the king of *the tribe of the house of Judah, and he brought him forth*[28] from prison. 28. And he spoke *good words*[29] with him, and he put his throne up above the *thrones*[30] of the kings who were with him in Babylon. 29. And he changed his prison garments, and he ate bread always before him all the days of his life. 30. And his portions, portions everyday, were being given to him from *before*[31] the king, a daily portion in his days, all the days of his life.

Notes, Chapter Twenty-Five (Cont.)

[26]MT: "the Maacathite."
[27]MT: "Judah."
[28]MT: "Judah."

[29]MT: "kindly" or "good" (plural).
[30]MT: "throne."
[31]MT: "with."

APPENDIX

An Index to Substantive Discussions of Texts in Smolar-Aberbach

In their *Studies in Targum Jonathan to the Prophets,* Leivy Smolar and Moses Aberbach provided important discussions of texts in Targum Jonathan of the Former Prophets. Their thematic method of presentation, however, made it difficult to find the specific discussions. Moreover, their index is not helpful, since it attempts to be very comprehensive and includes reference to Churgin's *Targum Jonathan to the Prophets.* Also, many references to 1–2 Samuel (and Isaiah) have been accidentally omitted.

To facilitate access to their important analyses of texts in Targum Jonathan of the Former Prophets, the following table gives references to their substantive treatments of the texts. The page numbers refer to *their* book, not ours. For our uses of their work, see the Index of Modern Scholars under "Aberbach" and the notes throughout this book. We urge that their book be used along with ours. The index should make such use easier.

Index of Ancient Sources

1. Hebrew Bible

2. Targum Jonathan of the Former Prophets

Other Rabbinic Sources

Index of Modern Scholars